GOLD COINS
of the WORLD

"All passes. Art alone
Enduring, stays with us.
The bust outlasts the throne,
The coin, Tiberius."

GOLD COINS of the WORLD

(THIRD EDITION)

COMPLETE FROM 600 A.D. TO THE PRESENT

An Illustrated Standard Catalogue with Valuations

by ROBERT FRIEDBERG

Revised and Edited by

JACK FRIEDBERG

THE COIN AND CURRENCY INSTITUTE, INC.

Book Publishers

393 SEVENTH AVENUE • NEW YORK, N. Y. 10001

OTHER BOOKS PUBLISHED BY
THE COIN AND CURRENCY INSTITUTE:

"PAPER MONEY OF THE UNITED STATES"
"COINS OF THE BRITISH WORLD"
"APPRAISING AND SELLING YOUR COINS" (U.S. and Canada)
"SO-CALLED DOLLARS" (U.S.)
"AMERICA'S FOREIGN COINS"

GOLD COINS OF THE WORLD
Complete from 600 A.D. to the present
An Illustrated Standard Catalogue with Valuations

Copyright, 1958, 1965, 1971, by
THE COIN AND CURRENCY INSTITUTE, INC., NEW YORK
Library of Congress catalog card no. 70-157937
ISBN 0-87184-303-X

Manufactured in the United States of America
by Hallmark Lithographers
Third Edition

Associate Editors
MANUEL E. AGUIAR
ARTHUR S. GOLDENBERG

CONTRIBUTORS

Our thanks and gratitude to the internationally known numismatists named below who have given graciously and generously of their precious time, their numismatic knowledge and their accumulated experience in helping with this revision of "Gold Coins of the World", and who, in many instances, helped with the preceding editions: —

RAOUL BAJOCCHI *Cairo*
ALBERT DELMONTE *Brussels*
JEAN-PAUL DIVO *Luxembourg*
GIUSEPPE DE FALCO *Naples*
DR. HELMUT H. HAHN *Freiburg*
HANS KOCHMANN *Sao Paulo*
D. G. LIDDELL *London*
LEO MILDENBERG *Zurich*
CHARLES K. PANISH *Norwalk*
JAMES C. RISK *New York*
HANS M. F. SCHULMAN *New York*
JACQUES SCHULMAN *Amsterdam*
PETER N. SCHULTEN *Frankfurt*
HERBERT A. and PETER SEABY *London*
DAVID SPINK *London*
HARVEY and NORMAN STACK *New York*
SIGMUND WERKNER *Innsbruck*

We are ever indebted to the following distinguished numismatists whose valuable assistance helped make possible the first and second editions of "Gold Coins of the World": —

L. M. BJORKQUIST *Stockholm*
EMILE BOURGEY *Paris*
ERICH and HERBERT A. CAHN *Basel*
HENRY CHRISTENSEN *Hoboken*
MAURICE GRENIER-LA FOREX *Paris*
LEONARD FORRER *Amsterdam*
KARL-LUDWIG GRABOW *Berlin*
HENRY GRUNTHAL *New York*
MORTIMER HAMMEL *New York*
HANS HOLZER *New York*
ERNST KRAUS *New York*
MARK M. SALTON-SCHLESSINGER *New York*
SIGMUND WERKNER *Innsbruck*

and to

THE AMERICAN NUMISMATIC SOCIETY OF NEW YORK
for use of their library

THE BRITISH MUSEUM *for furnishing certain illustrations*

CONTENTS

CONTENTS

PREFACE

INTRODUCTION TO GOLD COINS

The collecting of gold coins seems to have become a part of mankind almost since the first gold coins were struck by the ancient Greeks about 700 B.C.

Since then, gold coins have been struck by almost every government that has come into existence. The term government as used here, is an extension of any coining authority—permanent or provisional, secular or ecclesiastical, national or local, republican or royal.

Formidable quantities of gold coins have thus been struck over the centuries, and fortunately many have survived to enrich the culture of our times and provide the numismatist with a lifetime of pleasure and study.

That so many gold coins have survived since ancient times —generally in a choice state of preservation—is no accident, and can be attributed to the nature of gold itself as a metal and then to the love of mankind for the metal.

The chemical and physical properties of gold are too well known to require elaboration here. For the numismatist, however, it is important to remember that gold was selected as the supreme coinage because its rarity made it precious, because its color is unique and because its lustre will last forever. Gold coins which have been buried or otherwise secreted for hundreds or even for 2000 years, when finally discovered, were found to be in the same brilliant and untarnished condition as when they were first hidden.

It is this age-old tendency for gold to go underground that continually results in the unexpected discovery of new, unpublished coins, some of which may cast important light on a personage or place otherwise unknown or beclouded in history.

Mankind has learned to love the metal for good reason. His bitter experience has shown that in the face of war, invasion, revolution, panic, inflation, or other economic disaster, the gold coin, small as it is in size, has alone survived as the symbol of security when all other familiar standards of value have fallen in the general ruin.

Knowing this, the peoples of the world have developed an especial reverence for the gold coin, always preserving it, never melting it and in the face of any danger, hiding it. Sometimes, the original owners did not or could not reclaim their treasure and the coins have been lost to the world until accidentally exposed many years later, by a plough share, or a surging tide or by dynamite.

Even today the wealth of nations is measured in terms of gold, and since this is so, and to demonstrate how little the long history of gold has really changed, it will be noted that the governments of the world, as in the past, have hidden their monetary gold underground, where it is carefully kept in the safe control of their Central Banks,

under permanent armed guard and protected by the latest devices against theft, burglary or assault, and by heavy construction against all forms of disaster.

Although the literature of numismatics is extensive, there are no books in existence devoted to gold coins of the world as a class by themselves. Considering the passionate interest in gold coins, the author has found this condition remarkable. Having been a professional numismatist for most of his adult life, the author, as well as many thousands of other numismatists the world over, has sorely regretted the lack of such a book in the literature of numismatics.

In order to get a reference on any gold coin struck before the 20th century, it was necessary to hunt out the standard work (if it existed) on the country involved, which work, of course, was devoted also to silver and minor coins. Obviously, there are many hundreds of such books; most of them are printed in a foreign language and are out of print; many of them are rare and valuable and simply unobtainable.

It was thus a formidable undertaking looking up, or looking for, earlier issues of gold coins of the world, requiring special facilities or outside research assistance or many hours of tedious, and sometimes fruitless labors in the library.

The author had long dreamed of improving this condition by creating a single volume to encompass the entire gold coinage of the world, excluding ancient coins and coins of the Byzantine Empire. It seemed grandiose at first and impossible of ever bringing about, because of the colossal amount of coins to be found in 1300 years of coinage.

However, some preliminary calculations showed that with a certain economy of format, it would be possible to create a single, moderate size volume without sacrificing any vital information or the all-important illustrations.

Therefore, drawing on his own experience, and that of the valued contributors, the author spent over five years in gathering and collecting the information for this book which was first published in 1958.

THE SCOPE OF "GOLD COINS OF THE WORLD"

This book concerns itself with the gold coinage of the world that began when the coinage of antiquity ended and following the age of nomadic invasion, when new governments with recognizable names came into existence. The aim has been to start the coin issues of each place with the first distinctive coins that positively identify the place as we know its name today, thus making the coinage truly national in character; having determined the starting point for each place, the coinage has been treated chronologically until it comes to its natural end by the suspension of gold coinage of the particular place. Some of the issues continue up to the present time.

The earliest coins listed in this book are the Axumite issues of Ethiopia of about 300 A.D. Of the European issues the earliest coins are from around 600 A.D. and minted for the Italian city of Beneventum. Among the coins of the Western Hemisphere the earliest issues are the Spanish Colonial pieces of Colombia, about 1621.

THE GEOGRAPHY OF THIS BOOK

The proper national placement of certain place-names, which sometimes posed a dilemma, has been solved by arbitrarily focusing on a period of time best known to the present generation. The period between the two World Wars has thus been selected, (and 1937 as a normal year of that period), as a point of reference for the geo-political boundaries of the world. Therefore, the coins of a country in existence in 1937 have been listed under the name of that country, even though the coins may have been struck much earlier under foreign suzerainty.

Certain innovations have thus been made, as under this rule, the coinage of countries like Esthonia or Latvia are listed under their own names, rather than as a Swedish coinage, which is consistent, for example, with the traditional listing of Spanish-American coins under their American names, rather than under Spain.

The countries are arranged alphabetically. Under some of the countries — for example, Germany — a separate heading has been given to a state, principality, duchy or city that issued its own coinage. The index at the end of the book will be helpful in finding any locality which issued coins.

THE DESCRIPTIONS AND DATES

Every type of coin that falls within the scope of this book, and which the author could find, has been listed and described. The obverse of the coin is always described first. The description is followed by the various denominations and dates of that particular type. The use of a name only in the description indicates a standing figure. Otherwise, head, bust, etc. are used.

Coins without dates are followed by ND. In general, when a coin has from one to about four dates, all the dates have been listed; otherwise the first and last dates only have been used, but all years may not necessarily exist between these ultimate dates.

The author will be grateful for any omissions which are called to his attention, so that the coins can be included in future editions of this book.

THE ILLUSTRATIONS

About one half of the space in this book is devoted to the illustrations of the coins which are shown in actual size. At great additional expense, they have been incorporated within the text, where they belong, rather than at the end of the book as a separate section of plates. The description of the illustration is immediately below it.

An asterisk (*) alongside the denomination and date indicates that this is the coin illustrated above the description. In case there is only one denomination for the type of coin being illustrated, no asterisk has been used.

A variety of sizes of illustrations has purposely been used, as this will help to identify the denominations of those coins which are without the mark of value.

Most types from the very beginning have been illustrated — certainly since about 1700, the illustrations are virtually complete for all types. There are more than 2800 illustrations of gold coins in this book — more than have ever been illustrated in any one coin book of comparable size, and the author believes that almost all coins of general familiarity to numismatists have been shown.

THE VALUATIONS AND STATE OF PRESERVATION

The author publishes the valuations as a general guide to the value of the coins on the numismatic market. No one by himself can profess to know the numismatic value of every gold coin that has ever been struck. Hence, voluminous sales records have been consulted. These have been used in conjunction with the author's twenty years of experience in professional numismatics combined with the accumulated experience of the contributors, and it is believed that the present valuations reflect the true rarity, condition, demand and availability of the coins as of this printing.

These valuations represent an approximate figure at which the coins would change hands as between a well informed buyer and a well informed professional numismatist. They are based on recent sales records or are an extension into the present time of old sales records.

The valuation of rarities has been especially difficult because the coins have appeared so seldom. In some cases, they have not been valued at all and have been merely marked "rare." In other cases, the valuation has been determined by comparison of the coin with the known value of another coin of equal rarity or other similar attributes.

In any case, the valuation of a great rarity must be considered as purely nominal and at best can be an indication only that the coin is of extraordinary value. The author's experience in modern times has shown that when a great rarity has been put on the numismatic market, it has always tended to exceed its last known price because of an ever increasing demand for such coins.

In general, the numismatic value of a coin is determined partly by condition, partly by rarity and almost always by the inexorable law of supply and demand, which might sometimes cause a great divergence from the valuations in this book.

These valuations are for the average condition in which the coin is most frequently encountered, and for the commonest date or variety of the type. Coins in a superior condition or with rarer dates would command a higher price. In general, experience has shown that these average conditions are as follows:

For coins up to about 1800, the valuations are for fine specimens.

For coins from about 1800 to 1914, the valuations are for very fine specimens.

For coins from about 1914 to date, the valuations are for uncirculated (mint state) specimens or for choice specimens showing hardly any wear.

For coins marked "not placed in circulation," the valuations are for uncirculated or proof specimens.

Overseas readers would do well to consult the Foreign Exchange Table in the appendix, in relation to the valuations which are quoted in U. S. dollars.

PATTERNS, PROOFS, UNOFFICIAL ISSUES AND OFF-STRIKES

The author has attempted to include in the book all manner of gold coins which from time to time appear among numismatists. Among such coins are the fascinating series of patterns, proofs and essais. **These have been designated by the general term "not placed in circulation."** They are legitimate Government Mint issues and are among the rarest and most prized of gold coins, almost always appearing in proof condition.

Other coins have been plainly labelled as unofficially or privately made. These are not the official coins of any government and such coins have been manufactured exclusively for collectors, or for use in the gold markets of the world.

The question of including off-strikes in this book has posed a seemingly insoluble problem. (An off-strike is regarded as a coin struck in gold from the same die used to strike a non-gold coin). Off-strikes are generally the larger pieces of ducat coinage — from 3 Ducats up. Depending on what series was involved, they have sometimes been included, other times not, in keeping with traditional usage.

There is still no unanimity of opinion among numismatists whether to regard as legitimate, a gold coin weighing exactly what a 10 Ducat piece should weigh, but not bearing a mark of value and struck from the same die used to strike a silver Taler, similarly without the mark of value. Since most early gold coins are without the mark of value in any case (their true face value being their weight and purity), the question seems academic.

A BRIEF HISTORY OF THE LATIN MONETARY UNION

The Latin Monetary Union, which had a world-wide influence on the minting of gold coins, was formed in 1865 by France, Belgium, Italy and Switzerland. These countries were on a bimetallic monetary standard with a ratio between silver and gold of 15.5 to 1. This ratio was established by France in 1803 and had been adopted by Belgium, Italy and Switzerland for their coinage prior to forming the Union. Thus, the French monetary system was the predominating influence in the Union. The treaty provided that gold coins should continue to be struck with a fineness of .900 and that the denominations were to be of uniform weight and value.

Greece joined the Union in 1868. It, like the other

countries, had been minting gold coins on the French standard prior to becoming a member of the Union.

France, through the Union, attempted to establish a universal monetary system based on the French unit. Although France was not entirely successful in this endeavor, a number of non-member countries did base their gold coinage on the standards of the Latin Monetary Union. However, these countries retained their own monetary unit and struck the gold coins according to specified weight and fineness. For instance, the 20 Peso of Guatemala had the same value as the French 100 Franc coin.

The following countries struck gold coins based on the standards set by the Latin Monetary Union:

Albania	Peru
Argentina	Philippines
Belgium	Poland
Bulgaria	Roumania
Colombia	Russia
Finland	Salvador
France	San Marino
Greece	Serbia
Guatemala	Spain
Honduras	Switzerland
Italy	Tunis
Monaco	Venezuela
Montenegro	Yugoslavia

World War I had a serious effect on the currencies of many nations which resulted in the discontinuance of gold coins in these countries for several years. An aftermath of these difficulties was the final dissolvement of the Latin Monetary Union in 1926. Nevertheless, some countries struck gold coins after that date based on the weight and fineness established by the Union. Among these issues are coins of Liechtenstein, Luxembourg, Roumania and Switzerland.

ABBREVIATIONS USED IN THIS BOOK

ND for no date
mm for mint mark
Obv. for obverse
Rev. for reverse

R.F.
J.F.

Pour le Lecteur Français.

PREFACE

QUELQUES NOTES SUR LES MONNAIES D'OR

Il semble que la collection de pièces d'or fait partie de l'humanité dès que les premières monnaies d'or ont été frappées par les anciens grecs, vers l'an 700 av. J. C. environ.

Dès lors, des pièces d'or ont été frappées par presque tous les gouvernements qui virent le jour. Le terme de gouvernement, tel que nous l'employons ici, s'étend à toute autorité frappant de la monnaie, fût-elle permanente ou provisoire, séculaire ou éclésiastique, nationale ou locale, républicaine ou monarchique.

Des quantités énormes de pièces d'or ont ainsi été frappées au cours des siècles et heureusement un grand nombre

a été conservé pour enrichir la culture de notre époque et fournir au numismate une vie remplie de plaisir et d'étude.

Le fait que tant de pièces d'or ont survécu depuis les temps anciens, généralement dans un état de conservation excellent, n'est pas un accident, mais une consequence de la nature de l'or en tant que métal et de l'amour de l'humanité pour ce métal.

Les propriétés physiques et chimiques de l'or sont trop bien connues, elles ne seront plus traitées ici en profondeur. Pour le numismate il est toutefois important de se souvenir que l'or a été choisi comme métal suprême pour les monnaies, parce que sa rareté le rend précieux, parce que sa couleur est unique et parce que son lustre dure éternellement. Les pièces d'or qui furent enfouies sous terre ou cachées dans n'importe quel endroit pendant des siècles, même jusqu'à 2000 ans, se révélèrent enfin, lorsqu'on les découvrit, inaltérées dans leur condition, brillantes et non ternies, telles qu'on les avait cachées.

C'est cette vieille tendance de l'or à s'enfouir sous terre ce qui a pour résultat la découverte continuelle et inespérée de pièces nouvelles, inédites. Certaines d'entre elles peuvent jeter une lumière importante sur un personnage ou un endroit qui resterait sans cela inconnu ou embrumé dans le cours de l'histoire.

L'humanité a appris à aimer ce métal pour une bonne cause. L'expérience amère lui a montré qu'en face de la guerre, des invasions, des révolutions, de la panique, de l'inflation ou d'autres désastres économiques, la pièce d'or, toute petite qu'elle soit, n'est pas moins restéele seul symbole de la sécurité, alors que tous les autres standards de valeurs familiers se sont effondrés dans la ruine générale.

Sachant cela les peuples du monde entier ont développé une révérence spéciale pour la pièce d'or, la conservant toujours, refusant de la fondre, prêts à la cacher devant tout danger. Parfois les propriétaires ne voulaient ou ne pouvaient plus réclamer leur trésor et les pièces furent ainsi perdues et oubliées jusqu'à ce que, maintes années plus tard, elles aient été mises à jour par hasard, grâce au soc d'une charrue, au flot de la marée ou à la dynamite.

Aujourd'hui encore, la richesse des nations se mesure d'après la quantité d'or. Pour cette raison et afin de montrer combien la longue histoire de l'or a en réalité peu changé, on notera que les gouvernements du monde entier enfouissent aujourd'hui comme jadis leurs réserves d'or dans le sol. Il y reste conservé consciencieusement sous le contrôle sûr des Banques Centrales et des gardes permanents armés. On le protège avec les dispositifs les plus efficaces contre le vol, le cambriolage et l'attaque et par des constructions massives contre toute sorte de désastre.

Bien que la littérature numismatique soit abondante, il n'existe encore aucun livre consacré exclusivement aux monnaies d'or du monde entier. Etant donné l'ntérêt passionné pour ces pièces, l'auteur a trouvé cette situation pour le moins remarquable. Numismate professionnel pendant la plupart de sa vie, l'auteur, de même que des milliers d'autres numismates, a regretté vivement l'absence d'un tel livre dans littérature numismatique.

Afin d'obtenir des informations sur les pièces d'or frappées avant le 20ème siècle, il a fallu consulter les travaux standards (s'ils existaient) du pays en question. Ces travaux spécialisés, bien entendu, traitaient aussi les pièces d'argent et d'autres métaux. Il existent, évidement, de centaines de tels livres, la plupart écrits dans la langue du pays. L'édition en est très souvent épuisée et ils sont devenus rares et il est presque impossible de se les procurer.

C'était donc une entreprise formidable que de se mettre à étudier et à rechercher les émissions anciennes de monnaies d'or du monde entier. On avait besoin de privilèges spéciaux, d'assistants pour les recherches au dehors à part les longues heures de travail fastidieux et d'efforts parfois inutiles à la bibliothèque.

Depuis longtemps l'auteur rêvait d'améliorer cette situation en créant un seul volume qui comprendrait toutes les monnaies d'or du monde à l'exception des pièces antiques et de celles de tout l'empire byzantin. A première vue cette entreprise semblait prétentieuse et impossible à mener à bout, en vue de la quantité inouïe de pièces que l'on peut trouver au cours de 1300 ans.

Néanmoins quelques calculs préliminaires montrèrent qu'avec une certaine économie dans le format il serait pos-

sible de présenter un seul volume de dimensions modérées sans laisser de côté ni les renseignements essentiels, ni les illustrations très importantes.

Puisant dans sa propre expérience et dans celle de ses estimables collaborateurs, l'auteur a passé cinq années à réunir et sélectionner les renseignements pour ce volume, publié pour la première fois en 1958.

CADRE ET OBJET DE "PIÈCES D'OR DU MONDE"

Ce livre commence par les émissions de monnaies d'or à partir de la période des invasions nomades finissant l'antiquité, lorsque de nouveaux gouvernements avec de noms reconnaissables s'établirent. Le but livre était de commencer avec les toutes premières émissions distinctives de pièces de chaque endroit, qui identifient avec certitude chaque contrée telle que nous la connaissons aujourd'hui, ce qui donne à la monnaie un caractère vraiment national. Après avoir déterminé le point de départ pour chaque endroit, on a traité les monnaies dans l'ordre chronologique jusqu'à leur disparition naturelle par suspension de la frappe de monnaies en or en cet endroit particulier. Certaines émissions se poursuivent jusqu'à ce jour.

Les pièces les plus anciennes qui figurent dans ce livre sont les émissions Axumites d'Ethiopie de l'an 300 A.D. approximativement. Quant aux émissions européennes, les plus anciennes datent de l'an 600 A.D. environ; elles furent frappées pour la ville de Bénévent en Italie. Les premières monnaies de l'hémisphère occidental sont les pièces coloniales espagnoles de la Colombie, vers 1621.

LES DATES GÉOGRAPHIQUES DANS CE LIVRE

L'emplacement national correct de certains noms d'endroits problématiques a été fixée arbitrairement en tenant compte de la période la mieux connue par la génération actuelle. C'est ainsi que la période entre les deux guerres mondiales a été choisie (1937 étant considérée comme une année normale de cette période) comme point de référence des frontières géo-politiques du monde. En conséquence, les pièces d'un pays existant en 1937 ont été classées sous le nom de ce pays, bien que ces pièces auraient pu être frappées bien avant sous une suzeraineté étrangère.

On a fait quelques innovations suivant ce principe. C'est ainsi que les monnaies de pays tels que l'Esthonie ou la Lettonie sont classées sous leurs propres noms, et non parmi les monnaies suédoises, ce qui est cohérent, par exemple, avec le classement traditionnel des pièces hispano-américaines sous leurs noms américains et non sous la rubrique de l'Espagne.

Les pays se suivent dans l'ordre alphabéthique. Sous quelques rubriques—par exemple l'Allemagne—des en-têtes spéciaux introduisent chaque Etat, principauté, duché ou ville qui émit ses propres monnaies. L'index à la fin de ce livre servira à retrouver toute localité qui a frappé de la monnaie.

LES DESCRIPTIONS ET LES DATES

Chaque type de pièce que l'auteur a pu trouver et qui entre dans le cadre de ce livre, a été classé et décrit. Le côté face (Avers.) est toujours décrit en premier. La description est suivie des diverses dénominations et dates de ce type en particulier. Un nom seul dans la description indique un personnage debout. Autrement, on se sert des mots tête, buste, etc.

Les pièces sans date sont suivies de ND. En général, lorsqu'un même type a été émis avec une à quatre dates environ, on énumère toutes ces dates. Dans les autres cas on s'est servi de la première et de la dernière, mais toutes les années n'existent pas forcément entre ces dates mentionnées.

L'auteur sera reconnaissant de toute omission qui sera portée à son attention, de sorte que les pièces en question puissent figurer dans les éditions à venir.

LES ILLUSTRATIONS

A peu près la moitié de la capacité de ce livre a été consacrée aux illustrations des pièces représentées en grandeur naturelle. Avec de grands frais supplémentaires elles ont été incorporées dans le texte, au lieu de les placer à la fin du livre sous forme d'une section de planches séparées. La description de la monnaie suit immédiatement au-dessous de l'illustration.

Un astérisque (*) à côté de la dénomination et de la date indique qu'il s'agit de la pièce illustrée au-dessus de la description. Dans le cas où il y a seulement une dénomination pour le type de pièce illustré, on ne s'est pas servi d'astérisque.

Des illustrations de tailles différentes ont été utilisées à dessein, pour aider à identifier les dénominations des pièces sans marques de valeur.

Depuis le début la plupart des types se trouve illustré, et après 1700 environ, les illustrations sont virtuellement complètes pour tous les types. Il y a plus de 2800 illustrations de pièces d'or dans ce livre—plus qu'on n'a jamais représentées dans un seul volume numismatique de dimensions comparables, et l'auteur pense bien avoir publié presque toutes les pièces avec lesquelles les numismates sont généralement familiers.

LES ÉVALUATIONS ET L'ÉTAT DE CONSERVATION

L'auteur a mis les évaluations comme guide général pour la valeur des pièces sur le marché numismatique. Personne ne peut prétendre de connaître par lui tout seul la valeur numismatique de toutes les monnaies d'or qui ont été frappées. Par conséquent, des catalogues de vente ont été consultés. L'auteur s'en est servi ainsi que de l'expérience de ses collaborateurs, pour compléter sa propre expérience de 20 ans dans le domaine de la numismatique professionnelle. De cette manière ces évaluations donnent sans doute un tableau fidèle de la véritable rareté, de la condition, de la demande et des disponibilités des pièces à la date de la publication.

Ces évaluations veulent être approximatives et l'on suppose que les pièces sont échangées entre un acheteur et un numismate professionnel tous deux bien informés. Elles sont basées sur des actes de ventes récentes et représentent une mise à jour de vieux compte-rendus de ventes.

L'évaluation de pièces rares est particulierement difficile car de telles pièces n'apparaissent pas souvent sur le marché. Dans certains cas ces monnaies n'ont pas été évaluées du tout, on les a simplement étiquetées de "rare". Dans d'autre cas les évaluations ont été déterminées par comparaison avec la valeur connue d'une autre pièce de rareté égale ou qui présente des attributs similaires.

De toute manière, l'évaluation d'une pièce de grande rareté doit être considérée comme purement nominale et ne saurait être qu'une indication que la pièce est d'une valeur extraordinaire. L'expérience de l'auteur à l'époque actuelle a montrée que quand une pièce de grande rareté a été mise sur le marché, elle aura toujours la tendance à excéder son dernier prix connu car il y a une demande toujours croissante pour de telles pièces.

En général la valeur numismatique d'une pièce est déterminée d'une part par la condition, d'autre part par la rareté et presque toujours par la loi inexorable de l'offre et de la demande, ce qui peut causer parfois de larges divergences avec les évaluations de ce livre.

Ces évaluations s'entendent pour un état de conservation moyen et pour la date et la variété la plus commune de ce type. Des pièces de meilleure condition ou avec des dates plus rares demandent un prix plus élevé. La pratique a montré qu'en général ces conditions moyennes sont les suivantes:

Pour des pièces jusqu'a l'an 1800 environ les évaluations s'entendent pour des spécimens en bel état.

Pour des pièces allant de 1800 a 1914 environ, les évaluations s'entendent pour des spécimens en très bel état.

Pour des pièces allant de 1914 environ jusqu'à nos jours, les évaluations s'entendent pour des spécimens qui n'ont pas circulé (fleur de coin) ou pour des spécimens de choix qui n'ont guère circulé.

Pour des pièces marquées "non mises en circulation", les évaluations s'entendent pour des spécimens n'ayant pas circulé ou des spécimens d'épreuve (flan bruni).

Pour mieux s'informer sur les évaluations qui dans le livre sont données en dollars U.S., les lecteurs d'outre-mer voudront bien consulter la Foreign Exchange Table située dans l'appendice.

ESSAIS, ÉPREUVES, ÉMISSIONS NON-OFFICIELLES, FRAPPES HORS-SÉRIES

L'auteur a essayé de placer dans le livre toutes sortes de pièces d'or qui apparaissent de temps en temps chez les numismates. Parmi ces pièces figurent les séries fascinantes des épreuves et essais. **On les a designés avec le terme général "non mises en circulation".** Ce sont des émissions légitimes de la Monnaie du Gouvernement et elles comptent parmi les pièces d'or les plus rares et les plus recherchées, apparaissant presque toujours dans une condition exceptionnelle.

D'autres pièces ont été nettement reconnues non-officielles ou de facture privée. Aucun gouvernement n'a émis ces pièces officiellement. Elles ont été faites exclusivement pour les collectionneurs et pour les marchés mondiaux de l'or.

La question d'inclure les frappes hors-séries dans ce livre a posé un probleme qui semblait tout d'abord insoluble. (Une pièce hors-serie est une pièce en or frappée de la matrice qui avait été employée pour des monnaies d'autres métaux). Ces frappes sont généralement des multiples du ducat—3 ducats et plus. D'après les séries intéressées elles ont été parfois inclues et parfois exclues de la classification, suivant l'usage et la tradition.

L'opinion n'est pas toujours unanime parmi les numismates quand il s'agit de considérer comme légitime une pièce d'or qui pèse exactement 10 ducats sans toutefois porter aucune marque de valeur. Cette pièce a été frappée du même coin qui a servi pour frapper le taler d'argent, lui aussi sans marque de valeur. Etant donné que la plupart des pièces d'or ne portaient pas de marque de valeur (leur valeur réelle étant leur poids et leur pureté) la question semble purement académique.

BRÈVE HISTOIRE DE L'UNION MONÉTAIRE LATINE

L'Union Monétaire Latine qui a influencé la frappe de monnaies d'or à travers le monde a été formée en 1865 par la France, la Belgique, l'Italie et la Suisse. Ces pays basaient leur systeme monétaire bimetallique sur l'argent et l'or dans un rapport de 15.5 à 1. Ce rapport fut introduit en France en 1803 et l'Italie, la Suisse et la Belgique l'avaient adopté avant la fondation de l'Union. C'est pourquoi le système monétaire français a eu une influence prédominante dans l'Union. Le traité assurait la frappe de monnaies d'or dans une finesse de .900 demême que l'uniformité de la valeur et du poids de chaque dénomination.

La Grèce joignit l'Union en 1868. De même que les autres pays membres, la Grèce avait émis des monnaies d'or dans le standard français déjà avant de faire partie de l'Union.

En se servant de l'Union, la France tenta d'établir un système monétaire universel basé sur l'unité française. Elle n'a pas réussi entièrement à réaliser cette idée, pourtant de nombreux pays qui n'étaient pas membres adoptèrent le standard de l'Union Monétaire Latine comme base pour leurs monnaies d'or. Ces pays gardaient leur propre unité monétaire, mais ils frappèrent dorénavant les monnaies d'or d'après le poids et la finesse spécifiés. Par exemple, la pièce de 20 pesos de Guatemala avait la même valeur que celle de 100 francs français.

Les pays suivants ont frappé des monnaies d'or sur la base des standards fixés par l'Union Monétaire Latine:

Albanie	Monténégro
Argentine	Pérou
Belgique	Philippines
Bulgarie	Pologne
Colombie	Roumanie
Espagne	Russie
Finlande	Saint-Marin
France	Salvador
Grèce	Serbie
Guatemala	Suisse
Honduras	Tunisie
Italie	Vénézuela
Monaco	Yougoslavie

La première guerre mondiale a influencé profondément le système monétaire de bien de pays. Une discontinuité dans la frappe de monnaies d'or s'est manifestée dans ces pays pendant plusieurs années. Les difficultés se multiplièrent lorsque l'Union Monétaire Latine s'est effondrée en 1926. Pourtant après cette date quelques pays continuèrent à frapper des monnaies d'or en reconnaissant comme base le poids et la finesse fixés par l'Union. Parmi ces émissions se trouvent les pièces du Liechtenstein, du Luxembourg, de la Roumanie et de la Suisse.

ABRÉVIATIONS EMPLOYÉES DANS CE VOLUME
ND pour non daté
mm pour marque monétaire
Obv. pour côté face
Rev. pour revers

R.F.
J.F.

Für den deutschen Leser.

EINLEITUNG

EINFÜHRUNG ZU "GOLDMÜNZEN DER WELT"

Die ersten Goldmünzen wurden im 7. Jahrhundert vor Christus von den Griechen geprägt. Es hat wohl nicht lange gedauert, bis der Mensch begann, diese schönen und wertvollen Stücke zu sammeln.

Fast jede Regierung hat seither Goldmünzen geprägt. Der Begriff "Regierung" wird hier ausgedehnt auf jede Behörde, die Münzen prägen lässt, ob sie dauernd bestehe oder vorübergehend, ob sie weltlich sei oder geistlich, national oder regional, republikanisch oder königlich.

Riesige Mengen von Goldmünzen sind im Lauf der Jahrhunderte geschlagen worden, und glücklicherweise sind viele bis auf den heutigen Tag erhalten geblieben. Sie bereichern unsere Kultur und verschaffen dem Numismatiker ein Leben voll Freude und Arbeit.

Es ist kein Zufall, dass so viele Goldmünzen erhalten geblieben sind, im allgemeinen in ausgezeichnetem Zustand. Dies liegt an der unverwüstlichen Natur des Goldes und an der Liebe des Menschen zu diesem Metall. Es ist nicht nötig, sich hier mit den allgemein bekannten chemischen und physikalischen Eigenschaften des Goldes auseinander zu setzen. Der Numismatiker erinnere sich jedoch daran, dass das Gold als höchstgeschätzes Münzmaterial gewählt wurde, weil seine Seltenheit es wertvoll macht und seine Farbe und sein Glanz einzigartig sind. Goldmünzen können eingegraben, oder sonst auf irgendeine Weise versteckt während Jahrhunderten liegen oder sogar während 2000 und mehr Jahren: wenn sie entdeckt werden, glänzen sie makellos,

wie wenn sie eben erst versteckt worden wären.

Diese uralte Tendenz des Goldes, unter die Erde zu verschwinden, zeitigt immer wieder unerwartete Entdeckungen neuer, unveröffentlichter Münzen. Manche von ihnen werfen Licht auf eine historische Persönlichkeit oder eine historische Stätte, die sonst im Dunkel bleiben würden.

Die Menschen haben gelernt, das Metall zu lieben. Bittere Erfahrungen haben ihnen gezeigt, dass die kleinen Goldmünzen angesichts von Krieg, Invasion, Revolutionen, Panik, Inflation oder anderer wirtschaftlicher Katastrophen allein das Symbol der Sicherheit geblieben sind, wenn alle anden bekannten Wertbegriffe dem Ruin anheimfielen.

Weil sie das erkannten, haben die Völker der Welt gelernt, die Goldmünzen besonders zu verehren. Sie haben sie aufbewahrt, niemals eingeschmolzen und vor einer drohenden Gefahr versteckt. Manchmal haben die ursprünglichen Besitzer ihren Schatz nicht wieder gehoben oder konnten ihn nicht wieder in Besitz nehmen. Die Münzen waren dann für die Welt verloren, bis sie zufällig, nach vielen Jahren, von einer Pflugschar, einer Flutwelle oder durch Dynamit zum Vorschein gebracht wurden.

Auch heute noch wird der Wohlstand einer Nation an ihrem Goldbesitz gemessen. Dass dies so ist, beweist die Tatsache, dass die Regierungen, wie man das früher tat, ihr Münzgold unterirdisch verborgen halten, wo es sorgfältig unter der Kontrolle ihrer Zentralbanken aufbewahrt wird: es befindet sich unter der dauernden Obhut bewaffneter Wächter, geschützt durch alle Vorrichtungen gegen Diebstahl, Einbruch oder Ueberfall und durch solide Bauweise gegen alle Unglücksfälle. Dies alles zeigt, wie wenig sich eigentlich in der langen Geschichte des Goldes geändert hat.

Obwohl die numismatische Literatur gross ist, gibt es keine Bücher, welche die Goldmünzen der Welt als Gebiet für sich behandeln. Der Verfasser fand diesen Zustand angesichts des leidenschaftlichen Interesses an Goldmünzen merkwürdig. Er, der fast sein ganzes Leben lang ein berufsmässiger Numismatiker war, und viele tausende andere Numismatiker in der ganzen Welt haben das Fehlen eines solchen Buches in der numismatischen Literatur ausserordentlich bedauert. Um eine Auskunft über irgendeine Goldmünze zu erhalten, die vor dem zwanzigsten Jahrhundert geschlagen worden war, musste man das massgebende Werk des betreffenden Landes, falls ein solches existierte, ausfindig machen; dieses Buch war dann natürlich auch noch den Silbermünzen und dem Kleingeld gewidmet. Bekanntlich gibt es mehrere Hundert solcher Bücher; die meisten von ihnen sind in einer Fremdsprache geschrieben oder vergriffen. Viele von ihnen sind selten, wertvoll und nicht erhältlich. Es war also keine kleine Aufgabe, nach alten Büchern über Goldmünzen zu suchen und in ihnen die einschlägigen Stellen ausfindig zu machen. Oft erforderte diese Arbeit besondere Erlaubnisse oder Forschungsbeihilfen, sie zwang zu vielen Stunden von ermüdendem, oft erfolglosem Suchen in den Bibliotheken.

Der Verfasser träumte lange davon, diesem Umstand durch die Herausgabe eines einzigen Buches, welches die gesamten Goldmünzen der Welt — ausschliesslich der antiken und byzantinischen Münzen — umfassen sollte, Abhilfe zu schaffen. Dieses Unterfangen erschien zuerst vermessen, und, auch wegen der riesigen Menge von Münzen, die während 13 Jahrhunderten geschlagen worden waren, undurchführbar.

Die Vorbereitungen zeigten jedoch, dass es bei einer gewissen Sparsamkeit im Format möglich wäre, einen einzigen Band mässigen Ausmasses herauszubringen, ohne wesentliche Auskünfte oder wichtige Abbildungen zu opfern. Der Verfasser hat über fünf Jahre damit zugebracht, das Material für dieses Buch (1. Ausgabe 1958) zu sammeln und zu sichten.

DER INHALT DES WERKES "GOLDMÜNZEN DER WELT"

Dieses Buch befasst sich mit der Goldmünzenprägung der Welt vom Ende des Altertums an und folgt dann dem Zeitalter des Einbruchs der Nomaden, in dem neue Regierungen mit erkennbaren Namen entstanden. Dabei liess man die Münzprägung eines Ortes mit der ersten eindeutig von diesem Ort stammenden Münze beginnen, um so den nationalen und regionalen Charakter einer Münzserie deutlich zu machen. Innerhalb der Emission eines Ortes liess man die Münzen chronologisch aufeinander folgen, bis die betreffende Prägung eingestellt wurde. Einige Emissionen dauern bis heute an.

Die ältesten Münzen, die in diesem Buch aufgeführt werden, sind die axumitischen Prägungen vom Ende des 3. Jahrhunderts. Die ältesten europäischen Münzen wurden um 600 in der italienischen Stadt Benevent geprägt. Unter den Münzen der westlichen Hemisphäre sind die frühesten Prägungen die spanischen Kolonialmünzen von Kolumbien aus den Jahren um 1620.

DER GEOGRAPHISCHE BEREICH DES BUCHES

Es ist oft schwierig zu entscheiden, in welchem Land man einen Ort, der im Lauf der Geschichte ein oder mehrere Male die Herrschaft gewechselt hat, unterbringen soll. Man hat deshalb einen der heutigen Generation bekannten Zeitpunkt herausgegriffen, nämlich das Jahr 1937. Die geographische Lage in diesem Jahr wurde für die Zuteilung einzelner Orte an bestimmte Nationen massgebend.

In einigen Fällen ist man jedoch nicht nach diesem System verfahren. So wurden Estland und Lettland unter ihrem eigenen Namen aufgeführt und nicht unter Schweden, wie es auch üblich ist, die hispano-amerikanischen Münzen unter Amerika, und nicht unter Spanien, aufzuführen.

Die Länder sind alphabetisch geordnet. Bei einigen Ländern, zum Beispiel bei Deutschland, setzte man eine separate Ueberschrift für ein Land, ein Fürstentum, ein Herzogtum, eine Stadt, die eigene Münzen herausgaben. Das Verzeichnis am Schluss des Buches wird zum Auffinden jedes Ortes, der Münzen geprägt hat, gute Dienste leisten.

DIE BESCHREIBUNGEN UND DATEN

Jeder Münztypus, der in den Rahmen dieses Buches passt und der dem Verfasser bekannt ist, ist hier aufgeführt und beschrieben. Der Avers der Münze wird immer zuerst beschrieben. Der Beschreibung folgen die verschiedenen Werte und Daten des betreffenden Typs. Wenn in der Beschreibung von Figuren die Rede ist, sind stehende Figuren gemeint; andernfalls wird die Figur näher bezeichnet (Kopf, Büste usw.) Hinter undatierten Stücken steht der Vermerk "ND". Wenn eine Münze weniger als fünf Prägedaten aufweist, werden alle angegeben. Sind es mehr Daten, werden nur das erste und das letzte angegeben, was nicht heisst, dass alle dazwischen liegenden Jahre Prägedaten der betreffenden Münze sind. Der Autor ist dankbar für jeden Hinweis auf eine von diesem Buch noch nicht erfasste Münze, die in einer neuen Auflage aufgeführt werden kann.

DIE ABBILDUNGEN

Etwa die Hälfte des verfügbaren Raumes in diesem Buch ist den Abbildungen der Münzen in ihrer Originalgrösse gewidmet. Unter grossen Kosten wurden sie im Text, dort, wo sie hingehören, eingefügt. Ein separater Bildteil am Schluss des Buches konnte so umgangen werden. Die Beschreibung einer Münze befindet sich unmittelbar unter ihrer Abbildung. Ein Sternchen (*) neben Nennwert und Datum zeigt an, dass es sich in der Beschreibung um das abgebildete Stück handelt. Falls es von einer Münze nur einen Nennwert gibt, wird das Sternchen weggelassen.

Da die Münzen in ihrer Originalgrösse abgebildet sind, ist es möglich, den Wert der Stücke, die keine Angabe des Nennwertes aufweisen, ungefähr abzuschätzen.

Die meisten Münztypen, beginnend mit den ersten Prägungen, sind abgebildet. Von 1700 an sind alle Münztypen ausnahmslos abgebildet. Abbildungen von mehr als 2800 Goldmünzen sind in diesem Buch vereinigt. Das sind mehr, als je in einem Buch der gleichen Grössenordnung abgebildet wurden. Der Verfasser glaubt, dass fast alle Münzen, die dem Numismatiker im allgemeinen geläufig sind, auch im Bild gezeigt wurden.

BEWERTUNGEN UND ERHALTUNGSGRAD

Der Verfasser veröffentlicht die Schätzwerte als allgemeine Anleitung für den Wert der Münzen auf dem numismatischen Markt. Niemand kann behaupten, den numismatischen Wert jeder einzelnen Münze, die je geschlagen wurde, zu kennen. Aus diesem Grunde wurden umfangreiche Auktionsergebnisse zu Rate gezogen. Die Auswertung dieser Unterlagen und die zwanzigjährige berufsnumismatische Erfahrung des Verfassers und seiner Mitarbeiter erlaubten es, Schätzwerte, Seltenheit, Zustand, sowie Angebot und Nachfrage der einzelnen Stücke zu bestimmen und zwar nach dem derzeitigen Stand.

Diese Zahlen sind approximative Werte. Ungefähr zu diesen Preisen werden Münzen von Numismatikern angekauft. Sie basieren auf neueren Verkaufsverzeichnissen oder sind die Angleichungen alter Verkaufsergebnisse an den heutigen Stand.

Die Bewertung von Raritäten war besonders schwierig, weil es für solche Münzen keine Bewertungsgrundlagen gibt. In einigen Fällen konnten sie überhaupt nicht bewertet werden; die Stücke wurden dann nur mit "selten" bezeichnet. In anden Fällen bestimmte man den Wert einer Münze durch den Vergleich mit einer ähnlich seltenen oder ähnlich kostbaren Münze. Auf alle Fälle können die Schätzungen der seltenen Stücke nur als grobe Richtlinien gelten. Der Verfasser weiss aus Erfahrung, dass solche Raritäten, wenn sie einmal auf den Markt kommen, oft enorm hohe Preise erzielen, weil eine ständig wachsende Nachfrage danach besteht.

Im allgemeinen wird der Wert einer Münze teils durch ihren Zustand, teils durch ihre Seltenheit und meistens durch das unerbittliche Gesetz von Angebot und Nachfrage bestimmt. Letzteres ist der Grund für grössere Abweichungen der erzielten Preise von den Schätzungen in diesem Buch. **Diese Schätzungen gelten für Münzen in einem durchschnittlichen Erhaltungsgrad, so wie man ihnen am häufigsten begegnet, und zwar für das häufigste Datum und den gebräuchlichsten Typ.** Münzen von besserem Erhaltungsgrad und von seltenerem Datum würden einen höheren Preis erzielen. Erfahrungsgemäss gelten folgende Erhaltungsgrade als durchschnittlich:

Für Münzen bis 1800: der Grad "schön".

Für Münzen ungefähr von 1800 bis 1914: der Grad "sehr schön".

Von 1914 an: ungebrauchte Stücke oder solche, die kaum Abnützungsspuren aufweisen.

Die Bezeichnung "nicht im Umlauf befindlich" bezieht sich auch auf Stücke von polierter Platte.

Ausländischen Lesern gibt die Tabelle der Wechselkurse Auskunft über das Verhältnis der verschiedenen Währungen zueinander.

PROBESTÜCKE, STÜCKE VON POLIERTER PLATTE, UNOFFIZIELLE PRÄGUNGEN UND ABSCHLÄGE

Der Verfasser hat versucht, in diesem Buch alle Goldmünzen zu besprechen, die von Zeit zu Zeit bei einem Numismatiker auftauchen. Dazu gehören auch die attraktiven Serien der Proben und Stücke von polierter Platte. **Diese sind mit dem allgemeinen Begriff "nicht in Umlauf gesetzt" gekennzeichnet.** Es sind gesetzliche, ungebrauchte Regierungsausgaben; sie gehören zu den am meisten geschätzten und seltensten Goldmünzen.

Andere Münzen sind einfach als nicht offizielle oder als privat hergestellte Stücke bezeichnet. Sie sind keine offiziellen Münzen irgendeiner Regierung und sind ausschliesslich für Sammler oder zum Gebrauch auf Weltgoldmärkten hergestellt worden.

Ein Problem bildete die Frage, ob man Abschläge in dieses Buch aufnehmen sollte oder nicht. (Als Abschlag bezeichnet man eine Goldmünze, die mit einem Nicht-Goldmünzenstempel geprägt wurde.) Abschläge sind im allgemeinen die grösseren Stücke der Dukaten-Münzprägung, von 3 Dukaten an aufwärts. Je nach Tradition wurden sie manchmal als gängige Münzen aufgefasst, manchmal nicht.

Die Numismatiker sind sich noch immer nicht einig, ob eine Goldmünze vom Gewicht eines 10 Dukaten-Stückes,

ohne Nominalwert und mit dem Stempel eines Silbertalers geprägt, gesetzliches Zahlungsmittel ist oder nicht. Da die meisten frühen Goldmünzen sowieso ohne Wertbezeichnung sind (ihr Nominalwert resultiert aus ihrem Gewicht und ihrer Feinheit), ist dies eine rein akademische Frage.

KURZE GESCHICHTE DER LATEINISCHEN MÜNZUNION

Die lateinische Münzunion, die einen weltweiten Einfluss auf die Goldmünzprägung hatte, wurde 1865 von Frankreich, Belgien, Italien und der Schweiz gegründet. Diese Länder hatten ihre Währung auf einem Zweimetallsystem aufgebaut, wobei Gold und Silber wertmässig in einem Verhältnis 1:15,5 standen. Dieses Verhältnis war 1803 von Frankreich festgesetzt worden und von Belgien, Italien und der Schweiz schon vor der Gründung der Union übernommen worden. Der Einfluss Frankreichs auf die Union war somit vorherrschend. Der Vertrag der Union sah vor, dass die Goldmünzen, in eine Feinheit von .900 geprägt werden sollten und dass die Wertbezeichnungen einheitlichen Werten und Gewichten entsprechen sollten.

Griechenland trat der Union 1868 bei. Wie andere Länder hatte es auch Gold nach der französischen Norm geprägt, schon bevor es Mitglied der Union wurde.

Frankreich versuchte mit Hilfe der Union, ein auf der französischen Einheit basierendes, universales Münzsystem durchzusetzen. Obwohl Frankreich dies nicht ganz gelang, richteten doch viele Länder ihre Goldmünzprägungen nach den Abmachungen der Lateinischen Münzunion. Dennoch behielten diese Länder ihre eigenen Münzeinheiten bei und prägten ihr Gold nach dem festgesetzten Gewicht und Feinheit. Das 20 Peso-Stück von Guatemala, zum Beispiel, hatte den gleichen Wert wie das französische 100 Franken-Stück.

Die folgenden Länder prägten ihre Goldmünzen nach dem von der Lateinischen Münzunion eingeführten System:

Albanien	Montenegro
Argentinien	Peru
Belgien	Philippinen
Bulgarien	Polen
Finnland	Rumänien
Frankreich	Russland
Griechenland	Salvador
Guatemala	San Marino
Honduras	Schweiz
Italien	Serbien
Jugoslavien	Spanien
Kolumbien	Tunesien
Monaco	Venezuela

Die Auswirkungen des ersten Weltkrieges verursachten in manchen Ländern eine Unterbrechung der Goldmünzprägung von mehreren Jahren. Ein Nachspiel dieser Schweirigkeiten war schliesslich die Auflösung der Lateinischen Münzunion im Jahre 1926. Trotzdem gab es immer noch Länder, die nach diesem Zeitpunkt Goldmünzen mit Gewicht und Feinheit gemäss den Abmachungen der Union herausgaben. Darunter sind Münzen von Liechtenstein, Luxemburg, Rumänien und der Schweiz zu zählen.

ABKÜRZUNGEN

ND für ohne Jahr
mm für Münzkennzeichen
Obv. für Vorderseite
Rev. für Rückseite

R.F.
J.F.

PREFAZIONE

INTRODUZIONE ALLE MONETE AUREE

Raccogliere monete auree sembra sia stata una passione dell'uomo sin da quando le prime monete d'oro furono coniate dagli antichi greci, verso il 700 avanti Cristo.

Da allora, monete auree sono state coniate da quasi tutti i governi esistiti. Il termine governo, nel significato qui attribuitogli, si intende esteso ad ogni autorità che coniò monete, permanente o provvisoria, laica o ecclesiastica, nazionale o locale, repubblicana o monarchica.

Immense quantità di monete auree sono state così coniate attraverso i secoli. Fortunatamente molte sono a noi pervenute, contribuendo ad arricchire la cultura dei tempi odierni e fornendo al numismatico infinite possibilità di piacere e di studio.

Non è certo per caso che tante monete auree siano giunte fino a noi dai tempi antichi, generalmente in ottimo stato di conservazione. Ciò è dovuto alla natura dell'oro stesso ed all'amore dell'umanità per questo metallo.

Le proprietà fisiche e chimiche dell'oro sono troppo ben conosciute per essere qui ricordate. Per quanto riguarda la numismatica, è necessario ricordare che l'oro fu scelto come massimo simbolo monetario per il fatto che la sua rarità lo rese prezioso, per il suo colore singolare e per il suo splendore eterno.

Monete auree che furono sotterrate od altrimenti occultate per centinaia o migliaia di anni, quando furono ritrovate, erano ancora nelle identiche condizioni di quando furono nascoste.

E dobbiamo a questa vecchia tendenza dell'uomo a tesaurizzare, se continuamente abbiamo notizie di nuove, sconosciute monete, le quali in alcuni casi possono fornire importanti ragguagli su personaggi o luoghi altrimenti sconosciuti o avvolti nelle nebbie della storia.

L'uomo ha appreso ad amare l'oro per buone ragioni. La propria amara esperienza gli ha dimostrato che, di fronte alle guerre, invasioni, rivoluzioni, inflazioni o altri disastri economici, la moneta aurea, per quante piccole dimensioni possa avere, è sopravvissuta, unica, come simbolo di sicurezza, quanto tutti gli altri valori consueti erano trascinati nella rovina generale. Per questo motivo l'uomo ha sempre tenuto in speciale considerazione le monete auree, conservandole sempre, occultandole di fronte al pericolo, quasi mai fondendole. A volte, i possessori originari non vollero o non poterono reclamare i tesori che avevano nascosti e le monete furono sottratte alla circolazione, finché dopo molti anni vennero accidentalmente alla luce, per l'opera di un' aratro, di una marea, di un'alluvione o della dinamite.

Anche oggi la ricchezza di una nazione si misura in termini di oro, e per dimostrare quanto poco sia mutevole la storia di questo metallo sarà bene ricordare che i governi hanno, come nel passato sempre provveduto a cautelare le loro riserve auree nel sottosuolo, dove sono ben custodite sotto il controllo delle loro Banche Centrali, da guardie armate in permanenza e protette dagli ultimi ritrovati contro il furto, lo scasso a la rapina e da strutture resistenti ad ogni forma di disastro.

Sebbene le opere di letteratura numismatica siano innumerevoli, non esistono attualmente libri che si occupino delle monete di oro, come di una categoria a se stante.

Considerato il grande interesse delle emissioni auree, l'au-

tore ha trovato ciò alquanto sorprendente. Egli, numismatico professionista da molti anni, ha come migliaia di numismatici in tutto il mondo sentito la mancanza di tale opera nella letteratura numismatica. Per cercare un riferimento su una moneta d'oro coniata prima del 20mo secolo, era necessario trovare la letteratura esistente—se c'era—del paese in questione, la qual letteratura ovviamente era dedicata anche alle monete d'argento e di altri metalli. Come tutti sanno vi sono centinaia di tali libri; la maggior parte pubblicati in lingue straniere. Molti sono esauriti e perciò di grande valore e in alcuni casi introvabili. Pertanto lo studio delle emissioni auree si presentava compito alquanto arduo, e richiedeva mezzi speciali di ricerca o assistenza e molte ore di tedioso, spesso improduttivo lavoro di biblioteca.

L'autore rifletté a lungo sulla possibilità di migliorare tali condizioni creando un unico volume che comprendesse la totalità delle monete auree del mondo intero, eccezion fatta per quelle antiche greche e romane e per quelle bizantine.

Ciò sembrò a prima vista un progetto ambizioso, impossibile a realizzarsi, considerato l'enorme numero di monete coniate durante il periodo in esame.

Tuttavia calcoli preliminari dimostrarono che con una certa economia di formato, sarebbe stato possibile creare un solo volume, di dimensioni normali, senza sacrificare alcuna informazione vitale o le importantissime illustrazioni.

Attingendo alla propria esperienza, nonché a quella dei suoi stimati collaboratori, l'autore spese oltre cinquè anni per raccogliere tutti i dati necessari per questo libro, la cui prima edizione fu pubblicata nel 1958.

LO SCOPO DI "LE MONETE AUREE DEL MONDO"

Questo libro tratta le emissioni monetarie auree di tutto il mondo dalla caduta dell'Impero Romano di Occidente, escludendo quelle dell'Impero di Bisanzio e quelle dei popoli nomadi. Cioè da quando stati, dai nomi ben definiti, apparvero alla ribalta della scena mondiale. Scopo del libro è di prendere in considerazione le monete dei vari luoghi di emissione, catalogandole sotto il nome usato oggi per identificare tali luoghi. Determinata l'epoca di inizio per ciascuna zecca, le emissioni sono elencate in ordine cronologico, fino alla fine della coniazione dell'oro nella zecca stessa.

Le monete più antiche elencate in questo libro sono quelle di Axum (Etiopia) risalenti a circa il 300 dopo Cristo. Le più antiche fra quelle europee risalgono a circa il 600 dopo Cristo, e sono quelle coniate nella città italiana di Benevento. Tra le monete del continente americano, le più antiche qui elencate sono i pezzi coloniali della Colombia risalenti a circa il 1621.

CONSIDERAZIONI GEOGRAFICHE DEL PRESENTE VOLUME

I mutamenti geopolitici verificatisi nel corso dei secoli, hanno sollevato un notevole problema per l'esatto inquadramento geografico di talune zecche nel quadro di qualche nazione. Questo problema è stato risolto col fissare arbitrariamente un periodo di tempo ben conosciuto alla generazione presente. Si è quindi scelto il periodo tra le due guerre mondiali e il 1937 come punto di riferimento per i confini geopolitici del mondo. Perciò le monete di una nazione esistente nel 1937 sono state elencate sotto il nome di detta nazione, anche se quando furono coniate la nazione aveva un nome geografico differente. Secondo questa regola le monete di nazioni come l'Estonia o la Lituania, sono assegnate all'Estonia o alla Lituania, anziché di essere catalogate come monete svedesi. Così come tradizionalmente si usava per le monete ispano-americane che conservavano la loro denominazione nazionale invece di quella spagnola.

I Paesi sono elencati in ordine alfabetico. Sotto i titoli di alcuni Paesi—ad esempio la Germania—un capoverso a parte è stato dedicato ad uno Stato, Principato, Ducato, o Città che battè zecca propria. L'indice al termine del libro potrà servire a identificare ogni località che coniò moneta.

DESCRIZIONI E DATE

Tutti i tipi di monete che rientrino nella finalità dell'opera e che l'autore ha potuto trovare, sono stati elencati e descritti. Il diritto viene sempre descritto per primo. La descrizione è seguita dall'elenco dei valori e date riguardanti quel tipo particolare di moneta. Quando sulla moneta è rappresentata una figura stante questa viene descritta col solo nome, negli altri casi vengono indicati il busto, la testa ecc. Le monete senza data sono seguite da ND, quelle datate, quando il tipo non varia e si conoscono solo poche date, queste sono tutte elencate. Quando le date sono molte si riportano solo la prima e l'ultima. L'autore sarà grato a tutti coloro che segnaleranno le varie omissioni e gli errori, affinche possano essere incluse o corretti nelle future edizioni di questo libro.

LE ILLUSTRAZIONI

Circa la metà dello spazio di questo libro è dedicato alle illustrazioni delle monete, riprodotte a grandezza naturale. Nonostante una notevole spesa suppletiva, esse sono state incorporate nel testo, nei punti cui si riferiscono, anziché alla fine del libro. La descrizione delle illustrazioni è messa sotto la figura. L'asterisco che segue la denominazione e la data indica che la moneta è illustrata. Di proposito sono state usate illustrazioni di monete di varia grandezza per facilitare la identificazione di quelle prive di indicazione di valore. La maggior parte dei tipi sin dall'inizio dell'emissione è stato illustrato; dopo il 1700 circa, tutti i tipi sono riprodotti. Il volume comprende oltre 2800 fotografie, più di quante se ne trovino in un libro di simile argomento e formato corrispondente, e l'autore ritiene che quasi tutte le monete auree conosciute ai numismatici siano state raffigurate.

VALUTAZIONE E STATO DI CONSERVAZIONE

Per ogni moneta l'autore indica il prezzo di stima in dollari, secondo il mercato numismatico attuale. Sarebbe assurdo pretendere di conoscere il valore numismatico delle monete auree di tutti i tempi; per fornire delle valutazioni obiettive, sono stati consultati un'enorme numero di cataloghi e risultati di vendite all'asta. Questi dati sono stati usati congiuntamente alla lunga esperienza dell'autore e dei suoi collaboratori, e si ritiene che le valutazioni riportate riflettano esattamente l'andamento del mercato al momento della stampa e rappresentano il valore approssimativo di scambio tra un collezionista ben informato e un numismatico professionista. Quando mancavano riferimenti di prezzi attuali si sono aggiornati quelli di vendite passate.

La stima delle monete rare si è presentata molto difficile, in alcuni casi esse non sono state valutate affatto, ma definite semplicemente rare. In altri casi la stima è stata determinata comparando la moneta in questione col valore accettato di un'altra di pari rarità. La stima di un pezzo di grande rarità deve considerarsi puramente indicativa di un notevole valore. L'autore si è reso conto attraverso la sua esperienza che, quando una moneta di grande rarità è stata immessa sul mercato, il prezzo realizzato ha sempre superato l'ultimo prezzo conosciuto. Ciò è dovuto al fatto che la domanda per tali monete aumenta sempre.

Di regola il valore numismatico di una moneta è determinato in parte dallo stato di conservazione, in parte dalla rarità e quasi sempre dalla legge inesorabile della domanda e dell'offerta, che a volte può causare differenze apprezzabili con le valutazioni del presente volume.

Le valutazioni devono intendersi per monete in uno stato di conservazione normale e per i tipi e le date più comuni. Per monete di conservazione eccezionale o con date rare è giustificato un prezzo più alto. Il criterio adottato è stato il seguente:

Per monete fino al 1800 circa, le valutazioni si riferiscono ad esemplari di bella conservazione.

Per monete dal 1800 circa fino al 1914, le valutazioni si riferiscono ad esemplari di conservazione bellissima.

Per monete dal 1914 ad oggi, le valutazioni si riferiscono ad esemplari che non abbiano mai circolato o a pezzi scelti che non presentino usure.

Per monete indicate con la dizione "mai messe in circolazione" le valutazioni si riferiscono ad esemplari fior di conio o che siano fondo specchio.

Per comodità dei lettori stranieri in appendice si trova una tavola di comparazione tra le varie valute, questo perché, come si è detto prima, le valutazioni sono in dollari americani.

PROVE, FONDO SPECCHIO, EMISSIONI NON UFFICIALI E ANORMALI

L'autore ha cercato di includere nel testo ogni specie di monete auree che di tempo in tempo appaiano sul mercato. **Tra tali monete si trovano la serie affascinante delle "Prove" dei "Fondo specchio" e dei "Progetti", generalmente indicate col termine "Mai immesse in circolazione".** Devono essere considerate tra le più rare e pregiate e quasi sempre si trovano in perfetto stato di conservazione.

Altre monete sono state definite come emesse non ufficialmente, o privatamente, in quanto coniate esclusivamente per collezionisti o per uso nei mercati mondiali dell'oro.

L'includere i tipi a produzione anormale in questo volume ha creato un problema di ardua soluzione. (Esemplare di produzione anormale è considerata la moneta di oro battuta con un conio usato per monete di altro metallo). I numismatici non sono d'accordo se considerare ufficiale una moneta d'oro che pesi esattamente quanto un pezzo da 10 ducati, ma che non porti l'indicazione del proprio valore e che sia stata coniata con il conio usato per i talleri d'argento, ugualmente privo di indicazione di valore. Bisogna dire però che la maggior parte delle monete auree antiche non presenta l'indicazione del valore (essendo questo determinato dal peso e dalla purezza), la questione pertanto è puramente accademica.

BREVI CENNI SULL'UNIONE MONETARIA LATINA

L'Unione Monetaria Latina, che esercitò influenza mondiale nell' emissione delle monete auree, fu fondata nel 1865 dalla Francia, Belgio, Italia e Svizzera. Questi Paesi operavano in virtù di un sistema monetario bimetallico, con una proporzione tra argento ed oro di 15,5 a 1. Tale proporzione fu stabilita dalla Francia nel 1803, ed era stata adottata dal Belgio, Italia e Svizzera per le loro emissioni, anteriormente alla formazione dell'Unione. Quindi, il sistema monetario francese esercitava un'influenza predominante in seno all'Unione. Il trattato stabiliva che le monete auree continuassero a venir coniate con una purezza di 900 millesimi e che i nominali mantenessero peso e valore uniforme.

La Grecia aderì all'Unione nel 1868. Questo Paese, come le altre nazioni, aveva coniato monete auree in conformità al sistema francese ancor prima di divenire membro dell'Unione.

La Francia tentò di stabilire, a mezzo dell'Unione, un sistema monetario universale basato sull'unità francese. Sebbene la Francia non ottenesse un successo completo in questo campo, svariati Paesi non membri basarono le loro emissioni auree sul sistema vigente nell'Unione Monetaria Latina.

Comunque, questi Paesi mantennero le loro unità monetarie e coniarono le monete auree secondo peso e purezza specifici. Ad esempio, i 20 Pesos del Guatemala avevano lo stesso valore del pezzo da 100 Franchi francese.

I seguenti Paesi coniarono monete auree basate sul sistema adottato dall'Unione Monetaria Latina:

Albania	Monaco
Argentina	Montenegro
Belgio	Perù
Bulgaria	Polonia
Colombia	Romania
Filippine	Russia
Finlandia	San Marino
Francia	San Salvador
Grecia	Serbia
Guatemala	Spagna
Honduras	Svizzera
Italia	Tunisi
Iugoslavia	Venezuela

La prima guerra mondiale ebbe serie ripercussioni sui valori monetarii di molte nazioni, provocando l'interruzione dell'emissione di monete auree in questi Paesi per una durata di vari anni.

Queste difficoltà comportarono poi lo scioglimento definitivo dell'Unione Monetaria Latina, avvenuto nel 1926.

Ciononostante, alcuni Paesi coniarono monete auree anche dopo questa data, basandosi sul peso e purezza stabiliti dall'Unione. Tra queste emissioni si trovano le monete del Lichtenstein, Lussemburgo, Romania e Svizzera.

ABREVIAZIONI USATE NEL TESTO

ND — senza data
mm — segno di zecca
Obv. — diritto
Rev. — rovescio

R.F.
J.F.

Para el Lector de Habla Hispana.

PROLOGO

INTRODUCCION A MONEDAS DE ORO

El coleccionar monedas de oro pareciera haber interesado a la humanidad prácticamente desde que las primeras monedas fueron acuñadas por los griegos cerca de 700 años antes de Jesucristo. Desde entonces, casi todos los gobiernos que han existido, han acuñado monedas de oro. El término gobierno según se emplea aquí, se refiere a toda autoridad permanente o provisional, secular o eclesiástica, nacional o local, real o republicana encargada del cuño.

Cantidades formidables de monedas de oro han sido acuñadas a través de los siglos y afortunadamente muchas de ellas han sobrevivido enriqueciendo la cultura de nuestra época y proporcionando al numismático una fuente de estudio y placer permanentes.

No es en forma accidental que tantas monedas de oro han sobrevivido y llegado a nuestros días desde el fondo de los tiempos antiguos — generalmente en excelente estado de conservación — y esto puede atribuirse a la naturaleza del oro propiamente y al amor de la humanidad por este metal.

Las propiedades físicas y químicas del oro son bien conocidas y no vale la pena entrar en detalles sobre ellas en este artículo. Para el numismático sin embargo, es importante recordar que el oro fue seleccionado como el mejor material de cuño porque su escasez lo hacía precioso, porque su color es típico y porque su lustre y brillo son permanentes. Las monedas de oro que han sido enterradas u ocultadas por siglos y hasta por milenios, cuando son finalmente descubiertas se encuentran en la misma condición de brillo y lustre que tenían al ser escondidas.

Es esta vieja tendencia a enterrar el oro lo que resulta en inesperados descubrimientos de monedas nuevas y desconocidas, algunas de las cuales arrojan luz sobre algún sitio o personaje que de otra manera sería desconocido o permanecería envuelto en las nubes de la historia.

La humanidad ha aprendido a amar este metal por una buena razón: su amarga experiencia le ha demostrado que frente a guerras, invasiones, revoluciones, pánicos, inflación o cualquier otro desastre económico, la moneda de oro, pequeña como es en tamaño, ha sido única en sobrevivir como símbolo de seguridad cuando todos los otros estandards familiares de valores han sucumbido dentro de la ruina general.

Sabiendo ésto, los pueblos del mundo han desarrollado una especial reverencia por la moneda de oro, conservándola siempre, no fundiéndola y escondiéndola frente al peligro. Algunas veces, los dueños originales no pudieron reclamar o no reclamaron su tesoro y las monedas estuvieron perdidas para el mundo hasta que fueron accidentalmente expuestas muchos años después por un golpe de arado, una marea embravecida o una explosión de dinamita.

Aún hoy, la riqueza de las naciones se mide en términos de su oro, y ya que este es el caso y para demostrar lo poco que ha cambiado la larga historia del oro, llamamos la atención sobre el hecho de que los gobiernos del mundo en el pasado, han ocultado sus reservas de oro acuñado, bajo tierra, donde es cuidadosamente mantenido bajo el seguro control de sus Bancos Centrales, bajo permanente custodia armada y protegidos por las últimas novedades en aparatos preventores de robo o asalto así como por construcciones capaces de hacer frente a cualquier forma de desastre.

A pesar de que la literatura sobre numismática es extensa, no existen libros especiales sobre las monedas de oro en el mundo. Considerando el interés apasionado que existe sobre la materia, al autor le ha llamado mucho la atención este hecho. Habiendo sido un numismático profesional durante la mayor parte de su vida adulta, el autor, al igual que miles de otros numismáticos en el mundo entero, ha resentido, echando mucho de menos, la falta de un libro semejante en la literatura numismática.

Para poder obtener una referencia sobre cualquier moneda de oro acuñada antes del siglo veinte, era necesario ponerse a la búsqueda del material impreso estandard en el país de que se trataba, material que como es de suponer se refería también a monedas de plata y a otras monedas menores. Es obvio que existen cientos de estos libros, la mayor parte impresos en lenguas extranjeras y en ediciones agotadas; muchos constituyen ejemplares raros y valiosos y son inobtenibles.

Era por lo tanto una empresa formidable ponerse a buscar o consultar material de referencia sobre las monedas de oro en el mundo ya que ello requería facilidades especiales, asistencia de otros en las investigaciones o muchas horas de trabajo tedioso y muchas veces estéril, en las bibliotecas.

El autor había acariciado por mucho tiempo la idea de mejorar este estado de cosas con la creación de un solo volumen que abarcara en forma total la acuñación de moneda en el mundo, con excepción de lo referente a monedas antiguas y monedas del Imperio Bizantino. Esto parecía enorme al principio y de imposible realización a causa de la cantidad colosal de monedas encontradas en 1300 años de acuñación.

Sin embargo, algunos cálculos preliminares demostraron que con una cierta economía de formato sería posible crear un solo volumen de tamaño moderado sin sacrificar ninguna información vital ni las ilustraciones que son tan importantes.

Por lo tanto, usando la fuente de su propia experiencia y la de sus valiosos colaboradores, el autor dedicado alrededor de cinco años a la recolección y reunión de la información para este libro, que se publicó por primera vez en 1958.

LO QUE ABARCA "LAS MONEDAS DE ORO DEL MUNDO"

Este libro se refiere a la acuñación de oro en el mundo que comienza al terminar la acuñación de la antigüedad e inmediatamente después de la era de las invasiones nómadas, cuando comenzaron a existir nuevos gobiernos con nombres determinados. El propósito ha sido comenzar a catalogar las emisiones de moneda de cada lugar, con las primeras monedas distintivas que identifican positivamente el lugar al que damos hoy día un determinado nombre, haciendo la acuñación verdaderamente nacional en carácter. Habiendo establecido el punto de partida en el caso de cada sitio, la acuñación ha sido tratada cronológicamente hasta llegar a su fin natural por la suspensión de acuñamiento de oro en cada lugar en particular. Algunas de las emisiones llegan hasta el presente.

Las monedas más antiguas consignadas en este libro son las acuñadas por los Axumitas de Etiopía alrededor del año 300 D.C. Las primeras acuñaciones europeas fueron hechas alrededor del año 600 D.C., en la ciudad italiana de Beneventum. Las primeras monedas acuñadas en el Hemisferio Occidental son las de las colonias españolas emitidas en Colombia alrededor del año 1621.

LA GEOGRAFIA DE ESTE LIBRO

La apropiada ubicación nacional de ciertos nombres de lugares que muchas veces significaba un dilema, ha sido resuelta por medio del enfoque arbitrario sobre la época mejor conocida de la generación actual. El período entre las dos guerras ha sido seleccionado (y el año de 1937 como un año normal de ese período), como punto de referencia en lo que se refiere a los límites geopolíticos del mundo. Por lo tanto las monedas de un país en existencia en 1937 han sido incluídas bajo el nombre de ese país a pesar de que hayan sido acuñadas en épocas anteriores y bajo soberanía extranjera.

Algunas innovaciones han sido así llevadas a cabo ya que bajo este sistema la acuñacion de moneda de países como Estonia o Latvia aparece bajo su propio nombre en vez de aparecer como acuñación de Suecia, lo que es consistente por ejemplo con la forma tradicional de incluir las monedas hispanoamericanas bajo sus nombres americanos, en vez de incluirlas como acuñación de España. El índice geográfico en el libro ayudará a localizar cualquier acuñación.

Los países figuran por orden alfabético. Bajos algunos de ellos — como, por ejemplo, Alemania — se da un título aparte a algún estado, principado, ducado o ciudad que acuñó su propia moneda. El índice que figura al final del libro servirá de gran auxilio para hallar cualquier localidad que haya acuñado monedas.

DESCRIPCIONES Y FECHAS

Cada tipo de moneda que cae dentro de las categorías contempladas por este libro, y que el autor pudo encontrar, ha sido anotado y descrito. El anverso de la moneda siempre está descrito en primer lugar. Su descripción es seguida por las varias denominaciones y fechas de ese tipo en particular. El uso de un nombre solamente en la descripción, indica una figura de pie. De otra manera, son usadas las palabras cabeza, busto, etc.

Las monedas sin fecha van seguidas de las letras ND. Por lo general, cuando una moneda tiene de una a cuatro fechas, todas las fechas han sido anotadas; de lo contrario se habrán anotado solamente la primera y última fechas y ésto no querrá decir que existan todos los años comprendidos entre ambas.

En un trabajo de esta magnitud y complejidad y considerando que se trata de una primera edición, es inevitable que algunos tipos o denominaciones de monedas hayan escapado a la atención del autor y que no hayan sido anotados a pesar de lo dicho acerca de la total integridad del trabajo.

El autor agradecerá cualquiera de las omisiones que sea llevada a su atención de manera que las monedas en cuestión puedan ser incluídas en ediciones futuras de este libro.

LAS ILUSTRACIONES

Cerca de la mitad del espacio de este libro está dedicado a ilustraciones de las monedas, que son presentadas en tamaño natural. Con gasto adicional considerable han sido incorporadas dentro del texto, donde pertenecen, en vez de al final del libro como un conjunto de láminas adicionales. La descripción de las ilustraciones se encuentra al pie de las mismas.

Un asterisco (*) al lado de la denominación y la fecha indica que esta es la moneda ilustrada en el espacio anterior a la descripción. En el caso de que haya una sola denominación para el tipo de moneda que se ilustra, no se ha usado el asterisco.

Una variedad de tamaños ha sido usado a propósito para las ilustraciones ya que ésto ayudará a identificar la denominación de las monedas que carecen de la marca del valor.

La mayor parte de los tipos, aún los más antiguos, han sido ilustrados y ciertamente, después de 1700, las ilustraciones son virtualmente completas en todos los tipos. Este libro incluye más de 2800 ilustraciones de monedas de oro, más de las que han sido nunca ilustradas en ningún otro libro de tamaño comparable y el autor cree haber ilustrado casi todas las monedas con que está generalmente familiarizado el numismático.

LAS EVALUACIONES Y EL ESTADO DE CONSERVACION

El autor publica las evaluaciones como una guía general acerca del valor de las monedas en el mercado numismático. Nadie por sí mismo puede pretender conocer el valor numismático de cada moneda de oro que ha sido acuñada. Para presentar este trabajo se han consultado voluminosos registros de ventas. Estos han sido usados en conjunción con la experiencia de veinte años del autor, en numismática profesional, combinada con la experiencia acumulada de los colaboradores. El autor cree que las evaluaciones aquí presentadas reflejan la verdadera condición de curiosidad o rareza de la pieza, la condición, la demanda y la abundancia de las monedas hasta al imprimirse este libro.

Estas evaluaciones representan la cantidad aproximada en que las monedas cambiarían de mano entre un comprador bien informado y un numismático profesional. Están basadas en registros de ventas recientes o son una extensión dentro del tiempo presente de viejos registros de ventas.

La evaluación de piezas raras ha sido especialmente difícil porque las monedas han aparecido muy raras veces. En algunos casos no han sido evaluadas del todo y han sido marcadas simplemente "raras." En otros casos la evaluación ha sido determinada por comparación de la moneda con el valor conocido de otra moneda de igual rareza u otros atributos similares.

En todo caso, la evaluación de una verdadera rareza debe ser considerada como puramente nominal, y en el mejor de los casos puede ser solamente una indicación de que la moneda es de extraordinario valor. La experiencia del autor en los tiempos modernos le ha demostrado que cuando una verdadera rareza ha sido puesta en el mercado numismático, siempre ha tendido a exceder su último precio conocido a causa de la demanda siempre en aumento de esa clase de monedas.

En general el valor numismático de una moneda está determinado en parte por la condición, en parte por la rareza y casi siempre por la ley inexorable de la oferta y la demanda. Esta última puede a veces ser causa de gran divergencia entre los precios del momento y los anotados en este libro.

Estas evaluaciones se refieren a la condición corriente en que la moneda es más frecuentemente encontrada, y **para la más corriente fecha y variedad del tipo.** Las monedas en condición superior o con fechas más raras, exigirán un precio más elevado. En general la experiencia ha demostrado que estas condiciones corrientes son las siguientes:

Para monedas hasta cerca de 1800, las evaluaciones son para especímenes bien conservados.

Para monedas de cerca de 1800 a 1914, las evaluaciones son para especímenes muy bien conservados.

Para monedas de cerca de 1914, a esta fecha, las evaluaciones son para especímenes flor de cuño o para especímenes escogidos que casi no muestren señales, de desgaste.

Para monedas marcadas "no puestas en circulación," las evaluaciones son para "no circulante" o cospel bruñido.

Los lectores en el extranjero harían bien en consultar la Tabla de Cambio Extranjero en el apéndice, en relación con las evaluaciones que están cotizadas en dólares americanos.

ENSAYOS, PRUEBAS, EMISIONES NO OFICIALES Y ACUÑACIONES ESPECIALES

El autor ha intentado incluir en el libro toda clase de monedas de oro de las que de tiempo en tiempo aparecen entre los numismáticos. Entre esas monedas puede incluirse la fascinante serie de ensayos y pruebas. **Estas han sido designadas con el término general de "no puestas en circulación."** Son emisiones legítimas de las oficinas gubernamentales del cuño, y pueden contarse entre las más raras y más apreciadas monedas de oro. Aparecen casi siempre en la condición de cospel bruñido.

Otras monedas han sido simplemente marcadas como extraoficialmente o privadamente hechas. Estas no son monedas oficiales de ningún gobierno y han sido manufacturadas exclusivamente para coleccionistas o para uso en los mercados de oro del mundo.

La inclusión de acuñaciones especiales en este libro ha presentado un problema aparentemente insoluble. (Una acuñación especial es considerada como una moneda acuñada en oro de la misma matriz o cuño que se ha usado para acuñar una moneda de otro metal.) Las acuñaciones especiales son generalmente múltiplos de ducados, de 3 ducados en adelante. De acuerdo con el uso tradicional, unas veces han sido incluidas y otras no, según la serie de que se trate.

No hay unanimidad de opinión entre los numismáticos acerca de si debe considerarse como legítimo una moneda de oro que pese exactamente lo que debería pesar una moneda de 10 ducados pero que no lleve la marca del valor y acuñada con la misma matriz usada para un tálero de plata, igualmente sin la marca del valor. Dado que la mayor parte de las monedas de oro tempranas no llevan en ningún caso la marca del valor (siendo su valor facial el peso y la pureza), la cuestión resulta académica.

BREVE HISTORIA DE LA UNION MONETARIA LATINA

La Unión Monetaria Latina, que ha tenido influencia mundial en la acuñación de las monedas de oro, se formó en 1865 por Francia, Bélgica, Italia y Suiza. Estos países se hallaban bajo patrón monetario bimetálico, con una relación entre la plata y el oro de 15.5 a 1. Esta relación fue establecida por Francia en 1803, siendo después adoptada por Italia y Suiza para sus monedas antes de formarse la Unión. De esta manera, el sistema francés fue la influencia predominante en la Unión. El tratado dispuso que la acuñación de monedas de oro continuara con una ley de .900 y que las denominaciones debían tener el mismo peso y valor.

Grecia se adhirió a la Unión en 1868. Como los países ya en ella, había estado acuñando monedas bajo el sistema francés, antes de ser miembro de la Unión.

A través de la Unión, Francia intentó establecer un sistema monetario universal basado en la unidad francesa. Y aunque no triunfó por completo en su propósito, cierto número de países que no eran miembros de la Unión basaron sus monedas de oro en los tipos de la Unión Monetaria Latina. Sin embargo, estos países retuvieron su unidad monetaria propia y acuñaron sus monedas de acuerdo con peso y ley específicos. Por ejemplo, la moneda de 20 pesos de Guatemala tenía el mismo valor que la moneda francesa de 100 francos.

Los siguientes países acuñaron sus monedas de oro basados en los tipos establecidos por la Unión Monetaria Latina:

Albania	Italia
Argentina	Mónaco
Bélgica	Montenegro
Bulgaria	Perú
Colombia	Polonia
El Salvador	Rumanía
España	Rusia
Filipinas	San Marino
Finlandia	Serbia
Francia	Suiza
Grecia	Túnez
Guatemala	Venezuela
Honduras	Yugoeslavia

La Primera Guerra Mundial produjo un grave efecto sobre la circulación monetaria de varios países, los que discontinuaron las monedas de oro durante varios años. Resultado de estas dificultades fue, al fín, la disolución de la Unión Monetaria Latina en 1926. Sin embargo, algunos países acuñaron oro después de esa fecha basándose en el peso y la ley establecidos por la Unión. Entre estas acuñaciones se cuentan la de las monedas de Liechtenstein, Luxemburgo, Rumanía y Suiza.

ABREVIACIONES UTILIZADAS EN EL LIBRO

ND para sin fecha
mm para marca monetaria
Obv. para anverso
Rev. para reverso

R.F.
J.F.

GOLD COINS
of the WORLD

AFGHANISTAN

Prior to 1896, the type, style and workmanship of the coins were similar to those of Persia and the neighboring Indian states. The first modern style coins were the Dinars of 1896. This new denomination introduced for the first time the arms of Afghanistan, of which the dominant motif is the throne room.

Shahs of —

Seated Goddess. Rev. Legend. Struck during the period 1192-1300.

1. Stater ND 100.00

Arab legend on each side. Struck during the period 1725-1747 and with dates from about 1138-1160 A.H.

2. 2 Mohurs 225.00
3. 1 Mohur 100.00
4. ⅓ Mohur 45.00
5. ¼ Mohur 35.00

AHMED SHAH, 1747-1773
Arab legend on each side.

6. 1 Mohur 1160-86 A.H. (1747-72 A.D.) 100.00

TAIMUR SHAH, 1773-1793

Arab legend on each side.

7. 1 Mohur 1195-1209 A.H. (1780-94 A.D.) 100.00

ZAMAN SHAH, 1793-1801

Arab legend on each side. Struck by Dost Mohammed in the name of Zaman in 1835.

8. 3 Mohurs 1251 A.H. (1835 A.D.) ....*...... 500.00
9. 1 Mohur 1208-16 A.H. (1793-1801 A.D.) 200.00

MAHMUD SHAH, 1801-1829

Arab legend on each side.

10. 2 Mohurs 1217 A.H. (1802 A.D.) ....*...... 300.00
11. 1 Mohur 1217 A.H. (1802 A.D.) 100.00
12. 1 Dinar 1219 A.H. (1804 A.D.) 100.00

SHUJA SHAH, 1801, 1803-1809, 1839-1842

Arab legend on each side.

13. 2 Mohurs 1218 A.H. (1803 A.D.) 500.00
14. 1 Mohur 1223 A.H. (1808 A.D.) ....*...... 100.00

QUAISAR SHAH, 1803, 1807-1808
Arab legend on each side.

15. 1 Mohur 1218 A.H. (1803 A.D.) 300.00

AIYUB SHAH, 1818-1829
Arab legend on each side.

16. 1 Mohur 1238, 39 A.H. (1823, 24 A.D.) 200.00

SHER ALI, 1863-1866, 1868-1878

Arab legend on each side.

17. 1 Mohur 1285-88 A.H. (1868-71 A.D.) ....*...... 100.00
18. 1 Tilla 1283 A.H. (1866 A.D.) 80.00

ABDUR RAHMAN, 1880-1901

Arab legend on each side.

19. 1 Tilla 1298 A.H. (1880 A.D.) 80.00

Throne room. Rev. Toughra

19a. 1 Tilla 1313 A.H. (1895 A.D.) 250.00

Throne room. Rev. Toughra over crossed quivers.

20. 1 Dinar 1314, 16 A.H. (1896, 98 A.D.) 250.00

HABIBULLAH, 1901-1919

Throne room. Rev. Toughra over crossed quivers.

21. 1 Dinar 1319, 20 A.H. (1901, 02 A.D.) 150.00

AMANULLAH, 1919-1929

(The Afghanistan calendar was changed in 1920, when by Royal Decree, the corresponding A.H. year of 1338, was declared to be A.H. 1298).

Throne room in star. Rev. Legend in wreath.

22. 2 Amani 1298 A.H. (1920 A.D.) 135.00
23. 1 Amani 1337 A.H. (1919 A.D.). Swords below throne. 85.00
24. 1 Amani 1337 A.H. (1919 A.D.). Star below throne. *...... 85.00

Throne room in star. Rev. Toughra.

25. 5 Amani 1299 A.H. (1921 A.D.) ....*...... 750.00
26. 2 Amani 1299-1303 A.H. (1921-25 A.D.) 100.00
27. 1 Amani 1299 A.H. (1921 A.D.) 100.00
28. ½ Amani 1299 A.H. (1921 A.D.) ....*...... 60.00

Large plain throne room. Rev. Toughra.

29. 2½ Amani 1306 A.H. (1928 A.D.) 500.00
30. 1 Amani 1304-06 A.H. (1926-28 A.D.) ....*...... 75.00
31. ½ Amani 1304-06 A.H. (1926-28 A.D.) 60.00

HABIBULLAH GHAZI, 1929

(The name assumed by the Brigand Bacha-i-Saquao who held Kabul for nine months in 1929 but was captured and executed by Mohammed Nadir).

Throne room in star. Rev. Legend in wreath.

32. 30 Rupees 1347 A.H. (1929 A.D.) 500.00

MOHAMMED NADIR, 1929-1933
Large throne room. Rev. Toughra.

33. 20 Afghani 1347-50 A.H. (1929-32 A.D.) 500.00

ZAHIR SHAH, 1933—
Throne room. Rev. Inscription in wreath.

34. 1 Amani 1313 A.H. (1935 A.D.) 400.00
35. 1 Dinar or 8 Grams 1314 A.H. (1936 A.D.) 500.00
36. ½ Dinar or 4 Grams 1314 A.H. (1936 A.D.) 150.00

ALBANIA

Mints and mint marks:—R for Rome; V for Vienna. The 100 Franc pieces of 1928 and 1929 were unknown until about 1950. Albanian coinage is based on the Latin Monetary Union standard.

Presidents, and later, Kings of —

ZOG I, 1925-1939

Head with one, two or no stars below. Rev. Chariot.

1. 100 Francs 1926, 27 .... 300.00

Head. Rev. Eagle.

2. 20 Francs 1926, 27 .... 110.00
3. 10 Francs 1927 .... 100.00

Bust of Skanderbeg. Rev. Winged lion.

4. 20 Francs 1926. R mm. 100.00
5. 20 Francs 1926. Fasces mm. 150.00
6. 20 Francs 1927. V mm. ....*...... 90.00

Bare head to left. Rev. Eagle. Not placed in circulation.

7. 100 Francs 1928 .... 1250.00

Uniformed bust to right. Rev. Eagle. Not placed in circulation.

8. 100 Francs 1928 .... 1250.00

Bare head to left in wreath. Rev. Eagle. Not placed in circulation.

9. 100 Francs 1928 .... 1250.00

Bare head to left in wreath. Rev. Eagle with "Albania" added. Not placed in circulation.

10. 100 Francs 1929 .... 1250.00

Bare head. Rev. Arms and dates 1912-1937. On the 25th year of Independence.

11. 100 Francs 1937 .... 500.00
12. 20 Francs 1937 ....*...... 125.00

Bare head. Rev. Arms and date, "27. IV. 1938." On his wedding.

13. 100 Francs 1938 .... 450.00
14. 20 Francs 1938 ....*...... 115.00

Bare head. Rev. Arms and dates 1928-1938. On the 10th year
of his rule.

15.	100 Francs 1938	....	300.00
16.	50 Francs 1938	....	125.00
17.	20 Francs 1938	..........................*.....	100.00

ANNAM

The coins are dated in Annamese years. Most coins also exist in silver
and are struck from the same dies. This series maintains a great popularity in France.

Emperors of —
MING MANG, 1820-1841

Chinese legend on each side. Rectangular bars.

1.	100 Ounces (1833)	....	Rare
2.	50 Ounces (1837, 38)	....	Rare
3.	40 Ounces (1840), ND	....	Rare
4.	30 Ounces (1840)	....	Rare
5.	10 Ounces (1837)	....	3000.00
6.	5 Ounces (1837)	....	2000.00
7.	1 Ounce ND	....	500.00
8.	5/10 Ounce ND	..........................*.....	350.00
9.	4/10 Ounce ND	....	250.00
10.	3/10 Ounce ND	....	175.00
11.	2/10 Ounce ND	....	175.00
12.	1/10 Ounce ND	....	125.00

Four Chinese characters on each side around square central hole.

13.	½ Piastre ND	....	425.00

Four Chinese characters around radiant sun. Rev. Dragon.

14.	1 Piastre (1834)	....	800.00
15.	½ Piastre (1834)	..........................*.....	500.00

Four Chinese characters around radiant sun. Rev. Heavenly bodies.

16.	⅛ Piastre ND	....	150.00

Two vertical Chinese characters. Rev. Eight precious symbols.

17.	⅛ Piastre ND	....	225.00

Two vertical Chinese characters. Rev. Five precious symbols.

18.	⅛ Piastre ND	....	150.00

Two vertical Chinese characters. Rev. The Three Abundances.

19.	¼ Piastre ND	....	400.00

THIEU TRI, 1841-1847

Chinese legend on each side. Rectangular bars.

20.	100 Ounces ND	....	Rare
21.	50 Ounces ND	....	Rare
22.	10 Ounces ND	....	3000.00
23.	1 Ounce ND	.........................*.....	500.00
24.	5/10 Ounce ND	....	350.00
25.	4/10 Ounce ND	....	300.00
26.	3/10 Ounce ND	....	300.00
27.	2/10 Ounce ND	....	250.00
28.	1/10 Ounce ND	....	250.00

Sun between two dragons. Rev. Four Chinese characters. With
square central hole.

29.	7/10 Ounce ND	.............................*.....	650.00
30.	7/20 Ounce ND	....	300.00

Heavenly bodies flanked by four vertical characters. Rev. Long
legend in form of a quatrain. With square central hole.

31.	5/10 Ounce ND	....	650.00
32.	5/20 Ounce ND	....	325.00

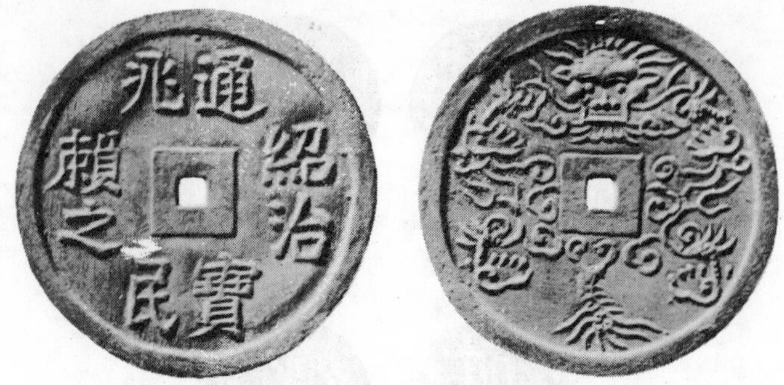

Eight Chinese characters. Rev. Facing dragon head. With square central hole.

33. 5/10 Ounce ND ....*...... 400.00
34. 5/20 Ounce ND 300.00

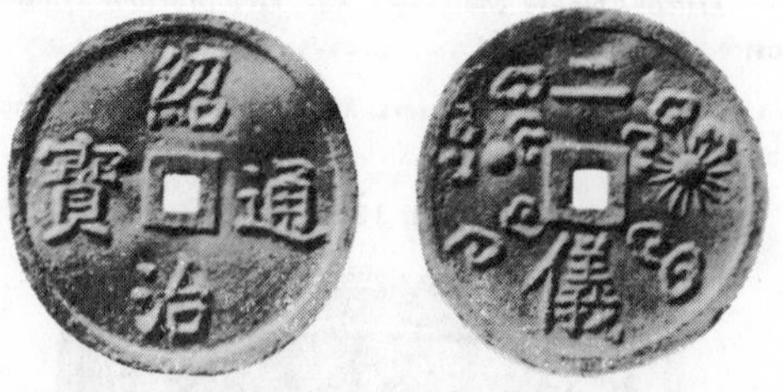

Four Chinese characters. Rev. Sun and moon between two vertical characters. With square central hole.

35. 1/4 Piastre ND 250.00

Four Chinese characters on each side around square central hole.

36. 1/2 Piastre ND 400.00

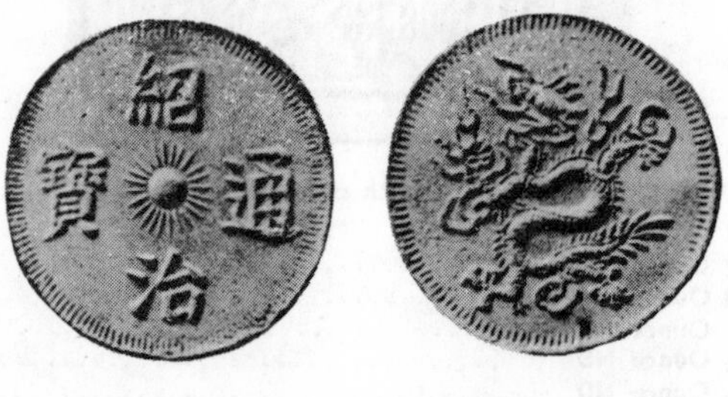

Four Chinese characters around radiant sun. Rev. Dragon.

37. 1 Piastre ND 600.00
38. 1/2 Piastre ND ....*...... 300.00

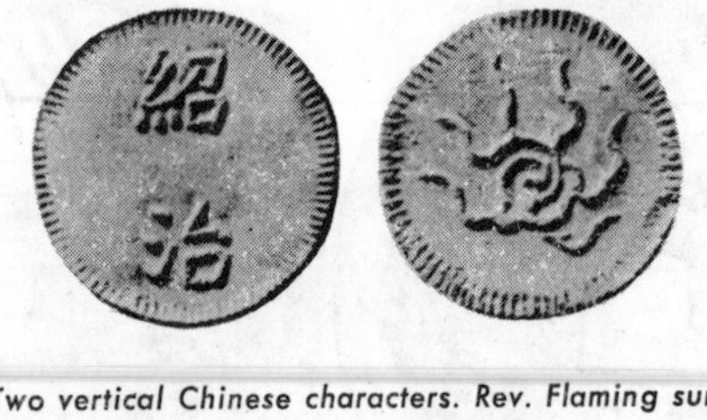

Two vertical Chinese characters. Rev. Flaming sun.

39. 1/8 Piastre ND 200.00

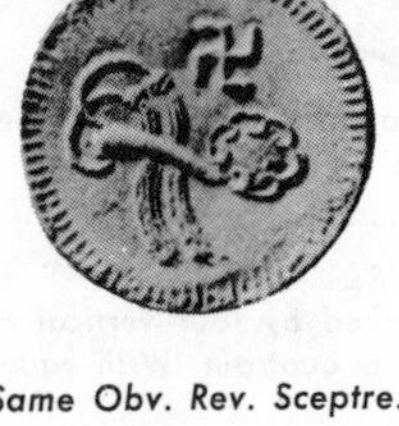

Same Obv. Rev. Sceptre.

40. 1/8 Piastre ND 200.00

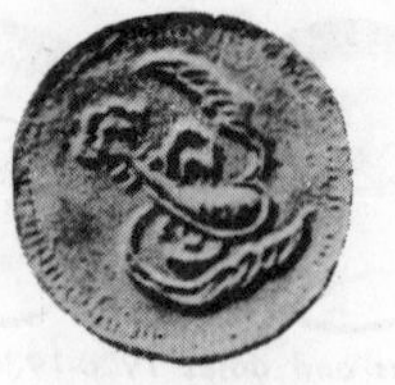

Same Obv. Rev. Guitar.

41. 1/8 Piastre ND 200.00

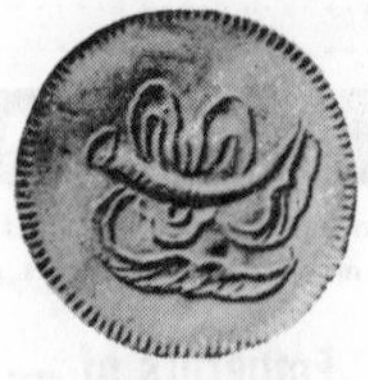

Same Obv. Rev. Trumpet.

42. 1/8 Piastre ND 200.00

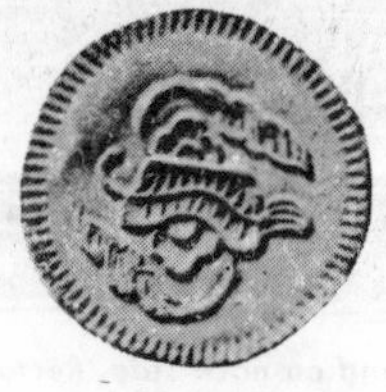

Same Obv. Rev. Fig leaves.

43. 1/8 Piastre ND 200.00

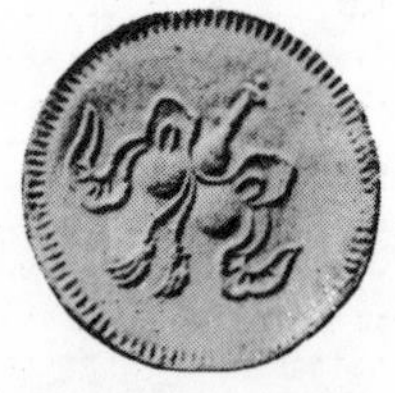

Same Obv. Rev. Gourde.

44. 1/8 Piastre ND 200.00

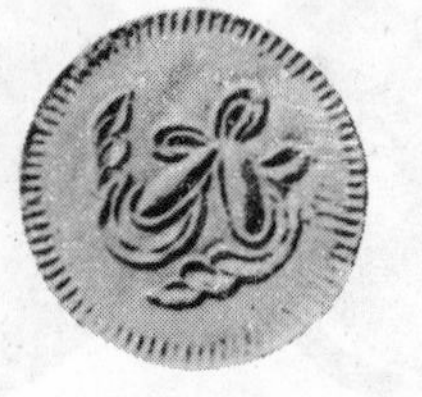

Same Obv. Rev. Castanets.

45. 1/8 Piastre ND 200.00

Same Obv. Rev. Tablets.

46. 1/8 Piastre ND 200.00

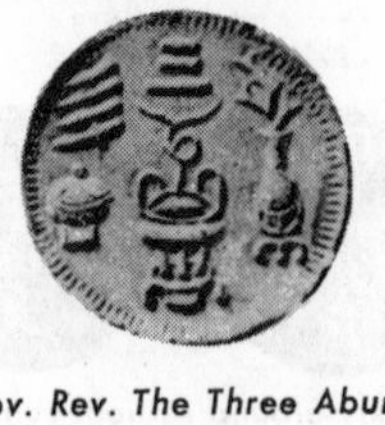

Same Obv. Rev. The Three Abundances.

47. 1/8 Piastre ND 200.00

TU DUC, 1847-1883

Four Chinese characters. Rev. The Four Perfections. With square central hole.

63. ½ Piastre ND. (The Rev. is shown) 500.00

Four Chinese characters. Rev. Five Chinese characters. Rectangular bars.

48.	10 Ounces ND	3000.00
49.	5 Ounces ND	2000.00
50.	1 Ounce ND	500.00
51.	5/10 Ounce ND	300.00
52.	4/10 Ounce ND ....*.....	150.00
53.	3/10 Ounce ND ....*.....	125.00
54.	2/10 Ounce ND ....*.....	125.00
55.	1/10 Ounce ND ....*.....	100.00

Sun between two dragons. Rev. Four Characters. With square central hole.

56. 7/10 Ounce ND 700.00

Four Chinese characters. Rev. The Five Happiness Symbols. With square central hole.

64. ¾ Piastre ND. (The Rev. is shown) 500.00

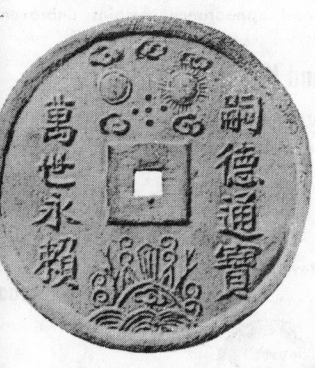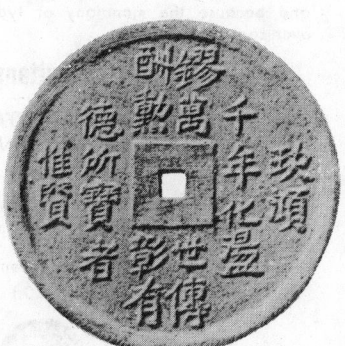

Heavenly bodies flanked by four vertical characters. Rev. Long legend in form of a quatrain. With square central hole.

57.	1 Ounce ND	800.00
58.	5/10 Ounce ND ....*......	925.00

Eight Chinese characters. Rev. Facing dragon head. With square central hole.

59. 5/10 Ounce ND 450.00

Legend on each side. With square central hole.

60.	½ Piastre ND	350.00
61.	¼ Piastre ND	250.00

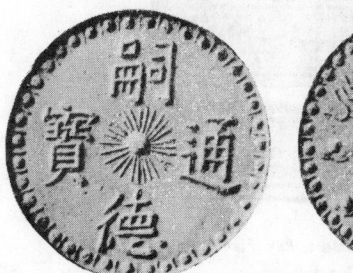

Four Chinese characters around radiant sun. Rev. Dragon.

65.	1 Piastre ND ....*......	900.00
66.	½ Piastre ND	500.00

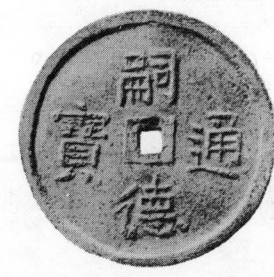

Four Chinese characters. Rev. The Three Longevities. With square central hole.

62. ½ Piastre ND 400.00

Four characters around sun with blunt rays. Rev. Dragon coiled around similar sun.

67.	1½ Piastres (37½ Grams) ND ....*......	1500.00
68.	1 Piastre (26 Grams) ND	800.00
69.	¾ Piastre (19 Grams) ND	600.00

DONG KHANH, 1885-1889

Five Chinese characters on each side.

70. 1 Ounce ND. Rectangular Bar 900.00

Four Chinese characters. Rev. Blank. With square central hole.

71. 1/16 Piastre ND 150.00

Four Chinese characters. Rev. Sun, moon and two constellations. With Square central hole.

72. 1/4 Piastre ND 600.00

THANH THAI, 1889-1905

Four Chinese characters. Rev. Five Chinese characters.

73. 1 Ounce ND. Rectangular bar 600.00

Heavenly bodies flanked by four vertical characters. Rev. Long legend in form of a quatrain. With square central hole.

74. 1 Ounce ND 900.00

Four Chinese characters. Rev. Clouds and symbols for cosmic evolution. With square central hole.

75. 1/8 Piastre ND. (The Rev. is shown) 250.00

Four Chinese characters around radiant sun. Rev. Dragon.

76. 1/3 Piastre (10½ Grams). ND 250.00

Four Chinese characters. Rev. Sun, moon and characters. With square central hole.

77. 1/4 Piastre ND 250.00

Four Chinese characters. Rev. The Three Longevities. With square central hole.

78. 1/3 Piastre ND 250.00

Four Chinese characters around radiant sun. Rev. The Four Perfections around radiant sun.

79. ½ Piastre ND 500.00

ARAB-ASIAN EMPIRES

The designation "Arab-Asian Empires" has been created especially for this book. Although they range over a vast expanse of earth, the coinages are basically similar in type, consisting mainly of native legends on each side of the coin. It was therefore felt that a single designation should encompass all such issues, except for those of Afghanistan, India, Persia and Turkey, which are catalogued separately.

Although it would have been possible to make a complete catalogue of the coins struck under each ruler (as has been done throughout this book), it was decided not to do so because all the coins look alike to to the average Western eye (except for those trained in Oriental studies), and because the monotony of type and appearance remains unbroken over centuries of issue.

Caliphs, Sultans and Khans of —

A. ANONYMOUS CALIPHS
(Earliest Issues of North Africa and Spain)

Cross potent. Rev. Legend.

1. 1/3 Solidus ND (630-720 A.D.) 150.00

Star. Rev. Legend.

2. 1/3 Solidus ND (630-720 A.D.) 150.00

Legend on each side.

3. 1/3 Solidus ND (630-720 A.D.) 150.00

Cross potent. Rev. Star.

4. 1/3 Solidus ND (630-720 A.D.) 150.00

B. THE OMAYYAD CALIPHS OF DAMASCUS, 660-750 A.D.
(Successors to the first four Caliphs after Mohammed)

Arab legend on each side. With dates from about 38-132 A.H.

5. 1 Dinar ....*...... 50.00
6. ½ Dinar 45.00
7. 1/3 Dinar ....*...... 40.00
8. 1/4 Dinar 40.00

C. THE ABBASID CALIPHS OF BAGHDAD, 750-1517 A.D.

(This coinage was superseded by that of the Ottoman Sultans of Turkey.)

Arab legend on each side. With dates from about 133-923 A.H.

9.	3	Dinars	500.00
10.	2	Dinars	350.00
11.	1½	Dinars	300.00
12.	1	Dinar ....*......	40.00
13.	½	Dinar	40.00
14.	¼	Dinar	35.00

Bull. Rev. Horseman.

15.	1 Dinar	Rare

D. THE ABBASID GOVERNORS OF EGYPT, 637-968 A.D.

(Including the lesser Dynasties of the Tulunuds, 868-905, and the Ikhshidis, 935-969).

Arab legend on each side. With dates from about 15-356 A.H.

16.	1 Dinar	50.00

E. THE FATIMIDE CALIPHS OF EGYPT, 969-1173 A.D.

Arab legend on each side. With dates from about 357-570 A.H.

17.	1	Dinar ....*......	40.00
18.	¾	Dinar	40.00
19.	½	Dinar	40.00
20.	¼	Dinar	35.00
21.	⅛	Dinar	35.00

F. THE AYUBITE SULTANS OF EGYPT, 1173-1250 A.D.

Arab legend on each side. With dates from about 570-650 A.H.

22.	2	Dinars	175.00
23.	1	Dinar ....*......	80.00

G. THE MAMELUKE SULTANS OF EGYPT, 1250-1517 A.D.

Arab legend on each side. With dates from about 650-923 A.H.

24.	2	Dinars	175.00
25.	1	Dinar ....*......	50.00

H. THE OMAYYAD CALIPHS OF CORDOVA, 756-1024 A.D.

(Northwest Africa and Spain)

Arab legend on each side. With dates from about 138-415 A.H.

26.	1	Dinar ....*......	150.00
27.	⅓	Dinar	100.00

I. THE ALMORAVIDE AMIRS OF SPAIN, 1056-1147 A.D.

(Northwest Africa and Spain)

Arab legend on each side. With dates from about 448-541 A.H.

28.	1	Dinar ....*......	120.00
29.	½	Dinar	100.00
30.	¼	Dinar	100.00

J. THE ALMOHADE CALIPHS OF SPAIN, 1130-1269 A.D.

(Northwest Africa and Spain)

Arab legend within square on each side. With or without dates from about 524-666 A.H.

31.	1	Dinar ....*......	100.00
32.	½	Dinar	100.00
33.	¼	Dinar	75.00

K. THE SELJUK SULTANS OF WESTERN ASIA, 1040-1308 A.D.

(Dynasties in Persia, Syria and Asia Minor)

Arab legend on each side. With or without dates from about 431-708 A.H.

34.	1 Dinar	60.00

L. THE MONGOL KHANS OF ASIA, 1251-1700 A.D.

Native legend on each side. With or without dates from about 750-1113 A.H.

35.	1 Dinar	60.00

M. THE MONGOL KHANS OF KHOKAND AND BOKHARA, 1700-1875 A.D.

Native legend on each side. With dates from about 1113-1319 A.H.

36.	1 Tilla	100.00

ARGENTINA

Mints and mint marks:—PTS monogram for Potosi; RA for Rioja. The 1 Escudo of 1813 remains unknown and its existence is in doubt. Many counterfeits exist of the large Rosas pieces. All gold coins of Argentina are considered rare except the 5 Peso piece, which is the equivalent of the 25 Franc piece struck on the Latin Monetary Union standard.

Radiant sun with human features. Rev. Arms.

1.	8 Escudos 1813. PTS mm.	....	**Rare**
2.	8 Escudos 1826-35. RA mm.	....	**800.00**
3.	4 Escudos 1813. PTS mm.	....	**Unknown**
4.	2 Escudos 1813. PTS mm.	....	**Unique**
5.	2 Escudos 1824, 25, 26. RA mm.	...........*	**350.00**
6.	1 Escudo 1813. PTS mm.	....	**Rare**

Uniformed bust of General Rosas. Rev. Mountain.

7.	8 Escudos 1836	....	**Rare**

Mountain with crossed flags below and with legend "Repub. Argentina Confederada R." Rev. Arms.

8.	8 Escudos 1838, 40	....	**900.00**

Similar Obv. but with legend "Republica Argentina R." Rev. Arms.

9.	8 Escudos 1840	....	**Rare**

Uniformed bust of General Rosas. Rev. Arms.

10.	8 Escudos 1842	....	**Rare**
11.	2 Escudos 1842	...................*	**300.00**

Sun over mountain. Rev. Arms.

12.	2 Escudos 1843	....	**225.00**

Shield. Rev. Arms.

13.	8 Escudos 1845	....	**1250.00**

Liberty head. Rev. Arms.

14.	5 Pesos 1881-89, 96	...............*	**85.00**
15.	2½ Pesos 1881	....	**2500.00**
16.	2½ Pesos 1884	....	**325.00**

AUSTRALIA

Mints and mint marks:—M for Melbourne; P for Perth; S for Sydney.

A. Early Issues of —

ADELAIDE ASSAY OFFICE

Crown and date. Rev. Value in beaded circle within two linear circles.

1.	1 Pound 1852	....	**1000.00**

Crown and date. Rev. Value in ornamental circle. The 5 Pound piece was not placed in circulation and no originals are known. The seven known pieces are re-strikes from the original dies.

2.	5 Pounds 1852	....	**Rare**
3.	1 Pound 1852	....................*	**500.00**

SOUTH AUSTRALIA GOLD INGOTS

Ingots of irregular shape stamped with a crown over SA and with other stamps denoting weight and fineness. Rev. Blank.

4.	Gold Ingot ND (1852)	....	**7500.00**

PORT PHILIP COINAGE

Kangaroo and date in circle. Rev. Large value in circle.

5.	2 Ounces 1853, 54 ....*	Rare
6.	1 Ounce 1853	Rare
7.	½ Ounce 1853	Rare
8.	¼ Ounce 1853 ....*	Rare

B. British Sovereigns of —

VICTORIA, 1837-1901

Young head. Rev. "Sydney Mint One Sovereign" or "Half."

9.	1 Sovereign 1855-70 ....*	75.00
10.	½ Sovereign 1855-66	60.00

(The remaining coins of Victoria and all those of the following rulers are of the same types as English gold coins, but with the distinguishing Australian mintmarks as indicated).

Young head. Rev. Arms, mintmark below.

11.	1 Pound 1871-87. S mm.	50.00
12.	1 Pound 1872-87. M mm.	65.00
13.	½ Pound 1871-87. S mm.	30.00
14.	½ Pound 1873-87. M mm.	30.00

Young head with mintmark below. Rev. St. George.

15.	1 Pound 1871-87. S mm.	45.00
16.	1 Pound 1872-87. M mm.	45.00

Jubilee head. Rev. St. George with mintmark on ground below horse.

17.	5 Pounds 1887. S mm.	Rare
18.	2 Pounds 1887. S mm.	2500.00
19.	1 Pound 1887-93. S mm.	30.00
20.	1 Pound 1887-93. M mm.	30.00

Jubilee head. Rev. Arms, mintmark below.

21.	½ Pound 1887, 93. M mm.	20.00
22.	½ Pound 1887, 89, 91. S mm.	20.00

Veiled head. Rev. Similar to above.

23.	1 Pound 1893-1901. S mm.	30.00
24.	1 Pound 1893-1901. M mm.	30.00
25.	1 Pound 1899-1901. P mm.	35.00
26.	½ Pound 1893-1901. M mm.	20.00
27.	½ Pound 1893, 97, 1900. S mm.	30.00
28.	½ Pound 1899, 1900. P mm.	20.00
29.	½ Pound 1893, 96, 99, 1900. M mm.	20.00

EDWARD VII, 1901-1911

Head. Rev. St. George with mintmark on ground below horse.

30.	5 Pounds 1902. S mm.	Rare
31.	2 Pounds 1902. S mm.	Rare
32.	1 Pound 1902-10. S mm.	25.00
33.	1 Pound 1902-10. M mm.	25.00
34.	1 Pound 1902-10. P mm.	25.00
35.	½ Pound 1902-10. S mm.	40.00
36.	½ Pound 1906-09. M mm.	20.00
37.	½ Pound 1904, 08, 09. P mm.	20.00

GEORGE V, 1910-1936

Head. Rev. St. George with mintmark on ground below horse.

38.	1 Pound 1911-26. S mm.	30.00
39.	1 Pound 1911-31. M mm.	25.00
40.	1 Pound 1911-31. P mm.	25.00
41.	½ Pound 1911-16. S mm.	20.00
42.	½ Pound 1915. M mm.	20.00
43.	½ Pound 1911, 15. P mm.	20.00

AUSTRIA

(See remarks under Holy Roman Empire.)

Mints and mint marks for period from about 1750-1916.

A	mm for Vienna.		M	mm for Milan
B, KB	mm for Kremnitz		V	mm for Venice
C	mm for Prague		W	mm for Vienna
D	mm for Salzburg			
E	mm for Karlsburg		Hand	mm for Antwerp
F	mm for Hall		Small head	mm for Brussels
G	mm for Nagybanya		Lion or lily	mm for Bruges
G.Y.F.	mm for Karlsburg (Hungarian)		Tower	mm for Tournai
H	mm for Gunzburg			

It will be seen that the series of coins struck under the Holy Roman Emperors is both long and extensive. It is regretted that lack of space did not permit a listing of the coinage of each mint, as has been done beginning with the reign of Joseph II. About 20 mints operated over a period of some 250 years, each with its own letter or symbol as a mint mark and a detailed listing of this formidable coinage would be beyond the scope of this book.

In many cases, some of the larger gold coins in the Austrian series are off-strikes. The denomination "Souverain" is traditionally applied to the coinage of the Austrian and Belgian Mints while its counterpart "Sovrano" is used for the coinage of the Milan and Venice Mints. The coins of Francis Joseph are especially noteworthy, since five different standards of gold coinage existed during his long reign, viz, Ducats, Sovranos, Krones, Florins and Corona.

A. Dukes of —

ALBERT II, 1330-1358

St. John. Rev. Lily.

1.	1 Goldgulden ND	175.00

RUDOLPH IV, 1358-1365
St. John. Rev. Lily.

2.	1 Goldgulden ND	500.00

B. Holy Roman Emperors and Archdukes —

ALBERT II, 1437-1439

Madonna. Rev. Orb in trilobe.

3.	1 Goldgulden ND	1250.00

FREDERICK III, 1439-1493
John the Baptist standing. Rev. Orb in trilobe.

4.	1 Goldgulden ND	900.00

ARCHDUKE SIGISMUND, 1439-1496
Ruler standing. Rev. Four shields and floriated cross.

5.	1 Goldgulden ND	90.00

MAXIMILIAN I, 1493-1519
St. Leopold. Rev. Arms.

6.	1 Goldgulden 1511	1000.00

St. Leopold. Rev. Cross and shield.

7.	1 Goldgulden 1514	500.00

St. Leopold. Rev. Five shields.

8.	1 Goldgulden 1517, 19, 20	500.00

Crowned bust. Rev. Carinthian shield.

9.	1 Goldgulden 1516, 19	450.00

Bust with hat. Rev. Carinthian shield.

10.	4 Ducats 1518	2500.00

FERDINAND I, 1521-1564
Bust. Rev. Legend.

11.	4 Ducats 1529. Square	2000.00
12.	3 Ducats 1529. Square	1500.00
13.	2 Ducats 1529. Square	1000.00

Bust. Rev. Cross and four shields.

14.	1½ Ducats 1529. Square	750.00
15.	1 Ducat 1529. Square ....*....	500.00
16.	½ Ducat 1529. Square	200.00

Austrian shield. Rev. Legend.

17.	½ Ducat 1529. Square	200.00

(The above seven coins were struck during the Siege of Vienna.)

Bust. Rev. Double eagle.

18.	12 Ducats 1532	Rare
19.	8 Ducats 1532	1500.00
20.	6 Ducats 1526	1000.00
21.	2 Ducats 1560	700.00

Bust. Rev. Arms.

22.	1 Ducat 1525	1000.00

Middle aged bust. Rev. St. Ladislas.

23.	1 Goldgulden 1531-58	125.00

Ruler standing. Rev. Floriated cross and four shields.

24.	1 Goldgulden ND	575.00

Ruler standing. Rev. Arms.

25.	2 Ducats ND	425.00
26.	1 Ducat ND	225.00
27.	1 Ducat 1565. Posthumous	125.00

Bust. Rev. Legend. On his burial.

28.	1 Ducat 1565	600.00

ARCHDUKE CHARLES, 1564-1590

Ruler standing. Rev. Arms.

29.	12 Ducats 1579	Rare
30.	10 Ducats 1572, 76	Rare
31.	2 Ducats 1576-87	450.00
32.	1 Ducat 1565-90 ....*...	150.00
33.	1 Ducat 1591, 92. Posthumous	150.00

Bust. Rev. Four shields.

34.	3 Ducats 1572	1000.00

Fortuna standing. Rev. Five shields.

35.	3 Ducats 1573	1250.00

ARCHDUKE FERDINAND, 1564-1595
Bust. Rev. Arms.

36.	3 Ducats ND	1350.00
37.	1 Ducat 1564-95	250.00
38.	½ Ducat 1591	450.00

Bust. Rev. Eagle.

39.	20 Ducats 1590	Rare
40.	1 Ducat 1569-83	175.00
41.	⅛ Ducat ND	150.00
42.	1 Gold Crown (Gulden) ND	750.00

Bust of Maximilian I, Charles V and Ferdinand I. Rev. Double eagle.

43.	10 Ducats 1590	1500.00
44.	8 Ducats ND	Rare
45.	5 Ducats 1590	900.00

RUDOLPH II, 1576-1612
Bust. Rev. Double eagle.

46.	10 Ducats 1589-1611	1000.00
47.	5 Ducats 1587-1611	475.00
48.	4 Ducats 1589-1604	475.00
49.	3 Ducats 1580-1607	350.00
50.	2 Ducats 1598-1611	275.00
51.	1 Ducat 1577-1611	90.00

Ruler standing. Rev. Double eagle.

52.	10 Ducats 1599-1610 ....*....	1000.00
53.	5 Ducats 1587-1611	475.00
54.	4 Ducats 1589-1604	475.00
55.	3 Ducats 1598-1606	350.00
56.	2 Ducats 1598-1611	250.00
57.	1 Ducat 1577-1611	90.00

Ruler standing. Rev. Arms.

59.	1 Ducat 1578-1608	90.00

Busts of Maximilian I, Charles V and Ferdinand I. Rev. Double eagle.

60.	10 Ducats ND	Rare
61.	5 Ducats ND	1000.00

MATTHIAS II, 1612-1619
Bust. Rev. Arms. Struck as Archduke.

62.	6 Ducats 1608-11	800.00
63.	5 Ducats 1608, 09	700.00
64.	1 Ducat 1609-11	175.00

Bust. Rev. Double eagle.

65.	25 Ducats 1615. Square		Rare
66.	20 Ducats 1612		Rare
67.	15 Ducats 1612, 17		2000.00
68.	10 Ducats 1611-19		1750.00
69.	8 Ducats 1612		1250.00
70.	5 Ducats 1612-19		650.00
71.	4 Ducats 1612		650.00
72.	3 Ducats 1613, 17		500.00
73.	2 Ducats 1613-19		375.00
74.	1 Ducat 1612-19		150.00

Armored bust. Rev. Busts of Maximilian I, Charles V and Ferdinand I.

75.	15 Ducats ND		Rare
76.	10 Ducats ND		Rare

ARCHDUKE MAXIMILIAN, 1612-1618
Ruler standing. Rev. Arms.

77.	1 Ducat ND		225.00

Armored bust. Rev. Cross.

78.	½ Ducat ND		300.00

ARCHDUKE FERDINAND, 1592-1618
Armored bust. Rev. Arms.

79.	8 Ducats 1618		1500.00
80.	1 Ducat 1617		150.00

Bust. Rev. Double eagle.

81.	5 Ducats 1602		900.00
82.	1 Ducat 1598-1616		175.00

Ruler standing. Rev. Arms.

83.	1 Ducat 1598-1617		175.00

FERDINAND II, 1618-1637
Ruler on throne. Rev. Double eagle.

84.	1 Ducat 1620-37		200.00

Armored bust. Rev. Double eagle.

85.	20 Ducats 1622, 36		Rare
86.	15 Ducats 1636		1750.00
87.	12 Ducats 1626		1500.00
88.	10 Ducats 1621-37		1250.00
89.	6 Ducats 1624, 27, 28		900.00
90.	5 Ducats 1621-37		750.00
91.	4 Ducats 1622-34		600.00
92.	3 Ducats 1637		475.00
93.	2 Ducats 1620-37		250.00
94.	1 Ducat 1620-37		100.00
95.	½ Ducat 1633, 36		175.00

Laureate bust. Rev. Silesian eagle.

96.	1 Ducat 1623		175.00

Armored bust. Rev. Arms.

97.	20 Ducats 1636		2250.00
98.	12 Ducats 1632		1750.00
99.	10 Ducats 1621-37		1100.00
100.	9 Ducats 1632		1100.00
101.	8 Ducats 1632		1100.00

102.	6 Ducats 1628, 32		600.00
103.	5 Ducats 1621-37	*	600.00
104.	4 Ducats 1627. Square		1000.00
105.	3 Ducats 1634. Square		800.00
106.	2 Ducats 1620-37		225.00
107.	1 Ducat 1620-37		100.00

Ruler standing. Rev. Arms.

108.	1 Ducat 1620-37		100.00

Bust facing. Rev. City view of Breslau, eagle above.

109.	10 Ducats 1626, 31		1750.00

Double eagle. Rev. Arms.

110.	4 Ducats 1621, 22		500.00

INTERREGNUM IN THE TYROL, 1618-1619
Tyrolian eagle shield. Rev. Arms of Austria.

111.	1 Goldgulden 1618, 19		550.00

ARCHDUKE LEOPOLD, 1619-1632
Busts of Leopold and Claudia. Rev. Eagle. Struck in 1626 on their marriage.

112.	20 Ducats ND		Rare
113.	8 Ducats ND		1250.00
114.	6 Ducats ND		900.00
115.	6 Ducats ND. Square		900.00
116.	5 Ducats ND		750.00

Ruler standing. Rev. St. Leopold.

117.	1 Ducat 1631		575.00

Tyrolian shield. Rev. Arms.

118.	½ Ducat ND		300.00

St. Leopold. Rev. Tyrolian shield.

119.	1 Ducat 1619		650.00

FERDINAND III, 1627-1657

Youthful bust. Rev. Arms.

120.	12 Ducats 1629		1650.00
121.	10 Ducats 1627-29	*	1500.00
122.	9 Ducats 1629		1250.00
123.	8 Ducats 1629		1000.00
124.	2 Ducats 1629-31		375.00
125.	1 Ducat 1629-36		150.00

Armored bust. Rev. Arms.

126.	15 Ducats 1641		2000.00
127.	12 Ducats 1641		1750.00
128.	10 Ducats 1638-57		1700.00
129.	8 Ducats 1638		1100.00
130.	7 Ducats 1638		1000.00
131.	6 Ducats 1638		900.00
132.	5 Ducats 1638-57		700.00
133.	4 Ducats 1638		600.00
134.	2 Ducats 1637-57		225.00
135.	1 Ducat 1637-57		125.00

Ruler on horseback. Rev. St. Leopold.

158.	3 Ducats 1642	1250.00
159.	2 Ducats 1642 ....*......	600.00

Ruler standing. Rev. St. Leopold.

160.	1 Ducat 1632-62, ND	275.00

Armored bust. Rev. Double eagle.

136.	20 Ducats 1645	2250.00
137.	10 Ducats 1638-57 ....*......	1500.00
138.	10 Ducats 1658. Posthumous	1500.00
139.	6 Ducats 1639-46	1000.00
140.	5 Ducats 1636-57	700.00
141.	4 Ducats 1645	600.00
142.	3 Ducats 1643, 56	600.00
143.	2 Ducats 1637-57	250.00
144.	1 Ducat 1637-57	125.00
145.	½ Ducat 1637-49	100.00

Laureate bust. Rev. Three shields.

146.	1 Ducat 1637, 38	200.00
147.	1 Ducat 1637, 38. Square	325.00

FERDINAND IV, 1646-1654
Legend. Rev. Altar.

161.	1 Ducat 1646	75.00

ARCHDUKE SIGISMUND FRANCIS, 1662-1665
Bust with long hair. Rev. Eagle.

162.	20 Ducats ND	Rare

Bust with long hair. Rev. Crowned arms.

163.	1 Ducat ND	900.00

Ruler standing. Rev. Double eagle.

148.	2 Ducats 1637-57 ....*......	350.00
149.	1 Ducat 1637-57	175.00

PROTESTANT ASSEMBLY OF SILESIA, 1633-1635
Armored bust of Ferdinand III. Rev. Double eagle.

150.	3 Ducats 1634	900.00
151.	1 Ducat 1634, 35	300.00

ARCHDUKE FERDINAND CHARLES, 1632-1662

LEOPOLD I (THE HOGMOUTH), 1658-1705
Two angels with crown. Rev. Globe under two hands. On his Coronation.

164.	4 Ducats 1658	800.00

Laureate bust. Rev. Tyrolian eagle.

165.	30 Ducats ND	Rare
166.	20 Ducats ND	Rare
167.	12 Ducats ND	1750.00
168.	4 Ducats ND ....*......	900.00

Bust. Rev. Eagle

152.	6 Ducats 1632-37	1500.00
153.	5 Ducats 1632-37, ND	1000.00
154.	2 Ducats 1632-62, ND ....*......	800.00

Bust. Rev. Arms.

155.	1 Ducat 1632-62 ....*......	425.00
156.	½ Ducat 1632-62	425.00

Bust with hat. Rev. Eagle.

157.	20 Ducats 1632-62	Rare

Laureate bust. Rev. Double eagle.

169.	12 Ducats 1674	1500.00
170.	10 Ducats 1658-1703 ....*......	1000.00
171.	10 Ducats 1694. Square	1500.00
172.	8 Ducats 1678	950.00
173.	6 Ducats 1669-1703	750.00
174.	5 Ducats 1659-1703	525.00
175.	5 Ducats 1694. Square	950.00
176.	4 Ducats 1692-1703	500.00

177.	4 Ducats 1696-98. Square		750.00
178.	3 Ducats 1694-1701		375.00
179.	2 Ducats 1659-1705		325.00
180.	2 Ducats 1660, 96. Square		600.00
181.	1 Ducat 1658-1705		85.00
182.	1 Ducat 1691, 95, 99. Square		175.00
183.	½ Ducat 1661-95		75.00
184.	⅓ Ducat 1675-98		75.00
185.	¼ Ducat 1669-1705		50.00
186.	⅙ Ducat 1669-99		50.00
187.	⅛ Ducat 1686-98		50.00
188.	1/12 Ducat 1675-99		60.00

Crowned bust. Rev. Double eagle.

189.	5 Ducats 1676-95		650.00
190.	3 Ducats 1665	*	550.00

Laureate bust. Rev. Arms.

191.	30 Ducats 1678		Rare
192.	20 Ducats 1670		Rare
193.	10 Ducats 1658-1703		1250.00
194.	6 Ducats 1662-1703		900.00
195.	5 Ducats 1659-1703		850.00
196.	4 Ducats 1658-95		500.00
197.	4 Ducats 1661. Square		600.00
198.	3 Ducats ND		375.00
199.	2 Ducats 1659-1705		275.00
200.	1 Ducat 1659-93	*	85.00
201.	¼ Ducat 1669, ND		35.00

Ruler on horseback. Rev. Double eagle.

202.	1 Ducat 1661		1000.00

JOSEPH I, 1705-1711
Bust. Rev. Tyrolian eagle.

203.	24 Ducats ND		Rare

Bust. Rev. Double eagle.

204.	10 Ducats 1705-09		1500.00
205.	5 Ducats 1706-08		900.00
206.	4 Ducats 1708		500.00
207.	3 Ducats 1706-11		500.00
208.	2 Ducats 1706-09. Round or square	*	325.00
209.	1 Ducat 1705-11		150.00
210.	½ Ducat 1706-10		90.00
211.	⅓ Ducat 1706		90.00
212.	¼ Ducat 1706-11		35.00
213.	⅙ Ducat 1706-11		35.00
214.	⅛ Ducat 1706-09		35.00
215.	1/12 Ducat 1705-11		35.00

Bust. Rev. Arms.

216.	10 Ducats 1706		1400.00
217.	3 Ducats 1710		575.00
218.	1 Ducat 1706, ND		150.00

Ruler standing. Rev. Double eagle.

219.	1 Ducat 1710, 11		175.00

Double Arms. Rev. Blank.

220.	⅛ Ducat 1710		75.00

CHARLES VI, 1711-1740

Armored bust. Rev. Double eagle.

221.	20 Ducats 1739		Rare
222.	12 Ducats 1740		1750.00
223.	10 Ducats 1712-40		1400.00
224.	6 Ducats 1714, 28		750.00
225.	5 Ducats 1713-39		750.00
226.	4 Ducats 1713-30		650.00
227.	3 Ducats 1717-38		600.00
228.	2 Ducats 1715-35		300.00
229.	2 Ducats 1734. Square		550.00
230.	1 Ducat 1712-40	*	60.00
231.	½ Ducat 1728-40		40.00
232.	¼ Ducat 1720-38		30.00
233.	⅙ Ducat 1731		30.00
234.	⅛ Ducat 1729		30.00
235.	1/16 Ducat 1729		30.00

Globe. Rev. Sceptre.

236.	1 Ducat 1716		135.00

Legend. Rev. Globe.

237.	1 Ducat 1723		90.00

Crowned bust with name and title as Charles III, King of Spain. Rev. Arms. With hand mint mark for Antwerp.

238.	2 Souverain d'or 1711		1250.00

Lion standing with same title. Rev. Arms. Hand mint mark.

239.	1 Souverain (Lion) d'or 1710		750.00

Crowned bust with name and title as Charles VI, Holy Roman Emperor. Rev. Eagle and shield. Hand mint mark.

240.	2 Souverain d'or 1719, 20.		1250.00

Laureate bust with titles as above. Rev. Arms. Hand mint mark.

241.	2 Souverain d'or 1724-26		750.00

(For additional coins of Charles VI, as well as of the rulers following, see under Italy-Milan.)

CHARLES VII, 1740-1745
(Elector of Bavaria with title of Holy Roman Emperor).
Eagle. Rev. Crown.

242.	1 Ducat 1742		350.00

MARIA THERESA, 1740-1780

Youthful bust. Rev. Elaborate arms.

243. 12 Ducats 1744 .... 1750.00
244. 10 Ducats 1742-45 .... 1400.00
245. 6 Ducats 1741-45 .... 950.00
246. 5 Ducats 1742-46 .... 850.00
247. 4 Ducats 1743 .... 800.00
248. 1 Ducat 1741-46 .... 100.00

Mature bust. Rev. Double eagle.

249. 10 Ducats 1748-61 ....*...... 1750.00
250. 7 Ducats 1758 .... 1200.00
251. 6 Ducats 1745-68 .... 1000.00
252. 5 Ducats 1746-65 .... 900.00
253. 4 Ducats 1759-65 .... 800.00
254. 3 Ducats 1754-61 .... 700.00
255. 2 Ducats 1746-65 .... 150.00
256. 1 Ducat 1746-65 .... 75.00
257. ½ Ducat 1748-65 ....*...... 65.00
258. ¼ Ducat 1749-65 .... 40.00
259. ⅙ Ducat 1752 .... 40.00
260. ⅛ Ducat 1749, 61 .... 35.00

Head. Rev. Double eagle.

261. ¼ Ducat 1749, 51 .... 40.00

Bust with widow's veil. Rev. Double eagle.

262. 5 Ducats 1777 .... 900.00
263. 4 Ducats 1778-80 .... 700.00
264. 2 Ducats 1767-80 .... 135.00
265. 1 Ducat 1765-80 .... 125.00
266. ½ Ducat 1765-80 .... 50.00
267. ¼ Ducat 1768-80 .... 40.00

Arms. Rev. Value and date.

268. ⅛ Ducat 1778 .... 50.00

Ruler standing. Rev. Crowned arms.

269. 1 Ducat 1744-65 .... 100.00

Bust. Rev. Bust of Francis.

270. 1 Ducat ND 175.00

Bust of the Imperial Couple. Rev. Crossed hammers.

271. 1 Mining Ducat 1751 .... 300.00

Bust with or without crown or veil. Rev. Arms.

272. 2 Souverain d'or 1756-80. W mm or without W 225.00
273. 2 Souverain d'or 1749-58. Hand mm. ....*...... 200.00
274. 2 Souverain d'or 1749-52. Lion mm. 225.00
275. 2 Souverain d'or 1758-80. Head mm. 200.00
276. 1 Souverain d'or 1749-57. Hand mm. 110.00
277. 1 Souverain d'or 1750-54. Lion mm. 125.00
278. 1 Souverain d'or 1757-77. Head mm. ....*...... 110.00

FRANCIS I, 1745-1765

Bust with long hair. Rev. Double eagle.

279. 6 Ducats 1747 .... 1250.00
280. 5 Ducats 1745, 47 .... 1000.00
281. 2 Ducats 1745, 46 .... 500.00
282. 1 Ducat 1745-65 ....*...... 90.00
283. 1 Ducat 1766-80. Posthumous 110.00
284. ¼ Ducat 1755-65 .... 35.00

Draped laureate bust. Rev. Double eagle.

284a. 10 Souverains d'or 1751. Hand mm 2000.00

JOSEPH II, 1765-1790

Youthful bust. Rev. Double eagle. Struck as co-regent with Maria Theresa, 1765-80.

285. 3 Ducats 1773, 76, 78 .... 525.00
286. 2 Ducats 1768-80 .... 175.00
287. 1 Ducat 1764-80 ....*...... 85.00
288. ¼ Ducat 1765, 77 .... 40.00

Draped laureate bust. Rev. Double eagle.

289. 4 Ducats 1786. A mm. 750.00
290. 1 Ducat 1781-84. C mm. 95.00
291. 1 Ducat 1781-86. F mm. ....*...... 85.00
292. 1 Ducat 1780, 82. A mm. 75.00
293. 1 Ducat 1781, 82. E mm. 75.00
294. 1 Ducat 1781, 82. G mm. 75.00

Laureate head. Rev. Double eagle.

295. 2 Ducats 1784, 86, 87. A mm. 100.00
296. 2 Ducats 1786, 87. B mm. 100.00

297.	2 Ducats 1781-87. E mm.	100.00
298.	2 Ducats 1786. M mm. ....*	750.00
299.	1 Ducat 1782-90. A mm.	50.00
300.	1 Ducat 1786-90. B. mm.	50.00
301.	1 Ducat 1783-90. E mm.	50.00
302.	1 Ducat 1787-90. F mm.	50.00
303.	1 Ducat 1783-90. G mm.	65.00
304.	1 Ducat 1786, 87, 88. M mm.	150.00
305.	½ Ducat 1787. A mm.	Rare

Laureate head. Rev. Circular shield over cross.

306.	1 Souverain d'or 1783-90. A mm.	175.00
307.	1 Souverain d'or 1786. F mm.	275.00
308.	1 Souverain d'or 1781-89. Head mm.	150.00
309.	½ Souverain d'or 1786-90. A mm. ....*	65.00
310.	½ Souverain d'or 1786-90. F mm.	85.00
311.	½ Souverain d'or 1786, 88. Head mm.	65.00
312.	1 Sovrano 1786-90. M mm. ....*	125.00
312a	1 Sovrano 1786. No mm. (Struck at Milan)	300.00
313.	½ Sovrano 1787-90. M mm.	150.00

LEOPOLD II, 1790-1792
Laureate head. Rev. Arms.

314.	1 Ducat 1790	225.00

Laureate head. Rev. Double eagle.

315.	4 Ducats 1790. A mm.	750.00
316.	2 Ducats 1790. A mm.	Rare
317.	1 Ducat 1790, 91. A mm. ....*	125.00
318.	1 Ducat 1791. B mm.	115.00
319.	1 Ducat 1791, 92. E mm.	100.00
320.	1 Ducat 1791, 92. F mm.	125.00
321.	1 Ducat 1791, 92. G mm.	100.00

Laureate head. Rev. Arms.

322.	1 Souverain d'or 1791. Head mm.	Rare
323.	1 Souverain d'or 1790, 91. A mm.	325.00
324.	1 Souverain d'or 1792. B mm.	325.00
325.	1 Souverain d'or 1792. E mm.	325.00
326.	1 Sovrano 1790, 91, 92. M mm. ....*	600.00
327.	½ Souverain d'or 1791, 92. A mm.	150.00
328.	½ Souverain d'or 1792. B mm.	175.00
329.	½ Souverain d'or 1792. E mm., F mm.	175.00
330.	½ Sovrano 1790, 91, 92. M mm. ....*	150.00
331.	¼ Sovrano 1791. M mm.	Rare

FRANCIS (II, 1792-1806; I, 1806-1835)
Laureate head. Rev. Arms.

332.	1 Ducat 1792. A mm.	350.00

Laureate bust. Rev. Double eagle.

333.	4 Ducats 1793-1830. A mm.	275.00

Laureate head. Rev. Double eagle.

334.	2 Ducats 1799-1804. A mm.	425.00
335.	1 Ducat 1792-1831. A mm.	60.00
336.	1 Ducat 1792-1830. B mm.	60.00
337.	1 Ducat 1797-1807. C mm.	125.00
338.	1 Ducat 1806, 08, 09. D mm.	150.00
339.	1 Ducat 1792-1830. E mm.	60.00
340.	1 Ducat 1793-1826. G mm. ....*	60.00
341.	1 Ducat 1819, 24. V mm.	200.00
342.	½ Ducat 1796. E mm.	425.00

Older laureate head. Rev. Double eagle.

343.	1 Ducat 1831-35. A mm.	50.00
344.	1 Ducat 1832-35. B mm.	55.00
345.	1 Ducat 1833, 34, 35. E mm.	60.00

Laureate head. Rev. Arms.

346.	1 Souverain d'or 1793. Head mm.	275.00
347.	1 Souverain d'or 1792-98. A mm.	125.00
348.	1 Souverain d'or 1794, 95, 96. B mm.	160.00
349.	1 Souverain d'or 1796. F mm.	225.00
350.	1 Souverain d'or 1793. H mm.	200.00
351.	1 Sovrano 1793-1800. M mm. ....*	175.00
352.	1 Sovrano 1793. V mm.	200.00
353.	1 Sovrano 1796. MM monogram mm. (Mantua)	1250.00
354.	½ Souverain d'or 1792-98. A mm.	140.00
355.	½ Souverain d'or 1794, 95. B mm.	165.00
356.	½ Souverain d'or 1795. E mm.	450.00
357.	½ Souverain d'or 1793-96. F mm.	165.00
358.	½ Souverain d'or 1793, 98. H mm.	200.00
359.	½ Sovrano 1800. M mm.	175.00
360.	½ Sovrano 1793. V mm.	225.00

Older laureate head. Rev. Double eagle.

361.	1 Sovrano 1822, 23, 31. A mm.	200.00
362.	1 Sovrano 1820-35. M mm. ....*........	165.00
363.	1 Sovrano 1822. V mm.	300.00
364.	½ Sovrano 1822, 23, 31. A mm.	135.00
365.	½ Sovrano 1820, 22, 31, 35. M mm.	125.00
366.	½ Sovrano 1822. V mm.	175.00

Ruler kneeling before St. Mark. Rev. Christ. Struck at Venice in the style of the old Venetian Ducats.

367.	1 Zecchino ND	275.00

FERDINAND I, 1835-1848

Laureate bust. Rev. Double eagle.

368.	4 Ducats 1835-48. A mm. ....*......	250.00
369.	4 Ducats 1848. E mm.	350.00

Laureate head. Rev. Double eagle.

370.	1 Ducat 1835-48. A mm.	40.00
371.	1 Ducat 1837-48. B mm.	40.00
372.	1 Ducat 1835-48. E mm.	40.00
373.	1 Ducat 1840-48. V mm.	135.00

Laureate head. Rev. Double eagle. The 1849-M ½ Sovrano is Posthumous.

374.	1 Sovrano 1837-47. A mm.	400.00
375.	1 Sovrano 1837-48. M mm.	400.00
376.	1 Sovrano 1837-47. V mm. ....*....	350.00
377.	½ Sovrano 1837. A mm. ....*...........Unknown
378.	½ Sovrano 1837-49. M mm. ....*....	350.00
379.	½ Sovrano 1837-47. V mm.	400.00

FRANCIS JOSEPH, 1848-1916

Young laureate bust. Rev. Double eagle.

380.	4 Ducats 1854-59. A mm. ....*......	275.00
381.	4 Ducats 1857. V mm.	750.00

Laureate bust with small side whiskers. Rev. Double eagle.

382.	4 Ducats 1860-65. A mm.	175.00
383.	4 Ducats 1864, 65. V mm.	500.00

Older bust with heavier whiskers. Rev. Double eagle.

384.	4 Ducats 1866-72	175.00

Oldest bust with thick whiskers. Rev. Double eagle.

385.	4 Ducats 1872-1914 ....*......	125.00
386.	4 Ducats 1915. Proof restrike ....*......	30.00

Young laureate head to left. Rev. Double eagle. With large date in legend and additional small date 1898. Struck in 1898 on the 50th year of his reign.

387.	1 Ducat 1848, 49, 50, 51	175.00

Young laureate head to right. Rev. Double eagle.

388.	1 Ducat 1852-59. A mm.	40.00
389.	1 Ducat 1853-59. B mm.	50.00
390.	1 Ducat 1853-59. E mm.	50.00
391.	1 Ducat 1858. M mm.	225.00
392.	1 Ducat 1854-59. V mm. ....*......	150.00

Laureate head with small side whiskers. Rev. Double eagle.

393.	1 Ducat 1860-65. A mm.	40.00
394.	1 Ducat 1860-65 B mm.	40.00
395.	1 Ducat 1860-65. E mm.	40.00
396.	1 Ducat 1860-65. V mm. ....*......	125.00

Older head with heavier whiskers. Rev. Double eagle.

397.	1 Ducat 1866-72. A mm.	....	35.00
398.	1 Ducat 1866, 67. B mm.	....	40.00
399.	1 Ducat 1866, 67.E mm.	....	40.00
400.	1 Ducat 1866. V mm.	....	150.00

Oldest head with thick whiskers. Rev. Double eagle.

401.	1 Ducat 1872-1914	....	20.00
402.	1 Ducat 1915. Proof restrike	..................*......	8.00
403.	1 Ducat 1951. Unofficial Mint error for 1915	....	50.00

Laureate head. Rev. Double eagle.

404.	1 Sovrano 1853, 55, 56. M mm.	..............*......	400.00
405.	1 Sovrano 1854, 55, 56. V mm.	..............*......	500.00
406.	½ Sovrano 1854, 55, 56. M mm.	..............*......	200.00
407.	½ Sovrano 1854, 55, 56. V mm.	..............*......	375.00

Laureate head. Rev. Value and date in wreath.

408.	1 Krone 1858-66. A mm.	.......................*......	250.00
409.	1 Krone 1859. B mm.	....	Rare
410.	1 Krone 1858. E mm.	....	250.00
411.	1 Krone 1859. M mm.	....	400.00
412.	1 Krone 1858, 59. V mm.	....	800.00
413.	½ Krone 1858-66. A mm.	....	150.00
414.	½ Krone 1859, 60, 61. B mm.	....	150.00
415.	½ Krone 1858, 59, 61. E mm.	....	150.00
416.	½ Krone 1858. V mm.	....	1000.00

Head in circle of shields. Rev. Double eagle. On the Vienna Shooting Match.

417.	4 Ducats 1873	....	500.00

Uniformed bust. Rev. Tourist Inn. On the building of the Charles Louis Inn on Mt. Raxalpe.

418.	6 Ducats 1877. (Same die as for the silver coin)	....	Rare

Head. Rev. Double eagle and values. Both originals and restrikes exist of the 8 and 4 Florins of 1892.

419.	8 Florins-20 Francs 1870-92	..................*......	35.00
420.	4 Florins-10 Francs 1870-92	....	30.00

Old laureate head. Rev. Double eagle.

421.	20 Corona 1892-1909	..................*......	30.00
422.	10 Corona 1892, 93	....	500.00
423.	10 Corona 1894-1909	....	20.00

Plain head. Rev. Double eagle. Both originals and restrikes exist of the 100 and 20 Corona of 1915 and the 10 Corona of 1912.

424.	100 Corona 1909-15	....	200.00
425.	20 Corona 1909-15	..................*......	75.00
426.	20 Corona 1916	....	125.00
427.	20 Corona 1916. Change in arms	....	100.00
428.	10 Corona 1909-12	....	20.00

Plain head. Rev. Female reclining on clouds. On the 60th year of reign.

429.	100 Corona 1908	....	300.00

Plain head. Rev. Double eagle. On the 60th year of reign.

430.	20 Corona 1908	....	80.00
431.	10 Corona 1908	..................*......	50.00

KARL I, 1916-1918
Head. Rev. Eagle.

432.	20 Corona 1918. Vienna Mint Cabinet	....	Unique

C. Republic of —

Large eagle. Rev. Value in circular wreath.

433.	100 Kronen 1923, 24	..................*......	500.00
434.	20 Kronen 1923, 24	....	175.00

Eagle. Rev. Value between branches.

435.	100 Schillings 1926-34	....	125.00
436.	25 Schillings 1926-34	.....................*......	35.00

Standing figure of the Maria Zell Madonna. Rev. Eagle.

437.	100 Schillings 1935-37	.....................*......	350.00
438.	100 Schillings 1938	....	2000.00

St. Leopold holding model of Church. Rev. Eagle.

439.	25 Schillings 1935-37	.....................*......	150.00
440.	25 Schillings 1938	....	1250.00

D. Cities of —

BRIXEN

Bishops of —

CHARLES OF AUSTRIA, 1613-1624
Bust. Rev. Arms.

441.	7 Ducats 1614	....	Rare
442.	3 Ducats 1614	....	600.00

Bust. Rev. Three shields and two hooks.

443.	1 Ducat 1614, 18	....	350.00
444.	½ Ducat 1618	....	275.00

CASPAR IGNATZ OF KUENIGL, 1702-1747

Bust. Rev. Two shields.

445.	1 Ducat 1717, 45	....	475.00

LEOPOLD MARIA JOSEPH OF SPAUR, 1747-1778
Bust. Rev. Arms.

446.	1 Ducat 1768	....	600.00

EGGENBERG

Princes —

JOHN CHRISTIAN AND JOHN SEYFRIED, 1649-1713
Two busts. Rev. Arms.

447.	15 Ducats 1652	....	Rare
448.	10 Ducats 1652, 54	....	2000.00
449.	5 Ducats 1652, 58	....	1250.00
450.	1 Ducat 1654	....	300.00

KEVENHULLER

Counts —

JOHN JOSEPH, 1742-1776

Bust. Rev. Arms.

451.	1 Ducat 1761	....	400.00

KLOSTERNEUBURG

Priors of —

THOMAS
St. Leopold. Rev. Castle.

452.	1 Ducat ND (1750)	....	Rare

MONTFORT

Counts —

ANTHONY III THE YOUNGER, 1693-1734

Crown over draped shield. Rev. Orb on eagle.

453.	1 Ducat 1715	....	1200.00

Bust. Rev. Crown over draped shield.

454.	1 Ducat 1718	.....................*......	1000.00
455.	½ Ducat 1722	....	600.00
456.	¼ Ducat 1722, 28, 30	.....................*......	250.00

ERNEST MAX JOSEPH, 1734-1758

Bust. Rev. Arms.

457.	1 Carolin 1735, 36	....	475.00
458.	½ Carolin 1734, 35	....	250.00
459.	1 Ducat 1745	.........................*......	800.00

Bust. Rev. Cross of four crossed monograms around central "X"

460.	1 Carolin 1735	.........................*......	850.00
461.	¼ Carolin 1736	....	300.00

FRANCIS XAVIER, 1758-1780

Bust. Rev. Arms.

462.	1 Ducat 1758	....	500.00

ORTENBURG

Counts —

CHRISTOPHER WIDMAN, 1640-1660
Bust. Rev. Arms.

463.	10 Ducats 1656	....	4000.00
464.	2 Ducats 1657	....	Rare
465.	1 Ducat 1658	....	500.00

PAAR

Princes —

JOHN WENZEL, 1741-1792
Bust. Rev. Arms.

465a.	1 Ducat 1771	....	250.00

SALZBURG

Archbishops of —

PILGRIM II, 1365-1396

Shield. Rev. St. John.

466.	1 Goldgulden ND	....	900.00

LEONARD, 1495-1519

Bust. Rev. Two shields, date below.

467.	4 Ducats 1513. Square	....	1500.00
468.	3 Ducats 1513. Square	.....................*......	900.00
469.	2 Ducats 1513. Square	....	600.00

Bust. Rev. Arms between divided date.

470.	6 Ducats 1513.	a. Square ..	1200.00	b. Round ..	750.00
471.	5 Ducats 1513.	a. Square ..	900.00	b. Round ..	575.00
472.	4 Ducats 1513.	a. Square ..	800.00	b. Round ..	450.00
473.	3 Ducats 1513, 19.	a. Square ..	450.00	b. Round ..	350.00

St. Rupert. Rev. Arms in enclosure.

474.	1 Ducat 1500-19	....	225.00

St. Rupert. Rev. Shield.

475.	1 Goldgulden 1500-10	....	175.00

MATTHEW LANG, 1519-1540

Bust. Rev. Two shields.

476.	3 Ducats 1521	....	800.00
477.	2 Ducats 1521	.........................*......	500.00

Bust. Rev. Saint standing.

478.	3 Ducats 1521	....	575.00
479.	2 Ducats 1521	.........................*......	425.00

Bust. Rev. Arms.

480.	10 Ducats 1522, 39	....	2250.00
481.	8 Ducats 1522, 39	....	2000.00
482.	8 Ducats 1522. Square	....	2000.00

483.	6 Ducats 1522, 39	1750.00
484.	5 Ducats 1522	1500.00
485.	5 Ducats 1522. Square	1750.00
486.	4 Ducats 1521, 22	900.00
487.	4 Ducats 1522. Square	1000.00
488.	3 Ducats 1522	700.00

Bust. Rev. Two saints seated.

489.	8 Ducats 1522	1500.00
490.	6 Ducats 1522	1100.00

Bust. Rev. Legend. On the end of rebellion.

491.	2 Ducats 1523. Square or round	725.00
492.	1 Ducat 1523. Square or round ....*......	325.00

Two saints seated. Rev. Arms

493.	10 Ducats 1539	1750.00
494.	6 Ducats 1539	1250.00

Saint standing. Rev. Arms.

495.	1 Ducat 1519-40	125.00

ERNEST DUKE OF BAVARIA, 1540-1554
Saint seated. Rev. Arms.

496.	10 Ducats 1540, 46	1750.00

Saint standing. Rev. Arms.

497.	8 Ducats 1540	1250.00
498.	4 Ducats 1540, 50	900.00
499.	1 Ducat 1541-54 ....*...	225.00

Two saints seated. Rev. Arms.

500.	2 Ducats 1547, 48, 49	500.00

Saint seated. Rev. Three shields.

501.	1 Goldgulden ND	225.00

MICHAEL, 1554-1560
Saint seated. Rev. Two shields.

502.	8 Ducats 1554, 59	1750.00
503.	6 Ducats 1555	1350.00
504.	4 Ducats 1559	825.00

Two saints seated. Rev. Arms.

505.	4 Ducats 1555	825.00
506.	3 Ducats 1555 ....*...	600.00

Saint standing. Rev. Arms.

507.	3 Ducats 1555	375.00
508.	2 Ducats 1555, 59	300.00
509.	1 Ducat 1555-59 ....*...	125.00

JOHN JACOB KHUEN, 1560-1586

Saint standing. Rev. Arms.

510.	4 Ducats 1561, 63	725.00
511.	3 Ducats 1561	500.00
512.	2 Ducats 1561-67 ....*...	300.00
513.	2 Ducats 1561. Thick flan.	300.00
514.	1 Ducat 1561-65	125.00

Two saints seated. Rev. Arms.

515.	20 Ducats 1565	Rare
516.	12 Ducats 1565	Rare
517.	10 Ducats 1565	1750.00
518.	6 Ducats 1565	800.00
519.	4 Ducats 1565	575.00

Saint seated with lions. Rev. Arms.

520.	20 Ducats 1572	**Rare**

Two saints seated. Rev. Two shields.

521.	8 Ducats ND	1400.00

Saint seated. Rev. Two shields.

522.	8 Ducats 1571	1250.00
523.	6 Ducats 1561, 63	800.00

Two saints seated. Rev. Three shields.

524.	5 Ducats ND	725.00
525.	4 Ducats ND	500.00

Saint seated. Rev. Three shields.

526.	3 Ducats 1565, 67 ....*......	600.00
527.	1 Goldgulden 1566	425.00

Saint seated with lions. Rev. St. Radiana with wolves.

528.	15 Ducats 1571	**Rare**

Double eagle. Rev. Arms.

529.	2 Ducats 1568, 69 ....*......	300.00
530.	1 Ducat 1568	175.00

Saint with shield. Rev. Double eagle.

531.	2 Ducats 1569-85	300.00
532.	1 Ducat 1569-82 ....*......	150.00

GEORGE, 1586-1587
Two saints seated. Rev. Arms.

533.	6 Ducats 1586	1750.00
534.	5 Ducats 1586	1750.00
535.	4 Ducats 1586	1400.00
536.	4 Ducats 1586. Square	1750.00
537.	3 Ducats 1586, ND	1200.00
538.	2 Ducats ND	950.00

Saint standing. Rev. Double eagle.

539.	2 Ducats 1586, 87 ....*......	750.00
540.	1 Ducat 1586	500.00

Saint seated. Rev. Three shields.

541.	1 Goldgulden 1586	500.00

WOLFGANG THEODORE, 1587-1612

Two saints seated. Rev. Arms.

542.	20 Ducats ND	**Rare**
543.	12 Ducats ND	**Rare**
544.	10 Ducats 1587	1750.00
545.	8 Ducats 1587, ND	1400.00
546.	7 Ducats ND	1200.00
547.	6 Ducats 1587, ND	900.00
548.	5 Ducats ND	700.00
549.	4 Ducats ND	575.00
550.	4 Ducats ND. Square	700.00
551.	3 Ducats ND	525.00
552.	3 Ducats ND. Square	575.00
553.	2 Ducats ND	300.00
554.	2 Ducats ND. Square ....*......	375.00

Saint seated. Rev. Arms.

555.	2 Ducats 1598-1611 ....*......	300.00
556.	2 Ducats 1600. Square	325.00
557.	1 Ducat 1600, 02	125.00
558.	1 Ducat 1600, 02. Square	200.00

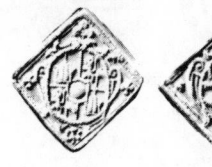

Arms. Rev. Shield.

559.	1 Ducat ND. Square	250.00
560.	½ Ducat 1603, ND. Square ....*......	250.00

Oval shield. Rev. Tower.

561.	14 Ducats 1590	**Rare**
562.	12 Ducats 1594	**Rare**
563.	12 Ducats 1594. Square	**Rare**
564.	10 Ducats 1590, 94	1750.00
565.	9 Ducats 1594	1400.00
566.	8 Ducats 1594	1200.00

Saint with shield. Rev. Tower

567.	16 Ducats 1593	**Rare**
568.	12 Ducats 1593	**Rare**
569.	10 Ducats 1593	1750.00
570.	10 Ducats 1593. Square	2000.00
571.	8 Ducats 1593	1250.00
572.	7 Ducats 1593	975.00
573.	7 Ducats 1593. Square	1250.00
574.	6 Ducats 1593	975.00
575.	5 Ducats 1593	600.00
576.	5 Ducats 1593, ND. Square	750.00
577.	4 Ducats 1593, ND ....*......	750.00
578.	4 Ducats ND. Square	850.00
579.	3 Ducats ND	375.00
580.	3 Ducats ND. Square	500.00

Saint with shield. Rev. Double eagle.

581.	2 Ducats 1587-97	300.00
582.	1 Ducat 1587-97 ....*......	150.00

Saint seated. Rev. Tower

583.	8 Ducats ND	1250.00
584.	5 Ducats ND	850.00
585.	4 Ducats ND	500.00
586.	4 Ducats 1587. Square	600.00
587.	3 Ducats ND	500.00

Four shields. Rev. Two shields.

588.	½ Ducat 1611. Square	300.00
589.	½ Ducat 1599/1611. Square hybrid ....*......	375.00
590.	¼ Ducat 1599/1559. Square hybrid	375.00

Four shields. Rev. Blank.

591.	¼ Ducat 1610. Square	250.00

MARCUS SITTICUS, 1612-1619

Bust. Rev. Two saints seated.

592.	14 Ducats 1612	**Rare**
593.	12 Ducats 1612	**Rare**
594.	8 Ducats 1613	1400.00

595.	6 Ducats 1615	1250.00
596.	5 Ducats 1615	950.00
597.	4 Ducats 1615, 16, 18 ....*....	850.00

Saint seated. Rev. Tower

598.	6 Ducats 1617	950.00

Saint seated. Rev. Arms.

599.	10 Ducats 1613. Square	2500.00
600.	10 Ducats 1617	1750.00
601.	8 Ducats 1613	1400.00
602.	7 Ducats 1618. Square	1400.00
603.	6 Ducats 1617, 18	950.00
604.	6 Ducats 1616, 17. Square	1100.00
605.	5 Ducats 1612	725.00
606.	5 Ducats 1612, 17. Square	900.00
607.	4 Ducats 1612, 14, 15, 17	650.00
608.	3 Ducats 1617	550.00
609.	3 Ducats 1612. Square	650.00
610.	2 Ducats 1612-16	325.00
611.	2 Ducats 1612-16. Square	400.00
612.	1 Ducat 1612-18	150.00
613.	1 Ducat 1613-18. Square	175.00

Two saints seated. Rev. Arms.

614.	2 Ducats ND. Square	300.00

Saint standing. Rev. Arms.

615.	1 Goldgulden 1619	475.00

Arms on each side.

616.	1 Ducat 1614, 15, 18. Square	175.00
617.	½ Ducat 1612, 14, 18. Square	175.00

PARIS, 1619-1653

Cathedral carried by two saints. Rev. Reliquary carried by eight Bishops.

618.	20 Ducats 1628	**Rare**
619.	16 Ducats 1628	**Rare**
620.	12 Ducats 1628	**Rare**
621.	10 Ducats 1628	900.00
622.	10 Ducats 1628. Square	1100.00
623.	8 Ducats 1628	725.00
624.	8 Ducats 1628. Square	850.00
625.	6 Ducats 1628	500.00
626.	5 Ducats 1628	500.00
627.	5 Ducats 1628. Square	650.00
628.	4 Ducats 1628 ....*....	375.00
629.	4 Ducats 1628. Square	425.00
630.	3 Ducats 1628	325.00

Saint standing. Rev. Madonna.

631.	10 Ducats 1628, 31	1750.00
632.	8 Ducats 1625, 28	1200.00
633.	6 Ducats 1628	900.00
634.	4 Ducats 1624. Square	900.00
635.	4 Ducats 1624, 25, 29, 38	600.00
636.	3 Ducats 1631, 38, 42	425.00
637.	3 Ducats 1624-42. Square	550.00
638.	2 Ducats 1626	375.00
639.	2 Ducats 1626. Square	425.00

Saint seated. Rev. Arms.

640.	8 Ducats 1620	1400.00
641.	5 Ducats 1620	750.00
642.	4 Ducats 1620	500.00
643.	4 Ducats 1620. Square	750.00
644.	3 Ducats 1620	500.00
645.	2 Ducats 1624-48	325.00
646.	2 Ducats 1634-51. Square	450.00
647.	1 Ducat 1620-53	150.00
648.	1 Ducat 1627-51. Square ....*......	200.00
649.	½ Ducat 1643-52	85.00
650.	½ Ducat 1643-50. Square	100.00
651.	¼ Ducat 1652	50.00

Arms. Rev. Arms on cross.

652.	½ Ducat 1634-46	85.00
653.	¼ Ducat 1624	50.00

GUIDOBALD, 1654-1668

Arms. Rev. Cathedral carried by two saints.

654.	50 Ducats 1654. Square	Rare
655.	24 Ducats 1654	Rare
656.	20 Ducats 1654	Rare
657.	16 Ducats 1654	Rare
658.	12 Ducats 1654	Rare
659.	10 Ducats 1654	1750.00
660.	8 Ducats 1654	1200.00
661.	6 Ducats 1654, 55	900.00
662.	5 Ducats 1654, 55 ....*......	650.00
663.	4 Ducats 1654, 55	500.00

Saint seated. Rev. Arms.

664.	2 Ducats 1654, 59, 62	250.00
665.	1 Ducat 1654-68 ....*......	100.00
666.	1 Ducat 1655, 57, 66. Square	125.00
667.	½ Ducat 1654-66	75.00
668.	¼ Ducat 1654-68	50.00

MAX GANDOLPH, 1668-1687

Arms. Rev. Five saints standing. On the 1100th year of Salzburg.

669.	12 Ducats 1682. Square ....*......	Rare
670.	10 Ducats 1682	1250.00
671.	10 Ducats 1682. Square	1600.00
672.	8 Ducats 1682. Square	1250.00
673.	7 Ducats 1682	950.00
674.	6 Ducats 1682	850.00
675.	5 Ducats 1682	700.00
676.	4 Ducats 1682	550.00
677.	3 Ducats 1682	375.00

Arms under triangle. Rev. Legend. On the 1100th year of Salzburg.

678.	3 Ducats 1682	350.00
679.	2 Ducats 1682 ....*......	275.00

Two saints seated with Church. Rev. Arms.

680.	44 Ducats 1668	Rare
681.	25 Ducats 1668	Rare
682.	25 Ducats 1668. Square	Rare
683.	20 Ducats 1668	Rare
684.	20 Ducats 1668. Square	Rare
685.	15 Ducats 1668	Rare
686.	12 Ducats 1668	Rare
687.	12 Ducats 1668. Square ....*......	Rare
688.	10 Ducats 1668	1500.00
689.	10 Ducats 1668. Square	1800.00
690.	9 Ducats 1668	1250.00
691.	8 Ducats 1668	1000.00
692.	6 Ducats 1668	650.00
693.	5 Ducats 1668	650.00
694.	4 Ducats 1668	475.00
695.	3 Ducats 1668	325.00

Saint standing. Rev. Arms.

696. 10 Ducats 1686 .... 1400.00

Saint seated. Rev. Arms.

697.	6 Ducats 1668	750.00
698.	5 Ducats 1668	550.00
699.	4 Ducats 1673. Square	600.00
700.	3 Ducats 1670, 73	375.00
701.	3 Ducats 1673. Square	500.00
702.	2 Ducats 1668, 73 ....*......	250.00
703.	2 Ducats 1673. Square	300.00
704.	1 Ducat 1668-87	125.00
705.	1 Ducat 1668-74. Square	150.00
706.	½ Ducat 1668-86	75.00
707.	½ Ducat 1668. Square	125.00
708.	¼ Ducat 1668-86	50.00

JOHN ERNEST, 1687-1709
Two saints seated with Church. Rev. Arms.

709.	50 Ducats 1687. Square	Rare
710.	20 Ducats 1687	Rare
711.	15 Ducats 1687	Rare
712.	12 Ducats 1687	Rare
713.	10 Ducats 1687	1400.00
714.	8 Ducats 1687	1200.00
715.	7 Ducats 1687	700.00
716.	6 Ducats 1687	600.00
717.	5 Ducats 1687	475.00
718.	4 Ducats 1687	350.00

Saint seated. Rev. Arms.

719.	10 Ducats 1687	1400.00
720.	3 Ducats 1690	375.00
721.	2 Ducats 1688, 1707, 08	300.00
722.	2 Ducats 1688. Square	325.00
723.	1 Ducat 1687-1708	150.00
724.	½ Ducat 1687-1707 ....*......	80.00
725.	¼ Ducat 1687-1707 ....*......	40.00

"WAS." Rev. "IRS." On the visit to Salzburg of Joseph I and Wilhelmina Amalia.

726.	1 Ducat 1699 ....*......	250.00
727.	¼ Ducat 1699	150.00

FRANCIS ANTHONY, 1709-1727
Bust. Rev. Arms.

728.	25 Ducats 1709	Rare
729.	20 Ducats 1709	Rare
730.	10 Ducats 1709, 11	1250.00
731.	5 Ducats 1709	600.00
732.	1 Ducat 1710-26	100.00

Bust. Rev. City view.

733.	25 Ducats 1711	Rare
734.	20 Ducats 1711	Rare

Bust. Rev. Horse in landscape.

735.	25 Ducats 1709	Rare
736.	20 Ducats 1709	Rare
737.	10 Ducats 1709	750.00
738.	5 Ducats 1718, ND	450.00

Saint seated. Rev. Arms.

739.	2 Ducats 1709. Square	375.00
740.	1 Ducat 1709-26 ....*......	100.00
741.	½ Ducat 1709-27	75.00
742.	¼ Ducat 1709-25	50.00

LEOPOLD ANTHONY, 1727-1744

Bust. Rev. Arms.

743. 1 Ducat 1728-44 .... 150.00

Saint seated. Rev. Arms.

744.	2 Ducats 1734, 35	325.00
745.	1 Ducat 1727-40	125.00
746.	½ Ducat 1728	75.00
747.	¼ Ducat 1728-40	40.00

JACOB ERNEST, COUNT LIECHTENSTEIN, 1745-1747
Bust. Rev. Arms.

748. 1 Ducat 1745, 46, 47 .... 325.00

Saint seated. Rev. Arms.

749.	1 Ducat 1745, 46	325.00
750.	¼ Ducat 1745	125.00

ANDREW JACOB, COUNT DIETRICHSTEIN, 1747-1753

Bust. Rev. Arms.

751.	2 Ducats 1750 ....*......	600.00
752.	1 Ducat 1748-51	200.00
753.	½ Ducat 1751	125.00
754.	¼ Ducat 1751	75.00

Saint seated. Rev. Arms.

755.	2 Ducats 1752	500.00
756.	1 Ducat 1747-52	200.00
757.	½ Ducat 1749	100.00
758.	¼ Ducat 1749	50.00

SIGISMUND III, 1753-1771
Bust. Rev. Arms.

759.	2 Ducats 1755	350.00
760.	1 Ducat 1754-63	150.00
761.	½ Ducat 1755, 61	100.00
762.	¼ Ducat 1755, 70	50.00

Bust. Rev. Saint seated.

763. 5 Ducats 1759 .... 1000.00

Bust. Rev. Two shields.

764. 2 Ducats 1764 ....*...... 200.00
765. 1 Ducat 1762-64 .... 100.00

Bust. Rev. Draped arms.

766. 2 Ducats 1765-71 ....*...... 250.00
767. 1 Ducat 1763-71, ND 125.00

Bust. Rev. Saint seated with small Madonna.

768. 6 Ducats 1760 .... 1000.00

Bust. Rev. View of the Mint.

769. 3 Ducats 1766 .... 500.00

Bust. Rev. City gate.

770. 10 Ducats 1767 .... 1800.00

Saint standing with small Madonna. Rev. Arms.

771. 1 Ducat 1763 .... 125.00

Saint seated. Rev. Arms.

772. 1 Ducat 1753 .... 125.00
773. ¼ Ducat 1753 .... 50.00

SEDE VACANTE, 1772

Saint seated. Rev. Arms.

774. 1 Ducat 1772 .... 125.00

JEROME, 1772-1803

Bust. Rev. Arms.

775. 2 Ducats 1773 .... 400.00
776. 1 Ducat 1772-1802 ....*.... 125.00
777. 1 Ducat 1803 .... 750.00
778. ½ Ducat 1776 .... 75.00
779. ¼ Ducat 1776, 77, 82 .... 50.00

Bust. Rev. Temple.

780. 2 Ducats 1782 .... 500.00
781. 1 Ducat 1782 .... 175.00

FERDINAND, PRINCE AND ELECTOR, 1803-1806

Bust. Rev. Draped arms.

782. 1 Ducat 1803, 04 .... 150.00

Bust. Rev. Crowned arms.

783. 1 Ducat 1805, 06 .... 150.00

FRANCIS II (I), HOLY ROMAN AND AUSTRIAN EMPEROR, 1806-1810

Head. Rev. Eagle.

784. 1 Ducat 1806, 09 .... 150.00

TRAUTSON-FALKENSTEIN

Counts, and later, Princes —

PAUL SIXTUS I, 1589-1621
Arms. Rev. Double eagle.

785. 1 Ducat ND 300.00

Bust. Rev. Arms.

786. 5 Ducats 1620 .... 700.00

JOHN FRANCIS, 1620-1663
Bust. Rev. Arms.

787. 10 Ducats 1638 .... 2750.00
788. 1 Ducat 1634, 38 .... 250.00
789. ¼ Ducat 1635 .... 125.00

FRANCIS EUSEBIUS, 1678-1728
Bust. Rev. Arms.

790. 1 Ducat 1708, 15 .... 250.00

JOHN LEOPOLD, 1663-1724
Bust. Rev. Arms.

791. 1 Ducat 1719 .... 250.00

VIENNA

Archbishops of —

CHRISTOPHER ANTHONY OF MIGAZZI, 1757-1803

Bust. Rev. Arms.

792. 1 Ducat 1781 .... 300.00

WINDISCHGRAETZ

Counts —

LEOPOLD VICTOR JOHN, 1727-1746
Bust. Rev. Arms.

793. 10 Ducats 1732 .... Rare
794. 1 Ducat 1733 .... 300.00

JOSEPH NICHOLAS, 1746-1802
Bust. Rev. Arms.

795. 5 Ducats 1777 .... 900.00
796. 1 Ducat 1777 .... 250.00

BAHAMAS

Head of Queen Elizabeth II. Rev. Columbus landing on San Salvador.

1. 100 Dollars 1967 .... 200.00

Head of Queen Elizabeth II. Rev. Columbus' flagship, the Santa Maria.

2. 50 Dollars 1967 .... 150.00

Head of Queen Elizabeth II. Rev. A lighthouse.

3. 20 Dollars 1967 .... 75.00

Head of Queen Elizabeth II. Rev. A fortress.

4. 10 Dollars 1967 .... 50.00

BAHRAIN

Bust of Isa Bin Sulman. Rev. Arms. On the opening of Isa Town.

1. 10 Dinars 1968 .... 200.00

BELGIUM

Mints and mint marks:—

Hand	mm for Antwerp
Small head	mm for Brussels
Lion or lily	mm for Bruges
Tower	mm for Tournai

Coins were struck at the above mints in the provinces of Brabant and Flanders when they were under Spanish and Austrian rule. Belgium became an independent country in 1830 and in 1832 it adopted the French monetary system for its coinage.

The coins listed as not being placed in circulation were all struck in proof condition and all are rare. Only 6 pieces were struck of the 100 Franc piece of 1912 with French legends and only 3 pieces of the same coin with Flemish legends.

A. United Provinces of —

Lion standing. Rev. Circle of eleven shields. Struck during the Insurrection against Austria.

1.   1 Lion d'or 1790 .... 1000.00

B. Kings of —

LEOPOLD I, 1831-1865

Laureate head. Rev. Value and date. This issue was not placed in circulation.

40 Francs 1834-41	....	1600.00
20 Francs 1835-41	.........................*......	700.00

Plain head. Rev. Arms

25 Francs 1847-50	....	200.00
10 Francs 1849, 50	....	225.00

Plain head. Rev. Conjoined heads of the Duke and Duchess of Brabant. On their marriage. Without the mark of value.

(100 Francs) 1853 .... 1000.00

Plain head. Rev. Value.

20 Francs 1865 .... 35.00

LEOPOLD II, 1865-1909

Head. Rev. Arms. The 10 Franc piece was not placed in circulation.

20 Francs 1866-82	....	22.50
10 Francs 1867	....	500.00

ALBERT, 1909-1934

Uniformed bust. Rev. Arms. Only the 20 Franc piece was placed in circulation. 100 Franc pieces dated 1911 were not officially struck. They exist with milled and plain edges.

10.	100 Francs 1912. French legends	...............*.....	3000.00
11.	100 Francs 1912. Flemish legends	....	3000.00
12.	20 Francs 1914. French legends	...............*......	65.00
13.	20 Francs 1914. Flemish legends	....	65.00
14.	10 Francs 1911, 12. French legends	....	350.00
15.	10 Francs 1911, 12. Flemish legends	....	350.00

C. Cities of —

BORNE

Lords of —

WALRAM, 1356-1378
Bust of Emperor Charles IV. Rev. Lion.

16. 1 Goldgulden ND 1500.00

BRABANT

Dukes of —

JOHN II, 1294-1312
St. John. Rev. Lily.

17. 1 Florin ND 1100.00

JOHN III, 1312-1355

Ruler on throne. Rev. Cross.

18.	1 Chaise d'or ND	....	350.00
19.	1 Chaise d'or ND. With name of Louis of Bavaria	.*......	275.00

St. John. Rev. Lily.

20. 1 Florin ND 200.00

JOAN AND WENCESLAS, 1355-1383
Bust of St. Peter. Rev. Cross.

21.	1 Peter d'or ND	300.00

Lamb. Rev. Cross.

22.	2 Mouton d'or ND		950.00
23.	1 Mouton d'or ND	*	350.00

Cavalier on horse. Rev. Cross.

24.	1 Cavalier d'or ND	275.00

St. Servais seated under Gothic dais. Rev. Shield.

25.	1 Florin ND	1600.00

St. John. Rev. Lily.

26.	1 Florin ND	150.00

JOAN AND PHILIP, 1384-1389
Two shields. Rev. Cross.

27.	1 Ecu d'or ND	2500.00

JOAN, 1383-1406

Knight on horse. Rev. Cross.

28.	1 Franc a cheval ND	400.00

Angel holding shield. Rev. Cross.

29.	1 Angel ND	4500.00

Church of St. Peter at Louvain. Rev. Cross.

30.	1 Tourelle d'or ND	4500.00

ANTHONY OF BURGUNDY, 1406-1415
Shield supported by lions. Rev. Cross.

31.	1 Lion d'or ND	3500.00
32.	½ Lion d'or ND	3500.00

JOHN IV, 1414-1427
Arms. Rev. Cross.

33.	1 Ecu d'or ND	300.00

Ruler on throne. Rev. Cross.

34.	1 Chaise d'or ND	350.00

St. John standing. Rev. Four shields.

35.	1 Florin ND	1250.00

Lamb. Rev. Cross.

36.	½ Mouton d'or ND	500.00

PHILIP OF ST. POL, 1420-1430
Ruler on throne. Rev. Cross.

37.	1 Chaise d'or ND	375.00

St. Peter standing. Rev. Five shields.

38.	1 Florin ND	1250.00

Bust of St. Peter over arms. Rev. Cross.

39.	1 Ecu d'or ND	750.00

PHILIP THE GOOD, 1430-1467
Ruler on throne. Rev. Cross.

40.	1 Chaise d'or ND	250.00

Bust of St. Peter over arms. Rev. Cross.

41.	1 Peter d'or ND	200.00

Ruler on horse. Rev. Cross.

42.	1 Cavalier d'or ND	225.00
43.	½ Cavalier d'or ND	450.00

Lion seated under dais. Rev. Arms.

44.	1 Lion d'or ND	*	225.00
45.	⅓ Lion d'or ND		450.00

St. Andrew standing with cross. Rev. Arms on cross.

46.	1 Florin ND	275.00

CHARLES THE BOLD, 1467-1477

St. Andrew standing with cross. Rev. Arms.

47.	1 Florin ND	*	200.00
48.	½ Florin ND		450.00

MARIE OF BURGUNDY, 1477-1482
St. Andrew standing with cross. Rev. Arms on cross.

49.	1 Florin ND	250.00

St. Andrew standing with cross. Rev. Shield.

50.	½ Florin ND	1750.00

MAXIMILIAN AND PHILIP, 1482-1496
Christ on throne. Rev. Four shields.

51.	1 Florin 1492	1600.00

Ruler standing in ship. Rev. Cross.

52.	½ Noble 1488	450.00

Maximilian standing. Rev. Arms on cross.

53.	2 Florins 1490	4000.00

St. Andrew standing with cross. Rev. Arms on cross.

54.	1 Florin 1482-89	750.00

St. Andrew standing with cross. Rev. Shield.

55.	½ Florin 1489, ND	1000.00

St. Andrew standing with open book. Rev. Arms on cross.

56.	1 Florin 1487	1750.00

PHILIP III, 1494-1506
St. Philip with shield. Rev. Cross.

57.	1 Florin 1499-1502, ND	200.00
58.	½ Florin 1500, ND	125.00

St. Philip standing. Rev. Four shields in angles of cross.

59. 1 Florin ND 350.00

Arms supported by lions. Rev. Cross.

60. 2 Souverain d'or 1499-1504 .... 1750.00

CHARLES V (CHARLES I OF SPAIN), 1506-1555
St. Philip with shield. Rev. Floriated cross.

61. 1 Florin (1506-55), ND 100.00
62. ½ Florin (1506-55), ND 100.00

Crowned bust. Rev. Arms on eagle.

63. 1 Real d'or ND ....*...... 250.00
64. ½ Real d'or ND 175.00

Crowned arms. Rev. Arms on floriated cross.

65. 1 Couronne d'or 1543-54, ND 125.00

Arms supported by lions. Rev. Cross.

66. 2 Souverain d'or 1513 .... 1500.00

PHILIP II OF SPAIN, 1555-1598

Bust. Rev. Arms.

67. 1 Real d'or (1555-98), ND ....*...... 250.00
68. ½ Real d'or (1555-98), ND 150.00

Arms. Rev. Floriated cross.

69. 2 Florins ND 1000.00
70. 1 Couronne d'or 1580-86, ND ....*...... 225.00

St. Andrew standing with cross. Rev. Arms.

71. 1 Florin 1567-69 .... 300.00

FRANCIS ALENCON, 1581-1584
Arms. Rev. Cross.

72. 1 Couronne d'or 1582 .... 1750.00

INDEPENDENT STATES OF BRABANT, 1584-1585

Lion seated under Gothic dais. Rev. Arms on cross.

73. 1 Lion d'or 1584, 85 .... 1000.00
74. ½ Lion d'or 1585 .... 1500.00

ALBERT AND ISABELLA OF SPAIN, 1598-1621
(Governors for the Crown).

Crowned busts facing each other. Rev. Arms.

75. 2 Ducats (1598-1621), ND ....*...... 300.00
76. 1 Ducat (1598-1621), ND 750.00

Arms. Rev. Cross.

77. 2 Albertins (⅔ Ducat) 1601-09 ....*...... 125.00
78. 1 Albertin (⅓ Ducat) 1601-04 .... 110.00
79. 1 Couronne d'or 1598-1621 .... 275.00

Albert and Isabella on thrones. Rev. Arms.

80. 2 Souverain d'or 1598-1621, ND 700.00

Conjoined busts. Rev. Arms.

81. 1 Souverain d'or ND 600.00

Crowned shield and crowned initials. Rev. Cross.

82. ½ Souverain d'or 1616, ND ....*...... 600.00
83. 1 Couronne d'or 1614, ND 400.00

Albert and Isabella walking to right. Rev. Arms.

84. ⅔ Souverain d'or ND 2250.00

PHILIP IV OF SPAIN, 1621-1665

Crowned bust. Rev. Arms.

85. 2 Souverain d'or 1623-65 .... 400.00

Crowned lion standing. Rev. Arms.

86. 1 Lion d'or (1621-65) 175.00

Cross. Rev. Arms.

87. 1 Couronne d'or 1623-65 .... 150.00

CHARLES II OF SPAIN, 1665-1700
Crowned child bust. Rev. Arms.

88. 2 Souverain d'or 1667-94 .... 750.00

Older bust with long curls. Rev. Arms.

89. 2 Souverain d'or 1686-99 .... 900.00

Lion standing. Rev. Arms.

90. 1 Lion d'or (1665-1700) 600.00

PHILIP V OF SPAIN, 1700-1712

Bust. Rev. Arms

91. 2 Souverain d'or 1700-12 .... 1500.00

AUSTRIAN RULERS

(For Austrian type coins struck at the Belgian Mints, see under Austria beginning with the year 1711).

BRUSSELS

Legend and "84". Rev. Blank. Square coins struck at Brussels while under siege by Alexander Farnese.

92. 4 Florins 1584 ....*......1750.00
93. 2 Florins 1584 .... 2000.00

FAGNOLLE

Counts —

CHARLES DE LIGNE, 1770-1803

Bust. Rev. Arms.

94. 1 Ducat ND 2000.00

FLANDERS

Counts of —

LOUIS DE CRECY, 1322-1346
St. John. Rev. Lily.

95. 1 Florin ND 450.00

LOUIS DE MALE, 1346-1384

Ruler seated on throne. Rev. Cross.

96. 1 Chaise d'or ND ....*...... 450.0
97. ½ Chaise d'or ND 425.0
98. ¼ Chaise d'or ND 175.0

Ruler on horse. Rev. Cross.

99. 1 Franc a Cheval ND .... 375.

Ruler standing. Rev. Initials and cross.

100. 1 Franc a Pied ND .... 350.

Lion seated. Rev. Initials and cross.

| 101. | 1 Lion d'or ND | ....*..... | 625.00 |
| 102. | ½ Lion d'or ND | .... | 400.00 |

Lamb. Rev. Cross.

| 103. | 1 Mouton d'or ND | .... | 375.00 |

Helmeted shield. Rev. Initials and cross.

| 104. | 1 Heaume d'or ND | ....*...... | 800.00 |
| 105. | ⅓ Heaume d'or ND | .... | 2500.00 |

PHILIP THE BOLD, 1384-1404
Ruler seated. Rev. Cross.

| 106. | 1 Chaise d'or ND | .... | 400.00 |

Ruler in ship. Rev. Cross.

| 107. | 1 Noble ND | .... | 800.00 |
| 108. | ½ Noble ND | .... | 1250.00 |

Angel with two shields. Rev. Cross.

| 109. | 1 Angel ND | .... | 1750.00 |

Two shields. Rev. Cross.

| 110. | 2 Heaume d'or ND | .... | 1300.00 |

JOHN, 1405-1419
Ruler in ship. Rev. Cross.

| 111. | 1 Noble ND | .... | 900.00 |

PHILIP THE GOOD, 1419-1467

Ruler in ship. Rev. Cross.

| 112. | 1 Noble ND | ....*...... | 500.00 |
| 113. | ½ Noble ND | .... | 700.00 |

Ruler on throne. Rev. Cross.

| 114. | 1 Chaise d'or ND | .... | 250.00 |
| 115. | ½ Chaise d'or ND | .... | 300.00 |

Ruler on horse. Rev. Arms on cross.

| 116. | 1 Cavalier d'or ND | .... | 200.00 |
| 117. | ½ Cavalier d'or ND | .... | 300.00 |

Lion seated. Rev. Arms on cross.

118.	1 Lion d'or ND	............................*......	225.00
119.	½ Lion d'or ND	....	125.00
120.	⅔ Lion d'or ND	....	450.00
121.	⅓ Lion d'or ND	....	400.00

St. Andrew. Rev. Arms on cross.

| 122. | 1 Florin ND | .... | 250.00 |

CHARLES THE BOLD, 1467-1477

St. Andrew. Rev. Arms.

| 123. | 1 Florin ND | .... | 200.00 |
| 124. | ½ Florin ND | .... | 300.00 |

MARIE OF BURGUNDY, 1477-1482

St. Andrew. Rev. Arms.

| 125. | 1 Florin ND | .... | 200.00 |

PHILIP THE HANDSOME, 1482-1506

St. John and lamb. Rev. Arms.

| 126. | 1 Florin ND | .... | 300.00 |

St. Andrew and arms. Rev. Eagle on shield.

| 127. | ½ Florin ND | .... | 600.00 |

St. Philip and arms. Rev. Arms.

128.	1 Florin ND	150.00
129.	½ Florin ND .... *	200.00

Arms supported by lions. Rev. Cross.

130.	1 Toison d'or ND	2750.00

CHARLES V (CHARLES I OF SPAIN), 1515-1555

Bust with sword and sceptre. Rev. Arms on eagle.

131.	1 Real d'or ND .... *	250.00
132.	1 Florin ND	150.00

Eagle on shield on cross. Rev. Arms.

133.	½ Real d'or ND	125.00

St. Philip and arms. Rev. Cross.

134.	1 Florin ND	150.00
135.	½ Florin ND	200.00

Arms between briquets. Rev. Cross.

136.	1 Couronne d'or 1545, 46	200.00

PHILIP II OF SPAIN, 1555-1598
Plain bust. Rev. Arms on floriated cross.

137.	2 Reales d'or 1586, ND	275.00

Crowned bust. Rev. Arms in golden fleece.

138.	1 Real d'or ND	275.00

Plain bust. Rev. Crowned arms.

139.	½ Real d'or ND	150.00

Arms. Rev. Floriated cross.

140.	1 Couronne d'or ND	375.00

ALBERT AND ISABELLA OF SPAIN, 1598-1621
Rulers on thrones. Rev. Arms.

141.	2 Souverain d'or 1613	1250.00

Initials and cross. Rev. Arms.

142.	1 Couronne d'or 1615, 20	750.00

PHILIP IV OF SPAIN, 1621-1665
Crowned bust. Rev. Arms.

143.	2 Souverain d'or 1646	400.00

Lion standing. Rev. Arms.

144.	1 Lion d'or 1648-62	175.00

CHARLES II OF SPAIN, 1665-1700

Bust. Rev. Arms supported by lions.

145.	8 Souverain d'or 1694 .... *	3000.00
146.	4 Souverain d'or 1696	2000.00

Lion standing. Rev. Arms.

147.	1 Lion d'or 1700	350.00

GHENT

Royal figure in ship. Rev. Cross.

148.	1 Noble 1581, 82, 83	500.00
149.	½ Noble 1581, 82, 83	350.00

GRONSFELD

Barons —

WILLIAM, 1558-1663

St. George on horse. Rev. Arms on cross.

150.	1 Florin ND	500.00

St. Martin. Rev. Lion.

151.	1 Florin ND	500.00

JUSTUS MAXIMILIAN, 1617-1667

Arms. Rev. Legend.

152.	1 Ducat 1642, 57, 64	350.00

Horseman. Rev. Arms.

153.	1 Florin ND	400.00

HAINAUT

Counts —

LOUIS OF BAVARIA, 1345-1347
Lamb. Rev. Cross.

154.	1 Mouton d'or ND	300.00

Ruler on throne. Rev. Cross.

155.	1 Chaise d'or ND	500.00

WILLIAM III, 1356-1389
Lamb. Rev. Cross.

156.	2 Mouton d'or ND	1250.00
157.	1 Mouton d'or ND	600.00

Ruler on horse. Rev. Cross.

158.	1 Grand Chevalier ND	750.00
159.	1 Franc a Cheval ND	450.00

Ruler standing. Rev. Cross.

160.	1 Royal ND	1000.00

ALBERT OF BAVARIA, 1389-1404

Arms. Rev. Cross.

161.	2 Couronne d'or ND	1000.00
162.	1 Couronne d'or ND .... *	350.00

WILLIAM IV, 1404-1417
Angel with shield. Rev. Cross.

163.	1 Angel ND	2000.00

Arms. Rev. Cross.

164.	1 Couronne d'or ND	175.00

JACQUELINE, 1417-1433
Round shield. Rev. Cross.

165.	2 Couronne d'or ND	700.00

JOHN IV, 1418-1427
Arms. Rev. Cross.

166.	1 Couronne d'or ND	750.00

PHILIP THE GOOD, 1433-1467

Ruler on horse. Rev. Arms on cross.

167.	1 Cavalier d'or ND	200.00

Lion. Rev. Arms on cross.

168.	1 Lion d'or ND .... *	225.00
169.	⅔ Lion d'or ND	750.00
170.	⅓ Lion d'or ND	400.00

St. Andrew. Rev. Arms on cross.

171.	1 Florin ND	300.00

PHILIP II AND THE STATES GENERAL, 1577-1599
Arms. Rev. Cross.

172.	2 Florins 1577	300.00
173.	1 Florin 1577	150.00

HOORN

Counts —

DIRK LOOF, 1358-1390
St. John. Rev. Lily.

174.	1 Ducat ND	600.00

WILLIAM VII, 1358-1415
Half length bust. Rev. Double eagle.

175.	1 Florin ND	900.00

PHILIP MONTMORENCY, 1540-1568
St. Martin. Rev. Arms.

176.	1 Florin ND	600.00

LIEGE

Bishops of —

ENGELBERT OF MARK, 1345-1364
St. John. Rev. Lily.

177.	1 Florin ND	150.00

JOHN D'ARCKEL, 1364-1378

Lamb. Rev. Cross.

178.	1 Mouton d'or ND	2000.00

St. Peter and shield. Rev. Cross.

179.	1 Ecu d'or ND	2500.00

ARNOLD, 1378-1389
Bishop under dais. Rev. St. John.

180.	1 Florin ND	2000.00

St. Peter under dais. Rev. Two shields.

181.	1 Florin ND	1500.00

JOHN OF BAVARIA, 1389-1418
Ruler on throne. Rev. Cross.

182.	1 Chaise d'or ND	2000.00

Ruler standing. Rev. Arms.

183.	1 Florin ND	700.00

St. John. Rev. Three shields.

184.	1 Florin ND	700.00

St. John. Rev. Five shields.

185.	1 Florin ND	700.00

Griffin and arms. Rev. Cross.

186.	1 Ecu d'or ND .... *	1000.00
187.	½ Ecu d'or ND	1200.00

JOHN HEINSBERG, 1419-1455
Ruler on throne. Rev. Cross.

188. 1 Chaise d'or ND 1500.00

Griffin and arms. Rev. Cross.

189. 1 Ecu d'or ND 1500.00

St. Peter with shield. Rev. Cross.

190. 1 Ecu d'or ND 2000.00

Angel with shield. Rev. Arms on cross.

191. 1 Ecu d'or ND ....*.....1750.00
192. ½ Ecu d'or ND 2000.00

St. Lambert standing. Rev. Arms.

193. 1 Florin ND 1250.00

LOUIS BOURBON, 1456-1482
Lion with arms. Rev. Arms on cross.

194. 1 Lion d'or ND 2500.00

Two lions with shield. Rev. Cross.

195. 1 Ecu d'or ND 1750.00

St. Lambert standing. Rev. Arms.

196. 1 Florin ND 400.00

Madonna. Rev. Arms on cross.

197. 1 Florin ND 2000.00

JOHN OF HOORN, 1484-1505
St. Lambert standing. Rev. Arms.

198. 1 Florin ND 150.00

Christ standing. Rev. Cross of four shields.

199. 1 Florin ND 225.00

EBERHARD OF MARK, 1506-1538
Arms. Rev. Cross.

200. 2 Florins 1512, 13 .... 800.00
201. 1 Florin 1512, 13 .... 300.00

St. Lambert standing. Rev. Arms.

202. 1 Florin ND 200.00

St. Lambert standing. Rev. Cross of four shields.

203. 1 Florin ND 150.00

CORNELIUS BERGHES, 1538-1544
St. Lambert standing. Rev. Arms.

204. 1 Florin ND 700.00

Christ on throne. Rev. Four shields.

205. 1 Florin ND 700.00

GEORGE OF AUSTRIA, 1544-1557
St. George and shield. Rev. Cross of four shields.

206. 1 Florin ND 800.00

GERHARD OF GROESBECK, 1564-1580
Arms. Rev. Double eagle.

207. 1 Florin 1568 .... 1000.00

Saint seated. Rev. Initials and cross.

208. 1 Florin ND 150.00

ERNEST OF BAVARIA, 1581-1612
Arms and three shields. Rev. Double eagle.

209. 1 Florin 1581, 85 .... 800.00

Bust. Rev. Arms.

210. 1 Ducat 1612, ND 1000.00

FERDINAND OF BAVARIA, 1612-1650
Bust. Rev. Arms.

211. 1 Ducat 1612, 13 .... 250.00

Arms. Rev. Legend on tablet.

212. 1 Ducat 1638, ND 250.00

Arms. Rev. Cross.

213. 2 Florins 1613 .... 375.00
214. 1 Florin 1613 .... 150.00

Arms. Rev. Initials and cross.

215. 1 Florin 1614, 35, 37 .... 125.00

Ruler seated. Rev. Arms.

216. 1 Florin ND 125.00

MAXIMILIAN HENRY OF BAVARIA, 1650-1688
Arms. Rev. Legend on tablet.

217. 1 Ducat 1651-53, 56-58 .... 250.00

Bust. Rev. Arms.

218. 1 Ducat 1663, 68, ND 400.00

JOHN LOUIS ELDERN, 1688-1694

Bust. Rev. Arms.

219. 2 Ducats 1690 ....*...... 1200.00
220. 1 Ducat 1690 .... 300.00

JOSEPH CLEMENT OF BAVARIA, 1694-1723
Bust. Rev. Arms.

221. 3 Ducats 1695, 1700 .... 1200.00

JOHN THEODORE OF BAVARIA, 1744-1763
Bust. Rev. Arms.

222. 1 Ducat 1749 .... 1000.00

SEDE VACANTE ISSUES
(Coins struck in the period between the death of one bishop and the coronation of another).

Bust of St. Lambert. Rev. Arms.

223. 2 Ducats 1688, 94, 1724 .... 850.00
224. 1 Ducat 1744, 63, 71, 84, 92 ....*...... 450.00
225. ½ Ducat 1724 .... 150.00

LOOS

Counts —

THEODORE III, 1336-1361
Lamb. Rev. Cross.

226. 1 Mouton d'or ND 1250.00

St. John. Rev. Lily.

227. 1 Florin ND 700.00

MEGEN

Counts —

MARIA, 1572-1580
Ruler on throne. Rev. Arms in rose.

228. 2 Souverain d'or ND 1750.00

Ruler in ship. Rev. Rose.

229. 1 Noble ND 1500.00

Ruler in ship. Rev. Cross.

230. 1 Noble ND 1500.00

RECKHEIM

Counts —

THE VLODORPS, 1562 AND LATER

St. Peter. Rev. Madonna.

231. 1 Florin ND 750.00

St. Victor. Rev. Madonna.

232. 1 Goldgulden ND 300.00

RUMMEN

Counts —

JOHN II, 1294-1312
Ruler on horse. Rev. Cross.

233. 1 Franc a Cheval ND 350.00

ARNOLD OREY, 1331-1364
Lamb. Rev. Cross.

234. 1 Mouton d'or ND 900.00

HENRY AND JOANNA, 1464-1474

Lamb. Rev. Cross.

235. 1 Mouton d'or ND ....*...... 350.00
236. ½ Mouton d'or ND 300.00

STAVELOT

Abbots of —

CHRISTOPHER MANDERSCHEID, 1546-1576
Arms. Rev. Double eagle.

237. 1 Ducat 1567, 68 .... 700.00

Ruler standing. Rev. Arms.

238. 1 Ducat ND 400.00

THOREN

Abbesses of —

MARGUERITE IV BREDERODE, 1531-1579
Madonna seated. Rev. Arms.

239. 1 Ducat ND 275.00

Bust of Ferdinand II. Rev. Madonna.

240. 1 Ducat ND 250.00

Bust of Ferdinand II. Rev. Arms.

241. 1 Ducat ND 400.00

St. Michael. Rev. Ship.

242. 1 Angel ND ....*...... 400.00
243. ½ Angel ND 750.00

TOURNAI

Gold coins were struck at the Tournai mint by the Kings of France (Charles VI and Charles VII) and by the Spanish rulers of the provinces of Brabant and Flanders (Philip II, Albert and Isabella, and Philip IV).

VALKENBERG (FALKENBERG)

Barons —

REINHALD SCHONFORST, 1354-1355
St. John. Rev. Lily.

244. 1 Florin ND 700.00

BERMUDA

Head of Queen Elizabeth II. Rev. Bird in flight.

1. 20 Dollars 1970 .... 75.00

BOHEMIA

This is the ancient Kingdom occupying the territory now known as Czechoslovakia.

A. Kings of —

WENCESLAS II, 1278-1305
W in shield. Rev. Lion.

1. 1 Florin ND 900.00

JOHN OF LUXEMBOURG, 1310-1346
St. John. Rev. Lily.

2. 1 Florin ND 350.00

CHARLES IV, 1346-1378

Bust facing. Rev. Lion.

3.	1 Goldgulden ND	250.00

WENCESLAS III, 1378-1419
Facing bust of St. Wenceslas. Rev. Lion.

4.	1 Ducat ND	950.00

Shield. Rev. Lion.

5.	1 Ducat ND	950.00

LADISLAS II, 1471-1516
St. Wenceslas. Rev. Lion in shield.

6.	1 Goldgulden ND	450.00

LOUIS II, 1516-1526
St. Wenceslas. Rev. Lion in shield.

7.	1 Ducat 1518, 21, ND	225.00

St. Wenceslas. Rev. Lion.

8.	1 Ducat ND	275.00

FERDINAND I, 1526-1564
St. Wenceslas. Rev. Lion.

9.	1 Goldgulden 1536-45, ND	175.00

MAXIMILIAN II, 1564-1576
Ruler standing. Rev. Arms.

10.	1 Ducat 1566, 73	175.00

RUDOLPH II, 1576-1612
Ruler standing. Rev. Arms.

11.	1 Ducat 1583	175.00

MATTHIAS II, 1612-1619
Bust. Rev. Legend.

12.	2 Ducats 1611	225.00
13.	1 Ducat 1611	125.00

Ruler standing. Rev. Double eagle.

14.	10 Ducats 1611-19	2000.00
15.	5 Ducats 1611-19	800.00
16.	2 Ducats 1611-19	200.00
17.	1 Ducat 1611-19	100.00

Ruler standing. Rev. St. Wenceslas.

18.	1 Ducat 1612-19	125.00

Stork. Rev. Legend.

19.	2 Ducats 1611	225.00

FREDERICK V OF PALATINATE, 1619-1620

Ruler standing. Rev. Arms.

20.	10 Ducats 1620 ....*......	Rare
21.	5 Ducats 1620	Rare
22.	1 Ducat 1620	1000.00

Bust. Rev. Lion

23.	1 Ducat 1620	600.00

Crowned bust. Rev. Arms on lion.

24.	2 Ducats 1620	1000.00
25.	1 Ducat 1620, ND ......*......	900.00

Lion. Rev. Three shields under hat.

26.	1 Goldgulden 1621	275.00

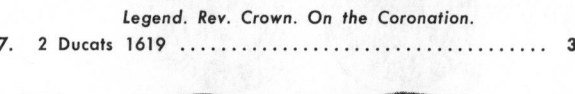

Legend. Rev. Crown. On the Coronation.

27.	2 Ducats 1619	350.00

Crowned initial. Rev. Legend. On the Coronation.

28.	1 Ducat 1619 ......*......	125.00
29.	½ Ducat 1619	100.00

NATIONAL ASSEMBLY OF BOHEMIA AND MORAVIA, 1619-1620
Crowned Moravian Eagle. Rev. Obelisk.

30.	25 Ducats 1620	Rare
31.	10 Ducats 1620	Rare
32.	5 Ducats 1620	Rare

NATIONAL ASSEMBLY OF MORAVIA AND SILESIA, 1621
Silesian Eagle. Rev. Blank.

33.	25 Taler 1621	Rare
34.	12½ Taler 1621. Round	Rare
35.	12½ Taler 1621. Square	Rare

FERDINAND II, 1619-1637

Ruler standing. Rev. Double eagle.

36.	12 Ducats 1632	Rare
37.	10 Ducats 1621-37 ......*......	1200.00
38.	5 Ducats 1621-37	700.00
39.	2 Ducats 1620-37	375.00
40.	1 Ducat 1620-37	175.00

Pax. Rev. Inscription.

41.	1 Peace Ducat 1635	500.00

FERDINAND III, 1637-1657

Bust in ruff collar. Rev. Bohemian Lion in shield.

42.	100 Ducats 1629	.............................*....12,000.00
43.	50 Ducats 1629	.... 5000.00
44.	40 Ducats 1629	.... 4000.00

CHARLES VI, 1711-1740

Ruler standing. Rev. Globe and owl. From gold of the Eule Mines.

45.	2 Ducats 1715-22	...........................*...... 850.00
46.	1 Ducat 1713-22	.... 375.00

Ruler standing. Rev. St. John on clouds. From gold of the Eule Mines.

47.	5 Ducats 1722. City view below St. John	......*...... 1000.00
48.	2 Ducats 1722-27	.... 400.00
49.	1 Ducat 1719-29	.... 175.00

MARIA THERESA, 1740-1780
Legend. Rev. Bohemian Lion. On the Coronation.

50.	1 Ducat 1743	.... 125.00

B. Cities of —

LOBKOWITZ

Princes —

FERDINAND AUGUST LEOPOLD, 1677-1715
Armored bust. Rev. Arms.

51.	1 Ducat ND	.... 500.00

OLMUTZ

Archbishops of —

FRANCIS OF DIETRICHSTEIN, 1599-1636

Madonna seated. Rev. Arms.

52.	1 Ducat 1626, 28, ND	.... 400.00

Shield of Dietrichstein. Rev. Arms.

53.	½ Ducat 1636	.... 200.00

LEOPOLD WILLIAM OF AUSTRIA, 1637-1662
Bust. Rev. Arms.

54.	10 Ducats 1656, 58	.... 2250.00
55.	4 Ducats 1656	.... 1000.00

Bust. Rev. Two shields.

56.	1 Ducat 1658	.... 200.00

CHARLES II OF LIECHTENSTEIN-CASTELCORN, 1664-1695

Bust. Rev. Arms.

57.	10 Ducats 1678	.... 1700.00
58.	8 Ducats 1678	.... 1350.00
59.	6 Ducats ND	.... 1100.00
60.	5 Ducats 1672, 76, 78	.... 1000.00

61. 2 Ducats 1680, 84, 91 ....*...... 500.00
62. 1 Ducat 1684, ND 200.00
63. ⅛ Ducat 1671, ND 100.00

CHARLES III, JOSEPH OF LORRAINE, 1695-1711
Bust. Rev. Arms.

64. 8 Ducats 1707 .... 1400.00
65. 5 Ducats 1703, 04, 05, 07, ND 1100.00
66. 3 Ducats 1707 .... 725.00
67. 2 Ducats 1703, ND 425.00
68. 1 Ducat ND 200.00
69. ⅛ Ducat ND 125.00

WOLFGANG SCHRATTENBACH, 1711-1738

Bust. Rev. Arms.

70. 5 Ducats 1722 ....*...... 1000.00
71. 4 Ducats 1713 .... 500.00
72. 3 Ducats 1717 .... 375.00
73. 1 Ducat 1725, 26, 28, ND 200.00

Bust with hat. Rev. Two shields.

74. 1 Ducat 1736, 37 .... 225.00

Bust and value. Rev. Three shields.

75. ¼ Ducat ND 100.00

JAMES ERNEST OF LIECHTENSTEIN-CASTELCORN, 1738-1745
Bust. Rev. Arms.

76. 1 Ducat 1739, 40 .... 150.00
77. ¼ Ducat ND 125.00

ANTHONY THEODORE COLLOREDO-WALLSEE, 1777-1811
Bust. Rev. Arms.

78. 1 Ducat 1779 .... 150.00

RUDOLPH JOHN OF AUSTRIA, 1819-1831
Bust. Rev. Arms.

79. 1 Ducat 1820 .... 225.00

ROSENBERG

Barons —

WILLIAM, 1581-1592
Bust right. Rev. Arms.

80. 4 Ducats 1585 .... 1200.00
81. 2 Ducats 1585 .... 1000.00

Arms. Rev. St. Christopher standing.

82. 2 Ducats 1584. Thick 1000.00
83. 1 Ducat 1582-88, 90 ....*...... 300.00

Arms. Rev. St. Christopher standing.

84. 1 Ducat 1592-95 .... 300.00

SCHLICK

Counts —

HENRY IV, 1612-1650

St. Anne and Virgin with shield. Rev. Eagle.

85. 10 Ducats 1627-46 ....*..... 2200.00
86. 5 Ducats 1634, 46, 49 .... 1100.00
87. 1 Ducat 1628-38 .... 400.00

FRANCIS ERNEST, 1652-1675
St. Anne above arms and Madonna. Rev. Eagle.

88. 5 Ducats 1661, 62 .... 1100.00

FRANCIS JOSEPH, 1675-1740
St. Anne. Rev. Eagle.

89. 1 Ducat 1716 .... 250.00

FRANCIS HENRY, 1740-1766
Madonna over arms. Rev. Eagle.

90. 1 Ducat 1759 .... 400.00

LEOPOLD HENRY, 1766-1770
Arms. Rev. Eagle.

91. 1 Ducat 1767 .,............................ 250.00

SCHWARZENBERG

Princes —

JOHN ADAM, 1641-1683

Bust. Rev. Arms.

92. 1 Ducat 1682 .... 450.00

FERDINAND WILLIAM EUSEBIUS, 1683-1703

Bust. Rev. Arms.

93.	5 Ducats ND ....*......	1100.00
94.	1 Ducat 1693, 95	350.00

ADAM FRANCIS, 1703-1732
Bust. Rev. Arms.

95.	1 Ducat 1710. Mint: Cologne	575.00
96.	1 Ducat 1721-32. Mint: Vienna	200.00

JOSEPH ADAM, 1732-1782

Bust. Rev. Arms.

97.	1 Ducat 1768	350.00

JOHN, 1782-1789

Bust. Rev. Arms.

98.	1 Ducat 1783	275.00

TESCHEN

Dukes of —

See under GERMANY (SILESIA-TESCHEN)

VISHEHRAD

Abbots of —

CHARLES JOSEPH MARTINITZ
Two shields. Rev. Legend.

99.	1 Ducat 1734	300.00

FERDINAND KINDERMANN SCHULSTEIN, 1782-1801
Arms. Rev. Legend.

100.	1 Ducat 1782	300.00

PROCOP BENEDICT HENNIGER EBERG, 1802
Shields and insignia. Rev. Legend.

101.	1 Ducat 1802	400.00

WALLENSTEIN

Duke of Friedland and Sagan

ALBERT WALLENSTEIN, 1625-1634
Facing bust. Rev. Arms with eagle.

102.	10 Ducats 1627, 29	4500.00
103.	5 Ducats 1627	2700.00
104.	2 Ducats 1627	1500.00
105.	1 Ducat 1627, 28, 29	400.00
106.	1 Goldgulden 1627, 28	1600.00

Bust right. Rev. Arms with eagle.

107.	10 Ducats 1628	4500.00
108.	5 Ducats 1628	2700.00
109.	1 Ducat 1628	1200.00

Facing bust. Rev. Arms. With title as Duke of Mecklenburg.

110.	10 Ducats 1630 (very rare), 31 ....*......	4000.00
111.	5 Ducats 1629-31, 33, 34	2500.00
112.	2 Ducats 1631, 33, 34	1700.00
113.	1 Ducat 1629-31, 33, 34 ....*......	500.00

BOLIVIA

Mints and mint marks: — PTS monogram for Potosi. The bust on No. 18 is the same type as Chile No. 28.

A. Spanish Kings of —

CHARLES III, 1759-1788

Bust. Rev. Arms.

1.	8 Escudos 1779-88	275.00
2.	4 Escudos 1778-88 ....*......	350.00
3.	2 Escudos 1778	450.00
4.	2 Escudos 1779-88	150.00
5.	1 Escudo 1780-87	125.00

CHARLES IV, 1788-1808
Bust of the previous King, Charles III. Rev. Arms.

6.	8 Escudos 1789, 90	250.00
7.	4 Escudos 1789, 90	Rare
8.	2 Escudos 1789, 90	225.00
9.	1 Escudo 1789, 90	225.00

Laureate bust. Rev. Arms.

10.	8 Escudos 1791	.............................*......	450.00
11.	4 Escudos 1791	....	750.00
12.	2 Escudos 1791	....	800.00
13.	1 Escudo 1791	....	250.00

Plain bust. Rev. Arms.

14.	8 Escudos 1791-1808	....	225.00
15.	4 Escudos 1792-1808	....	500.00
16.	2 Escudos 1793-1808	....	150.00
17.	1 Escudo 1793-1808	....	125.00

FERDINAND VII, 1808-1824
Uniformed bust. Rev. Arms.

18.	8 Escudos 1809	....	Rare

Laureate head. Rev. Arms.

19.	8 Escudos 1817, 22, 23, 24	...................*......	275.00
20.	1 Escudo 1822, 23, 24	....	150.00

B. Republic of —

Uniformed bust of Bolivar. Rev. Arms.

21.	8 Escudos 1831-40	...........................*......	300.00
22.	4 Escudos 1834	....	750.00
23.	2 Escudos 1834, 35, 39	....	150.00
24.	1 Escudo 1831-39	....	100.00
25.	½ Escudo 1834, 39, 40	....	85.00

Small laureate head of Bolivar to right, his name below. Rev. Arms.

26.	8 Escudos 1841-47	...........................*......	300.00
27.	4 Escudos 1841	....	1250.00
28.	2 Escudos 1841	....	500.00
29.	1 Escudo 1841, 42	....	150.00
30.	½ Escudo 1841-47	....	75.00

Plain head of Bolivar to left. Rev. Arms.

31.	8 Escudos 1851	....	600.00
32.	1 Escudo 1851	.... Unknown

Laureate head of Bolivar to left, his name on neck. Rev. Arms.

33.	8 Escudos 1852	....	750.00

Laureate head of Bolivar to right, his name on neck. Rev. Arms.

34.	8 Escudos 1852-57	....	300.00
35.	1 Escudo 1852-56	.........................*......	125.00
36.	½ Escudo 1852-56	....	125.00

Arms. Rev. Value, weight and fineness in wreath.

37.	1 Onza 1868	..............................*......	Rare
38.	1 Escudo 1868	....	300.00
39.	½ Escudo 1868	....	175.00

Special Issue of 1952

These coins commemorate the revolution of October 31, 1952. The values are expressed by weight in grams. All coins are dated 1952. The reverses of all coins show the National arms. The obverses are as follows:

40. 35 Grams. Head of Villaroel	150.00
41. 14 Grams. Head of Busch	100.00
42. 7 Grams. Miner	60.00
43. 3½ Grams. Head of worker	35.00

BRAZIL

Mints and mint marks:—

B or BBBB	mm for Bahia
R or RRRR	mm for Rio de Janeiro
PPPP	mm for Pernambuco
M or MMMM	mm for Minas Geraes

Brazilian gold coins were extensively counterstamped during the 18th and 19th centuries for use in other localities. Such coins may be found under Bahamas, Bermuda, British Guiana (Essequibo & Demerara), Grenada and Barlovento Islands, Guadeloupe, Jamaica, Martinique, Nevis, Saint Martin, Saint Vincent, Tobago, Trinidad, Virgin Islands and also under Portugal (1834, Mary II).

Under the Portuguese Kings, the coins on the Colonial or Decimal standard (20000, 10000, 4000, 2000, 1000 and 400 Reis) show the denominations, whereas the coins on the National or Escudo standard (12800, 6400, 3200, 1600 and 800 Reis) are without the marks of value.

The first gold coin under the Empire, the "Coronation Piece" of 6400 Reis, 1822-R, was not approved for circulation by the Emperor, Peter I, and of the 64 originally struck, only 15 have survived.

The 10000 Reis pieces dated 1833-1840 have the same intrinsic value as the 6400 Reis pieces of similar head (Peter II as a child at the age of 7) dated 1832 and 1833, but are smaller and thicker.

It is interesting to note that of the two gold types of the Republic, 20000 and 10000 Reis, 1889-1922, only the 10000 Reis piece shows the mark of value.

A. Dutch Government of Pernambuco, 1630-1654

G.W.C. monogram and value. Rev. Name and date. Square necessity coins struck by the Dutch West India Company (Geoctroyerde Westindische Compagnie).

1. XII Guilders 1645, 46	2250.00
2. VI Guilders 1645, 46 ....*	1500.00
3. III Guilders 1645, 46 ....*	1500.00

B. Brazil — Colony, 1500-1818

ALFONSO VI, 1656-1667; PETER, PRINCE REGENT, 1667-1683, AND PETER II, 1683-1706

Primitive Brazilian counterstamps over Portuguese 4, 2 and 1 Cruzado pieces from the reigns of Philip I, II and III; John IIII (IV) and Peter, Prince Regent.

Crown bearing numeral of value (in Cruzados) counterstamped on reverse of Portuguese coins.

4. Crowned 4 over 4 Cruzados ....*	1200.00
5. Crowned 2 over 2 Cruzados	1100.00
6. Crowned 1 over 1 Cruzado	1250.00

Portuguese counterstamps (value in Reis) for Portugal and Colonies.

7. Crowned 4400 over 4 Cruzados ....*	1250.00
8. Crowned 2200 over 2 Cruzados	1250.00
9. Crowned 1100 over 1 Cruzado	1500.00

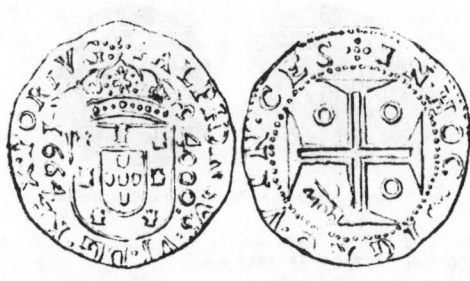

Conjoined counterstamps (values in Cruzados and Reis) on the Cruzado coinage of Portugal.

10. Crowned 4 and 4400 over 4 Cruzados ....*	1400.00
11. Crowned 2 and 2200 over 2 Cruzados	1300.00
12. Crowned 1 and 1100 over 1 Cruzado	1500.00

Two or three counterstamps on the Cruzado coinage of Portugal; one counterstamp being a crowned globe, the others being the value in Cruzados and/or the value in Reis.

13. Crowned Globe, 4 and/or 4400 over 4 Cruzados	1600.00
14. Crowned Globe, 2 and/or 2200 over 2 Cruzados	1500.00
15. Crowned Globe, 1 and/or 1100 over 1 Cruzado	1500.00

PETER II, 1683-1706

Arms and value. Rev. Plain cross in quadrilobe.

BAHIA.

16. 4000 Reis 1695. Large crown. No mm.	120.00
17. 4000 Reis 1696-98. No mm. ....*	100.00
18. 2000 Reis 1695. Large crown. No mm.	1000.00
19. 2000 Reis 1696, 97. No mm.	80.00
20. 1000 Reis 1696, 97. No mm.	500.00

RIO.

21. 4000 Reis 1699, 1700. No mm.	90.00
22. 2000 Reis 1699, 1700. No mm.	75.00
23. 1000 Reis 1699, 1700. No mm.	60.00

PERNAMBUCO.

24. 4000 Reis 1702. PPPP mm.	700.00

Arms and value. Rev. Cross of Jerusalem.

RIO.

25.	4000 Reis 1703-07. RRRR mm. ....*		350.00
26.	2000 Reis 1703. RRRR mm.		400.00

JOHN V, 1706-1750

Arms and value. Rev. Cross of Jerusalem.

RIO.

27.	4000 Reis 1707-27, RRRR mm.	175.00
28.	2000 Reis 1723, 25, 26. RRRR mm.	150.00
29.	1000 Reis 1708, 26. RRRR mm.	200.00

BAHIA.

30.	4000 Reis 1714-27. BBBB mm.	200.00
31.	2000 Reis 1714-25. BBBB mm. ....*	125.00
32.	1000 Reis 1714-26. BBBB mm.	275.00

MINAS GERAES.

33.	20000 Reis 1724-27. MMMM mm.	750.00
34.	10000 Reis 1724-27. MMMM mm.	500.00
35.	4000 Reis 1724-27. MMMM mm.	450.00
36.	2000 Reis 1724-27. MMMM mm.	300.00
37.	1000 Reis 1724-27. MMMM mm.	250.00

Crowned name and value. Rev. Cross of Jerusalem.

RIO.

38.	400 Reis 1730. RRRR mm.	400.00

MINAS GERAES.

39.	400 Reis 1724-26. MMMM mm. ....*	250.00

Laureate head. Rev. Oval arms.

RIO.

40.	12800 Reis 1727-31. R mm.	450.00
41.	6400 Reis 1727-31. R mm.	700.00
42.	3200 Reis 1727, 29. R mm.	500.00
43.	1600 Reis 1727-30. R mm.	400.00
44.	800 Reis 1727, 30. R mm.	175.00

Laureate head. Rev. Italic arms

RIO.

45.	12800 Reis 1731-33. R mm.	600.00
46.	6400 Reis 1732-50. R mm.	225.00

47.	3200 Reis 1739, 41, 49. R mm.	400.00
48.	1600 Reis 1736. R mm.	350.00
49.	800 Reis 1734, 36, 49. R mm.	175.00

BAHIA.

50.	12800 Reis 1727-32. B mm.	750.00
51.	6400 Reis 1727-50 (1727-34 rare). B mm. ....*	250.00
52.	3200 Reis 1727-50. B mm.	500.00
53.	1600 Reis 1727-50. B mm.	400.00
54.	800 Reis 1727-51. B mm.	250.00

MINAS GERAES.

55.	12800 Reis 1727-33. M mm.	450.00
56.	6400 Reis 1727, 32-34. M mm.	600.00
57.	3200 Reis 1727-33. M mm.	400.00
58.	1600 Reis 1727-33. M mm.	200.00
59.	800 Reis 1727-34. M mm.	100.00

Laureate head. Rev. Crown over date.

RIO.

60.	400 Reis 1734. R mm. ....*	65.00

MINAS GERAES.

61.	400 Reis 1730, 32-34. M mm.	65.00

Arms and value. Rev. Plain cross in quadrilobe. Without mint mark. Struck at Lisbon for the state of Maranhão.

LISBON.

62.	4000 Reis 1749. No mm.	150.00
63.	2000 Reis 1749. No mm.	100.00
64.	1000 Reis 1749. No mm.	75.00

JOSEPH I, 1750-1777

Laureate head. Rev. Arms.

RIO.

65.	6400 Reis 1751-77. R mm.	125.00
66.	3200 Reis 1755-73. R mm. ....*	275.00
67.	1600 Reis 1752, 63, 72. R mm.	200.00
68.	800 Reis 1752, 63. R mm.	250.00

BAHIA.

69.	6400 Reis 1751-77. B mm.	175.00
70.	3200 Reis 1752-74. B mm.	350.00
71.	1600 Reis 1752-77. B mm.	250.00
72.	800 Reis 1752-77. B mm.	250.00

Arms and value. Rev. Plain cross in quadrilobe. With IOSEPHUS or JOSEPHUS; DOMINVS or DOMINUS. Without mint mark. Struck at Lisbon, Rio and Bahia.

73.	4000 Reis 1751-77. No mm. ....*	125.00
74.	2000 Reis 1752-73. No mm.	75.00
75.	1000 Reis 1749 (Rev. of John V), 52, 71, 74. No mm.	65.00

MARY I AND PETER III, 1777-1786

Conjoined busts. Rev. Arms.

RIO.
76.   6400 Reis 1777-86. R mm. . . . .* 125.00

BAHIA.
77.   6400 Reis 1777-86. B mm. 200.00
78.   3200 Reis 1780-86. B mm. 400.00
79.   1600 Reis 1780-84. B mm. 400.00
80.   800 Reis 1782, 86. B mm. 450.00

Arms and value. Rev. Plain cross in quadrilobe. Without mint mark.

RIO.
81.   4000 Reis 1778. No mm. 125.00

LISBON, RIO.
82.   4000 Reis 1779, 81, 83, 86. No mm. 150.00
83.   2000 Reis 1778, 81-83 (1781-83 rare). No mm. 100.00
84.   1000 Reis 1778, 79, 81, 82 (rare). No mm. 80.00

MARY I, 1786-1805

Bust with widow's veil. Rev. Arms.

RIO.
85.   6400 Reis 1786-89. R mm. 175.00

BAHIA.
86.   6400 Reis 1787-90. B mm. . . . . * 225.00

Bust in decorative headdress. Rev. Arms.

RIO.
87.   6400 Reis 1789-1805. R mm. . . . .* 125.00

BAHIA.
88.   6400 Reis 1790-1804 (1790 rare). B mm. 175.00

Arms and value. Rev. Plain cross in quadrilobe. Without mint mark.

LISBON, RIO.
89.   4000 Reis 1787, 90, 92 (1790, 92 rare). No mm. 120.00
90.   2000 Reis 1787, 92, 93. No mm. . . . .* 100.00
91.   1000 Reis 1787. No mm. 70.00

BAHIA.
92.   4000 Reis 1801-05. No mm. 100.00

JOHN, PRINCE REGENT, 1805-1818

Laureate bust. Rev. Arms.

RIO.
93.   6400 Reis 1805-17 (1815-17 rare). R mm . . . .* 125.00
94.   6400 Reis 1816, with BRAS. ET. ALG. R mm. 900.00

Arms and value. Rev. Plain cross in quadrilobe. Without mint mark. Pieces from the Rio Mint have the date between two small flowers; those from the Bahia Mint have the date between two points (1805-11) or between two small flowers but cruder coinage (1811-16).

RIO.
95.   4000 Reis 1808-17. No mm. . . . .* 100.00
96.   4000 Reis 1816, with BRAS. ET. ALG. No mm. 400.00

BAHIA.
97.   4000 Reis 1805-16. No mm. 125.00

C. Brazil — United Kingdom, 1818-1822

JOHN VI, 1818-1822 (Brazil)

Laureate bust. Rev. Arms.

RIO.
98.   6400 Reis 1818-20, 21, 22 (1821, 22 rare). R mm. 750.00

Arms and value. Rev. Plain cross in quadrilobe. Without mint mark. Pieces from the Rio Mint have the date between two small flowers or between two small crosses (1819); those from the Bahia Mint have the date between two small crosses but cruder coinage.

RIO.

99. 4000 Reis 1818-22. No mm. . . . .*. 150.00

BAHIA.

100. 4000 Reis 1819, 20. No mm. 500.00

Crudely shaped rectangular gold bars, 1778-1833 (Colony, United Kingdom and Empire), issued as current money at Cuiabá, Goiás, Mato Grosso, Rio das Mortes, Sabará, Serro Frio and Vila Rica, assay offices in Brazil, and punched with various stamps, including arms and globe, date, weight, fineness and the assayer's monogram.

101. Gold Bar—Cuiabá 2000.00
102. Gold Bar—Goiás 1800.00
103. Gold Bar—Mato Grosso 2000.00
104. Gold Bar—Rio das Mortes 1800.00
105. Gold Bar—Sabará 1600.00
106. Gold Bar—Serro Frio 1700.00
107. Gold Bar—Vila Rica and 960 . . . .*. 1600.00

D. Brazil — Empire, 1822-1889

PETER I, 1822-1831

Laureate head with "Z. FERREZ" below. Rev. Arms. Without the mark of value. Coronation piece, not placed in circulation.

RIO.

108. 6400 Reis 1822. R mm. 7500.00

Bust in naval uniform. Rev. Arms.

RIO.

109. 6400 Reis 1823-30. R mm. 1000.00
110. 4000 Reis 1823-27. R mm. . . . .*. 350.00

BAHIA.

111. 6400 Reis 1825, 26, 28. B mm. 1000.00
112. 4000 Reis 1825, 26, 28. B mm. 650.00

PETER II, 1831-1889

Child head. Rev. Arms. With and without the engraver's name. The 10000 Reis piece is without the mark of value.

RIO.

113. 6400 Reis 1832. R mm. AZEVEDO F. below bust 500.00
114. 4000 Reis 1832. R mm. AZEVEDO F. below bust 4000.00
115. 6400 Reis 1832, 33. R mm. 250.00
116. 4000 Reis 1832, 33. R mm. 1000.00
117. 10000 Reis 1833-40 . . . .*. 250.00

Bust in naval uniform. Rev. Arms. Without the mark of value.

118. 10000 Reis 1841-48 . . . . 300.00

Bust in Coronation Robe (Papo Tucano). Rev. Arms. Without the mark of value.

119. 20000 Reis 1849-51 . . . .*. 225.00
120. 10000 Reis 1849-51 . . . . 175.00

Bearded head. Rev. Arms. Without the mark of value.

121. 20000 Reis 1851-89 . . . . 125.00
122. 10000 Reis 1853-89 . . . . 90.00
123. 5000 Reis 1854-59 . . . .*. 75.00

E. Brazil — Republic, 1889-

Liberty head. Rev. The Stars of the Southern Cross. Without the mark of value.

124. 20000 Reis 1889-1922 . . . . 325.00

Liberty head. Rev. Arms of the Republic.

25. 10000 Reis 1889-1922 .... 325.00

BRITISH COLUMBIA

The two coins listed are of extreme rarity. They were struck in British Columbia as trials for a proposed coinage, but the actual issuance of the coins was forbidden by England.

Crown. Rev. Value and date. These coins were not placed in circulation.

    20 Dollars 1862 .... Rare
    10 Dollars 1862 ....*...... Rare

BRITISH GUIANA

Brazilian gold coins of the period 1727-1804 counterstamped ED (Essequibo and Demerara) and with or without other counterstamps.

. 6400 Reis 1727-1804 .... 750.00

BULGARIA

Bulgarian coinage is based on the Latin Monetary Union standard, excepting the Ducat coinage. The coins of 1894 are rare in perfect uncirculated condition; the coinage of that year is as follows: 100 Leva, 7500 pieces; 20 Leva, 175,000 pieces; 10 Leva, 75,000 pieces.

Kings of —

IVAN-ASSEN II, 1218-1241

Ruler and St. Dimitar. Rev. Christ standing. On the victory over the Byzantine Empire in the battle of Klokotnitza.

1.   1 Solidus ND .... Rare

FERDINAND, 1887-1918

Head. Rev. Arms.

2.   100 Leva 1894 .... 600.00
3.   20 Leva 1894 ....*...... 65.00
4.   10 Leva 1894 ....*...... 60.00

Head. Rev. Crowned oval shield. On the 25th year of reign. The date 1912 is in very small numerals under the shield.

5.   100 Leva 1912 .... 500.00
6.   20 Leva 1912 ....*...... 75.00

SPECIAL ISSUES

Uniformed bust. Rev. Arms with small crown counterstamped at bottom.
7.   4 Ducats 1910, 12 .... 600.00

BORIS III, 1918-1943

Uniformed bust. Rev. Arms with small crown counterstamped at bottom.
8.   4 Ducats 1926 .... 600.00

Republic of —

Standing figures of Saints Cyril and Methodius. Rev. Value above shield. On the 1100th anniversary of the Slavic alphabet.

9.	20 Leva 1963	..............................*......	175.00
10.	10 Leva 1963	....	100.00

Head of Premier Dimitrov. Rev. Flag above value. On the 20th anniversary of the People's Republic.

11.	20 Leva 1964	...............................*......	150.00
12.	10 Leva 1964	....	85.00

BURMA

Kings of —

MINDON MIN, 1852-1878

Burmese type lion. Rev. Legend in wreath.

1.	8 Rupees 1878	....	450.00
2.	4 Rupees 1878	........................*......	250.00
3.	2 Rupees 1866	........................*......	150.00
4.	1 Rupee 1852	....	125.00

THEBAW, 1878-1885

Peacock. Rev. Legend in wreath.

5.	5 Rupees ND (1880)	....	400.00
6.	2 Rupees 1880	....	175.00
7.	1 Rupee 1880	......................*......	125.00

CAMBODIA

The bird Hamsa. Rev. Legend.

1.	1 Fuang ND (1846)	....	250.0

Head of King Norodom I. Rev. Arms. Souvenir gold coins struck from dies used for silver coins.

2.	1 Piastre 1860	....	1500.0
3.	2 Francs 1860	.......................*......	450.0
4.	1 Franc 1860	....	300.0
5.	50 Centimes 1860	....	225.0
6.	25 Centimes 1860	....	150.0

CANADA

EDWARD VII, 1901-1910

Head. Rev. St. George. As the English Pound but with the distinguishing mintmark C on ground below horse.

1.	1 Pound 1908-10 (1908 rare)	....	125.0

GEORGE V, 1910-1936

Head. Rev. St. George. As the English Pound but with the distinguishing mintmark C on ground below horse.

2.	1 Pound 1911-19 (1913, 16 rare)	....	40.0

Crowned head. Rev. Arms.

3.	10 Dollars 1912-14	....	225.
4.	5 Dollars 1912-14 (1914 rare)	....	95.

QUEEN ELIZABETH II, 1952-

Head. Rev. Arms. On the 100th Anniversary of Confederation.

5.	20 Dollars 1967	....	80.

CEYLON

Ruler standing. Rev. Ruler seated. Crude style. Struck during the period 840-1295 A.D.

1.	1 Stater ND	............................*......	225.00
2.	½ Stater ND	....	115.00
3.	¼ Stater ND	....	75.00
4.	⅛ Stater ND	....	60.00

Ruler kneeling. Rev. Legend. Crude style.

| 5. | 1 Mas ND (840-1295 A.D.) | .... | 75.00 |

Ruler standing. Rev. Legend. Crude style.

| 6. | 1 Mas ND (840-1295 A.D.) | .... | 75.00 |

"C" (For Colombo) and "VOC" monogram (Dutch East India Company) counterstamped on continental Dutch gold coins.

| 7. | 2 Ducats 1691 | .... | Unique |

Standing god. Rev. Granular surface.

| 8. | 1 Pagoda ND (1760-94) | .... | 100.00 |

CHILE

Mints and mint marks: — S topped by small o for Santiago.
On the coins from 1846-1851, the Grecian helmet worn by Liberty in earlier years, is replaced by the Liberty Cap.

A. Spanish Kings of —

PHILIP V, 1700-1746

Bust. Rev. Arms. This issue was not placed in circulation. The last two coins were struck during the reign of Ferdinand VI.

1.	8 Escudos 1744	....	Rare
2.	4 Escudos 1744	....	Rare
3.	2 Escudos 1758	....	Rare
4.	1 Escudo 1754	....	Rare

FERDINAND VI, 1746-1760

Small bust. Rev. Arms.

5.	8 Escudos 1750-60	......................*......	500.00
6.	4 Escudos 1749-52	....	750.00
7.	1 Escudo 1754, 59	....	500.00

Large bust. Rev. Arms.

| 8. | 8 Escudos 1760 | .... | 450.00 |

CHARLES III, 1759-1788

Bust of the previous King, Ferdinand VI. Rev. Arms.

| 9. | 8 Escudos 1760-63 | ....*...... | 500.00 |
| 10. | 1 Escudo 1761, 62 | .... | 400.00 |

Bust. Rev. Arms without value.

11.	8 Escudos 1764-72	....	400.00
12.	4 Escudos 1763	..............................*......	750.00
13.	2 Escudos 1764	....	Rare
14.	1 Escudo 1763, 64, 66	....	300.00

Bust. Rev. Arms with value.

15.	8 Escudos 1772-89	..........................*......	200.00
16.	4 Escudos 1773-89	....	400.00
17.	2 Escudos 1773-88	....	200.00
18.	1 Escudo 1772-88	....	150.00

CHARLES IV, 1788-1808

Bust of the previous King, Charles III with title as "Carol IV." Rev. Arms.

19.	8 Escudos 1789, 90	..........................*......	225.00
20.	4 Escudos 1789, 90	....	450.00
21.	2 Escudos 1790	....	750.00
22.	1 Escudo 1790	....	150.00

Bust of the previous King, Charles III with title as "Carol IIII." Rev. Arms.

23.	8 Escudos 1791-1808	..................*......	250.00
24.	2 Escudos 1791-1808	....	200.00
25.	1 Escudo 1791	....	125.00

Hand on the book of the Constitution. Rev. Arms.

37.	8 Escudos 1835-38	..................*.....	200.00
38.	4 Escudos 1836, 37	....	300.00
39.	2 Escudos 1837, 38	....	150.00
40.	1 Escudo 1838	....	75.00

Bust of Charles IV. Rev. Arms.

26.	4 Escudos 1791-1808	....	500.00
27.	1 Escudo 1791-1808	....	125.00

FERDINAND VII, 1808-1821

Large uniformed bust. Rev. Arms.

28.	8 Escudos 1808-11	....	275.00

Liberty as Pallas Athene standing at altar. Rev. Arms. The 8 Escudos from 1839-43 has a striated edge; from 1843-51 it has the month of issue inscribed on the edge.

41.	8 Escudos 1839-51	..................*......	200.00
42.	4 Escudos 1839, 41	....	1000.00
43.	2 Escudos 1839-51	....	75.00
44.	1 Escudo 1839-51	....	50.00

Bust of the previous King, Charles IV. Rev. Arms.

29.	8 Escudos 1812-17	....	250.00
30.	4 Escudos 1810-17	..................*......	400.00
31.	2 Escudos 1811-17	....	300.00
32.	1 Escudo 1811-18	....	150.00

Liberty standing at altar. Rev. Arms.

45.	10 Pesos 1851-92	..................*......	125.00
46.	5 Pesos 1851-73	....	50.00
47.	2 Pesos 1857-75	....	35.00

B. Republic of —

Liberty standing at altar. Rev. Value in wreath.

48.	1 Peso 1860-73	....	30.00

Head of Liberty wearing cap. Rev. Arms.

49.	10 Pesos 1895	..................*......	65.00
50.	5 Pesos 1895, 96	....	40.00

Sun, mountains and volcanos. Rev. Crossed flags.

33.	8 Escudos 1818-34	..................*......	200.00
34.	4 Escudos 1824-34	....	350.00
35.	2 Escudos 1818-34	....	125.00
36.	1 Escudo 1824-34	....	75.00

Draped Liberty head with coiled hair. Rev. Arms.

51. 20 Pesos 1896-1917	....................*......	75.00
52. 10 Pesos 1896, 98, 1901	....................*......	50.00
53. 5 Pesos 1898, 1900	....	40.00

Liberty head with coiled hair. Rev. Arms. Two values appear on these coins.

54. 100 Pesos—10 Condores 1926-58	...............*......	55.00
55. 50 Pesos— 5 Condores 1926	....	40.00
56. 20 Pesos— 2 Condores 1926	...............*......	40.00

CHINA

The seventeen coins listed are the only ones which can be regarded as authentic Chinese gold coins, and of these seventeen, only numbers 4, 5, 10, 11 and 12 circulated to any extent. The many other Chinese "gold coins" which exist are either gold impressions from dies for silver coins or are outright fantasies.

A. Emperors of China

KUANG HSU, 1875-1908

Large dragon. Rev. Legend. The coins with reeded edge were reportedly not struck officially.

1. 1 Tael 1906, 07. Plain edge	....	1500.00
2. 1 Tael 1906, 07. Reeded edge	....	1250.00

B. Republic of China

Head of President Yuan Shi Kai. Rev. Dragon with Chinese legend reading "Empire of China."

3. 10 Yuans 1916	....	1000.00

Head of President Yuan Shi Kai. Rev. Legend and wreath.

4. 20 Yuans 1919	.................*......	600.00
5. 10 Yuans 1919	....	400.00

C. Republican Provinces of China

SHANTUNG

Dragon and Phoenix. Rev. Legend.

6. 20 Yuans 1926	...................—	2500.00
7. 10 Yuans 1926	.................*......	2000.00

YUNNAN

Five vertical characters flanked on each side by five dots. Rev. Blank.

8. 10 Yuans ND (1917)	....	300.00
9. 5 Yuans ND (1917)	....	300.00

Facing head of General Tang Chi Yao. Rev. Crossed flags.

10. 10 Yuans 1919. Numeral "1" below flags	......*......	300.00
11. 10 Yuans 1919. Without numeral	....	500.00
12. 5 Yuans 1919. Numeral "2" below flags	......*......	250.00

Four characters around central dot. Rev. One character within grain wreath.

13. 10 Yuans ND (1925)	....	600.00
14. 5 Yuans ND (1925)	....	600.00

D. Nationalist China

Head of Dr. Sun Yat-sen. Rev. Value in floral wreath. On the 100th anniversary of his birth.

15. 2000 Yuan 1965 (Year 54)	.................*......	125.00
16. 1000 Yuan 1965 (Year 54)	.................*......	75.00

Bust of Chiang Kai-shek. Rev. Two cranes and flowers. On his 80th birthday.

17. 2000 Yuan 1966 (Year 55) 125.00

COLOMBIA

Mints and mint marks: — Under the Spanish Kings, NR for Bogota; P or PN for Popayan; SF or FS for Santa Fe de Bogota. Under the Republic, the mints of Bogota, Popayan and Medellin used their names in full on the coins, with an occasional B or P for the first two.

All 5 Peso pieces of the 19th century are rare. During the latter part of the 19th century, the coinage was based on the Latin Monetary Union standard and in the 20th century, on that of the English Pound.

A. Spanish Kings of —

PHILIP IV, 1621-1665
Arms. Rev. Cross. Crude Cob type.

1. 2 Escudos ND, 1628, 33-35, 40-42, 50, 52-54. .... 250.00

CHARLES II, 1665-1700
Arms. Rev. Cross. Cob type.

2. 2 Escudos ND or partial date. 225.00
3. 2 Escudos 1672, 87, 1701. .... 500.00
4. 1 Escudo ND. 275.00

PHILIP V, 1700-1746
Arms. Rev. Cross. Cob type.

5. 8 Escudos 1744, 46. SF or FS mm. .... Rare
6. 4 Escudos 1740, 45. FS mm. 1000.00
7. 2 Escudos 1719, 20, 26, 30, 33, 35, 37, 43. FS or SF mm. 350.00
8. 1 Escudo 1736, 46. FS mm. 200.00

FERDINAND VI, 1746-1760
Arms. Rev. Cross. Cob type.

8a. 8 Escudos 1754-56. SF or FS mm. 2000.00

Bust. Rev. Arms.

9. 8 Escudos 1756-59. NR mm. 500.00
10. 8 Escudos 1758, 59, 60. P or PN mm. 500.00
11. 4 Escudos 1757, 59. NR mm. 550.00
12. 4 Escudos 1758. NR mm. 1200.00
13. 4 Escudos 1758-60. P or PN mm. 475.00
14. 2 Escudos 1756-59. NR mm. ....*...... 225.00
15. 2 Escudos 1758-61. P or PN mm. 225.00
16. 1 Escudo 1756-59. NR mm. 125.00
17. 1 Escudo 1758, 59. P or PN mm. 125.00

CHARLES III, 1759-1788

Bust of the previous King, Ferdinand VI. Rev. Arms.

18. 8 Escudos 1760-62. NR mm. 450.00
19. 8 Escudos 1760-71. P or PN mm. 450.00
20. 4 Escudos 1760. NR mm. 750.00
21. 4 Escudos 1760-69. P or PN mm. 450.00
22. 2 Escudos 1760-62. NR mm. 175.00
23. 2 Escudos 1760-71. P or PN mm. ....*..... 200.00
24. 1 Escudo NR mm. .... Unknown
25. 1 Escudo 1760-69. P or PN mm. 100.00

Bust with name as "Carolus." Rev. Arms without value. This type was not struck at the Popayan Mint.

26. 8 Escudos 1763-71. NR mm. 450.00
27. 4 Escudos 1769-71. NR mm. 750.00
28. 2 Escudos 1762-71. NR mm. ....*...... 275.00
29. 1 Escudo 1767. NR mm. 200.00

Bust with name as "Carol." Rev. Arms with value.

30. 8 Escudos 1772-89. NR mm. 250.00
31. 8 Escudos 1772-89. P or PN mm. 250.00
32. 4 Escudos 1775-87. NR mm. 500.00
33. 4 Escudos 1771-86. P or PN mm. 450.00
34. 2 Escudos 1772-89. NR mm. 150.00
35. 2 Escudos 1771-89. P or PN mm. ....*..... 150.00
36. 1 Escudo 1772-89. NR mm. 100.00
37. 1 Escudo 1772-89. P or PN mm. 100.00

CHARLES IV, 1788-1808

Bust of the previous King, Charles III. Rev. Arms.

38. 8 Escudos 1789-91. NR mm. 200.00
39. 8 Escudos 1789-91. P or PN mm. 200.00
40. 4 Escudos 1789, 90. NR mm. 300.00
41. 4 Escudos 1789, 90. P or PN mm. 300.00
42. 2 Escudos 1789, 90. NR mm. 150.00
43. 2 Escudos 1789-91. P or PN mm. ....*..... 125.00
44. 1 Escudo 1790. NR mm. 75.00
45. 1 Escudo 1789, 90. P or PN mm. 90.00

Bust. Rev. Arms.

46.	8 Escudos 1791-1808. NR mm.	200.00
47.	8 Escudos 1791-1808. P or PN mm.	200.00
48.	4 Escudos 1792-1807. NR mm.	450.00
49.	4 Escudos 1792-1801. P or PN mm.	300.00
50.	4 Escudos 1807, 08. P or PN mm.	1200.00
51.	2 Escudos 1790-1805. NR mm.	125.00
52.	2 Escudos 1791-1805. P or PN mm. ....*	125.00
53.	1 Escudo 1792-1808. NR mm.	75.00
54.	1 Escudo 1792-1808. P or PN mm.	75.00

FERDINAND VII, 1808-1824

Bust of the previous King, Charles IV. Rev. Arms.

55.	8 Escudos 1808-20. NR mm.	200.00
56.	8 Escudos 1808-20. P or PN mm. ....*	200.00
57.	4 Escudos 1818, 19. NR mm.	450.00
58.	2 Escudos 1808-17. NR mm.	150.00
59.	2 Escudos 1817-19. P or PN mm.	150.00
60.	1 Escudo 1808-20. NR mm.	65.00
61.	1 Escudo 1808-19. P or PN mm.	75.00

B. Republic of —

I. Coinage of the Republic of Colombia

Liberty head. Rev. Fasces within a double cornucopia and above, "Bogota" or "Popayan," the place of minting.

62.	8 Escudos 1822-37. Bogota	225.00
63.	8 Escudos 1822-36. Popayan.	200.00
64.	4 Escudos 1826. Bogota.	900.00
65.	2 Escudos 1824-36. Bogota.	75.00
66.	1 Escudo 1823-33. Bogota.	40.00
67.	1 Escudo 1823-36. Popayan. ....*	40.00
68.	1 Peso 1825-36. Bogota.	40.00

II. Coinage of the Republic of New Granada

Draped Liberty head. Rev. Arms and "Bogota" or "Popayan"

69.	16 Pesos 1837-46. Bogota	200.00
70.	16 Pesos 1837-46. Popayan.	200.00
71.	2 Pesos 1838-46. Popayan. ....*	75.00
72.	1 Peso 1837-46. Bogota. ....*	40.00

Plain Liberty head. Rev. Arms with the value of the coins expressed by their weight in grams.

73.	16 Pesos 1848-53 Bogota. 25.8064 grams. ......*	750.00
74.	10 Pesos 1854-57. Bogota. 16.400 grams.	400.00
75.	10 Pesos 1853. Popayan. 16.400 grams.	400.00
76.	2 Pesos 1849, 51. Bogota. 3.2258 grams.	125.00

Liberty head and "Nueva Granada." Rev. Value in wreath with B or P as mint marks.

77.	5 Pesos 1856, 57, 58. B mm. ....*	225.00
78.	2 Pesos 1857, 58. P mm.	125.00
79.	1 Peso 1856, 58. B mm.	150.00

Liberty head and "Republica de la Nueva Granada." Rev. Arms with place of minting below.

| 80. | 10 Pesos 1857, 58. Bogota. ....* | 750.00 |
| 81. | 10 Pesos 1856, 57, 58. Popayan. | 275.00 |

III. Coinage of the Granadine Confederation

Liberty head. Rev. Arms and place of minting.

82.	20 Pesos 1858, 59. Bogota.	Rare
83.	10 Pesos 1859-61. Bogota. ....*	200.00
84.	10 Pesos 1858-62. Popayan.	250.00
85.	5 Pesos 1859. Popayan.	675.00

Liberty head. Rev. Value in wreath.

86.	5 Pesos 1862. Medellin.	Rare
87.	2 Pesos 1859, 60. Popayan ....*	100.00
88.	1 Peso 1862. Medellin.	150.00

IV. Coinage of the United States of Colombia

Liberty head with "Colombia" only in legend. Rev. Value and date in wreath. Medellin Mint.

89.	5 Pesos 1862, 63, 64. ....*......	450.00
90.	1 Peso 1863, 64.	100.00

Liberty head with "Estados Unidos de Colombia" in legend. Rev. Value in wreath. Medellin Mint.

91.	5 Pesos 1863 ....*......	Rare
92.	2 Pesos 1863	175.00
93.	1 Peso 1863	150.00

Liberty head. Rev. Arms and place of minting.

94.	20 Pesos 1862-77. Bogota.	300.00
95.	20 Pesos 1862-75. Popayan.	400.00
96.	20 Pesos 1868-72. Medellin.	375.00
97.	10 Pesos 1862, 63. Bogota.	175.00
98.	10 Pesos 1863-67. Popayan.	200.00
99.	10 Pesos 1863-76. Medellin. ....*......	175.00
100.	5 Pesos 1885. Medellin	1500.00
101.	2 Pesos 1871-76. Medellin.	50.00
102.	1 Peso 1872, 73. Medellin.	45.00

Liberty head. Rev. Condor and place of minting.

103.	1 Peso 1872. Medellin.	65.00
104.	1 Peso 1871-78. Bogota. ....*......	40.00

V. Coinage of the Republic of Colombia (again)

Workman chipping at rock. Rev. Arms.

105.	5 Pesos 1913-19.	35.00
106.	2½ Pesos 1913.	50.00

Large head of Bolivar. Rev. Arms.

107.	10 Pesos 1919-24.	75.00
108.	5 Pesos 1919-24.	50.00
109.	2½ Pesos 1919, 20. ....*......	60.00

Small head of Bolivar. Rev. Arms.

110.	5 Pesos 1924-30. ....*......	50.00
111.	2½ Pesos 1924-28.	50.00

COSTA RICA

Sun and five mountain peaks. Rev. Tree. The 2, 1 and ½ Escudo pieces come with or without a counterstamped lion.

1.	8 Escudos 1828, 33, 37.	900.00
2.	4 Escudos 1828-50.	500.00
3.	2 Escudos 1828-50. ....*......	125.00
4.	1 Escudo 1825-49.	75.00
5.	½ Escudo 1825-49.	50.00

Small star on larger radiant star. Rev. Tree.

6.	1 Escudo 1842.	275.00

Indian leaning against column. Rev. Arms.

7.	½ Onza 1850. ....*......	175.00
8.	2 Escudos 1850-63.	125.00
9.	1 Escudo 1850-55.	50.00
10.	½ Escudo 1850-64.	35.00

Arms. Rev. Value spelled out.

11. 10 Pesos 1870, 71, 72. Large size. 100.00
12. 5 Pesos 1867-70. Large size. 75.00
13. 5 Pesos 1873, 75. Small size. 125.00
14. 2 Pesos 1866-68. Large size. ....*...... 40.00
15. 1 Peso 1864-71. Large size. 30.00
16. 1 Peso 1871, 72. Small size. 30.00

Arms. Rev. Value expressed in numerals.

17. 20 Pesos 1873. .... 1500.00
18. 5 Pesos 1873. ....*...... 600.00

Head of Columbus. Rev. Arms.

19. 20 Colones 1897-1900. ....*...... 200.00
20. 10 Colones 1897-1900. ....*...... 85.00
21. 5 Colones 1899, 1900. .... 60.00
22. 2 Colones 1897-1928. .... 50.00

COURLAND

Dukes of —

JAMES
Bust. Rev. Arms.

1. 1 Ducat 1646 .... 1000.00

FREDERICK CASIMIR, 1682-1698

Bust. Rev. Eagle.

2. 1 Ducat 1689 .... 800.00

ERNEST JOHN
Bust. Rev. Arms.

3. 1 Ducat 1764 .... 400.00

PETER BIRON, 1769-1795

Head. Rev. Two shields.

4. 1 Ducat 1780 .... 500.00

CROATIA

Head of the Duke of Aosta as king. Rev. Value over shield.
This coin was not placed in circulation. 12 pieces struck.

1. 500 Kuna 1941 ....   Rare

CUBA

The coinage was struck at the Philadelphia Mint, and is without a mint mark. The 20 pesos of 1916 is extremely rare as proof specimens only were struck and only a few are known. Cuban coinage is based on the U. S. gold standard.

Head of Marti. Rev. Arms.

1. 20 Pesos 1915. .... 250.00
2. 20 Pesos 1916. ....   Rare
3. 10 Pesos 1915, 16. .... 75.00
4. 5 Pesos 1915, 16. ....*...... 45.00
5. 4 Pesos 1915, 16. ....*...... 125.00
6. 2 Pesos 1915, 16. ....*...... 75.00
7. 1 Peso 1915, 16. .... 125.00

CURACAO

Gold coins of Brazil and Portugal with five round counterstamps on Obv. — GI, L, MH and B close to border, and GH in center. Rev. W stamped within a line circle.

1. 6400 Reis 1776. Rio mint 1250.00
2. 6400 Reis 1781. .... 1250.00

CYPRUS

The gold coinage of Cyprus belongs to the series of the Crusader Kings.

Kings of—

JOHN I, 1184-1185
King standing. Rev. Christ seated.

1. 1 Bezant ND 750.00

HUGH I, 1205-1218

King standing. Rev. Christ seated.

2. 1 Bezant ND 600.00

HENRY I, 1218-1253
King standing. Rev. Christ seated.

3. 1 Bezant ND 450.00

HENRY II, 1285-1324
King standing. Rev. Christ seated.

4. 1 Bezant ND 450.00

CZECHOSLOVAKIA

(Formerly the ancient kingdom of Bohemia, which see).

Half-length figure of St. Wenceslas. Rev. Shield.

1. 2 Ducats 1923-38, 51 ....*...... 80.00
2. 1 Ducat 1923-38, 51 .... 35.00
3. 1 Ducat 1923. With a number from 1 to 1,000 next to date. 70.00

St. Wenceslas on horse. Rev. Shield.

4. 10 Ducats 1929-38, 51 .... 300.00
5. 5 Ducats 1929-38, 51 ....*...... 175.00

COMMEMORATIVES AND SPECIAL ISSUES

Saint holding plow drawn by Devil. Rev. Arms. On the 10th year of the Republic.

6. 4 Ducats 1928 ....*...... 135.00
7. 2 Ducats 1928 .... 90.00

Standing figure with banner. Rev. Knight on horse. On the 1000th year of the introduction of Christianity into Bohemia.

8. 5 Ducats 1929 ....*...... 300.00
9. 4 Ducats 1929 .... 225.00
10. 1 Ducat 1929 .... 100.00

Head of Dr. Miroslav Tyrs. Rev. Eagle. On the Sokol movement.

11. 1 Ducat 1932 .... 75.00

Head of Dr. Antonin Svehla. Rev. Sower. Homage issue.

12. 1 Ducat 1933 .... 75.00

St. Elizabeth praying. Rev. Mining scenes. On the reopening of the Kremnica Mines.

13. 10 Ducats 1934 ....*...... 600.00
14. 5 Ducats 1934 .... 400.00
15. 2 Ducats 1934 .... 200.00
16. 1 Ducat 1934 .... 125.00

Bust of Wallenstein. Rev. Crowned shield. To commemorate the ancient Wallenstein coinage.

17. 10 Ducats 1934 .... 600.00
18. 5 Ducats 1934 .... 400.00

DANISH WEST INDIES

(Now the U. S. Virgin Islands.)

Head of Christian IX of Denmark. Rev. Seated female. Two values appear on these coins.

1. 10 Daler—50 Francs 1904. .... 1000.00
2. 4 Daler—20 Francs 1904, 05 ....*...... 175.00

DANZIG

A. Polish Kings of —

SIGISMUND I, 1506-1548

Bust. Rev. City arms.

1. 1 Ducat 1546, 47, 48 .... 400.00

SIGISMUND II, 1548-1572

Bust right or left. Rev. City arms.

2. 1 Ducat 1549-58 .... 400.00

Bust. Rev. City arms.

3.   1 Ducat 1578-87 .... 300.00

Christ standing. Rev. City arms.

4.   1 Siege Ducat 1577 .... 500.00

SIGISMUND III, 1587-1632

Bust. Rev. City arms.

5. 10 Ducats 1613, 14 .... 1250.00
6.   5 Ducats 1614, ND 800.00
7.   4 Ducats 1617 .... 800.00
8.   3 Ducats 1617 .... 600.00
9.   2 Ducats 1619 .... 350.00
10.   1 Ducat 1588-1632 ....*...... 175.00

LADISLAS IV, 1632-1648

Bust. Rev. City arms.

11.   4   Ducats 1640, 41 ....*...... 1000.00
12.   3   Ducats 1640, 41 .... 650.00
13.   2   Ducats 1634-47 .... 400.00
14.   1½ Ducats 1634, 47 .... 350.00
15   1   Ducat 1633-48 .... 200.00

Bust. Rev. City view.

16. 10 Ducats 1644, ND 1200.00
17.   8 Ducats 1644 .... 1000.00
18.   6 Ducats ND 1000.00
19.   5 Ducats 1645 .... 1000.00
20.   4 Ducats 1645 .... 750.00
21.   3 Ducats 1634-47 ....*...... 650.00

JOHN CASIMIR, 1648-1668

Plain or crowned bust. Rev. City arms.

22.   2   Ducats 1652-58, ND ....*...... 750.00
23.   1½ Ducats 1661 .... 400.00
24.   1   Ducat 1649-68 .... 250.00

Plain or crowned bust. Rev. City view.

25. 12 Ducats 1650 .... 2500.00
26. 10 Ducats 1651 .... 5000.00
27.   6 Ducats ND ....*...... 1000.00
28.   5 Ducats 1654, 56, ND 600.00
29.   4 Ducats 1650, ND 450.00
30.   3 Ducats 1650, 58, ND 450.00
31.   2 Ducats 1651 .... 300.00

MICHAEL KORYBUT, 1669-1673

Bust. Rev. City arms.

32.   1 Ducat 1670-73 .... 375.00

Crowned bust. Rev. City view.

33.   3 Ducats ND 500.00

JOHN SOBIESKI, 1674-1696

Plain or crowned bust. Rev. City arms.

34.   4 Ducats 1692 .... 1000.00
35.   2 Ducats 1692, ND 600.00
36.   1 Ducat 1676-92 ....*...... 300.00

Bust. Rev. City view.

37.   5 Ducats ND 1000.00
38.   4 Ducats ND 800.00
39.   3 Ducats ND 600.00

AUGUST II OF SAXONY, 1697-1733

Bust. Rev. City arms.

40.	2 Ducats 1698	600.00
41.	1 Ducat 1698 ....*......	275.00

AUGUST III OF SAXONY, 1733-1763
Bust. Rev. City arms.

42.	1 Ducat 1734	375.00

B. Free City of —

The 25 Gulden pieces of both 1923 and 1930 were struck in proof condition only. 1000 specimens were struck in 1923 and 4000 in 1930, but the later issue was not placed in circulation, and very few are known.

Neptune with trident. Rev. Arms between two columns.

43.	25 Gulden 1923	650.00

Neptune with trident. Rev. Arms supported by lions.

44.	25 Gulden 1930	2000.00

DENMARK

It will be noted that some of the earlier coins are in imitation of English, German or Hungarian types.

Kings of —

(For additional coins of the Danish Kings, see under Norway).

HANS, 1481-1513

Ruler on throne. Rev. Arms.

1.	3 Nobles 1496 ....*......	**Rare**
2.	2 Nobles 1502	**Rare**
3.	1 Noble 1496, 1502	**Rare**

Ruler standing. Rev. Triple lion shield.

4.	1 Goldgulden ND	1500.00
5.	½ Goldgulden ND	1000.00

CHRISTIAN II, 1513-1523
Ruler on throne. Rev. Arms.

6.	1 Noble 1516, 18	**Rare**

Ruler standing. Rev. Triple lion shield.

7.	1 Goldgulden ND, Square	1200.00

Ruler on throne. Rev. Crowned shield. Posthumously struck in 1535 and 1536.

8.	2 Goldgulden ND ....*......	1750.00
9.	1 Goldgulden ND	800.00

FREDERICK I, 1523-1533

Ruler standing. Rev. Four shields around central shield.

10.	1 Goldgulden 1527	1100.00

Small crowned bust. Rev. Triple lion shield.

11.	1 Goldgulden 1531	1000.00

Busts of the King and Queen. Rev. Arms.

12.	1 Noble 1532	**Rare**

Ruler on throne. Rev. Arms.

13.	1 Noble ND	**Rare**

St. Andrew standing with cross. Rev. Cross of shields. Struck for Schleswig.

14.	1 Goldgulden 1531, ND	1200.00

CHRISTIAN III, 1534-1559

Crowned head. Rev. Arms.

15.	1 Goldgulden 1557	1250.00

Cross of arms. Rev. Orb in circle. Struck for Schleswig.

16.	1 Goldgulden ND	1000.00

St. Andrew standing with cross. Rev. Cross of shields. Struck for Schleswig.

17.	2 Goldgulden 1546	1500.00
18.	1 Goldgulden 1536, 46, ND ....*......	900.00

FREDERICK II, 1559-1588
Crowned F. Rev. Value.

19.	1 Goldgulden 1563. Square	1750.00
20.	1 Krone 1563. Square	3000.00

Crowned F. Rev. Fortuna standing on globe.

21.	1 Goldgulden 1563. Crudely shaped	1500.00

Arms. Rev. Value.

22.	1 Ducat 1564. Square	2000.00
23.	1 Krone 1564. Square	2000.00
24.	1 Goldgulden 1564. Square	2000.00

FS monogram crowned. Rev. Value.

25.	1 Portugaloser 1584	4000.00
26.	1 Rosenoble 1584 ....*.....	3000.00
27.	2 Ducats 1584	1500.00
28.	1 Angelot 1584	1500.00
29.	1 Krone 1584	1200.00
30.	1 Goldgulden 1584 ....*.....	1200.00
31.	1 Hungarian Gulden 1584	1200.00

CHRISTIAN IV, 1588-1648
Ruler standing. Rev. Arms.

32.	1 Goldgulden 1591, 92, 93, 1607	400.00

Ruler standing. Rev. Triple lion shield.

33.	1 Goldgulden 1603, 07, 08, 11 ......*......	400.00
34.	1 Ducat 1637	450.00

Ruler standing. Rev. Thirteen shields around central arms.

35.	3 Goldgulden 1608	2250.00
36.	2 Goldgulden 1608 ....*......	1250.00

Ruler standing. Rev. Legend in square.

37.	1 Ducat 1640, 42, 46	425.00

Ruler standing. Rev. Hebrew legend.

38.	2 Ducats 1644, 45, 46, 48 ....*......	500.00
39.	1 Ducat 1644, 45, 46, 47, 48	300.00
40.	½ Ducat 1644, 45, 46, 47	125.00
41.	¼ Ducat 1646, 47, 48	100.00

Ruler standing. Rev. C4 crowned.

42.	¼ Ducat ND	100.00

Large crowned bust. Rev. Triple lion shield.

43.	1 Goldgulden 1604-32	400.00

Crowned bust. Rev. Value.

44.	8 Daler 1604. Square	3500.00
45.	6 Daler 1604. Square ....*......	3000.00
46.	4 Daler 1604. Square	2000.00
47.	3 Daler 1604. Square	800.00

Large crowned bust. Rev. Elephant.

48.	1 Rosenoble 1611-29	1500.00
49.	½ Rosenoble 1611	1750.00

Plain bust. Rev. Two figures holding crown over arms and C4.

50.	Gold coin, 22.64 Grams ND	1250.00
51.	Gold coin, 10.75 Grams ND	600.00
52.	Gold coin, 8.1 Grams ND	500.00

Crowned bust. Rev. Similar to above.

53.	Gold coin, 4.65 Grams ND	450.00

Triple lion shield. Rev. Crown.

54. 2 Kroner 1619-48 ....*.....	800.00
55. 1 Krone 1619	425.00
56. ½ Krone 1619	300.00

C4 crowned. Rev. Arms.

57. 2 Ducats 1627	750.00
58. 1 Ducat 1627	475.00

C4 crowned. Rev. Legend.

59. ½ Ducat 1642	150.00
60. ¼ Ducat 1647, ND	125.00

Large cross. Rev. Arms.

61. 2 Portugalosers 1592	Rare
62. 1 Portugaloser 1591, 92	2000.00
63. ½ Portugaloser 1591, 92, 93	1000.00
64. ¼ Portugaloser 1592, 93 ....*.....	700.00

Ruler on throne. Rev. Arms.

65. 1 Portugaloser 1603	2500.00

Ruler standing. Rev. Fortuna on globe. Struck for Gluckstadt.

66. 1 Portugaloser 1623	2250.00

Large cross. Rev. Crowned heart.

67. ¼ Portugaloser 1629	600.00

Ruler on horse. Rev. Arms.

68. 1 Portugaloser ND	2250.00

Large bust. Rev. Ruler on horse in circle of shields.

69. 1 Portugaloser ND	2500.00
70. ¼ Portugaloser ND	1250.00

FREDERICK III, 1648-1670

Laureate bust. Rev. Vase with flowers.

71. 5 Ducats 1648. Square	2250.00
72. 4 Ducats 1648. Square	1750.00
73. 3 Ducats 1648. Square	1500.00
74. 2 Ducats 1648. Square	1250.00
75. 1 Ducat 1648. Square ....*.....	500.00
76. ½ Ducat 1648. Square	250.00

Laureate bust. Rev. Legend in circle.

77. 1 Ducat 1649, 50, 51, 53 ....*.....	200.00
78. ½ Ducat 1652	150.00

Laureate bust. Rev. Fortuna on globe.

79. 1 Ducat 1660-69	400.00

Laureate bust. Rev. Arms.

80. 1 Portugaloser 1666	1750.00
81. 5 Ducats 1665	1000.00
82. 1 Ducat 1667, 68, 69 ....*.....	375.00
83. 1 Krone 1667	375.00

Laureate bust. Rev. Large crown.

84. 5 Ducats 1665, 66	1100.00
85. 3 Ducats 1667	850.00
86. 2 Ducats 1657	600.00
87. 2 Kroner 1666 ....*.....	600.00
88. 1 Krone 1666	300.00

Laureate bust. Small oval arms on cross.

89. 2 Portugalosers 1666	Rare
90. ½ Portugaloser 1665, 67	1500.00
91. 12 Ducats 1665	2750.00

Laureate bust. Rev. Crown and value.

92. 18 Marks 1668	800.00

Laureate bust. Rev. Three shields on cross within circle of shields.

93. 2 Portugalosers ND	Rare
94. 10 Ducats 1669. Thick	1750.00

Laureate head. Rev. Double cross formed by F3 monogram.

95. 2 Ducats 1670	750.00

Laureate bust. Rev. Crown and orb between sceptre and sword.

96. 2 Ducats ND	350.00

Crowned bust. Rev. Square formed by four F's. The diameter of these coins is the same, the value being determined by the thickness and corresponding weight.

97.	10 Ducats 1653	....	3750.00
98.	5 Ducats 1653, 62	....	2250.00
99.	3 Ducats 1662	....	1100.00
100.	2 Ducats 1653, 62	....	750.00
101.	1 Ducat 1653-66, ND	..............*.....	200.00
102.	½ Ducat 1659, 64	....	150.00
103.	¼ Ducat 1660, 64	....	150.00

Laureate head. Rev. Similar to above.

104.	1 Ducat 1664, 67	....	300.00

Crowned bust. Rev. Circle of shields around central arms.

105.	1 Portugaloser 1653, 55, 56	....	1750.00
106.	½ Portugaloser 1653, 55, 57, 61	.....	1200.00
107.	3 Ducats 1661	....	1100.00

Crowned bust. Rev. Cross of crowned F's.

108.	1 Ducat 1653	....	700.00

Crowned bust. Rev. Three shields on crowned cross.

109.	1 Ducat 1669, 70	....	500.00

Crowned bust. Rev. Ship.

110.	4 Ducats 1657, 58, 64	...........*.....	1200.00
111.	3 Ducats 1666, 67	....	1000.00
112.	2 Ducats 1657-67	....	750.00

Crowned bust. Rev. Crowned shield on cross.

113.	1 Portugaloser 1662, 63, 64	....	1750.00
114.	½ Portugaloser 1663, 64	....	1250.00
115.	5 Ducats 1662	............*.....	1250.00
116.	4 Ducats 1663	....	1100.00
117.	2 Ducats 1662, 63	....	750.00

Crowned bust. Rev. View of Fort Aggershus.

118.	1 Portugaloser ND	....	2750.00

Triple lion shield. Rev. Crown.

119.	2 Kroner 1657, 59	....	325.00
120.	1 Krone 1655, 57, 59, 60	........*.....	250.00

Triple lion shield. Rev. Crowned F3 over lion.

121.	½ Portugaloser 1658	....	1250.00

Crowned F3. Rev. Sword cutting off hand reaching for crown.

122.	2 Portugalosers 1659	....	3500.00
123.	1 Portugaloser 1659	............*.....	2250.00
124.	½ Portugaloser 1659	....	1250.00
125.	6 Ducats 1659	....	1250.00
126.	4 Ducats 1659	....	900.00
127.	3 Ducats 1659	....	700.00

Crowned F3. Rev. Value.

128.	6 Marks 1669	....	375.00
129.	3 Marks 1665, 68, 70	....	175.00

Crown over double F3 monogram. Rev. Arms.

130.	¼ Ducat 1670	....	150.00

Crossed sword and sceptre between crown and orb. Rev. Cross of St. Andrew.

131.	1 Portugaloser 1663	....	2750.00
132.	6 Ducats 1663	....	1250.00

CHRISTIAN V, 1670-1699

Crowned bust. Rev. Three crowns over triple C5 monogram.

133.	2 Ducats 1673	....	425.00
134.	1 Ducat 1672, 73, 74, 76	..........*.....	275.00

Laureate bust. Rev. Crowned C5 monogram.

135.	5 Ducats 1692	850.00
136.	2 Ducats 1670, 92, 94, ND ....*......	450.00
137.	1 Ducat 1672-94, ND	225.00
138.	½ Ducat 1675	150.00
139.	¼ Ducat 1675	125.00

Laureate bust. Rev. Three shields on cross.

140.	1 Ducat 1671-92	375.00

Laureate bust. Rev. Three crowns over triple C5 monogram.

141.	1 Ducat 1679, 80, 85	250.00

Laureate bust. Rev. C's and 5's around radiate triangle.

142.	5 Ducats 1692	1500.00
143.	2 Ducats 1692, 94 ....*......	900.00
144.	1 Ducat 1694	600.00

Laureate bust. Rev. Long cross over arms.

145.	1 Ducat 1692	375.00

Laureate bust. Rev. Six crowns around C5 monograms.

146.	2 Ducats ND	475.00

Armored bust. Rev. Crowned arms.

147.	1 Ducat 1681, 83	375.00

Bust. Rev. Fortress.

148.	1 Ducat 1682	350.00

Long haired bust. Rev. Arms in circle of shields.

149.	10 Ducats 1691	3000.00
150.	5 Ducats 1687	1100.00
151.	3 Ducats 1687	600.00
152.	2 Ducats 1687	750.00
153.	1 Ducat 1687, ND ....*......	450.00

Long haired bust. Rev. Crowned oval arms.

154.	2 Ducats 1691	500.00
155.	1 Ducat 1691, 92 ....*......	175.00

Long haired bust. Rev. Triple C5 monogram.

156.	1 Ducat 1691, 92, 93, 96, ND	200.00

Bust. Rev. Large crown.

157.	10	Ducats 1693, 96	2250.00
158.	3	Ducats 1694	500.00
159.	2½	Ducats 1696	500.00
160.	2	Ducats 1693, 94, 96	400.00
161.	1	Ducat 1693, 94, 96 ....*......	175.00
162.	½	Ducat 1694, 96	150.00
163.	¼	Ducat 1694	125.00

Bust. Rev. Legend. From gold of the Koenigsberg Mines.

164.	2 Ducats 1697 ....*......	1100.00
165.	1 Ducat 1697	750.00

Helmited bust. Rev. View of Fort Christiansborg in Guinea, Africa.

166.	4 Ducats 1688	....	1750.00
167.	2 Ducats 1688	...............................*......	1250.00
168.	1 Ducat 1688	....	750.00

Bust. Rev. Ship in Christiansborg harbor.

169.	2 Ducats 1699	...............................*......	900.00
170.	1 Ducat 1699	....	375.00

Laureate head. Rev. Elephant.

171.	3 Ducats 1678	....	1100.00
172.	2 Ducats 1673	...............................*......	950.00

Laureate head. Rev. Value and date.

173.	3 Marks (¼ Ducat) 1676	....	175.00

*Laureate head. Rev. Six crowns around C5 monograms. The Rev.
is shown.*

174.	3 Ducats 1678	....	550.00
175.	2 Ducats 1678	...............................*......	450.00

Ruler standing. Rev. Fortuna on globe.

176.	1 Ducat 1682	....	400.00

Ruler standing. Rev. C5 monogram crowned.

177.	10 Ducats ND	....	1750.00

Ruler on horse. Rev. Elephant.

178.	3 Ducats 1673	....	900.00
179.	2 Ducats 1673	....	650.00

Ruler on horse. Rev. Crowned circular arms.

180.	1 Rider 1696	...............................*......	350.00
181.	2 Ducats ND	....	350.00
182.	1 Ducat 1696	....	250.00
183.	½ Ducat 1696	....	150.00

Ruler on horse. Rev. Triple C5 monogram.

184.	4 Ducats ND	....	650.00
185.	2 Ducats ND	....	450.00
186.	1 Ducat 1692, ND	...............................*......	225.00
187.	½ Ducat ND	....	200.00

Ruler on horse. Rev. Conjoined knight and lion. Without any legends.

188.	2½ Ducats ND	....	450.00
189.	1 Ducat ND	....	350.00
190.	½ Ducat ND	....	125.00

Ruler on horse. Rev. Double C5 monogram. Without any legends.

191.	2 Ducats ND	....	375.00
192.	1 Ducat ND	....	175.00
193.	½ Ducat ND	....	125.00

Ruler on horse. Rev. Six crowns around C5 monograms. Without any legends.

194.	4 Ducats ND	....	600.00
195.	2 Ducats ND	....	375.00
196.	1½ Ducats ND	....	225.00

Crown over C5. Rev. Elephant.

197.	4 Ducats 1683	....	1100.00
198.	2 Ducats 1673	...............................*......	750.00
199.	1½ Ducats 1673	....	550.00
200.	1 Ducat 1673	....	300.00

Crown over double C5 monogram. Rev. Crowned arms.

201.	1 Ducat 1691	....	225.00

Crown over initials. Rev. Value and date.

202.	3 Marks 1675	....	150.00

Six crowns around C5 monograms. Rev. Elephant.

203.	3 Ducats 1673	....	500.00

Pyramid with or without base. Rev. View of Copenhagen harbor.

204. 2 Ducats ND ....*...... 500.00
205. 1 Ducat ND 250.00

FREDERICK IV, 1699-1730

*Bust. Rev. Bust of Christian V. Coronation coins struck in 1699.
The indicated 3 Ducat piece is 28 millimetres, all the others
are 21 millimetres and of varying thickness, the value being
determined by weight.*

206. 4 Ducats ND 1250.00
207. 3 Ducats ND (size 21) 950.00
208. 3 Ducats ND (size 28) 1250.00
209. 2 Ducats ND 600.00
210. 1 Ducat ND ....*...... 400.00

Bust. Rev. Three shields and three monograms around star.

211. 2 Ducats 1708, 09 .... 525.00
212. 1 Ducat 1708, 09, ND ....*...... 175.00

Bust. Rev. Three shields and three monograms around radiate triangle.

213. 10 Ducats 1699 .... 2250.00
214. 5 Ducats 1699, 1700 .... 900.00
215. 4¾ Ducats, 1699 .... 900.00
216. 2 Ducats 1708 .... 500.00
217. 1 Ducat 1708, 09, ND 200.00

Bust. Rev. Crown over DMA, and below "Christiansborg".

218. 18 Marks 1701 .... 7000.00

Bust. Rev. Large crown and value (for the "Rixdalers").

219. 1 Ducat 1705, 06 ....*...... 150.00
220. 4 Rixdaler (2 Courant Ducats) 1714 .... 600.00
221. 2 Rixdaler (1 Courant Ducat) 1714, 15, 16 .... 300.00
222. 1 Rixdaler (½ Courant Ducat) 1715 .... 175.00

Bust. Rev. Crowned arms in wreath.

223. 2 Ducats 1709 .... 350.00
224. 1 Ducat 1709, 23, 26 ....*...... 175.00
225. ½ Ducat 1719 .... 125.00

Bust. Rev. Crowned circular arms.

226. 1 Ducat 1718, 19 .... 175.00
227. ½ Ducat 1710, 19 ....*...... 125.00

Bust. Rev. Double F4 monogram.

228. 3 Ducats 1700 ....*...... 725.00
229. 2 Ducats 1701, 04 .... 550.00
230. 1 Ducat 1700, ND 250.00
231. ½ Ducat ND 135.00
232. ¼ Ducat ND 250.00

Ruler on horse. Rev. Cross of three shields and three monograms.

233. 2 Ducats ND 425.00
234. 1 Ducat 1702, ND ....*...... 250.00
235. ½ Ducat ND 135.00
236. ¼ Ducat ND 110.00

Ruler on horse. Rev. Arms.

237. 2 Ducats 1710, 11 ....*...... 425.00
238. 1 Ducat 1710, 11 .... 250.00

Ruler on horse. Rev. Double F4 monogram.

239. 2 Ducats ND 425.00
240. 1 Ducat ND 250.00
241. ½ Ducat ND 150.00
242. ¼ Ducat ND 110.00

Bust. Rev. View of Fort Christiansborg.

243. 2 Ducats 1701, 04 .... 1250.00
244. 1 Ducat 1701, 02, 04, 08, 25, ND 450.00

Bust. Fortress and ship at Christiansborg.

245. 1 Ducat 1701 .... 550.00

Bust. Rev. Ship and radiate sun, and below, "Christiansborg".

246. 5 Ducats 1704 .... 2250.00

*Bust. Rev. Radiate sun over ship and below, "SOC. IND. OCC."
(The Danish West Indies Company).*

247. 2 Ducats 1708 .... 1750.00

CHRISTIAN VI, 1730-1746

Double C6 monogram. Rev. Fortress at Christiansborg.

248. 1 Ducat 1730, 38, 40 .... 250.00

Bust. Rev. Arms on cross.

249. 1 Ducat 1732 .... 375.00

Bust. Rev. Bust of Frederick IV.

250. 1 Ducat 1730 .... 425.00

FREDERICK V, 1746-1766

Bust. Rev. Bust of Christian VI. Coronation coins struck in 1746.

251. 2 Ducats ND 475.00
252. 1 Ducat ND 250.00

*Bust. Rev. Crowned arms with ornaments and below, "EX AURO
SINICO". Struck from Chinese gold.*

253. 2 Ducats 1746 .... 850.00
254. 1 Ducat 1746 ....*...... 475.00

Laureate head. Rev. Type as above. Struck from Chinese gold.

255. 2 Ducats 1746 .... 850.00
256. 1 Ducat 1746 .... 475.00

Bust. Rev. Ancient galley with banner. Struck from Chinese gold.

257. 2 Ducats 1746 .... 850.00
258. 1 Ducat 1746 ....*...... 400.00

Laureate head. Rev. Type as above. Struck from Chinese gold.

259. 1 Ducat 1746 .... 400.00

Bust. Rev. Crowned oval arms.

260. 2 Ducats 1747 .... 425.00

Bust. Rev. Draped arms and below "EBEN EZER".

261. 1 Ducat 1758 .... 350.00

Bust in helmet. Rev. Crown and value.

262. 12 Marks 1757, 58 .... 150.00

Laureate head. Rev. Fortress and ship at Christiansborg.

263. 2 Ducats 1746 .... 400.00
264. 1 Ducat 1746 ....*...... 250.00

Laureate head. Rev. Crowned oval arms.

265. 2 Ducats 1747 .... 350.00
266. 1 Ducat 1747 .... 225.00

Laureate head. Rev. Ship.

267. 2 Ducats 1753 .... 475.00
268. 1 Ducat 1753, 54, 56 ....*...... 200.00

Head. Rev. Crown and value.

269. 12 Marks 1757-65 .... 125.00

Ruler standing. Rev. Crowned oval arms.

270. 2 Ducats 1747 .... 350.00
271. 1 Ducat 1747 ....*...... 200.00

Ruler standing. Rev. Fortress at Christiansborg.

272.   2 Ducats 1747 .... 425.00
273.   1 Ducat 1747 ....*...... 300.00

Ruler on horse. Rev. Embellished arms with initials DWC for
Danish West Indies Company.

274.   2 Ducats 1749 ....*...... 450.00
275.   1 Ducat 1749 .... 275.00

Ruler on horse. Rev. Double F5 monogram.

276.   2 Ducats 1748 .... 350.00
277.   1 Ducat 1748 ....*...... 200.00

F's and V's around triangle. Rev. Crown and value.

278. 12 Marks 1757, 63 .... 150.00

CHRISTIAN VII, 1766-1808

Bust. Rev. Crowned C7 monograms around triangle.

279.   1 Christian d'or 1775, ND 400.00

Bust. Rev. "29 Januarii" in wreath.

280.   1 Ducat 1771 .... 350.00

Bust. Rev. Crown and value.

281. 12 Marks 1781, 82, 83, 85 .... 200.00

Wild man standing. Rev. Legend in square.

282.   1 Ducat 1771 .... 500.00

Wild man standing. Rev. Value, weight and fineness in square tablet.

283.   1 Species Ducat 1791, 92, 94, 1802 .... 200.00

FREDERICK VI, 1808-1839

Head. Rev. Value.

284.   2 Frederick d'or 1826, 27 .... 350.00
285.   1 Frederick d'or 1827 ....*...... 175.00

Head. Rev. Arms flanked by value.

286.   2 Frederick d'or 1828-36 .... 400.00
287.   1 Frederick d'or 1828-38 ....,..... 175.00

Head. Rev. Arms supported by wild men.

288.   2 Frederick d'or 1836, 37, 38, 39 .... 375.00

CHRISTIAN VIII, 1839-1848

Head. Rev. Arms supported by wild men.

289.   2 Christian d'or 1841-47 .... 350.00
290.   1 Christian d'or 1843-47 ....*...... 200.00

FREDERICK VII, 1848-1863

Head. Rev. Arms supported by wild men.

291.   2 Frederick d'or 1850-63 ....*...... 300.00
292.   1 Frederick d'or 1853 .... 600.00

CHRISTIAN IX, 1863-1906

Head. Rev. Arms supported by wild men.

293.	2 Christian d'or 1866, 67, 69, 70 ....*......	400.00
294.	1 Christian d'or 1869	600.00

Head. Rev. Seated female.

295.	20 Kroner 1873-1900 ....*......	50.00
296.	10 Kroner 1873-1900	55.00

FREDERICK VIII, 1906-1912

Head. Rev. Arms.

297.	20 Kroner 1908-12 ....*......	45.00
298.	10 Kroner 1908, 09	60.00

CHRISTIAN X, 1912-1947

Head. Rev. Arms.

299.	20 Kroner 1913-17 ....*......	45.00
300.	10 Kroner 1913, 17	60.00

DOMINICAN REPUBLIC

The 30 Peso is unique in that it is the only gold coin of the Americas, the face value of which is based on the present-day value of gold, viz, $35.00 per ounce. The coin was originally issued at a premium, the amount over 30 Pesos reverting to the Government.

Head of Trujillo. Rev. Arms. On the 25th year of his rule.

1.	30 Pesos 1955.	60.00

ECUADOR

Mints: — Quito and Birmingham. The unique 50 Franc piece of 1862 was discovered in 1956.

Liberty head. Rev. Sun over two mountain peaks. Issued while Ecuador was part of Colombia.

1.	2 Escudos 1833-35	150.00
2.	1 Escudo 1833-35.	100.00

Liberty head. Rev. Sun and Zodiac over three mountain peaks.

3.	8 Escudos 1838-43.	400.00
4.	4 Escudos 1836-41. ....*......	200.00

Head of Bolivar to right. Rev. Arms.

5.	8 Escudos 1844.	Rare

Larger head of Bolivar to left. Rev. Flag-draped arms, the poles showing below.

6.	8 Escudos 1845.	650.00

Type as above but the flagpoles do not show below the arms.

7.	8 Escudos 1845.	750.00

Head of Bolivar. Rev. Flag-draped oval arms.

8.	8 Escudos 1847-56.	325.00

Head of Bolivar. Rev. Arms.

9.   50 Francs 1862. . . . .   **Unique**

Head of General Sucre. Rev. Arms.

10.   10 Sucres 1899, 1900. . . . .   **70.00**

Head of Bolivar. Rev. Arms.

11.   1 Condor 1928. . . . .   **125.00**

EGYPT

A. French Occupation of —

*Toughra and accession date 1203 in Arabic (1789 A.D.).
Rev. Arab legend and regnal year 13 or Arabic letter B
(for Bonaparte). Struck during the rule of Selim III following Napoleon's invasion of Egypt.*

1.   1 Sequin. Size 21 millimetres . . . .*. 90.00
2.   ½ Sequin. Size 19 millimetres . . . .*. 400.00
3.   ¼ Sequin. Size 17 millimetres 80.00

B. Turkish Sultans —

(Earlier coins were of the same types as those of Turkey).

MAHMUD II, 1808-1839
*Toughra. Rev. Dates and Mint. Coin bears the accession
date 1223 and regnal year in Arabic numerals.*

4.   100 Piastres. Year 31 (1839) 75.00

ABDUL MEJID, 1839-1861

*Toughra and value in plain field. Rev. Legend and date.
All coins bear the accession date 1255 in Arabic numerals in addition to other Arabic numerals for the
regnal year, which indicate the precise date of coinage.*

5.   100 Piastres . . . .*. 55.00
6.   50 Piastres 35.00
7.   20 Piastres 25.00
8.   10 Piastres 20.00
9.   5 Piastres 17.50

ABDUL AZIZ, 1861-1876

*Same type as above. All coins bear the accession date
1277 in Arabic numerals in addition to other Arabic numerals for the regnal year, which indicate the precise
date of coinage.*

10.   500 Piastres 500.00
11.   100 Piastres . . . .*. 60.00
12.   50 Piastres 35.00
13.   20 Piastres 22.50
14.   10 Piastres 17.50
15.   5 Piastres 12.50

MURAD V, 1876
*Same type as preceding coins but bearing the toughra of
Murad V and accession date 1293 (not to be confused
with the next ruler's coins which bear the same accession
date).*

15a.   100 Piastres 700.00

ABDUL HAMID, 1876-1909

*Same type as above. All coins bear the accession date
1293 in Arabic numerals in addition to other Arabic numerals for the regnal year, which indicate the precise
date of coinage. Only seven pieces were reported struck
of number 17.*

16.   500 Piastres. Year 1 (1876) . . . .*. 400.00
17.   500 Piastres. Year 6 (1881) 850.00
18.   100 Piastres 60.00
19.   50 Piastres 35.00
20.   20 Piastres 22.50
21.   10 Piastres 17.50
22.   5 Piastres 12.50

*Toughra in lobed floral circle, value below. Rev. Legend
and date. On larger flan than the preceding 100 Piastre
pieces.*

23.   100 Piastres. Year 12 (1888) 80.00

C. Independent Sultans —

HUSEIN KAMIL, 1915-1917

Arab legend. Rev. Value and date in English.

24. 100 Piastres 1916 .... 75.00

D. Kings of—

FUAD, 1917-1936

Civilian bust to right. Rev. Legend.

25.	500 Piastres 1922. Red gold		500.00
26.	500 Piastres 1922. Yellow gold		400.00
27.	100 Piastres 1922. Red gold ....*......		75.00
28.	100 Piastres 1922. Yellow gold		65.00
29.	50 Piastres 1923-29		50.00
30.	20 Piastres 1923-29		35.00

Military bust to left. Rev. Legend.

31.	500 Piastres 1929-32 ....*......		700.00
32.	100 Piastres 1929, 30		85.00
33.	50 Piastres 1929, 30		50.00
34.	20 Piastres 1929, 30		40.00

FAROUK, 1937-1952

Military bust. Rev. Legend.

35.	500 Piastres 1938		750.00
36.	100 Piastres 1938		100.00
37.	50 Piastres 1938 ....*......		70.00
38.	20 Piastres 1938		50.00

E. Republic of (1953-1958) —

Ancient chariot and small Arabic date 1952. Rev. Legend and dates 1955 and 1374 in Arabic. On the Flight of Farouk and the formation of the Republic in 1952.

39.	5 Pounds 1955. Yellow gold		400.00
40.	1 Pound 1955. Yellow gold ....*.....		75.00
41.	5 Pounds 1957. Red gold		400.00
42.	1 Pound 1957. Red gold		75.00

F. United Arab Republic (1958-   ) —

Same design as coin numbers 39-42 above.

43. ½ Pound 1958 .... 50.00

Aswan Dam. Rev. Inscription.

44.	5 Pounds 1960 ....*.....		350.00
45.	1 Pound 1960		70.00

Diversion of the Nile. Rev. Inscription. The weight of the Pound was reduced in 1964 from 8.5 grams to 5.2 grams. The 10 Pound coin struck in that year weighs 52 grams and is the heaviest gold coin minted since 1915.

46.	10 Pounds 1964. Reduced weight ....*........		300.00
47.	5 Pounds 1964. Reduced weight		225.00

Koran on globe. Rev. Inscription in circle. On the 1400th Anniversary of the Koran.

48. 5 Pounds 1968 .... 175.00

Bust of Gamal Abdel Nasser. Rev. Legend and value. in honor of the late President.

49.	5 Pounds 1970	125.00
50.	1 Pound 1970	50.00

ESTHONIA (REVAL)

Swedish Rulers of —

CHRISTINA, 1632-1654

Bust. Rev. City shield.

1.	1 Ducat 1650	1000.00

ETHIOPIA

The coins of the Axumite Kings of Ethiopia of about 300 A.D. are the earliest coins that appear in this book. This historical but little known coinage has been listed here since these coins are not included in the standard reference works on ancient coins. The ancient Kingdom of Axum was under Pagan rule until the period of Ousanas I, who converted to Christianity about 350 A.D.

A. Axumite Kings of —

ENDYBIS, ABOUT 300 A.D.

Helmeted bust on each side.

1.	½ Aureus ND	550.00

AFILAS, ABOUT 300 A.D.

Crowned bust. Rev. Helmeted bust.

2.	½ Aureus ND	400.00

Helmeted bust. Rev. Legend.

3.	¹⁄₁₀ Aureus ND	Rare

(Type: — The coins of the following kings of Axum are all of the same type and show a crowned bust on the obverse, and a helmeted bust on the reverse.)

OUSANAS I, ABOUT 350 A.D.

4.	⅓ Solidus ND	400.00

WAZEBA, ABOUT 375 A.D.

5.	⅓ Solidus ND	Rare

EZANAS AND/OR EZANA, ABOUT 400 A.D.

6.	⅓ Solidus ND	400.00

ANAFEON, ABOUT 500 A.D.

7.	⅓ Solidus ND	400.00

ESBEL OR ESBENA, ABOUT 550 A.D.

8.	⅓ Solidus ND	500.00

CALEB, ABOUT 575 A.D.

9.	⅓ Solidus ND	500.00

NEZANA, ABOUT 600 A.D.

10.	⅓ Solidus ND	600.00

OUSANAS II, ABOUT 600 A.D.

11.	⅓ Solidus ND	Rare

OUSAS, ABOUT 600 A.D.

12.	⅓ Solidus ND	400.00

ALALMIRYIS, ABOUT 650 A.D.

13.	⅓ Solidus ND	Rare

ELLA GABAZ, ABOUT 700 A.D.

14.	⅓ Solidus ND	600.00

JOEL, ABOUT 700 A.D.

15.	⅓ Solidus ND	600.00

ISRAEL, ABOUT 750 A.D.

16.	⅓ Solidus ND	400.00

JATHLIA, ABOUT 750 A.D.

17.	⅓ Solidus ND	600.00

GERSEM, ABOUT 850 A.D.

18.	⅓ Solidus ND	600.00

B. Modern Emperors of —

MENELIK II, 1889-1913

Crowned bust. Rev. Lion of Judah. Posthumously struck in 1916.

19.	2 Warks ND	400.00
20.	1 Wark ND	*…… 200.00
21.	½ Wark ND	150.00
22.	¼ Wark ND	125.00
23.	⅛ Wark ND	75.00

EMPRESS ZAUDITU, 1916-1930

Crowned bust. Rev. Lion of Judah.

24.	4 Warks ND. Size 31 millimetres	1000.00
25.	2 Warks ND. Size 25 millimetres ....*......	500.00
26.	1 Wark ND. Size 20 millimetres	400.00

HAILE SELASSIE, 1930-1936 AND 1941-

Bust Facing. Rev. Arms.

27.	4 Warks 1930	300.00

   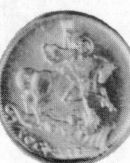

Head. Rev. St. George slaying dragon.

28.	1 Wark 1931	600.00
29.	½ Wark 1931	300.00

FINLAND

A. Coinage under the Czars of Russia

Crowned eagle. Rev. Value. Struck under different Czars as indicated.

1.	20 Markkaa 1878-80. Alexander II ....*......	100.00
2.	20 Markkaa 1891. Alexander III	125.00
3.	20 Markkaa 1903, 04, 10-13. Nicholas II	90.00
4.	10 Markkaa 1878, 79. Alexander II ....*......	85.00
5.	10 Markkaa 1881, 82. Alexander III	75.00
6.	10 Markkaa 1904, 05, 13. Nicholas II	75.00

B. Coinage of the Republic

Lion. Rev. Value.

7.	200 Markkaa 1926 ....*......	350.00
8.	100 Markkaa 1926	325.00

FRANCE

Additional coins of the French Kings will be found under some of the Italian States over which France had suzerainty.

Mints and mint marks for the period 1806-1870: — (Later coinage was struck only at the Paris Mint).

A	mm for	Paris
B	mm for	Rouen
BB	mm for	Strasbourg
CL	mm for	Genoa (Italy)
D	mm for	Lyon
H	mm for	La Rochelle
I	mm for	Limoges
K	mm for	Bordeaux
L	mm for	Bayonne
M	mm for	Toulouse
MA	monogram for	Marseille
Q	mm for	Perpignan
R	Crowned mm for	Rome (Italy)
R	(1815 only) for	London (England)
T	mm for	Nantes
U	mm for	Turin (Italy)
W	mm for	Lille
Fish and Mast	mm for	Utrecht (Netherlands)

The French gold Franc, first issued in 1803, was the standard adopted by the Latin Monetary Union. France maintained this standard for its gold coins until 1914. It was not until 1929 that the first coins appeared based on the revaluation of the gold Franc.

A. Kings of —

(The coins from St. Louis IX through Henry IV are followed by an L and a number. These numbers identify the same coins in the French work by Lafaurie).

ST. LOUIS IX, 1226-1270
Shield in lobed circle. Rev. Floriated cross.

1.	1 Ecu d'or ND. L-197	Rare

PHILIP IV, 1285-1314

King on Gothic throne. Rev. Floriated cross in quadrilobe.

2.	1 Chaise d'or ND. L-213	3000.00

King seated. Rev. Floriated cross in quadrilobe.

3.	1 Masse d'or ND. L-212	1500.00

King seated. Rev. Floriated cross.

4. 1 Petit Royal d'or ND. L-217 .... 2500.00
5. 1 Denier d'or ND. L-214 ....*... 2500.00

King standing. Rev. Floriated cross in quadrilobe.

6. 1 Petit Royal d'or ND. L-215 .... 5000.00

Lamb. Rev. Floriated cross in quadrilobe.

7. 1 Agnel d'or ND. L-216 .... 850.00

LOUIS X, 1314-1316

Lamb. Rev. Floriated cross in quadrilobe.

8. 1 Agnel d'or ND. L-240 .... 1500.00

PHILIP V, 1316-1322

Lamb. Rev. Floriated cross in quadrilobe.

9. 1 Agnel d'or ND. L-241 .... 750.00

CHARLES IV, 1322-1328

King standing under Gothic dais. Rev. Floriated cross in quadrilobe.

10. 1 Royal d'or ND. L-244 ....*...... 600.00
11. ½ Royal d'or ND. L-245 .... Rare

Lamb. Rev. Floriated cross in quadrilobe.

12. 1 Agnel d'or ND. L-243 .... 500.00

PHILIP VI, 1328-1350

King seated on Gothic throne. Rev. Floriated cross in quadrilobe.

13. 1 Parisis d'or ND. L-252 .... 3000.00

King seated on Gothic throne, a lion at feet. Rev. Floriated cross in quadrilobe.

14. 1 Lion d'or ND. L-253 .... 1500.00

King seated on throne under draped pavillion. Rev. Floriated cross in quadrilobe, diamond in center.

15. 1 Pavillion d'or ND. L-254 .... 1350.00

King with two sceptres on Gothic throne under dais. Rev. Floriated cross in enclosure.

16. 1 Double d'or ND. L-256 ....*..... 1500.00
17. 1 Single d'or ND .... Unknown

King on Gothic throne. Rev. Floriated cross in quadrilobe, diamond in center.

18. 1 Chaise d'or ND. L-261 .... 500.00

Armored King with shield on Gothic throne. Rev. Floriated cross in quadrilobe.

19. 1 Ecu d'or ND. L-262 .... 300.00

King standing under Gothic dais. Rev. Floriated cross in quadrilobe.
20.   1 Royal d'or ND. L-251 ....   **400.00**

St. George on horse. Rev. Floriated cross in quadrilobe.
21.   1 George-Florin ND. L-260 ....   **7000.00**

Angel standing. Rev. Floriated cross in quadrilobe.
22.   1 Ange d'or ND. L-258 ....*...... **1250.00**
23.   ½ Ange d'or ND ....Unknown

Large crown. Rev. Floriated cross in quadrilobe.
24.   1 Couronne d'or ND. L-255 .... **5000.00**

JOHN THE GOOD, 1350-1364
Armored King with shield on Gothic throne. Rev. Floriated cross in quadrilobe.
25.   1 Ecu d'or ND. L-292 ....   **350.00**

King standing under dais flanked by lis. Rev. Floriated cross in quadrilobe.
26.   1 Denier d'or ND. L-293 ....   **Rare**

King standing under dais. Rev. Floriated cross, diamond in center.
27.   1 Royal d'or ND. L-296 ....   **450.00**

Armored King on horse. Rev. Floriated cross in quadrilobe.
28.   1 Franc a Cheval ND. L-297 ....   **400.00**

Lamb. Rev. Floriated cross in ornate circle.
29.   1 Mouton d'or ND. L-294 ....*......   **350.00**
30.   ½ Mouton d'or ND. L-295 .... **5000.00**

St. John standing. Rev. Fleur-de-lis.
31.   1 Florin ND. L-358 ....   **250.00**

CHARLES V, 1364-1380
King standing under dais. Rev. Floriated cross, diamond in center.
32.   1 Royal d'or ND. L-369 .... **3000.00**

King standing under dais. Rev. Floriated cross in ornate circle.
33.   1 Franc a Pied ND. L-371 ....   **275.00**

Armored King on horse. Rev. Floriated cross in quadrilobe.
34.   1 Franc a Cheval ND. L-370 ....   **400.00**

CHARLES VI, 1380-1422

King on throne, two lions at feet. Rev. Floriated cross in ornate enclosure.
35.   1 Chaise d'or ND. L-428 ....*...... **7500.00**
36.   ½ Chaise d'or ND. L-429 ....   **Rare**

Arms between madonna and angel. Rev. Roman cross.

37. 1 Salut d'or ND. L-413 ....*...... 4000.00
38. ½ Salut d'or ND ....Unknown

Lamb. Rev. Floriated cross in ornate enclosure.

39. 1 Mouton d'or ND. L-380 .... 400.00

Crowned arms. Rev. Floriated cross in quadrilobe.

40. 1 Ecu d'or ND. L-378 ....*...... 250.00
41. ½ Ecu d'or ND. L-379 .... Rare

Crowned arms flanked by two coronets. Rev. Floriated cross in quadrilobe.

42. 1 Ecu d'or ND. L-426 .... 400.00

Crowned helmet over shield. Rev. Cross in ornate enclosure.

43. 1 Heaume d'or ND. L-398 .... Rare
44. ½ Heaume d'or ND. L-399 ....*...... 2500.00

HENRY V OF ENGLAND, 1415-1422
Lamb. Rev. Floriated cross in ornate enclosure.

45. 1 Mouton d'or ND. L-434 .... 3500.00

Arms between madonna and angel. Rev. Roman cross.

46. 1 Salut d'or ND. L-437 .... 7500.00
47. ½ Salut d'or ND ....Unknown

HENRY VI OF ENGLAND, 1422-1453

Angel over two shields. Rev. Roman cross

48. 1 Angelot ND. L-488 .... 1250.00

Madonna and angel over two shields. Rev. Roman cross.

49. 1 Salut d'or ND. L-447 .... 400.00

CHARLES VII, 1422-1461
Armored king on horse. Rev. Floriated cross in quadrilobe.

50. 1 Franc a Cheval ND. L-455 .... Rare

King standing. Rev. Floriated cross in quadrilobe.

51. 1 Royal d'or ND. L-459 .... 450.00

Lamb. Rev. Floriated cross in ornate enclosure.

52. 1 Mouton d'or ND ....Unknown

Arms between madonna and angel. Rev. Roman cross.

53. 1 Salut d'or ND. L-461 .... 4500.00

Large crowned shield. Rev. Floriated cross in quadrilobe.

54. 1 Ecu d'or ND. L-457 .... 250.00

Crowned shield flanked by two lis or crowns. Rev. Floriated cross, a crown in each angle.

55. 1 Ecu Neuf ND. L-510 .... 200.00
56. ½ Ecu Neuf ND. L-511. (Crowns not in angles) 225.00

Crowned shield flanked by two lis. Rev. Floriated cross,
a crown or briquette in each angle.

57. 1 Ecu Briquette ND. L-512 .... **400.00**

LOUIS XI, 1461-1483

St. Michael slaying dragon. Rev. Floriated cross.

58. 3 Angelots ND. L-526 .... **Rare**
59. ½ Angelot ND. L-528 .... **8000.00**

Crowned arms flanked by crowned lis. Rev. Floriated cross in quadrilobe.

60. 1 Ecu d'or ND. L-524 .... **175.00**

Crowned arms. Rev. Large floriated cross.

61. ½ Ecu d'or ND. L-525 .... **200.00**

Crowned arms, small radiate sun above. Rev. Floriated cross.

62. 1 Ecu au Soleil ND. L-529 ....*...... **150.00**
63. ½ Ecu au Soleil ND. L-530 .... **275.00**

Quartered arms of Dauphine. Rev. Ornate cross.

64. 1 Ecu Delphinil ND. L-531 .... **6000.00**

CHARLES VIII, 1483-1498

Crowned arms, small radiate sun above. Rev. Floriated cross.

65. 3 Ecus au Soleil ND. L-555 .... **Rare**
66. 1 Ecu au Soleil ND. L-554 ....*..... **150.00**
67. ½ Ecu au Soleil ND. L-556 ....*..... **150.00**

Crowned arms flanked by two ermines, sun above. Rev. Ornate cross.

68. 1 Ecu au Soleil de Bretagne ND. L-557 ....*...... **250.00**
69. ½ Ecu au Soleil de Bretagne ND. L-557bis **4000.00**

Arms of Dauphine. Rev. Floriated cross

70. 1 Ecu au Soleil du Dauphine ND. L-558 .... **225.00**

LOUIS XII, 1498-1515

Crowned arms, small radiate sun above. Rev. Floriated cross.

71. 1 Ecu d'or au Soleil ND. L-592 .... **150.00**
72. ½ Ecu d'or au Soleil ND. L-593 .... **175.00**

Crowned arms flanked by two porcupines. Rev. Cross

73. 1 Ecu d'or au Porcepic ND. L-598 ....*...... **225.00**
74. ½ Ecu d'or au Porcepic ND. L-599 .... **1750.00**

Crowned arms flanked by two ermines, sun above. Rev. Ornate cross.

75. 1 Ecu au Soleil de Bretagne ND. L-594 ....*...... **200.00**
76. ½ Ecu au Soleil de Bretagne ND. L-595 ....:...... **1750.00**

Crowned arms flanked by two ermines, a porcupine below.
Rev. Ornate cross.

77. 1 Ecu au Porcepic de Bretagne ND. L-600a **225.00**

Arms of France and Dauphine quartered, sun above. Rev. Floriated cross.

78. 1 Ecu au Soleil du Dauphine ND. L-597 .... **300.00**

Arms of France and Dauphine flanked by two porcupines. Rev. Cross.
79. 1 Ecu au Porcepic du Dauphine ND. L-601 . . . . 500.00

Crowned arms, small radiate sun above. Rev. Cross of Jerusalem.
80. 1 Ecu au Soleil de Provence ND. L-596 . . . . 4000.00

FRANCIS I, 1515-1547

Crowned arms flanked by two lis. Rev. Two crowns and two F's in angles of cross.
81. 1 Ecu d'or au Soleil ND. L-638 . . . . 175.00

Crowned arms flanked by two crowned F's. Rev. Two F's and two lis in angles of cross.
82. 1 Ecu d'or au Soleil ND. L-642 . . . . 500.00

Crowned arms flanked by a G and a lis. Rev. Two F's and two lis in angles of cross.
83. 1 Ecu d'or au Soleil ND. L-644 . . . . 450.00

Crowned arms, sun above, mint mark below. Rev. Floriated cross.
84. 1 Ecu d'or au Soleil ND. L-739 . . . .*. 150.00
85. ½ Ecu d'or au Soleil ND. L-740 . . . . 600.00

Crowned arms, sun above, mint mark below. Rev. Two F's and two lis in angles of cross.
86. 1 Ecu d'or au Soleil ND. L-741 . . . . 150.00
87. ½ Ecu d'or au Soleil ND. L-742 . . . . 200.00

Crowned arms, small radiate sun above. Rev. Floriated cross.
88. 1 Ecu d'or au Soleil ND. L-634 . . . .*. 150.00
89. ½ Ecu d'or au Soleil ND. L-635 . . . . 200.00

Crowned arms, small radiate sun above. Rev. Two crowned F's in angles of cross.
90. 1 Ecu d'or au Soleil ND. L-636 . . . .*. 175.00
91. ½ Ecu d'or au Soleil ND. L-637 . . . . 550.00
92. 1 Ecu d'or au Soleil ND. The F's not crowned. L-644 bis . 600.00

Crowned arms, small radiate sun above. Rev. Two F's and two lis in angles of cross.
93. 1 Ecu d'or au Soleil ND. L-639 . . . .*. 150.00
94. ½ Ecu d'or ND. L-640 . . . . 300.00

Same type as above but with a small cross added to both the Obv. and Rev.
95. 1 Ecu d'or a la Petite Croix ND. L-746 . . . . 225.00
96. ½ Ecu d'or a la Petite Croix ND. L-747 . . . . 600.00

Crowned arms, small radiate sun above. Rev. Four F's in angles of cross.
97. 1 Ecu d'or au Soleil ND. L-641 . . . . 400.00

Crowned arms flanked by two salamanders. Rev. Two F's and two salamanders in angles of cross.
98. 1 Ecu d'or au Salamanders ND. L-744, 745 . . . . 500.00

Crowned arms. Rev. Plain cross.
99. 1 Ecu d'or a la Croisette ND. L-749 . . . .*. 150.00
100. ½ Ecu d'or a la Croisette ND. L-750 . . . . 500.00

Crowned arms flanked by two F's. Rev. Plain cross. This coin is doubtful.
101. 1 Ecu d'or a la Croisette ND. L-751 . . . . .Unknown

Arms of France and Dauphine. Rev. Floriated cross.

102. 1 Ecu d'or du Dauphine ND. L-645 .... 150.00

Arms of France and Dauphine. Rev. Two crowned F's in angles of cross.

103. 1 Ecu d'or du Dauphine ND. L-646 .... 150.00

Arms of France and Dauphine. Rev. One dolphin and one lis in angles of cross.

104. 1 Ecu d'or du Dauphine ND. L-647 .... 300.00

Arms of France and Dauphine. Rev. Two crowns in angles of cross.

105. 1 Ecu d'or du Dauphine ND. L-648 .... 150.00

Arms of France and Dauphine. Rev. Crowned F and dolphin in angles of cross.

106. 1 Ecu d'or du Dauphine ND. L-649 .... 150.00

Arms of France and Dauphine. Rev. Two dolphins in angles of cross.

107. 1 Ecu d'or du Dauphine ND. L-650 .... 150.00

Crowned arms of France and Dauphine. Rev. Two F's and two lis in angles of cross.

108. 1 Ecu d'or du Dauphine a la Petite Croix ND. L-753 .. 3000.00

Same arms as above. Rev. Floriated cross.

109. 1 Ecu d'or du Dauphine. L-752 .... 3500.00

Arms of France and Dauphine. Rev. Plain cross.

110. 1 Ecu d'or du Dauphine a la Croisette L-754 .... 1000.00

Crowned arms flanked by two ermines. Rev. Two F's and two ermines in angles of cross.

111. 1 Ecu d'or de Bretagne ND. L-651 .... 500.00

Crowned arms flanked by an F and an ermine. Rev. Two F's and two ermines in angles of cross.

112. 1 Ecu d'or de Bretagne ND. L-652 .... 350.00

HENRY II, 1547-1559

Crowned bust. Rev. Crowned arms.

113. 1 Ecu d'or 1549. L-807 ....*...... 2500.00
114. ½ Ecu d'or 1549. L-808 .... 2750.00

Bust. Rev. Cross of four H's with two crescents and two lis in angles (see also under Frances II and Charles IX).

115. 2 Henri d'or 1553-62. L-809 .... 1250.00
116. 1 Henri d'or 1550-62. L-810 ....*...... 1000.00
117. ½ Henri d'or 1550-60. L-811 .... 650.00

Bust. Rev. Cross of four H's, with four lis in angles (see also under Francis II and Charles IX).

118. 2 Henri d'or 1550-61. L-812 .... 1250.00
119. 1 Henri d'or 1550-59. L-813 ....*...... 850.00

Laureate bust. Rev. Gallia seated.

120. 2 Henri d'or ND. L-816 .... 6000.00
121. 1 Henri d'or ND. L-817 .... 3500.00
122. ½ Henri d'or ND. L-818 ....*...... 3000.00

Crowned arms flanked by two crescents. Rev. Two H's and two crescents in angles of cross. The ½ Ecu is known only as an Essai in double thickness. The normal weight ½ Ecu is unknown.

123. 1 Ecu d'or aux Croissants 1552. L-814 ....*...... **3000.00**
124. ½ Ecu d'or aux Croissants 1552 ....**Unknown**

Crowned arms. Rev. Plain cross.

125. 1 Ecu d'or a la Croisette ND. L-806 .... **1000.00**

FRANCIS II, 1559-1560

(There are no distinctive coins of Francis II. During his short reign of seventeen months, the coinage of Henry II was continued without change. Therefore, coins dated 1559 or 1560 actually bear the name or portrait of Henry II, although they may have been struck under Francis II).

CHARLES IX, 1560-1574

(The early coins of this reign are not distinctive, in that like those of Francis II, they continue to bear the name or portrait of Henry II. Therefore, certain coins dated 1560, 1561 or 1562, although they purport to be coins of Henry II, were actually struck under Charles IX. The distinctive coinage of Charles IX follows).

Crowned arms. Rev. Floriated cross. (The coins dated 1575 were struck under Henry III although they bear the name of Charles IX).

126. 1 Ecu d'or 1562-75. L-890 ....*...... **200.00**
127. ½ Ecu d'or 1561-75. L-891 .... **175.00**

Arms of France and Dauphine. Rev. Floriated cross.

128. 1 Ecu d'or du Dauphine 1562-74. L-893 ......*...... **300.00**
129. ½ Ecu d'or du Dauphine ....**Unknown**

Crowned arms without the King's name. Rev. Floriated cross. Struck by the Protestants in Rouen.

130. 1 Ecu au Soleil 1562. L-890c **300.00**

HENRY III, 1574-1589

Crowned arms flanked by two H's. Rev. Ornate floriated cross. (For certain coins dated 1575, see under Charles IX).

131. 2 Ecu d'or 1589. L-959 .... **Rare**
132. 1 Ecu d'or 1578, ND. L-963 ....*...... **500.00**
133. ½ Ecu d'or 1578. L-964 .... **1250.00**

Crowned arms. Rev. Lobed floriated cross.

134. 1 Ecu d'or 1575-89. L-960 ....*...... **200.00**
135. ½ Ecu d'or 1575-89. L-961 .... **350.00**

Crowned arms. Rev. Floriated cross, mint mark in center.

136. 1 Ecu d'or 1575, 88. L-960x, 962 .... **200.00**

CHARLES X, 1589-1590

Crowned arms. Rev. Floriated cross. (Coins with his name dated after 1590 were struck during the reign of Henry IV).

137. 1 Ecu d'or 1590-95. L-1015 .... **250.00**
138. ½ Ecu d'or 1590-94. L-1016 ....*...... **600.00**

HENRY IV, 1589-1610

Crowned arms flanked by two H's. Rev. Two H's and two lis in angles of floriated cross.

139. 2 Ecu d'or 1589. L-1047 .... **Rare**

Crowned arms. Rev. Lobed, floriated cross.

140. 1 Ecu d'or 1590-1610. L-1048 ....*...... 750.00
141. ½ Ecu d'or 1590-1610. L-1049 .... 750.00

Crowned arms. Rev. Floriated cross with an H under each of the four lis.

142. 1 Ecu d'or 1589-1604. L-1051 ....*...... 1000.00
143. ½ Ecu d'or 1589-1603. L-1052 .... 1100.00

Crowned arms in beaded circle. Rev. Floriated cross in beaded circle.

144. 1 Ecu d'or 1589-1610. L-1054 ....*...... 1200.00
145. ½ Ecu d'or 1589-1603 .... Unknown

LOUIS XIII, 1610-1643

Crowned arms. Rev. Lobed floriated cross.

146. 1 Ecu d'or 1626, 1637-43 ....*...... 200.00
147. ½ Ecu d'or 1615-40 .... 175.00

Crowned arms in circle. Rev. Floriated cross in circle.

148. 1 Ecu d'or 1615 ....*...... 200.00
149. ½ Ecu d'or 1615 .... 300.00

Crowned arms. Rev. Floriated cross.

150. 1 Ecu d'or ND. 150.00

Arms of France and Dauphine. Rev. Floriated cross.

151. 1 Ecu d'or 1641. .... 1750.00
152. ½ Ecu d'or 1641. .... 2000.00

Draped, laureate bust. Rev. Cross of eight L's.

153. 10 Louis d'or 1640. .... 18,000.00

Laureate head. Rev. Cross of eight L's.

154. 10 Louis d'or 1640. .... 10,000.00
155. 8 Louis d'or 1640. .... 8500.00
156. 4 Louis d'or 1640. .... 9000.00
157. 2 Louis d'or 1640-43. .... 1500.00
158. 1 Louis d'or 1640-43. ....*...... 500.00
159. ½ Louis d'or 1640-43. .... 275.00

LOUIS XIV, 1643-1715

Crowned arms. Rev. Lobed, floriated cross.

160. 1 Ecu d'or au Soleil 1643-51. .... 250.00
161. ½ Ecu d'or au Soleil 1643-51. .... 1000.00

Child head with short curl. Rev. Cross of eight L's.

162. 2 Louis d'or 1644. .... 4000.00
163. 1 Louis d'or 1644. .... 400.00
164. ½ Louis d'or 1644. ....*...... 500.00

Child head with long curl. Rev. Cross of eight L's.

165. 2 Louis d'or 1644-52. .... 3000.00
166. 1 Louis d'or 1644-53. ....*...... 500.00
167. ½ Louis d'or 1644-46. .... 650.00

Youthful laureate head. Rev. Cross of eight L's.

168. 1 Louis d'or 1659-68. ....*...... 450.00
169. ½ Louis d'or 1660-68. .... 1200.00

Youthful plain head. Rev. Cross of eight L's.

170.	1 Louis d'or 1668-80.	..........................*	400.00
171.	1 Louis d'or 1688. Older head.	....	400.00
172.	½ Louis d'or 1669-80.	....	1200.00

Older laureate head. Rev. Cross of eight L's.

173.	1 Louis d'or 1683-89.	....	700.00

Old laureate head. Rev. Crowned arms.

174.	2 Louis d'or 1690-93.	....	1250.00
175.	1 Louis d'or 1690-93.	......................*	325.00
176.	½ Louis d'or 1690-93.	....	350.00

Old laureate head. Rev. Arms of France and Navarre-Bearn.

177.	1 Louis d'or 1690.	....	4500.00

Old laureate head. Rev. Four L's around mint mark.

178.	2 Louis d'or 1693-95.	.......................*	1000.00
179.	1 Louis d'or 1693-95.	....	225.00
180.	½ Louis d'or 1693-95.	....	300.00

Old laureate head. Rev. Eight L's over crossed insignia.

181.	2 Louis d'or 1701, 02.	....	800.00
182.	1 Louis d'or 1701, 02.	....	275.00
183.	½ Louis d'or 1701, 02.	.......................*	300.00

Old laureate head. Rev. Four lis in angles of crossed insignia.

184.	2 Louis d'or 1704-09.	....	1200.00
185.	1 Louis d'or 1704-09.	.......................*	325.00
186.	½ Louis d'or 1704-09.	....	400.00

Old laureate head. Cross of eight L's, sun in center.

187.	2 Louis d'or 1709-11.	....	1200.00
188.	1 Louis d'or 1709-11.	.......................*	300.00
189.	½ Louis d'or 1709-11.	....	350.00

Cross of four lis. Rev. Two angels holding arms.

190.	1 Lis d'or 1656.	....	1500.00

LOUIS XV, 1715-1774
Child head. Rev. Cross of eight L's.

191.	1 Louis d'or 1715.	....	4000.00
192.	½ Louis d'or 1715.	....	3000.00

Child head. Rev. Crowned arms over crossed insignia.

193.	2 Louis d'or 1716.	....	3000.00
194.	1 Louis d'or 1716.	.......................*	1000.00
195.	½ Louis d'or 1716.	....	1750.00

Crowned child head. Rev. Cross of four shields.

196.	2 Louis d'or 1717, 18.	......................*	1000.00
197.	1 Louis d'or 1717, 18.	....	1250.00
198.	½ Louis d'or 1717, 18.	....	1000.00

Young laureate head. Rev. Maltese cross.

199. 1 Louis d'or 1718, 19. .... 500.00
200. ½ Louis d'or 1718, 19. ....*...... 1500.00

Laureate head. Rev. Crown over two L's.

201. 2 Louis d'or 1720, 22. .... 1500.00
202. 1 Louis d'or 1720, 22. ....*...... 600.00
203. ½ Louis d'or 1720, 22. .... 1250.00

Laureate head. Rev. Two script L's in palms, crown above.

04. 2 Louis d'or 1723-25. .... 1750.00
05. 1 Louis d'or 1723-25. ....*...... 450.00
06. ½ Louis d'or 1723-25. .... 1500.00

Draped bust. Rev. Crown over two shields.

07. 1 Louis d'or 1726-39 ....*...... 175.00
08. ½ Louis d'or 1726-39 .... 150.00

Large head with band. Rev. Crown over two shields.

09. 2 Louis d'or 1740-65. .... 400.00
10. 1 Louis d'or 1740-65. .... 200.00
11. ½ Louis d'or 1740-65. ....*...... 150.00

Old laureate head. Rev. Crown over two shields.

212. 2 Louis d'or 1765-74. ....*...... 750.00
213. 1 Louis d'or 1765-74. .... 350.00

LOUIS XVI, 1774-1793

Uniformed bust. Rev. Crowned arms within palms.

214. 1 Louis d'or 1774. .... 1000.00

Uniformed bust. Rev. Crown over two oval shields.

215. 2 Louis d'or 1775-84. .... 750.00
216. 1 Louis d'or 1774-84. ....*...... 250.00
217. ½ Louis d'or 1775-84. .... 600.00

Bare head. Rev. Crown over two oval shields. This coin was not placed in circulation.

218. 1 Louis d'or 1785. .... 1500.00

Bare head. Rev. Crown over two square shields.

219. 2 Louis d'or 1786-92. ....*...... 225.00
220. 1 Louis d'or 1785-92 .... 125.00
221. 1 Louis d'or 1786. Horn on head. BB mm. 500.00

Bare head. Rev. Angel writing.

222. 24 Livres (Louis d'or) 1792, 93. .... 1250.00

THE FIRST REPUBLIC

Angel writing. Rev. Value in wreath.

223. 24 Livres 1793. .... 1250.00

NAPOLEON BONAPARTE, 1801-1815

Bare head with title of First Consul. Rev. Value and "Republique Francaise." Struck under the First Republic.

224.	40 Francs. Years 11, 12 (1803, 04). ....*......	175.00
225.	20 Francs. Years 11, 12 (1803, 04).	110.00

Bare head with title of Emperor. Rev. Value and "Republique Francaise."

226.	40 Francs. Years 12, 13, 14, 1806, 07. A mm. *......	150.00
227.	40 Francs. 1806, 07. I mm.	200.00
228.	40 Francs. 1807. M mm.	300.00
229.	40 Francs. Year 14, 1806, 07. U mm.	185.00
230.	40 Francs. Year 14, 1806, 07. W mm.	300.00
231.	20 Francs. Years 12, 13, 14, 1806, 07. A mm.	75.00
232.	20 Francs. Years 13, 14, 1806. I mm.	125.00
233.	20 Francs. 1807. M mm.	200.00
234.	20 Francs. Years 13, 14, 1806. Q mm.	250.00
235.	20 Francs. Year 14, 1806, 07. U mm.	400.00
236.	20 Francs. Year 14, 1806, 07. W mm.	150.00

Laureate head with title of Emperor. Rev. Value and "Republique Francaise."

237.	40 Francs 1807, 08. A mm.	150.00
238.	40 Francs 1808. H mm.	185.00
239.	40 Francs 1808. M mm.	225.00
240.	40 Francs 1808. U mm.	750.00
241.	40 Francs 1808. W mm.	185.00
242.	20 Francs 1807, 08. A mm. ....*......	60.00
243.	20 Francs 1808. K mm.	500.00
244.	20 Francs 1808. M mm.	80.00
245.	20 Francs 1808. Q mm.	750.00
246.	20 Francs 1808. U mm.	350.00
247.	20 Francs 1808. W mm.	125.00

Laureate head with title of Emperor. Rev. Value and "Empire Francais."

248.	40 Francs 1809-13. A mm.	125.0
249.	40 Francs 1809, 10, 12. W mm.	125.0
250.	40 Francs 1809. M mm.	400.0
251.	40 Francs 1809. U mm.	750.0
252.	40 Francs 1810, 11. K mm.	200.0
253.	40 Francs 1813. CL mm.	250.0
254.	20 Francs 1809-15. A mm.	55.0
255.	20 Francs 1809-15. L mm.	80.0
256.	20 Francs 1809-13. K mm.	125.0
257.	20 Francs 1809, 10, 11. H mm.	200.0
258.	20 Francs 1809-15. W mm.	60.0
259.	20 Francs 1809-12. M mm.	175.0
260.	20 Francs 1809-13. U mm. ....*	200.0
261.	20 Francs 1810-14. Q mm.	125.0
262.	20 Francs 1812, 13. R mm.	125.0
263.	20 Francs 1813, 14. CL mm.	350.0
264.	20 Francs 1813. Fish and mast mm.	100.0

LOUIS XVIII, 1814-1824

Uniformed bust. Rev. Arms.

265.	20 Francs 1814, 15. A mm.	45.0
266.	20 Francs 1814, 15. L mm.	60.0
267.	20 Francs 1814, 15. K mm.	60.0
268.	20 Francs 1814, 15. W mm.	75.0
269.	20 Francs 1814, 15. Q mm.	75.0
270.	20 Francs 1815. B mm.	125.0
271.	20 Francs 1815. R mm. (London) ....*	100.0

Bare head. Rev. Arms.

272.	40 Francs 1816-24. A mm. ....*......	135.00
273.	40 Francs 1816, 17. L mm.	300.00
274.	40 Francs 1822. H mm.	700.00
275.	40 Francs 1816, 18, 19. W mm.	135.00
276.	40 Francs 1816. Q mm.	175.00
277.	40 Francs 1816. B mm.	700.00
278.	20 Francs 1816-24. A mm.	45.00
279.	20 Francs 1816, 17, 18. L mm.	55.00
280.	20 Francs 1816, 17. K mm.	55.00
281.	20 Francs 1822. H mm.	125.00
282.	20 Francs 1816-24. W mm.	45.00
283.	20 Francs 1824. MA monogram mm.	225.00
284.	20 Francs 1818, 19, 20. T mm.	75.00
285.	20 Francs 1816-24. Q mm.	55.00
286.	20 Francs 1816. B mm.	55.00

CHARLES X, 1824-1830

Head. Rev. Arms.

287.	40 Francs 1824-30. A mm. ....*......	125.00
288.	40 Francs 1830. MA monogram mm.	225.00
289.	20 Francs 1825-30. A mm.	65.00
290.	20 Francs 1825-30. W mm.	75.00
291.	20 Francs 1828. T mm.	125.00
292.	20 Francs 1826. Q mm.	125.00

LOUIS PHILIPPE I, 1830-1848

Bare head. Rev. Value and date.

293.	20 Francs 1830, 31. A mm.	60.00
294.	20 Francs 1831. B mm.	60.00
295.	20 Francs 1831. T mm.	225.00
296.	20 Francs 1831. W mm. ....*......	60.00

Laureate head. Rev. Value and date.

297.	40 Francs 1831-39. A mm. ....*......	110.00
298.	40 Francs 1834, 35. L mm.	125.00
299.	40 Francs 1832, 33. B mm.	150.00
300.	20 Francs 1832-48. A mm.	45.00
301.	20 Francs 1834, 35. L mm.	65.00
302.	20 Francs 1832-46. W mm.	50.00
303.	20 Francs 1832. T mm.	175.00
304.	20 Francs 1832-35. B mm.	50.00

LOUIS NAPOLEON BONAPARTE, PRESIDENT, 1848-1852

(President of the Second Republic, and later Emperor Napoleon III)

Bare head. Rev. Value and date.

305.	20 Francs 1852	50.00

NAPOLEON III, 1852-1870

Bare head. Rev. Arms (100, 50 Francs); Value (20, 10, 5 Francs).

306.	100 Francs 1855-59. A mm. ....*......	200.00
307.	100 Francs 1855-60. BB mm.	225.00
308.	50 Francs 1855-59. A mm.	125.00
309.	50 Francs 1855-60. BB mm.	150.00
310.	20 Francs 1853-60. A mm. ....*......	30.00
311.	20 Francs 1855, 56. D mm.	35.00
312.	20 Francs 1855-60. BB mm.	30.00
313.	10 Francs 1854-60. A mm.	30.00
314.	10 Francs 1855-60. BB mm.	30.00
315.	5 Francs 1854-60. A mm.	40.00
316.	5 Francs 1859, 60. BB mm.	40.00

Laureate head. Rev. Arms (100, 50, 20 Francs); Value (10, 5 Francs).

317.	100 Francs 1862-70. A mm.	350.00
318.	100 Francs 1862-69. BB mm.	375.00
319.	50 Francs 1862-68. A mm.	150.00
320.	50 Francs 1862-69. BB mm.	175.00
321.	20 Francs 1861-70. A mm. ....*......	25.00
322.	20 Francs 1861-70. BB mm.	27.50
323.	10 Francs 1861-68. A mm.	30.00
324.	10 Francs 1861-69. BB mm.	30.00
325.	5 Francs 1862-68. A mm.	40.00
326.	5 Francs 1862-69. BB mm.	40.00

SECOND AND THIRD REPUBLICS—1848-1852 and 1870-1940

Angel writing. Rev. Value and date.

327.	100 Francs 1878-1913	225.00
328.	50 Francs 1878-1904	500.00
329.	20 Francs 1848, 49 (2nd Rep.)	45.00
330.	20 Francs 1871-98 (3rd Rep.) ....*..	25.00

Head of Ceres. Rev. Value in circle.

331.	20 Francs 1849,50, 51 (2nd Rep.) ....*......	30.00
332.	10 Francs 1850, 51 (2nd Rep.)	40.00
333.	10 Francs 1878, 89 (3rd Rep.)	850.00
334.	10 Francs 1895, 96, 99	40.00
335.	5 Francs 1878, 89	500.00

Head of the Republic. Rev. Rooster.

336.	20 Francs 1899-1915 ....*......	25.00
337.	10 Francs 1899-1915	17.50

Winged head of the Republic. Rev. Value.

338.	100 Francs 1929, 33, 35, 36	350.00

B. Cities and Provinces of —

AQUITAINE

A. English Rulers of —

EDWARD III, 1317-1355

Ruler walking. Rev. Cross.

339. 1 Guyennois ND 850.00

Ruler seated. Rev. Cross.

340. 1 Ecu d'or ND 450.00

St. John. Rev. Lily.

341. 1 Florin ND 525.00

Leopard. Rev. Cross.

342. 1 Leopard ND 500.00

EDWARD, THE BLACK PRINCE, 1355-1375

Ruler standing under dais. Rev. Cross.

343. 1 Pavillion d'or ND ....*...... 1250.00
344. ½ Pavillion d'or ND 3500.00

Ruler walking. Rev. Cross

345. 1 Guyennois ND 900.00

Ruler seated. Rev. Cross.

346. 1 Chaise d'or ND 900.00

Crowned bust facing. Rev. Cross.

347. 1 Hardi ND 900.00

Leopard. Rev. Cross.

348. 1 Leopard ND 900.00

RICHARD II, 1377-1399
Crowned bust facing. Rev. Cross.

349. 1 Hardi ND 1000.00
350. ½ Hardi ND 2500.00

HENRY IV, 1399-1413
Crowned bust facing. Rev. Cross.

351. 1 Hardi ND. 3000.00

HENRY V, 1417-1422
Lamb. Rev. Cross.

352. 1 Mouton d'or ND. 600.00

Virgin and angel with shields. Rev. Cross.

353. 1 Salut d'or ND. 2500.00

HENRY VI, 1422-1436

Angel over two shields. Rev. Cross.

354. 1 Angelot ND. 850.00

Virgin and angel over two shields. Rev. Cross.

355. 1 Salut d'or ND. 375.00

B. French Rulers of —

CHARLES, 1468-1474
Ruler on horse. Rev. Cross.

356. 1 Franc a Cheval ND. 2500.00

Crowned bust facing. Rev. Cross.

357. 1 Hardi ND. 750.00
358. ½ Hardi ND. 3000.00

Ruler standing with leopard. Rev. Arms on cross.

359. 1 Fort d'or ND. 4000.00

ARLES

Archbishops of —

GAILLARD DE SAUMATE, 1317-1323
St. John. Rev. Lily. G. Arel Archp.

360. 1 Florin ND. 450.00

STEPHAN DE LA GARDE, 1350-1359
St. John. Rev. Lily. S. Arel Archp.

361. 1 Florin ND. 275.00

WILLIAM II DE LA GARDE, 1360-1374
Ruler standing. Rev. Cross.

362. 1 Franc a Pied ND. 2000.00

JOHN FERRER, 1499-1521
Arms. Rev. Cross.

363. 1 Ecu d'or ND. 2000.00

AVIGNON

Popes of Rome at —

JOHN XXII, 1316-1334

St. John. Rev. Lily.

364. 1 Florin ND. 600.00

INNOCENT VI, 1352-1362
Pope seated. Rev. Crossed Keys.

365. 1 Zecchino ND. 1000.00

URBAN V, 1362-1370

St. John. Rev. Lily.

366. 1 Florin ND. 450.00

CLEMENT VII, 1378-1394
Tiara and arms. Rev. St. Peter.

367. 1 Zecchino ND. 600.00

Tiara. Rev. Crossed Keys.

368. 1 Zecchino ND. 1000.00

JOHN XXIII, 1410-1415
Tiara. Rev. Cross.

369. 1 Zecchino ND. 750.00

Pope seated. Rev. Tiara over arms.

370. 1 Ecu d'or ND. 850.00

Pope seated. Rev. Cross.

371. 1 Zecchino ND. 850.00

MARTIN V, 1417-1431

Tiara over shield. Rev. Crossed Keys.

372. 1 Zecchino ND. 900.00

SIXTUS IV, 1471-1484
Tiara over arms. Rev. St. Peter.

373. 1 Zecchino ND. 1000.00

Tiara. Rev. Two keys.

374. ½ Ecu d'or ND. 1000.00

INNOCENT VIII, 1484-1492
Tiara. Rev. Crossed keys.

375. 1 Zecchino ND. 850.00

JULIUS II, 1503-1513

Legate's shield and arms. Rev. Cross.

376. 1 Ecu d'or ND. 800.00

JULIUS III, 1550-1555
Papal arms. Rev. Legate's arms.

377. 1 Ecu d'or ND. 850.00

PIUS IV, 1555-1559
Papal arms. Rev. Legate's arms.

378. 1 Ecu d'or 1562. With name of Alexander Farnese as legate 1000.00
379. 1 Ecu d'or ND. With name of Charles Bourbon as legate 1000.00

ST. PIUS V, 1565-1572
Pope seated. Rev. Cross.

380. 1 Ecu d'or ND. 800.00

Papal arms. Rev. Legate's arms.

381. 1 Ecu d'or ND 1000.00

Two shields. Rev. View of Avignon.

382. 1 Ecu d'or 1570 .... 1500.00

GREGORY XIII, 1572-1585
Two shields. Rev. View of Avignon.

383. 1 Ecu d'or ND. 1500.00

Pope seated. Rev. Cross.

384. 1 Ecu d'or ND. 800.00

Papal arms. Rev. Two shields.

385. 1 Ecu d'or ND. 650.00

CLEMENT VIII, 1592-1605
Legate's arms. Rev. View of Avignon.

386. 8 Ecu d'or 1596 ....15,000.00
387. 4 Ecu d'or 1590 .... 4500.00

Bust. Rev. Legate's arms.

388.	10 Zecchini 1599	....	12,000.00
389.	4 Ecu d'or 1597, 98, 1602	....................*	5000.00
390.	2 Ecu d'or 1596, 98, 1600	....	2000.00

PAUL V, 1605-1621

Bust. Rev. Legate's arms.

391.	4 Ecu d'or 1611	...........................*	4000.00
392.	2 Ecu d'or 1608	....	2000.00

GREGORY XV, 1621-1623
Bust. Rev. Arms.

393.	8 Ecu d'or 1622	....	5000.00

URBAN VIII, 1623-1644

Bust. Rev. Arms.

394.	4 Ecu d'or 1632-43	........................*	1750.00
395.	2 Ecu d'or 1640	....	650.00

INNOCENT X, 1644-1655
Bust. Rev. Legate's arms.

396.	4 Ecu d'or 1644-50	....	1500.00
397.	2 Ecu d'or 1644	....	800.00

ALEXANDER VII, 1655-1667

Bust. Rev. Legate's arms.

398.	4 Ecu d'or 1657, 58, 62, 63	................*	1500.00
399.	2 Ecu d'or 1664	....	800.00

BAR

Dukes of —

ROBERT, 1352-1411
St. John standing. Rev. Lily.

399a.	1 Florin ND	....	500.00

EDWARD III, 1411-1415
Crowned bust facing. Rev. Lily.

400.	1 Florin ND	....	750.00

BEARN

Counts —

GASTON, 1436-1471
Ruler on horse. Rev. Cross.

401.	1 Ecu d'or ND	....	800.00

St. John. Rev. Lily.

402.	1 Florin ND	....	200.00

FRANCIS PHOEBUS, 1479-1483

Arms. Rev. Cross.

403.	1 Ecu d'or ND	........................*	800.00
404.	½ Ecu d'or ND	....	3000.00

CATHERINE, 1483-1484
Arms. Rev. Cross.

405.	1 Ecu d'or ND	....	750.00

BESANCON

CHARLES V (CHARLES I OF SPAIN), 1515-1556
Coins were struck in his name as late as 1673.

Ruler standing. Rev. Cross.

406.	1 Florin 1541	....	Unknown

Laureate head. Rev. Eagle.

407.	4 Pistolets 1579, 80	....	2500.00
408.	2 Pistolets 1579-1673	....................*	1200.00

Crowned bust. Rev. Eagle.

409.	1 Pistolet 1578, 1653, 54	....	275.00

Ruler standing. Rev. Eagle.

410.	2 Pistolets 1664	1500.00

Ruler standing. Rev. Legend in cartouche.

411.	2 Ducats 1642, 54	350.00
412.	1 Ducat 1655	150.00
413.	½ Ducat 1655	125.00

PHILIP IV OF SPAIN, 1621-1665
Armored bust. Rev. Name and date.

414.	4 Pistolets 1664	2500.00

BOUILLON

Dukes of —

WILLIAM ROBERT DE LA MARCK, 1574-1588

Arms. Rev. Cross.

415.	1 Pistole 1587	1000.00

CHARLOTTE, 1589-1591
Arms. Rev. Plain or elaborate cross.

416.	1 Ecu d'or 1589, 91	1250.00
417.	1 Pistole 1591	750.00

HENRY DE LA TOUR AND CHARLOTTE, 1591-1594
Arms. Rev. Cross of four towers.

418.	1 Pistole 1592	1000.00

HENRY DE LA TOUR, 1591-1623
Bust. Rev. Arms.

419.	1 Ecu d'or 1614	350.00

Crowned arms. Rev. Cross of four towers.

420.	1 Ecu d'or 1597	350.00

Crowned arms. Rev. Cross.

421.	2 Ecu d'or 1610, 14, ND	1000.00
422.	1 Ecu d'or 1598, 1610, ND	300.00

GEOFFREY MAURICE, 1652-1691
Bust. Rev. Arms.

423.	1 Souverain d'or (1652-1691)	450.00
424.	½ Souverain d'or (1652-1691)	350.00

BRITTANY

Dukes of —

PERIOD 800-1000
Bust. Rev. Cross.

425.	Electrum 1 Sou ND	600.00

CHARLES DE BLOIS, 1341-1364
Ruler standing. Rev. Cross.

426.	1 Royal d'or ND	1000.00

JOHN IV, 1345-1399
Ruler on horse. Rev. Cross.

427.	1 Ecu d'or ND	1000.00

JOHN V, 1399-1442
Ruler on horse. Rev. Cross.

428.	1 Ecu d'or ND	600.00

FRANCIS I, 1442-1450

Ruler on horse. Rev. Cross.

429.	1 Ecu d'or ND	400.00

FRANCIS II, 1458-1488
Ruler on horse. Rev. Cross.

430.	1 Ecu d'or ND	400.00

ANNE, 1488-1491

Duchess on throne. Rev. Cross.

431.	1 Ecu d'or ND	2500.00

BURGUNDY

Dukes of —

EUDES IV, 1315-1350

St. John. Rev. Lily.

432.	1 Florin ND	250.00

Ruler standing. Rev. Cross.

433.	1 Ecu d'or ND	2000.00

PHILIP I, 1350-1361
St. John. Rev. Lily.

434.	1 Florin ND	200.00

PHILIP III, 1419-1467
Horseman. Rev. Arms on cross.

435.	1 Ecu d'or ND	500.00

CAMBRAI

A. Archbishops of —

GUY IV, 1342-1348

St. John. Rev. Lily. "FLOR PSV CA or FLOR EPI CA."
436. 1 Florin ND 175.00

PETER IV, 1349-1368

Lamb. Rev. Floriated cross.
437. 1 Agnel d'or ND 1000.00

Ruler on horse. Rev. Cross.
438. 1 Franc a cheval ND 400.00

Ruler standing. Rev. Cross.
439. 1 Royal d'or ND 1000.00

ROBERT OF GENEVA, 1368-1372

Ruler standing. Rev. Cross.
440. 1 Franc a pied ND 600.00

Ruler on horse. Rev. Cross.
441. 1 Franc a cheval ND 400.00

GERARD III, 1372-1378
Ruler on horse. Rev. Cross.
442. 1 Franc a cheval ND 1000.00

MAXIMILIAN BERGHES, 1556-1570

Arms. Rev. Cross.
443. 1 Ecu d'or ND 300.00

Double eagle. Rev. Eagle shield.
444. 1 Goldgulden ND 125.00

LOUIS BERLAYMONT, 1570-1596
Eagle shield. Rev. Double eagle.
445. 1 Goldgulden 1578 .... 400.00

B. Cathedral Chapter of —

St. John. Rev. Lily. "FLOR. CAPI. CA."
446. 1 Florin ND 150.00

CHATEAU-RENAUD

Princes —

FRANCIS AND LOUISE MARGUERITE, 1605-1614
Bust of Francis. Rev. Arms.
447. 1 Florin ND 200.00

LOUISE MARGUERITE, 1614-1631
Arms between two crosses of Jerusalem. Rev. Cross.
448. 1 Ecu d'or ND 850.00

CHATELET-VAUVILLERS

NICHOLAS II, 1525-1562
Arms. Rev. Cross.
449. 1 Ecu Sol 1554, ND 2000.00

DOLE (DOLA)

Spanish Kings of —

PHILIP II, 1556-1598
Crowned arms. Rev. Floriated cross.
450. 1 Ecu Pistolet 1563 .... 2000.00

PHILIP IV, 1621-1665
Floriated cross. Rev. Crowned arms between two small crowns.
451. 1 Corona or Ducat 1632 .... 2000.00

DOMBES

Princes —

JOHN II, 1459-1482

Bust. Rev. Prince on horse.
452. 1 Franc a Cheval ND 2000.00

PETER II, 1482-1503
Bust. Rev. Prince on horse.

453.　1 Franc a Cheval ND 1000.00

LOUIS II, 1560-1582

Crowned arms. Rev. Cross.

454.　2 Ecu d'or or 1 Pistole 1574, 78 ....　600.00
455.　1 Ecu d'or or ½ Pistole 1574, 75 ....*......　350.00

FRANCIS II, 1582-1592
Prince kneeling before St. Mark. Rev. Christ.

456.　1 Zecchino ND 1500.00

Arms. Rev. Cross.

457.　1 Pistole 1587 .... Unknown

MARIE, 1608-1626
Arms. Rev. Cross.

458.　1 Ecu d'or 1616 .... 1000.00
459.　½ Ecu d'or 1611 .... 1000.00

GASTON AND MARIE, 1626-1627
Arms. Rev. Cross.

460.　1 Ecu d'or 1627 .... 1000.00

GASTON, 1627-1650

Crowned shield. Rev. Lobed, floriated cross.

461.　2 Ecu d'or 1640 ....　500.00
462.　1 Ecu d'or 1640, 41 ....*......　300.00

Laureate bust. Rev. Cross of eight L's. Posthumous issue.

463.　2 Louis d'or 1652 ....*......　3000.00
464.　1 Louis d'or 1652 .... 3000.00

ANNE MARIE LOUISE DE MONTPENSIER, 1650-1693
Ruler and Saint standing. Rev. Christ. Venetian style.

465.　1 Ducat ND ....　500.00

EVREUX

Counts —

CHARLES OF NAVARRE, 1343-1387
Ruler standing before Gothic canopy. Rev. Cross.

466.　1 Ecu d'or ND ....　600.00

LIGNY

Counts —

JOHN, 1353-1364
Bust of St. Peter with lion shield. Rev. Cross.

467.　1 Ecu d'or ND ....　600.00

GUY, 1364-1371

Ruler standing under dais. Rev. Cross.

468.　1 Ecu d'or ND ....　500.00

WALERAN III, 1371-1415
Lamb. Rev. Cross.

469.　1 Agnel d'or ND 1500.00

Ruler standing under dais. Rev. Cross.

470.　1 Ecu d'or ND ....　900.00

LORRAINE

Dukes of —

JOHN I, 1346-1389

St. John standing. Rev. Lily.

471.　1 Florin ND ....　500.00

RENE II, 1473-1508
St. Nicholas. Rev. Arms.

472.　1 Goldgulden ND ....　450.00
473.　½ Goldgulden ND ....　450.00

ANTHONY, 1508-1544
Bust. Rev. Arms.

474.　6 Ducats ND 3000.00
475.　1 Goldgulden 1526, 33 .... 1000.00

CHARLES III, 1545-1608
Arms. Rev. Cross.

476.　2 Pistoles 1587 ....　600.00
477.　1 Pistole 1587 ....　300.00
478.　½ Pistole 1587 ....　300.00

Crowned bust. Rev. Arms.

479.　½ Pistole ND ....　500.00

Plain bust. Rev. Arms.

480.	4 Pistoles 1587	1250.00
481.	2 Pistoles 1587, 88 ....*.....	700.00
482.	1 Ducat 1566-88	700.00
483.	½ Ducat ND	500.00

Bust. Rev. Circle of seven shields.

484.   1 Ducat 1588 ....   600.00

HENRY II, 1608-1624
St. Nicholas. Rev. Arms.

485.   1 Goldgulden ND 200.00
486.   ½ Goldgulden ND 400.00

Bust. Rev. Arms.

487.   1 Goldgulden 1611, ND 400.00

CHARLES IV, 1625-1670

Arms. Rev. Cross.

488.   2 Pistoles 1631 ....*......   750.00
489.   1 Pistole 1639, ND 600.00

Laureate head. Rev. Interlinked C's.

490.   1 Pistole 1661, 62, 68, 69 ....   400.00

LEOPOLD I, 1697-1729
Laureate head. Rev. Two L's.

491.   5 Taler 1702 ....   400.00

Laureate head. Rev. Arms.

492.	10 Taler 1720, 24 ....*......	750.00
493.	5 Taler 1719	400.00
494.	2½ Taler 1718	400.00

FRANCIS III, 1729-1736

Bust. Rev. Arms supported by eagles.

495.	2 Ducats 1736 ....*......	850.00
496.	1 Ducat 1736	400.00

METZ

St. Stephan standing. Rev. Arms.

497.   1 Goldgulden 1620-45, ND 150.00

Bust of St. Stephan. Rev. Arms.

498.   1 Goldgulden 1639, 45, ND 800.00

MONTELIMART

Barons —

GAUCHER ADEMAR, 1346-1369
St. John. Rev. Lily.

499.   1 Florin ND 2000.00

MONTPELLIER

Barons —

SANCHO OF MAJORCA, 1311-1324

Ruler seated. Rev. Double cross.

500.   1 Petit Royal d'or ND 1500.00

NAVARRE

Kings of —

CHARLES II, 1349-1387
Crowned bust. Rev. Floriated cross.

501. 1 Gold Real ND 1500.00

JOHN II, 1441-1479

Arms. Rev. Cross.

502. 1 Ecu d'or ND 500.00
503. ½ Ecu d'or ND ....*...... 400.00

FRANCIS PHOEBUS, 1479-1483
Crowned bust. Rev. Arms.

504. 1 Ecu d'or ND 1000.00
505. ½ Ecu d'or ND 600.00

JOHN AND CATHERINE, 1484-1512

Arms. Rev. Small cross in quadrilobe.

506. 1 Ecu d'or ND ....*...... 300.00
507. ¼ Ecu d'or ND 600.00

Two busts facing each other. Rev. Arms.

508. 1 Ducat ND 700.00

Crown over initials "I-K." Rev. Cross.

509. ½ Ecu d'or ND 600.00

FERDINAND II OF ARAGON, 1512-1516
Crowned bust. Rev. Crowned arms.

510. 4 Ducats ND 1000.00
511. 2 Ducats ND 700.00
512. 1 Ducat ND 300.00
513. ½ Ducat ND 250.00

HENRY OF ALBRET, 1516-1555
Crowned arms. Rev. Floriated cross.

514. 1 Ecu au Soleil ND 400.00

Crowned arms. Rev. Short cross.

515. 1 Ecu d'or ND 600.00

JOAN, 1562-1572
Cross. Rev. Crowned arms.

516. 1 Ecu au Soleil 1561 .... 500.00

Crowned S between two I's. Rev. Crowned arms.

517. 1 Ecu d'or 1565 .... 2000.00

HENRY II, 1572-1610

Busts of Henry and Margaret. Rev. crowned arms.

518. 2 Ducats 1577 ....*...... 1400.00
519. 1 Ducat 1576, 77 .... 1000.00

Crowned arms. Rev. Cross and four H's.

520. 1 Ecu d'or 1575-78 .... 400.00

NICE

Arms. Rev. Legend. Siege coin.

521. 1 Scudo d'oro 1543 .... 1500.00

ORANGE

Princes —

RAYMOND III AND IV, 1335-1393
St. John. Rev. Lily.

522. 1 Florin ND 150.00

Ruler standing. Rev. Cross.

523. 1 Franc a Pied ND 300.00

JOHN II, 1475-1502
Helmet. Rev. Cross.

524. 1 Ecu d'or ND 850.00

PHILIP WILLIAM, 1584-1618

Armored bust. Rev. Arms.

525. 1 Pistole 1616 .... 1100.00
526. ½ Pistole 1617 .... 1000.00
527. 4 Ecu d'or 1616 ....*...... 1500.00

MAURICE, 1618-1625
Bust. Rev. Arms.

528. 1 Grand Ecu d'or 1618 .... 1500.00

FREDERICK HENRY, 1625-1647

Bust. Rev. Arms.

529. 1 Grand Ecu d'or 1641, 45, ND ....*...... 750.00
530. ½ Grand Ecu d'or 1640, 43, ND 1000.00

Knight standing. Rev. Tablet. Dutch type.

531. 1 Ducat (1625-47) 975.00

WILLIAM HENRY, 1650-1702

Prince kneeling before Christ. Rev. Madonna.

532. 1 Zecchino ND .... 550.00 •

PERPIGNAN

French Kings of —

LOUIS XI, 1461-1483

Arms of France. Rev. Cross and P.

533. 1 Ecu au Soleil ND 200.00

CHARLES VIII, 1483-1498

Arms of France. Rev. Cross and P.

534. 1 Ecu au Soleil ND 300.00

PROVENCE

Counts —

CHARLES I OF ANJOU, 1246-1285

Bust. Rev. Arms.

535. 1 Augustale d'or ND 1250.00

K. Rev. Arms.

536. 1 Sou d'or ND 300.00

K. Rev. Cross.

537. 1 Double Tarin ND 200.00

The Annunciation. Rev. Arms.

538. 1 Salut d'or ND 200.00
539. ½ Salut d'or ND ....*...... 600.00

CHARLES II OF ANJOU, 1285-1309

The Annunciation. Rev. Arms.

540. 1 Salut d'or ND 200.00

JOANNA OF NAPLES, 1343-1352

Ruler standing. Rev. Cross.

541. 1 Franc a Pied ND 200.00

Crowned bust facing. Rev. Arms.

542. 1 Florin ND 1750.00

St. John. Rev. Arms.

543. 1 Florin ND 125.00

St. John. Rev. Lily.

544. 1 Florin ND 100.00

Crown. Rev. Cross.

545. 1 Florin ND 600.00

LOUIS AND JOANNA, 1347-1382

St. John. Rev. Lily.

546. 1 Florin ND 100.00

LOUIS I, 1382-1384

Crowned arms. Rev. Cross in enclosure.

547. 1 Ecu d'or ND 100.00

Ruler standing. Rev. Cross.

548. 1 Franc a Pied ND 250.00

St. John. Rev. Arms.

549. 1 Florin ND 125.00

RENE, 1434-1480
Crowned arms. Rev. Cross of Jerusalem.

550.	1 Ecu d'or ND	750.00
551.	½ Ecu d'or ND	750.00
552.	¼ Ecu d'or ND	375.00

Bust of St. Magdalene. Rev. Cross.

553.	1 Magdalin ND	325.00

CHARLES III, 1480-1482
St. Magdalene standing. Rev. Cross with two bars.

554.	1 Magdalin (½ Ecu) ND	1000.00

Bust of St. Magdalene. Rev. Cross with two bars.

555.	1 Magdalin ND	350.00

RETHEL

Counts —

LOUIS III DE MALE, 1346-1384

Lamb. Rev. Cross.

556.	1 Mouton d'or ND	1000.00

CHARLES II GONZAGA, 1601-1637
Bust and date. Rev. Crowned arms.

557.	Gold 1 Ecu 1608	2500.00

Ruler standing. Rev. Crowned arms.

558.	1 Florin ND	700.00

Ruler standing. Rev. Legend in cartouche.

559.	1 Florin ND	700.00

Arms. Rev. Double eagle.

560.	1 Florin ND	600.00

Crowned arms. Rev. Cross of Jerusalem.

561.	1 Florin 1608	500.00

ROUSILLON

Spanish Kings of —

FERDINAND II, 1479-1516
Crowned bust. Rev. Crowned arms between P-P.

562.	1 Principat ND	750.00

CHARLES AND JOHANNA, 1516-1556
Crowned busts facing each other. Rev. Crowned arms between P-P.

563.	2 Ducats 1522	2500.00

SAINT POL

Counts —

GUY VI, 1360-1371
Count on horse. Rev. Cross and name of Count of Saint Pol.

564.	1 Franc a Cheval ND	1250.00

STRASBOURG

Madonna. Rev. Orb.

565.	2 Goldgulden ND (1600)	300.00
566.	1 Goldgulden ND (1600) ....*......	200.00

Inscription. Rev. Inscription. On the Centennial of the Reformation.

567.	1 Ducat 1617. Square	300.00

Arms. Rev. Legend in wreath.

568.	4 Ducats ND (1650)	650.00
569.	1 Ducat ND (1650)	200.00

Madonna. Rev. Arms. Issued by the Cathedral Chapter.

570.	1 Ducat 1632	300.00

Seated female and child. Rev. Arms over three shields. Issued under Bishop John v. Manderscheid, 1569-1592.

571.	6 Goldgulden 1575	Unique

Bust. Rev. Arms on mantle. Issued under Bishop Louis Constantin de Rohan, 1756-1779.

572.	2 Ecu d'or 1759	Rare
573.	1 Ecu d'or 1759	2000.00
574.	½ Ecu d'or 1759	2000.00

VERDUN

Bishops of —

ERIC OF LORRAINE, 1593-1611
Bust. Rev. Arms.

575.	1 Florin 1608	600.00

CHARLES OF LORRAINE-CHALIGNY, 1611-1622
Bust. Rev. Arms.

576.	1 Florin 1613	600.00

VIENNOIS

Dauphins of —

GUIGES VIII, 1319-1333
St. John. Rev. Lily.

577.	1 Florin ND	300.00

HUMBERT II, 1333-1349
St. John. Rev. Lily.

578.	1 Florin ND	250.00

CHARLES V, 1349-1364
St. John. Rev. Lily.

579.	1 Florin ND	250.00

Ruler on horse. Rev. Cross.

580. 1 Franc a Cheval ND 400.00

CHARLES VI, 1380-1409
Crowned arms. Rev. Elaborate cross.

581. 1 Ecu d'or ND 500.00

CHARLES VII, 1422-1440
Crowned arms. Rev. Cross.

582. 1 Ecu d'or ND ....Unknown

LOUIS, 1440-1456
Arms. Rev. Cross.

583. 1 Ecu d'or ND 250.00

GERMAN EAST AFRICA

Elephant. Rev. Eagle.

1. 15 Rupees 1916 .... 200.00

GERMAN NEW GUINEA

The two gold coins of this colony have always been popular and in demand. 1500 specimens were struck of the 20 Mark piece and 2000 of the 10 Mark piece.

Bird of Paradise. Rev. Value.

1. 20 Marks 1895 .... 1750.00
2. 10 Marks 1895 .... 1500.00

GERMANY

Mints and mint marks for the coinage of the German Empire from 1871 to 1918: —

    A mm for Berlin
    B mm for Hanover
    C mm for Frankfort
    D mm for Munich
    E mm for Dresden
    F mm for Stuttgart
    G mm for Karlsruhe
    H mm for Darmstadt
    J mm for Hamburg

The colossal coinage of Germany is no way better evidenced than that it comprises about one third of this book. It must be remembered that Germany until 1871 was not a unified country and for hundreds of years consisted of a multitude of independent coin issuing localities, each one of which merits the same numismatic attention as a sovereign nation. This mingled secular coinage has been further enlarged by the extensive issues of many ecclesiastical rulers.

Even the issues of the German Empire from 1871-1918 were similar only in denominations for they still bore the heads and titles of the many different rulers whose states formed the Empire.

As a matter of fact, it can truly be said that there is no such thing as a "German" gold coin—only a Prussian coin or a Cologne coin, etc. Actually, it was not until the formation of the German Republic after World War I that a truly national German coinage came into existence, and under this coinage, there were unfortunately no gold coins.

A. Empire of —, 1871-1918
General Types for all the States

Obverse: Head of the ruler except for the free cities of Bremen, Hamburg and Lubeck, which have the city arms.

Reverse: "Deutsches Reich," value, date and eagle. Three varieties of this reverse design were used and the date on the coin automatically indicates the type of reverse:

FIRST REVERSE, 1871-1873 inclusive: Small eagle, and below, both the date and abbreviated value.

SECOND REVERSE, 1874-1889 inclusive: Small eagle, and below, the complete value with the date appearing at the right.

THIRD REVERSE, 1890-1915 inclusive: Large eagle.

(The illustrations above show a typical obverse as well as the three reverses in their correct numerical order.)

NOTE: The valuations in this section are for Uncirculated specimens of the commonest dates.

ANHALT

Dukes of —
FREDERICK I, 1871-1904

1. 20 Marks 1875 .... 150.00
2. 20 Marks 1896, 1901 .... 175.00
3. 10 Marks 1896, 1901 .... 175.00

FREDERICK II, 1904-1918

4. 20 Marks 1904 .... 135.00

BADEN

Grand Dukes of —
FREDERICK I, 1852-1907

5. 20 Marks 1872, 73 .... 60.00
6. 20 Marks 1874 .... 60.00
7. 20 Marks 1894, 95 .... 60.00
8. 10 Marks 1872, 73 .... 50.00
9. 10 Marks 1875-81, 88 .... 50.00
10. 10 Marks 1890, 91, 93, 96, 97, 98, 1900, 01. Head left.. 50.00
11. 10 Marks 1902-07. Head right 50.00
12. 5 Marks 1877 .... 110.00

FREDERICK II, 1907-1918

13. 20 Marks 1911-14 .... 60.00
14. 10 Marks 1909-13 .... 50.00

BAVARIA

Kings of —
LOUIS II, 1864-1886

15. 20 Marks 1872, 73 .... 65.00
16. 20 Marks 1874-76, 78 .... 65.00
17. 10 Marks 1872, 73 .... 45.00
18. 10 Marks 1874-81 .... 45.00
19. 5 Marks 1877, 78 .... 125.00

OTTO, 1886-1913

20. 20 Marks 1895, 1900, 05, 13 .... 55.00
21. 10 Marks 1888 .... 75.00
22. 10 Marks 1890, 93, 96, 98, 1900. "Von" in title 55.00
23. 10 Marks 1901-07, 09-12. "V" in title 60.00

LOUIS III, 1913-1918

24. 20 Marks 1914 .... 275.00

BREMEN

Free City of —

25.	20 Marks 1906	200.00
26.	10 Marks 1907	175.00

BRUNSWICK

Dukes of —

WILLIAM, 1831-1884

27.	20 Marks 1875	125.00

HAMBURG

Free City of —

28.	20 Marks 1875-81, 83, 84, 87, 89	45.00
29.	20 Marks 1893-95, 97, 99, 1900, 13	45.00
30.	10 Marks 1873	300.00
31.	10 Marks 1874. Arms of 1873	250.00
32.	10 Marks 1875-80, 1888. New type arms	45.00
33.	10 Marks 1890, 93, 96, 98, 1900-03, 05-13	45.00
34.	5 Marks 1877	125.00

HESSE

Grand Dukes of —

LOUIS III, 1848-1877

35.	20 Marks 1872, 73	75.00
36.	20 Marks 1874	95.00
37.	10 Marks 1872-73	55.00
38.	10 Marks 1875-77	65.00
39.	5 Marks 1877	150.00

LOUIS IV, 1877-1892

40.	20 Marks 1892	200.00
41.	10 Marks 1878-80. H mm	110.00
42.	10 Marks 1888. A mm	110.00
43.	10 Marks 1890	150.00
44.	5 Marks 1877	175.00

ERNEST LOUIS, 1892-1918

45.	20 Marks 1893. Young head	150.00
46.	20 Marks 1896-1901, 03. Older head with one S in title	100.00
47.	20 Marks 1905, 06, 08, 11. With 2 S's in title	90.00
48.	10 Marks 1893. Young head	150.00
49.	10 Marks 1896, 98. Older head	135.00

LUBECK

Free City of —

50.	10 Marks 1901, 04. Small arms	225.00
51.	10 Marks 1905, 06, 09, 10. Large arms	225.00

MECKLENBURG-SCHWERIN

Grand Dukes of —

FREDERICK FRANCIS II, 1842-1883

52.	20 Marks 1872	165.00
53.	10 Marks 1872	350.00
54.	10 Marks 1878	225.00

FREDERICK FRANCIS III, 1883-1897

55.	10 Marks 1890	150.00

FREDERICK FRANCIS IV, 1897-1918

56.	20 Marks 1901	475.00
57.	10 Marks 1901	350.00

MECKLENBURG-STRELITZ

Grand Dukes of —

FREDERICK WILLIAM, 1860-1904

58.	20 Marks 1873	850.00
59.	20 Marks 1874	850.00
60.	10 Marks 1873	950.00
61.	10 Marks 1874, 80	725.00

ADOLPH FREDERICK, 1904-1914

62.	20 Marks 1905	800.00
63.	10 Marks 1905	900.00

OLDENBURG

Grand Dukes of —

NICHOLAS FREDERICK PETER, 1853-1900

64.	10 Marks 1874	550.00

PRUSSIA

Emperors of Germany and Kings of —

WILLIAM I, 1861-1888

65.	20 Marks 1871-73. A mm	45.00
66.	20 Marks 1872, 73. B mm	45.00
67.	20 Marks 1872, 73. C mm	45.00
68.	20 Marks 1874-79, 81-88. A mm	45.00
69.	20 Marks 1874, 75, 77. B mm	55.00
70.	20 Marks 1874, 76-78. C mm	45.00
71.	10 Marks 1872, 73. A mm	40.00
72.	10 Marks 1872, 73. B mm	40.00
73.	10 Marks 1872, 73. C mm	40.00
74.	10 Marks 1874, 75, 77-80, 82, 83, 86, 88. A mm	40.00
75.	10 Marks 1874-78. B mm	40.00
76.	10 Marks 1874-79. C mm	50.00
77.	5 Marks 1877, 78. A mm	115.00
78.	5 Marks 1877. B mm	115.00
79.	5 Marks 1877. C mm	115.00

FREDERICK III, 1888

80.	20 Marks 1888	55.00
81.	10 Marks 1888	50.00

WILLIAM II, 1888-1918

82.	20 Marks 1888, 89	65.00
83.	20 Marks 1890-1913. A mm ....*	40.00
84.	20 Marks 1905, 06, 08, 09, 10, 12. J mm	40.00
85.	20 Marks 1913-15. Uniformed bust	45.00
86.	10 Marks 1889	500.00
87.	10 Marks 1890, 92-1907, 09-12 ....*	50.00

REUSS-OLDER LINE

Princes of —

HENRY XXII, 1859-1902

88.	20 Marks 1875	1750.00

REUSS-YOUNGER LINE

Princes of —

HENRY XIV, 1867-1913

89.	20 Marks 1881	500.00
90.	10 Marks 1882	850.00

SAXONY

Kings of —

JOHN, 1854-1873

91.	20 Marks 1872, 73	65.00
92.	10 Marks 1872, 73	60.00

ALBERT, 1873-1902

93.	20 Marks 1874, 76-78	65.00
94.	20 Marks 1894, 95	65.00

95.	10 Marks 1874, 75, 77, 78, 79, 81, 88	55.00
96.	10 Marks 1891, 93, 96, 98, 1900, 01, 02	55.00
97.	5 Marks 1877	115.00

GEORGE, 1902-1904

98.	20 Marks 1903	65.00
99.	10 Marks 1903, 04	50.00

FREDERICK AUGUST III, 1904-1918

100.	20 Marks 1905, 13, 14	50.00
101.	10 Marks 1905-07, 1909-12	55.00

SAXONY ALTENBURG

Dukes of —

ERNEST, 1853-1908

102.	20 Marks 1887	375.00

SAXONY-COBURG-GOTHA

Dukes of —

ERNEST II, 1844-1893

103.	20 Marks 1872	1750.00
104.	20 Marks 1886	375.00

ALFRED, 1893-1900

105.	20 Marks 1895	350.00

CARL EDWARD, 1900-1918

106.	20 Marks 1905	350.00
107.	10 Marks 1905	275.00

SAXONY-MEININGEN

Dukes of —

GEORGE II, 1866-1914

108.	20 Marks 1872	1250.00
109.	20 Marks 1882. Head right	900.00
110.	20 Marks 1889. Head left	600.00
111.	20 Marks 1900, 05	900.00
112.	20 Marks 1910, 14. New older head	900.00
113.	10 Marks 1890, 98	575.00
114.	10 Marks 1902, 09, 14. New older head	575.00

SAXONY-WEIMAR

Grand Dukes of —

CARL ALEXANDER, 1853-1901

115.	20 Marks 1892, 96	350.00

WILLIAM ERNEST, 1901-1918

116.	20 Marks 1901	400.00

SCHAUMBURG-LIPPE

Princes of —

ADOLPH GEORGE, 1860-1893

117.	20 Marks 1874	1500.00

GEORGE, 1893-1911

118.	20 Marks 1898, 1904	475.00

SCHWARZBURG-RUDOLSTADT

Princes of —

GUNTHER, 1890-1918

119.	10 Marks 1898	475.00

SCHWARZBURG-SONDERSHAUSEN

Princes of —

CHARLES GUNTHER, 1880-1909

120.	20 Marks 1896	550.00

WALDECK

Princes of —

FREDERICK, 1893-1918

121.	20 Marks 1903	750.00

WURTTEMBERG

Kings of —

CHARLES, 1864-1891

122.	20 Marks 1872, 73	55.00
123.	20 Marks 1874, 76	75.00
124.	10 Marks 1872, 73	60.00
125.	10 Marks 1874-81, 1888	60.00
126.	10 Marks 1890, 91	60.00
127.	5 Marks 1877, 78	125.00

WILLIAM II, 1891-1918

128.	20 Marks 1894, 97, 98, 1900, 05, 13, 14	55.00
129.	10 Marks 1893, 96, 98, 1900-07, 09-13	50.00

B. Republic of —

Private Commemorative Issues, 1955-1958

A series of large handsome coins struck on the old Ducat standard to commemorate the anniversaries of various cities or of historical events. They are dated 1955, 1956, 1957 or 1958 and about ten different types have been struck.

130.	30 Ducat pieces	400.00
131.	20 Ducat pieces	300.00
132.	10 Ducat pieces	150.00
133.	4 Ducat pieces	50.00

C. Coinage of the German Cities and States before the Empire.

AACHEN (AIX)

Seated Madonna with name of Reynald of Julich. Rev. Charlemagne standing.

134.	½ Goldgulden ND. (1402-23)	Rare

Madonna standing with name of Reynald of Julich. Rev. Charlemagne standing.

135.	½ Goldgulden ND. (1402-23)	Rare

Charlemagne seated. Rev. Church

136.	5 Ducats ND (1500)	1250.00

Charlemagne seated. Rev. Eagle with name of Maximilian II.

137.	1 Goldgulden 1572	600.00

Charlemagne seated. Rev. Eagle with name of Rudolph II.

138.	1 Goldgulden 1582, 85, 91, 92	500.00

Charlemagne seated. Rev. Eagle with name of Ferdinand II.

139.	1 Goldgulden 1634	400.00
140.	1 Goldgulden 1634, square	500.00

Bust of Charlemagne. Rev. Ferdinand III standing.

141.	1 Ducat 1641, 43, 45	250.00

Ferdinand III standing. Rev. Value in tablet.

142.	1 Ducat 1646	200.00

Bust of Charlemagne. Rev. Madonna standing.

143.	1 Ducat ND. (1637-57)	Rare

Madonna standing. Rev. Value in tablet.

144.	1 Ducat ND	500.00

Emperor Francis standing. Rev. Value in tablet.

145. 1 Ducat 1753 .... 350.00

ANHALT

Princes of —

WOLDEMAR VI AND BROTHERS, 1471-1508
St. Anne standing. Rev. Arms.

146. 1 Goldgulden ND .... Rare

JOHN GEORGE AND BROTHERS, 1603-1618
Two busts. Rev. Three busts.

147. 4 Ducats 1614 .... 1500.00
148. 3 Ducats 1614, 16 .... 900.00

Three helmets. Rev. Arms.

149. 1 Ducat 1615, 16, 18, ND 350.00
150. ½ Ducat 1616, 18 .... 200.00

ANHALT-BERNBURG

Dukes of —

VICTOR FREDERICK, 1721-1765
Arms. Rev. Bear on wall.

151. 1 Ducat 1730-61 .... 200.00

Bust. Rev. Arms.

152. 5 Taler 1744 .... 300.00
153. 2½ Taler 1744 .... 300.00

ALEXIUS FREDERICK CHRISTIAN, 1796-1834

Bust. Rev. Arms.

154. 5 Taler or 1 Pistole 1796 .... 300.00

Bear on wall. Rev. Value and date.

155. 1 Harz-gold Ducat 1825 .... 350.00

ANHALT-COETHEN

Dukes of —

AUGUST LOUIS, 1728-1755
Arms supported by bears. Rev. Bear with shield.

156. 1 Ducat 1747, 51 .... 200.00

Head. Rev. Bear with shield.

157. 1 Ducat 1751 .... 250.00

ANHALT-PLOETZKAU

Dukes of —

AUGUST, 1603-1653
Altar with Phoenix. Rev. Fountain.

158. 3 Goldgulden 1620 .... 850.00
159. 2 Goldgulden 1620 .... 600.00
160. 1 Goldgulden 1615, 17, 20 .... 375.00

ANHALT-ZERBST

Princes of —

CHARLES WILLIAM, 1667-1718
Bust. Rev. C.W.

161. ½ Ducat ND 175.00

JOHN LOUIS AND CHRISTIAN AUGUST, 1742-1747

Two busts. Rev. Arms.

162. 1 Ducat 1742 ....*...... 200.00
163. 1 Ducat 1745. On the marriage of Catherine II of
　　 Russia, and with different legend 375.00

FREDERICK AUGUST, 1747-1793
Bust. Rev. Arms.

164. 1 Ducat 1764 .... 250.00

ARENBERG

Dukes of —

LOUIS ENGELBERT, 1778-1820

Head. Rev. Arms.

165. 1 Ducat 1783 .... 550.00

ASPREMONT

Barons —

FERDINAND
Ruler standing. Rev. Arms.

166. 1 Ducat ND (1650) 450.00

AUGSBURG

A. City Coinage

Legend. Rev. Ship. On the Reformation.

167. 1 Ducat 1717 .... 150.00

City View. Rev. Legend. On the Augsburg Confession.

168. 1 Ducat 1730 .... 125.00

B. Coinage with the heads or names of the Holy Roman Emperors.

St. Udalric seated. Rev. Orb. Name of Maximilian I.

169. 1 Goldgulden 1515 .... 500.00

Bust of Charles V. Rev. Arms.

170. 1 Goldgulden 1527, 31 .... 500.00

St Udalric seated. Rev. Orb. Name of Charles V.

171. 1 Goldgulden 1520 .... 500.00

Eagle. Rev. Arms. Name of Charles V.

172. 1 Goldgulden ND (1517-58) 150.00

Bust of Ferdinand I. Rev. Arms.

173. 1 Goldgulden 1558 .... 500.00

Eagle. Rev. Arms. Name of Ferdinand I.

174. 1 Goldgulden 1562, 63 .... 400.00

Bust of Maximilian II. Rev. Arms.

175. 1 Goldgulden 1562, 66 .... 400.00

Bust of Rudolph II. Rev. Arms.

176. 1 Goldgulden 1582 .... 400.00

Eagle. Rev. Pyre. Name of Rudolph II.

177. 1 Goldgulden 1609 .... 375.00

Seated female. Rev. Eagle. Name of Matthias II.

178. 1 Goldgulden 1613 .... 200.00

Bust of Ferdinand II. Rev. Arms.

179. 1 Goldgulden 1619 .... 350.00

Eagle. Rev. Arms. Name of Ferdinand II.

180. 1 Goldgulden 1623, 28 .... 350.00

St. Afra and St. Ulric standing. Rev. Eagle. Name of Ferdinand II.

181. 2 Ducats 1626 .... 500.00

St. Afra and pyre. Rev. Eagle. Name of Ferdinand II.

182. 4 Ducats 1630 .... 1000.00
183. 1 Ducat 1629-38 .... 175.00

St. Afra and St. Ulric standing. Rev. Double eagle. Name of Ferdinand II.

184. 1 Goldgulden 1627, 28 .... 400.00

Bust of Ferdinand III. Rev. Arms.

185. 2 Ducats 1641, 43 .... 400.00
186. 1 Ducat 1637-57 ....*...... 175.00

Busts of Ferdinand III and Eleanor. Rev. Arms.

187. 2 Ducats 1657 .... 500.00

St. Afra and pyre. Rev. Eagle. Name of Ferdinand III.

188. 1 Ducat 1638, 39, 42 .... 250.00

Bust of Ferdinand IV. Rev. Legend in wreath. On his coronation.

189. 1 Ducat 1653 .... 400.00

Legend. Rev. Eagle and trophies. Homage for Ferdinand IV.

190. 1 Ducat 1653 .... 100.00

Sceptre and palms. Rev. Inscription.

191. 1 Ducat 1653 .... 100.00

Bust of Leopold I. Rev. Arms.

192. 1 Ducat 1658-77 .... 200.00

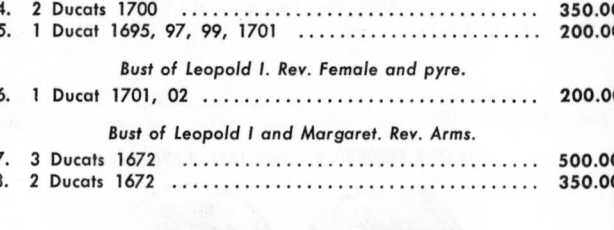

Bust of Leopold I. Rev. Pyre in wreath.

193. 1 Ducat 1677-92 .... 200.00

Bust of Leopold I. Rev. Arms between river gods.

194. 2 Ducats 1700 .... 350.00
195. 1 Ducat 1695, 97, 99, 1701 .... 200.00

Bust of Leopold I. Rev. Female and pyre.

196. 1 Ducat 1701, 02 .... 200.00

Bust of Leopold I and Margaret. Rev. Arms.

197. 3 Ducats 1672 .... 500.00
198. 2 Ducats 1672 .... 350.00

Bust of Leopold I. Rev. Bust of Eleanor.

199. 1 Ducat 1689, 90 .... 200.00

Busts of Leopold and Eleanor. Rev. Arms.

200. 3 Ducats 1691 .... 500.00
201. 2 Ducats 1691 .... 400.00

Bust of Joseph I. Rev. Crown and insignia. On his coronation.

202. 1 Ducat 1690 .... 100.00

Bust of Joseph I. Rev. Eagle.

203. 1 Ducat 1690 .... 100.00

Two genii over legend. Rev. Sword. Joseph I as Emperor.

204. 1½ Ducats 1690 .... 150.00

Two genii over legend. Rev. Crown. Joseph I as Crown Prince.

205. 1 Ducat 1690 .... 125.00

Bust of Joseph I. Rev. Female and pyre.

206. 1 Ducat 1705, 07 .... 200.00

Bust of Joseph I. Rev. Pyre between river gods and eagle.

207. 1 Ducat 1708, 11 .... 200.00

Bust of Charles VI. Rev. Pyre between river gods and eagle.

208. 1 Ducat 1711 .... 200.00

Bust of Charles VI. Rev. Pyre between river gods and eagle.

209. 1 Ducat 1714, 15 .... 200.00

Bust of Charles VI. Rev. Flying eagle. On his coronation.

210. 1 Ducat 1711 .... 150.00

Bust of Charles VI. Rev. Pyre between river gods.

211. 2 Ducats 1738 .... 400.00
212. 1 Ducat 1737, 38 .... 200.00

Bust of Charles VI. Rev. Female and pyre.

213. 1 Ducat 1726 ....*...... 200.00
214. ½ Ducat 1717 .... 125.00

Bust of Charles VII. Rev. Female and pyre.

215. 1 Ducat 1742 .... 250.00

Bust of Charles VII. Rev. Arms.

216. 1 Ducat 1743 .... 250.00

Bust of Francis I. Rev. As indicated.

217. 3 Ducats 1745. City view 500.00
218. 2 Ducats 1745. City view 400.00
219. 3 Ducats 1745. Arms 400.00
220. 2 Ducats 1745. Arms 250.00

Bust of Francis I. Rev. Eagle and pyre between river gods.

221. 1 Ducat 1745 .... 250.00

Bust of Francis I. Rev. Arms.

222. 1 Ducat 1762, 63 .... 225.00

Bust of Joseph II. Rev. Arms.

223. 1 Ducat 1767 .... 225.00

C. Bishops of —

ALEXANDER SIGISMUND OF THE PALATINATE, 1690-1737

Bust. Rev. Two shields.

224. 2 Ducats 1708 ....*...... 600.00
225. 1 Ducat 1708 .... 300.00

JOSEPH OF HESSE, 1740-1768

Bust with cap. Rev. Two shields.

226. 1 Ducat 1744 .... 350.00

D. Swedish Kings of —

Conjoined heads of Gustav Adolphe and Queen. Rev. Two shields.

227. 2 Ducats 1632 .... 1000.00

Facing or profile bust of Gustav Adolphe. Rev. Arms.

228. 1 Ducat 1632, 33, 34, 35 .... 200.00

BADEN

Margraves, and later, Grand Dukes of —

A. The Baden Line (Baden-Baden)

CHRISTOPHER, 1475-1527

St. Peter. Rev. Four shields and cross.

229. 1 Goldgulden ND ....*...... 250.00
230. 1 Goldgulden 1505-09 .... 300.00

St. Bernard standing. Rev. Arms.
231. 1 Goldgulden 1513, 18, 19 .... 800.00

WILLIAM, 1622-1677
St. George on horse. Rev. Circle of arms.
232. 1 Goldgulden ND 1000.00

Bust. Rev. Arms.
233. 1 Ducat 1674 .... 600.00

LOUIS GEORGE AND FRANCISCA SIBYLLA AUGUSTA, 1707-1761

Conjoined busts. Rev. Two shields. On the Peace of Rastatt.
234. 1 Ducat 1714 .... 250.00

B. The Durlach Line (Baden-Durlach)

GEORGE FREDERICK, 1604-22

Bust. Rev. Quartered Arms.
235. 10 Ducats 1610 ....*..... 3000.00
236. 2 Ducats 1610 .... 850.00
237. 1 Goldgulden 1609 .... 600.00

Ruler standing. Rev. Arms.
238. 1 Ducat 1622 ....Unknown

CHARLES WILLIAM, 1709-1738

Armored Bust. Rev. Arms supported by griffins.
239. 1 Ducat 1721 .... 275.00
240. ½ Ducat 1721 ....*...... 200.00

Bust. Rev. Four shields and four initials around central shield.
241. 1 Carolin 1733, 34 .... 500.00
242. ½ Carolin 1734 .... 300.00

Large bust. Rev. Draped arms.
243. 1 Ducat 1736 .... 350.00
244. 1 Carolin 1734, 35 .... 500.00

Arms. Rev. Legend in square tablet.
245. 2 Ducats 1737 .... 600.00

Arms. Rev. Legend in circle.
246. 1 Ducat 1737 .... 200.00

Arms. Rev. Legend in cartouche.
247. ½ Ducat 1737 .... 150.00

CHARLES AUGUST AND MAGDALENE WILHELMINA, 1738-1745

Crowned oval shield. Rev. Two shields surmounted by vase.
248. 1 Ducat 1738 .... 125.00

Crowned oval shield. Rev. Two shields surmounted by flame.
249. 1 Ducat 1738 .... 125.00

Crowned oval shield. Rev. Three line legend and date.
250. 1 Ducat 1738 .... 250.00

Crowned oval shield. Rev. Standing female and column.
251. 1 Ducat 1738 .... 125.00

CHARLES FREDERICK, 1746-1811
Large armored bust. Rev. Arms surrounded by legend and
date.
252. 1 Ducat 1747 .... 300.00

Large armored bust. Rev. Arms flanked by date.
253. 1 Ducat 1751 .... 225.00

Large armored bust. Rev. Two shields crowned.
254. ½ Ducat 1747 .... 225.00

Crowned shield. Rev. Legend and date in circle.
255. ¼ Ducat 1747 .... 125.00

Large Head. Rev. Shield with supporters.
256. 1 Rhine-gold Ducat 1765, 67, 68 .... 800.00

Bust of Amalie Frederika of Hesse. Rev. Two shields. On the birth of twin princesses.

257. 1 Ducat 1776 .... 250.00

Two baby heads facing each other. Rev. Legend. On the birth of twin princesses.

258. 1 Ducat 1776 .... 225.00

Bust. Rev. Draped arms. On the birth of Prince Charles.

259. 1 Ducat 1786 .... 250.00

Head. Rev. River god.

260. 1 Rhine-gold Ducat 1807 .... 400.00

LOUIS, 1818-1830

Head. Rev. Arms.

261. 10 Gulden 1819, 21, 23, 24, 25 ....*...... 350.00
262. 5 Gulden 1819, 21, 22, 24-28 ....*..... 200.00
263. 5 Taler or 500 Kreuzer 1830 .... 250.00

LEOPOLD, 1830-1852

Obv. as indicated. Rev. Arms.

264. 1 Rhine-gold Ducat 1832-42. Small head 275.00
265. 1 Rhine-gold Ducat 1843-46. Larger head 275.00
266. 1 Rhine-gold Ducat 1847-52. Largest head 275.00

FREDERICK, 1852-1907

Head. Rev. Arms.

267. 1 Rhine-gold Ducat 1854 .... 300.00

BAMBERG

A. City of —

Two females standing. Rev. Legend. On the Union with Bavaria.

268. 1 Ducat 1802 .... 200.00

B. Bishops of —

GEORGE III SCHENK, 1505-1522

St. Henry standing. Rev. Two shields.

269. 1 Goldgulden 1506, 11, 12, 13, 14 .... 600.00

St. Henry and St. Kunigunde with church model. Rev. Two shields.

270. 1 Goldgulden 1507, ND 600.00

JOHN PHILIP, 1599-1609

St. Henry and St. Kunigunde with church model. Rev. Two shields.

271. 2 Ducats 1601 ....*...... 1000.00
272. 1 Ducat 1600, 01, 02 ....*...... 350.00

JOHN GODFREY, 1609-1622
Arms. Rev. Legend. On his death.

273. 1 Goldgulden 1622 .... 400.00

JOHN GEORGE II FUCHS, 1623-1633
Bust. Rev. St. Henry and St. Kunigunde with church model.

274. 1 Ducat 1628, 31 .... 350.00
275. 1 Goldgulden 1624, 28 .... 250.00

FRANCIS, 1633-1642

Madonna seated. Rev Arms.

276. 1 Ducat 1635, 37, 38, 40 .... 300.00

MELCHIOR OTTO VOIT, 1642-1653

Bust. Rev. Arms.

277. 1 Ducat 1647 .... 300.00

PHILIP VALENTINE VOIT, 1653-1672
Bust. Rev. Two shields.

278. 1 Ducat 1657 .... 250.00

LOTHAR FRANCIS, 1693-1729
(See under Mayence.)

FREDERICK CHARLES, 1729-1746
(See under Wurzburg.)

JOHN PHILIP ANTHONY, 1746-1753
Bust. Rev. Arms.

279. 1 Ducat 1750 .... 250.00

Knight standing. Rev. Arms.

280. 1 Ducat 1746 .... 250.00

FRANCIS CONRAD, 1753-1757

Bust. Rev. Arms. On the Homage of Bamberg.

281. 1 Ducat 1753 .... 250.00

ADAM FREDERICK, 1757-1779

Bust. Rev. Knight standing. On the Homage of Bamberg.

282. 1 Ducat 1757 .... 250.00

FRANCIS LOUIS, 1779-1795

Bust. Rev. Female and pyramid. On the Homage of Bamberg.

283. 1 Ducat 1779 .... 275.00

CHRISTOPHER FRANCIS, 1795-1802

Bust over legend. Rev. Female at altar. On the Homage of Bamberg.

284. 1 Ducat 1795, ND 175.00

BAVARIA

Dukes, and later, Kings of —

LOUIS IV, 1413-1447
Arms on cross. Rev. Three shields.

285. 1 Goldgulden ND 150.00

Lamb. Rev. Floriated cross.

286. 1 Mouton d'or ND 500.00

Ruler on throne. Rev. Cross.

287. 1 Chaise d'or ND 300.00

ALBERT IV, 1465-1508
Duke kneeling before Madonna standing. Rev. Arms.

288. 1 Goldgulden 1506 .... 250.00

Duke kneeling before Madonna seated. Rev. Arms.

289. 1 Goldgulden 1506 .... 250.00

WILLIAM IV, 1508-1550
Duke kneeling before Madonna seated. Rev. Arms. With titles of Albert.

290. 1 Goldgulden 1508, 09, 10 .... 250.00

WILLIAM IV AND LOUIS X, 1516-1545
Madonna seated. Rev. Arms.

291. 1 Goldgulden ND 500.00

Madonna standing. Rev. Arms.

292. 1 Goldgulden 1525, 32 .... 500.00

ALBERT V, 1550-1579
Bust. Rev. Arms.

293. 2 Ducats 1565, 68 .... 500.00

Bust with hat. Rev. Arms.

294. 1 Ducat ND 250.00

Duke kneeling. Rev. Lion with arms.

295. 2 Ducats ND 500.00
296. 1 Ducat ND 250.00

WILLIAM V, 1579-1598
Arms. Rev. Date. On his wedding.

297.   1 Ducat 1568 ....   250.00

St. Henry standing. Rev. Arms.

298.   1 Ducat 1596 ....   300.00

MAXIMILIAN I, 1598-1651

Elector before Madonna. Rev. Arms.

299.   2 Ducats 1642, 44, 45, 47 ....*......   400.00
300.   1 Ducat 1638, 42-47 ....   250.00

Madonna. Rev. Arms.

301.   2 Ducats 1618 ....*......   375.00
302.   1 Goldgulden 1625 ....   250.00
303.   1 Ducat 1632, 40 ....   200.00

Elector standing. Rev. View of Munich.

304.   5 Ducats 1640 ....*......   500.00
305.   1 Ducat 1645 ....   200.00

Elector standing. Rev. Madonna.

306.   2 Ducats 1645 ....   300.00
307.   1 Ducat 1644, 46 ....   200.00

Elector at table. Rev. Madonna over view of Munich.

308.   4 Ducats 1610 ....   600.00

FERDINAND MARIA, 1651-1679
Elector standing. Rev. Madonna and shield.

309.   1 Ducat 1655-71 ....   150.00

Elector standing. Rev. View of Munich.

310.   1 Ducat 1677, 78 ....   250.00

Bust. Rev. Madonna and shield.

311.   1 Goldgulden 1674-79 ....   200.00

Bust. Rev. Arms.

312.   ½ Ducat 1672, 78 ....   120.00
313.   ¼ Ducat 1672, 73, 76 ....   100.00

Busts of Ferdinand and Adelaide. Rev. Arms. On their wedding.

314.   3 Ducats 1652 ....   600.00

Madonna. Rev. Shield. On the birth of Prince Max Emanuel.

315.   ½ Ducat 1662 ....   100.00

Bust of Adelaide. Rev. Arms. On the birth of Princess Louise.

316.   1 Ducat 1663 ....   150.00

Family kneeling. Rev. Two shields. On the birth of Prince Louis Amadeus.

317.   4 Ducats 1665 ....   400.00

Sun, moon and earth. Rev. Three shields. On the birth of Prince Cajetan Maria.

318.   2 Ducats 1670 ....   250.00

St. Nicholas seated. Rev. Arms. On the birth of Prince Joseph Clemens.

319.   1 Ducat 1671 ....   200.00

Two shields. Rev. Column. On the birth of Princess Violanta Beatrix.

320.   2 Ducats 1673 ....   250.00

MAXIMILIAN EMANUEL, 1679-1726

Bust. Rev. Madonna standing.

321.   2 Ducats 1685, 87 ....*........   500.00
322.   1 Ducat 1687, 97 ....   250.00

Bust. Rev. Madonna over arms.

323.   1 Goldgulden 1691, 98 ....   200.00

Bust. Rev. Bust of Madonna over arms.

324.   1 Goldgulden 1699, 1700, 02, 03, 15 ....*......   200.00
325.   1 Goldgulden 1704. With pyre under bust. (Occupation of Augsburg) 400.00

Head. Rev. Arms. Struck for the Lowlands.

326. 2 Souverain d'or 1712 .... 600.00

Head. Rev. Madonna seated.

327. 2 Max d'or 1717 .... 175.00
328. 1 Max d'or 1715-26 ....*...... 100.00
329. ½ Max d'or 1715-25 .... 75.00

Palm tree. Rev. Shields of Bavaria and Poland. On the birth
   of Prince Charles Albert.

330. 2 Ducats 1697 .... 250.00

Three sunflowers. Rev. Legend. On the birth of Prince
   Ferdinand Maria.

331. 2 Ducats 1699 .... 200.00

Crowned lion. Rev. Arms. Struck for the Lowlands.

332. 1 Souverain d'or 1711-13 .... 250.00

CHARLES ALBERT, 1726-1744

Head. Rev. Madonna seated.

333. 1 Carolin 1726-32 ....*...... 150.00
334. ½ Carolin 1726-31 .... 125.00
335. ¼ Carolin 1726-31 .... 75.00

Bust. Rev. Madonna seated.

336. 1 Carolin 1732-35 .... 175.00
337. ½ Carolin 1732-37 .... 100.00
338. ¼ Carolin 1732-35 .... 75.00

Bust. Rev. Arms supported by lions.

339. 1 Ducat 1737 .... Unknown

Head. Rev. Eagle. On the Vicariat.

340. 2 Goldgulden 1740 .... 300.00
341. 1 Goldgulden 1740 .... 200.00

Bust. Rev. Eagle. On the Vicariat.

342. 1 Ducat 1740 .... 250.00

Madonna. Rev. Arms supported by lions.

343. 2 Ducats 1737 .... Unknown
344. 1 Ducat 1737, 39 ....*...... 200.00

"AB". Rev. Legend. On his wedding.

345. 1 Ducat 1722 .... 150.00

MAXIMILIAN III JOSEPH, 1745-1777

Bust. Rev. Eagle. On the Vicariat.

346. 1 Ducat 1745 .... 250.00

Bust. Rev. Madonna.

347. 1 Max d'or 1747, 51 .... 300.00

Busts of Maximilian and Marie Anne. Rev. Landscape. On
   their wedding.

348. 1 Ducat 1747 .... 250.00

Bust. Rev. Carriage. Homage of the representatives of the people.

349. 1 Ducat 1747 .... 200.00

Bust of Maximilian and Marie Anne. Rev. Bavaria before Pyramid.

350. 5 Ducats 1747 .... 600.00

Bust. Rev. River god.

351. 1 Danube-gold Ducat 1756, 60, 62 .... 400.00
352. 1 Inn-gold Ducat 1756, 60, 62 .... 400.00
353. 1 Isar-gold Ducat 1756, 60, 62 .... 500.00

Bust. Rev. Arms supported by lions.

354. 1 Ducat 1755-75 .... 200.00

CHARLES THEODORE, 1777-1799

Head. Rev. Arms.

355. 3 Ducats 1787 .... 600.00
356. 2 Ducats 1787 .... 400.00
357. 1 Ducat 1778-98 ....*...... 150.00

Head. Rev. River god, city in background.

358. 1 Danube-gold Ducat 1779, 80, 93 .... 450.00
359. 1 Inn-gold Ducat 1779, 80, 93, 98 .... 450.00
360. 1 Isar-gold Ducat 1779, 80, 93, 98 .... 500.00

Head. Rev. Double Eagle. On the Vicariat.

361. 3 Ducats 1790, 92 ....*...... 600.00
362. 2 Ducats 1790, 92 .... 400.00
363. 1 Ducat 1790, 92 .... 200.00

MAXIMILIAN JOSEPH (IV, 1799-1806), (I, 1806-1825)
Head. Rev. Arms.

364. 1 Ducat 1799-1805 .... 175.00

Head. Rev. Wurzburg shield under palm tree.

365. 1 Goldgulden 1803 .... 250.00

Bust or head. Rev. Arms supported by lions.

366. 1 Ducat 1806. Bust 200.00
367. 1 Ducat 1811-25. Head 150.00

Head. Rev. Wurzburg city view.

368. 1 Goldgulden 1815 .... 300.00

Head. Rev. Wurzburg shield.

369. 1 Goldgulden 1817, ND 250.00

Head. Rev. River god.

370. 1 Danube-gold Ducat 1821 .... 250.00
371. 1 Inn-gold Ducat 1821 .... 250.00
372. 1 Isar-gold Ducat 1821 .... 300.00

Head. Rev. Speyer city view.

373. 1 Rhine-gold Ducat 1821 .... 250.00

LOUIS I, 1825-1848

Head. Rev. Arms supported by lions.

374. 1 Ducat 1826-48 .... 150.00

Head. Rev. River god.

375. 1 Danube-gold Ducat 1830 .... 350.00
376. 1 Inn-gold Ducat 1830 .... 350.00
377. 1 Isar-gold Ducat 1830 .... 350.00

Young or old head. Rev. Speyer city view.

378. 1 Rhine-gold Ducat 1830, 42, 46 .... 250.00

Head. Rev. Legend.

379. 1 Goldgulden 1826 .... 250.00

Head. Rev. Wurzburg city view.

380. 1 Goldgulden ND (1827, 43) 250.00

Head. Rev. Wurzburg shield.

381. 1 Goldgulden ND (1843) 250.00

MAXIMILIAN II, 1848-1864

Head. Rev. Arms.

382. 1 Ducat 1849-56 .... 150.00

Head. Rev. Wurzburg shield.

383. 1 Goldgulden ND (1850) 250.00

Head. Rev. Wurzburg city view.

384. 1 Goldgulden ND (1850) 250.00

Head. Rev. Speyer city view.

385. 1 Rhine-gold Ducat 1850-56, 63 .... 300.00

Head. Rev. Arms.

386. 1 Mining-Ducat 1855. Goldkronach 1250.00

Head. Rev. Value.

387. 1 Krone 1857-64 .... 750.00
388. ½ Krone 1857-63 ....*...... 300.00
389. ½ Krone 1864 .... 1000.00

LOUIS II, 1864-1886

Head. Rev. Value.

390. 1 Krone 1864-69 ....*...... 750.00
391. ½ Krone 1864-69 .... 300.00

Head. Rev. Wurzburg city view.

392. 1 Goldgulden ND (1864) 200.00

Head. Rev. Wurzburg shield.

393. 1 Goldgulden ND (1864) 200.00

Head. Rev. Crown in wreath.

394. 1 Ducat ND (1864) 125.00

BENTHEIM

Counts —

MAURICE, 1625-1674
Bust. Rev. Arms.

395. 1 Ducat 1656 .... 750.00

ERNEST WILLIAM, 1643-1693
Arms. Rev. Value.

396. 2 Ducats 1669 .... 750.00
397. 1 Ducat 1669 .... 350.00

BRANDENBURG-ANSBACH

Margraves of —

JOACHIM ERNEST, 1603-1625

Margrave standing. Rev. Arms.

398. 4 Ducats 1622 ....*...... 1500.00
399. 2 Ducats 1622 .... 1000.00
400. 1 Ducat 1609, 19, 20, 23, 24 .... 200.00

Facing armored bust. Rev. Arms.

401. 1 Goldgulden 1610, 11, 19-21, 23, 24 .... 250.00

Margrave on horse. Rev. Cross and five shields.

402. 1 Goldgulden 1623 .... 300.00

FREDERICK, ALBERT AND CHRISTIAN, 1625-1634
Three busts. Rev. Arms.

403. 1 Ducat 1625-30, 32 .... 200.00

ALBERT, 1634-1667
Bust. Rev. Arms.

404. 2 Ducats 1660 .... 600.00
405. 1 Ducat 1651, 52, 63 .... 200.00

JOHN FREDERICK, 1667-1686
Bust. Rev. Arms.

406. 3 Ducats 1672 .... 750.00
407. 2 Ducats 1672, 77, 83 .... 350.00
408. 1 Ducat 1672 .... 250.00
409. 1 Ducat 1680, 83. PIETATE ET IVSTITIA 175.00

Bust. Rev. Crossed initials.

410. 1 Ducat 1684 .... 250.00

Arms. Rev. Piety and Justice.

411. 2 Ducats 1683 .... 400.00
412. ⅝ Ducat 1674 .... 250.00
413. ¼ Ducat 1680, 84 .... 75.00

WILLIAM FREDERICK, 1703-1723
Bust. Rev. Arms.

414. 1 Ducat 1715 .... 300.00

Bust. Rev. Two shields.

415. ¼ Ducat 1717 .... 150.00

CHRISTIANE CHARLOTTE, 1723-1729

Bust. Rev. Crown over linked C's.

416. 1 Ducat 1726 .... 300.00

CHARLES WILLIAM FREDERICK, 1729-1757
Bust. Rev. Eagle.

417.	2 Ducats 1729. Thick or broad	350.00
418.	1 Ducat 1729	250.00

Bust. Rev. Two shields.

419.	1 Ducat 1740, 47, 50	200.00

Bust. Rev. Eagle with shield.

420.	1 Ducat 1744	200.00

Bust. Rev. Eagle over arms.

421.	1 Ducat 1753	200.00

Falconier on horse. Rev. Falcon.

422.	1 Hunting Ducat ND	300.00

Bust. Rev. Arms.

423.	1 Carolin 1734, 35	350.00
424.	½ Carolin 1734, 35	250.00

ALEXANDER, 1757-1791
Two shields. Rev. Legend. On his wedding.

425.	2 Ducats 1754	300.00
426.	1 Ducat 1754	200.00

Bust. Rev. Eagle shield.

427.	1 Ducat 1757	200.00

Bust. Rev. Arms.

428.	1 Ducat 1762	200.00

Bust. Rev. Crown above three arms.

429.	1 Ducat 1763	200.00
430.	1 Ducat 1777 ....*......	275.00

Bust. Rev. Star of Order.

431.	1 Ducat 1779	200.00

Bust. Rev. Eagle shield with chain of Order.

432.	1 Carolin 1758, 66	350.00

Margrave on horse. Rev. Shields and trophies.

433.	1 Ducat 1765	200.00

Head. Rev. Eagle with two shields. On the union of Ansbach and Culmbach.

434.	1 Ducat 1769	200.00

Busts of Alexander and George Frederick. Rev. Altar. On the union of Ansbach and Culmbach.

435.	1 Ducat 1769	200.00

Knight at altar. Rev. Legend. On the homage.

436.	1 Ducat 1769	200.00

BRANDENBURG-BAYREUTH

Margraves of —

CHRISTIAN, 1603-1655
Margrave standing. Rev. Arms.

437.	4 Ducats 1609	600.00
438.	2 Ducats 1609	350.00
439.	1 Ducat 1609,28-32	200.00

Bust. Rev. Arms.

440.	1 Ducat 1631, 41, 42, 44, ND	200.00

Bust. Rev. Arms. On the 50th year of his reign.

441.	1 Ducat 1653	350.00

CHRISTIAN ERNEST, 1655-1712
Bust. Rev. Arms.

442.	1 Ducat 1659, 62, 77, 94, 1708, ND	200.00
443.	½ Ducat 1685	150.00

Busts of the Margrave and his wife. Rev. View of Cronach Mine.

444.	2 Ducats 1695	1250.00

GEORGE WILLIAM, 1712-1726
Bust. Rev. Arms.

445.	2 Ducats 1720	900.00
446.	1 Ducat 1720-22	450.00

Bust. Rev. Legend. On his death.

447.	2 Ducats 1726	650.00
448.	1 Ducat 1726	250.00

GEORGE FREDERICK CHARLES,1726-1735
Swan and tree. Rev. Legend. On the homage.

449.	1 Ducat 1727	200.00

FREDERICK, 1735-1763
Bust. Rev. Arms.

450.	1 Ducat 1735, 46	200.00

Margrave on horse. Rev. Order.

451.	1 Ducat 1746	200.00

FREDERICK CHRISTIAN, 1763-1769
Bust. Rev. Arms.

452.	1 Ducat 1763	200.00

Bust. Rev. Bible, cross and sword. On his birthday.

453.	1 Ducat 1764	200.00

Margrave on horse. Rev. Crown over Order.

454. 1 Ducat 1767 .... 200.00

BRANDENBURG-FRANCONIA

Margraves of —

FREDERICK V, 1361-1397

Arms in enclosure. Rev. St. John.

455. 1 Goldgulden ND 350.00

JOHN III, 1404-1420

Arms in enclosure. Rev. St. John.

456. 1 Goldgulden ND 1000.00

FREDERICK VI, 1404-1440

Eagle. Rev. St. John.

457. 1 Goldgulden ND 600.00

ALBERT ACHILLES, 1464-1486

St. John. Rev. Cross with five shields.

458. 1 Goldgulden ND. Mint: Schwabach 100.00

FREDERICK AND SIGISMUND, 1486-1495

St. John. Rev. Cross with four shields.

459. 1 Goldgulden ND. Mint: Schwabach 100.00

FREDERICK IV, 1495-1515

St. John. Rev. Cross with four shields.

460. 1 Goldgulden 1497-1515, ND. Mint: Schwabach 125.00

CASIMIR AND GEORGE, 1515-1527

St. John. Rev. Cross with four shields.

461. 1 Goldgulden 1515-26. Mint: Schwabach 125.00

GEORGE, 1527-1536

Cross with five shields. Rev. St. John.

462. 1 Goldgulden 1528-35 .... 175.00

GEORGE AND ALBERT, 1536-1543

Cross with five shields. Rev. St. John.

463. 1 Goldgulden 1538, 40, 41 .... 250.00

ALBERT ALCIBIADES, 1527-1554

Eagle. Rev. Blank. Square necessity coin.

464. 1 Ducat 1553 .... 600.00

Armored bust. Rev. Cross with five shields.

465. 1 Goldgulden 1549 .... 800.00

GEORGE FREDERICK, 1543-1603

Margrave standing. Rev. Arms.

466. 1 Ducat 1557. Mint: Schwabach 1000.00

Facing bust. Rev. Cross with five shields.

467. 1 Goldgulden 1571. Mint: Schwabach 1000.00

Margrave standing. Rev. Eagle.

468. 1 Ducat 1587-91, 94-97. Mint: Koenigsberg 150.00

BRANDENBURG-PRUSSIA

(See under Prussia)

BRAUNAU

Arms. Rev. Blank. Octagonal siege coins of the Austrian War of Succession.

469. 2 Ducats 1743 .... 1000.00
470. 1 Ducat 1743 .... 375.00
471. ½ Ducat 1743 .... 250.00

BREISACH

Legend. Rev. Imperial orb over three shields.

472. 1 Ducat 1633. Square siege coin 1250.00

BREMEN

A. City Coins with the heads or names of the Holy Roman Emperors

Eagle. Rev. Arms. Charles V.

473. 1 Goldgulden 1542, 46, 49 .... 750.00

Eagle. Rev. Arms. Matthias II.

474. 1 Goldgulden 1613 .... 650.00

Eagle. Rev. Arms supported by lions. Ferdinand II.

475. 1 Goldgulden 1635, 37 .... 250.00

Eagle. Rev. Arms. Ferdinand II.

476. 1 Goldgulden 1627, 35 .... 250.00

Ferdinand II standing. Rev. Arms.

477. 2 Ducats 1640, 52 .... 350.00
478. 1 Ducat 1640-52 ....*...... 200.00

130

Eagle. Rev. Arms supported by lions. Ferdinand III.

479. 2 Goldgulden 1649 ....* 1000.00
480. 1 Goldgulden 1640 .... 300.00

Key. Rev. St. Peter. Leopold I.

481. ¼ Ducat ND 100.00

Eagle. Rev. Arms supported by lions. Leopold I.

482. 5 Ducats 1661 .... 600.00
483. 3 Ducats 1667 .... 500.00

Leopold I standing. Rev. Arms.

484. 5 Ducats ND 1000.00
485. 3 Ducats 1659 .... 1000.00
486. 2 Ducats 1659, 67 .... 400.00
487. 1 Ducat 1659, 67 ....* 200.00

Head of Leopold I. Rev. Arms.

488. 1 Ducat 1672 .... 375.00

Bust of Leopold I. Rev. Arms supported by lions.

489. 4 Ducats ND 1250.00

Eagle. Rev. Arms supported by lions. Joseph I.

490. 1 Ducat 1710 .... 250.00

Eagle. Rev. Arms supported by lions. Charles VI.

491. 1 Ducat 1723 .... 250.00

Eagle. Rev. Arms supported by lions. Francis I.

492. 2 Ducats 1746 .... 350.00
493. 1 Ducat 1745, 46 ....* 200.00

B. Archbishops of —

HENRY II OF SCHWARZBURG, 1463-1497

St. Peter standing. Rev. Arms on cross.

494. 1 Goldgulden ND 350.00

JOHN III RODE, 1497-1511
St. Peter standing. Rev. Arms on cross.

495. 1 Goldgulden ND 300.00
496. ½ Goldgulden ND 300.00

St. Peter seated. Rev. Arms.

497. 1 Goldgulden ND 300.00

CHRISTOPHER OF BRUNSWICK, 1511-1558
St. Peter standing. Rev. Arms on cross.

498. 1 Goldgulden ND 300.00

St. Peter seated. Rev. Arms.

499. 1 Goldgulden 1521 .... 350.00

GEORGE OF BRUNSWICK, 1558-1566
St. Peter standing. Rev. Arms.

500. 1 Goldgulden ND 300.00

HENRY III OF LAUENBURG, 1567-1585
Bust. Rev Arms.

501. 1 Ducat 1583 .... 400.00

St. Peter. Rev. Arms.

502. 1 Goldgulden 1584, ND 350.00

JOHN FREDERICK OF HOLSTEIN-GOTTORP, 1596-1634
Bust. Rev. Cross.

503. 10 Ducats ND 1250.00

St. Peter standing. Rev. Arms.

504. 1 Goldgulden 1612, 18 .... 300.00

BREMEN AND VERDEN

Swedish Rulers of —

Bust of Christina. Rev. Arms.

505. 10 Ducats 1650 ....10,000.00

BRESLAU

A. City of —

St. Wenceslas. Rev. Lion.

506. 1 Goldgulden 1517-31, ND 250.00

St. John. Rev. Arms.

507. 1 Goldgulden 1531, 34 .... 250.00

St. Wenceslas. Rev. Arms.

508. 2 Ducats 1542 .... 750.00
509. 1 Ducat 1531-60 ....* 200.00

Arms. Rev. Shield of Pfintzig. On the Shooting Fete.

510. 2 Ducats 1560 .... 500.00

Maximilian II standing. Rev. Arms.

511. 1 Ducat 1572, 73 .... 200.00

Rudolph II standing. Rev. Arms.

512.	1 Ducat 1577	250.00

Louis II standing. Rev. Arms.

513.	1 Ducat 1577	225.00

Arms. Rev. Legend. On the Shooting Fetes.

514.	3 Ducats (1527-1614) Round	750.00
515.	3 Ducats (1527-1614) Square	500.00
516.	2 Ducats 1527, 77, 1614	325.00
517.	1 Ducat 1614 ....*......	200.00

Bust of Matthias II. Rev. Arms.

518.	5 Ducats 1612	800.00
519.	5 Ducats 1612. Square	1200.00
520.	4 Ducats 1612 ....*......	900.00
521.	3 Ducats 1612	750.00
522.	3 Ducats 1612. Square	900.00
523.	2 Ducats 1611-13	375.00
524.	2 Ducats 1612, 13. Square	450.00
525.	1 Ducat 1611-13	200.00

Bust of Matthias II. Rev. Crowned F over arms.

526.	2 Ducats 1617. Round and broad	300.00
527.	2 Ducats 1617. Square and smaller ....*......	350.00
528.	1 Ducat 1617	200.00

Bust of Frederick V of Bohemia. Rev. Arms.

529.	2 Ducats 1620	1000.00

Bust of Frederick V. Rev. Lion.

530.	1 Ducat 1620	375.00

Bust of Ferdinand II. Rev. Arms.

531.	3 Ducats 1622	500.00
532.	1 Ducat 1622	200.00
533.	½ Ducat 1622	150.00

Bust of Ferdinand II. Rev. Scales.

534.	2 Ducats 1630	300.00
535.	1 Ducat 1630 ....*......	200.00

Bust of Ferdinand III. Rev. Arms.

536.	5 Ducats 1651	600.00

B. Bishops of —

JACOB, 1520-1539

St. John. Rev. Arms.

537.	1 Ducat 1524-39	300.00

Bust. Rev. Arms.

538.	3 Ducats 1531	750.00

BALTHASAR, 1539-1562
Bust with hat. Rev. Arms.

539.	5 Ducats 1551	1800.00

St. John. Rev. Three shields.

540.	1 Ducat 1540-60	200.00

CASPAR, 1562-1574

St. John. Rev. Arms.

541.	1 Ducat 1562-73	250.00

MARTIN GERSTMANN, 1574-1585
St. John. Rev. Arms.

542.	2 Ducats 1574-77	600.00
543.	1 Ducat 1574-85	200.00

ANDREW JERIN, 1585-1596

St. John. Rev. Arms.

544.	1 Ducat 1585-92, ND	200.00

JOHN VI, 1600-1608

St. John. Rev. Arms.

545.	3 Ducats 1603. Square	....	775.00
546.	2 Ducats 1603. Square	....	325.00
547.	1 Ducat ND	........................*......	225.00

CHARLES OF AUSTRIA, 1608-1624

Bust. Rev. Two shields.

| 548. | 1 Ducat 1611, 12 | .... | 300.00 |

Two shields. Rev. Legend. On the Shooting Fete.

549.	3 Ducats 1612	....	375.00
550.	2 Ducats 1612	....	325.00
551.	1 Ducat 1612	..........................*.....	225.00

Bust. Rev. Three shields.

552.	10 Ducats 1615, 18	....	1250.00
553.	7 Ducats 1614, 18	....	850.00
554.	6 Ducats 1614	....	750.00
555.	5 Ducats 1616	....	650.00
556.	4 Ducats 1618	....	650.00
557.	3 Ducats 1614, 18	....	500.00
558.	1 Ducat 1614	....	175.00

Bust. Rev. Arms.

| 559. | 1 Ducat 1618 | .... | 225.00 |
| 560. | ½ Ducat 1618 | .... | 100.00 |

Bust. Rev. Arms and two small shields.

561.	5 Ducats ND	....	750.00
562.	2 Ducats ND	....	475.00
563.	1 Ducat ND	....	175.00

CHARLES FERDINAND OF POLAND, 1625-1655

Bust right or left. Rev. Two shields or arms.

564.	15 Ducats 1631, 32		Rare
565.	10 Ducats 1631, 38, 39, 42	....	2000.00
566.	6 Ducats 1632, 39	....	1250.00
567.	6 Ducats 1632. Square	....	1500.00
568.	5 Ducats 1632, 39	....	900.00
569.	5 Ducats 1632. Square	....	1250.00
570.	4 Ducats 1632	.......................*......	750.00
571.	3 Ducats 1632, 53. Round. 800.00 Octagonal	....	900.00
572.	2 Ducats 1632, 53. Round. 450.00 Octagonal	....	500.00
573.	1 Ducat 1635	....	200.00

SEBASTIAN OF ROSTOCK, 1664-1671
Bust. Rev. Arms.

574.	10 Ducats 1667	....	2000.00
575.	2 Ducats 1655	....	600.00
576.	1 Ducat 1655	....	375.00

FREDERICK OF HESSE, 1671-1682

Bust. Rev. Arms.

577.	3 Ducats 1674	....	600.00
578.	2 Ducats 1679-82	........................*......	500.00
579.	1 Ducat 1679-82	....	300.00

FRANCIS LOUIS OF NEUBURG, 1683-1732

Bust. Rev. Arms.

580.	10 Ducats 1701	....	2000.00
581.	6 Ducats 1730	....	1200.00
582.	2 Ducats 1690, 93	....	500.00
583.	1 Ducat 1686-1732	......................*......	300.00
584.	¼ Ducat ND	....	150.00
585.	⅛ Ducat ND	....	100.00

PHILIP OF SINZENDORF, 1732-1749

Bust. Rev. Arms.

| 586. | 8 Ducats 1733 | .... | 1500.00 |
| 587. | 1 Ducat 1738 | ....*...... | 300.00 |

PHILIP GOTTHARD SCHAFFGOTSCH, 1747-1795
Bust. Rev. Arms.

| 588. | 5 Ducats 1748 | .... | 1000.00 |
| 589. | 1 Ducat 1748-77 | .... | 250.00 |

JOSEPH OF HOHENLOHE, 1795-1817

Bust. Rev. Arms.

| 590. | 1 Ducat 1796 | .... | 250.00 |

BRETZENHEIM

Princes —
CHARLES AUGUST, 1769-1823

Bust. Rev. Arms on cross.

591. 1 Ducat 1790 .... 400.00

BRUNSWICK

City of —

Double Eagle. Rev. Lion.

592. 1 Goldgulden 1622, 29, 30 .... 400.00
593. 1 Ducat 1627, 48, 49, ND 250.00

Double Eagle. Rev. Arms.

594. 1 Goldgulden 1628, 31 .... 400.00

Double Eagle. Rev. Value.

595. 1 Ducat 1626 .... 400.00

Double Eagle. Rev. Value on tablet.

596. 1 Ducat 1628-60 .... 375.00

BRUNSWICK-CALENBERG

Dukes of —

ERIC I, 1491-1540
Arms. Rev. Double Eagle.

597. 1 Goldgulden 1539 .... 600.00

BRUNSWICK-GRUBENHAGEN

Dukes of —

WOLFGANG AND PHILIP II, 1567-1595
Arms. Rev. Bear and date.

598. 1 Goldgulden 1588 .... 500.00

BRUNSWICK-LUNEBURG

Dukes of —

JULIUS ERNEST OF DANNENBERG, 1598-1636
Bust. Rev. Arms.

599. 1 Goldgulden 1619 .... 600.00
600. 1 Ducat 1625 .... 500.00

CHRISTIAN OF MINDEN, 1599-1633

Bust. Rev. Arms.

601. 1 Goldgulden 1621-1633 .... 300.0

St. Andrew. Rev. Arms. Struck from Andreasberg gold.

602. 1 Goldgulden 1624, 29 .... 375.0

AUGUST, 1610-1636
Bust. Rev. Arms.

603. 1 Ducat 1634 .... 600.0

Ruler on horse. Rev. Arms.

604. 1 Goldgulden 1618 .... 375.0

Standing ruler. Rev. Arms.

605. 1 Goldgulden ND 375.0

FREDERICK, 1636-1648

Standing ruler. Rev. Arms.

606. 1 Ducat 1636-48, ND 250.0

Armored bust. Rev. Arms.

607. 1 Ducat 1647, 48, ND 250.0

GEORGE OF CALENBERG, 1635-1641

Bust. Rev. Arms.

608. 1 Ducat 1635, 36, 37, 38, ND 300.0

Arms. Rev. Orb.

609. 1 Goldgulden 1635 .... 500.0

CHRISTIAN LOUIS OF CELLE, 1646-1665
Bust. Rev. Arms.

610. 1 Ducat 1646 .... 600.0

Arms. Rev. Horse.

611. 1 Ducat 1650, 61 .... 200.0

GEORGE WILLIAM OF CELLE, 1665-1705
Bust. Rev. Horse.

612. 4 Ducats 1688 .... 1000.0
613. 2 Ducats 1685, 88, 90, 99 .... 300.0
614. 1 Ducat 1685, 90 .... 200.0
615. ½ Ducat 1685, 90 .... 150.0
616. ¼ Ducat 1690 .... 100.0

Bust. Rev. Arms.

617. 10 Ducats 1665 .... 1750.0
618. 2 Ducats 1675, 99 .... 300.0
619. 1 Ducat 1664, 75 .... 600.0

Arms. Rev. Horse.

620.	4 Ducats 1681	1000.00
621.	2 Ducats 1675, 99, 1700	300.00
622.	1 Ducat 1684-97, ND ....*......	200.00
623.	½ Ducat 1685-90	100.00

JOHN FREDERICK OF CALENBERG, 1665-1679
Bust. Rev. Arms.

624.	1 Ducat 1659-1685	500.00

Bust. Rev. Palm tree on rock.

625.	4 Ducats 1673	1000.00
626.	2 Ducats 1673	400.00
627.	1 Ducat 1668-79 ....*......	500.00

ERNEST AUGUST, 1692-1698
Bust. Rev. Landscape.

628.	20 Ducats 1680	Rare

Bust. Rev. Arms.

629.	10 Ducats 1681, 85	2000.00
630.	1 Ducat 1681, 85, 94	500.00

Bust. Rev. Arms under hat.

631.	2 Ducats 1694, 95	600.00
632.	1 Ducat 1694, 98 ....*......	250.00

Bust. Rev. Horse.

633.	2 Ducats 1695	400.00
634.	1 Ducat 1695, 98	200.00
635.	½ Ducat 1695	150.00
636.	¼ Ducat 1695	100.00

Bust. Rev. Legend. On his death.

637.	1 Ducat 1698	250.00

GEORGE I OF ENGLAND, 1698-1727

Bust. Rev. Arms.

638.	2 Ducats 1698	450.00
639.	1 Ducat 1712-23 ....*......	200.00
640.	1 Harz-gold Ducat 1712, 14	350.00

Laureate bust. Rev. Four shields crossed.

641.	2 Ducats 1716, 18	400.00
642.	1 Ducat 1715-27 ....*......	200.00
643.	1 Harz-gold Ducat 1715-27	350.00

Laureate bust. Rev. Legend. On his death.

644.	4 Ducats 1727	650.00
645.	2 Ducats 1727	400.00

Laureate head. Rev. Horse.

646.	1 Ducat 1713	250.00
647.	½ Ducat 1724	150.00
648.	¼ Ducat 1724	100.00

Arms. Rev. Horse.

649.	5 Taler 1699 .... Unknown
650.	2½ Taler 1699 .... Unknown
651.	2 Ducats 1698-1707	350.00
652.	1 Ducat 1698-1714	250.00
653.	1 Harz-gold Ducat 1710, 13, 14, 15 ....*......	300.00

Four shields crossed. Rev. Wild man.

654.	1 Ducat 1726	200.00

GEORGE II OF ENGLAND, 1727-1760

Bust. Rev. Four shields crossed.

655.	1 Harz-gold Ducat 1729	350.00

Bust. Rev. Arms.

656.	1 Ducat 1730, 32, 47	250.00
657.	1 Harz-gold Ducat 1730, 47 ....*......	350.00
658.	½ Ducat 1730, 34, 37 ....*......	175.00
659.	¼ Ducat 1737	100.00

Head or Arms. Rev. Two values as indicated.

660.	4 Goldgulden or 8 Taler 1749-52	300.00
661.	2 Goldgulden or 4 Taler 1749-55 ....*......	200.00
662.	1 Goldgulden or 2 Taler 1749-55	125.00

663. ½ Goldgulden or 1 Taler 1749-56 .... 100.00
664. ¼ Goldgulden or ½ Taler 1754-57 .... 75.00

Bust. Rev. Value.

665. 1 Ducat 1751 .... 275.00

Bust. Rev. Horse.

666. ¼ Ducat 1737 .... 100.00

Arms. Rev. Horse.

667. 1 Ducat 1730-38 .... 200.00
668. 1 Harz-gold Ducat 1730-56 ....*...... 350.00

Arms. Rev. Value.

669. 5 Taler 1758 .... 200.00

Horse. Rev. Value.

670. 1 Harz-gold Ducat 1751 .... 350.00

Four shields crossed. Rev. Horse.

671. 1 Ducat 1728, 30 .... 200.00
672. 1 Harz-gold Ducat 1727, 29 .... 350.00

Crowned initials. Rev. Horse.

673. ¼ Ducat 1730 .... 75.00

GEORGE III OF ENGLAND, 1760-1820
Bust. Rev. Arms.

674. The coin previously listed does not exist. ——————
675. 5 Taler 1768 .... 300.00

Arms. Rev. Horse.

676. 1 Harz-gold Ducat 1767-1818 .... 350.00

Arms. Rev. Value.

677. 5 Taler 1813, 14, 15 .... 200.00

Horse. Rev. Value.

678. 1 Pistole 1803 ....*...... 250.00
679. 10 Taler 1813, 14 .... 300.00
680. 5 Harz-gold Taler 1814 .... 500.00
681. 2½ Taler 1814, 15 ....*...... 175.00
682. 1 Harz-gold Ducat 1815, 18 ....*...... 250.00

(For coins of the succeeding English Kings, see under Hanover and under Charles II of Brunswick-Wolfen-buttel.)

BRUNSWICK-WOLFENBUTTEL

Dukes of —

(Old Line, 1514-1634 and New Line, 1635-1884.)

HENRY II, 1514-1568

Bust. Rev. Fortuna standing.

683. 1 Goldgulden 1558 .... 300.00

Bust. Rev. Arms.

684. 1 Ducat 1558 .... 300.00

Arms. Rev. Wild man.

685. 1 Ducat 1558 .... 400.00

JULIUS, 1568-1589
Busts of Julius and Hedwig. Rev. Arms.

686. 2 Ducats ND 600.00

FREDERICK ULRIC, 1613-1634

Bust. Rev. Arms.

687. 1 Goldgulden 1625, 26 .... 500.00

Half length figure. Rev. Arms and wild man.

688. 10 Ducats 1615 .... Rar

Standing ruler. Rev. Arms.

689. 1 Goldgulden 1630 .... 300.00

Wild man and tree. Rev. Arms.

690. 1 Goldgulden 1615-31 .... 250.00
691. 1 Goldgulden 1621 .... 500.00

CHRISTIAN OF HALBERSTADT, 1616-1626
Armored arm with sword. Rev. Legend.

692. 10 Ducats 1622 .... Rar
693. 2 Ducats 1622 .... Rar
694. 1 Ducat 1622 .... 1250.00

AUGUST, 1635-1666

Armored bust. Rev. Arms.

95. 1 Ducat 1638, 39 .... 250.00

Facing bust with cap. Rev. Arms.

96. 1 Ducat 1658 .... 250.00

RUDOLPH AUGUST, 1666-1704

Armored bust. Rev. Galley.

97. 1 Ducat 1680 .... 800.00

Bust. Rev. Legend. On his death.

98. 1 Ducat 1704 .... 250.00
99. ¾ Ducat 1704 .... 150.00

Arms. Rev. Horse.

700. 2 Ducats 1669 .... 375.00
701. 1 Ducat 1669, 79 .... 200.00

RUDOLPH AUGUST AND ANTHONY ULRIC, 1685-1704

Two busts. Rev. Arms.

702. 1 Ducat 1691, 99 .... 300.00

Bust on each side.

703. 1 Ducat 1698, 99, 1701, ND 300.00

ANTHONY ULRIC, 1704-1714
Bust. Rev. Arms.

704. 1 Ducat 1705 .... 250.00

Bust. Rev. Horse.

705. 2 Ducats 1707, 11 .... 400.00
706. 2 Harz-gold Ducats 1712 .... 750.00
707. 1 Ducat 1707, 11, 12 ....*...... 200.00
708. 1 Harz-gold Ducat 1710 .... 300.00
709. ½ Ducat 1708, 09 ....*...... 400.00

Initials. Rev. Horse.

710. 1 Ducat 1707, 09, 11 .... 200.00

---

711. ½ Ducat 1708, 09 ....*...... 100.00
712. 2 Harz-gold Ducats 1712 .... 600.00
713. 1 Harz-gold Ducat 1710, 12 .... 400.00

Prince Anthony Ulric in cradle. Rev. Legend.

714. 2 Ducats 1714 .... 300.00

ELIZABETH JULIANA, 1656-1704
Bust. Rev. Legend. On her death.

715. 1 Ducat 1704 .... 250.00

Bust. Rev. Salzdahlum Castle. On her death.

716. 2 Ducats 1704 .... 450.00

FERDINAND ALBERT I, DIED 1687

Bust. Rev. Arms.

717. 2 Ducats 1678 ....*...... 500.00
718. 1 Ducat 1680 .... 350.00

LOUIS RUDOLPH, 1714-1735

Bust. Rev. Angel over city view of Blankenburg. On the Reformation.

719. 1 Ducat 1717 .... 250.00

Bust. Rev. Horse and city view of Blankenburg.

720. 1 Ducat 1720 .... 250.00

Bust. Rev. Arms.

721. 1 Ducat 1714 .... 250.00

Bust. Rev. Horse.

722. 12 Ducats 1715 .... Rare
723. 1 Ducat 1725-34 .... 200.00
724. 1 Harz-gold Ducat 1732, 33, 34 .... 400.00

Bust of Albert Ernest of Oettingen. Rev. Legend.

725. 1 Friendship Ducat ND 300.00

Head. Rev. Helmet and horse.

726. 1 Ducat 1726 .... 250.00

Head. Rev. Helmet.

727. 1 Ducat 1718-33 ....*...... 200.00
728. 1 Harz-gold Ducat 1731, 32 .... 400.00

Head. Rev. Star.

729. 1 Ducat 1726, 30, 33 .... 250.00

Bust or head. Rev. Wild man with or without arms.

730.	2 Ducats 1731, 32, 33, ND	350.00
731.	1 Ducat 1733 ....*......	200.00

Head. Rev. Legend. On his death.

732.	1 Ducat 1735	200.00

Arms. Rev. Horse.

733.	1 Ducat 1715	200.00

Arms. Rev. Wild man.

734.	1 Ducat 1717-27	200.00

Initials. Rev. Horse.

735.	1 Ducat 1715, 18 ....*......	200.00
736.	1 Ducat 1726	300.00
737.	½ Ducat 1715	100.00
738.	¼ Ducat 1717-34, ND	75.00

Initials. Rev. Wild man.

739.	1 Ducat 1720	200.00
740.	½ Ducat 1718-28 ....*......	100.00
741.	½ Ducat ND. Square ....*......	200.00
742.	¼ Ducat 1728, ND	75.00

Horse. Rev. Wild man.

743.	1 Ducat 1733	300.00

Initials. Rev. Helmet.

744.	½ Ducat 1726, 27	125.00

AUGUST WILLIAM, 1714-1731

Bust. Rev. Horse.

745.	2 Ducats 1716, 19, 22, 28 ....*......	350.00

746.	1 Harz-gold Ducat 1719, 21, 28, 29, 30	300.00
747.	1 Ducat 1714-30	200.00

Bust. Rev. Legend.

748.	2 Ducats 1730. Birthday issue	375.00
749.	1 Ducat 1731. Death issue	200.00

Bust. Rev. Legend. On the Reformation.

750.	1 Ducat 1717, 28	200.00

Arms. Rev. Wild man.

751.	1 Ducat 1725, 28	200.00

Arms. Rev. Horse.

752.	1 Harz-gold Ducat 1730	500.00

Wild man. Rev. Legend. On the jubilee of the dynasty.

753.	2 Ducats 1730	400.00

Initials. Rev. Horse.

754.	2 Harz-gold Ducats 1727 ....*......	Rare
755.	1 Ducat 1716	200.00
756.	½ Ducat 1715-21 ....*......	100.00
757.	¼ Ducat 1717, 18	75.00

Bust. Rev. Legend. On the Augsburg Confession.

758.	1 Ducat 1730	350.00

FERDINAND ALBERT II, 1735

Bust. Rev. Horse.

759.	1 Ducat 1735 ....*......	500.00
760.	1 Harz-gold Ducat 1735	600.00

Bust. Rev. Legend. On his death.

761. 1 Ducat 1735 .... 350.00

Initials. Rev. Horse.

762. 1 Ducat 1735 .... 250.00

Arms. Rev. Horse.

763. 1 Ducat 1735 .... 750.00

ELIZABETH CHRISTINA, 1733-1797

Initials. Rev. Legend. On her wedding.

764. 1 Ducat 1733 .... 200.00

CHARLES I, 1735-1780

Armored bust. Rev. Arms.

765. 10 Taler 1742 .... 375.00
766. 5 Taler 1742 ....*..... 250.00

Armored bust. Rev. Horse.

767. 1 Harz-gold Ducat 1736 .... 300.00
768. 1 Ducat 1736, 39 ....*..... 250.00
769. 10 Taler 1742-64 .... 300.00
770. 5 Taler 1742-75 .... 200.00
771. 2½ Taler 1742-77 .... 150.00

Head. Rev. Horse.

772. 1 Ducat 1737-65 ....*..... 200.00
773. 1 Harz-gold Ducat 1737, 39, 49 ..... 300.00

774. 2 Pistoles 1767, 77. (10 Taler) 400.00
775. 1 Pistole 1767, 76-78. (5 Taler) 200.00
776. ½ Pistole 1767, 77. (2½ Taler) 125.00

Initials. Rev. Legend. On his wedding.

777. 1 Ducat 1733 .... 125.00

CHARLES WILLIAM FERDINAND, 1780-1806

Arms. Rev. Value.

778. 1 Ducat 1780 .... 200.00
779. 1 Harz-gold Ducat 1781-1801 ....*..... 250.00
780. 10 Taler 1781-1806 .... 300.00
781. 5 Taler 1780-1806 ....*..... 200.00
782. 2½ Taler 1781-1806 ....*..... 150.00

FREDERICK WILLIAM, 1806-1815

Arms. Rev. Value.

783. 10 Taler 1813, 14 .... 300.00
784. 5 Taler 1814, 15 ....*..... 200.00
785. 2½ Taler 1815 .... 275.00
786. 1 Harz-gold Ducat 1814, 15 .... 350.00

CHARLES II, 1815-1830

Arms. Rev. Value. Struck during the regency of George IV of England. The coinage before 1822 shows his name as George only. The coinage of 1822 shows his name as George IV. Other coins of George IV will be found under Hanover.

787. 10 Taler 1817-22 .... 300.00
788. 5 Taler 1816-23 ....*..... 175.00
789. 2½ Taler 1816-22 .... 125.00

Arms. Rev. Value. Without the name of George and showing the title of Charles II as Duke.

790. 10 Taler 1824-30 ....*..... 300.00
791. 5 Taler 1824-30 .... 200.00
792. 2½ Taler 1825-28 .... 125.00
793. 1 Harz-gold Ducat 1825 ....*..... 300.00

Uniformed bust. Rev. Arms.

794. 10   Taler 1827-29 ....* 400.00
795. 2½ Taler 1829 .... 225.00

WILLIAM, 1831-1884

Horse. Rev. Value.

796. 10 Taler 1831 .... 250.00

Arms supported by wild men. Rev. Value.

797. 10   Taler 1831-34 ....* 350.00
798. 5   Taler 1832, 34 .... 450.00
799. 2½ Taler 1832 .... 275.00

Head. Rev. Arms.

800. 10   Taler 1850-57 ....* 300.00
801. 2½ Taler 1851 .... 175.00

Head. Rev. Value.

802. 1 Krone 1857, 58, 59 .... 250.00

BUCHEIM

Counts —

JOHN CHRISTIAN, 1619-1657
Bust. Rev. Arms.

803. 1 Ducat 1650 .... 400.00

COLOGNE

A. City coinage

Arms (Uniface).

804.   Gold Bracteate ND (1300) .... Unknown

Christ on throne. Rev. Orb.

805. 1 Goldgulden ND (1400-1500) 200.00

Christ seated. Rev. Arms.

806. 1 Goldgulden 1515-34 .... 175.00

The three Magi. Rev. St. Ursula in ship.

807. 6 Ducats ND (1600) 1200.00
808. 4 Ducats 1612 .... 1200.00

St. Ursula standing. Rev. Shield on cross.

809. 1 Goldgulden ND (1600) 200.00

Value on tablet. Rev. Arms.

810. 1 Ducat 1634 .... 200.00

B. Coinage with the heads or names of the Holy Roman Emperors.

Eagle. Rev. Arms. Maximilian II.

811. 1 Goldgulden 1567-73 .... 250.00

Eagle. Rev. Arms. Rudolph II.

812. 1 Goldgulden 1577-1611 .... 200.00

Eagle. Rev. Arms. Ferdinand II.

813. 1 Goldgulden 1619-34 .... 200.00

Ferdinand II standing. Rev. Arms.

814. 1 Ducat 1634-36 .... 200.00

Ferdinand III standing. Rev. Arms.

815. 1 Ducat 1643-57 .... 225.00

Bust of Leopold I. Rev. Arms.

816. 1 Ducat 1661-72 .... 250.00

Leopold I standing. Rev. Arms.

817. 1 Ducat 1689, 93 .... 200.00

Eagle. Rev. Wine glass. Leopold I.

818. 1 Ducat 1672 .... 250.00

Bust of Joseph I. Rev. Arms.

819. 1 Ducat 1705, 08 .... 300.00

Eagle. Rev. Arms. Joseph I.

820. 1 Ducat 1705 .... 250.00

Bust of Charles VI. Rev. Eagle.

821. 1 Ducat 1724 .... 275.00

Bust of Charles VI. Rev. Arms.

822. 1 Ducat 1717-39 .... 250.00

Bust of Charles VI. Rev. Arms with supporters.

823.	12 Ducats 1727	Rare
824.	1 Ducat 1727, 31	300.00

Arms. Rev. Eagle. Charles VI.

825.	1 Ducat 1716	250.00

Arms. Rev. Wine bottle. Charles VI.

826.	1 Ducat 1716	250.00

Bust of Charles VII. Rev. Two shields.

827.	1 Ducat 1742	500.00

Bust of Francis I. Rev. Arms.

828.	1 Ducat 1750, 53, ND	250.00

Bust of Joseph II. Rev. Arms.

829.	1 Ducat 1767	300.00

C. Archbishops of —

WALRAM, 1346-1349
Ruler on throne. Rev. Cross.

830.	1 Ecu d'or ND	750.00

St. John. Rev. Lily.

831.	1 Florin ND	250.00

WILLIAM, 1349-1362
St. John. Rev. Lily.

832.	1 Florin ND	175.00
833.	½ Florin ND	150.00
834.	¼ Florin ND	125.00

ADOLPH II, 1363-1364
St. John. Rev. Lily.

835.	1 Florin ND	400.00

ENGELBERT III, 1364-1368
St. John. Rev. Lily.

836.	1 Florin ND	250.00

KUNO, 1368-1371
St. John on throne. Rev. Arms.

837.	1 Goldgulden ND	175.00

St. Peter. Rev. Arms.

838.	1 Goldgulden ND	175.00

St. Peter under canopy. Rev. Arms.

839.	1 Goldgulden ND	175.00

FREDERICK III, 1371-1414
St. Peter under canopy. Rev. Arms.

840.	1 Goldgulden ND	100.00

St. Peter on throne. Rev. Arms.

841.	1 Goldgulden ND	100.00

St. John. Rev. Arms and two shields.

842.	1 Goldgulden ND	100.00

St. John. Rev. Arms.

843.	1 Goldgulden ND	100.00

THEODORE II, 1414-1463
Ruler standing. Rev. Arms.

844.	1 Goldgulden 1458, ND	100.00

Christ. Rev. Four shields.

845.	1 Goldgulden ND	100.00

St. Peter. Rev. Arms.

846.	1 Goldgulden ND	100.00

St. John. Rev. Arms.

847.	1 Goldgulden ND	100.00

Arms on cross. Rev. Three shields.

848.	1 Goldgulden ND	100.00
849.	1 Goldgulden 1436-56	100.00

RUPERT, 1463-1480
Christ on throne. Rev. Cross and four shields.

850.	1 Goldgulden ND	100.00

Christ standing. Rev. Four shields.

851.	1 Goldgulden ND	100.00

Ruler standing. Rev. Arms.

852.	1 Goldgulden ND	100.00

HERMAN IV, 1480-1508
St. Peter. Rev. Arms.

853.	1 Goldgulden ND	150.00

Christ on throne. Rev. Arms.

854.	1 Goldgulden 1491-1508	150.00

PHILIP II, 1508-1515
Christ on throne. Rev. Arms.

855.	1 Goldgulden 1508-15, ND	200.00

HERMAN V, 1515-1546

Christ on throne. Rev. Arms.

856.	1 Goldgulden 1515-31 ....*......	200.00
857.	½ Goldgulden 1516	250.00

ADOLPH III, 1547-1556
Christ on throne. Rev. Arms.

858.	1 Goldgulden 1547-49	250.00

ANTHONY, 1556-1558
Christ on throne. Rev. Arms.

859.	1 Goldgulden 1556, 57	250.00

JOHN GEBHARD, 1558-1562
Christ on throne. Rev. Arms.

860.	1 Goldgulden 1558	350.00

FREDERICK IV, 1562-1567
Christ on throne. Rev. Arms.

861.	1 Goldgulden 1563, 64, 65	250.00

SALENTIN, 1567-1577
Bust with long beard. Rev. Arms.

862.	2 Ducats 1577	750.00
863.	1 Ducat 1573, 75	300.00
864.	1 Goldgulden 1575	400.00

St. Peter standing. Rev. Arms.

865.	1 Goldgulden 1570	400.00

GEBHARD, 1577-1583
Bust. Rev. Arms.

866.	1 Goldgulden 1583	475.00

St. Peter. Rev. Arms.

867. 1 Goldgulden 1581, 82, 83 .... 300.00

ERNEST, 1583-1612
St. Peter. Rev. Arms.

868. 1 Goldgulden ND 250.00

FERDINAND, 1612-1650
Arms of Bavaria. Rev. Shield.

869. 1 Goldgulden 1634, 37 .... 250.00

Madonna. Rev. Arms.

870. 1 Ducat ND 300.00

Arms. Rev. Value in square.

871. 1 Ducat 1640 .... 250.00

MAX HENRY, 1650-1688
Bust. Rev. Arms.

872. 1 Ducat 1644, 65, ND 300.00

JOSEPH CLEMENT, 1688-1723

Joseph and Mary with the three Magi. Rev. Arms. Struck
from Westphalian gold.

873. 3 Ducats 1696 .... 1000.00

Bust. Rev. Arms.

874. 1 Ducat 1694, 1722 .... 250.00

Bust with hat. Rev. Arms.

875. 1 Ducat 1715 .... 300.00

Bust. Rev. Madonna seated.

876. 1 Ducat 1694, 98 .... 300.00

Bust. Rev. The three Magi.

877. 1 Ducat 1723 .... 350.00

CLEMENT AUGUST, 1723-1761
Bust. Rev. Adoration of the three Magi.

878. 1 Ducat 1726, 42, 44 .... 250.00

Bust. Rev. Seven shields on mantle.

879. 1 Carolin 1735 .... 500.00
880. ½ Carolin 1735, 36 .... 300.00

Bust. Rev. Madonna seated.

881. 1 Ducat 1750 .... 350.00

Facing or profile bust. Rev. Sun and legend.

882. 1 Ducat 1750 .... 300.00

CONSTANCE

A. City of —

Eagle and CONST. Rev. Orb. Name of Maximilian.

883. 1 Goldgulden ND. (1486-1508) 500.00

Eagle and CONSTANC. Rev. Similar to above.

884. 1 Goldgulden ND. (1486-1508) 500.00

Arms. Rev. Double eagle. Name of Ferdinand II or III.

885. 2 Ducats ND. (1618-57). Square 1500.00
886. 1 Ducat 1629, 52, ND. Round or square 500.00

B. Bishops of —

JOHN FRANCIS II SCHENK, 1704-1740

Two shields. Rev. Arms.

887. 2 Ducats 1737 .... 750.00
888. 1 Ducat 1737 ....*...... 450.00

FRANCIS CONRAD, 1750-1775
Bust. Rev. Arms.

889. 1 Ducat 1761 .... 300.00

CORVEY

Abbots of —

CHARLES BLITTERSDORF, 1722-1737
St. Vitus. Rev. Arms.

890. 1 Ducat 1724, ND 400.00

CASPAR BOSELAGER, 1737-1758

St. Vitus. Rev. Arms.

891. 1 Ducat 1743, 53 .... 300.00

PHILIP SPIEGEL, 1758-1776
St. Vitus. Rev. Arms.

892. 1 Ducat 1758, 59 .... 300.00

COSEL

(Several so-called "Love Ducats" were struck under Saxon auspices, but they are more jetons than coins.)

DARMSTADT

Legend on each side. On the Reformation.

893. 1 Ducat 1817 .... 175.00

DIEPHOLT

St. Stephen. Rev. Eagle.

894. 1 Goldgulden ND. (1600) 275.00

DIETRICHSTEIN

Princes —

FERDINAND, 1655-1698
Bust with wig. Rev. Arms.

895. 10 Ducats 1695 .... Rare
896. 1 Ducat 1695, 96 .... 375.00

CHARLES LOUIS, DIED 1732
Bust. Rev. Arms.

897. 1 Ducat 1726 .... 375.00

DORTMUND

(Coinage with the names, heads or standing figures of the Holy Roman Emperors.)

St. John standing. Rev. Orb. Name of Sigismund.

898. 1 Goldgulden ND (1410-39) 375.00

Frederick III standing. Rev. Orb.

899. 1 Goldgulden ND (1470-80) 250.00

Maximilian standing. Rev. Orb.

900. 1 Goldgulden ND (1500) 300.00

Ferdinand II standing. Rev. Orb.

901. 1 Ducat 1632 .... 400.00

Ferdinand III standing. Rev. Arms.

902. 1 Ducat 1636, 37, 39 .... 400.00

Ferdinand III standing. Rev. Eagle over legend.

903. 1 Ducat 1635-55 .... 400.00

Leopold I standing. Rev. Eagle.

904. 1 Ducat 1660, 63 .... 400.00

Bust of Charles VI. Rev. Eagle.

905. 1 Ducat 1717 .... 500.00

Bust of Charles VII. Rev. Eagle.

906. 2 Ducats 1742. Square .... *...... 1000.00
907. 1 Ducat 1742. Square 400.00

EAST FRISIA

Counts, and later, Princes of —

UDO, 1421-1433

St. Luderus. Rev. Lion shield.

908. 1 Goldgulden ND (1433) 750.00

ULRIC, 1441-1466
St. Peter. Rev. Orb.

909. 1 Goldgulden ND 175.00

St. John. Rev. Orb.

910. 1 Goldgulden ND 175.00

ENNO I, 1446-1491
St. John. Rev. Orb.

911. 1 Goldgulden ND 175.00

EDZARD 1, 1491-1528
St. John. Rev. Orb.

912. 1 Goldgulden ND 150.00

ENNO II, 1528-1540
Christ with globe. Rev. Harpyrie shield.

913. 1 Goldgulden ND 175.00

St. John. Rev. Orb.

914. 1 Goldgulden ND 150.00

Bust with hat. Rev. Arms.

915. 1 Goldgulden 1529 .... 350.00

EDZARD II AND JOHN, 1566-1591
Bust of Emperor Maximilian II. Rev. Arms.

916. 1 Goldgulden 1568, 69 .... 250.00

Bust of Emperor Rudolph II. Rev. Arms.

917. 1 Goldgulden 1571-90 .... 200.00

Charlemagne standing. Rev. Arms.

918. 1 Goldgulden 1574 .... 275.00

Charlemagne on throne. Rev. Cross.

919. 1 Goldgulden ND 275.00

EDZARD II, 1591-1599
Bust of Emperor Rudolph II. Rev. Arms.

920. 1 Goldgulden 1594 .... 300.00

St. Luderus. Rev. Arms.

921. 1 Goldgulden ND 250.00

ENNO III, 1599-1625
Bust. Rev. Cross.

922. 1 Goldgulden 1615 .... 300.00

Christ standing. Rev. Arms.

923. 1 Goldgulden ND 200.00

Arms. Rev. Cross.

924. ½ Ducat ND 175.00

CHRISTIAN EBERHARD, 1690-1708
Bust. Rev. Arms.

925. 1 Ducat 1702 .... 300.00

GEORGE ALBERT, 1708-1734

Bust. Rev. Arms.

926. 1 Ducat 1715, 30, 31 .... 300.00

CHARLES EDZARD, 1734-1744
Armored bust. Rev. Arms.

927. 1 Ducat 1737 .... 300.00

EICHSTAETT

Bishops of —

GABRIEL, 1496-1535
St. Walburga standing. Rev. Arms.

928. 1 Goldgulden 1511, 12 .... 1200.00

MARTIN, 1560-1590

St. Willibald standing. Rev. Arms.

929. 4 Goldgulden 1560 .... Rare
930. 1 Goldgulden 1560 ....*...... 500.00

St. Willibald standing. Rev. Eagle and name of Maximilian II.

931. 2 Ducats 1570 .... 750.00

JOHN CONRAD, 1595-1612
Arms. Rev. Eagle and name of Rudolph II.

932. 14 Ducats 1596 .... Rare
933. 8 Ducats 1596 .... Rare
934. 6 Ducats 1596 .... 1500.00

JOHN CHRISTOPHER, 1612-1636
St. Willibald standing. Rev. 2 shields.

935. 1 Ducat 1633, 34 .... 300.00

St. Walburga standing. Rev. 2 shields.

936. 1 Ducat 1633 .... 250.00

Saint standing. Rev. eagle and name of Ferdinand II.

937. 1 Ducat 1635 .... 300.00

JOHN EUCHARIUS SCHENK, 1685-1697
Bust. Rev. Arms supported by lions.

938. 6 Ducats 1694 .... 700.00

Bust. Rev. Eagle flying over arms.

939. 10 Ducats ND .... Rare

FRANCIS LOUIS SCHENK, 1725-1736
Bust. Rev. Arms. Oval shaped.

940. 1 Ducat 1736 .... 450.00

JOHN ANTHONY II, 1736-1757
Bust. Rev. Arms.

941. 1 Ducat 1755 .... 325.00

St. Willibald standing. Rev. Arms.

942. 1 Ducat 1738 .... 300.00

St. Walburga standing. Rev. Arms.

943. 1 Ducat 1738 .... 225.00

EINBECK

City gate. Rev. Double eagle. Name of Ferdinand II.

944. 1 Goldgulden 1629 .... 750.00

ELBING

A. Swedish Kings of —

Bust of Gustav Adolphe. Rev. Arms.

945. 1 Ducat 1630 .... 750.00

Bust of Charles X. Rev. Arms.

946. 1 Ducat 1657 .... 1000.00

B. Polish Kings of —

Bust of John Casimir. Rev. Arms.

947. 1 Ducat 1661 .... 375.00

Bust of Michael Korybut. Rev. Arms.

948. 2 Ducats 1672 .... 750.00
949. 1 Ducat 1671 .... 375.00

EMDEN

St. Peter. Rev. Orb.

950. 1 Goldgulden ND. (1470) 250.00

Knight standing. Rev. Value in tablet or cartouche.

951. 2 Ducats 1694 .... 750.00
952. 1 Ducat 1635-98, ND ....*...... 250.00

View of the city. Rev. Hand and sceptre.

953. 3¼ Ducats ND 750.00
954. 2½ Ducats 1737, 43, 46 .... 350.00
955. 2¼ Ducats 1750 .... 350.00
956. 2 Ducats ND 300.00

Arms. Rev. Hands with bundle of arrows.

957. 4 Ducats ND. (1700) 750.00

ERFURT

A. City of —

Wheel and date. Rev. Arms.

958. 1 Goldgulden 1620, 22, 70, ND 350.00

B. Swedish Kings of —

Radiant Jehovah in Hebrew characters. Rev. Long legend.

959. 10 Victory Ducats 1631. Struck by Gustav Adolphe 4000.00

King in bed. Rev. King in triumphal chariot. On the death of Gustav Adolphe.

960. 4 Ducats 1634 .... 1200.00

Bust of Gustav Adolphe. Rev. Crown over legend.

961. 1 Ducat 1632, 33, 34 .... 200.00

Bust of Gustav Adolphe. Rev. Arms.

962. 8 Ducats 1632 ....*...... 4000.00
963. 1 Ducat 1634 .... 300.00

ESSEN

Abbesses of —

ANNA SALOME, 1646-1688
Arms. Rev. Madonna.

964. 1 Ducat 1672 .... 900.00

FRANCES CHRISTINE, 1717-1776

Arms. Rev. Madonna.

965. 1 Ducat 1754 .... 800.00

FRANKFURT

A. City coinage

Angel. Rev. Legend. On the Reformation.

966. 1 Goldgulden 1617 ....*...... 200.00
967. 1 Goldgulden 1617. Square 300.00

Two hands in prayer. Rev. Comet. On the appearance of a comet.

968. 1 Ducat 1618. Square 300.00

Eagle. Rev. Value on tablet, in cartouche or plain.

969.	2 Ducats 1633-37	....	350.00
970.	1 Ducat 1633-1749, ND	....	150.00
971.	½ Ducat 1740	....	100.00

Eagle. Rev. View of the city in a storm.

972.	2 Ducats 1705, 10	....	350.00

Eagle. Rev. Tower in a stormy sea.

973.	2 Ducats 1710, 11	...............*	350.00
974.	1 Ducat 1710, 11	....	250.00

Bible on rock at sea. Rev. Legend. On the Reformation.

975.	1 Ducat 1717	....	250.00

Eagle. Rev. Floriated cross.

976.	1 Ducat 1762	....	250.00

City view. Rev. Legend. Struck under French occupation.

977.	1 Ducat 1796	....	175.00

Legend on each side. On the Reformation.

978.	1 Ducat 1817	....	100.00

Eagle. Rev. Value.

979.	1 Ducat 1853, 56	....	125.00

B. Coinage with the heads or names of the Holy Roman Emperors

St. John. Rev. Lily. Charles IV.

980.	1 Florin ND (1347-78)	....	350.00

St. John. Rev. Eagle on shield. Rupert of Palatinate.

981.	1 Goldgulden ND. (1400-10)	....	350.00

St. John. Rev. Orb. Sigismund.

982.	1 Goldgulden ND. (1410-33)	....	175.00

Charlemagne standing. Rev. Arms. Sigismund.

983.	1 Goldgulden ND. (1410-33)	....	400.00

St. John. Rev. Orb. Albert II.

984.	1 Goldgulden ND. (1438-39)	....	200.00

St. John. Rev. Orb. Frederick III.

985.	1 Goldgulden ND	....	125.00
986.	1 Goldgulden 1491, 92, 93	....	175.00

St. John. Rev. Orb. Maximilian I.

987.	1 Goldgulden 1494-1515, ND	....	125.00

St. John. Rev. Lily. Charles V.

988.	1 Goldgulden 1521, 22	....	250.00

St. John. Rev. Orb. Charles V.

989.	1 Goldgulden 1527	....	250.00

St. John. Rev. Eagle. Rudolph II.

990.	1 Goldgulden 1611, 12	....	250.00

Bust of Matthias II. Rev. Crown.

991.	3 Ducats 1612	....	500.00
992.	2 Ducats or Goldgulden 1612	...............*	350.00
993.	1 Goldgulden 1612	....	175.00

Matthias II on horse. Rev. Eagle.

994.	10 Ducats ND. (1612)	....	1500.00
995.	5 Ducats ND. (1612)	....	900.00

Matthias II on horse. Rev. Circle of shields.

996.	5 Ducats ND. (1612)	....	900.00
997.	3 Ducats ND. (1612)	....	400.00

St. John. Rev. Eagle. Matthias II.

998.	1 Goldgulden 1617, 18, 19	....	175.00

Ferdinand II on throne. Rev. Crown.

999.	3 Ducats 1619	....	350.00
1000.	1 Goldgulden 1619	........................*	175.00

Eagle. Rev. Legend. On the coronation of Charles VII.

1019.	1 Ducat 1742	....	175.00

Bust of Ferdinand II. Rev. Wreath over crown.

1001.	2 Ducats ND. Square	....	400.00

Legend. Rev. Arm with Crown. Ferdinand II.

1002.	2 Ducats 1619	....	375.00
1003.	1 Ducat 1619	....	175.00

Bust of Francis I. Rev. Insignia on table.

1020.	1 Ducat 1745	....	150.00

Eagle. Rev. Legend. On the election of Francis I.

1021.	1 Ducat 1745	....	150.00

Altar. Rev. Legend. On the coronation of Francis I.

1022.	1½ Ducats 1745	....	175.00
1023.	¾ Ducat 1745	....	150.00

Crowned F. Rev. Legend. Ferdinand II.

1004.	½ Ducat 1619	....	75.00

St. John. Rev. Eagle. Ferdinand II.

1005.	1 Goldgulden 1620, 21, 22	....	250.00

St. John. Rev. Orb. Ferdinand II.

1006.	1 Goldgulden 1620, 21, 24, 25	....	250.00

Hand with sceptre and arm with sword. Rev. Legend. On the coronation of Leopold I.

1007.	4 Ducats 1658	....	600.00
1008.	2 Ducats 1658	....	375.00
1009.	1 Ducat 1658	....	175.00
1010.	½ Ducat 1658	....	125.00

Bust of Charles VI. Rev. Insignia.

1011.	2 Ducats 1711	....	250.00

Globe. Rev. Legend. Charles VI.

1012.	1½ Ducats 1711	....	200.00
1013.	¾ Ducat 1711	....	150.00

Bust of Joseph II. Rev. Peace standing near fallen soldier.

1024.	2 Ducats 1764	............................*	175.00
1025.	1 Ducat 1764	....	100.00

Globe. Rev. Legend. On the coronation of Joseph II.

1026.	1½ Ducats 1764	....	175.00
1027.	¾ Ducat 1764	....	150.00

Head of Leopold II. Rev. Altar.

1028.	2 Ducats 1790	....	200.00
1029.	1 Ducat 1790	....	120.00

Crossed insignia. Rev. Legend. On the coronation of Leopold II.

1030.	1½ Ducats 1790	....	200.00
1031.	¾ Ducat 1790	....	125.00

Head of Francis II. Rev. Altar.

1032.	2 Ducats 1792	....	275.00
1033.	1 Ducat 1792	....	150.00

Bust. Rev. Two figures.

1034.	1 Ducat ND	....	150.00

Crossed insignia. Rev. Legend. On the coronation of Francis II.

1035.	1½ Ducats 1792	....	275.00
1036.	¾ Ducat 1792	....	150.00

Legend. Rev. City view. On the election of Charles VI.

1014.	2 Ducats 1711	....	350.00

Bust of Charles VII. Rev. Female at altar.

1015.	4 Ducats 1742	....	500.00
1016.	2 Ducats 1742	....	350.00
1017.	1 Ducat 1742	....	200.00

Bust of Charles VII. Rev. Bust of Maria Amalia.

1018.	1 Ducat ND. (1742)	....	200.00

FREIBURG

Madonna. Rev. Arms.

1037.	1 Goldgulden 1622	....	2000.00

Two shields and eagle. Rev. City view.

1038.   1 Ducat 1717 ....   500.00

FREISING

Bishops of —

JOHN FRANCIS, 1695-1727

St. Corbianus. Rev. Arms. On the Milennium.

1039.   2 Ducats 1724 ....   600.00

CLEMENT WENCESLAS, 1763-1768

Bust. Rev. Arms.

1040.   1 Ducat 1765, 66 ....   350.00

FUERSTENBERG

Princes —

JOSEPH, 1704-1762

Bust with wig. Rev. Arms with owl below.

1041.   1 Ducat 1750, 51 ....   450.00

CHARLES EGON I, DIED 1788

Bust. Rev. Arms.

1042.   1 Ducat 1772 ....   400.00

FUGGER

Counts —

ANTHONY, 1493-1560

Arms. Rev. Eagle.

1043.   1 Goldgulden ND 450.00

MAXIMILIAN, 1619-1637

Arms. Rev. Eagle.

1044.   13 Ducats 1621 ....   Rare
1045.   10 Ducats 1621 ....   Rare
1046.   1 Goldgulden ND 500.00

Three shields. Rev. Eagle.

1047.   1 Ducat 1622 ....   500.00

FULDA

Bishops of —

BALTHASAR, 1570-1606

Eagle. Rev. Arms and name of Rudolph II.

1048.   20 Ducats 1606 ....   Rare

BERNARD GUSTAVE, 1671-1678

St. Boniface. Rev. Initials.

1049.   2 Ducats 1672 ....   600.00
1050.   1 Ducat 1672 ....   400.00
1051.   ½ Ducat 1672 ....*......   250.00
1052.   ¼ Ducat 1672 ....   150.00

PLACIDUS, 1678-1700

Bust with hat. Rev. Arms.

1053.   10 Ducats 1680 ....   1250.00
1054.   8 Ducats 1688 ....   1000.00
1055.   7 Ducats 1688 ....   900.00
1056.   2 Ducats 1692 ....   600.00
1057.   1 Ducat 1692 ....   300.00

CONSTANTINE, 1714-1726

Bust. Rev. Arms.

1058.   1 Ducat 1715-26 ....   350.00

Bust. Rev. Two shields.

1059.   1 Ducat 1716, 21 ....   350.00

ADOLPH, 1726-1737

Bust. Rev. Arms.

1060.   2 Ducats 1728, 30 ....*......   500.00
1061.   1 Ducat 1726, 28, 30 ....   350.00

Bust. Rev. Crossed initials.

1062.   1 Carolin or 10 Gulden 1734, 35 ....   500.00
1063.   ½ Carolin or 5 Gulden 1734 ....   300.00

AMANDUS, 1737-1756

Bust. Rev. Arms.

1064.	8 Ducats 1738	1200.00
1065.	1 Ducat 1738 ....*......	400.00

Bust. Rev. Sun and legend. On the Jubilee.

1066.	1 Ducat 1744	350.00

ADALBERT, 1756-1759

Bust. Rev. Arms.

1067.	2 Ducats 1759	600.00

HENRY VIII, 1759-1788

Arms. Rev. Legend.

1068.	1 Ducat 1779	750.00

Bust. Rev. Legend.

1069.	1 Ducat 1779	350.00

Bust. Rev. Arms.

1070.	1 Ducat 1779	350.00

FURTH

Swedish Kings of —

Gustave Adolphe standing. Rev. Arms.

1071.	1 Ducat 1632	3000.00

GLATZ

Counts —

JOHN, 1537-1549

Two shields. Rev. Bohemian lion.

1072.	1 Ducat 1540, 41, 44, 46	375.00

ERNEST, 1549-1554
Three shields. Rev. Bohemian lion.

1073.	1 Ducat 1549, 50, 54	375.00

GOSLAR

Arms under helmet. Rev. Double eagle. Name of Ferdinand II.

1074.	1 Goldgulden 1628, ND	750.00

Bust of Ferdinand II. Rev. Arms.

1075.	1 Ducat ND. (1620)	375.00

Ferdinand II standing. Rev. Arms.

1076.	1 Ducat ND. (1620)	1500.00

GOTTINGEN

Double Eagle. Rev. Arms.

1077.	4 Ducats 1660	Rare

HAGENAU

Rose in shield. Rev. Double eagle. Name of Rudolph II.

1078.	1 Goldgulden 1604, 08, 10, 11	2000.00

St. John. Rev. Eagle.

1079.	1 Goldgulden ND	3000.00

HALBERSTADT

CATHEDERAL CHAPTER OF THE BISHOPRIC
St. Stephan standing. Rev. Arms.

1080.	1 Goldgulden 1628, 29, ND	300.00

St. Stephan standing. Rev. Shield.

1081.	2 Goldgulden 1631	500.00

HALL-IN-SUEBIA

Bust of Joseph I. Rev. Three shields.

1082.	1 Ducat 1705	300.00

Bust of Charles VI. Rev. Three shields.

1083.	1 Ducat 1712	300.00

Three shields. Rev. Legend. On the Peace of Baden.

1084.	1 Ducat 1714	150.00
1085.	¼ Ducat 1714	75.00

Bust of Charles VII. Rev. Three shields.

1086.	1 Ducat 1742	350.00

Bust of Francis I. Rev. Three shields.

1087. 1 Ducat 1746 .... 350.00

Bust of Joseph II. Rev. Three shields.

1088. 1 Ducat 1777, ND 300.00

HAMBURG

A. City coinage

City gate. Rev. Cross.

1089. 10   Ducats or 1 Portugaloser ND. (1553-1673) 1500.00
1090. 5   Ducats or ½ Portugaloser ND. (1553-1673) .*..... 1000.00
1091. 2½ Ducats or ¼ Portugaloser ND. (1553-1673) 600.00

Christ blessing couple. Rev. The Wedding at Cana.

1092. 10 Ducats ND 1750.00

Madonna on each side.

1093. 2 Ducats 1649, 60, 66 .... 400.00
1094. 1 Ducat 1497-1667, ND 150.00

Madonna. Rev. Arms.

1095. 2 Ducats 1669-94 ....* 300.00
1096. 1 Ducat 1668-75 .... 125.00
1097. ½ Ducat 1675 .... 150.00

Madonna. Rev. Annunciation.

1098. ¼ Ducat ND (1700) 75.00

Elbe River god. Rev. Father Time.

1099. 1 Ducat ND. (1700) 200.00

Hammonia standing. Rev. Tablet.

1100. 1 Ducat 1807 .... 200.00

City gate. Rev. Tablet.

1101. 2 Ducats 1808, 09, 10 ....*...... 250.00
1102. 1 Ducat 1808-11 .... 175.00

Knight standing. Rev. Tablet.

1103. 1 Ducat 1811-50. Old style 85.00
1104. 1 Ducat 1851-72. New style ....*...... 75.00

B. Coinage with the heads or names of the Holy Roman Emperors

St. Peter. Rev. Orb. Sigismund I.

1105. 1 Goldgulden ND. (1435-37) 200.00

St. Peter. Rev. Orb. Frederick III.

1106. 1 Goldgulden ND. (1440-93) 200.00

St. Peter. Rev. Orb. Maximilian I.

1107. 1 Goldgulden ND. (1495-1519) 225.00

St. Peter. Rev. Orb. Charles V.

1108. 1 Goldgulden 1553 .... 250.00

St. Peter. Rev. Orb. Ferdinand I.

1109. 1 Goldgulden 1553, 61 .... 225.00

St. Peter. Rev. Orb. Maximilian II.

1110. 1 Goldgulden 1566 .... 250.00

St. Peter. Rev. Orb. Rudolph II.

1111. 1 Goldgulden 1581-89, ND 200.00

St. Peter. Rev. Orb. Matthias II.

1112. 1 Goldgulden 1617, 19 .... 200.00

St. Peter. Rev. Orb. Ferdinand II.

1113. 1 Goldgulden 1628 .... 275.00

Eagle. Rev. Arms. Leopold I.

1114. 5 Ducats 1696 .... 800.00
1115. 2 Ducats 1689-1707 .... 175.00
1116. ½ Ducat ND. (1692-1704) 80.00
1117. ¼ Ducat 1680, ND 70.00
1118. 1 Goldgulden 1675 .... 250.00

Madonna. Rev. Eagle. Leopold I.

1119. 2½ Ducats ND. (1692-1705) 375.00

Madonna and shield. Rev. Eagle. Leopold I.

1120. 1 Ducat 1694, 1702 .... 150.00

Bust of Joseph I. Rev. Arms.

1121. 2 Ducats 1705 .... 450.00
1122. 1 Ducat 1705-10 .... 200.00

Eagle. Rev. Arms. Joseph I.

1123.	2 Ducats 1705	375.00
1124.	1 Ducat 1706-11	150.00
1125.	¼ Ducat 1729	75.00

Eagle. Rev. Arms. Charles VI.

1126.	2 Ducats 1713-40	250.00
1127.	1 Ducat 1713-40	150.00

Eagle. Rev. Arms. Charles VII.

1128.	2 Ducats 1742, 44, 45	400.00
1129.	1 Ducat 1742, 43, 44, 45	250.00

Eagle. Rev. Arms. Francis I.

1130.	2 Ducats 1746-64	250.00
1131.	1 Ducat 1746-65	150.00

Eagle. Rev. Arms. Joseph II.

1132.	2 Ducats 1764-72	250.00
1133.	1 Ducat 1765-72	125.00

Eagle. Rev. Tablet. Joseph II.

1134.	2 Ducats 1766-90	250.00
1135.	1 Ducat 1773-90	125.00

Eagle. Rev. Tablet. Leopold II.

1136.	2 Ducats 1790-92	300.00
1137.	1 Ducat 1791, 92	200.00

Eagle. Rev. Arms. Francis II.

1138.	4 Ducats 1797	1500.00

Eagle. Rev. Tablet. Francis II.

1139.	2 Ducats 1793-1806	*	225.00
1140.	1 Ducat 1793-1806		125.00

HAMLIN

City church. Rev. Double eagle. Name of Leopold I.

1141.	1 Goldgulden 1638-68	500.00

Ferdinand III standing. Rev. City church.

1142.	1 Ducat 1656	500.00

HANAU-LICHTENBERG

Counts —

JOHN REINHARD I, 1599-1625

Arms. Rev. Double Eagle.

1143.	1 Goldgulden 1613, 14, 17, 18, ND	350.00

FREDERICK CASIMIR, 1641-1685
Jehova and wreath. Rev. Arms.

1144.	1 Ducat 1647	350.00

Arms. Rev. Legend in cartouche.

1145.	1 Ducat 1647	300.00

PHILIP REINHARD, 1666-1712
Bust. Rev. Arms.

1146.	1 Ducat ND	400.00

JOHN REINHARD II, 1712-1736
Bust. Rev. Arms.

1147.	1 Ducat 1733, ND	350.00

WILLIAM IX, 1736-1785
Bust. Rev. Arms.

1148.	1 Ducat 1737	300.00

Bust of Wilhelmine of Denmark. Rev. Inscription.

1149.	1 Marriage Ducat 1764	500.00

HANOVER

A. City of —

Castle gate. Rev. Legend.

1150.	3½ Goldgulden 1590	1000.00

Castle gate. Rev. Eagle.

1151.	3 Ducats 1666		600.00
1152.	3 Goldgulden 1654		600.00
1153.	1 Ducat 1640, 66, 67	*	250.00
1154.	1 Goldgulden 1616-33		300.00

B. English Kings of —

(For earlier issues of the English Kings, see under Brunswick-Luneburg).

GEORGE IV, 1820-1830

Head. Rev. Value.

1155.	10 Taler 1821-30	*	300.00
1156.	5 Taler 1821-30		250.00
1157.	2½ Taler 1821-30		250.00

Horse. Rev. Value.

1158. 5 Harz-gold Taler 1821 .... 375.00
1159. 1 Harz-gold Ducat 1821, 24, 27 .... 300.00

(For other coins with the name and title of George IV, see under Charles II of Brunswick-Wolfenbuttel.)

WILLIAM IV, 1830-1837

Head. Rev. Arms.

1160. 10 Taler 1832-37 .... 325.00
1161. 5 Taler 1835 ....*..... 450.00
1162. 2½ Taler 1832-37. Rev. Value ....*...... 125.00

Horse. Rev. Value.

1163. 1 Harz-gold Ducat 1831 .... 300.00

C. Hanoverian Kings of —

ERNEST AUGUST, 1837-1851

Small head. Rev. Arms in circle.

1164. 10 Taler 1837, 38. B mm 275.00
1165. 10 Taler 1839, 44. S mm 225.00
1166. 5 Taler 1839. S mm ....*..... 175.00
1167. 2½ Taler 1839, 40, 43. S mm 125.00

Large head. Rev. Plain arms. All with B mm.

1168. 10 Taler 1846-51 .... 325.00
1169. 5 Taler 1845-51 ....*...... 150.00
1170. 5 Harz-gold Taler 1849, 50 ....*...... 300.00
1171. 2½ Taler 1845-50 .... 150.00

GEORGE V, 1851-1866

Head. Rev. Arms.

1172. 10 Taler 1853-56 .... 400.00

1173. 5 Taler 1853, 55, 56 ....*...... 175.00
1174. 5 Harz-gold Taler 1853 ....*...... 400.00
1175. 2½ Taler 1853, 55 .... 175.00

Head. Rev. Value.

1176. 1 Krone 1857-66 .... 325.00
1177. ½ Krone 1857-65 .... 175.00

HATZFELD

Princes —

SEBASTIAN, 1569-1631
Bust. Rev. Two virtues standing.

1178. 1 Ducat 1597 .... 400.00

HERMAN, 1631-1677

Bust. Rev. Madonna.

1179. 1 Ducat ND 500.00

MELCHIOR, 1631-1658
Bust of Ferdinand II. Rev. Madonna seated.

1180. 1 Ducat ND 600.00

HESSE-CASSEL

A. Landgraves, and later, Electors of —

WILLIAM II, 1493-1509
St. Elizabeth. Rev. Five shields crossed.

1181. 1 Goldgulden 1506-08 .... 800.00

WILLIAM I AND PHILIP
St. Elizabeth. Rev. Five shields crossed.

1182. 1 Goldgulden 1510 .... 1000.00

PHILIP, 1509-1567
St. Elizabeth. Rev. Lion shield within four small shields.

1183. 1 Goldgulden 1510, 11 .... 800.00

Arms. Rev. Legend.

1184. ½ Goldgulden 1564 .... 250.00

MAURICE, 1592-1632
Bust. Rev. Flags and symbols.

1185. 1 Goldgulden 1618 .... 350.00

Arms. Rev. Four shields.

1186. 1 Ducat 1624 .... 750.00
1187. 1 Goldgulden 1624, 26 ....*...... 600.00

Lion. Rev. Two flags.

1188. 4 Ducats 1627 .... 1000.00

Legend. Rev. Crossed flags. On his death.

1189. 2 Ducats 1632 .... 600.00
1190. 1 Ducat 1632 .... 275.00

WILLIAM V, 1627-1637
Bust. Rev. Arms.

1191. 1 Goldgulden 1627 .... 600.00

Arms. Rev. Willow tree in storm.

1192. 2 Ducats 1632 .... 375.00
1193. 1 Goldgulden 1628-34 ....* 250.00

Lion. Rev. Willow tree in storm.

1194. 2 Goldgulden 1637 .... 600.00
1195. 1 Goldgulden 1635-37 ....* 250.00

Lion. Rev. Willow tree.

1196. 2 Ducats 1637 .... 375.00
1197. 1 Ducat 1637 .... 200.00

Legend. Rev. Willow tree. On his death.

1198. 2 Ducats 1637 .... 400.00
1199. 1 Ducat 1637 .... 225.00

AMALIA ELIZABETH, REGENT, DIED 1651
Arms. Rev. Rock in storm.

1200. 1 Mining Ducat ND 600.00

Legend. Rev. Rock. On her death.

1201. 2 Ducats 1651 .... 900.00

WILLIAM VI, 1637-1663
Bust. Rev. Arms.

1202. 1 Ducat 1661, 63 .... 600.00

Bust. Rev. Legend. On his death.

1203. 1 Ducat 1663 .... 350.00

Lion. Rev. Willow tree in storm.

1204. 1 Goldgulden 1638 .... 350.00

Arms. Rev. Ship.

1205. 1¼ Ducats 1654 .... 375.00
1206. 1 Goldgulden 1652, 53 .... 325.00

HEDWIG SOPHIA, 1649-1683
Arms. Rev. Legend. On her death.

1207. 2 Ducats 1683 .... 350.00

ELIZABETH HENRIETTA, DIED 1683
Bust. Rev. Crown on pedestal. On her death.

1208. 2 Ducats 1683 .... 350.00

WILLIAM VII, 1663-1670
Arms. Rev. Legend. On his death.

1209. 1 Ducat 1670 .... 350.00

CHARLES, 1670-1730
Bust. Rev. Spring.

1210. ½ Ducat ND 125.00

Bust. Rev. Lion and "Eddergold".

1211. ½ Edder-gold Ducat ND 375.00

Head. Rev. Lion on pedestal with book.

1212. 2 Ducats ND 450.00
1213. 1 Ducat 1720, ND ....* 200.00
1214. 1 Ducat 1720. Without book on Rev. 200.00
1215. ¼ Ducat 1720 .... 110.00

Head. Rev. Arms.

1216. 2 Ducats ND 400.00
1217. 1 Ducat 1724, 25, ND ....* 200.00

Head. Rev. Swan.

1218. ¼ Ducat ND 75.00

Arms. Rev. Swan.

1219. 1 Ducat 1686 .... 375.00

Legend. Rev. Edder River Landscape.

1220. 1 Edder-gold Ducat 1677 .... 1000.00

FREDERICK I
(See next page under B. Swedish Kings of—)

WILLIAM VIII, 1751-1760
Bust. Rev. Arms.

1221. 1 Ducat 1751, 54 .... 250.00

Initials. Rev. Lion.

1222. ¼ Ducat 1752 .... 75.00

FREDERICK II, 1760-1785

Head. Rev. Star of Order.

1223. 2 Louis d'Or 1773, 75-77, 80, 85 .... 350.00
1224. 1 Louis d'Or 1771, 77, 78, 83, 84, 85 ....* 200.00

Armored bust. Rev. Landscape with river-god.

1225. 1 Edder-gold Ducat 1775 .... 750.00

GEORGE WILLIAM, PRINCE
Bust. Rev. Arms.

1226. 1 Ducat 1768 .... 225.00

Bust of Wilhelmine Caroline. Rev. Legend.

1227. 1 Ducat 1764 .... 300.00

WILLIAM IX (I), 1785-1821
Head. Rev. Star of Order.

1228. 1 Louis d'Or 1786, 87, 88, 90 .... 225.00

Head. Rev. Lion and trophies.

1229. 5 Taler 1791-1801 .... 275.00
1230. 5 Taler 1803, 05, 06. With title as elector William I..*.. 250.00

Head. Rev. Arms.

1231. 5 Taler 1814-20 .... 400.00

WILLIAM II, 1821-1831

Bust. Rev. Arms.

1232. 5 Taler 1821-29 .... 300.00

WILLIAM II AND FREDERICK WILLIAM, 1831-1847

Arms. Rev. Value.

1233. 10 Taler 1838, 40, 41 .... 300.00
1234. 5 Taler 1834-47 ....*...... 150.00

Legend on each side.

1235. ½ Edder-gold Ducat 1835 .... 300.00

FREDERICK WILLIAM I, 1847-1866

Head. Rev. Arms.

1236. 5 Taler 1851 .... 200.00

B. Swedish Kings of —
FREDERICK I, 1730-1751

Bust. Rev. Swedish arms.

1237. 1 Ducat 1731, 46, 49, 50 .... 300.00

Head. Rev. Swedish arms.

1238. 1 Ducat 1737, 46 .... 375.00

Crown over linked FR. Rev. Lion-shield.

1239. 1 Ducat 1737 .... 375.00

Crown over linked FR. Rev. Swedish arms.

1240. 1 Ducat 1737 .... 400.00

Head. Rev. Lion standing.

1241. ½ Edder-gold Ducat 1731 ....*...... 300.00
1242. ½ Ducat 1748 ....*...... 200.00
1243. ¼ Ducat ND 150.00

Bust. Rev. Lion standing.

1244. ½ Edder-gold Ducat 1731 .... 400.00

Crown over linked FR. Rev. Lion standing.

1245. ¼ Ducat 1744, 50 .... 100.00

HESSE-DARMSTADT

Landgraves, and later, Grand Dukes of —

LOUIS V, 1596-1626
Arms. Rev. Three helmets.

1246. 1 Goldgulden 1621 .... 600.00
1247. 1 Ducat 1623 .... 600.00

GEORGE II, 1626-1661
Bust. Rev. Arms.

1248. 1 Ducat 1651, 55, 56, 58 .... 300.00
1249. 1 Goldgulden 1656 .... 300.00

Oak tree. Rev. Legend. On his death.

1250.	1 Ducat 1661	500.00
1251	½ Ducat 1661	250.00

Legend. Rev. Laurel tree. On his death.

1252.	½ Ducat 1661	150.00

LOUIS VI, 1661-1678
Bust. Rev. Arms.

1253.	1 Ducat 1675	400.00

ERNEST LOUIS, 1678-1739
Bust. Rev. Arms.

1254.	2 Ducats 1703, 06-10. Arms supported by lions	375.00
1255.	2 Ducats 1704. Arms with 5 helmets	375.00
1256.	1 Ducat 1702-06, 17, 18. Arms supported by lions	200.00
1257.	½ Ducat 1703. Arms supported by lions	100.00
1258.	½ Ducat 1703. Arms between branches	100.00
1259.	¼ Ducat 1705	75.00

Bust. Rev. Female at altar. On the Reformation.

1260.	1 Ducat 1717	250.00

Bust. Rev. Crossed initials.

1261.	4 Ducats 1717	1000.00
1262.	2 Ducats ND	300.00
1263.	1 "Alchemy" Ducat ND	375.00
1264.	1 Carolin 1733, ND ....*.....	300.00
1265.	½ Carolin 1733, ND	150.00
1266.	¼ Carolin 1733, ND	100.00

Arms. Rev. Value.

1267.	¼ Ducat 1703 ....*.....	75.00
1268.	⅛ Ducat 1705	60.00

Lion. Rev. Value.

1269.	½ Ducat 1710	200.00

LOUIS VIII, 1739-1768
Crossed initials. Rev. Lion.

1270.	1 Ducat 1740, 41	200.00

Monogram. Rev. Lion with arms.

1271.	1 Ducat 1742, 43, 53, ND	250.00

Initials. Rev. Lion recumbent.

1272.	1 Ducat ND	250.00

Bust. Rev. Arms with palm-branches.

1273.	1 Ducat 1746, 48, 49, 51, 53, 55, ND	250.00

Bust. Rev. Lion with arms.

1274.	1 Ducat 1746	250.00

Crossed initials. Rev. Lion-shield within 7 shields.

1275.	2 Ducats 1760	400.00
1276.	1 Ducat 1760, 61 ....*......	250.00

Monogram. Rev. Horse and city view.

1277.	1 Ducat ND	300.00

Monogram. Rev. Lion with monogram-shield.

1278.	1 Ducat ND	250.00

Horse and city view. Rev. Lion with monogram-shield.

1279.	1 Ducat 1741	300.00

Stag and hunter. Rev. Stag and 3 dogs.

1280.	2 Ducats ND	750.00

Crossed initials. Rev. Stag.

1281.	1 Ducat ND	350.00

Crossed initials. Rev. Boar.

1282.	1 Ducat ND	300.00

Monogram NB. Rev. Legend ALLES IN DER WELT etc.

1283.	1 Ducat ND	225.00

LOUIS IX, 1768-1790
Bust. Rev. Arms, lions and value.

1284.	1 Ducat 1758, 72	250.00

LOUIS X (I), 1790-1830

Head. Rev. Arms.

1285.	10 Gulden 1826, 27	300.00

Inscription. Rev. Inscription.

1286.	1 Reformation Jubilee Ducat 1817	100.00

LOUIS II, 1830-1848

Head. Rev. Arms.

1287.	10 Gulden 1840, 41, 42	300.00
1288.	5 Gulden 1835, 40, 41 ....*......	150.00
1289.	5 Rhine-gold Gulden 1835 ....*......	750.00

HESSE-HOMBURG

Landgraves of —

FREDERICK II, DIED 1708
Bust. Rev. Mountain.

1290.   1 Ducat 1690, ND (3 different bust-dies) 500.00

HESSE-MARBURG

Landgraves of —

LOUIS III, 1567-1604
Bust. Rev. Arms.

1291.   1 Goldgulden 1591 .... 750.00

HILDESHEIM

A. City of —

Bust of Charles V with hat. Rev. Arms.

1292.   5 Ducats 1528 .... 800.00

Bust of Charles V. Rev. Arms.

1293.   4½ Goldgulden 1605, ND 800.00

Orb. Rev. Arms.

1294.   1 Goldgulden 1573 .... 300.00

Arms. Rev. Eagle. Name of Rudolph II.

1295.   1 Goldgulden 1602, 03, 06 .... 250.00

Rudolph II on horse. Rev. Eagle.

1296.   10 Goldgulden ND (1576-1610) .... **Rare**

Madonna. Rev. Arms.

1297.   1 Goldgulden 1624 ....:. 250.00

Arms. Rev. Eagle. Name of Ferdinand II.

1298.   4 Goldgulden 1626 .... 750.00
1299.   1 Goldgulden 1623, 27, 28 .... 250.00
1300.   ½ Goldgulden 1623, 27 .... 200.00

Arms. Rev. Eagle. Name of Leopold I.

1301.   1 Goldgulden 1672 .... 300.00

B. Bishops of —

JODOCUS EDMUND, 1688-1702
Bust. Rev. Arms.

1302.   1 Ducat 1694 .... 300.00

SEDE VACANTE, 1761-1763
Arms. Rev. Value in cartouche.

1303.   ½ Pistole 1763 .... 250.00

FREDERICK WILLIAM, 1763-1789

Bust right or left. Rev. Arms and value.

1304.   10 Taler or 2 Pistoles 1766 .... 800.00
1305.   5 Taler or 1 Pistole 1764, 65 ....*...... 400.00
1306.   1 Ducat 1778 .... 250.00

Arms. Rev. Value in cartouche.

1307.   ½ Pistole 1763 .... 200.00

Arms. Rev. Value.

1308.   1 Ducat 1784 .... 200.00

HOHENLOHE

Counts, and later, Princes —

ANONYMOUS
Bust of Rudolph II. Rev. Arms.

1309.   1 Ducat 1608 .... 750.00

Arms. Rev. Eagle.

1310.   1 Goldgulden 1615 .... 500.00

JOHN FREDERICK I OF OHRINGEN, 1676-1702

Knight on horse. Rev. Arms.

1311.   2 Ducats 1699 .... 500.00
1312.   1 Ducat 1699 ....*...... 300.00

WOLFGANG JULIUS OF NEUENSTEIN, 1676-1698

Bust. Rev. Knight on horse.

1313.   1 Ducat 1697 .... 300.00

CHARLES LOUIS OF WEICKERSHEIM, 1708-1756
Bust. Rev. Arms.

1314.   1 Ducat 1737 .... 300.00

JOHN FREDERICK II OF OHRINGEN, 1708-1765
Bust. Rev. Three shields.

1315.   1 Ducat 1760 .... 300.00

CHARLES PHILIP OF NEUENSTEIN, 1733-1763
Bust. Rev. Arms.

1316.   1 Goldgulden 1735 .... 300.00

Bust. Rev. Phoenix over arms.

1317.   1 Ducat 1747 .... 300.00

PHILIP ERNEST OF SCHILLINGSFUERST, 1697-1753
Bust. Rev. Arms.

1318.   1 Ducat 1750 .... 300.00

JOSEPH ANTHONY OF PFEDELBACH, 1745-1764
Bust. Rev. Phoenix.

1319.	1 Ducat 1747	300.00

LOUIS GOTTFRIED OF PFEDELBACH, 1685-1728
Arms. Rev. Legend. On the Reformation.

1320.	1 Ducat 1717	300.00

LOUIS OF LANGENBURG, 1715-1765
Legend. Rev. Three female figures.

1321.	1 Ducat 1751	300.00

LOUIS FREDERICK CHARLES OF OHRINGEN, 1765-1805
Bust. Rev. Arms.

1322.	1 Ducat 1770	300.00

FREDERICK LOUIS OF INGELFINGEN, 1796-1806
Bust. Rev. Value.

1323.	1 Ducat 1796	300.00

HOHENZOLLERN-HECHINGEN

Princes —

FREDERICK WILLIAM, 1671-1735

Bust. Rev. Arms.

1324.	1 Carolin 1734, 35 ....*......	500.00
1325.	½ Carolin 1734, 35	300.00

INGELHEIM

St. John. Rev. Orb. With name of Frederick III.

1326.	1 Goldgulden ND (1470-90)	300.00

ISENBURG

Princes —

WOLFGANG ERNST I, 1596-1628
Arms. Rev. Double eagle.

1327.	2 Ducats 1618,19	1000.00

CHARLES, 1803-1815
Head. Rev. Arms and value.

1328.	2 Ducats 1811	750.00

JULICH-CLEVE-BERG

A. Dukes of Julich

WILLIAM I, 1356-1361
St. John. Rev. Lily.

1329.	1 Goldgulden ND	350.00

WILLIAM II, 1361-1393
St. John. Rev. Lily.

1330.	1 Goldgulden ND	350.00

Bust over arms. Rev. Two shields.

1331.	1 Goldgulden ND	350.00

Bust over two shields. Rev. Eagle.

1332.	1 Goldgulden ND	400.00

WILLIAM III, 1393-1402
Duke on throne. Rev. Cross.

1333.	1 Ecu d'or ND	800.00

REYNALD IV, 1402-1423
Two angels with shield. Rev. Duke on horse.

1334.	1 Goldgulden ND	150.00

St. John. Rev. Four or five shields.

1335.	1 Goldgulden ND	150.00

B. Dukes of Cleve

JOHN, 1347-1368
St. John. Rev. Lily.

1336.	1 Florin ND	400.00

ADOLPH VII, 1394-1448
Helmeted arms on each side.

1337.	1 Goldgulden ND	350.00

JOHN I, 1448-1481
Madonna. Rev. Helmet over two shields.

1338.	½ Goldgulden ND	350.00

Standing ruler. Rev. Shield on cross.

1339.	1 Goldgulden ND	300.00

JOHN II, 1481-1521
Standing ruler. Rev. Shield on cross.

1340.	1 Goldgulden ND	250.00

Half length bust. Rev. Cross and four shields.

1341.	1 Goldgulden ND	250.00

Bust of St. John. Rev. Five shields.

1342.	1 Goldgulden 1511, 17	350.00

St. John. Rev. Cross.

1343.	1 Philips-gulden 1501	600.00

St. John. Rev. Helmeted arms.

1344.	1 Goldgulden ND	250.00

St. John. Rev. Arms on cross.

1345.	1 Goldgulden ND	250.00

St. Martin standing. Rev. Arms.

1346.	1 Goldgulden 1503	600.00

C. Dukes of Berg

WILLIAM II, 1360-1408
Half length bust. Rev. Shield.

1347.	1 Goldgulden ND	375.00

ADOLPH IX, 1408-1423
St. John. Rev. Four shields.

1348.	1 Goldgulden ND	250.00

D. Dukes of Julich - Berg

ADOLPH IX, 1423-1437
St. John. Rev. Orb. Name of Sigismund I

1349. 1 Goldgulden ND 250.00

GERHART II, 1437-1475
St. John. Rev. Orb.

1350. 1 Goldgulden ND 250.00

WILLIAM IV, 1475-1511
Arms on cross. Rev. Three shields.

1351. 1 Goldgulden ND 250.00

Bust of St. Hubert. Rev. Arms on cross.

1352. 1 Goldgulden 1501, ND 200.00

St. Hubert standing. Rev. Arms.

1353. 1 Goldgulden 1503 .... 200.00

St. Hubert standing. Rev. Five shields. The last three dates are posthumous.

1354. 1 Goldgulden 1511, 12, 14 .... 200.00

E. Dukes of Julich, Cleve and Berg

JOHN III, 1511-1539
St. Hubert. Rev. Arms.

1355. 1 Goldgulden 1511-16 .... 300.00

WILLIAM V, 1539-1592
Five shields. Rev. Double eagle.

1356. 1 Goldgulden 1567, 68, 72, 81, 87, 89 .... 300.00

JOHN WILLIAM I, 1592-1609
Five shields. Rev. Double eagle.

1357. 1 Goldgulden 1592, 93, 98, 1604, 05, 08, 09 .... 300.00

INTERREGNUM, 1609-1624
Five shields. Rev. Double eagle.

1358. 1 Goldgulden 1613, ND 400.00

SIEGE OF JULICH, 1610
Eight punch marks. Rev. Blank. Octagonal necessity coin.

1359. 40 Taler 1610 .... Rare

F. Palatine Dukes of Julich, Cleve and Berg

WOLFGANG WILLIAM, 1624-1653

Bust. Rev. Arms and value.

1360. 1 Ducat 1636, 43, 50 .... 300.00

PHILIP WILLIAM, 1653-1679

Bust. Rev. Arms.

1361. 1 Ducat 1654-77 .... 300.00

Bust. Rev. Sun over legend.

1362. 1 Ducat 1676 .... 300.00

JOHN WILLIAM II, 1679-1716

Bust. Rev. Orb on Shield.

1363. 1 Ducat 1682-1710 ....*...... 300.00
1364. ¼ Ducat 1710, 11 .... 100.00

Bust. Rev. Circle of nine shields.

1365. 2 Ducats 1707 ....*...... 500.00
1366. 1 Ducat 1707, 08 .... 300.00

Bust. Rev. Three shields.

1367. 2 Ducats 1708, 09, 11 .... 500.00
1368. 1 Ducat 1708, 09, 11 .... 300.00

Head. Rev. Two shields on double eagle. Vicariat issue.

1369. 5 Ducats 1711 .... 800.00
1370. 3 Ducats 1711 .... 600.00
1371. 2 Ducats 1711 ....*...... 350.00
1372. 1 Ducat 1711 .... 200.00

Bust. Rev. Bust of Marie Anne.

1373. 2 Ducats ND 300.00

CHARLES PHILIP, 1716-1742
Bust. Rev. Initials.

1374. 10 Ducats 1717 .... Rare
1375. 5 Ducats 1717 .... 1500.00
1376. 1 Ducat 1720 .... 300.00
1377. 1 Goldgulden 1718 .... 500.00

Head. Rev. Five shields.

1378. 1 Carolin 1732 .... 575.00

Head. Rev. Arms.

1379. 1 Carolin 1733 ....*...... 450.00
1380. ½ Carolin 1733 .... 350.00
1381. ¼ Carolin 1735 .... 200.00

CHARLES THEODORE, 1742-1799

Bust. Rev. Arms.

1382.	1 Ducat 1749, 50	....	400.00

Bust. Rev. Three shields.

1383.	2 Ducats 1750	....	500.00

Bust. Rev. Cross of St. Hubert.

1384.	1 Ducat 1750	....	350.00

KAUFBEUREN

Bust of Charles V. Rev. Orb.

1385.	1 Goldgulden ND (1517-58)	....	350.00

Charles V standing. Rev. Pillars of Hercules.

1386.	1 Ducat 1542, 43	....	600.00

Orb. Rev. Arms.

1387.	1 Goldgulden 1541, 46	....	600.00

Arms. Rev. Cross.

1388.	1 Gold Crown ND (1545)	....	300.00

Seated female. Rev. Legend. On the Augsburg Confession.

1389.	1 Ducat 1730	....	250.00

KEMPTEN

A. Abbots of —

RUPERT, 1678-1728

Four helmeted shields. Rev. St. Hildegarde in shield.

1390.	2 Ducats 1693	...............*......	600.00
1391.	1 Ducat 1692, 95	....	300.00

ANSELM, 1728-1747
Bust. Rev. Horse and arms.

1391a.	1 Ducat 1729	....	Rare

ENGELBERT, 1747-1760
Bust. Rev. Arms.

1392.	2 Ducats 1748	....	600.00
1393.	1 Ducat 1748	....	400.00

B. City of —

St. Magnus standing. Rev. Double eagle.

1394.	1 Goldgulden 1511-48	....	400.00

Angel. Rev. Legend. On the Reformation.

1395.	1 Ducat 1717	....	200.00

Obelisk. Rev. Sun over castle. On the Augsburg Confession.

1396.	1 Ducat 1730	....	200.00

KOENIGSEGG

Counts —

FRANCIS HUGO

Armored bust. Rev. Arms.

1397.	1 Ducat 1756	....	500.00

LANDAU

Arms, legend and punch marks. Rev. Blank. Square with clipped corners. Struck while besieged by the French.

1398.	4 Doppia 1713	...................*....10,000.00
1399.	2 Doppia 1713	.... 4500.00
1400.	1 Doppia 1713	...................*..... 2500.00

LEININGEN

Counts —

EMICHO V, 1375-1442

Half length figure under canopy. Rev. Arms in cartouche.

1401.	1 Goldgulden ND	....	2000.00

LEININGEN-WESTERBURG

Counts —

LOUIS, 1597-1622

Bust. Rev. Arms.

1402.	1 Goldgulden 1614, 17, 18, 19	....	450.00

LEIPZIG

Bust of Frederick the Bellicose. Rev. City view. On the 300th year of the Academy.
1403. 1 Ducat 1709 . . . . 250.00

Bust of Martin Luther. Rev. Altar. On the Reformation.
1404. 2 Ducats 1717 . . . . 300.00
1405. 1 Ducat 1717 . . . . 150.00

LEUTKIRCH

City View. Rev. Church.
1406. 1 Peace Ducat 1748 . . . . 500.00

LIMBURG-SONTHEIM

Barons —

FREDERICK, 1530-1596
Armored bust. Rev. Ship.
1407. 2 Ducats ND 600.00

LIPPE-DETMOLD

(The coinage of Lippe-Schaumburg will be found under Schaumburg-Lippe.)

Counts —

SIMON VII, 1613-1627

Eagle. Rev. Arms. Name of Matthias.
1408. 1 Goldgulden 1619 . . . . 750.00

SIMON HENRY, 1666-1697
Bust. Rev. Arms.
1409. 3   Ducats 1685, 92 . . . . 1000.00
1410. 1½ Ducats 1685, 92 . . . . 500.00
1411. 1   Ducat 1673, 85 . . . . 400.00

FREDERICK ADOLPH, 1697-1718
Bust. Rev. Arms.
1412. 10 Ducats 1712, 15 . . . . Rare
1413. 5 Ducats 1711, 15, 16 . . . . 1250.00
1414. 2 Ducats 1714 . . . . 600.00
1415. 1 Ducat 1711-16, ND 250.00

Bust. Rev. Legend.
1416. 1 Ducat 1710, ND 375.00

Bust. Rev. Value.
1417. ¼ Ducat 1714, 15 . . . . 100.00

SIMON HENRY ADOLPH, 1718-1734
Bust. Rev. Arms.
1418. 4 Ducats 1719 . . . . 1000.00
1419. 1 Ducat 1718, 19 . . . . 300.00

SIMON AUGUST, 1734-1782
Head. Rev. Arms.
1420. 1 Ducat 1765. Birthday issue 350.00
1421. 1 Ducat 1767 . . . . 350.00

Busts of the Count and Countess. Rev. Two hands. On their wedding.
1422. 1 Ducat 1769 . . . . 350.00

FREDERICK WILLIAM LEOPOLD, 1782-1802
Two shields. Rev. Legend. On the birth of the Crown Prince.
1423. 1½ Ducats 1796 . . . . 375.00

LOEWENSTEIN-ROCHEFORT

Princes —

MAXIMILIAN CHARLES, 1672-1718
Flying eagle. Rev. Legend. On the birth of Leopold.
1424. 1 Ducat 1716 . . . . 450.00

Bust. Rev. Arms.
1425. 1 Ducat 1692 . . . . 500.00

CHARLES THOMAS, 1735-1789

Bust. Rev. Arms.
1426. 1 Ducat 1754 . . . . 300.00

LOEWENSTEIN-WERTHEIM

Princes —

CHARLES LOUIS, 1737-1779

Bust. Rev. Arms.
1427. 1 Ducat 1767 . . . . 300.00

JOHN LOUIS WOLRAD, 1730-1790
Bust. Rev. Lion.
1428. 1 Ducat ND 375.00
1429. ¼ Ducat ND 125.00

Bust. Rev. Arms.
1430. 1 Ducat 1768, 69, 71 . . . . 300.00

Bust. Rev. Figure kneeling at altar. On the 50th year of reign.
1431. 1 Ducat 1780 . . . . 400.00

DOMINICK CONSTANTINE, 1789-1806
Bust. Rev. Allegory. On his birthday.
1432. 1 Ducat 1791 . . . . 300.00

FREDERICK CHARLES, 1799-1806

Bust. Rev. Arms.

433.	2 Ducats 1799. Thick flan	....	600.00
434.	1 Ducat 1799	..................*	300.00

LUBECK

A. City of —

Double eagle. Rev. Blank.

435. ½ Ducat or Bracteate ND (1300) 750.00

"English" king in ship. Rev. Sun and eagle.

436. 1 Rosenoble ND (1327-77) 750.00

St. John. Rev. Lily.

1437. 1 Ducat ND (1400-1500) 175.00

St. John. Rev. Emperor seated.

1438. 1½ Ducats ND (1400-1500) 1500.00

St. John. Rev. Madonna.

1438. 1 Ducat 1497 .... 750.00

St. John on each side.

1439. 1 Ducat ND (1500) 175.00

Orb. Rev. Double eagle.

1440. 1 Goldgulden 1583-1675 .... 200.00
1441. ¼ Ducat ND (1650) 100.00

Double eagle. Rev. Arms.

1442. 1 Goldgulden 1589-1637 .... 200.00

Birth of Christ. Rev. The Resurrection.

1443. 10 Ducats ND (1619-27) 1500.00
1444. 5 Ducats ND (1619-27) 750.00

St. John. Rev. Cross.

1445. ½ Portugaloser or 5 Ducats 1636 .... 1500.00

Royal figure seated. Rev. Double eagle.

1446. ½ Portugaloser or 5 Ducats 1628 .... 1500.00

Royal figure standing. Rev. Double eagle.

1447. 4 Ducats 1638 .... 1000.00

1448.	2 Ducats 1656-1716	.............*	350.00
1449.	1 Ducat 1631-1759	....	200.00
1450.	½ Ducat 1679-1714	....	100.00
1451.	¼ Ducat 1679-1728	....	75.00

Rock on sea. Rev. All-seeing eye.

1452. 1 Ducat 1707 .... 200.00

Double eagle. Rev. Legend. On the Reformation.

1453. 2 Ducats 1717 .... 250.00
1454. 1 Ducat 1717 ....* 125.00

Bust of Charles VI. Rev. Double eagle.

1455. 1 Ducat 1729, 30 .... 200.00

Religion standing. Rev. Double eagle. On the Augsburg Confession.

1456. 1 Ducat 1730 .... 200.00

Tablet. Rev. Double eagle. With names of the Holy Roman Emperors.

1457. 1 Ducat 1790-1801 .... 150.00

B. Bishops of —

EBERHARD, 1567-1586
Bust. Rev. Arms.

1458. 10 Ducats ND .... Rare

JOHN ADOLPH, 1585-1596
Arms. Rev. Cross.

1459. 1 Portugaloser or 10 Ducats ND ..... Rare
1460. ½ Portugaloser or 5 Ducats ND 1000.00

JOHN FREDERICK, 1607-1634
St. Peter. Rev. Arms.

1461. 1 Goldgulden 1612 .... 750.00

Bust. Rev. Arms.

1462. 1 Portugaloser or 10 Ducats ND ...... Rare

CHRISTIAN ALBERT, 1655-1666
Armored bust. Rev. Arms. Posthumously struck.

1463. 1 Ducat 1689 .... 350.00

AUGUST FREDERICK, 1666-1705
Armored bust. Rev. Arms.

1464. 1 Ducat 1688, 89 .... 300.00

CHRISTIAN AUGUST, 1705-1726
Armored bust. Rev. Lion.

1465.   1 Ducat 1724, 26 .... 300.00

FREDERICK AUGUST, 1750-1785
Bust. Rev. Arms. For illustration, see Oldenburg No. 1808.

1466.   1 Pistole 1776 .... 300.00

LUNEBURG

St. John. Rev. Orb.

1467.   2 Goldgulden 1592 .... 600.00
1468.   1 Goldgulden ND (1419-1500) ....* 200.00
1469.   1 Goldgulden 1581-99 .... 250.00

St. John. Rev. Double eagle.

1470.   2 Goldgulden 1600 .... 500.00
1471.   1 Goldgulden 1600-35 .... 200.00

St. John. Rev. Arms on cross.

1472.   3   Goldgulden ND (1600-50) 600.00
1473.   2½ Goldgulden ND (1600-50) 500.00

Bust of St. John. Rev. Orb.

1474.   1 Goldgulden 1626, 29 .... 200.00

St. John. Rev. Face in crescent.

1475.   2 Goldgulden ND (1650) 600.00
1476.   1 Goldgulden ND (1650) ....*..... 200.00
1477.   1 Ducat 1645, 47 .... 250.00

St. John. Rev. Crescent, hunters and fishermen.

1478.   6 Ducats ND (1650) 1000.00

Castle gate. Rev. Double cross.

1479.   ½ Portugaloser 1567, ND 1000.00

Castle gate. Rev. Double eagle.

1480.   2 Goldgulden ND (1576-1610) 600.00

Lion. Rev. Double eagle.

1481.   1 Goldgulden ND (1576-1610) 250.00

MAGDEBURG

A. General City coinage

Arms. Rev. Inscription.

1482.   ½ Siege Ducat 1551 square 1000.00

Arms. Rev. Cross.

1483.   10 Ducats ND (1573-1606) 4000.00
1484.   5 Ducats ND (1573-1606) 1500.00

Emperor Otto I on horse. Rev. Eagle.

1485.   10 Ducats 1599 .... 2500.00
1486.   4 Ducats 1599 .... 1750.00

Arms. Rev. Value in square.

1487.   1 Ducat 1673 .... 375.00

City view. Rev. Arms.

1488.   2 Ducats 1675 .... 750.00

B. Coinage with the names of the Holy Roman Emperors

Female over city gate. Rev. Eagle. Maximilian II.

1489.   1 Goldgulden 1571, 74, 76 .... 350.00

Female over city gate. Rev. Eagle. Rudolph II.

1490.   2 Goldgulden 1594 .... 750.00
1491.   1 Goldgulden 1571, 85, 1600, 05, 06 ..... 375.00

Female over city gate. Rev. Eagle. Matthias.

1492.   1 Goldgulden 1617 .... 500.00

Arms with helmet. Rev. Eagle. Matthias.

1493.   1 Goldgulden ND 600.00

Arms with helmet. Rev. Eagle. Ferdinand II.

1494.   1 Goldgulden 1624 .... 450.00

Female over city gate. Rev. Eagle. Ferdinand II.

1495.   1 Goldgulden 1622, 24, 26-30 .... 200.00

Female over city gate. Rev. Eagle. Ferdinand III.

1496.   2 Ducats 1639 .... 350.00

Eagle. Rev. Value on tablet. Ferdinand III.

1497.   1 Ducat 1638, 41, 42 .... 250.00

C. Archbishops of —

JOACHIM FREDERICK, 1566-1598
Bust. Rev. Arms.

1498.   2 Ducats 1590 .... 800.00

Eagle. Rev Arms.

1499.   1 Goldgulden 1586 .... 700.00

CHRISTIAN WILLIAM, 1598-1631
Bust. Rev. Arms.

1500.   1 Goldgulden 1615, 23, ND 600.00
1501.   ½ Goldgulden ND 300.00

Bust. Rev. Three shields in circle of fourteen shields.

1502.   2 Goldgulden ND 600.00

CATHEDRAL CHAPTER, 1638

St. Mauritius. Rev. Arms.

1503.   1 Ducat 1638 .... 350.00

AUGUST, 1638-1680
Legend. Rev. St. Mauritius. On his enthronement.

1504.   1 Ducat 1638 .... 250.00

Facing bust. Rev. Arms of Magdeburg.

1505.   1 Ducat 1640, 41 .... 250.00

Bust. Rev. Arms of Saxony.

1506. 1 Ducat 1671 .... 300.00

Initials. Rev. Legend. On the death of Anna Marie.

1507. 1 Ducat 1669 .... 250.00

MANSFELD

Counts —

A. The Vorderort Line BORNSTEDT

BRUNO II, WILLIAM I AND JOHN GEORGE IV, 1604-1607
Three shields. Rev. St. George.

1508. 1 Goldgulden 1606 .... 400.00

BRUNO II, WILLIAM I, JOHN GEORGE IV AND VOLRAT VI, 1605-1615
Three shields. Rev. St. George.

1509. 1 Goldgulden 1611 .... 400.00

BRUNO II, WILLIAM I, JOHN GEORGE IV, VOLRAT VI AND JOBST, 1609-1615
Three shields. Rev. St. George.

1510. 1 Goldgulden 1615, ND 250.00

WOLFGANG III AND JOHN GEORGE II, 1631-1638

St. George. Rev. Value on tablet.

1511. 1 Ducat 1631, 32, 35, 38 .... 250.00

CHARLES ADAM, 1638-1662
St. George. Rev. Value on tablet.

1512. 1 Ducat 1656 .... 300.00

FRANCIS MAXIMILIAN, 1644-1692
St. George. Rev. Arms and value.

1513. ¼ Ducat 1670, 71 .... 100.00

FRANCIS MAXIMILIAN AND HENRY FRANCIS, 1644-1692

St. George. Rev. Crowned arms.

1514. 1 Ducat 1687 .... 250.00

HENRY, PRINCE OF FONDI, 1717-1780
Armored bust. Rev. Crowned arms.

1515. 1 Ducat 1747 .... 500.00

Crowned arms on mantle. Rev. St. George.

1516. 1 Ducat 1774 .... 250.00

FRANCIS GUNDACAR, 1780-1806
Crowned arms on mantle. Rev. St. George.

1517. 1 Ducat 1792 .... 250.00

B. The Vorderort Line EISLEBEN

JOHN GEORGE I, PETER ERNEST I AND CHRISTOPHER II, 1558-1579
St. George. Rev. Three shields.

1518. 1 Goldgulden ND 200.00

JOHN GEORGE II, 1619-1647
St. George. Rev. Three shields.

1519. 1 Goldgulden 1632, 35-37 .... 250.00

C. The Vorderort Line FRIEDEBURG

PETER ERNEST I, BRUNO II, HOYER CHRISTOPHER, GEBHARD VIII AND JOHN GEORGE IV, 1579-1587
Three shields. Rev. St. George.

1520. 1 Goldgulden 1587 .... 300.00

PETER ERNEST I, BRUNO II, GEBHARD VIII AND JOHN GEORGE IV, 1587-1601
Three shields. Rev. St. George.

1521. 1 Goldgulden 1597 .... 300.00

PETER ERNEST I, BRUNO II, WILLIAM I AND JOHN GEORGE IV, 1601-1604
Three shields. Rev. St. George.

1522. 1 Goldgulden 1603 .... 300.00

D. The Vorderort Line ARTERN

VOLRAT VI, JOBST II AND WOLFGANG III, 1615-1617
Three shields. Rev. St. George.

1523. 1 Goldgulden 1616, 17 .... 250.00

VOLRAT VI, JOBST II, WOLFGANG III AND BRUNO III, 1616-1619
Three shields. Rev. St. George.

1524. 1 Goldgulden 1617, 18 .... 250.00

VOLRAT VI AND JOBST II
St. George. Rev. Three shields.

1525. 1 Goldgulden 1619 .... 250.00

VOLRAT VI, WOLFGANG III AND JOHN GEORGE II, 1620-1627

St. George. Rev. Three shields.

1526. 1 Goldgulden 1620, 21, 28 ....*...... 225.00
1527. ½ Goldgulden 1620 .... 450.00

PHILIP ERNEST, WOLFGANG III AND JOHN GEORGE II
St. George. Rev. Three shields.

1528. 1 Goldgulden 1630 .... 300.00

E. The Hinterort Line

VOLRAT V, JOHN I AND CHARLES I, 1560-1566
Arms. Rev. Helmet.

1529. 1 Goldgulden 1563 .... 800.00

DAVID, 1603-1628
St. George. Rev. Crowned arms.

1530. 1 Ducat 1619 .... 600.00

St. George. Rev. Legend above arms.

1531. 1 Goldgulden 1606, 18 .... 600.00

Arms with helmet. Rev. St. George.

1532. 1 Goldgulden 1622 .... 750.00

ERNEST VI AND FREDERICK CHRISTOPHER, 1579 AND 1603-1611
Arms with helmet. Rev. St. George. Title of Rudolph II.

1533. 1 Goldgulden 1607 .... 600.00

FREDERICK CHRISTOPHER AND DAVID, 1620-1628
St. George. Rev. Arms with helmet.

1534. 1 Ducat 1622 .... 750.00

CHRISTIAN FREDERICK, 1632-1666
St. George. Rev. Value on tablet.

1535. 1 Ducat 1644, 47, 52 .... 375.00

MAYENCE (MAINZ)

A. Archbishops of —

GERLACH, 1346-1371
St. John. Rev. Lily.

1536.	1 Goldgulden ND	125.00
1537.	1 Goldgulden ND. Mint: Eltville	350.00

Archbishop standing. Rev. Arms in enclosure.

1538.	1 Goldgulden ND. Mint: Bingen	125.00

Archbishop standing. Rev. Rupert of Palatinate standing.

1539.	1 Goldgulden ND. Mint: Bingen	450.00

SEDE VACANTE, 1371
St. Martin standing. Rev. Wheel shield in enclosure.

1540.	1 Goldgulden ND. Mint: Bingen	250.00

JOHN I, 1371-1373
Archbishop standing. Rev. Arms in enclosure.

1541.	1 Goldgulden ND. Mint: Bingen	150.00

Archbishop on throne. Rev. Wheel shield in enclosure.

1542.	1 Goldgulden ND. Mint: Hoechst	150.00

ELECTION DISPUTE AFTER THE DEATH OF JOHN I, 1373
St. Martin on throne. Rev. Wheel shield in enclosure.

1543.	1 Goldgulden ND (Anonymous). Mint: Bingen	150.00

ADOLPH I, 1373-1390

St. Martin on throne. Rev. Wheel shield in enclosure.

1544.	1 Goldgulden ND. Mints: Bingen, Hoechst	150.00

St. John standing. Rev. 4 Arms in enclosure.

1545.	1 Goldgulden ND. Mints: Bingen, Hoechst	150.00
1546.	1 Goldgulden ND. Mint: Udenheim	350.00

Archbishop standing. Rev. Arms in enclosure.

1547.	1 Goldgulden ND. Mint: Oberlahnstein	500.00

CONRAD II, 1390-1396
Archbishop on throne. Rev. Wheel shield in enclosure.

1548.	1 Goldgulden ND. Mint: Bingen	100.00

St. John standing. Rev. Wheel shield in enclosure.

1549.	1 Goldgulden ND. Mint: Bingen	100.00

St. John standing. Rev. Arms of Mainz-Nassau in enclosure.

1550.	1 Goldgulden ND. Mint: Bingen	100.00

St. John standing. Rev. 4 Arms in enclosure.

1551.	1 Goldgulden ND. Mints: Bingen, Hoechst	100.00

ELECTION DISPUTE, 1396-1397
St. Martin on throne. Rev. Wheel shield in enclosure.

1552.	1 Goldgulden ND. Mints: Bingen, Hoechst	100.00

JOHN II, 1397-1419
Archbishop on throne. Rev. Wheel shield in enclosure.

1553.	1 Goldgulden ND. Mint: Bingen	100.00

St. John standing. Rev. Arms of Mainz-Nassau and small arms of Cologne and Trier.

1554.	1 Goldgulden ND. Mints: Bingen, Hoechst	100.00

St. John standing. Rev. 5 Arms in enclosure.

1555.	1 Goldgulden ND. Mints: Bingen, Hoechst	100.00

St. Peter standing. Rev. 5 Arms in enclosure.

1556.	1 Goldgulden ND. Mints: Bingen, Hoechst	100.00

Bust of St. Peter under canopy. Rev. 5 Arms in enclosure.

1557.	1 Goldgulden ND	100.00

St. Martin on throne. Rev. Wheel shield in enclosure.

1558.	1 Goldgulden ND. Mint: Hoechst	100.00

CONRAD III, 1419-1434
Archbishop standing. Rev. Wheel shield in enclosure.

1559.	1 Goldgulden ND. Mints: Bingen, Hoechst	100.00

St. Peter standing. Rev. 5 Arms in enclosure.

1560.	1 Goldgulden ND. Mints: Bingen, Hoechst	100.00

St. Peter standing. Rev. 4 Arms in enclosure.

1561.	1 Goldgulden ND. Mint: Bingen	100.00

THEODORE I, 1434-1459
Archbishop standing. Rev. Wheel shield in enclosure.

1562.	1 Goldgulden ND. Mints: Bingen, Hoechst	100.00

Arms on cross. Rev. 3 shields.

1563.	1 Goldgulden 1436-38, ND. Mints: Bingen, Hoechst	100.00

THEODORE II, 1459-1461 and 1475-1482
Christ on throne. Rev. Floriated cross with 4 shields.

1564.	1 Goldgulden ND. (1459-61). Mint: Mayence	150.00

Arms on cross. Rev. 3 shields.

1565.	1 Goldgulden ND. (1475-82). Mints: Mayence, Hoechst, Rhenish	150.00

ADOLPH II, 1461-1475
Christ on throne. Rev. Floriated cross with 4 shields.

1566.	1 Goldgulden ND. Mint: Mayence	150.00

BERTHOLD, 1484-1504
Arms on cross. Rev. Christ on throne.

1567.	1 Goldgulden 1490. Mint: Rhenish	180.00

4 Arms in enclosure. Rev. Christ on throne.

1568.	1 Goldgulden 1491-1504	180.00

JAMES, 1504-1508
4 Arms in enclosure. Rev. Christ on throne.

1569.	1 Goldgulden 1504-08	150.00

URIEL, 1508-1514
4 Arms in enclosure. Rev. Christ on throne over wheel shield.

1570.	1 Goldgulden 1506, 09, 12, 14, ND	150.00

Christ on throne over family shield. Rev. 4 Arms in enclosure.

1571.	1 Goldgulden ND	200.00

ALBERT, 1514-1545
Christ on throne. Rev. 4 Arms in enclosure.

1572.	1 Goldgulden 1515, 34-43, ND	300.00

DANIEL BRENDEL, 1555-1582
Arms. Rev. Floriated cross and 4 shields.

1573.   1 Goldgulden 1571, 72 ....   **500.00**

WOLFGANG, 1582-1601
Arms. Rev. 4 Arms in enclosure.

1574.   1 Goldgulden 1586, 87, 88, 93, 95 ....   **250.00**

Arms with infulae. Rev. 4 Arms in enclosure.

1575.   1 Goldgulden 1596 ....   **450.00**

GEORGE FREDERICK, 1626-1629

Arms. Rev. Floriated cross, 3 shields and orb.

1576.   1 Goldgulden 1626, 27 ....   **450.00**

Arms. Rev. St. Martin on horse.

1577.   1 Goldgulden 1628 ....   **400.00**

Arms. Rev. Value in tablet.

1578.   1 Ducat 1628, 29 ....   **200.00**
1579.   1 Ducat 1628. Square **500.00**

ANSELM CASIMIR, 1629-1647
Facing bust. Rev. Arms.

1580.   2 Ducats 1629 (from the ducat die) **500.00**
1581.   1 Ducat 1629 ....   **250.00**

Facing bust. Rev. Crowned arms.

1582.   2 Ducats 1642 ....   **350.00**

Bust right. Rev. Crowned arms.

1583.   2 Ducats 1642, 44, 46, 47 ....   **300.00**
1584.   1 Ducat 1633, 38, 44, ND **150.00**

Bust right. Rev. Arms.

1585.   2 Ducats 1636 (from the ducat die) **350.00**
1586.   1 Ducat 1636, 38 ....   **150.00**

Bust right. Rev. Arms with 3 helmets.

1587.   2 Ducats 1642 ....   **300.00**

Arms with 3 helmets. Rev. Legend in wreath.

1588.   2 Ducats 1638, 39, ND **300.00**

Arms. Rev. Legend on tablet.

1589.   1 Ducat 1636, 41 ....   **200.00**

Crowned arms. Rev. Legend between branches.

1590.   1 Ducat 1642, 46 ....   **200.00**

Crowned arms in wreath. Rev. Legend between branches.

1591.   1 Ducat 1645, 46 ....   **150.00**

JOHN PHILIP, 1647-1673
Facing bust. Rev. Arms.

1592.   1 Ducat 1648-66 ....   **275.00**

Bust right or left. Rev. Arms.

1593.   1 Ducat 1654, 67, 68, 70, 71 ....   **150.00**

LOTHAR FREDERICK, 1673-1675
Bust. Rev. Arms.

1594.   1 Ducat 1673 ....   **375.00**

DAMIAN HARTARD, 1675-1678
Bust. Rev. Arms.

1595.   1 Ducat 1676 ....   **300.00**

ANSELM FRANCIS, 1679-1695

Bust. Rev. Arms.

1596.   2 Ducats 1680 ....* **400.00**
1597.   1 Ducat 1684 ....   **250.00**

LOTHAR FRANCIS, 1695-1729
Concordia seated. Rev. Arms under canopy. On the Peace of Ryswick.

1598.   2 Ducats ND (1696) **300.00**
1599.   1 Ducat ND (1696) **175.00**

Arms. Rev. Altar and value.

1600.   2 Ducats 1696 ....   **350.00**
1601.   1 Peace Ducat 1696 ....* **175.00**

Minerva standing. Rev. Arms. On the Peace of Ryswick.

1602.   2 Ducats 1696 ....* **300.00**
1603.   1 Ducat 1696 ....   **150.00**

Bust. Rev. Arms.

1604.   1 Ducat 1716, 28 ....   **275.00**
1605.   ¾ Ducat 1712 ....   **150.00**

FRANCIS LOUIS, 1729-1732
Bust. Rev. Lion being led by hand from heaven.

1606.   1 Ducat 1730 ....   **250.00**

PHILIP CHARLES, 1731-1743
Bust. Rev. Arms.

1607.   2 Ducats 1738 ....   **375.00**
1608.   1 Ducat 1738 ....   **250.00**

JOHN FREDERICK CHARLES, 1743-1763
Bust. Rev. Arms.

1609.   2 Ducats 1745, 48 ....   **350.00**
1610.   1 Ducat 1745, 47, 53 ....   **250.00**

Bust. Rev. Arms supported by dogs.

1611.   2 Ducats 1760 ....* **350.00**
1612.   1 Ducat 1759, 60 ....   **250.00**

EMERIC JOSEPH, 1763-1774
Bust. Rev. Arms.

1613. 1 Ducat 1768, 69, 71 .... 250.00

Bust. Rev. Legend.

1614. 1 Rhine-gold Ducat 1772 .... 500.00

FREDERICK CHARLES JOSEPH, 1774-1802

Bust. Rev. Arms.

1615. 1 Ducat 1795 .... 200.00

Bust. Rev. City view.

1616. 1 Ducat 1795 .... 250.00

CHARLES, 1802-1813
(See under Rhine Confederation.)

B. Abbey of St. Alban —

St. Martin on horse and S-M-E. Rev. Shield with wheel in enclosure.

1617. 1 Goldgulden ND (1300-1400) 800.00

St. Martin on horse and S-M-E. Rev. Arms.

1618. 1 Goldgulden ND 600.00
1619. ½ Goldgulden ND 600.00

St. Martin on horse. Rev. Shield with wheel in enclosure.

1620. 2 Goldgulden ND (shield with ornaments) 1000.00
1621. 2 Goldgulden ND (Smaller shield) 1000.00
1622. 1 Goldgulden ND 600.00

St. Martin on horse. Rev. Angel with arms.

1623. 1 Goldgulden 1584, ND 600.00

C. Swedish Rulers of —

Facing bust of Christina. Rev. Arms.

1624. 2 Ducats ND (1634) 1250.00

(Note: For the coinage of St. Alban in Mayence, see under Saint Alban.)

MECKLENBURG

Dukes of —

JOHN ALBERT, 1547-1576
Bust with hat. Rev. Cross with five arms.

1625. 1 Ducat 1554 .... 450.00

MECKLENBURG-GUSTROW

Dukes of —

JOHN ALBERT II, 1611-1636
Duke standing. Rev. Arms.

1626. 3 Ducats 1633 .... 600.00
1627. 2 Ducats 1633 .... 450.00
1628. 1 Ducat 1633 .... 250.00

GUSTAVE ADOLPH, 1636-1695

Bust. Rev. Arms.

1629. 1 Ducat 1666, 68. Mint: Wismar ....*...... 250.00
1630. 1 Ducat 1671, 72, 74, 75, 80, 85-89. Mint: Gustrow .. 250.00

MECKLENBURG-SCHWERIN

Dukes, and later Grand Dukes of —

ADOLPH FREDERICK, 1592-1658
Bust. Rev. Arms.

1631. 1 Goldgulden 1615 .... 300.00

Half length bust. Rev. Arms.

1632. 1 Goldgulden 1616 .... 300.00

Bust. Rev. Arms.

1633. 1 Goldgulden 1625 .... 250.00

Facing bust. Rev. Arms.

1634. 1 Ducat 1639 .... 250.00

CHRISTIAN LOUIS I, 1658-1692
Bust. Rev. Arms.

1635. 2 Ducats 1681 .... 500.00
1636. 1 Ducat 1670, 71, 81, 88 .... 300.00

FREDERICK WILLIAM, 1692-1713
Initials. Rev. Arms.

1637. 1 Ducat 1696. NON EST MORTALE QVOD OPTO 375.00
1638. 1 Ducat 1703. PROVIDE ET CONSTANTER 250.00

Bust. Rev. Arms.

1639. 2 Ducats 1703. PROVIDE ET CONSTANTER 400.00
1640. 1 Ducat 1696. NON EST MORTALE QVOD OPTO 350.00
1641. 1 Ducat 1701. QVO DEVS ET FORTVNA DVCVNT 175.00
1642. 1 Ducat 1703, 05. PROVIDE ET CONSTANTER ..*...... 175.00

Bust. Rev. Initials.

1643. 1 Ducat 1696 .... 375.00

Arms. Rev. Ox head.

1644. 1 Ducat 1701 ....*...... 200.00
1645. ¼ Ducat 1701 .... 100.00

Bust. Rev. The Duke and Duchess in boat.

1646. 2 Ducats 1704 .... 375.00
1647. 1 Ducat 1703, 04 ....*...... 175.00

Bust. Rev. Value.

1648. ¼ Ducat ND 100.00

CHRISTIAN LOUIS II, 1747-1756
Bust. Rev. Arms.

1649. 2 Pistoles 1752 .... 350.00
1650. 1 Pistole 1754 .... 250.00

Bust. Rev. Value.

1651. ¼ Ducat 1756 .... 75.00

FREDERICK, 1756-1785

Bust. Rev. Value.

1652. 2 Taler 1769, 78, 82, 83 .... 100.00

FREDERICK FRANCIS, 1785-1837

Arms. Rev. Value.

1653. 2 Taler 1792, 97 .... 100.00

Head. Rev. Arms.

1654. 10   Taler 1828, 31, 32, 33 .... 275.00
1655. 5   Taler 1828, 31-33, 35 ....*...... 150.00
1656. 5   Taler 1828. Mint visit 400.00
1657. 2½   Taler 1831, 33, 35 .... 150.00
1658. 2   Taler 1830 .... 400.00
1659. 1   Ducat 1830 ....*...... 400.00

Head. Rev. Arms.

1660. 10   Taler 1839 ....*...... 350.00
1661. 5   Taler 1840 .... 200.00
1662. 2½   Taler 1840 ....*...... 125.00

MECKLENBURG-STRELITZ

Dukes of —

ADOLPH FREDERICK III, 1708-1752

Bust. Rev. Faith before temple. On the Reformation.

1663. 1 Ducat 1717. A DEO 375.00

Bust. Rev. Jerusalem on mountain. On the Reformation.

1664. 1 Ducat 1717. NEC INGENS etc. 400.00

Bust. Rev. City on rock in ocean. On the Reformation.

1665. 1 Ducat 1717. CONSILIO STAT etc. 400.00

Bust. Rev. Arms.

1666. 5 Taler 1747, 49 .... 200.00

Initials. Rev. Ox head.

1667. 5 Taler 1748 .... 200.00

Initials. Rev. Value.

1668. 2 Taler 1746, 47 .... 150.00
1669. 1 Taler 1746, 47, 49 .... 125.00

ADOLPH FREDERICK IV, 1752-1794

Head. Rev. Arms.

1670.	1 Pistole 1754	300.00

Bust. Rev. Arms.

1671.	1 Pistole 1754	300.00

MEMMINGEN

City view. Rev. Inscription. On the centennial of Peace of Westphalia.

1672.	1 Ducat 1748	300.00

MINDEN

Bishops of —

HERMAN, 1566-1582
Arms. Rev. Double eagle.

1673.	1 Goldgulden ND	1500.00

ANTHONY, 1585-1599
Arms. Rev. Double eagle.

1674.	1 Goldgulden 1589, 95, ND	750.00

MOERS

Counts —

FREDERICK II, 1375-1417
Three shields in enclosure. Rev. St. John.

1675.	1 Goldgulden ND	1250.00

FREDERICK III, 1417-1448
Five shields in enclosure. Rev. St. John.

1676.	1 Goldgulden ND	750.00

Arms in enclosure. Rev. St. John.

1677.	1 Goldgulden ND. Mint: Falkenberg	1000.00

Arms in enclosure. Rev. St. Andrew over shield.

1678.	1 Goldgulden ND. Mint: Moers	1000.00

MUNSTER

Bishops of —

JOHN III, 1457-1466
Bust of St. Paul. Rev. Arms on cross.

1679.	1 Goldgulden ND	1000.00

HENRY III, 1466-1496

St. Paul seated. Rev. Three shields.

1680.	1 Goldgulden ND	450.00

CONRAD II, 1497-1508
St. Paul standing. Rev. Eagle shield in enclosure.

1681.	1 Goldgulden ND	600.00
1682.	½ Goldgulden ND	375.00

St. Paul seated. Rev. Three shields.

1683.	1 Goldgulden ND	400.00
1684.	½ Goldgulden ND	300.00

ERIC I, 1508-1522
Knight on horse. Rev. Arms in enclosure.

1685.	1 Goldgulden ND	1000.00

FRANCIS, 1532-1553
St. Peter and St. Paul. Rev. Four shields in enclosure.

1686.	1 Goldgulden ND	500.00

St. Paul seated. Rev. Four shields in enclosure.

1687.	1 Goldgulden ND	500.00

JOHN IV, 1566-1574
St. Paul standing. Rev. Four shields in enclosure.

1688.	1 Goldgulden 1570	500.00

FERDINAND, 1612-1650

Arms. Rev. Value.

1689.	2 Ducats 1640. Square	500.00
1690.	1 Ducat 1638-47 ....*.........	250.00

St. Paul standing. Rev. Arms.

1691.	1 Ducat 1633, 34	250.00

CHRISTOPHER BERNARD, 1650-1678
Madonna. Rev. Arms.

1692.	2 Ducats ND	450.00
1693.	1 Ducat ND	325.00

Arms. Rev. Value.

1694.	1 Ducat 1652, 65	250.00

Arms. Rev. Legend. On his death.

1695.	1 Goldgulden 1678	300.00

FREDERICK CHRISTIAN, 1688-1706
Bust. Rev. Arms.

1696.	1 Ducat 1695	300.00

FRANCIS ARNOLD, 1704-1718

Bust. Rev. Arms.

1697.	2 Ducats 1717 ....*......	500.00
1698.	1 Ducat 1717	300.00

NASSAU

Counts, and later, Dukes of —

RUPERT, 1355-1390
St. John. Rev. Lily.

1699.	1 Goldgulden ND	500.00

WALRAM, 1370-1393
St. Paul standing. Rev. Arms in enclosure.

1700.	1 Goldgulden ND	500.00

PHILIP, 1371-1429

St. John. Rev. Arms in enclosure.

1701. 1 Goldgulden ND 600.00

HENRY OF DILLENBURG, 1662-1702

Bust. Rev. Arms.

1702. 1 Ducat 1688 .... 500.00

CHARLES AUGUST, 1719-1753

Arms. Rev. Prince standing.

1703. 1 Ducat 1750 .... 250.00

Bust. Rev. Arms.

1704. 1 Ducat 1750 .... 350.00

FREDERICK AUGUST AND FREDERICK WILLIAM, 1803-1816

Arms. Rev. Value on tablet.

1705. 1 Ducat 1809 .... 250.00

WILLIAM, 1816-1839

Head. Rev. Arms.

1706. 1 Ducat 1818 .... 300.00

NOERDLINGEN

St. John. Rev. Orb. With name of Holy Roman Emperor as indicated.

1707. 1 Goldgulden ND. Sigismund 125.00
1708. 1 Goldgulden 1491-93, ND. Frederick III 125.00
1709. 1 Goldgulden 1494-1501, 06-08, 11, 13, 16. Maximilian I 125.00

NORDHAUSEN

Theodosius seated. Rev. Arms.

1710. 1 Goldgulden 1619 .... 750.00

NOSTIZ

Counts —

ANTHONY JOHN, 1683-1736

Bust. Rev. Arms supported by griffins.

1711. 1 Ducat 1719 .... 450.00

NUREMBERG

A. General City Coinage

St. Sebaldus. Rev. Arms in trefoil.

1712. 1 Goldgulden ND (1429) 400.00

St. Lawrence. Rev. Eagle.

1713. 3 Goldgulden 1612 .... 1500.00
1714. 2 Goldgulden ND (1552), 1614, 86 .... 1000.00
1715. 1 Goldgulden ND (1429-1506), 1506-1686 ....* 250.00

St. Lawrence. Rev. Arms.

1716. 1 Goldgulden 1614-23 .... 200.00

Two shields. Rev. Legend. On the Shooting Match.

1717. 1 Goldgulden 1579 .... 350.00

St. Sebaldus with church model. Rev. Eagle.

1718. 1 Goldgulden 1623-86 .... 250.00

St. Sebaldus with church model. Rev. Arms.

1719. 1 Goldgulden 1629-30 .... 250.00

Eagle. Rev. Two shields.

1720. 1 Ducat 1635, 40 .... 150.00

Eagle. Rev. Genius standing with two shields.

1721.	1 Peace Ducat 1635	....	175.00
1722.	1 Ducat 1637-86	.........................*......	150.00

Arms. Rev. Tablet.

1723.	1 Ducat 1635-45	....	150.00

Legend and arms. Rev. Two hands over globe. On the Peace.

1724.	4 Ducats 1650. Square	....	850.00
1725.	3 Ducats 1650	....	750.00
1726.	3 Ducats 1650. Square	....	800.00
1727.	2 Ducats 1650	.........................*......	200.00
1728.	1 Ducat 1650	....	125.00

Eagle and hand. Rev. Legend.

1729.	1 Ducat 1650	....	175.00

Arms. Rev. Tablet.

1730.	1 Goldgulden 1660	....	750.00

Genius with two shields. Rev. City view.

1731.	5 Ducats 1677	....	600.00

Light and screen. Rev. Legend. On the Reformation.

1732.	2 Ducats 1717. Square	.....................*......	300.00
1733.	1 Ducat 1717	....	200.00
1734.	1 Goldgulden 1617	....	150.00

Three shields. Rev. City view.

1735.	½ Ducat 1773	....	150.00

B. Coinage with the heads of the Holy Roman Emperors

Bust of Maximilian II. Rev. Two shields.

1736.	2 Goldgulden 1570	....	1000.00
1737.	1 Goldgulden 1570	....	600.00

Bust of Rudolph II. Rev. Two shields.

1738.	1 Goldgulden 1580	....	350.00

Busts of Matthias and Anna. Rev. Three shields.

1739.	2 Goldgulden 1612	....	800.00
1740.	1 Goldgulden 1612	.....................*......	200.00

Ferdinand II on horse. Rev. Genius with two shields.

1741.	10 Ducats 1630	....	1750.00

Bust of Leopold I. Rev. Three shields.

1742.	1 Goldgulden 1658	....	600.00

Bust of Leopold I. Rev. Genius with two shields.

1743.	10 Ducats ND (1670)	....	1750.00
1744.	6 Ducats ND (1670)	....	1250.00
1745.	5 Ducats ND (1670)	.....................*......	900.00
1746.	4 Ducats ND (1670)	....	800.00

City view. Rev. Pax with two genii.

1747.	5 Ducats 1698	....	500.00

Bust of Charles VI. Rev. Three shields.

1748.	1 Ducat 1711	....	750.00

Bust of Charles VI. Rev. Altar.

1749.	1 Ducat 1712	....	200.00

Bust of Charles VII. Rev. Noris standing.

1750. 1 Ducat 1742 .... 500.00

Bust of Francis I. Rev. Noris standing.

1751. 1 Ducat 1745 .... 250.00

Bust of Joseph II. Rev. Arms.

1752. 1 Ducat 1766 .... 250.00

Bust of Leopold II. Rev. City view.

1753. 1 Ducat 1790 .... 250.00

Bust of Francis II. Rev. City view.

1754. 1 Ducat ND (1792) 250.00

C. The Lamb Coinage of Nuremberg

Arms. Rev. Lamb on globe.

1755.	2 Ducats 1632	.............................*......	300.00
1756.	1 Ducat 1632	....	200.00
1757.	½ Ducat 1700. Square	....	75.00
1758.	¼ Ducat ND. Round	....	60.00
1759.	¼ Ducat ND. Square	....	40.00
1760.	⅛ Ducat ND. Round	....	40.00
1761.	⅛ Ducat ND. Square	....	30.00
1762.	1/16 Ducat ND. Round	....	30.00
1763.	1/16 Ducat ND. Square	....	30.00
1764.	1/32 Ducat ND.	....	30.00

Arms. Rev. Lamb under cross from heaven.

1765.	3 Ducats 1649. Square	....	500.00
1766.	1 Ducat 1633. Round	...................*......	200.00

Three shields. Rev. Lamb.

1767.	2 Ducats 1649	....	300.00
1768.	1 Ducat 1649	..........................*......	150.00
1769.	½ Ducat 1692	....	75.00

Three shields. Rev. Lamb on globe.

1770.	5 Ducats 1703	....	600.00
1771.	4 Ducats 1703	....	450.00
1772.	3 Ducats 1703. Round	.....................*......	400.00
1773.	3 Ducats 1700. Square	....	300.00
1774.	2 Ducats 1700. Round	....	200.00
1775.	2 Ducats 1700. Square	....	200.00
1776.	1 Ducat 1700. Round	....	100.00
1777.	1 Ducat 1700. Square	...................*......	100.00
1778.	½ Ducat 1700. Round	....	50.00
1779.	½ Ducat 1700. Square	....	50.00
1780.	¼ Ducat 1700. Square	....	30.00

City view. Rev. Lamb.

1781.	2 Ducats 1806. With laurel wreath	....	1000.00
1782.	1 Ducat 1806	..........................*......	375.00

D. Nuremberg Coinage of the Swedish Kings
GUSTAVE ADOLPHE, 1611-1632

Bust facing. Rev. Arms.

1784.	2 Ducats 1631. Thick	....	1500.00
1785.	1 Ducat 1631	..........................*......	1000.00

Bust right. Rev. Arms.

1786.	6 Ducats 1632	2500.00
1787.	2 Ducats 1632. Thick ....*	1250.00
1788.	1 Ducat 1632	200.00

Bust. Rev. Legend in wreath.

1789.	1 Ducat 1632	375.00

King standing. Rev. Arms.

1790.	1 Ducat 1632	800.00

Bust facing. Rev. Legend in square. On his death.

1791.	2 Ducats 1632	1250.00

OBERSTEINBACH

Two shields. Rev. Altar. On the Reformation.

1792.	1 Ducat 1717	250.00

OETTINGEN

Counts, and later, Princes —

WOLFGANG I AND JOACHIM, 1477-1520
Arms. Rev. St. Wolfgang

1793.	1 Goldgulden 1519, 20	1500.00

CHARLES WOLFGANG AND LOUIS XV, 1522-1549
Arms. Rev. Adoration of the three Magi.

1794.	1 Goldgulden 1522, 29, 34, 40, 41	1500.00

CHARLES WOLFGANG AND MARTIN, 1522-1549
Arms. Rev. Adoration of the three Magi.

1795.	1 Goldgulden 1529, 40	750.00

MARTIN, 1520-1549

Half length bust of Charles V. Rev. Arms.

1796.	1 Goldgulden 1541	1250.00

CHARLES WOLFGANG, LOUIS XV AND MARTIN, 1522-1549
Arms. Rev. Double eagle. Name of Charles V.

1797.	2 Goldgulden 1546	1500.00
1798.	1 Goldgulden 1546	1200.00

OETTINGEN-OETTINGEN

Princes —

ALBERT ERNEST I, 1659-1683
Bust. Rev. Arms.

1799.	2 Goldgulden 1677	1500.00
1800.	1 Ducat 1675	350.00

Bust. Rev. Legend and arms.

1801.	1 Goldgulden 1677	900.00

Monogram. Rev. Arms.

1802.	½ Ducat ND. Square	600.00
1803.	¼ Ducat ND	250.00

ALBERT ERNEST II, 1683-1731

Armored bust. Rev. Arms.

1804.	1 Ducat ND	850.00

Bust. Rev. Legend. On his death.

1805.	1 Ducat ND (1731)	500.00

OLDENBURG

Counts, and later, Dukes of —
ANTHONY GUNTHER, 1603-1667

Bust. Rev. Arms.

1806.	3 Ducats 1660. Facing bust	1000.00
1807.	1 Ducat 1664. Profile bust	300.00

FREDERICK AUGUST, 1773-1785

Bust. Rev. Arms. This is the same coin as Lubeck No. 1466.

1808.   1 Pistole 1776 ....   350.00

OSNABRUCK

A. Bishops of —

JOHN III, 1424-1437
St. Peter standing. Rev. Arms.

1809.   1 Goldgulden ND 2500.00

CONRAD IV, 1482-1508
St. Peter on throne. Rev. Arms in enclosure.

1810.   1 Goldgulden ND 250.00

St. Peter standing. Rev. Arms in enclosure.

1811.   1 Goldgulden ND ....*......   250.00
1812.   ½ Goldgulden ND 300.00

ERIC II, 1508-1532
St. Peter on throne. Rev. Arms in enclosure.

1813.   1 Goldgulden 1515, 23, 30 ....   400.00

St. Peter on throne. Rev. Cross with four arms.

1814.   1 Goldgulden ND. Mint: Wiedenbruck 500.00

FRANCIS WILLIAM, 1625-1661
St. Peter standing. Rev. Arms.

1815.   1 Ducat 1637 ....   400.00

Three shields on each side.

1816.   1 Ducat ND 400.00

ERNEST AUGUST I, 1662-1698

Bust. Rev. Arms.

1817.   1 Ducat 1666-98 ....   350.00

Bust. Rev. Horse.

1818.   ¼ Ducat 1695 ....   75.00

Bust. Rev. Horse and pillar.

1819.   2 Ducats ND 350.00

B. Swedish Kings of —

Bust of Gustave Adolphe II. Rev. Crown over legend.

1820.   1 Ducat 1633 ....   250.00

PADERBORN

Bishops of —

THEODORE ADOLPH, 1650-1660
Facing bust. Rev. Arms.

1821.   1 Ducat 1651, 53 ....   375.00

FERDINAND II, 1661-1683
Bust. Rev. Arms.

1822.   1 Ducat 1674 ....   350.00

HERMAN WERNER, 1683-1704
Bust. Rev. Arms.

1823.   1 Ducat 1684, 93 ....   350.00

FRANCES ARNOLD, 1704-1718
Bust. Rev. Arms.

1824.   1 Ducat 1713 ....   350.00

CLEMENT AUGUST, 1719-1761

Bust. Rev. Madonna and arms.

1825.   1 Goldgulden 1720 ....   300.00

WILLIAM ANTHONY, 1763-1782

Bust. Rev. Arms.

1826.   5 Taler or 1 Pistole 1767 ....*......   350.00
1827.   1 Ducat 1776, 77 ....   300.00

PALATINATE (PFALZ)

Electors of the —

RUPERT I, 1353-1390

St. John. Rev. Lily.

1828.   1 Goldgulden ND. Mints: Bacharach, Heidelberg 125.00

St. John. Rev. Arms in enclosure.

1829.   1 Goldgulden ND. Mints: Bacharach, Heidelberg,
         Oppenheim 125.00

RUPERT II, 1390-1398

St. John. Rev. Lion and wheel shield in enclosure.
1830. 1 Goldgulden ND. Mint: Neustadt 200.00

St. John. Rev. 4 arms in enclosure.
1831. 1 Goldgulden ND. Mints: Bacharach, Oppenheim 175.00

RUPERT III, 1398-1410

St. John. Rev. 5 arms in enclosure.
1832. 1 Goldgulden ND. Mints: Bacharach, Neustadt 250.00

St. John. Rev. Eagle over 2 shields.
1833. 1 Goldgulden ND. Mint: Heidelberg 375.00

LOUIS III, 1410-1436
St. Peter. Rev. 4 arms in enclosure.
1834. 1 Goldgulden ND. Mints: Bacharach, Heidelberg 150.00

St. Peter. Rev. 5 arms in enclosure.
1835. 1 Goldgulden ND. Mints: Bacharach, Heidelberg,
     Oppenheim 150.00

Christ on throne. Rev. Cross with 4 arms.
1836. 1 Goldgulden ND. Mint: Bacharach 150.00

Elector standing. Rev. Arms in enclosure.
1837. 1 Goldgulden ND. Mints: Bacharach, Heidelberg,
Neustadt (rare), Oppenheim, Ruesselsheim (rare) 150.00

LOUIS IV, 1436-1449

Arms on cross. Rev. Three shields.
1838. 1 Goldgulden 1436-38, ND. Mint: Bacharach 150.00

FREDERICK I, 1449-1476
Christ on throne. Rev. Cross with 4 arms.
1839. 1 Goldgulden ND. Mints: Bacharach, Heidelberg 125.00

Arms on cross. Rev. Three shields.
1840. 1 Goldgulden ND. Mint: Bacharach 125.00

Elector standing. Rev. Arms in enclosure.
1841. 1 Goldgulden ND. Mint: Bacharach 200.00

PHILIP, 1476-1508
Christ on throne. Rev. Arms on cross.
1842. 1 Goldgulden 1490, ND 300.00

Christ on throne. Rev. 4 arms in enclosure.
1843. 1 Goldgulden 1492, 93, 97 .... 400.00

Madonna on crescent. Rev. Three shields.
1844. 1 Goldgulden 1500, 02, 05 .... 400.00

Shield on cross. Rev. Three shields.
1845. 1 Goldgulden ND. Mint: Bacharach 200.00

Shield with 3 arms on cross. Rev. Three shields.
1846. 1 Goldgulden ND 200.00

LOUIS V, 1508-1544
Madonna. Rev. Three shields.
1847. 1 Goldgulden 1508 .... 600.00

Christ on throne. Rev. 4 shields in enclosure.
1848. 1 Goldgulden 1509, 13, 15 .... 200.00

OTTO HENRY AND PHILIP, 1505-1556
Madonna on crescent. Rev. Arms in enclosure.
1849. 1 Goldgulden 1515. Mint: Neuburg 600.00

Bust of Madonna. Rev. Arms.
1850. 1 Ducat 1516 .... 600.00

FREDERICK II, 1508-1566

Half length bust. Rev. 4 arms in enclosure.

1851.　1 Goldgulden ND. Mint: Heidelberg 1000.00

FREDERICK III, 1557-1576

Half length bust. Rev. Arms and 3 shields.

1852.　1 Goldgulden 1567. Mint: Heidelberg 750.00

Bust. Rev. Arms.

1853.　1 Goldgulden 1575 .... 750.00

LOUIS VI, 1576-1592
Bust. Rev. Arms.

1854.　2 Goldgulden 1583 .... 1500.00

FREDERICK IV, 1592-1610

Half length bust. Rev. Three shields.

1855.　1 Goldgulden 1608 .... 600.00

FREDERICK V, 1610-1632

Elector on horse. Rev. Three shields.

1856.　4 Ducats 1612 ....* 1250.00
1857.　2 Ducats 1612 .... 1000.00
1858.　1 Ducat 1612 .... 550.00

Lion. Rev. Three shields.

1859.　1 Goldgulden 1621. Mint: Heidelberg 350.00

Lion. Rev. Arms.

1860.　1 Goldgulden 1621. Mint: Heidelberg 350.00

CHARLES LOUIS, 1648-1680
Bust. Rev. Three shields. On the Vicariat.

1861.　1 Ducat 1657 .... 300.00

Bust. Rev. Three shields.

1862.　1 Ducat 1659, 62, 73 ....* 375.00
1863.　½ Rhine-gold Ducat 1674 .... 500.00
1864.　½ Ducat 1673 .... 200.00
1865.　¼ Rhine-gold Ducat 1674 .... 350.00

CHARLES, 1680-1685
Bust. Rev. Three shields.

1866.　1 Ducat 1682 .... 600.00

JOHN WILLIAM, 1690-1716
Bust. Rev. Ten shields.

1867.　2 Ducats 1707 .... 400.00
1868.　2 Ducats 1707. "Hoc Bellonae Stipendium" 400.00
1869.　1 Ducat 1707 .... 300.00
1870.　1 Ducat 1707. "Hoc Bellonae Stipendium" 300.00

Bust. Rev. Imperial globe in shield.

1871.　1 Ducat 1708 .... 300.00
1872.　¼ Ducat 1711 .... 175.00

Bust. Rev. Three shields.

1873.　1 Ducat 1708 .... 375.00

Bust. Rev. Double eagle. On the Vicariat.

1874.　3 Ducats 1711 .... 750.00
1875.　2 Ducats 1711 .... * 500.00
1876.　1 Ducat 1711 .... 300.00
1877.　¼ Ducat 1711 .... 150.00

Bust. Rev. Arms.

1878.　1 Ducat 1683, 86, 1703 .... 300.00
1879.　½ Ducat 1705, 08 .... 150.00

Bust. Rev. Value.

1880.　¼ Ducat 1708 .... 150.00

Head Rev. Imperial globe in shield.

1881.　¼ Ducat 1710 .... 150.00

CHARLES PHILIP, 1716-1742

Young bust of Prince Philip August. Rev. The Prince standing. Struck by the city of Mannheim.

1882.   1 Ducat 1725 ....   350.00

Head. Rev. Three shields.

1883.   1 Ducat 1737 ....   450.00

Bust. Rev. Double Eagle. On the Vicariat.

1884.   1 Ducat 1740 ....   350.00

Bust. Rev. City view of Mannheim.

1885.   1 Rhine-gold Ducat ND 400.00

Bust. Rev. Three shields.

1886.   1 Ducat 1721 ....   300.00

Elector on horse. Rev. Five shields crossed.

1887.   1 Ducat 1721, 26 ....   300.00

Head. Rev. Five shields crossed between four initials.

1888.   1 Carolin 1732 ....   500.00
1889.   ½ Carolin 1732 ....   300.00

Head. Rev. Arms.

1890.   1 Carolin 1733, 35 ....*......   300.00
1891.   ½ Carolin 1733, 36 ....   200.00
1892.   ¼ Carolin 1735, 36 ....   150.00

Head. Rev. Crown over three arms supported by lions.

1893.   1 Carolin 1733 ....   800.00

Bust. Rev. Crown over three arms supported by lions.

1894.   ½ Carolin 1732 ....   800.00

CHARLES THEODORE, 1743-1799

Bust. Rev. Four initials and arms.

1895.   1 Carolin 1748, 49 (very rare), 50 ....   350.00

Bust. Rev. Three shields.

1896.   2 Ducats 1750. (Dusseldorf) 600.00

Bust. Rev. Arms.

1897.   1 Ducat 1749 (rare), 50, 51 ....   300.00

Bust. Rev. St. Hubertus Order.

1898.   1 Ducat 1750 ....   300.00

Head. Rev. Arms.

1899.   1 Ducat 1764 ....   400.00

Head. Rev. Three shields.

1900.   1 Ducat 1769 ....   250.00

Head or bust. Rev. City view of Mannheim.

1901.   1 Rhine-gold Ducat 1763, 64, 67, 78 ....   300.00

Conjoined heads of Charles and Elizabeth Augusta. Rev. Two shields.

1902.   1 Ducat 1742. Struck at Mannheim 250.00

Small bust. Rev. Fortuna.

1903. 1 Lottery Ducat ND 400.00

Arms of Heidelberg. Rev. Long legend.

1904. 1 Homage Ducat 1746 .... 200.00

City shield of Mannheim. Rev. Legend.

1905. 1 Homage Ducat 1744 .... 200.00

City shield of Mannheim. Rev. Legend. On the 50th year of reign.

1906. 1 Ducat 1792 .... 200.00

(For other coins of Charles Theodore, see under BAVARIA)

PALATINATE-BIRKENFELD-ZWEIBRUCKEN

Counts —

CHRISTIAN IV, 1735-1775
Bust. Rev. Arms.

1907. 1 Ducat 1747, 51 .... 750.00

CHARLES AUGUST, 1775-1795
Head. Rev. Arms.

1908. 2 Ducats 1788 .... 750.00

Head. Rev. Arms supported by lions.

1909. 1 Ducat 1788, 90 .... 450.00

PALATINATE-MOSBACH

Counts —

OTTO II, 1461-1499

Madonna. Rev. Arms.

1910. 1 Goldgulden 1496 .... 800.00

PALATINATE-NEUBURG

Counts —

PHILIP WILLIAM, 1653-1690

Bust. Rev. Sun. On his daughter's marriage.

1911. 1 Ducat 1676 .... 350.00

Bust. Rev. Arms.

1912. 1 Ducat 1654 .... 400.00

PALATINATE-SIMMERN

Counts —

STEPHAN, 1410-1453

Count standing. Rev. Arms in enclosure.

1913. 1 Goldgulden ND. Mints: Simmern, Wachenheim (rare) .. 300.00

FREDERICK I, 1453-1480

Count standing. Rev. Arms in enclosure.

1914. 1 Goldgulden ND 400.00

RICHARD, 1569-1598

Count standing. Rev. Arms and value.

1915.	2 Ducats 1576	800.00
1916.	1 Ducat 1576-79, 87 ....*......	125.00

PALATINATE-SULZBACH

Counts —

CHRISTIAN AUGUST, 1632-1708
Bust. Rev. Arms.

1917.	1 Ducat 1682	450.00

Arms. Rev. Resurrection of Christ.

1918.	¼ Ducat ND	150.00

PALATINATE-VELDENZ

Counts —

GEORGE GUSTAVE, 1592-1634
Count standing. Rev. Arms.

1919.	1 Ducat 1596	600.00

LEOPOLD LOUIS, 1634-1694
Bust. Rev. Arms.

1920.	1 Ducat 1673	600.00

PALATINATE-ZWEIBRUCKEN

Counts —

LOUIS, 1459-1489
Count standing. Rev. Arms in enclosure.

1921.	1 Goldgulden ND. Mint: Wachenheim	400.00

Arms on cross. Rev. Three shields.

1922.	1 Goldgulden ND. Mint: Wachenheim	500.00

JOHN II, 1604-1635

Arms. Rev. Double Eagle.

1923.	1 Goldgulden 1611, 16-19, 24, ND	200.00

PASSAU

Bishops of —

VIGILIUS FROESCHL, 1500-1517
St. Stephan. Rev. Cross.

1924.	1 Goldgulden 1508	800.00

ERNEST, 1517-1540
St. Stephan. Rev. Arms.

1925.	1 Ducat 1522, 37	700.00

URBAN, 1561-1598
St. Stephan. Rev. Double eagle.

1925a.	4 Ducats 1563	Rare
1926.	2 Ducats 1567	800.00
1927.	1 Ducat 1570	500.00

SEBASTIAN, 1673-1689

1928.	¼ Ducat 1674	100.00
1929.	⅛ Ducat 1674	100.00

JOHN PHILIP, 1689-1712

Bust. Rev. Arms.

1930.	2 Ducats 1698, 1701	500.00
1931.	1 Ducat 1698, 1705, 06, 09 ....*......	250.00

Monogram. Rev. Arms.

1932.	½ Ducat 1709	150.00

RAYMOND FERDINAND, 1713-1722
Bust. Rev. Arms.

1933.	1 Ducat 1716	250.00

Initials. Rev. Fox with arms.

1934.	½ Ducat 1716	150.00

JOSEPH DOMINIC, 1723-1761

Bust. Rev. Arms.

1935.	1 Ducat 1747	250.00

LEOPOLD ERNEST, 1763-1783

Bust. Rev. Arms.

1936.	1 Ducat 1779	250.00

POMERANIA

A. Dukes of —

BOGISLAUS X, 1474-1523
Madonna. Rev. Arms on cross.
1937. 1 Goldgulden 1499, ND 750.00

JOHN FREDERICK, 1569-1600
Half length bust. Rev. Arms.
1938. 1 Ducat 1594, 96 .... 250.00

PHILIP JULIUS, 1592-1625
Bust. Rev. Arms.
1939. 1 Goldgulden 1609, 11 .... 300.00

PHILIP II, 1606-1618
Bust. Rev. Arms.
1940. 1 Goldgulden 1612, 13 .... 250.00

Arms supported by wild men. Rev. David with his harp.
1941. 2 Goldgulden 1614 .... 400.00

Bust. Rev. David with his harp.
1942. 2 Goldgulden 1614 .... 400.00

Bust. Rev. Crossed sword and pen.
1943. 1 Goldgulden 1614, 15 .... 225.00

Bust. Rev. Light.
1944. 2 Goldgulden 1615 .... 400.00
1945. 1 Goldgulden 1615 .... 300.00

Bust. Rev. Stag.
1946. 2 Goldgulden 1615 .... 600.00
1947. 1 Goldgulden 1615, 16 .... 300.00

Bust. Rev. Snail.
1948. 2 Goldgulden 1617 .... 600.00
1949. 1 Goldgulden 1617, 18 .... 300.00

Bust. Rev. Wreath with SOLI DEO GLORIA.
1950. 2 Goldgulden 1616 .... 400.00
1951. 1 Goldgulden 1616-18 .... 200.00

Bust. Rev. Legend. On the Reformation.
1952. 1 Goldgulden 1617 .... 400.00
Man with lamb. Rev. Legend. On the Reformation.
1953. 1 Goldgulden 1617 .... 400.00

FRANCIS, 1618-1620
Bust. Rev. Griffin.
1954. 1 Goldgulden 1618 .... 400.00

BOGISLAUS XIV, 1620-1637
Bust. Rev. Griffin in shield.
1955. 1 Goldgulden 1632 .... Rare

Bust. Rev. Arms.
1956. 1 Goldgulden 1628 .... 225.00

Bust and helmet. Rev..Griffin.
1957. 1 Goldgulden 1629 .... 225.00

Duke standing. Rev. Arms.
1958. 1 Ducat 1629, 31, 33-36, ND 200.00

Duke standing. Rev. Arms with three helmets.
1959. 1 Ducat 1633, ND 200.00

Legend. Rev. Skull. On his burial.
1960. 1 Ducat 1654 .... 200.00
1961. ½ Ducat 1654 .... 125.00

B. Swedish Rulers of —

CHRISTINA, 1632-1654

Facing bust. Rev. Christ over arms.
1962. 1 Ducat 1641 .... 500.00

Facing half length bust. Rev. Arms.
1963. 1 Ducat 1642 .... 600.00

Facing bust. Rev. Arms.
1964. 1 Ducat 1642, 46, 53 .... 300.00

Bust. Rev. Arms.
1965. 2½ Ducats 1653 .... 2500.00

CHARLES X, 1654-1660

Bust. Rev. Arms.
1966. 2 Ducats 1658 .... 2000.00

King standing. Rev. Arms.
1967. 1 Ducat 1654, 56, 58, 59 .... 1500.00

CHARLES XI, 1660-1697

Small bust in circle. Rev. Arms supported by wild men.
1968. 2 Ducats 1661 ....*...... 1200.00
1969. 1 Ducat 1662 .... 1200.00

Large bust not in circle. Rev. Arms supported by wild men.
1970. 3 Ducats 1674 .... 1500.00

1971. 2 Ducats 1684, 90 .... 1000.00
1972. 1 Ducat 1672-75, 82, 84, 86, 89, 90, 95, 97 ..*...... 900.00
1973. 1 Ducat 1666. Without the wild men ....*...... 1500.00

Large bust. Rev. Crown, orb and crossed swords over sheaf.
1974. 2 Ducats 1692-94, 96, 97, ND 900.00

CHARLES XII, 1697-1718

Half length bust. Rev. Lion between falling and broken columns.
1975. 2 Ducats 1706 .... 1000.00

Half length bust. Rev. Five line legend in wreath.
1976. 2 Ducats 1706 .... 900.00

Bust with long hair. Rev. Arms.
1977. 1 Ducat 1706 .... 400.00

Bust with short hair. Rev. Arms.
1978. 1 Ducat 1706, 09 .... 400.00

ADOLPH FREDERICK, 1751-1771

Head. Rev. Griffin and value.
1979. 10 Taler 1759 .... 1200.00
1980. 5 Taler 1758 (very rare), 59 ....*...... 750.00

PRUSSIA

A. Brandenburg, Electors of —

JOACHIM AND ALBERT, 1499-1514
St. Paul standing. Rev. Cross and five shields.
1981. 1 Goldgulden ND. Mint: Brandenburg 1200.00
1982. 1 Goldgulden ND. Mint: Berlin 900.00

JOACHIM I, 1499-1535
St. Paul standing. Rev. Cross and five shields.
1983. 1 Goldgulden 1516, 18, 19, 21. Mint: Frankfurt (Oder) .. 1000.00

St. John standing. Rev. Cross and five shields.
1984. 1 Goldguden 1526. Mint: Frankfurt (Oder) 1200.00

JOACHIM II, 1535-1571
St. John. Rev. Cross and five shields.
1985. 2 Goldgulden 1540 .... 3000.00
1986. 1 Goldgulden 1538-40 .... 2500.00

Eagle. Rev. Double eagle.
1987. 1 Goldgulden 1552 .... 1750.00

Five shields. Rev. Double eagle.
1988. 1 Goldgulden 1557 .... 1750.00

Bust. Rev. Arms.
1989. 2 Ducats 1560 .... 3000.00
1990. 1 Ducat 1560, 66 .... 1600.00

Arms. Rev. Cross.
1991. 10 Ducats 1570 .... 6000.00

JOHN GEORGE, 1571-1598
Eagle. Rev. Five shields.
1992. 1 Goldgulden 1573, 87 .... 1500.00

Armored bust. Rev. Arms and legend.
1993. 2 Ducats 1584 .... 3000.00

Armored bust. Rev. Cross and shields.
1994. 10 Ducats 1584, 87 .... 6000.00
1995. 5 Ducats 1590 .... 5000.00

Armored bust. Rev. Arms.
1996. 1 Ducat 1590 .... 1500.00

JOACHIM FREDERICK, 1598-1608
Elector standing. Rev. Eagle.
1997. 2 Ducats 1606 .... 2500.00
1998. 1 Ducat 1605, 06 .... 1000.00

Half length bust. Rev. Cross.
1999. 10 Ducats 1605 .... 6000.00

JOHN SIGISMUND, 1608-1619
Bust. Rev. Arms.
2000. 1 Goldgulden 1615 .... 800.00

Facing bust. Rev. Arms.
2001. 1 Goldgulden 1614, 17 .... 600.00

Half length bust. Rev. Arms.
2002. 1 Goldgulden 1617 .... 1000.00

Bust. Rev. Arms.
2003. 1 Ducat ND 1500.00

Elector standing. Rev. Eagle.
2004. 1 Ducat 1611, 12, 14 .... 750.00

Elector standing. Rev. Arms.
2005. 2 Ducats 1615 .... 1600.00

Bust. Rev. Cross.
2006. 10 Ducats 1612 .... 6000.00
2007. 5 Ducats 1611, 13, 14 .... 5000.00

GEORGE WILLIAM, 1619-1640
I. Berlin Mint with or without Mintmaster's Initials LM
Elector on horse. Rev. Sceptre within two circles of 24 shields.
2008. 10 Ducats 1620 (LM) 6000.00

Bust. Rev. Sceptre shield.
2009. 1 Goldgulden 1620 (LM) 2400.00

Bust. Rev. Arms with 7 fields.
2010. 1 Goldgulden 1622 .... 800.00

Bust. Rev. Arms with 12 fields.
2011. 2 Goldgulden 1621 .... 1500.00

Elector standing before desk with helmet. Rev. Five Arms.
2012. 1 Ducat 1620 (LM) 2400.00

Elector standing before desk with helmet. Rev. Sceptre within circle of 8 shields.
2013. 2 Ducats 1620 (LM) 800.00

Elector standing before desk with helmet. Rev. Arms.
2014. 2 Ducats ND (LM) 1500.00

II. Cologne Mint with Mintmaster's Initials LM or IP
Bust in elector's robes. Rev. Arms with 12 fields.
2015. 2 Ducats 1626 (IP) from the ducat die 2000.00
2016. 1 Ducat 1626 (IP) 1500.00
2017. 1 Goldgulden 1628 (LM) 1500.00

Elector standing. Rev. Sceptre within circle of shields.
2018. 1 Ducat 1639 (LM) 600.00

Armored bust with sceptre. Rev. Arms.
2019. 1 Goldgulden 1628 (LM) 600.00

Bust in elector's robes with sceptre. Rev. Arms.
2020. 2 Goldgulden ND (LM) 1600.00

Bust in elector's robes with sceptre. Rev. Arms under elector's hat.
2021. 2 Goldgulden 1628 (LM) 1600.00

Elector standing at desk with helmet. Rev. Arms.
2022. 2 Ducats 1634 (LM), 36 (LM) 450.00

Elector standing at desk with helmet. Rev. Oval arms.
2023. 2 Ducats 1635 (LM) 750.00

Elector standing at desk with helmet. Rev. Eagle with shields.
2024. 2 Ducats 1637 (LM), 38, 40 .... 400.00

Elector on horse. Rev. Eagle with 14 shields.
2025. 10 Ducats 1634 (LM) 5000.00
2026. 5 Ducats 1634 (LM) 4000.00

III. Koenigsberg Mint with Initials DK or a heart
Elector standing. Rev. Arms under elector's hat.
2027. 1 Ducat 1625 .... 800.00

Elector standing. Rev. Arms with 12 fields.
2028. 1 Ducat 1627 (heart) 800.00

Elector standing. Rev. Arms with 5 fields under elector's hat.
2029. 1 Ducat 1631, 32 (heart) 800.00

Bust with elector's hat. Rev. Arms with 5 fields under elector's hat.
2030. 2 Ducats 1634 (heart) 1600.00
2031. 1 Ducat 1633, 34 (heart) 500.00
2032. 1 Ducat 1635-40 (DK) 250.00

Bust with elector's hat. Rev. Arms with 9 fields under elector's hat.
2033. 1 Ducat 1635 (DK and heart) .... *...... 300.00
2034. 1 Ducat 1638, 39 (DK) 300.00

Bust. Rev. Arms with 9 fields under elector's hat.
2035. 1 Ducat 1639 (DK) 750.00

FREDERICK WILLIAM, 1640-1688
I. Berlin Mint with initials LM, AB, LCS, CT, IL, or CS
Half length bust in elector's robes with sceptre. Rev. Arms with 25 fields.
2036. 5 Ducats 1650 (CT) 1500.00

Elector standing at desk with helmet. Rev. Arms with 25 fields.
2037. 5 Ducats 1652, 53, 55, 57 (CT) 1500.00

Elector standing at desk with helmet. Rev. Arms with 10 fields.
2038. 4 Ducats 1666 (IL) 1750.00

Armored half length bust with sceptre. Rev. Arms with 25 fields.
2039. 5 Ducats 1653 (CT) 1200.00

Armored bust. Rev. Sceptre shield with the ribbon of the Order of the Garter between branches.
2040. 4 Ducats 1675 (CS) 6500.00

Elector standing. Rev. Eagle with 12 shields.
2041. 2 Ducats 1641 (LM) 1250.00

Elector standing in wreath of flowers. Rev. Arms with 12 fields in wreath of flowers.
2042. 2 Ducats 1641 (sometimes with LM) 450.00

Elector standing. Rev. Arms with 23 fields.
2043. 2 Ducats 1643, 44 (AB) 450.00
2044. 2 Ducats 1646 (CT) 450.00

Elector standing. Rev. Arms with 25 fields under elector's hat.
2045. 2 Ducats 1650, 54 (CT) 450.00

Armored half length bust. Rev. Arms with 25 fields under elector's hat.
2046. 2 Ducats 1654 (CT), 1665 (IL) 1000.00

Bust. Rev. Arms between palm-branches.
2047. 2 Ducats 1669 .... 750.00

Bust with elector's hat. Rev. Arms between palm-branches.
2048. 2 Ducats 1670 .... 1000.00

Elector standing at desk. Rev. 6 shields and sceptre.
2049. 1 Ducat 1641 (LM) 600.00

Elector standing at desk. Rev. Arms with 9 fields.
2050. 1 Ducat 1641 (LM) 600.00

Elector standing at desk. Rev. Arms with 12 fields.
2051. 1 Ducat 1643 (AB) 600.00

Elector standing at desk. Rev. Arms with 14 fields under elector's hat.
2052. 1 Ducat 1651 (CT) 600.00

Elector standing knee-length. Rev. Arms with 14 fields under elector's hat.
2053. 5 Ducats 1654 (CT, from the ducat die) 1750.00
2054. 1 Ducat 1654, 56 (CT) 600.00

Armored bust. Rev. Sceptre shield surrounded by 13 shields.
2055. 1 Ducat 1662 (AB) 275.00
2056. 1 Ducat 1665, 66 (IL) 600.00

Bust. Rev. Sceptre shield surrounded by 13 shields.
2057. 1 Ducat 1667 (IL) 500.00

Draped bust. Rev. Sceptre shield between branches.
2058. 1 Ducat 1668, 73, 74 (IL), 75 (CS), 77 (CS) 500.00

Naked bust. Rev. Sceptre shield between branches.
2059. 1 Ducat 1669-72 (IL) 400.00

Armored bust. Rev. Sceptre shield between branches.
2060. 1 Ducat 1679-82 (CS) 400.00
2061. 1 Ducat 1683-85 (LCS) 300.00

Armored and draped bust. Rev. Sceptre shield between branches.
2062. 1 Ducat 1685, 86 (LCS) 300.00

Armored half length bust. Rev. Sceptre shield between branches.
2063. 1 Ducat 1686, 87 .... 500.00

Bust in elector's robes. Rev. Sceptre shield.

2064. ¾ Ducat 1656 (CT) 750.00

Bust in elector's robes. Rev. Sceptre shield between branches.

2065. ½ Ducat ND 750.00

Bust in elector's robes. Rev. Arms with 14 fields.

2066. ½ Ducat 1655 (CT) 150.00

Helmeted head. Rev. Crown over flying eagle.

2067. ½ Ducat 1668 (IL) 200.00
2068. ¼ Ducat 1668 (IL) 200.00

Bust. Rev. Crown over flying eagle.

2069. ¼ Ducat 1675 (IL) 200.00

Bust. Rev. Ship. Trade coins for Guinea, Africa.

2070. 1 Ducat 1682 (CS) 400.00
2071. 1 Ducat 1682, 83, 85, 86 (LCS) ....*...... 400.00

Armored half length bust. Rev. Ship. For Guinea.

2072. 1 Ducat 1686-88 (LCS) 400.00

Facing bust. Rev. Legend. On his 35th birthday and on the birth of Prince Charles Emil.

2073. 4 Ducats 1655 (AB) 750.00
2074. 3 Ducats 1655 (CT) 500.00
2075. 2 Ducats 1655 (with or without elector's hat) 350.00

Bust. Rev. City view of Stettin; above eagle and griffin. On the conquest of Stettin.

2076. 2 Ducats 1677 (CS). FORTIOR HIS SIGNIS 200.00
2077. 2 Ducats 1677 (CS). LUCE RESURGO NOVA 200.00

Elector on horse. Rev. Legend. On the conquest of Stettin.

2078. ½ Ducat 1677 .... 150.00

Bust with elector's hat. Rev. Arms.

2079. 1 Ducat 1646 (CT). For Prussia 250.00

Elector standing knee length. Rev. Crowned arms.

2080. 1 Ducat 1665 (IL). For Prussia 600.00

Bust. Rev. Crowned arms.

2081. 1 Ducat 1665 (IL). For Prussia 750.00

II. Halberstadt Mint with initials LCS
Bust. Rev. Sceptre between branches.

2082. 1 Ducat 1679 (LCS) 1500.00

III. Koenigsberg Mint with initials DK, HM, TT, CV, HS, BA, CM, CG, DS, NB
Bust. Rev. Arms.

2083. 5 Ducats ND (1657, DK) 2000.00
2084. 4 Ducats ND (1657, DK) 1750.00

Elector on horse. Rev. Rose in circle of shields.

2085. 5 Ducats ND 1750.00
2086. 3 Ducats ND 1000.00
2087. 2 Ducats ND ....*...... 400.00

Head. Rev. Head of Prince Charles Emil. On the 14th birthday of the Prince.

2088. 2 Ducats 1669 (CG) 500.00

Bust. Rev. Crowned arms.

2089. 2 Ducats 1670-72 (TT) 500.00
2090. 2 Ducats 1673, 74 (CV) 500.00
2091. 2 Ducats 1675, 79, 82-84 (HS) 450.00
2092. 2 Ducats 1686 (BA) 600.00

Bust with elector's hat. Rev. Arms.

2093. 1 Ducat 1641, 48, 49 (DK) 300.00

Facing bust. Rev. Arms.

2094. 1 Ducat 1643 (DK) 500.00

Bust. Rev. Arms.

2095. 1 Ducat 1651 (CM) 350.00
2096. 1 Ducat 1657 (DK), 1660 over 1657 .... 300.00

Bust in elector's robes. Rev. Arms.

2097. 1 Ducat 1657 (NB), 1658 (without NB) 350.00

Armored bust. Rev. Arms.

2098. 1 Ducat 1661-63 (HM) 300.00

Crowned bust with sword. Rev. Arms with 5 fields.

2099. 1 Ducat 1664-66 ....*...... 300.00
2100. 1 Ducat 1667 (CG) 300.00

Bust. Rev. Eagle.

2101. 1 Ducat 1668 (CG and DS) 400.00
2102. 1 Ducat 1673, 74 (CV) 750.00
2103. ½ Ducat 1670, 71 (TT), 1685 (HS) ....*...... 150.00

Head. Rev. Crowned arms.

2104. 1 Ducat 1669 (CG and DS) 250.00

Bust. Rev. Crowned arms.

2105. 1 Ducat 1670-72 (TT) 350.00
2106. 1 Ducat 1679, 81, 82 (HS) 400.00

Bust. Rev. Crowned oval arms.

2107. 1 Ducat 1676, 83, 84 (HS) 350.00
2108. 1 Ducat 1685, 86 (BA) 400.00

Bust. Rev Crowned round arms.

2109. 1 Ducat 1687 (HS) 400.00

IV. Magdeburg Mint with initials IE
Bust. Rev. Arms.

2110. 5 Ducats 1683 (IE) 2000.00

V. Luenen Mint
Facing bust. Rev. Arms with 4 fields.

2111. 1 Ducat 1659 (M-M for Moneta Marcana) 1500.00

Bust. Rev. Arms with 4 fields.

2112. 1 Ducat 1660, 62 .... 750.00

Facing bust. Rev. Arms with 6 fields.

2113. 1 Ducat 1664 .... 750.00

VI. Minden Mint with initials HB
Bust in elector's robes. Rev. Arms with 26 fields.

2114. 1 Ducat 1652 (HB) 800.00

Bust. Rev. Arms with 5 fields.

2115. 1 Ducat 1670 (HB) 600.00

VII. Ravensberg Mint struck at Bielefeld
Arms. Rev. Value on tablet.

2116. 1 Ducat 1648 .... 1250.00

Bust in elector's robes. Rev. Arms with 6 fields.

2117. 1 Ducat 1648 .... 600.00

FREDERICK III, 1688-1701 (I, 1701-1713)
I. Berlin Mint with initials LCS, S or RF
Bust. Rev. Crossed initials.

2118. 1 Ducat 1688 .... 750.00
2119. 1 Ducat 1697 (RF and LCS) 400.00
2120. 1 Ducat 1697 (RF and LCS). Without Order of the Garter 750.00

Bust. Rev. Sceptre in shield.

2121. 1 Ducat 1689, 90 (LCS) 400.00
2122. 1 Ducat 1696 (LCS). Without Order of the Garter 400.00

Head. Rev. Crossed initials.

2123. 2 Ducats 1698-1700 (RF and LCS) 600.00
2124. 1 Ducat 1698, 99 (RF and LCS) 400.00

Bust with mantle. Rev. Ship. Trade coin for Guinea, Africa.

2125. 1 Ducat 1688, 90 (LCS) 400.00

Bust. Rev. Ship. Trade coin for Guinea.

2126. 1 Ducat 1692, 94-96 (S and LCS) 400.00

II. Koenigsberg Mint with initials HS, SD or CG
Laureate bust. Rev. Arms.

2127. 1 Ducat 1691, 93 (HS) 600.00
2128. 1 Ducat 1695, 97 (SD) 700.00
2129. 1 Ducat 1700 (CG) 700.00

Laureate bust. Rev. Eagle.

2130. ½ Ducat 1700 (CG) 250.00

III. Magdeburg Mint with initials ICS
Bust. Rev. Sceptre in shield.

2131. 1 Ducat 1692 (ICS) 750.00

IV. Minden Mint with initials BH
Bust. Rev. Arms with 25 fields.

2132. 1 Ducat 1691 (BH) 750.00

Bust. Rev. Sceptre in shield and eagle with crown.

2133. 1 Ducat 1695 (BH) 750.00

Bust. Rev. Sceptre in shield.

2134. ½ Ducat 1695 (BH) 400.00

(The coinage of Frederick III continues directly below under B,
as Frederick I, King of Prussia.)

B. Kings of —

FREDERICK I, 1701-1713
*Mints and the initials of the mint masters or engravers
as they appear on the coins.*
Berlin Mint: LCS, CS, L, CFL, M, R
Koenigsberg Mint: CG, GWM
Magdeburg Mint: HFH
Minden Mint: BH

Head. Rev. Cross of initials.

2135. 2 Ducats 1701. Thick. LCS 1250.00
2136. 1 Ducat 1701. LCS ....*....... 400.00

Bust over legend. Rev. Crown. On his Coronation.

2137. 1 Ducat 1701. Koenigsberg Mint 250.00

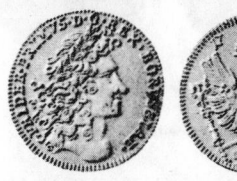

Head. Rev. Crowned eagle.

2138. 1 Ducat 1701. CS ....*...... 400.00
2139. 1 Ducat 1703, 04. CFL and CS 250.00

Bust. Rev. Initials in chain of Order.

2140. 1 Ducat 1705-12. L and CS 250.00
2141. 1 Ducat 1707-09. HFH 800.00
2142. 1 Ducat 1706. BH 800.00

Head. Rev. Flying eagle.

2143. 2 Ducats 1701. Thick. R and CS 1250.00
2144. 2 Ducats 1712. HFH 600.00
2145. 1 Ducat 1710. R and CS 800.00
2146. ½ Ducat 1712. HFH 200.00

Bust. Rev. Eagle shield.

2147. 2 Ducats 1713. CG 1200.00
2148. 2 Ducats 1703, 04. Thick. CG 1000.00
2149. 1 Ducat 1702-12. CG ....*...... 200.00
2150. 1 Ducat 1713. GWM and CG 800.00

Head. Rev. Crowned arms. Struck for Neuchatel.

2151. 1 Ducat 1713. JP 800.00

Bust. Rev. Crown on altar. On his death.

2152. 1 Ducat 1713. L with or without CS 200.00

FREDERICK WILLIAM AND SOPHIA DOROTHEA, 1706

*Busts. Rev. Legend. On their wedding. Magdeburg Mint with
initials HFH.*

2153. 2 Ducats 1706 .... 500.00

2154.	1 Ducat 1706 ....*	250.00
2155.	½ Ducat 1706, 12	150.00
2156.	¼ Ducat 1706, 12	100.00
2157.	¼ Ducat 1706. With legend "Frid:Wilh:D.G.Rex. Boruss"	200.00

FREDERICK WILLIAM I, 1713-1740

*Mints and the initials of the mint masters or engravers
as they appear on the coins.*

**Berlin Mint: IFS, IGN, EGN, L, M
Koenigsberg Mint: CG, M
Magdeburg Mint: HFH**

Bust. Rev. Eagle flying to sun.

2158.	1 Ducat 1713. L and IFS	250.00
2159.	¼ Ducat 1713. HFH	100.00

Bust. Rev. Eagle.

2160.	1 Ducat 1714. HFH	500.00
2161.	1 Ducat 1733. EGN	200.00

Laureate head. Rev. Eagle flying to sun.

2162.	2 Ducats 1713. HFH	900.00
2163.	1 Ducat 1713. CG with or without M or L ....*	250.00
2164.	1 Ducat 1713. HFH	250.00
2165.	½ Ducat 1713. HFH	150.00
2166.	¼ Ducat 1713. HFH	150.00

Bust. Rev. Initials and crown in chain of Order.

2167.	1 Ducat 1714. L and IFS	375.00

Bust. Rev. Arms with five fields.

2168.	1 Ducat 1714. L and IFS	600.00

Bust. Rev. Arms with six fields.

2169.	1 Ducat 1715, 16. L and IFS	400.00
2170.	1 Ducat 1714-17. CG with M or L	250.00
2171.	1 Ducat 1714. HFH	250.00

Bust. Rev. Arms with twelve fields.

2172.	1 Ducat 1714. HFH	400.00

Bust. Rev. Arms with forty fields.

2173.	1 Ducat 1714. HFH	250.00
2174.	¼ Ducat 1715. HFH	75.00

Laureate head. Rev. Arms with forty fields.

2175.	½ Ducat 1714. HFH	100.00
2176.	¼ Ducat 1715. HFH	75.00

Bust. Rev. Star of Order with legend.

2177.	1 Ducat 1717. L and IFS	200.00
2178.	1 Ducat 1733-40. EGN	200.00
2179.	1 Ducat 1714. HFH	200.00

Bust. Rev. Star of Order without legend.

2180.	1 Ducat 1714-16. IFS	200.00
2181.	1 Ducat 1714. CG and M	600.00
2182.	1 Ducat 1715. No initials	600.00
2183.	1 Ducat 1714, 16. Plain bust. HFH ....*	200.00
2184.	1 Ducat 1717. Laureate bust. HFH	225.00
2185.	¼ Ducat 1716. HFH	75.00

Laureate head. Rev. Star of Order.

2186.	½ Ducat 1714. HFH	100.00
2187.	¼ Ducat 1714, 16. HFH	75.00

Bust with pigtail. Rev. Oval Arms.

2188.	1 Ducat 1718-28. CG with or without M	200.0
2189.	1 Ducat 1718. HFH with or without L	200.0

Bust with pigtail. Rev. Star of Order with legend.

2190.	1 Ducat 1717, 18. HFH with or without M	200.0

Bust with or without L. Rev. Oval arms with six fields.

2191.	2 Ducats 1724. IGN	800.0
2192.	2 Ducats 1732. EGN	1000.0
2193.	1 Ducat 1716. M and IFS	250.0
2194.	1 Ducat 1717, 18. IFS	250.0
2195.	1 Ducat 1719-25. IGN	200.0
2196.	1 Ducat 1725-32. EGN	200.0
2197.	½ Ducat 1726. EGN	200.0

Bust. Rev. Flying eagle.

2198.	2 Ducats 1733. EGN	800.0
2199.	1 Ducat 1733, 34. EGN	200.0

Bust. Rev. Cross of initials.

2200.	1 William D'or 1737-40. EGN on Obv. or Rev. .*	450.0
2201.	½ William D'or 1738-40. EGN	250.0

FREDERICK II, THE GREAT, 1740-1786

*Mints, mint marks and the initials of mint masters or
mint officials as they appear on the coins.*

**Berlin Mint: A mm, EGN, CHI, ALS
Breslau Mint: B mm, AHE, AE
Cleve Mint: C mm
Aurich Mint: D mm**

Head. Rev. Justice standing. On the Homage of Koenigsberg.

2202.	1 Ducat 1740. No initials	125.00

Head. Rev. Legend. On the Homage of Berlin.

2203.	1 Ducat 1740. No initials	125.00

Armored bust. Rev. Crowned eagle shield.

2204.	1 Ducat 1741-45. EGN	250.0
2205.	1 Ducat 1743-48. AHE	250.0

Armored bust. Rev. Crowned initials in chain of Order.

2206.	1 Ducat 1745. EGN	250.0

Armored bust. Rev. Flying eagle over trophies.

2207.	1 Ducat 1745-49. EGN	250.0
2208.	1 Ducat 1749. CHI	250.0

Armored bust. Rev. Eagle on globe over branches.

2209.	2 Ducats 1749. EGN	800.0
2210.	1 Ducat 1749. EGN	600.0

Armored bust. Rev. Eagle over trophies and value.

2211.	1 Ducat 1753, 54. A mm	200.0

Bare bust. Rev. Eagle over trophies and value.

2212. 1 Ducat 1754, 57. B mm 250.00

Armored bust. Rev. Cross of initials.

2213. 1 Frederick D'or 1744-48. AE 300.00

Armored bust. Rev. Crowned eagle between trophies. The last coin was struck in lower grade gold during the Seven Year War.

2214. 2 Frederick D'or 1749. ALS 400.00
2215. 2 Frederick D'or 1750-52. A mm 400.00
2216. 2 Frederick D'or 1747-49. W on shield. AHE 500.00
2217. 1 Frederick D'or 1741-46. EGN 200.00
2218. 1 Frederick D'or 1750-52, 59. A mm ....*..... 150.00
2219. 1 Frederick D'or 1749. Bust left. ALS 300.00
2220. 1 Frederick D'or 1746-49. W on shield. AHE or AE ... 250.00
2221. 1 Frederick D'or 1750. AE 250.00
2222. 1 Frederick D'or 1750, 64. B on shield. B mm or AE .. 225.00
2223. ½ Frederick D'or 1749 CHI 125.00
2224. ½ Frederick D'or 1750-52. A mm 100.00
2225. 1 Frederick D'or 1755, 56. A mm 300.00

Head. Rev. Crowned eagle shield.

2226. 1 Frederick D'or 1750. A mm 300.00

Armored bust. Rev. Eagle and lion's head between trophies.

2227. 1 Frederick D'or 1752, 53. D mm 850.00

Head. Rev. Crowned eagle between trophies.

2228. 2 Frederick D'or 1753, 55. A mm 450.00

Head. Rev. Eagle between trophies. The last three coins were struck in lower grade gold during the Seven Year War.

2229. 1 Frederick D'or 1752-58, 63. A mm 150.00
2230. ½ Frederick D'or 1752-56. A mm 100.00
2231. 2 Frederick D or 1756, 57. A mm 750.00
2232. 1 Frederick D'or 1755, 56, 57. A mm 175.00
2233. ½ Frederick D'or 1755. A mm 600.00

Head. Rev. Crown over Two F's.

2234. ½ Frederick D'or 1750. A mm 175.00

Armored bust. Rev. Eagle over trophies.

2235. 2 Frederick D'or 1751, 52. B mm 400.00
2236. 2 Frederick D'or 1752, 53. C mm 750.00
2237. 1 Frederick D'or 1750-57. B mm 200.00
2238. 1 Frederick D'or 1751-53. C mm ....*..... 300.00
2239. ½ Frederick D'or 1750-53. B mm ....*..... 150.00
2240. ½ Frederick D'or 1753. C mm 300.00

Head. Rev. Eagle over trophies.

2241. 1 Frederick D'or 1754, 55. C mm 750.00

Young laureate head. Rev. Eagle over trophies.

2242. 2 Frederick D'or 1764-71, 75. A mm 400.00

2243. 1 Frederick D'or 1764-76. A mm 225.00
2244. 1 Frederick D'or 1764-75. B mm 200.00
2245. ½ Frederick D'or 1765, 69, 70, 72-74. A mm 100.00
2246. ½ Frederick D'or 1765-75. B mm 150.00

Old laureate head. Rev. Eagle over trophies.

2247. 2 Frederick D'or 1776. A mm 350.00
2248. 1 Frederick D'or 1775-86. A mm 150.00
2249. 1 Frederick D'or 1776-78, 80-86. B mm 200.00
2250. 1 Frederick D'or 1781. With date "D.20.August." B mm 3000.00
2251. ½ Frederick D'or 1784, 86. A mm 100.00
2252. ½ Frederick D'or 1776, 77. B mm 350.00

FREDERICK WILLIAM II, 1786-1797
Bust. Rev. Eagle above trophies.

2253. 1 Frederick D'or 1786, 88-97. A mm 125.00
2254. 1 Frederick D'or 1787-97. B mm 125.00

Crowned eagle shield. Rev. Value.

2255. 1 Ducat 1787, 90. A mm 200.00

FREDERICK WILLIAM III, 1797-1840

Eagle shield. Rev. Legend, "Fuerstenzeche."

2256. 1 Rhine-gold Ducat 1803. B mm 2000.00

Bust. Rev. Eagle above trophies.

2257. 2 Frederick D'or 1800-02, 06, 11, 13, 14. A mm *...... 250.00
2258. 1 Frederick D'or 1798-1813, 16. A mm 150.00
2259. 1 Frederick D'or 1800-05. B mm 375.00
2260. ½ Frederick D'or 1802-04, 06, 14, 16. A mm 100.00

Bust. Rev. Eagle.

2261. 1 Frederick D'or 1797, 98. A mm 125.00

Bust in uniform. Rev. Eagle above trophies.

2262. 1 Frederick D'or 1817-19, 22. A mm 125.00
2263. ½ Frederick D'or 1817. A mm 100.00

Head. Rev. Eagle above trophies.

2264.	2 Frederick D'or 1825-32, 36-40. A mm	200.00
2265.	1 Frederick D'or 1825, 27-34, 36-40. A mm	125.00
2266.	½ Frederick D'or 1825, 27-29, 32, 33, 37-40. A mm ...	100.00

FREDERICK WILLIAM IV, 1840-1861

Head. Rev. Eagle above trophies.

2267.	2 Frederick D'or 1841-46, 48, 49, 52. A mm ..*......	200.00
2268.	1 Frederick D'or 1841-52. A mm	125.00
2269.	½ Frederick D'or 1841-46, 49. A mm ....*......	100.00

Older head. Rev. Eagle above trophies.

2270.	2 Frederick D'or 1853-55. A mm	200.00
2271.	1 Frederick D'or 1853-55. A mm ....*......	125.00
2272.	½ Frederick D'or 1853. A mm	100.00

Older head. Rev. Value in wreath.

2273.	1 Krone 1858, 59, 66. A mm	350.00
2274.	½ Krone 1858. A mm	300.00

WILLIAM I, 1861-1888

Head. Rev. Value in wreath. The B mm is for Hanover.

2275.	1 Krone 1861-64, 66-68, 70. A mm ....*......	400.00
2276.	1 Krone 1868. B mm	400.00
2277.	½ Krone 1862-64, 66-68. A mm	300.00
2278.	½ Krone 1867. B mm	500.00

QUEDLINBURG

Abbesses of —

DOROTHEA SOPHIA, 1618-1645

Arms of Quedlinburg. Rev. Arms of Saxony.

2279.	1 Ducat ND	500.00

Crowned arms of Quedlinburg. Rev. Crowned arms of Saxony.

2280.	1 Ducat ND	350.00

ANNE DOROTHEA, 1685-1704

Bust. Rev. Ship. On her death.

2281.	2 Ducats 1704	450.00

Bust. Rev. Setting sun. On her death.

2282.	1 Ducat 1704	300.00

RANTZAU

Counts —

CHRISTIAN I, 1650-1663

Bust. Rev. Arms.

2283.	2 Ducats 1656	1000.00
2284.	1 Ducat 1655, 56, 58 ....*......	400.00

DETLEF, 1663-1697
Bust. Rev. Arms.

2285.	1 Ducat 1689	500.00

RATZEBURG

Bishops of —

AUGUST OF BRUNSWICK, 1610-1636

Duke on horse. Rev. Arms.

2286.	1 Goldgulden 1618	500.00

Duke standing. Rev. Arms.

2287.	1 Ducat ND	400.00

Bust. Rev. Arms.

2288.	1 Ducat 1634	500.00

REGENSBURG (RATISBON)

A. General City Coinage

Arms. Rev. St. Wolfgang.

2289. 1 Goldgulden 1512 .... 1250.00

Trinity Church. Rev. Inscription.

2290. 1 Ducat 1627 .... 200.00

Arms. Rev. Legend. In honor of Bernard of Saxony.

2291. 1 Ducat 1633 .... 375.00

Arms. Rev. City view.

2292. 1 Ducat 1634 .... 350.00

Legend and arms. Rev. Light and hands. On the Reformation.

2293. 2 Ducats 1642 .... 200.00

Arms. Rev. Light. On the Reformation.

2294. 1 Ducat 1642 .... 150.00

Double eagle. Rev. Wreath.

2295. 1 Ducat 1653 .... 400.00

Arms. Rev. Double eagle.

2296. 1 Ducat 1658 ....* 375.00
2297. ½ Ducat ND. Square ....*...... 150.00
2298. ¼ Ducat ND 100.00
2299. ¼ Ducat ND. Square 100.00
2300. ⅛ Ducat ND. Square 75.00
2301. ⅛ Ducat ND. Square 75.00

Lamb on column. Rev. Legend. On the Reformation.

2302. 1 Ducat 1717 .... 150.00

Arms over legend. Rev. Vine. On the Reformation.

2303. 1 Ducat 1742 .... 175.00

Crossed keys. Rev. Crowned R.

2304. 1⁄16 Ducat ND (1750) 75.00
2305. 1⁄32 Ducat ND (1750) 50.00

Crossed keys. Rev. Double eagle.

2306. 1⁄32 Ducat ND (1750) 50.00

B. Coinage with the heads or names of the Holy Roman Emperors

Arms. Rev. Double eagle. Matthias.

2307. 1 Goldgulden 1617, 18 .... 350.00

Arms. Rev. Double eagle. Ferdinand II.

2308. 2 Ducats 1632 .... 500.00
2309. 1 Ducat 1632 .... 350.00

Inscription. Rev. Scales.

2310. 2 Ducats 1636 .... 300.00

Arms. Rev. Double eagle. Ferdinand III.

2311. 1 Ducat 1637-57 .... 250.00

Inscription. Rev. Inscription. Ferdinand IV.

2312. 1 Ducat 1653 .... 250.00

Arms. Rev. Double eagle. Leopold I.

2313. 6 Ducats 1667 .... 1000.00
2314. 4 Ducats 1664 .... 600.00
2315. 2 Ducats ND 450.00
2316. 1 Ducat 1659-96 ....*...... 250.00
2317. ½ Ducat ND 250.00

Arms. Rev. Double eagle. Joseph I.

2318. 5 Ducats ND 1000.00
2319. 1 Ducat 1706 .... 250.00

Bust of Charles VI. Rev. Arms.

2320. 2 Ducats ND 400.00
2321. 1 Ducat 1712 .... 250.00
2322. ½ Ducat ND 175.00

Bust of Charles VI. Rev. City View.

2323. 1 Ducat 1737, ND 300.00

Arms. Rev. Double eagle. Charles VI.

2324. 3 Ducats ND (1740) 600.00
2325. ½ Ducat ND (1740) 175.00

Bust of Charles VII. Rev. City view.

2326. 2 Ducats ND (thick) ....*...... 1000.00
2327. 1 Ducat ND 300.00

Bust of Charles VII. Rev. Arms.

2328. 2 Ducats ND (1742-45) 600.00
2329. ½ Ducat ND (1742-45) 250.00

Bust of Francis I. Rev. City view.

2330.	3 Ducats ND (1745-65)	..................*......	750.00
2331.	2 Ducats ND (1745-65)		400.00
2332.	1 Ducat ND (1745-65)		250.00
2333.	½ Ducat ND (1745-65)		150.00
2334.	¼ Ducat ND (1745-65)		100.00

Bust of Francis I. Rev. Eagle flying over arms.

2335.	3 Ducats ND (1745-65)		750.00
2336.	2 Ducats ND (1745-65)		600.00

Bust of Joseph II. Rev. Arms.

2337.	3 Ducats ND (1765-90)		600.00
2338.	1 Ducat ND (1765-90)		250.00

Bust of Joseph II. Rev. City view.

2339.	1 Ducat ND (1765-90)		250.00
2340.	½ Ducat ND		150.00
2341.	¼ Ducat ND		100.00

City view. Rev. Double eagle. Joseph II.

2342.	8 Ducats ND		1000.00
2343.	5 Ducats ND		600.00
2344.	2 Ducats ND (1765-90)		400.00

Head of Leopold II. Rev. City view.

2345.	1 Ducat ND (1790-92)		275.00

City view. Rev. Double eagle. Francis II.

2346.	1 Ducat ND (1792-1806)		250.00

C. Bishops of —

JOHN III, 1507-1538
Arms. Rev. St. Peter standing.

2347.	1 Goldgulden 1523		1000.00

Arms. Rev. Madonna.

2348.	1 Ducat 1526		1000.00

DAVID, 1567-1579
Arms. Rev. Double eagle.

2349.	1 Goldgulden ND		1000.00

ANTHONY IGNACE, 1769-1787
Bust. Rev. Arms.

2350.	1 Ducat 1770		350.00

CHARLES, 1804-1817
Bust. Rev. Arms.

2351.	1 Ducat 1809		300.00

REUSS

Counts, and later, Princes —

A. Older Line

HENRY III, 1733-1768
Bust. Rev. Arms.

2352.	1 Ducat 1764		200.00

B. Younger Line

HENRY II, 1572-1635
Arms. Rev. Two helmets.

2353.	1 Goldgulden 1619, 22		300.00

HENRY XII, 1744-1784

Initials. Rev. Arms. On the Peace of Hubertusburg.

2354.	1 Ducat 1763		200.00

Bust. Rev. Arms.

2355.	1 Ducat 1764		250.00

REUSS-RODENTHAL

Counts —

HENRY V, 1668-1698
Bust. Rev. Arms.

2356.	1 Ducat 1679		600.00

RHINE (CONFEDERATION)

CHARLES, ARCHBISHOP OF MAYENCE, 1802-1813

Bust. Rev. Arms.

2357.	1 Ducat 1809		250.00

ROSTOCK

(The coinage is with the names of the Holy Roman Emperors.)

Griffin. Rev. Double eagle. Rudolph II.

2358.	1 Goldgulden 1606, 08-11, ND		200.00

Griffin. Rev. Double eagle. Matthias.

2359.	1 Goldgulden 1613-17		300.00

Griffin. Rev. Double eagle. Ferdinand II.

2360.	2 Goldgulden 1623		1000.00
2361.	1 Goldgulden 1625-31		200.00

Arms. Rev. Double eagle. Ferdinand II.

2362.	1 Ducat 1632-34, 36		150.00

Tablet and value. Rev. Double eagle. Ferdinand III.

2363.   2 Ducats 1639 ....   350.00

Arms. Rev. Double eagle. Ferdinand III.

2364.   1 Ducat 1636, 39, 46, 55 ....   175.00

Arms. Rev. Double eagle. Leopold I.

2365.   2 Ducats 1661, 95 ....   600.00
2366.   1 Ducat 1661, 64, 65, 72, 77, 82, 94 ....   300.00

Griffin. Rev. Double eagle. Leopold I.

2367.   ½ Ducat 1695 ....   175.00

Griffin. Rev. Double eagle. Leopold I.

2368.   1 Wedding Ducat 1704 ....   400.00

Griffin. Rev. Value. Leopold II.

2369.   ¼ Ducat 1696 ....   175.00

Arms. Rev. Double eagle. Francis I.

2370.   1 Ducat 1762 ....   350.00

Arms. Rev. Double eagle. Joseph II.

2371.   1 Ducat 1783 ....   200.00

Arms. Rev. Double eagle. Francis II.

2372.   1 Ducat 1796 ....   150.00

ROTHENBURG

Legend. Rev. Fortress. On the Reformation.

2373.   1 Ducat 1717 ....   350.00

ROTTWEIL

Eagle. Rev. Orb in enclosure. Maximilian I.

2374.   1 Goldgulden ND (1486-1519) 2000.00

ST. ALBAN

(In Mayence)

St. Alban standing. Rev. Shield and donkey.

2375.   1 Goldgulden 1597 ....   400.00

2376.   1 Goldgulden 1712, 16, 20, 25, 44, 78, 79, 80 * 300.00

SALM-DHAUN

CURATORIAL COINAGE, 1606-1617
Arms. Rev. Double eagle. Matthias.

2377.   1 Goldgulden 1617 ....   500.00

WOLFGANG FREDERICK, DIED 1638
Arms. Rev. Double eagle. Matthias.

2378.   1 Goldgulden 1619 ....   500.00

SALM-KYRBURG

Counts, and later, Princes —

OTTO I, DIED 1607
Arms. Rev. Double eagle. Rudolph II.

2379.   2 Ducats ND 800.00

JOHN PHILIP, OTTO LOUIS, JOHN CASIMIR AND OTTO
Arms with lion. Rev. Double eagle. Ferdinand II.

2380.   1 Goldgulden ND 700.00

FREDERICK III, 1779-1794
Head. Rev. Arms.

2381.   1 Carolin 1782 ....   500.00
2382.   1 Ducat 1780, 82 ....   325.00

SAXONY

(The Albertine Line)

Electors, and later, Kings of —

ALBERT, 1464-1500
Orb in trefoil. Rev. St. John.

2383.   1 Goldgulden ND 150.00

Shield on cross. Rev. Shield with double eagle supported by lions. Struck for Frisia.

2384.   1 Goldgulden ND 600.00

GEORGE, 1500-1539
St. John. Rev. Orb in trefoil.

2385.   1 Goldgulden ND 400.00

Arms. Rev. St. Boniface. Struck for Frisia.

2386.   1 Goldgulden ND 600.00

GEORGE AND HENRY, 1500-1505
St. John. Rev. Orb in trefoil.

2387.   1 Goldgulden ND 400.00

MAURICE, 1547-1553
Arms. Rev. Legend. On the Siege of Leipzig.

2388.   10 Ducats 1547. Round 3000.00
2389.   4 Ducats 1547. Square 1200.00
2390.   2 Ducats 1547. Square 600.00
2391.   1 Ducat 1547. Square 375.00

Shield. Rev. Arms.

2392.   2 Ducats 1552 ....   800.00
2393.   1 Ducat ND 400.00

Elector standing. Rev. Five shields in quatrefoil.

2394.   1 Goldgulden 1548 ....   750.00

AUGUST, 1553-1586
Bust with sword. Rev. Arms.

2395.   2 Goldgulden 1554 ....   800.00

Bust with sword. Rev. Helmeted shield with lion.

2396.   1 Goldgulden 1558 ....   450.00

Bust with sword. Rev. Two shields and orb.

2397. 10 Goldgulden 1585 .... 3000.00

Bust. Rev. Arms.

2398. 1 Goldgulden ND 400.00

Half length figure. Rev. Arms.

2399. 1¼ Ducats ND 800.00
2400. 1 Goldgulden ND 400.00

Half length figure. Rev. Five shields.

2401. 1 Goldgulden 1585, ND 200.00

Arms within orb. Rev. Value.

2402. 1 Goldgulden 1584 .... 350.00
2403. 1 Goldgulden 1584. Square 400.00

CHRISTIAN I, 1586-1591

Armored bust. Rev. Cross and four shields.

2404. 10 Ducats 1587, 90 .... 2500.00
2405. 5 Ducats 1587 .... 1500.00
2406. 2½ Ducats 1587 .... 900.00
2407. 2 Ducats 1587, 90 ....*...... 750.00
2408. 1 Ducat 1590 .... 350.00

Duke standing. Rev. Arms.

2409. 1 Ducat 1589, 90 .... 300.00

FREDERICK WILLIAM, REGENT, 1591-1601
Bust. Rev. Arms.

2410. 1 Ducat 1594 .... 400.00

SOPHIA, 1582-1622

Initials. Rev. "IHS".

2411. 1 Ducat 1616 .... 75.00

CHRISTIAN II, 1601-1611
Half length figure. Rev. Cross and circle of shields.

2412. 20 Ducats 1610 .... 2000.00
2413. 10 Ducats 1606, 10 .... 1250.00
2414. 8 Ducats 1606 .... 1000.00

JOHN GEORGE I, 1611-1656
Half length figure with sword, before helmet. Rev. Cross within circle of shields.

2415. 5 Ducats 1614 .... 1000.00

Half length figure with sword, a helmet in front. Rev. Arms.

2416. 2 Ducats 1616 (swan) 300.00
2417. 2 Ducats 1625 (HI) 300.00
2418. 2 Goldgulden 1620 (swan) 800.00
2419. 1 Goldgulden 1615 .... 400.00
2420. 1 Goldgulden 1618-20 (swan) ....*...... 225.00

2421. 1 Goldgulden 1625, 32 (HI) 400.00
2422. 1 Goldgulden 1641 (CR) 400.00

Elector standing. Rev. Arms.

2423. 2 Ducats 1620 (swan) 300.00
2424. 2 Ducats 1628, 29, 32 (HI) ....*...... 300.00
2425. 2 Ducats 1635 (CM) 400.00
2426. 2 Ducats 1636-39 (SD) 300.00
2427. 2 Ducats 1640-46, 52, 54 (CR) 300.00
2428. 1 Ducat 1622 (swan) 150.00
2429. 1 Ducat 1627-30, 32-34 (HI) 125.00
2430. 1 Ducat 1635 (CM) 150.00
2431. 1 Ducat 1635-40 (SD) 125.00
2432. 1 Ducat 1640-46, 48, 49, 52, 53, 55 (CR) 125.00
2433. ½ Ducat 1651-53, 55 (CR) 150.00
2434. ¼ Ducat 1651 (CR) 175.00

Bust of John George I. Rev. Bust of Frederick III. On the Reformation.

2435. 2 Ducats 1617 .... 250.00
2436. 1 Ducat 1617 .... 150.00

Elector on horse over arms. Rev. Legend. On the Vicariat.

2437. 5 Ducats 1619 .... 600.00
2438. 2 Ducats 1619 .... 250.00
2439. 1 Ducat 1619 .... 150.00

Arms. Rev. St. George. On the baptism of Prince Henry.

2440. 2 Ducats 1622 .... 450.00
2441. 1 Ducat 1622 .... 200.00

Bust of John George I. Rev. Bust of John. On the Augsburg Confession.

2442. 10 Ducats 1630 .... 750.00
2443. 5 Ducats 1630 .... 500.00
2444. 2 Ducats 1630 ....*...... 250.00
2445. 1 Ducat 1630 .... 150.00

Legend. Rev. Patience standing. On the Peace of Prague.

2446. 1 Ducat 1635 .... 300.00

Facing bust with sword. Rev. Legend. On his death.

2447. 2 Ducats 1656 .... 400.00

JOHN GEORGE II, 1656-1680

Elector on horse. Rev. Legend. On the Vicariat.

2448. 2 Ducats 1657 .... 300.00
2449. 1 Ducat 1657 .... 150.00

Bust with sword; in front, elector's hat. Rev. Arms.

2450. 2 Ducats 1659, 60, 62 .... 250.00
2451. 1 Ducat 1659, 60, 62, 64, 65, 72 ....*...... 125.00
2452. ½ Ducat 1659, 60, 62, 64, 65, 66 .... 100.00

Bust. Rev. Arms.

2453. 1 Goldgulden 1669 .... 450.00

Elector on horse. Rev. Shield on obelisk.

2454. 1 Ducat 1669 .... 200.00

Elector on horse. Rev. Arms.

2455. 1 Goldgulden 1670 .... 600.00

Bust. Rev. Arms on palm branches.

2456. 3 Ducats 1675, 79 .... 500.00
2457. 2 Ducats 1675, 76 ....*...... 300.00

JOHN GEORGE III, 1680-1691

Bust. Rev. Arms on palm branches.

2458. 4 Ducats 1688 .... 800.00
2459. 2 Ducats 1681, 83, 85, 86, 88, 89, 91 .... 300.00
2460. 1½ Ducats 1681, 83, 84, 90, 91 ....*...... 200.00

Bust with sword; in front, elector's hat. Rev. Arms on palm branches.

2461. 1 Ducat 1681, 83, 84, 86, 87, 90, 91 ....*...... 200.00
2462. ½ Ducat 1683, 84, 88, 90, 91 .... 100.00

Half length figure with sword, before elector's hat. Rev. Arms.

2463. 2 Ducats 1685 .... 500.00

Half length figure with sword. Rev. Arms.

2464. 2 Ducats 1685 .... 500.00

Bust. Rev. Crossed swords and four arms.

2465. 1 Ducat 1686 .... 200.00

Bust with sword, before helmet. Rev. Arms.

2466. 2 Ducats 1691 .... 500.00

Legend. Rev. Arms in clouds with flag. On his death.

2467. 1 Ducat 1691 .... 350.00

JOHN GEORGE IV, 1691-1694

Bust with sword, before elector's hat. Rev. Arms.

2468. 1 Ducat 1691-94 .... 250.00
2469. ½ Ducat 1691-94 .... 150.00

Bust. Rev. Crossed swords and four arms.

2470. 3 Ducats 1692 .... 500.00
2471. 2 Ducats 1692-94 .... 300.00
2472. 1½ Ducats 1692, 93 .... 325.00

ANNA SOPHIA, DIED 1717

Ship. Rev. Legend under crown. On her death.

2473. 1 Ducat 1717 .... 300.00

FREDERICK AUGUST I (AUGUST II), 1694-1733

A. Coinage of the Dresden Mint.

Bust with sword. Rev. Arms.

2474. 2 Ducats 1695 (IK) 450.00
2475. 1 Ducat 1694 (IK) 200.00

Bust with sword. Rev. Lion with sword and arms.

2476. 1 Ducat 1695-97 (IK) 200.00
2477. ¼ Ducat 1696 (IK) 100.00

Bust. Rev. Lion with sword and arms.

2478. ½ Ducat 1696 (IK) 100.00
2479. ¼ Ducat 1696 (IK) 100.00

Elector standing to right, before desk. Rev. Elector's hat over two arms.

2480. 2 Ducats 1696 .... 300.00

Elector standing to left, before desk. Rev. Altar.

2481. 2 Ducats 1696 .... 300.00

Bust. Rev. Crowned arms.

2482. 2 Ducats 1698, 1700-02, 04, 07, 11, 14 (ILH) 300.00
2483. 2 Ducats 1717, 23, 27, 33 (IGS) 450.00
2484. 1 Ducat 1698-1704, 06, 07, 10, 11, 13, 14 (ILH) 175.00
2485. 1 Ducat 1716-18, 20-33 (IGS) 175.00
2486. 1 Ducat 1733 from the ½ ducat die (IGS) 250.00
2487. ½ Ducat 1669, 1701, 07, 10 (ILH) 125.00
2488. ½ Ducat 1716, 17, 26, 29, 33 (IGS) 125.00
2489. ¼ Ducat 1700, 10 (ILH) 75.00
2490. ¼ Ducat 1717, 20-22, 27, 29, 33 (IGS) 75.00

Head. Rev. Crowned arms.

2491. 1 Ducat 1721 .... 450.00

Bust. Rev. Crowned initials.

2492. 2 Ducats 1708, 09 (ILH) 300.00
2493. 1 Ducat 1708, 09 (ILH) 200.00

Crowned initials. Rev. Crowned arms.

2494. 2 Ducats 1710 .... 450.00
2495. 1 Ducat 1710 .... 375.00
2496. ½ Ducat 1710 .... 125.00
2497. ¼ Ducat 1710 from the ½ ducat die 175.00
2498. ¼ Ducat 1710 .... 100.00

B. Coinage of the Leipzig Mint.

Elector on horse. Rev. Arms on drapery.

2499. 1½ Ducats 1697 (EPH) 400.00
2500. 1 Ducat 1697 (EPH) 200.00
2501. 1 Ducat 1697 (EPH) from the ½ ducat die 250.00
2502. 1 Ducat 1697 (EPH) from the ¼ ducat die 250.00
2503. ½ Ducat 1697 (EPH) 175.00
2504. ¼ Ducat 1697 (EPH) 100.00

King on horse. Rev. Arms on trophies.

2505. 2 Ducats 1702, 12 (EPH) 300.00
2506. 1 Ducat 1702, 12 (EPH) 175.00

Bust. Rev. Crown over two arms.

2507. 2 Ducats 1709 (EPH) from the ducat die 350.00

| 2508. | 1 Ducat 1702, 09 (EPH) | 175.00 |
| 2509. | ½ Ducat 1702 (EPH) | 125.00 |

Bust. Rev. Arms on star.

| 2510. | 2 Ducats 1702 | 300.00 |

Crowned bust on post. Rev. Crown over three arms.

| 2511. | 1 Ducat 1702 (EPH) | 600.00 |

Crowned bust on post. Rev. Crowned initials and three arms.

2512.	1 Ducat 1703 (EPH)	300.00
2513.	1 Ducat 1703 (EPH) from the ½ ducat die	450.00
2514.	½ Ducat 1703 (EPH)	400.00

C. Coinage on the Vicariat.

Elector on horse. Rev. Altar with insignia.

| 2515. | 2 Ducats 1711 | 300.00 |

Elector on horse. Rev. Two desks with insignia.

| 2516. | 2 Ducats 1711 (ILH) | 300.00 |
| 2517. | 1 Ducat 1711 ....*.... | 175.00 |

Elector on horse. Rev. Sword and sceptre crossed.

| 2518. | 1 Ducat 1711 | 150.00 |

D. Commemorative Coinage.

Elector on horse. Rev. Arms on drapery. Expedition to Hungary.

| 2519. | 2 Ducats 1695 | 400.00 |
| 2520. | 1 Ducat ND (1695), 1695 | 150.00 |

King on horse. Rev. Crown over legend. On the Coronation.

| 2521. | 2 Ducats 1697 | 250.00 |
| 2522. | 1 Ducat 1697 (O) | 150.00 |

Bust. Rev. Crown. On the Coronation.

2523.	2 Ducats 1697. FRID-AVG-etc.	250.00
2524.	2 Ducats 1697. FRIDERICVS AVGVST etc.	250.00
2525.	1 Ducat 1697	150.00

Arm with Polish sabre. Rev. Crown over legend. On the Coronation.

| 2526. | 1 Ducat 1697 (IK) | 150.00 |

Bust, AVGVSTVS-II:REX POLONIAE. Rev. Crown. On the Coronation.

| 2527. | 1 Ducat ND. (1697) from the ½ ducat die | 300.00 |
| 2528. | ½ Ducat ND (1697) | 125.00 |

Bust of Frederick the Warlike with elector's hat and sword. Rev. City view of Leipzig. Jubilee of the University.

| 2529. | 2 Ducats 1709 | 350.00 |
| 2530. | 1 Ducat 1709 | 175.00 |

Rock and seven planets. Rev. Legend. From gold of the Freiberg mines.

| 2531. | 1 Ducat 1701 | 300.00 |

Rock and triangle. Rev. Legend. From gold of the Freiberg mines.

| 2532. | 1 Ducat 1709, 14 | 300.00 |

Head. Rev. Crown on cushion. Treaty of Lublin.

| 2533. | 1 Ducat 1715 | 250.00 |

Legend. Rev. Two hearts. On the wedding of his son to Maria Josepha of Austria.

2534.	3 Ducats 1719 (IGS)	400.00
2535.	2 Ducats 1719 (IGS)	300.00
2536.	1 Ducat 1719 (IGS)	150.00

FREDERICK AUGUST II, 1733-1763

A. Coinage of the Dresden Mint.

Bust. Rev. Crowned arms.

2537.	2 Ducats 1735-39 (FWoF)	750.00
2538.	1 Ducat 1734 (IGS)	250.00
2539.	1 Ducat 1735-45, 48-51, 55, 56 (FWoF)	125.00
2540.	1 Ducat 1757 (IDB)	150.00
2541.	1 Ducat 1760-63 (FWoF)	125.00
2542.	1 Ducat 1757 (IDB) with FR (Fridericus Rex)	300.00
2543.	½ Ducat 1735-37, 40, 43, 56 (FWoF)	75.00
2544.	½ Ducat 1750. (AVGVSTVS III REX POL)	375.00
2545.	¼ Ducat 1734 (IGS)	75.00
2546.	¼ Ducat 1735-37, 39, 40, 43 (FWoF)	60.00

B. Coinage of the Leipzig Mint.

Crowned bust. Rev. Crowned arms.

2547.	2 Ducats 1753, 54 (EDC)	250.00
2548.	1 Ducat 1752 (IGG)	150.00
2549.	1 Ducat 1753, 54, 56 (EDC)	150.00
2550.	10 Taler 1753 (G)	225.00
2551.	10 Taler 1754, 55, 56 (EDC)	225.00
2552.	5 Taler 1753 (G)	175.00
2553.	5 Taler 1754-56, 58 (EC)	150.00
2554.	2½ Taler 1753 (G)	125.00

C. Coinage on the Vicariat.

Bust. Rev. Double eagle with arms.

| 2555. | 1 Ducat 1740 | 200.00 |

Elector on horse. Rev. Throne.

| 2556. | 1 Ducat 1741, 42 | 150.00 |

Bust. Rev. Crown over two arms.

| 2557. | 1 Ducat 1745 | 200.00 |

Elector on horse. Rev. Flying eagle.

| 2558. | 1 Ducat 1745 | 150.00 |

FREDERICK CHRISTIAN, 1763

Hymen floating. Rev. Legend. On his wedding with Antonia of Bavaria.

| 2559. | 1 Ducat 1747 | 250.00 |

Bust. Rev. Crowned arms.

| 2560. | 1 Ducat 1763 (FWoF) | 250.00 |

XAVIER, 1763-1768

Bust. Rev. Arms.

| 2561. | 1 Ducat 1766-68 (EDC) | 250.00 |

FREDERICK AUGUST III (I, FROM 1806), 1763-1827

A. Coinage of the Dresden Mint.

Head. Rev. Arms.

| 2562. | 1 Ducat 1764-78 (EDC) | 150.00 |
| 2563. | 1 Ducat 1779-90 (IEC) | 150.00 |

Bust. Rev. Arms.

| 2564. | 1 Ducat 1791-1804 (IEC) | 150.00 |
| 2565. | 1 Ducat 1805, 06 (SGH) | 150.00 |

Armored bust. Rev. Two arms.

| 2566. | 10 Taler 1777, 78 (EDC) | 250.00 |
| 2566a. | 10 Taler 1779 (IEC) | 275.00 |

Head. Rev. Two arms.

2567.	10 Taler 1779-87, 90 (IEC)	250.00
2568.	5 Taler 1777, 78 (EDC)	150.00
2569.	5 Taler 1779, 82 (IEC)	150.00

Armored bust. Rev. Arms on branches.

2570.	10 Taler 1791-1803 (IEC)	250.00
2571.	10 Taler 1804-1806 (SGH)	250.00
2572.	5 Taler 1802 (IEC)	500.00
2573.	5 Taler 1805-06 (SGH)	200.00

B. Coinage of the Leipzig Mint.

Head. Rev. Arms.

2574.	1 Ducat 1764 (IFoF)	150.00

C. Coinage on the Vicariat.

Bust. Rev. Double eagle with arms.

2575.	1 Ducat 1792	175.00

D. Coinage as Frederick August I.

Head. Rev. Arms.

2576.	10 Taler 1806-17 ....*......	350.00
2577.	5 Taler 1806-17	250.00
2578.	1 Ducat 1806-22	200.00
2579.	1 Ducat 1806. Without D in the D.G. of legend.*......	250.00

Uniformed bust. Rev. Arms.

2580.	10 Taler 1818, 25-27	300.00
2581.	5 Taler 1818, 25-27 ....*......	250.00
2582.	1 Ducat 1823-27	200.00

ANTHONY, 1827-1836
Head. Rev. Arms.

2583.	10 Taler 1828-36	400.00
2584.	5 Taler 1827-36	200.00
2585.	1 Ducat 1827-36	175.00

Bust of Frederick. Rev. Inscription. On Leipzig University Jubilee.

2586.	1 Ducat 1829	150.00

FREDERICK AUGUST II, 1836-1854
Head. Rev. Arms in wreath.

2587.	1 Ducat 1836-38	150.00

Head. Rev. Inscription.

2588.	1 Hunting Ducat 1847	300.00

Head. Rev. Draped arms.

2589.	10 Taler 1836-53	300.00
2590.	5 Taler 1837-54 ....*......	250.00
2591.	2½ Taler 1842-54	150.00

JOHN, 1854-1873

Head. Rev. Value.

2592.	1 Krone 1857-63, 65, 67, 68, 70, 71	500.00
2593.	½ Krone 1857, 58, 62, 66, 68, 70 ....*......	350.00

SAXONY-ALTENBURG

Dukes of —
JOHN PHILIP AND HIS BROTHERS, 1602-1639

Four busts. Rev. Arms.

2594.	1 Goldgulden 1614, 19, 22	200.00

JOHN PHILIP AND FREDERICK WILLIAM II
Bust of John Philip. Rev. Arms.

2595.	2 Ducats 1637, 38	300.00

Bust of John Philip. Rev. Bust of Frederick William.

2596.	1 Ducat 1638	200.00

JOHN PHILIP

Bust. Rev. Legend. On his death.

2597.	1 Ducat 1639	300.00

FREDERICK WILLIAM II, 1639-1669

Armored bust. Rev. Arms.

2598.	1 Ducat 1640, 41, 42	200.00

Initials of Magdalene Sybil. Rev. Legend. On her death.

2599.	1 Ducat 1668	150.00

Armored bust. Rev. Legend. On his death.

2600. 1 Ducat 1669 .... 300.00

SAXONY-COBURG-GOTHA

Dukes of —

ERNEST, 1826-1844

Head. Rev. Value and Arms.

2601. 1 Ducat 1831, 36, 42 .... 250.00

SAXONY-EISENACH

Dukes of —

JOHN WILLIAM, 1690-1729

Armored bust. Rev. Arms and four initials.

2602. 1 Ducat 1700 .... 350.00

Arms and four initials. Rev. Crane.

2603. 1 Ducat 1716 .... 200.00

SAXONY-EISENBERG

Dukes of —

CHRISTIAN, 1675-1707

Armored bust. Rev. Two arms in clouds and heart on altar.

2604. 1 Ducat 1682 .... 350.00

Bust. Rev. Arms.

2605. 2 Ducats 1682 .... 600.00
2606. ½ Ducat 1683. Thick 150.00
2607. ¼ Ducat 1683, ND ....*...... 100.00

Armored bust. Rev. Table with sword and palm.

2608. 1 Ducat 1686 .... 400.00

Bust. Rev. Oval arms.

2609. 2 Ducats 1697. Thick 500.00
2610. 1 Ducat 1697 ....*...... 300.00
2611. ½ Ducat ND 125.00

Arms. Rev. Palm tree. "Alchemical" gold issue.

2612. 1 Goldgulden 1684 .... 400.00

SAXONY-ERNESTINE

Electors of —

FREDERICK II, 1428-1464
St. John. Rev. Orb in trefoil.

2613. 1 Goldgulden ND .... Unknown

FREDERICK III, ALBERT AND JOHN
St. John. Rev. Orb in quatrefoil.

2614. 1 Goldgulden 1498-1500, ND 250.00

FREDERICK III, GEORGE AND JOHN, 1498-1507
St. John. Rev. Orb.

2615. 1 Goldgulden 1498, 99, ND 250.00

FREDERICK III, JOHN AND GEORGE
St. John. Rev. Orb.

2616. 1 Goldgulden 1500, ND 250.00

FREDERICK III, 1486-1525
Bust with hat. Rev. Cross.

2617. 2 Ducats 1522 .... 750.00

JOHN FREDERICK, 1532-1553
Bust. Rev. Double eagle. Name of Charles V.

2618. 2 Goldgulden 1552 .... 800.00

SAXONY-GOTHA

Dukes of —
A. Old Gotha

JOHN FREDERICK, 1554-1595
Arms. Rev. Two angels with wreath.

2619. 1 Ducat 1566, ND 750.00

Arms and date. Rev. Blank. On the Siegé of Gotha.

2620. 1 Ducat 1567. Square 400.00

JOHN CASIMIR, 1572-1633

Armored bust. Rev. Legend. On his death.

2621. 2 Ducats 1633 .... 350.00

JOHN ERNEST, 1572-1638
Bust. Rev. Arms.

2622. 1 Ducat 1635, 36, 37 .... 125.00
2623. 1 Ducat 1637, 38. With GOTT BESS etc. 125.00

Bust. Rev. Legend. On his death.

2624. 1 Ducat 1638 .... 175.00

B. New Gotha

ERNEST, 1640-1675

Name of Jehovah over legend. Rev. Arms over legend.
On the Peace of Westphalia.

2625.	2 Ducats 1650	200.00
2626.	1 Ducat 1650	150.00
2627.	½ Ducat 1650 ....*......	125.00

Arms. Rev. Legend.

2628.	½ Ducat 1673	150.00
2629.	¼ Ducat 1675 ....*......	75.00

Bust. Rev. Legend. On his death.

2630.	1 Ducat 1675	250.00

FREDERICK I, 1675-1691
Bust. Rev. Arms.

2631.	1 Ducat 1681	250.00

Laureate head of Magdalene Sybil. Rev. Legend. On her death.

2632.	1 Ducat 1681	400.00

Fortuna on globe. Rev. Arms.

2633.	1 Goldgulden 1684	250.00

Bust. Rev. Four arms and four initials.

2634.	1 Ducat 1689	250.00
2635.	½ Ducat 1689, 90	150.00

Head with wig. Rev. Ship.

2636.	1 Ducat 1690	250.00
2637.	½ Ducat 1690	150.00

Head. Rev. Star of the Elephant Order, crossed initials and arms.

2638.	1 Ducat 1690	375.00

Bust. Rev. Arms.

2639.	¼ Ducat 1682, 84	100.00

Armored bust. Rev. Legend. On his death.

2640.	1 Ducat 1691	150.00

FREDERICK II AND JOHN WILLIAM, 1691-1707

Busts of Bernard and Henry. Rev. Two hands in clouds.

2641.	1 Ducat 1692. Homage of Gotha	250.00

FREDERICK II, 1691-1732
Bust. Rev. Arms.

2642.	2 Ducats 1699, 1707	500.00
2643.	1 Ducat 1694, 98, 99, 1707	250.00
2644.	½ Ducat 1702	75.00

Bust. Rev. Legend. On the Reformation.

2645.	2 Ducats 1717	325.00

Bust. Rev. Oak tree. On the Reformation.

2646.	1 Ducat 1717	250.00

Bust. Rev. Legend. On the Augsburg Confession.

2647.	2 Ducats 1730	350.00

FREDERICK III, 1732-1772

Bust. Rev. Arms.

2648.	1 Ducat 1732	250.00

Armored bust. Rev. Legend. On the religious peace.

2649.	2 Ducats 1755	375.00

Armored bust. Rev. Arms. On the religious peace.

2650.	1 Ducat 1755	225.00

SAXONY-GOTHA-ALTENBURG

FREDERICK IV, 1822-1825
Bust. Rev. Inscription. On Gotha Gymnasium.

2651.	1 Ducat 1824	150.00

SAXONY-HILDBURGHAUSEN

Dukes of —

ERNEST FREDERICK, 1715-1724
Bust. Rev. Legend. On the Reformation.

2652.	½ Ducat 1717	200.00

ERNEST FREDERICK CHARLES, 1745-1780
Bust. Rev. Arms.

2653. 1 Ducat 1771 .... 375.00

SAXONY-LAUENBURG

Dukes of —

FRANCIS II, 1581-1619
Bust. Rev. Arms.

2654. 1 Goldgulden 1609, 11, 12 .... 750.00

JULIUS HENRY, 1656-1665

Bust. Rev. Arms.

2655. 2 Ducats 1662 .... 650.00
2656. 1 Ducat 1657, 62 ....*...... 300.00

Bust. Rev. Madonna.

2657. 1 Ducat 1659 .... 450.00

JULIUS FRANCIS, 1666-1689

Bust. Rev. Arms.

2658. 2 Ducats 1673, 78-83, ND 500.00
2659. 1 Ducat 1670, 73, ND ....*...... 350.00

FREDERICK AUGUST (1689-?)
Bust. Rev. Lion with shield.

2660. ¼ Ducat 1696 .... 150.00

SAXONY-MEININGEN

Dukes of —

BERNARD, 1680-1706
Armored bust. Rev. Arms.

2661. 1 Ducat 1687, 88 .... 250.00

Armored bust. Rev. Meiningen Castle.

2662. 2 Ducats 1692 .... 400.00
2663. 1 Ducat 1692 .... 250.00

ERNEST LOUIS I, 1706-1724

Busts of the Duke and his wife. Rev. Two shields.

2664. 1 Ducat 1714. On the Marriage 250.00
2665. 1 Ducat 1717. On the Reformation ....*...... 250.00

CHARLES, 1763-1782
Two shields. Rev. Inscription.

2666. 2 Wedding Ducats 1780 .... 600.00

Initials. Rev. Inscription.

2667. 1 Wedding Ducat 1780 .... 400.00

SAXONY-ROEMHILD

Dukes of —

HENRY, 1680-1710
Bust. Rev. Arms.

2668. 1 Ducat 1698. Three varieties of the Rev. 500.00

SAXONY-SAALFELD

Dukes of —

JOHN ERNEST VIII, 1680-1729
Armored bust. Rev. Arms.

2669. 1 Ducat 1698, 1720, 21, 27 .... 250.00
2670. ½ Ducat 1725, 27, 28 .... 150.00
2671. ¼ Ducat 1725, 27, 28 .... 125.00

Armored bust. Rev. Bust of Luther. On the Reformation.

2672. 2 Ducats 1717 .... 375.00
2673. 1 Ducat 1717 .... 200.00

Armored half length bust. Rev. City view of Reichmansdorf.

2674. 1 Mining Ducat 1717, 19, 21, 22, 26-28 .... 350.00

CHRISTIAN ERNEST AND FRANCIS JOSIAS, 1729-1745

Initials in shields. Rev. Arms supported by lions.

2675. 1 Ducat 1740 .... 225.00

Duke kneeling. Rev. Bust of his brother.

2676. 1 Ducat 1745 .... 250.00

Initials. Rev. Arms.

2677. ¼ Ducat 1738, 43 .... 75.00

CHRISTIAN ERNEST, 1729-1745

Duke kneeling. Rev. Eagle and sun. On his death.

2678. 2 Ducats ND 200.00
2679. 1 Ducat ND ....*...... 100.00

FRANCIS JOSIAS, 1745-1764

Lion with initials in shield. Rev. Arms.

2680.   1 Ducat 1746, 49 ....   200.00

Initials in shield. Rev. Arms.

2681.   ¼ Ducat 1752 ....   75.00

ERNEST FREDERICK, 1764-1800

Bust. Rev. City view of Reichmansdorf.

2682.   1 Mining Ducat 1766 ....   500.00

SAXONY-WEIMAR

Dukes of —

JOHN ERNEST AND HIS SEVEN BROTHERS, 1605-1640
Four busts on each side.

2683.   1 Goldgulden 1613-15, 17, 19 ....   125.00

JOHN ERNEST AND HIS FIVE BROTHERS

Arms. Rev. Shield.

2684.   1 Goldgulden 1623 ....   200.00

BERNARD, DIED 1639
Arms. Rev. Christ standing.

2685.   1 Goldgulden 1634 ....   600.00

WILLIAM, 1630-1662
Arms. Rev. Jehovah and legend.

2686.   1 Ducat 1651   ....   175.00
2687.   ½ Ducat 1651, 52 ....   100.00
2688.   ¼ Ducat 1651 ....   60.00

Bust. Rev. Trophies and legend.

2689.   2 Ducats 1654 ....   600.00
2690.   ½ Ducat 1654 ....*......   100.00

Arms. Rev. Legend.

2691.   1 Ducat 1651 ....   225.00

2692.   ½ Ducat 1651, 56 ....*......   175.00
2693.   ¼ Ducat 1658 ....   150.00

Arms of Henneberg. Rev. Legend.

2694.   1 Ducat 1661 ....   350.00

Bust. Rev. Jena Castle.

2695.   1 Ducat 1661 ....   250.00

Bust. Rev. Arms.

2696.   ¼ Ducat 1662 ....   75.00

WILLIAM ERNEST, 1683-1728
Bust. Rev. Weimar Castle.

2697.   1 Ducat 1717 ....   175.00

Table with book and lamp. Rev. Legend. On the Reformation.

2698.   2 Ducats 1717 ....   400.00
2699.   1 Ducat 1717 ....*......   150.00

ERNEST AUGUST, 1728-1748
Hercules and lion. Rev. Mountain.

2700.   1 Ducat ND 150.00

Initials in shield. Rev. Legend.

2701.   1 Ducat 1745 ....   200.00

Bust amid trophies. Rev. Rose bush and sheep.

2702.   1 Ducat ND 250.00

FREDERICK III, ADMINISTRATOR
Bust. Rev. Felicitas standing.

2703.   1 Ducat 1752 ....   225.00

Bust. Rev. Arms.

2704.   1 Ducat 1754 ....   225.00

ERNEST AUGUST CONSTANTINE, 1756-1758
Bust. Rev. City view of Eisenach.

2705.   1 Ducat 1756. Homage of Eisenach 225.00

Bust. Rev. Hilarity.

2706.   1 Ducat 1756 ....   225.00

Initials. Rev. Hilarity standing.

2707.   1 Ducat 1756 ....   225.00

Armored bust. Rev. Arms and value.

2708.   1 Pistole ND 750.00

ANNE AMALIA, 1758-1775
Bust. Rev. Arms.

2709.   1 Ducat 1764 ....   750.00

Bust. Rev. Arms and value.

2710.   1 Pistole 1764 ....   750.00

SAXONY-WEISSENFELS

Dukes of —

JOHN ADOLPH, 1680-1697
Initials of Joan Magdalene, his wife. Rev. Legend. On her death.

2711.   1 Ducat 1686 ....   400.00

JOHN GEORGE, 1697-1712
Duke standing. Rev. Arms.

2712. 1 Ducat 1698 .... 500.00

Bust. Rev. Two shields.

2713. 1 Ducat ND 450.00

CHRISTIAN, 1712-1736
Bust. Rev. Stag.

2714. 1 Ducat 1726, ND 300.00

Bust. Rev. Luther kneeling. On the Reformation.

2715. 1 Ducat 1717 .... 300.00

SAYN-SAYN

Counts —

HENRY, 1568-1606
Arms. Rev. Double eagle. Rudolph II.

2716. 2 Goldgulden 1592 .... 1000.00
2717. 1 Goldgulden 1590 .... 500.00

SAYN-WITTGENSTEIN

Counts —

LOUIS, 1605-1634

Arms. Rev. Double eagle. Ferdinand II.

2718. 1 Goldgulden ND 400.00

Arms. Rev. Orb.

2719. 1 Goldgulden ND. (Zwitter) 500.00
2720. 1 Goldgulden ND. Title of Ferdinand II. 400.00

Three shields. Rev. Double eagle. Ferdinand II.

2721. 1 Goldgulden ND 400.00

Three shields. Rev. Orb.

2722. 1 Goldgulden ND. SI DEUS PRO NOBIS etc. 600.00
2723. 1 Goldgulden ND. Title of Ferdinand II. 500.00

Two shields. Rev. Orb. Ferdinand II.

2724. 1 Goldgulden ND 400.00

JOHN, 1634-1657

Bust. Rev. Arms.

2725. 1 Ducat 1654 .... 750.00

GUSTAVE, 1657-1701
Bust with wig. Rev. Castle, rock and goat.

2726. 2 Ducats 1687 .... 1000.00

SCHAUENBURG

Counts —

ADOLPH XIII, 1576-1601
Count on horse. Rev. Arms.

2727. 20 Ducats 1592 .... 3000.0

Three shields. Rev. Orb. Rudolph II.

2728. 1 Goldgulden 1589, 92, 93, 95, 1600 .... 500.0

ERNEST III, 1601-1622
Arms. Rev. Double eagle.

2729. 1 Goldgulden 1603, 04, 08, 10, 12. Rudolph II. 500.0
2730. 1 Goldgulden 1616. Matthias 500.0

Count on horse. Rev. Dragon over wall.

2731. 20 Ducats ND 3500.0

Count on horse. Rev. Arms.

2732. 20 Ducats ND 3500.0
2733. 10 Ducats ND. 45 or 51 millimetres 1500.0
2734. 5 Ducats ND 1000.0

SCHAUMBURG-LIPPE

Counts, and later, Princes —

WILLIAM, 1748-1777

Head. Rev. Arms.

2735. 10 Taler 1763 .... 500.0
2736. 1 Ducat 1762 ....*...... 275.0

PHILIP ERNEST, 1777-1787
Arms. Rev. Legend.

2737. 1 Ducat 1777 .... 275.0

Bust. Rev. Tablet.

2738. 1 Ducat 1783 .... 300.0

GEORGE WILLIAM, 1807-1860

Head. Rev. Arms.

2739. 10 Taler 1829 .... 600.0

SCHLESWIG-HOLSTEIN

(See under Denmark, period 1523-1559)

SCHLESWIG-HOLSTEIN-GLUCKSBURG

Dukes of —

PHILIP ERNEST, 1698-1729

Arms. Rev. Initials.

2740. 1 Ducat 1716 .... 300.0

SCHLESWIG-HOLSTEIN-GOTTORP

Dukes of —

JOHN ADOLPH, 1590-1616
Duke standing. Rev. Arms.

2741. 1 Ducat 1601 .... 300.00

FREDERICK III, 1616-1659

Bust. Rev. Arms.

2742. 1 Goldgulden 1619 .... 350.00
2743. 1 Ducat 1642 .... 300.00

Duke standing. Rev. Arms.

2744. 1 Goldgulden 1627 .... 300.00

CHRISTIAN ALBERT, 1659-1694
Bust. Rev. Arms.

2745. 5 Ducats 1674 .... 1000.00
2746. 1 Ducat 1664, 74, 89 .... 300.00

Bust. Rev. Orb.

2747. 1 Goldgulden 1664 .... 350.00

Bust. Rev. Mountain.

2748. 1 Ducat 1689 .... 300.00

FREDERICK IV, 1694-1702

Arms and lions. Rev. Holm Fortress.

2749. 1 Ducat 1698 .... 350.00

Bust. Rev. Arms with two lions.

2750. 1 Ducat 1698, 1700 .... 300.00

Bust. Rev. Arms.

2751. 1 Ducat 1698 .... 375.00

Bust. Rev. Lions in shield and six arms.

2752. 1 Ducat 1698 .... 325.00

CHARLES FREDERICK, 1702-1739
Head. Rev. Lion shield.

2753. ¼ Ducat 1711 .... 150.00

Head. Rev. Arms supported by lions.

2754. 1 Ducat 1705 .... 300.00

Head. Rev. Arms.

2755. 1 Ducat 1706 .... 300.00

Bust. Rev. Arms.

2756. 1 Ducat 1712 .... 300.00

Bust. Rev. Lion shield.

2757. 1 Ducat 1710, 11, ND 300.00

Arms. Rev. Initials.

2758. 1 Ducat 1710 .... 300.00

Lion shield. Rev. Initials.

2759. ¼ Ducat 1708 .... 125.00

SCHLESWIG-HOLSTEIN-PLOEN

Dukes of —

JOHN ADOLPH, 1671-1704
Arms. Rev. Initials.

2760. 1 Ducat 1677 .... 400.00

Bust. Rev. Arms.

2761. 1 Ducat 1690 .... 400.00

FREDERICK CHARLES, 1722-1761

Bust. Rev. Arms.

2762. 1 Ducat 1760. Year under arms ....*...... 350.00
2763. 1 Ducat 1760. Value under arms 350.00

SCHLESWIG-HOLSTEIN-SONDERBURG

Dukes of —

JOHN THE YOUNGER, 1564-1622
Bust. Rev. Orb.

2764. 1 Goldgulden 1619 .... 350.00

ALEXANDER, 1622-1627
Arms. Rev. Orb.

2765. 1 Goldgulden 1624 .... 300.00

SCHWARZBURG

Counts —

THE SONS OF ALBERT VII, 1605-1613
Three helmets. Rev. Arms.

2766. 1 Goldgulden 1606 .... 350.00

Three helmets. Rev. Cross and five shields.

2767. 1 Goldgulden 1606, 08. Mint: Erfurt 250.00
2768. 1 Goldgulden 1611, 13, 16, 18. Mint: Saalfeld 250.00

SCHWARZBURG-RUDOLSTADT

Princes —

GUNTHER XLIII, 1718-1740

Arms. Rev. Legend. From gold of the Goldisthal Mines.

2769. 1 Ducat 1737 .... 650.00

LOUIS FREDERICK II, 1793-1807

Double eagle. Rev. Value.

2770. 1 Ducat 1803 .... 250.00

SCHWARZBURG-SONDERSHAUSEN

Princes —

CHRISTIAN WILLIAM, 1666-1721

Bust. Rev. Shield.

2771. ¼ Ducat 1684, 86 .... 100.00

Bust. Rev. Arms between wild man and wild woman.

2772. 1 Ducat 1679, 84, 89 .... 250.00

ANTHONY GUNTHER II, 1697-1716

Bust. Rev. Arms.

2773. 1 Ducat 1680 .... 350.00

SILESIA

Protestant States of —

Silesian eagle. Rev. "Jehova" beneath radiate clouds.

2774. 1 Ducat 1634 .... 400.00

SILESIA-JAEGERNDORF

Dukes of —

GEORGE FREDERICK, 1543-1603

Duke standing. Rev. Arms.

2775. 4 Ducats 1592. Thick 2500.00
2776. 2 Ducats 1592. Thick 1500.00
2777. 1 Ducat 1561, 92, 95, 96 .... 900.00

Arms. Rev. Double eagle. Name of Ferdinand I.

2778. 1 Ducat 1563 .... 800.00

Arms. Rev. Double eagle. Name of Rudolph II.

2779. 1 Ducat 1578 .... 800.00

JOHN GEORGE, 1606-1621

Half-length bust. Rev. Oval arms with three helmets.

2780. 12 Ducats ND 4000.00
2781. 10 Ducats ND 3500.00
2782. 5 Ducats ND 2000.00
2783. 4 Ducats ND 2000.00

Half-length bust to right. Rev. Arms with three helmets.

2784. 10 Ducats 1611 .... 3500.00
2785. 8 Ducats 1611 .... 3000.00
2786. 7 Ducats 1611 .... 3000.00
2787. 5 Ducats 1611. Two sizes 2000.00
2788. 4 Ducats ND 1500.00

Bust. Rev. Arms with three helmets.

2789. 4 Ducats 1610 .... 2000.00
2790. 3 Ducats 1610 .... 1500.00

Half-length bust facing. Rev. Arms with three helmets.

2791. 10 Ducats 1611 .... 3500.00

Duke standing. Rev. Crowned oval arms.

2792. 3 Ducats ND 1000.00
2793. 2 Ducats 1618, 20, 21, ND ....*...... 350.00

Duke standing. Rev. Arms with three helmets.

2794. 1 Ducat 1610 .... 600.00

Duke standing. Rev. Crowned arms.

2795. 1 Ducat 1611 .... 600.00

Half-length bust. Rev. Crowned arms.

2796. 1 Ducat 1612, 20 .... 350.00
2797. 1 Ducat 1614, 16, 17. With oval arms. 350.00

Crowned arms. Rev. Legend.

2798. 2 Ducats 1617. Thick 700.00
2799. 1 Ducat 1620. Thick 400.00
2800. ½ Ducat 1615, 17, 20-22 ....*...... 200.00

SILESIA-LIEGNITZ-BRIEG

Dukes of —

WENCESLAS, 1348-1364

Lily. Rev. St. John.

2801. 1 Goldgulden ND 200.00

FREDERICK II, 1488-1547

Bust. Rev. Arms.

2802. 5 Ducats 1545 .... 1500.00
2803. 1 Ducat 1543, 44 .... 300.00

JOACHIM FREDERICK, 1587-1602

Bust. Rev. Arms.

2804. 1 Ducat 1600 .... 250.00

Bust. Rev. Legend. On his death.

2805. 5 Ducats 1602 .... 1200.00
2806. 2 Ducats 1602 .... 600.00

JOHN CHRISTIAN AND GEORGE RUDOLPH, 1602-1621

Two busts facing. Rev. Crowned arms.

2807. 1 Ducat 1604-06 .... 200.00

Two busts facing each other. Rev. Crowned arms.

2808.	2 Ducats 1608. Square	....	400.00
2809.	2 Ducats 1609	...........................*......	300.00
2810.	1 Ducat 1606-09	....	200.00
2811.	½ Ducat ND	....	150.00

Two busts facing each other. Rev. Arms with three helmets.

2812.	10 Ducats 1609, 10, 17, 19	....	1500.00
2813.	7 Ducats 1610	....	900.00
2814.	6 Ducats 1607, 17, 19, 21	....	750.00
2815.	5 Ducats 1608-10, 19, 21	....	600.00
2816.	4 Ducats 1605, 07, 09, 10	...........*......	450.00
2817.	3 Ducats 1610, 13	....	350.00
2818.	1 Ducat 1620	....	250.00
2819.	½ Ducat 1620	....	175.00

Half-length bust to right over two arms. Rev. Half-length bust to left of George Rudolph over two arms.

2820. 10 Ducats 1609 .... 1500.00

Bust to right between two arms. Rev. Bust of George Rudolph to left between two arms.

2821.	10 Ducats 1611	....	1500.00
2822.	6 Ducats 1611	....	750.00
2823.	5 Ducats 1611, 17	....	600.00
2824.	4 Ducats 1611	.....................*......	450.00
2825.	4 Ducats 1610, 11. Square	....	600.00
2826.	3 Ducats 1611, 17, 19	....	350.00
2827.	3 Ducats 1610. Square	....	500.00
2828.	2 Ducats 1609-11	....	300.00
2829.	2 Ducats 1610. Square	....	350.00
2830.	1 Ducat 1610, 11, 19	....	200.00

Crowned arms. Rev. Legend.

2831.	1 Ducat 1610. Thick	....	350.00
2832.	½ Ducat 1610. Legend in 6 lines	..........*......	125.00
2833.	½ Ducat 1610. Legend in 5 lines	....	150.00

Two busts facing each other. Rev. Crown over two arms.

2834. 1 Ducat 1612 .... 250.00

Two busts facing each other over two arms. Rev. Legend.

2835.	1 Ducat 1619. Thick	....	325.00
2836.	½ Ducat 1619	....	175.00
2837.	½ Ducat 1619. Square	....	250.00

Crown over two arms. Rev. Legend.

2838.	¼ Ducat 1619	....	250.00
2839.	¼ Ducat 1619. Square	....	250.00

Bust to right between two arms. Rev. Bust of George Rudolph to left between two arms. Struck at Reichenstein.

2840.	4 Ducats 1614	....	850.00
2841.	2 Ducats 1614	....	650.00
2842.	1 Ducat 1614	....	450.00

Two busts facing. Rev. Arms with three helmets. Struck at Reichenstein.

2843.	10 Ducats 1617	....	1500.00
2844.	8 Ducats 1617	....	1250.00
2845.	6 Ducats 1615, 16	....	1000.00
2846.	5 Ducats 1615, 16	....	600.00

JOHN CHRISTIAN, DIED 1639
Bust. Rev. Arms with three helmets.

2847.	7 Ducats 1621	....	900.00
2848.	5 Ducats 1622. Kreuzberg	....	700.00
2849.	4 Ducats 1622	....	600.00
2850.	3 Ducats 1622	....	600.00
2851.	3 Ducats 1622. Square	....	700.00

GEORGE RUDOLPH, DIED 1653
Bust. Rev. Crowned arms.

2852.	5 Ducats 1621	....	750.00
2853.	3 Ducats 1622	....	600.00
2854.	2 Ducats 1622	....	350.00

Bust. Rev. Arms with three helmets.

2855.	8 Ducats 1621	....	1000.00
2856.	7 Ducats 1621	....	900.00
2857.	6 Ducats 1621	....	800.00
2858.	1 Ducat 1621	....	175.00

Facing bust. Rev. Legend. On his death.

2859. 2 Ducats 1653 .... 375.00

GEORGE, LOUIS AND CHRISTIAN, 1639-1663

Three half-length busts. Rev. Arms with three helmets.

2860.	5 Ducats 1656, 58, 59	750.00
2861.	4 Ducats 1652, 58, 59	850.00
2862.	3 Ducats 1651, 58, 60	650.00
2863.	2 Ducats 1651, 53, 57-59 ....*	350.00
2864.	1 Ducat 1651-62	200.00
2865.	½ Ducat 1651, 52, 52/53, 52/54, 56	100.00

GEORGE III, 1639-1664

Crowned bust. Rev. Arms with three helmets.

2866.	1 Ducat 1660 ....*	250.00
2867.	1 Ducat 1664. Reichenstein	300.00

Facing bust. Rev. Legend. On his death.

2868.	2 Ducats 1664	350.00

LOUIS, 1653-1663

Crowned bust. Rev. Arms with three helmets.

2869.	1 Ducat 1661 ....*	300.00
2870.	1 Ducat 1662. With DUCES	300.00

CHRISTIAN, 1639-1673

Crowned bust. Rev. Arms with three helmets.

2871.	1 Ducat 1660. With DUCES ....*	300.00
2872.	1 Ducat 1661. Two different legends on Rev.	300.00

Bust. Rev. Eagle.

2873.	10 Ducats 1666	1500.00
2874.	5 Ducats 1672	1000.00
2875.	3 Ducats 1666	750.00
2876.	2 Ducats 1666, 70, 72 ....*	350.00
2877.	1 Ducat 1666, 70, 72	250.00

LOUISE, DIED 1680

Facing bust. Rev. Two arms.

2878.	¼ Ducat 1674	150.00

GEORGE WILLIAM, 1672-1675

Bust. Rev. Eagle.

2879.	2 Ducats 1675	750.00
2880.	1 Ducat 1674, 75 ....*	250.00
2881.	¼ Ducat 1675	100.00

Facing bust. Rev. Eagle.

2882.	1 Ducat 1675. Thick	375.00
2883.	½ Ducat 1675 ....*	150.00

Bust. Rev. Legend. On his death.

2884.	2 Ducats 1675	600.00

SILESIA-MUENSTERBERG

Duke of —

JOHN WEIKHARD, 1654-1677
Facing bust. Rev. Arms.

2885.	1 Ducat ND	400.00

SILESIA-MUENSTERBERG-OELS

Dukes of —

ALBERT AND CHARLES, 1498-1511

St. James standing. Rev. Arms on cross.

2886.	1 Goldgulden ND	600.00

St. James standing. Rev. Cross and four arms.

2887.	1 Goldgulden 1510, 11	400.00

CHARLES I, 1498-1536
Bust. Rev. Arms.

2888.	2 Ducats 1528	900.00

St. James standing. Rev. Cross and four arms.

2889.	1 Goldgulden 1512-19 ....*	200.00
2890.	1 Goldgulden 1515, 22, ND. With name on Rev.	300.00

Arms. Rev. St. Christopher.

2891. 1 Ducat 1520-22, 26-36 .... 250.00

JOACHIM, HENRY II, JOHN AND GEORGE, 1536-1558

Arms. Rev. St. Christopher.

2892. 1 Ducat 1537-53 .... 250.00

JOACHIM, HENRY III AND CHARLES II, 1552-1562

Arms. Rev. St. Christopher.

2893. 1 Ducat 1553-58, 60-62 .... 250.00

JOHN, DIED 1565

Bust. Rev. Arms.

2894. 1 Ducat 1553-62 .... 300.00

Bust. Rev. Five shields.

2895. 1 Ducat 1563, 64, 65 .... 300.00

HENRY III AND CHARLES II, 1562-1587

Five shields. Rev. St. Christopher.

2896. 1 Ducat 1563-70 .... 250.00

Arms. Rev. St. Christopher.

2897. 1 Ducat 1569 .... 250.00

CHARLES II, 1548-1617

Bust. Rev. Arms.

2898. 2 Ducats 1593. Thick 750.00
2899. 1 Ducat 1593 ....*...... 300.00

Bust. Rev. Arms with three helmets.

2900. 10 Ducats 1612, 13, 16 .... 1500.00
2901. 9 Ducats 1612 .... 1500.00
2902. 6 Ducats 1611, 15, 16 .... 1200.00
2903. 5 Ducats 1611-13, 15, 16 ....*..... 900.00
2904. 4 Ducats 1613, 15 .... 750.00
2905. 3 Ducats 1613, 14 .... 600.00
2906. 2 Ducats 1614, 15 .... 375.00

Bust. Rev. Five shields.

2907. 4 Ducats 1612 .... 900.00
2908. 3 Ducats 1612 .... 750.00

Bust. Rev. Crowned arms.

2909. 2 Ducats 1612 .... 900.00
2910. 1 Ducat 1611-16 .... 250.00

Eagle. Rev. Four shields.

2911. ½ Ducat 1612 .... 150.00

Eagle. Rev. Crowned arms.

2912. ½ Ducat 1616 .... 150.00

Bust over arms. Rev. Legend. On his death.

2913. 12½ Ducats 1617 .... 2000.00
2914. 10 Ducats 1617 .... 1500.00
2915. 6 Ducats 1617 .... 850.00

Bust. Rev. Legend. On his death.

2916. 2 Ducats 1617 .... 600.00

HENRY WENCESLAS AND CHARLES FREDERICK, 1617-1639

Two busts facing each other. Rev. Arms with three helmets.

2917. 5 Ducats 1620, 21 .... 900.00
2918. 4 Ducats 1619, 21 .... 750.00
2919. 3 Ducats 1619, 21, 22 ....*...... 600.00

Half-length bust to right. Rev. Half-length bust of Charles
Frederick to left. Five shields are on each side.

2920.	6 Ducats 1619	1000.00
2921.	4 Ducats 1620	750.00
2922.	3 Ducats 1620, 21	600.00
2923.	2 Ducats 1621	300.00

Bust to right. Rev. Bust of Charles Frederick to left.

2924.	1 Ducat 1619, 20, 21	275.00

SILESIA-SCHWEIDNITZ

Dukes of —

BOICO II, 1326-1368
Lily. Rev. St. John.

2925.	1 Goldgulden ND	350.00

SILESIA-TESCHEN

Dukes of —

ADAM WENCESLAS, 1579-1617
Half-length bust. Rev. Helmeted eagle-shield supported by
angels.

2926.	5 Ducats 1611	1200.00

Half-length bust. Rev. Eagle.

2927.	8 Ducats 1609	1500.00
2928.	5 Ducats 1609	1200.00

Bust. Rev. Eagle.

2929.	3 Ducats 1613. Square	850.00

ELISABETH LUCRETIA, 1625-1653
Facing bust. Rev. Arms.

2930.	10 Ducats 1650	2000.00
2931.	5 Ducats 1650	1500.00

SILESIA-TROPPAU

Dukes of —

PRZEMISLAW, 1366-1433
Arms. Rev. Duke standing with flag and sword.

2932.	1 Goldgulden ND	1250.00

SILESIA-WURTTEMBERG-OELS

Counts —

SYLVIUS FREDERICK, 1673-1697

Bust. Rev. Arms.

2933.	2 Ducats 1677	850.00
2934.	1 Ducat 1674, 75, 76 ....*......	350.00

Bust. Rev. Bust of Eleonore Charlotte. On their wedding.

2935.	1 Ducat ND (1672)	350.00

CHRISTIAN ULRIC, 1673-1704
Bust. Rev. Helmeted arms.

2936.	1 Ducat 1679, 98, 1701, 03	750.00

Bust. Rev. Crowned arms.

2937.	1 Ducat 1681, 83	750.00
2938.	½ Ducat 1683	375.00
2939.	¼ Ducat 1685 ....*......	200.00

Bust. Rev. Five shields and four initials crossed.

2940.	1 Ducat 1696	600.00

Bust of Sybil Marie. Rev. Blank.

2941.	½ Ducat ND. Square	150.00

Bust. Rev. Bust of Anne.

2942.	¼ Ducat ND. (1680)	150.00

Bust. Rev. Bust of Sophia of Mecklenburg. On his wedding.

2943.	1 Ducat ND. (1700) Two different dies	275.00

CHARLES OF JULIUSBURG, 1684-1745
Bust. Rev. Arms.

2944.	1 Ducat 1705	750.00

CHARLES FREDERICK, 1704-1744
Bust. Rev. Arms.

2945.	1 Ducat 1708, 11, 13, 14	750.00
2946.	¼ Ducat 1711	150.00

Arms. Rev. Initials.

2947.	¼ Ducat 1708	100.00

SINZENDORF

Counts —

GEORGE LOUIS, 1632-1680
Bust with cap. Rev. Arms.

2948.	1 Ducat 1676	600.00

PHILIP LOUIS, 1687-1742
Bust. Rev. Arms.

2949.	1 Ducat 1726	350.00

JOHN WILLIAM, 1742-1766

Bust. Rev. Arms.

2950.	1 Ducat 1753	350.00

SOLMS-LAUBACH

Counts —

CHRISTIAN AUGUST, 1738-1784
Bust. Rev. Arms and value.

2951.	1 Ducat 1761	500.00

SOLMS-LICH

Counts —

ERNEST I, EBERHARD AND HERMAN ADOLPH, 1588-1590
Arms. Rev. Double eagle. Name of Rudolph II.

2952.	1 Goldgulden 1589	700.00

HERMAN ADOLPH, GEORGE EBERHARD, ERNEST II AND PHILIP, 1590-1610
Arms. Rev. Double eagle. Name of Rudolph II.

2953.   1 Goldgulden 1601 ....   600.00

ERNEST II, 1602-1619
Arms. Rev. Double eagle. Name of Matthias.

2954.   1 Goldgulden 1615 ....   700.00

PHILIP, DIED 1631
Arms. Rev. Double eagle. Name of Matthias.

2955.   1 Goldgulden 1616 ....   300.00

Arms. Rev. Double eagle. Name of Ferdinand II.

2956.   1 Goldgulden 1623 ....   300.00

Arms. Rev. Emperor Matthias standing.

2957.   1 Ducat 1613 ....   700.00

PHILIP REINHARD I, 1613-1635
Arms. Rev. Initials of Christian IV of Denmark.

2958.   2 Ducats 1627 ....   1000.00
2959.   1 Ducat 1627 ....   700.00

CHARLES, DEPOSED 1918
Arms. Rev. Wreath.

2960.   1 Ducat 1908, 12 ....   100.00

SOLMS-ROEDELHEIM

Counts —

JOHN AUGUST AND HIS BROTHERS, 1632-1665
Arms. Rev. Value in wreath.

2961.   1 Ducat 1656 ....   650.00

JOHN AUGUST, 1665-1680
Bust. Rev. Arms.

2962.   1 Ducat 1680 ....   700.00

SPEYER

Bishops of —

PHILIP CHRISTOPHER, 1610-1652
Arms. Rev. Madonna.

2963.   2 Goldgulden 1612 ....   1500.00

LOTHAR FREDERICK, 1652-1675
Bust. Rev. Arms.

2964.   1 Ducat 1665 ....   600.00

HENRY HARTARD, 1711-1719
Bust. Rev. Arms.

2965.   2 Ducats 1711 ....   900.00

DAMIAN HUGO, 1719-1743

Arms. Rev. City view of Bruchsal.

2966.   2 Ducats 1726 ....   750.00
2967.   1 Ducat 1726 ....*......   350.00

FRANCIS CHRISTOPHER, 1743-1770

Bust. Rev. Seated and kneeling figures.

2968.   1 Ducat 1745 ....   350.00

AUGUST, 1770-1797

Three shields. Rev. Minerva with four genii.

2969.   1 Ducat 1770 ....   300.00

STETTIN

Swedish Kings of —

Facing bust of Gustave Adolphe. Rev. Arms.

2970.   1 Ducat 1632 ....   375.00

STOLBERG

Counts, and later, Princes —
A. The Stolberg Line (Stolberg-Stolberg)

LOUIS II AND HIS BROTHERS, 1555-1571
Arms. Rev. Double eagle. Name of Charles V.

2971.   1 Goldgulden ND 1200.00

LOUIS II, 1535-1574
Arms. Rev. Double eagle. Name of Ferdinand I.

2972.   1 Goldgulden 1560. Mint: Augsburg 750.00

Five shields in enclosure. Rev. Double eagle. Name of Maximilian II.

2973.   1 Goldgulden 1567. Mint: Frankfurt 800.00

Five shields. Rev. Orb. Name of Maximilian II.

2974.   1 Goldgulden ND. Mint: Noerdlingen 800.00

JOHN AND HENRY XXII, 1607-1612
Stag. Rev. Arms.

2975.   1 Goldgulden 1607, 09 ....   450.00

Stag and column. Rev. Arms.

2976.   1 Goldgulden 1612 ....   450.00

JOHN, 1606-1612
Stag. Rev. Legend. On his death.

2977.   1 Goldgulden 1612 ....   450.00

HENRY XXII AND WOLFGANG GEORGE, 1612-1615
Stag. Rev. Arms.

2978.   1 Goldgulden 1613, 14, ND 275.00

WOLFGANG GEORGE, 1615-1631
Arms. Rev. Stag.

2979. 1 Goldgulden 1619, 25, 26 .... 250.00

CHRISTOPHER II AND HENRY VOLRAD, 1618-1632
Stag. Rev. Double eagle. Name of Matthias.

2980. 1 Goldgulden 1619 .... 600.00

JOHN MARTIN, 1638-1669
Stag. Rev. Arms.

2981. 2 Ducats 1646 .... 800.00

Stag and column. Rev. Value on tablet.

2982. 1 Ducat 1647, 49, 53 .... 250.00

CHRISTOPHER FREDERICK AND JOST CHRISTIAN, 1704-1738
Stag and column. Rev. Arms.

2983. 2 Ducats 1725 .... 400.00
2984. 1 Ducat 1706, 23, 25, 34 .... 250.00
2985. ¼ Ducat 1706 .... 125.00

Martin Luther at table. Rev. Legend. On the Reformation.

2986. 1 Ducat 1717 .... 200.00

CHRISTOPHER FREDERICK, 1704-1738
Initials. Rev. Stag and column.

2987. ½ Ducat 1715 .... 75.00
2988. ¼ Ducat ND 50.00
2989. ⅛ Ducat ND 50.00

JOST CHRISTIAN, 1704-1739
Initials. Rev. Stag and column.

2990. ¼ Ducat ND 50.00
2991. ⅛ Ducat ND 100.00

Stag and column. Rev. Arms.

2992. ¼ Ducat ND 50.00

CHRISTIAN LOUIS II AND FREDERICK BOTHO, 1739-1761

Stag and column. Rev. Arms.

2993. 4 Ducats 1743 .... 1000.00
2994. 2 Ducats 1743 .... 350.00
2995: 1 Ducat 1740, 42, 43, 48, 50, 57 ....*..... 250.00
2996. ½ Ducat 1745, 48, 50 .... 100.00
2997. ¼ Ducat ND 75.00
2998. ⅛ Ducat ND 50.00

CHRISTOPHER LOUIS II, 1738-1761
Initials. Rev. Stag and column.

2999. ¼ Ducat ND 75.00
3000. ⅛ Ducat ND 50.00
3001. 1⁄16 Ducat ND 50.00
3002. 1⁄32 Ducat ND 50.00

FREDERICK BOTHO AND CHARLES LOUIS, 1761-1768

Stag and column. Rev. Arms.

3003. 2 Ducats 1764 .... 750.00
3004. 1 Ducat 1762, 64, 66 ....*..... 250.00
3005. ½ Ducat 1762, 66 .... 125.00

FREDERICK BOTHO, 1739-1768
Initials. Rev. Stag and column.

3006. ¼ Ducat ND 75.00
3007. ⅛ Ducat ND 60.00

CHARLES LOUIS AND HENRY CHRISTIAN FREDERICK, 1768-1810

Stag and column. Rev. Arms.

3008. 1 Ducat 1768, 70, 88, 93, 96 ....*......, 250.00
3009. ½ Ducat 1768. From the ducat die 450.00
3010. ½ Ducat 1768. (very rare), 70 .... 200.00

CHARLES LOUIS, 1796-1810
Bust. Rev. Arms.

3011. 1 Ducat 1796 .... 300.00

B. The Wernigerode Line

LOUIS GEORGE, DIED 1618
Arms. Rev. Stag and column. On the Reformation.

3012. 1 Goldgulden 1617 .... 400.00

HENRY ERNEST, 1638-1672
Stag. Rev. Arms.

3013. 1 Ducat 1661 .... 500.00

ERNEST, DIED 1710
Bust. Rev. Legend. On his death.

3014. 1 Ducat 1710 .... 375.00

FREDERICK CHARLES, 1710-1767
Head. Rev. Stag and column.

3015. 1 Ducat 1719 .... 450.00

CHRISTIAN ERNEST, 1710-1771
Stag. Rev. Arms.

3016. 1 Ducat 1742, 59 .... 250.00

Bust. Rev. Stag.

3017. 1 Ducat 1768 .... 250.00

Bust. Rev. Arms.

3018. 1 Ducat 1730 .... 250.00

HENRY ERNEST II, 1771-1778
Head. Rev. Stag.

3019. 1 Ducat 1778 .... 250.00

CHRISTIAN FREDERICK, 1778-1824
Stag. Rev. Value on tablet.

3020. 1 Ducat 1784, 95 .... 250.00

Stag. Rev. Value and date in wreath. On the golden wedding.

3021. 1 Ducat 1818 .... 225.00

HENRY XII, 1824-1854
Bust. Rev. Stag and value.

3022. 1 Ducat 1824 .... 200.00

STRALSUND

City emblem. Rev. Orb. Ferdinand II.

3023. 1 Goldgulden 1628-31 .... 300.00

City emblem. Rev. Double eagle. Ferdinand II.

3024. 1 Ducat 1632, 33, 35, ND 300.00

City emblem. Rev. Double eagle. Ferdinand III.

3025. 1 Ducat ND, 1638, 40, 41, 44, 55 .... 300.00

City emblem. Rev. Double eagle. Leopold I.

3026. 1 Ducat 1658, 62, 64, 66, 71, 77, 81 .... 300.00

SUEBIAN LEAGUE

Arms. Rev. Two shields.

3027. 1 Ducat 1737 .... 600.00

TEUTONIC ORDER

Grand Masters of —
A. Coinage in Prussia

HENRY VON PLAUEN, 1410-1413
Arms on cross. Rev. Madonna.

3028. 1 Ducat ND 1500.00

Grand Master standing. Rev. Madonna standing.

3029. 1 Ducat ND 1500.00

ALBERT OF BRANDENBURG, 1511-1525
Arms on cross. Rev. Madonna with shield.

3030. 2 Goldgulden 1521 .... 2500.00

Arms on cross. Rev. Madonna over shield.

3031. 1 Goldgulden ND 1500.00

B. Coinage in Mergentheim

WALTER VON CRONBERG, 1526-1543
Three shields. Rev. Madonna.

3032. 1 Goldgulden 1531 .... 1250.00

HENRY VON BOBENHAUSEN, 1572-1590
Three shields. Rev. Madonna.

3033. 1 Ducat 1575 .... 1250.00

MAXIMILIAN OF AUSTRIA, 1590-1618
Grand Master standing. Rev. Arms.

3034. 2 Ducats ND 600.00
3035. 1 Ducat 1597, ND 250.00

CHARLES OF AUSTRIA, 1619-1624
Head. Rev. Arms between arms of Brixen and Breslau.

3036. 1 Ducat ND 300.00

Armored bust. Rev. Arms.

3037. 2 Ducats ND 500.00

JOHN EUSTACE VON WESTERNACH, 1624-1627
Three shields. Rev. Double eagle.

3038. 1 Ducat 1626 .... 375.00

JOHN CASPAR I VON STADION, 1627-1641
Madonna. Rev. Arms.

3039. 1 Ducat ND .... Rare

JOHN CASPER II VON AMPRINGEN, 1664-1684
Armored bust. Rev. Madonna.

3040. 1 Ducat 1673 .... 375.00

Arms. Rev. Madonna.

3041. 2 Ducats 1666 .... 900.00
3042. 1 Ducat 1666 .... 250.00

FRANCIS LOUIS OF THE PALATINATE-NEUBURG, 1694-1732
Bust. Rev. Arms.

3043. 1 Ducat 1696 .... 400.00

Armored bust. Rev. Five shields.

3044. 1 Ducat 1699, 1701 .... 400.00

CHARLES ALEXANDER OF LORRAINE, 1761-1780
Bust. Rev. Arms.

3045. 1 Ducat 1765 .... 300.00

THURN AND TAXIS

Princes —

ANSELM FRANCIS, 1714-1739
Bust. Rev. Arms and lions.

3046. 1 Ducat 1734 .... 500.00

TRIER (TREVES)

Archbishops of —

BOEMUND, 1354-1362

Lily. Rev. St. John.

3047. 1 Goldgulden ND 200.00

CONRAD, 1362-1388
A. Coinage of the Coblenz Mint.
Lily. Rev. St. John standing.

3048. 1 Goldgulden ND 100.00

Arms in octofoil. Rev. St. John standing.

3049. 1 Goldgulden ND 100.00

Arms in trefoil. Rev. St. John standing.

3050. 1 Goldgulden ND 100.00

St. Peter on throne. Rev: Arms in octofoil.

3051. 1 Goldgulden ND 100.00

St. Peter on throne over shield of Minzenberg. Rev. Arms in trefoil.

3052. 1 Goldgulden ND 100.00

St. Peter on throne over shields of Minzenberg and Saarwerden. Rev. Arms in trefoil.

3053. 1 Goldgulden ND 150.00
3054. 1 Goldgulden ND. Arms in sexfoil 100.00

St. Peter on throne over shields of Minzenberg. Rev. Arms in sexfoil.

3055. 1 Goldgulden ND 100.00

St. Peter on throne over shield of Minzenberg. Rev. Two shields in sexfoil.

3056. 1 Goldgulden ND 100.00

St. Peter on throne over shields of Trier and Minzenberg. Rev. Arms in sexfoil.

3057. 1 Goldgulden ND 100.00

St. John standing. Rev. Arms and three shields in trefoil.

3058. 1 Goldgulden ND 100.00

B. Coinage of the Wesel Mint.
St. Peter standing under architecture. Rev. Arms in trefoil.

3059. 1 Goldgulden ND 100.00

St. John standing. Rev. Arms and three shields in trefoil.

3060. 1 Goldgulden ND 150.00

C. Coinage of the Trier Mint.
Arms with four shields in sexfoil. Rev. St. Peter on throne over crossed keys.

3061. 1 Goldgulden ND 100.00

St. Peter on throne over crossed keys. Rev. Arms in sexfoil.

3062. 1 Goldgulden ND 100.00

St. John standing. Rev. Arms and three shields in trefoil.

3063. 1 Goldgulden ND 125.00

D. Coinage of the Deutz Mint.
Arms in sexfoil. Rev. Half-length bust of St. Peter under canopy over shield of Minzenberg.

3064. 1 Goldgulden ND. With title as Coadjutor of Cologne   125.00
3065. 1 Goldgulden ND. With title as Administrator 150.00
3066. 1 Goldgulden ND. With title as Vicarius 175.00

St. Peter standing under architecture over shield of Minzenberg. Rev. Arms in sexfoil.

3067. 1 Goldgulden ND. With title as Vicarius 150.00
3068. 1 Goldgulden ND. With title as Administrator 150.00

WERNER, 1388-1418
A. Coinage of the Coblenz Mint.
St. John standing. Rev. Arms and three shields in trefoil.

3069. 1 Goldgulden ND 150.00
3070. 1 Goldgulden ND. Eagle under St. John. 100.00

St. John standing over eagle. Rev. Arms in trefoil.

3071. 1 Goldgulden ND 100.00

St. John standing over cross. Rev. Five shields in quatrefoil.

3072. 1 Goldgulden ND 100.00

Half-length bust of St. Peter over shield of Minzenberg under architecture. Rev. Arms in sexfoil.

3073. 1 Goldgulden ND 150.00

Half-length bust of St. Peter over shield of Minzenberg under architecture. Rev. Arms in trefoil.

3074. 1 Goldgulden ND 100.00
3075. 1 Goldgulden ND. Without name of Werner 150.00

St. Peter standing under architecture. Rev. Arms in trefoil.

3076. 1 Goldgulden ND 100.00

St. John standing. Rev. Angel over arms, two shields and ornament in trefoil.

3077. 1 Goldgulden ND 100.00
3078. 1 Goldgulden ND. Without angel 100.00

B. Coinage of the Wesel Mint.
St. John standing. Rev. Arms and three shields in trefoil.

3079. 1 Goldgulden ND 100.00

St. John standing. Rev. Arms in trefoil.

3080. 1 Goldgulden ND 100.00

St. John standing. Rev. Five shields in quatrefoil.

3081. 1 Goldgulden ND 100.00

St. Peter standing and shield of Minzenberg under architecture. Rev. Arms in trefoil.

3082. 1 Goldgulden ND 125.00

Half-length bust of St. Peter over shield of Minzenberg under architecture. Rev. Arms in trefoil.

3083. 1 Goldgulden ND 100.00

St. Peter standing. Rev. Arms in trefoil.

3084. 1 Goldgulden ND 100.00

St. John standing. Rev. Angel over arms and two shields (and sometimes ornament) in trefoil.

3085. 1 Goldgulden ND 150.00
3086. 1 Goldgulden ND. Without angel 100.00

C. Coinage of the Trier Mint.
Arms in sexfoil. Rev. St. Peter on throne over shield of Minzenberg.

3087. 1 Goldgulden ND 100.00

Half-length bust of St. Peter over shield of Minzenberg under architecture. Rev. Arms in trefoil.

3088. 1 Goldgulden ND 100.00

D. Coinage of the Offenbach Mint.
St. Peter standing under architecture. Rev. Arms in trefoil.

3089. 1 Goldgulden ND 100.00

St. John standing. Rev. Arms, two shields and ornament in trefoil.

3090. 1 Goldgulden ND 100.00

OTTO, 1418-1430
A. Coinage of the Coblenz Mint.
Half-length bust of St. Peter over shield of Ziegenhain under architecture. Rev. Arms in trefoil.

3091. 1 Goldgulden ND 100.00

St. Peter standing behind shield of Ziegenhain. Rev. Arms and four shields in quatrefoil.

3092. 1 Goldgulden ND 100.00

Archbishop standing. Rev. Arms in trefoil.

3093. 1 Goldgulden ND 150.00

B. Coinage of the Wesel Mint.
Half-length bust of St. Peter over shield of Ziegenhain under architecture. Rev. Arms in trefoil.

3094. 1 Goldgulden ND 150.00

St. Peter standing behind shield of Ziegenhain. Rev. Arms and four shields in quatrefoil.

3095. 1 Goldgulden ND 100.00

C. Coinage of the Trier Mint.
St. Peter standing behind shield of Ziegenhain. Rev. Arms and four shields in quatrefoil.

3096. 1 Goldgulden ND 150.00
3097. 1 Goldgulden ND. With three shields and rosette 150.00

D. Coinage of the Offenbach Mint.
Archbishop standing. Rev. Arms in trefoil.

3098. 1 Goldgulden ND 100.00

ULRIC, 1430-1436
Half-length bust of St. Peter over shield of Manderscheid. Rev. Arms in trefoil.

3099. 1 Goldgulden ND. Mint: Coblenz 150.00

RABAN, 1436-1439
Arms on cross. Rev. Three shields.

3100. 1 Goldgulden 1436, 37, 38, ND. Mint: Coblenz 100.00

JAMES, 1439-1456
Arms on cross. Rev. Three shields.

3101. 1 Goldgulden ND. Mint: Coblenz 100.00

JOHN II, 1456-1503
Arms on cross. Rev. Three shields.

3102. 1 Goldgulden ND. Mint: Coblenz 200.00
3103. 1 Goldgulden 1491, 1502. Mint: Wesel 200.00

Christ on throne over shield of Baden. Rev. Cross and four shields.

3104. 1 Goldgulden ND. Mint: Coblenz 175.00

Arms and three shields in trefoil. Rev. Christ on throne over arms.

3105. 1 Goldgulden 1491, 1502. Mint: Coblenz 400.00

JAMES II, 1503-1511
Arms and three shields in trefoil. Rev. Christ on throne over arms.

3106. 1 Goldgulden 1503, 04, 05 .... 750.00

RICHARD GREIFFENKLAU, 1511-1531
Arms and three shields in trefoil. Rev. Christ on throne over arms.

3107. 1 Goldgulden 1511 .... **750.00**

Christ standing. Rev. Arms and three shields in trefoil.

3108. 1 Goldgulden ND **750.00**

Christ on throne. Rev. Arms and three shields in trefoil.

3109. 1 Goldgulden 1518 .... **800.00**

JOHN III, 1531-1540
Arms and three shields in trefoil. Rev. Christ on throne over arms.

3110. 1 Goldgulden 1538 .... **800.00**

JOHN VI, 1556-1567
Christ on throne over arms. Rev. Arms and three shields in trefoil.

3111. 1 Goldgulden 1563, 64 .... **800.00**

JAMES III, 1567-1581
Christ on throne over arms. Rev. Arms and three shields in trefoil.

3112. 1 Goldgulden 1571 .... **800.00**

JOHN VII, 1581-1599
Christ on throne. Rev. Arms and three shields in trefoil.

3113. 1 Goldgulden 1587, 90, 93-95 .... **300.00**

LOTHAR, 1599-1623
Christ on throne over arms. Rev. Arms and three shields in trefoil.

3114. 1 Goldgulden 1601, 05, 08, 09, 13, 17-19, ND. Mint: Coblenz **200.00**

Bust of St. Peter over arms. Rev. Arms and three shields in trefoil.

3115. 1 Goldgulden 1619. Mint: Coblenz **225.00**
3116. 1 Goldgulden 1662. Kipper **500.00**

St. Helen standing. Rev. Five shields in quatrefoil.

3117. 1 Goldgulden 1608, 10, 11. Mint: Trier **225.00**

PHILIP CHRISTOPHER, 1623-1652
Arms. Rev. Madonna.

3118. 1 Goldgulden 1632. Philipsburg **750.00**

CHARLES CASPAR, 1652-1676
Facing bust. Rev. Arms.

3119. 1 Ducat 1654, 56 .... **300.00**

JOHN HUGO, 1676-1711
Bust. Rev. Arms.

3120. 2 Ducats 1703 .... **750.00**
3121. 1 Ducat 1680, 84, 91, 92, 99 .... **500.00**
3122. ½ Ducat ND **175.00**

Bust. Rev. Three shields.

3123. 1 Ducat 1690 .... **600.00**

St. Peter and value. Rev. Three shields.

3124. 1 Goldgulden 1684, 94, 1700, 01 .... **250.00**

FRANCIS LOUIS, 1716-1729
Bust. Rev. Arms.

3125. 1 Ducat 1720, 22 .... **375.00**

Bust. Rev. Lion.

3126. 1 Ducat 1721 .... **350.00**

FRANCIS GEORGE, 1729-1756
Bust. Rev. Arms supported by lions.

3127. 2 Ducats 1735, 45, 50, 52 .... **500.00**

3128. 1 Ducat 1735, 50, 52 .... **300.00**

JOHN PHILIP, 1756-1768
Bust. Rev. Arms supported by lions.

3129. 1 Ducat 1759. With VNIONE MIRIFICA SPLENDESCO .. **850.00**
3130. 1 Ducat 1760, 61, 62 .... **300.00**

CLEMENT WENCESLAS, 1768-1803
Bust. Rev. Arms.

3131. 1 Ducat 1770 .... **300.00**

ULM

Arms. Rev. Book. On the Reformation.

3132. 2 Ducats 1617 .... **500.00**

Tablet. Rev. Arms.

3133. 1 Ducat 1635, 36, 38, ND **300.00**

Wreath. Rev. Arms.

3134. 2 Ducats 1639 .... **800.00**
3135. 1 Ducat 1639 .... **300.00**

Bust of Joseph I. Rev. Arms.

3136. 1 Ducat 1705 .... **500.00**

Arms. Rev. Legend. Necessity coins.

3137. 6 Goldgulden 1704. Square **1750.00**
3138. 1 Goldgulden 1704 ....*...... **350.00**

Arms. Rev. Legend. On the Reformation.

3139. 1 Ducat 1717 .... **300.00**
3140. ½ Ducat 1717 .... **200.00**

Arms. Rev. Altar or Book. On the Augsburg Confession.

3141. 2 Ducats 1730. Rev. Altar ....*...... **375.00**
3142. 1 Ducat 1730. Rev. Book **250.00**
3143. ½ Ducat 1730. Rev. Book **150.00**

Bust of Charles VII. Rev. Arms.

3144. 1 Ducat 1742 .... **500.00**

WALDECK

Counts, and later, Princes —

CHRISTIAN AND WOLRAD IV, 1588-1640

Arms. Rev. Double Eagle.

3145. 1 Goldgulden 1615-17, 22, ND **600.00**

GEORGE FREDERICK, JOHN AND HENRY WOLRAD, 1645-1664

Arms. Rev. Palm tree.

3146.　1 Ducat 1654 .... 600.00

CHARLES AUGUST FREDERICK, 1728-1763
Head. Rev. Arms.

3147.　1 Ducat 1731, 32, 36, 42, 50 .... 400.00
3148.　½ Ducat 1736 .... 250.00
3149.　¼ Ducat 1741, 60, 61 .... 100.00
3150.　1 Carolin 1734. Head right 750.00
3151.　1 Carolin 1750. Head left 750.00
3152.　2 Ducats 1750. Head left 750.00

Bust left. Rev. Arms.

3153.　10 Ducats 1752 .... 1750.00
3154.　1 Ducat 1762 .... 350.00

Bust right. Rev. Arms.

3155.　1 Ducat 1762 .... 350.00

Head. Rev. Cross of initials.

3156.　1 Carolin 1734 .... 650.00

Head. Rev. Arms and initials.

3157.　½ Carolin 1734 .... 350.00

Bust. Rev. Cross of initials.

3158.　½ Carolin 1735 .... 750.00
3159.　¼ Carolin 1735 .... 300.00

FREDERICK, 1763-1812
Head. Rev. Arms.

3160.　1 Ducat 1781 .... 750.00

WALLMODEN-GIMBORN

Counts —

LOUIS, DIED 1811

Initials. Rev. Value.

3161.　1 Ducat 1802 .... 500.00

WERDEN AND HELMSTAEDT

Abbots of —

HENRY IV DUECKER, 1646-1667

Arms. Rev. Value.

3162.　1 Ducat 1647 .... 700.00

WESTPHALIA

Kings of —

JEROME NAPOLEON, 1807-1813

Arms. Rev. Value.

3163.　10 Taler 1810 .... 350.00
3164.　5 Taler 1810 ....*..... 250.00

Laureate head. Rev. Value.

3165.　10 Taler 1811-13 ....*...... 400.00
3166.　5 Taler 1811, 12 .... 300.00

Laureate head. Rev. Value in wreath.

3167.　40 Francs 1813, Restrike 1000.00
3168.　20 Francs 1808-11 ....*...... 250.00
3169.　10 Francs 1813. Without wreath. 150.00
3170.　5 Francs 1813. Without wreath. 150.00

WIED

Counts —

FREDERICK ALEXANDER, 1737-1791

Bust. Rev. Tree and all seeing eye.

3171.　1 Ducat 1744 .... 350.00

Bust. Rev. Peacock.

3172.　1 Goldgulden 1751 .... 350.00

Bust. Rev. City view of Neuwied.

3173.　2 Ducats 1752 .... 750.00
3174.　1 Pistole 1752. Rev. Arms. ....*...... 600.00

WISMAR

St. Lawrence. Rev. City arms.
3175. 1 Goldgulden 1558 .... 750.00

St. Lawrence. Rev. Double eagle. Name of Rudolph II.
3176. 1 Goldgulden 1587, 91, 97, 1604, ND 600.00

St. Lawrence. Rev. Double eagle. Name of Matthias.
3177. 1 Goldgulden 1616 .... 600.00

St. Lawrence. Rev. Double eagle. Name of Ferdinand II.
3178. 1 Goldgulden 1626, 29, 32 .... 600.00

Arms. Rev. Double eagle. Struck under Swedish rule.
3179. 1 Ducat 1672, 76 .... 1200.00
3180. 1 Ducat 1743 ....*...... 550.00

WORMS

A. City of —

Bust of Madonna over shield. Rev. Double eagle.
3181. 1 Goldgulden 1510, ND 750.00

Dragon with shield. Rev. Double eagle.
3182. 1½ Goldgulden 1571. Square 850.00
3183. 1   Goldgulden ND (1519-56) 650.00
3184. 1   Goldgulden 1614-22 ....*...... 250.00
3185. 1   Ducat 1651, 55 .... 750.00

B. Bishops of —

GEORGE, 1580-1595
St. John. Rev. Lily.
3186. 1 Goldgulden 1588-93 .... 700.00

WURTTEMBERG

Dukes, and later, Kings of —

ULRIC, 1498-1550

Duke standing. Rev. Arms.
3187. 2 Goldgulden ND 1250.00

3188. 1 Goldgulden ND ....*...... 300.00

Bust. Rev. Arms.
3189. 2 Ducats 1513 .... 1250.00

Bust with hat. Rev. Arms.
3190. 2 Ducats 1537 .... 1250.00
3191. 1 Ducat 1537 .... 600.00

AUSTRIAN OCCUPATION, 1519-1534
Bust of Charles V. Rev. Cross and four shields.
3192. 2 Goldgulden 1520 .... 1500.00
3193. 1 Goldgulden 1520 .... 750.00

CHRISTOPHER, 1550-1568
Arms. Rev. Eagle. Charles V.
3194. 1 Goldgulden 1554, 55 .... 500.00

LOUIS, 1568-1593
Arms. Rev. Eagle. Maximilian II.
3195. 2 Goldgulden 1575. Square 1000.00
3196. 1 Goldgulden 1575 .... 500.00

Armored bust. Rev. Arms. Rudolph II.
3197. 2 Goldgulden 1592. Bust right 1000.00
3198. 1 Goldgulden 1592. Bust right 800.00
3199. 1 Goldgulden 1593. Bust left 700.00

FREDERICK, 1593-1608
Half length armored bust. Rev. Arms.
3200. 2 Ducats 1597 .... 1000.00
3201. 1 Ducat 1603, 05 .... 600.00

Armored bust. Rev. Arms on cross.
3202. 2 Goldgulden 1606 .... 1000.00
3203. 1 Goldgulden 1597, 1606 .... 600.00

JOHN FREDERICK, 1608-1628
Half length bust. Rev. Arms under eagle.
3204. 2 Ducats 1609, 15 .... 800.00

Half length bust. Rev. Arms on cross.
3205. 1 Goldgulden 1609 .... 600.00

Bust. Rev. Four shields around orb.
3206. 1 Goldgulden 1614, 20, 21 .... 600.00

Half length figure. Rev. Arms under eagle.
3207. 2½ Ducats 1621 .... 1000.00

Half length figure. Rev. Arms.
3208. 1 Ducat 1621 .... 600.00

Duke on horse. Rev. Three wreaths.
3209. 2 Ducats 1623, 24, 27 .... 600.00

EBERHARD III, 1628-1674

Armored facing bust. Rev. Arms.
3210. 2 Ducats 1640, 44, 48, 51 .... 600.00

Bust right. Rev. Arms.
3211. 1¼ Ducats 1631. Square 800.00
3212. 1   Ducat 1639, 44, 51, 59, 68, 69 .... 500.00
3213. ½ Ducat 1659 .... 250.00

Armored facing bust. Rev. Palm tree. On the peace.
3214. 2 Ducats 1650 .... 500.00

Three shields. Rev. Flag.
3215. ½ Ducat ND 250.00

FREDERICK CHARLES, 1677-1693
Armored bust. Rev. Arms.
3216. 2 Ducats 1681, 83 .... 700.00

3217.	1 Ducat 1681, 88	400.00

Head. Rev. Arms.

3218.	½ Ducat 1688	350.00

EBERHARD LOUIS, 1693-1733
Bust. Rev. Arms.

3219.	4 Ducats 1699, 1707	1000.00
3220.	3 Ducats 1699	800.00

Bust. Rev. Crowned arms.

3221.	2 Ducats 1694, 1706	600.00
3222.	1 Ducat 1694-97	350.00
3223.	½ Ducat ND	250.00

Bust. Rev. Helmeted arms.

3224.	2 Ducats 1699, 1707, ND ....*......	500.00
3225.	1 Ducat 1732, 33, ND	350.00

Duke on horse. Rev. Arms.

3226.	1 Goldgulden ND	350.00

Bust. Rev. Shield in chain of Order.

3227.	1 Carolin 1731, 32, 33	350.00
3228.	½ Carolin 1731, 32, 33	150.00
3229.	¼ Carolin 1731, 32, 33	110.00

CHARLES ALEXANDER, 1733-1737
Bust. Rev. Five shields.

3230.	1 Ducat 1736	500.00

Bust. Rev. Arms. Homage issue.

3231.	2 Ducats 1733	600.00

Bust. Rev. Arms.

3232.	1 Carolin 1734, 35, 36 ....*......	350.00
3233.	½ Carolin 1734, 35, 36	150.00
3234.	¼ Carolin 1734, 35, 36	150.00
3235.	1 Ducat 1733. Helmeted arms	400.00
3236.	1 Ducat 1735, ND	400.00
3237.	½ Ducat ND	300.00

CHARLES RUDOLPH, 1737-1738
Bust. Rev. Arms.

3238.	1 Ducat 1737	500.00
3239.	½ Ducat ND	350.00
3240.	¼ Ducat ND	300.00

CHARLES FREDERICK, 1738-1744
Bust. Rev. Arms.

3241.	1 Ducat 1739, 42 ....*......	400.00
3242.	½ Ducat ND	300.00
3243.	¼ Ducat ND	250.00

CHARLES EUGENE, 1744-1793
Bust. Rev. Crowned arms.

3244.	1 Ducat 1744, 47-50, 62, 90, 91, ND	350.00

Bust. Rev. Helmeted arms.

3245.	1 Ducat 1746	350.00

FC in shield. Rev. Altar. On his wedding.

3246.	1 Ducat 1749	300.00

LOUIS EUGENE, 1793-1795
Bust. Rev. Arms.

3247.	1 Ducat 1794	400.00

FREDERICK, 1795-1816
Bust. Rev. Legend. Struck in the presence of the king.

3248.	1 Ducat 1803, 04	600.00

Draped bust. Rev. Arms.

3249.	1 Ducat 1804. Bust right	400.00
3250.	1 Ducat 1808. Bust left	400.00

Head. Rev. Arms.

3251.	1 Frederick d'or 1810	500.00
3252.	1 Ducat 1813 ....*......	350.00

WILLIAM, 1816-1864

Head Rev. Large supported arms without legend.

3253.	1 Ducat 1818	350.00

Head. Rev. Small supported arms with legend.

3254.	1 Ducat 1840-48	125.00

Head. Rev. Arms.

3255.	10 Gulden 1824, 25	600.00
3256.	5 Gulden 1824, 25, 35, 36, 39	250.00

Head. Rev. Date and four line legend. On the King's visit to the mint.

3257. 10 Gulden 1825 .... 1200.00

Head. Rev. Seated female and children. On the 25th year of reign.

3258. 4 Ducats 1841 .... 450.00

Head. Rev. The Mint in Stuttgart. On the King's visit.

3259. 4 Ducats 1844. The value is on the edge 1000.00

WURZBURG

A. Bishops of —

GERHARD, 1372-1400
Arms. Rev. St. John standing.

3260. 1 Goldgulden ND 900.00

LAWRENCE, 1495-1519

St. Kilian. Rev. Arms.

3261. 2 Goldgulden 1506 .... 1000.00
3262. 1 Goldgulden 1506, 07, 08, 13, ND ....*...... 250.00

MELCHIOR ZOBEL, 1544-1558
Three shields. Rev. Eagle.

3263. 2 Goldgulden 1553 .... 1000.00
3264. 1 Goldgulden 1553 .... 600.00

FREDERICK, 1558-1573
Three shields. Rev. Eagle.

3265. 1 Goldgulden 1572 .... 600.00

JULIUS ECHTER, 1573-1617

St. Kilian over arms. Rev. Madonna over eagle.

3266. 4 Goldgulden ND 800.00
3267. 2 Ducats ND 700.00
3268. 1 Ducat ND ....*...... 300.00

Three shields. Rev. Legend. Homage issue.

3269. 1 Goldgulden 1583 .... 300.00

St. Kilian standing. Rev. Date over arms. Name of Rudolph II.

3270. 2 Goldgulden 1575, 78, 79 .... 500.00
3271. 1 Goldgulden 1575 .... 300.00

St. Kilian standing. Rev. Arms with 3 helmets. Name of Rudolph II.

3272. 2 Goldgulden 1581, 83, 85, 89, 90, 1608, 11, 13, ND 500.00
3273. 1 Goldgulden 1581, 83, 86, 89, 90, 92, 94,
     1601, 08, 11 ....*..... 300.00
3274. 1 Goldgulden 1613, 15. Name of Matthias II 300.00

Arms with 3 helmets. Rev. Legend. On his death.

3275. 2 Goldgulden 1617 .... 600.00
3276. 1 Goldgulden 1617 .... 300.00

JOHN GODFREY, 1617-1622

Arms. Rev. Legend around shield.

3277. 2 Goldgulden ND. Square. AUGUSTUM PATRIAE etc. *. 700.00
3278. 1 Goldgulden ND. AUGUSTUM PATRIAE etc. 350.00
3279. 1 Goldgulden ND. ORE ET CORDE, etc. 350.00
3280. 1 Goldgulden 1617, 18, 19 .... 350.00

Arms with 4 helmets. Rev. Legend. On his death.

3281. 1 Goldgulden 1622 .... 350.00

PHILIP ADOLPH, 1623-1631

St. Kilian. Rev. Arms.

3282. 2 Goldgulden ND 800.00
3283. 1 Goldgulden 1626, ND ....*...... 350.00

Arms. Rev. Legend. On his death.

3284.   1 Goldgulden 1631 .... **350.00**

FRANCIS, 1631-1642
Arms. Rev. Wreath.

3285.   1 Goldgulden 1631, ND **375.00**

Arms. Rev. Legend. On his death.

3286.   1 Ducat 1642 .... **375.00**

JOHN PHILIP I, 1642-1673
Bust right over arms. Rev. Three mountain peaks.

3287.   2 Ducats ND **500.00**
3288.   1 Ducat ND **300.00**

Facing bust over arms. Rev. Three mountain peaks.

3289.   2 Ducats ND **500.00**
3290.   1½ Ducats ND ....*...... **350.00**
3291.   1 Ducat ND **300.00**

Bust right over arms. Rev. Legend over shield.

3292.   1 Goldgulden ND **350.00**

Facing bust over arms. Rev. Legend over shield.

3293.   1 Goldgulden ND **300.00**

Arms. Rev. Legend over shield.

3294.   1 Goldgulden ND **375.00**

JOHN HARTMANN, 1673-1675
Bust over arms. Rev. Legend over shield.

3295.   1 Goldgulden ND **375.00**

PETER PHILIP, 1675-1683
Bust. Rev. Legend over shield.

3296.   1 Goldgulden ND **375.00**

CONRAD WILLIAM, 1683-1684
Bust. Rev. Arms.

3297.   1 Ducat ND **325.00**

JOHN GODFREY II, 1684-1689
Facing bust. Rev. Legend over shield.

3298.   1 Goldgulden ND **375.00**

Arms. Rev. Flag in cartouche.

3299.   1 Goldgulden ND **375.00**

JOHN PHILIP II, 1699-1719
Bust. Rev. Three Saints.

3300.   1 Ducat 1702 .... **300.00**

Bust. Rev. Arms with 3 helmets.

3301.   2 Ducats 1705 .... **500.00**
3302.   1 Ducat 1700 .... **300.00**

Bust. Rev. Coat of arms.

3303.   2 Ducats 1705 .... **500.00**

Bust. Rev. Tree.

3304.   1 Ducat 1703 .... **300.00**

Bust. Rev. Madonna over arms.

3305.   3 Ducats 1707 .... **600.00**
3306.   2 Ducats 1707 ....*...... **400.00**

Arms. Rev. Flag in shield.

3307.   1 Goldgulden ND **250.00**

Arms supported by lions. Rev. Madonna over shield.

3308.   1 Goldgulden ND **250.00**

JOHN PHILIP FRANCIS, 1719-1724
Bust. Rev. Lion with sword and scales before city view.

3309.   2 Ducats ND **600.00**
3310.   2 Ducats ND. Without the city view **700.00**

Bust. Rev. Arms.

3311.   2 Ducats ND **600.00**
3312.   2 Ducats 1719. On his election **600.00**

Bust. Rev. Arms in cartouche.

3313.   1 Ducat ND **300.00**

Bust. Rev. Altar with Wurzburg shield.

3314.   1 Goldgulden ND **250.00**
3315.   1 Goldgulden ND. With "QUIA TU ES" etc. **250.00**

CHRISTOPHER FRANCIS, 1724-1729
Arms. Rev. St. Christopher. With D.G.EL.EP.

3316.   2 Ducats ND **350.00**
3317.   1 Ducat ND **175.00**

Arms. Rev. Ship entering harbor. With D.G.EL.EP.

3318.   1 Ducat ND **300.00**

Bust. Rev. St. Christopher. With D.G.EP.

3319.   2 Ducats ND **400.00**

Arms. Rev. St. Christopher. With D.G.EP.

3320. 1 Ducat ND 100.00

Arms. Rev. Initials on mantle.

3321. 1 Ducat 1725, 27, 28 .... 250.00

Arms. Rev. Sword and stola.

3322. ½ Ducat ND 75.00

Arms. Rev. Mountain. "NON FULMEN" etc.

3323. 1 Goldgulden ND 200.00

Arms. Rev. Mountain and city view. "FELIX A DEO" etc.

3324. 1 Goldgulden 1724. With flag-shield 200.00
3325. 1 Goldgulden 1724. With flag and sceptre crossed ... 200.00

FREDERICK CHARLES, 1729-1746

Bust. Rev. Arms.

3326. 10 Gulden or 1 Carolin 1735, 36 ....*...... 500.00
3327. 5 Gulden or ½ Carolin 1735 .... 300.00
3328. 2½ Gulden or ¼ Carolin 1735, 36 .... 200.00

Bust. Rev. Initials on mantle.

3329. 10 Gulden or 1 Carolin 1735, 36 .... 500.00
3330. 5 Gulden or ½ Carolin 1735 .... 300.00
3331. 2½ Gulden or ¼ Carolin 1736 .... 200.00

Bust. Rev. Arms supported by lions.

3332. 2 Ducats 1729, 30, 31 .... 450.00

Bust. Rev. Arms.

3333. 1 Ducat 1731, 32, 33 .... 300.00

Arms supported by lions. Rev. Initials on mantle.

3334. 1 Ducat 1729, 30 .... 250.00

Arms. Rev. Franconia standing and lion.

3335. 2 Goldgulden 1729 .... 500.00
3336. 1 Goldgulden 1729 .... 250.00

Bust. Rev. Flag shield.

3337. 1 Goldgulden ND 250.00
3338. 1 Goldgulden ND. Shield with flowers ....*...... 250.00

Arms. Rev. Initials on mantle.

3339. ½ Ducat 1729 .... 125.00

ANSELM FRANCIS, 1746-1749

Arms. Rev. Hands over city shield.

3340. 1 Goldgulden ND 250.00

Angel and 3 lambs. Rev. Legend.

3341. 1 Ducat 1747. On his consecration 350.00

CHARLES PHILIP, 1749-1754

Bust over arms. Rev. Arms with 3 helmets.

3342. 1 Goldgulden ND 250.00

Arms with 3 helmets. Rev. Griffin.

3343. 1 Goldgulden ND 250.00

ADAM FREDERICK, 1755-1779

Bust. Rev. Arms and legend.

3344. 1 Goldgulden 1755 .... 250.00

Bust. Rev. Arms without legend.

3345. 1 Ducat 1755-70 .... 250.00

Bust in square. Rev. Arms in square.

3346. 1 Ducat 1772 .... 250.00

Bust in square. Rev. Madonna in square.

3347. 1 Ducat 1773-79 .... 250.00

Bust and arms. Rev. Palm tree and shield.

3348. 1 Goldgulden 1773, 74, 77, 78 .... 250.00

Fame over arms. Rev. Three females.

3349. 1 Goldgulden ND (1755). Homage issue 250.00

Bust over arms. Rev. Franconia standing and dove. On the Peace of Hubertusburg.

3350. 1 Goldgulden 1764 .... 250.00

FRANCIS LOUIS, 1779-1795

Bust over arms. Rev. Palm tree and shield.

3351. 1 Goldgulden 1779 .... 200.00

Bust over arms. Rev. Arms.

3352. 1 Goldgulden 1786, 91, 94 .... 200.00

Bust. Rev. Three Saints over arms.

3353. 1 Ducat 1785 .... 200.00

Bust. Rev. St. Kilian standing and value.

3354. 2 Goldgulden 1786 ....*...... 350.00
3355. 1 Goldgulden 1786 .... 200.00

Bust. Rev. St. Burkhard standing and value.

3356. 1 Goldgulden 1790 .... 250.00

GEORGE CHARLES, 1795-1803
Bust. Rev. Arms and value.

3357. 1 Carolin 1795 .... 500.00

Arms. Rev. Palm tree and shield.

3358. 1 Goldgulden 1795 .... 200.00

Bust. Rev. City view and value.

3359. 1 Goldgulden 1798............................. 200.00

FERDINAND, GRAND DUKE, 1806-1814

Bust. Rev. Palm tree and shield.

3360. 1 Goldgulden 1807, 09 .... 200.00

Head. Rev. Shield and value.

3361. 1 Goldgulden 1812, 13 .... 250.00

Head. Rev. Altar and shield.

3362. 1 Goldgulden 1814 .... 300.00

B. Swedish Rulers of —

Bust of Gustav Adolphe. Rev. Arms.

3363. 1 Ducat 1631, 32 .... 275.00

GREAT BRITAIN

The English gold Pound enjoyed enormous popularity and prestige during its years of issue and was known and accepted throughout the world. In order to identify themselves more closely with this unit of currency, many other countries struck their own local coins in the same weight and fineness as the Pound. Such coins can be noted in the appendix under "the principal gold coins of the world."

Additional English type gold coins will be found among the various parts of the British Empire, namely, Canada, Australia, India, and South Africa. These coins bear the distinguishing mint mark of the issuing country. The coinage of the London Mint is without a mint mark.

Kings of —

OFFA, KING OF MERCIA, 757-796

Arabic legend. Rev. Arabic legend and "OFFA REX." Struck in the style of the contemporary Arabian Dinars.

1. 1 Dinar ND .... Unique

Bust. Rev. Standing figure.

2. Gold Penny ND .... Unique

WIGMUND, ARCHBISHOP OF YORK, 837-854

Facing bust. Rev. Cross in wreath.

3. 1 Solidus ND .... Unique

AETHELRED II, 979-1016

Bust in helmet. Rev. Long cross.

4. 1 Gold Penny ND .... Unique

EDWARD THE CONFESSOR, 1042-1066
Diademed bust. Rev. Cross.

5. 1 Gold Penny ND .... Unique

HENRY III, 1216-1272

Ruler on throne. Rev. Long cross.

6. 1 Gold Penny ND 12,000.00

EDWARD III, 1327-1377

Ruler on throne. Rev. Ornamental cross.

7. 1 Florin ND ....   **Rare**

Crowned leopard with banner. Rev. Ornamental cross.

8. ½ Florin or Leopard ND ....   **Rare**

Leopard on helm. Rev. Ornamental cross.

9. ¼ Florin or Helm ND ....   **Rare**

Ruler in ship. Rev. Ornamental cross.

10. 1 Noble ND ....* 550.00
11. ½ Noble ND 175.00

Arms. Rev. Ornamental cross.

12. ¼ Noble ND 110.00

RICHARD II, 1377-1399

Ruler in ship. Rev. Ornamental cross.

13. 1 Noble ND 425.00
14. ½ Noble ND ....* 250.00

Arms. Rev. Ornamental cross.

15. ¼ Noble ND 175.00

HENRY IV, 1399-1413

Ruler in ship. Rev. Ornamental cross. The heavy Nobles weigh 120 grains, the light Nobles 108 grains. The smaller coins are in proportion.

16. 1 Noble ND. Heavy type 4000.00
17. 1 Noble ND. Light type ....* 1400.00
18. ½ Noble ND. Heavy type ....   Rare
19. ½ Noble ND. Light type ....   Rare

Arms. Rev. Ornamental cross.

20. ¼ Noble ND. Heavy type ....* ......   Rare
21. ¼ Noble ND. Light type 450.00

HENRY V, 1413-1422

Ruler in ship. Rev. Ornamental cross.

22. 1 Noble ND 300.00
23. ½ Noble ND ....* 300.00

Arms. Rev. Ornamental cross.

24. ¼ Noble ND 150.00

HENRY VI, 1422-1461

Ruler in ship. Rev. Ornamental cross.

25. 1 Noble ND 275.00
26. ½ Noble ND ....* 125.00

Arms. Rev. Ornamental cross.

27. ¼ Noble ND 100.00

HENRY VI RESTORED, 1470-1471

St. Michael slaying dragon. Rev. Cross and arms on ship.
Restoration coinage.

28. 1 Angel ND ....*...... 500.00
29. ½ Angel (Angelet) ND 600.00

EDWARD IV, 1461-1470 AND 1471-1483
Ruler in ship. Rev. Ornamental cross.

30. 1 Noble ND. Heavy type .... Rare
31. 1 Noble ND. Light type .... Unique

Ruler in ship, rose at side. Rev. Radiate rose within royal emblems.

32. 1 Rose Noble or Ryal ND ....*...... 250.00
33. ½ Rose Noble or ½ Ryal ND 200.00

Arms. Rev. Radiate rose.

34. ¼ Ryal ND 150.00

St. Michael slaying dragon. Rev. Cross and arms on ship.

35. 1 Angel ND ....*...... 150.00
36. ½ Angel (Angelet) ND 200.00

EDWARD V, 1483

St. Michael slaying dragon. Rev. Cross and arms on ship.

37. 1 Angel ND. Mint mark boar's head ....*..... Rare
38. ½ Angel ND .... Rare

RICHARD III, 1483-1485

St. Michael slaying dragon. Rev. Cross and arms on ship.

39. 1 Angel ND 600.00
40. ½ Angel ND ....*...... 3000.00

HENRY VII, 1485-1509

Ruler on throne. Rev. Arms on large rose.

41. 2 Sovereigns ND .... Rare
42. 1 Sovereign ND ....*...... 4000.00

Ruler in ship. Rev. Shield on large rose.

43. 1 Ryal ND .... Rare

St. Michael slaying dragon. Rev. Cross and arms on ship.

44. 1 Angel ND ....*...... 150.00
45. ½ Angel ND 175.00

HENRY VIII, 1509-1547
Ruler on throne. Rev. Arms on large rose.

46. 1 Sovereign ND 2500.00

Ruler on throne. Rev. Arms with supporters.

47. 1 Sovereign ND ....* 2500.00
48. ½ Sovereign ND 150.00

St. Michael slaying dragon. Rev. Cross and arms on ship.

49. 1 Angel ND 125.00
50. ½ Angel ND ....* 125.00
51. ¼ Angel ND 200.00

St. George on horse. Rev. Cross and rose on ship.

52. 1 George Noble ND ....* 5000.00
53. ½ George Noble ND .... Rare

Crowned arms. Rev. Rose, initials and floriated cross.

54. 1 Crown of the Rose ND .... Rare

Crown over double rose. Rev. Crowned arms.

55. 1 Crown ND ....* 125.00
56. ½ Crown ND 150.00

EDWARD VI, 1547-1553

Ruler on throne. Rev. Arms with supporters. With name and title of Henry VIII, although the figure is that of Edward VI.

57. ½ Sovereign ND 150.00

Ruler on throne. Rev. Arms on large rose. With his own name and title.

58. 2 Sovereigns ND .... **Rare**
59. 1 Sovereign ND ....* 5000.00

Ruler on throne. Rev. Arms with supporters. With his own name and title.

60. 1 Sovereign ND 950.00

Half length figure. Rev. Arms.

61. 1 Sovereign ND ....* 600.00
62. ½ Sovereign ND 225.00
63. 1 Crown ND 450.00
64. ½ Crown ND 450.00

Crowned child bust. Rev. Arms.

65. ½ Sovereign ND ....* 200.00

66.　1 Crown ND 450.00
67.　½ Crown ND 450.00

Child bust without crown. Rev. Arms.

68.　½ Sovereign ND 200.00
69.　1 Crown ND 450.00
70.　½ Crown ND 450.00

Crowned bust with King's name on each side.

71.　½ Sovereign ND .... Rare

Crown over double rose, with name of Henry VIII. Rev. Crowned arms.

72.　1 Crown ND 250.00
73.　½ Crown ND 250.00

St. Michael slaying dragon. Rev. Cross and arms on ship.

74.　1 Angel ND 2500.00
75.　½ Angel ND .... Unique

MARY, 1553-1554

Queen on throne. Rev. Arms on large rose.

76.　1 Sovereign 1553, 54, ND 1100.00

Queen in ship. Rev. Radiate rose.

77.　1 Ryal 1553, ND 5000.00

St. Michael slaying dragon. Rev. Cross and arms on ship.

78.　1 Angel ND ....*...... 400.00
79.　½ Angel ND 1500.00

PHILIP AND MARY, 1554-1558

St. Michael slaying dragon. Rev. Cross and arms on ship.

80.　1 Angel ND ....*...... 1000.00
81.　½ Angel ND .... Rare

ELIZABETH I, 1558-1603

Queen on throne. Rev. Arms on large rose.

82.　1 "Fine" Sovereign ND 850.00

Queen in ship. Rev. Radiate rose.

83.　1 Ryal ND 2400.00

St. Michael slaying dragon. Rev. Cross and arms on ship.

84.　1 Angel ND ....*..... 150.00
85.　½ Angel ND 150.00
86.　¼ Angel ND 150.00

Crowned bust. Rev. Crowned arms.

87.　1 Sovereign ND. Hammered coinage 375.00
88.　½ Sovereign ND. Hammered coinage 200.00
89.　½ Sovereign ND. Milled coinage ....*..... 500.00
90.　1 Crown ND. Hammered coinage 200.00
91.　1 Crown ND. Milled coinage 1000.00
92.　½ Crown ND. Hammered coinage ....*..... 200.00
93.　½ Crown ND. Milled coinage 1500.00

JAMES I, 1603-1625

Ruler on throne. Rev. Arms on large rose.

94. 1 Rose Ryal ND 600.00

Ruler on throne. Rev. XXX over arms.

95. 30 Shillings (Rose Ryal) ND 750.00

Ruler in ship. Rev. Radiate rose.

96. 1 Spur Ryal ND 2500.00

Crowned bust. Rev. Crowned arms. With "Exurgat" legend.

97. 1 Sovereign ND 850.00
98. ½ Sovereign ND ....*...... 1000.00

Crowned bust. Rev. Crowned arms. With "Tueatur Venita Deus" legend.

99. 1 Crown ND 750.00
100. ½ Crown ND ....*...... 500.00

Crowned bust. Rev. Crowned arms. With "Faciam Eos" legend.

101. 1 Unite (20 Shillings) ND 100.00
102. ½ Unite (10 Shillings) ND 75.00
103. 1 Crown ND 50.00
104. ½ Crown ND 50.00

Laureate bust. Rev. Crowned arms.

105. 1 Laurel (Unite) ND 100.00
106. ½ Laurel ND ....*...... 75.00
107. ¼ Laurel ND 60.00

St. Michael slaying dragon. Rev. Arms.

108. ¼ Angel ND .... Rare

St. Michael slaying dragon. Rev. Large arms on ship.

109. 1 Angel ND ....*...... 1000.00
110. ½ Angel ND .... Rare

St. Michael slaying dragon. Rev. Large ship with three masts.

111. 1 Angel ND 1250.00

Crowned facing lion over arms with XV. Rev. Radiate rose.

112. 15 Shillings (Spur Ryal) ND 2400.00

Crowned rose. Rev. Crowned thistle.

113. 1 Thistle Crown or 4 Shillings ND 100.00

CHARLES I, 1625-1649

St. Michael with or without X for value in field. Rev. Three masted ship.

114. 10 Shillings (1 Angel) ND ....*..... 850.00
115. 10 Shillings ND. Smaller size and finer style.
     By Nicholas Briot .... Unique

Crowned bust. Rev. Scroll type legend. (The Declaration). The 20 and 10 Shilling values are indicated by Roman numerals on the Obv.

116. 3 Pounds (Triple Unite) 1642-44. Oxford Mint ..*...... 2000.00
117. 3 Pounds 1642. Shrewsbury Mint .... Rare
118. 20 Shillings (1 Unite) 1642-46. Oxford Mint 250.00
119. 20 Shillings 1645. Bristol Mint .... Rare
120. 10 Shillings (½ Unite) 1642-44. Oxford Mint 450.00
121. 10 Shillings 1645. Bristol Mint .... Rare

Crowned bust and Roman numerals for value. Rev. Arms.

122. 20 Shillings ND. Tower Mint 125.00
123. 20 Shillings ND. Briot's coinage 600.00
124. 20 Shillings ND. Chester Mint .... Unique
125. 20 Shillings ND. Truro Mint .... Rare
126. 20 Shillings ND. Weymouth Mint .... Rare
127. 20 Shillings ND. Salisbury Mint .... Unique
128. 10 Shillings ND. Tower Mint ....*..... 100.00
129. 10 Shillings ND. Tower Mint. Briot's coinage 600.00
130. 5 Shillings ND. Tower Mint 100.00
131. 5 Shillings ND. Tower Mint. Briot's coinage ....*...... Rare

CIVIL WAR
Siege of Colchester

Castle, date and value. Rev. Blank.

132. 10 Shillings 1648 .... Unique

Siege of Pontefract

Crown over CR. Rev. Castle.

133. 1 Unite 1648 .... Rare

Crown over legend. Rev. Castle in circle, with name of Charles II.

134. 1 Unite 1648 .... Rare

THE COMMONWEALTH OF ENGLAND, 1649-1660

Shield of St. George. Rev. Shields of St. George and Ireland. With Roman numerals for value.

135. 20 Shillings 1649-60 .... 200.00
136. 10 Shillings 1649-60 ....*...... 200.00
137. 5 Shillings 1649-60 .... 175.00

OLIVER CROMWELL, 1656-1660

Laureate head. Rev. Arms.

138. 50 Shillings 1656 .... Rare
139. 1 Broad 1656 .... 600.00
140. ½ Broad 1656 ....*...... 1000.00

CHARLES II, 1660-1685

Laureate head with or without value as indicated. Rev. Arms.

141. 20 Shillings ND. Without value ....*...... 300.00
142. 20 Shillings ND. With value 200.00
143. 10 Shillings ND. Without value 400.00
144. 10 Shillings ND. With value ....*...... 250.00
145. 5 Shillings ND. Without value 300.00
146. 5 Shillings ND. With value 300.00

Laureate head. Rev. Cross of four shields. With or without the various symbols below the head as indicated.

5 Guineas

47.	1668-84. No symbol	650.00
48.	1668, 69, 75. Elephant	750.00
49.	1675-84. Elephant and castle	850.00

2 Guineas

50.	1664-84. No symbol	300.00
51.	1664, 78. Elephant	300.00
52.	1676-84. Elephant and castle	400.00

1 Guinea

53.	1663-84. No symbol	125.00
54.	1663-78. Elephant ....*.	250.00
55.	1674-84. Elephant and castle	200.00

½ Guinea

56.	1669-84. No symbol	120.00
57.	1676-84. Elephant and castle	200.00

JAMES II, 1685-1688

Laureate head. Rev. Cross of four shields. With or without the various symbols below the head as indicated.

5 Guineas

58.	1686, 87, 88. No symbol ....*.	700.00
59.	1687, 88. Elephant and castle	900.00

2 Guineas

60.	1687, 88. No symbol	425.00

1 Guinea

61.	1685-88. No symbol	125.00
62.	1685-88. Elephant and castle	150.00

½ Guinea

63.	1686, 87, 88. No symbol	125.00
64.	1686. Elephant and castle	250.00

WILLIAM AND MARY, 1688-1694

Conjoined heads. Rev. Crowned arms. With or without the various symbols below the heads as indicated.

5 Guineas

65.	1691-94. No symbol	750.00
66.	1691-94. Elephant and castle	900.00

2 Guineas

167.	1693, 94. No symbol	300.00
168.	1691, 93, 94. Elephant and castle	450.00

1 Guinea

169.	1689-94. No symbol	125.00
170.	1692. Elephant	400.00
171.	1689-94. Elephant and castle	250.00

½ Guinea

172.	1689-94. No symbol	150.00
173.	The coin previously listed does not exist.	
174.	1691, 92. Elephant and castle ....*.	150.00

WILLIAM III, 1694-1702

Laureate head. Rev. Cross of four shields. With or without the various symbols below the head as indicated.

5 Guineas

175.	1699, 1700, 01. No symbol	750.00
176.	1699. Elephant and castle	1100.00

2 Guineas

177.	1701. No symbol ....*.	450.00

1 Guinea

178.	1695-1701. No symbol	125.00
179.	1695-1701. Elephant and castle	400.00

½ Guinea

180.	1695-1701. No symbol	80.00
181.	1695, 96, 98. Elephant and castle	120.00

ANNE, 1702-1714

Draped bust. Rev. Cross of four shields. With or without the various symbols below the bust as indicated.

5 Guineas

182.	1705-14. No symbol	1250.00
183.	1703. Vigo	8000.00

2 Guineas

184.	1709-14. No symbol	325.00

1 Guinea

185.	1702-14. No symbol	150.00
186.	1703. Vigo ....*.	1500.00
187.	1707, 08, 09. Elephant and castle	400.00

½ Guinea

188.	1702-14. No symbol	100.00
189.	1703. Vigo	1000.00

GEORGE I, 1714-1727

Laureate head. Rev. Cross of four shields. With or without the symbol below the head as indicated.

5 Guineas

190.	1716, 17, 20, 26. No symbol	1500.00

2 Guineas

191.	1717, 20, 26. No symbol	350.00

1 Guinea

192.	1714-27. No symbol	125.00
193.	1721, 22, 26. Elephant and castle ....*	400.00

½ Guinea

194.	1715-27. No symbol	100.00
195.	1721. Elephant and castle	1000.00

¼ Guinea

196.	1718. No symbol	60.00

GEORGE II, 1727-1760

Laureate head. Rev. Crowned arms. With or without "E.I.C." or "Lima" below the head as indicated.

5 Guineas

197.	1729-41. Young head, plain	650.00
198.	1729. Young head, E.I.C.	650.00
199.	1748, 53. Old head, plain	650.00
200.	1746. Old head, Lima	750.00

2 Guineas

201.	1734-39. Young head, plain	175.00
202.	1739, 40. Middle aged head, plain	175.00
203.	1748, 53. Old head, plain	250.00

1 Guinea

204.	1727-38. Young head, plain ....*	100.00
205.	1729, 31, 32. Young head, E.I.C.	250.00
206.	1739-46. Middle aged head, plain	150.00
207.	1739. Middle aged head, E.I.C. ....*	250.00
208.	1745. Middle aged head, Lima	400.00
209.	1747-60. Old head, plain ....*	125.00

½ Guinea

210.	1728-39. Young head, plain	125.00
211.	1729-39. Young head, E.I.C.	250.00
212.	1740-46. Middle aged head, plain	150.00
213.	1745. Middle aged head, Lima	400.00
214.	1747-60. Old head, plain	75.00

GEORGE III, 1760-1820

Laureate head. Rev. Arms.

5 Guineas

215.	1770, 73, 77. Patterns only	10,000.00

2 Guineas

216.	1768, 73, 77. Patterns only	4,000.00

1 Guinea

217.	1761. 1st young head ....*	350.00
218.	1763, 64. 2nd young head. Longer, curlier hair	350.00
219.	1765-73. 3rd young head. Laurel divides legend	120.00
220.	1774-79, 81-86. 4th head. Larger head; laurel divides legend ....*	75.00

Laureate head. Rev. Spade shaped shield.

221.	1787-99. 5th head, smaller. "Spade Guinea"	75.00

Laureate head. Rev. Arms within the Order of the Garter.

222.	1813. 6th head, smaller. "Military Guinea"	100.00

Laureate head. Rev. Arms.

½ Guinea

223.	1762, 63. 1st young head	250.00
224.	1764-66, 68, 69, 72-75. 2nd young head. Laurel divides legend ....*	100.00
225.	1774, 75. 3rd head. Laurel in legend	250.00
226.	1775-79, 81, 84-86. 4th head. Hair on both shoulders	75.00
227.	1787-98, 1800. 5th head. "Spade" shield rev.	50.00
228.	1801-03. 6th type, long hair. "Garter" rev.	50.00
229.	1804, 06, 08-11, 13. 7th type, short hair. "Garter" rev.	50.00

Laureate head. Rev. Crown.

⅓ Guinea

230.	1797-1800. 1st head. Date in legend ....;....*	40.00
231.	1801-03. 1st head. Date below crown	40.00
232.	1804, 06, 08-11, 13. 2nd head, short hair. Date below crown ....*	30.00

¼ Guinea

233.	1762. Type similar to No. 224	50.00

Laureate head. Rev. St. George slaying dragon.

234.	5 Pounds 1820. Plain or lettered edge. Patterns only	10,000.00
235.	2 Pounds 1820. Plain or lettered edge. Patterns only	2,000.00
236.	1 Sovereign 1817-20. (1819 rare) ....*	85.00

Laureate head. Rev. Arms.

237. ½ Sovereign 1817, 18, 20 . . . .   50.00

GEORGE IV, 1820-1830

Bare head. Rev. Arms.

238. 5 Pounds 1826. Proofs only 1500.00
239. 2 Pounds 1825, 26. Proofs only . . . . *. 1200.00

Bare head. Rev. St. George slaying dragon.

240. 2 Pounds 1823 . . . .   200.00

Laureate head. Rev. St. George slaying dragon.

241. 1 Sovereign 1821-25 . . . .   75.00

Bare head. Rev. Arms.

242. 1 Sovereign 1825-30 . . . .   75.00

Laureate head. Rev. Arms.

243. ½ Sovereign 1821. Ornately garnished shield . . . . .*. 200.00
244. ½ Sovereign 1823-25. Plain shield . . . .*. 75.00
245. ½ Sovereign 1826-28. Bare head. Type similar to No. 242. . .   75.00

WILLIAM IV, 1830-1837

Head. Rev. Arms.

246. 5 Pounds 1831. Proofs only 10,000.00
247. 2 Pounds 1831. Proofs only . . . .*. . . .   750.00
248. 1 Sovereign 1831-33, 35-37 . . . .   100.00
249. ½ Sovereign 1834. Small size 125.00
250. ½ Sovereign 1835-37. Large size 100.00

VICTORIA, 1837-1901

Young head. Rev. Una and the lion.

251. 5 Pounds 1839. Plain and lettered edge. Proofs only 3000.00

Young head. Rev. Arms.

252. 1 Sovereign 1838, 39, 41-66, 68-74 . . . .   50.00

Young head. Rev. St. George slaying dragon.

253. 1 Sovereign 1871-74, 76, 78-80, 84, 85 . . . .   32.50
Young head. Rev. Arms.
254. ½ Sovereign 1838, 39, 41-67, 69-80, 83-85 . . . .   27.50

Jubilee bust. Rev. St. George slaying dragon.

255. 5 Pounds 1887 . . . .   375.00
256. 2 Pounds 1887 . . . .   225.00
257. 1 Sovereign 1887-92 . . . .*. 25.00
258. ½ Sovereign 1887-93. Rev. Arms 20.00

Old veiled bust. Rev. St. George slaying dragon.

259.	5 Pounds 1893 ....*.....	400.00
260.	2 Pounds 1893	275.00
261.	1 Sovereign 1893-96, 98-1901	25.00
262.	½ Sovereign 1893-1901	20.00

EDWARD VII, 1901-1910

Head. Rev. St. George slaying dragon.

263.	5 Pounds 1902	375.00
264.	2 Pounds 1902	225.00
265.	1 Sovereign 1902-10 ....*......	25.00
266.	½ Sovereign 1902-10	17.50

GEORGE V, 1910-1936

Head. Rev. St. George slaying dragon.

267.	5 Pounds 1911. Proofs only	750.00
268.	2 Pounds 1911. Proofs only	350.00
269.	1 Sovereign 1911-17, 25 ....*......	25.00
270.	½ Sovereign 1911-15	17.50

GEORGE VI, 1936-1952

Head. Rev. St. George slaying dragon.

271.	5 Pounds 1937. Proof ....*......	750.00
272.	2 Pounds 1937. Proof	225.00
273.	1 Sovereign 1937. Proof	200.00
274.	½ Sovereign 1937. Proof	100.00

ELIZABETH II, 1952-

Head. Rev. St. George slaying dragon. A few specimen sets of 5 Pound, 2 Pound, Sovereign and ½ Sovereign pieces were struck in 1953 for presentation and to maintain the series. None was made available and all are now in official custody.

275.	1 Sovereign 1957-59, 62-	17.5

GREECE

Greek coinage is based on the Latin Monetary Union standard. T coins of 1852 are of extraordinary rarity. Although 8 specimens we struck of the 40 Drachmai piece and 32 specimens of the 20 Drachm piece, the author knows of only one 40 Drachmai coin and none of t 20 Drachmai.

Only 76 pieces were struck of the 100 Drachmai piece of 1876 ar 182 pieces of the 50 Drachmai.

A. Kings of —

OTTO, 1831-1863

Young head. Rev. Arms.

1.	20 Drachmai 1833	225.0

Head with moustache. Rev. Arms. Not placed in circulation.

2.	40 Drachmai 1852 ....*......	Rare
3.	20 Drachmai 1852	Rare

GEORGE I, 1863-1913

Young head. Rev. Arms. Coins dated 1875 are Essais.

4.	100 Drachmai 1876	2500.00
5.	50 Drachmai 1876 ....*......	1250.00
6.	20 Drachmai 1869 (Rare), 76	125.00

Young head. Rev. Value and date.

7.   10 Drachmai 1876 .... 175.00
8.   5 Drachmai 1869 (Rare), 76 .... 175.00

Old head. Rev. Arms.

9.   20 Drachmai 1884 .... 65.00

GEORGE II, 1935-1947

Head. Rev. Value. On the re-establishment of the Kingdom. Not placed in circulation.

10.   100 Drachmai 1935 ....* 1500.00
11.   20 Drachmai 1935 .... 500.00

CONSTANTINE II, 1964-

Phoenix bird and soldier. Rev. Arms and value. Issued in 1970 by the Bank of Greece to mark the 1967 revolution.

12.   100 Drachmai 1967 ....* 150.00
13.   20 Drachmai 1967 .... 50.00

B. Cities and Islands of —

CHIOS

A. Genoese Doges of —

MARTIN AND BENEDICT II ZACCHARIA, 1319-1324

Shield. Rev. Cross.

14.   ¼ Zecchino ND 900.00

Cross. Rev. Christ on throne.

15.   ¼ Zecchino ND 900.00

THE CAMPOFREGOSI, 1415-1421 AND 1436-1458

Ruler kneeling before St. Lawrence. Rev. Christ.

16.   1 Zecchino ND 500.00

B. Milanese Dukes of —

PHILIP MARIA, 1421-1436

Ruler kneeling before St. Peter. Rev. Christ.

17.   1 Zecchino ND. S mm for Chios 500.00
18.   1 Zecchino ND. P mm for Pera ....* 800.00

C. French Kings of —

CHARLES VII, 1458-1461

Ruler kneeling before St. Lawrence. Rev. Christ.

19.   1 Zecchino ND 800.00

D. Venetian Coinage for —

LEONARDO LOREDANO, 1501-1521
Ruler kneeling before St. Mark, legend completely around. Rev. Christ.

20.   1 Zecchino ND 400.00

FOKIA (PHOCAEA)

Mytilene Lords of —
DORINO GATTILUSIO, 1400-1449

Ruler kneeling before Saint. Rev. Christ.

21.   1 Zecchino ND 800.00

MYTILENE

Lords of —
THE GATTILUSI, 1376-1462

Ruler kneeling before Saint. Rev. Christ.

22.   1 Zecchino ND 700.00

GRENADA

Gold coins of Brazil counterstamped three times along the outer edge of the obverse with a G and with or without a plugged hole in the center.

1. 6400 Reis 1727-1804 .... **750.00**

GUADELOUPE

Gold coins of Brazil or Portugal counterstamped with a "G" (plain or crowned) and with or without a fleur-de-lis or "82.10."

1. 82 Livres, 10 Sous 1727-1804 .... **1000.00**

GUATEMALA

Mints and mint marks:—G or NG (New Guatemala) for Guatemala. Almost every coin issued under the Spanish Kings is a rarity.

During the latter part of the 19th century, the coinage was based on the Latin Monetary Union standard, and is unique in that so many denominations were struck—the equivalent of 100, 80, 50, 40, 25, 20, 10, 5 and 2½ Franc pieces (20 Pesos to 4 Reales). Of all the countries in the Union, only Guatemala struck so tiny a coin as the 2½ Franc equivalent.

The only coins of the 20th century were struck in 1926 and are based on the U.S. gold dollar. In the 1926 issues, 49,000 pieces were reported struck of the 20 Quetzals, 18,000 of the 10 Quetzals, and 48,000 of the 5 Quetzals.

A. Spanish Kings of —

PHILIP V, 1700-1746
Bust. Rev. Arms.

1. 8 Escudos 1733-45 .... **Rare**

FERDINAND VI, 1746-1760

Crude bust of the previous King, Philip V. Rev. Arms.

2. 8 Escudos 1750 .... **Rare**
3. 1 Escudo 1751 .... **1000.00**

Bust. Rev. Arms with star hanging at bottom.

4. 8 Escudos 1754, 55 ....*...... **2000.00**
5. 1 Escudo 1755 .... **600.00**

Bust. Rev. Arms with the Golden Fleece hanging at bottom.

6. 8 Escudos 1756, 57 ....*...... **1500.00**
7. 1 Escudo 1757 .... **500.00**

CHARLES III, 1759-1788
Crude small bust. Rev. Arms.

8. 8 Escudos 1761 .... **Rare**

Crude large bust. Rev. Arms without value.

9. 8 Escudos 1765, 68, 70 .... **Rare**

Normal style bust. Rev. Arms with value.

10. 8 Escudos 1778-87 ....*...... **1500.00**
11. 4 Escudos 1778, 81, 83 .... **1750.00**
12. 2 Escudos 1783, 85 .... **600.00**
13. 1 Escudo 1778, 83 .... **400.00**

CHARLES IV, 1788-1808

Bust of the previous King, Charles III. Rev. Arms.

14. 8 Escudos 1789, 90 ....*...... **1250.00**
15. 4 Escudos 1789 .... **1500.00**
16. 2 Escudos 1789 .... **Rare**
17. 1 Escudo 1789, 90, 91 .... **450.00**

Bust. Rev. Arms.

18. 8 Escudos 1794, 97, 1801 ....* 1000.00
19. 4 Escudos 1794, 97, 1801 .... 650.00
20. 2 Escudos 1794 .... 600.00
21. 1 Escudo 1794, 97, 1801 .... 325.00

FERDINAND VII, 1808-1822

Laureate head. Rev. Arms.

22. 8 Escudos 1811, 17 .... 850.00
23. 4 Escudos 1813, 17 ....* 850.00
24. 2 Escudos 1808, 11, 17 .... 500.00
25. 1 Escudo 1817 .... 225.00

B. Republic of —

Sun over five mountain peaks. Rev. Tree.

26. 8 Escudos 1824, 25 .... 2500.00
27. 4 Escudos 1824, 25, 26 .... 2000.00
28. 2 Escudos 1825-46 ....* 200.00
29. 1 Escudo 1824, 25 .... 200.00
30. ½ Escudo 1824-26, 43 .... 75.00

Head of Carrera with title as "PTE" (President). Rev. Arms.

31. 16 Pesos 1863. Size 35½ millimetres .... Rare
32. 16 Pesos 1864, 65, 67. Size 33 millimetres ....* .... Rare
33. 8 Pesos 1864 .... 400.00
34. 4 Pesos 1861, 62 .... 200.00
35. 2 Pesos 1859 .... 75.00

Obv. similar to above. Rev. Value in wreath.

36. 1 Peso 1859, 60 .... 40.00
37. 4 Reales 1860-64 .... 25.00

Head of Carrera with title as "Fundator" (Founder). Rev. Arms.

38. 20 Pesos 1869 .... 250.00
39. 16 Pesos 1869 .... 600.00
40. 10 Pesos 1869 .... 125.00
41. 8 Pesos 1869 .... 300.00
42. 5 Pesos 1869 ....* 100.00
43. 4 Pesos 1866, 68, 69 .... 110.00

Liberty head with flowing hair. Rev. Arms.

44. 20 Pesos 1877-78 .... 3000.00
45. 5 Pesos 1872-78 ....* 150.00

Liberty head with coiled hair. Rev. Arms. These coins were not placed in circulation.

46. 10 Pesos 1894 .... 4500.00
47. 5 Pesos 1894 ....* 4000.00

Quetzal on column. Rev. Arms.

48. 20 Quetzals 1926 .... 350.00
49. 10 Quetzals 1926 .... 225.00
50. 5 Quetzals 1926 ....* 125.00

HAWAII

Head of King Kalakua. Rev. Arms. Souvenir gold and platinum coins struck from dies used for silver coins.

1. ½ Dollar 1884. Gold .... Rare
2. ½ Dollar 1884. Platinum .... Rare
3. ¼ Dollar 1884. Gold .... Rare
4. ¼ Dollar 1884. Platinum .... Rare
5. ⅛ Dollar 1883. Gold .... Rare
6. ⅛ Dollar 1883. Platinum .... Rare

(The two coins following were privately struck in England by Reginald Huth).

Head of Queen Liliuocalania to right. Rev. Map of the islands.

7. 20 Dollars 1893 .... Rare

Head of Queen Liliuocalania to left. Rev. Crown over value and date.

8. 20 Dollars 1893 .... Rare

HEJAZ

Kings of —

HUSEIN IBN ALI, 1916-1924

Arab legend in panels on each side.

1. 1 Dinar 1923 .... **75.00**

HOLY ROMAN EMPIRE

(See under Austria, Bohemia and Hungary).

For the sake of as much simplicity as could be gained, this most complicated and involute of all coinage systems has been divided among Austria, Bohemia and Hungary. Necessity has forced this arrangement, since the Holy Roman Empire was a political concept and not a geographical entity with clearly defined borders.

Under Austria will be found those coins of the Hapsburg Emperors which are of similar type, whether the coins were struck in Austria proper or in the various mints of Bohemia or Hungary (including Transylvania). These similar type coins differ from each other only in the minor aspect of mint marks, mint symbols or in variations of the armorial devices or legends.

Under Bohemia and Hungary will be found the coins of these same Hapsburg Emperors, but of types which are peculiar only to their own areas, and these coins differ markedly in design from those listed under Austria.

Other coins, with either the portraits or names of the Holy Roman Emperors will be found throughout the cities and states of Germany, as well as in several other European countries.

The coinage of the Holy Roman Empire as such ended in 1806, at which time the incumbent Emperor Francis II became Francis I of the newly created Austro-Hungarian Empire, which in turn lasted until the First World War.

HONDURAS

The coinage of Honduras was based on the Latin Monetary Union standard and 20 Pesos were equivalent to 100 Francs.

Arms. Rev. Tree. With plain or reeded edges. These coins were not placed in circulation.

1. 10 Pesos 1871 ....*...... **Rare**
2. 5 Pesos 1871 .... **Rare**

Liberty head. Rev. Arms. Most coins have overstruck dates.

3. 20 Pesos 1888 .... **Rare**
4. 10 Pesos 1889 .... **Rare**
5. 5 Pesos 1883, 88, 95-97, 1913 ....*..... **600.00**
6. 1 Peso 1871, 88, 89, 95, 96, 1902, 13, 19, 22 ......*...... **250.00**
7. 1 Peso 1912 .... **Rare**

HUNGARY

The Hungarian Goldgulden and Ducat of the standing Emperor type were among the most popular coins of Europe and were circulated and accepted throughout the Continent. Many cities and states imitated this type for their own local coinage.

The St. George coins of Kremnitz have always been carried on the person to bring good luck to the bearer and keep him from harm. The coins of Transylvania are notable for the striking portraits and costuming that appear on them.

A. Kings of —

CHARLES ROBERT, 1308-1342
St. John. Rev. Lily.

1. 1 Goldgulden ND **125.00**

LOUIS I, 1342-1382

St. John. Rev. Lily.

2. 1 Goldgulden ND **75.00**

St. John. Rev. Arms.

3. 1 Goldgulden ND **75.00**

St. Ladislas. Rev. Arms.

4. 1 Ducat ND **75.00**

MARIA, 1382-1387
St. Ladislas. Rev. Arms.

5. 1 Ducat ND **100.00**

SIGISMUND, 1387-1437

St. Ladislas. Rev. Quartered arms.

6. 1 Ducat ND **100.00**

ALBERT OF AUSTRIA, 1438-1439
St. Ladislas. Rev. Quartered arms.

7. 1 Ducat ND **100.00**

LADISLAS OF POLAND, 1440-1449
St. Ladislas. Rev. Quartered arms.

8. 1 Ducat ND **100.00**

JOHN HUNYAD, 1446-1452
St. Ladislas. Rev. Quartered arms.

9. 1 Ducat ND **100.00**

LADISLAS V, 1452-1457
St. Ladislas. Rev. Quartered arms.

10. 1 Ducat ND **100.00**

MATTHIAS CORVINUS, 1458-1490

St. Ladislas. Rev. Quartered arms.

11. 1 Ducat ND **75.00**

St. Ladislas. Rev. Madonna seated.

12.   1 Ducat ND **75.00**

LADISLAS II, 1495-1516

St. Ladislas. Rev. Madonna seated.

13.   1 Ducat 1507, ND **100.00**

St. Ladislas. Rev. Madonna standing.

14.   1 Ducat 1510-16 .... **100.00**

St. Ladislas on horseback. Rev. Arms.

15. 10 Ducats 1506 .... **1250.00**
16.   8 Ducats 1506 .... **1500.00**

LOUIS II, 1516-1526
Ruler on horse. Rev. Madonna seated.

17.   2 Ducats 1525 .... **600.00**

St. Ladislas. Rev. Madonna standing.

18.   1 Ducat 1518-23 .... **100.00**

Youthful King seated. Rev. Legend.

19.   5 Ducats 1544 ....*...... **300.00**
20.   3 Ducats 1544 .... **200.00**
21.   2 Ducats 1544 .... **150.00**

JOHN ZAPOLYA, 1526-1540
Madonna seated. Rev. Arms.

22.   1 Ducat 1539 .... **100.00**

St. Ladislas. Rev. Arms.

23.   1 Ducat 1540 .... **100.00**

St. Ladislas. Rev. Madonna standing.

24.   1 Ducat 1527-40 .... **100.00**

FERDINAND I, 1521-1564
St. Ladislas. Rev. Madonna standing.

25.   2 Ducats 1535-60 .... **225.00**
26.   1 Ducat 1521-64 .... **125.00**
27.   1 Ducat 1565. Posthumous **150.00**

St. Ladislas. Rev. Arms.

28.   1 Ducat 1545-58 .... **100.00**

MAXIMILIAN II, 1564-1576
St Ladislas. Rev. Madonna standing.

29.   2 Ducats 1567, 72 .... **200.00**
30.   1 Ducat 1564-76 .... **125.00**
31.   1 Ducat 1577, 78. Posthumous **200.00**

Ruler standing. Rev. St. Ladislas.

32.   1 Ducat 1564-76 .... **150.00**

RUDOLPH II, 1576-1612
St. Ladislas. Rev. Madonna standing.

33.   3 Ducats 1580 .... **400.00**
34.   1 Ducat 1578-1608 .... **100.00**

MATTHIAS II, 1612-1619

Ruler standing. Rev. Madonna.

35.   5 Ducats 1614 ....*..... **650.00**
36.   2 Ducats 1612-19 .... **275.00**
37.   1 Ducat 1612-19 .... **125.00**
38. ¼ Ducat 1615 .... **50.00**

Bust. Rev. Double eagle between K-B or N-B.

39. 15 Ducats 1617 .... **1750.00**
40.   5 Ducats 1617 .... **600.00**

FERDINAND II, 1618-1637

Ruler standing. Rev. Madonna.

41.   5 Ducats 1632 .... **600.00**
42.   2 Ducats 1622-37 .... **200.00**
43.   1 Ducat 1620-37 ....*...... **100.00**
44. ¼ Ducat 1630-35 .... **60.00**

Bust. Rev. Double eagle between K-B or N-B.

45. 10 Ducats 1626-35 ....*...... **1250.00**
46.   5 Ducats 1632-37 .... **600.00**

FERDINAND III, 1627-1657
Ruler standing. Rev. Madonna.

47.   2 Ducats 1637-57 .... **225.00**
48.   1 Ducat 1637-57 .... **150.00**
49.   1 Ducat 1658, 59. Posthumous **200.00**

Bust. Rev. Double eagle between K-B or N-B.

50. 10 Ducats 1629-57 .... **1000.00**

LEOPOLD I, (THE HOGMOUTH), 1658-1705

Ruler standing. Rev. Madonna.

51.   1 Ducat 1658-1704 .... **75.00**

Laureate bust. Rev. Madonna on crescent.

52.	10 Ducats	1687	1500.00
53.	8 Ducats	1695	1200.00
54.	5 Ducats	1675, 87	750.00
55.	4 Ducats	1687, 95	750.00
56.	3 Ducats	1695	500.00
57.	2 Ducats	1695	300.00

Laureate bust. Rev. Madonna seated, two shields below.

58.	1 Ducat	1675	175.00

Bust and value. Rev. Madonna.

59.	¼ Ducat	1684-99	*	40.00
60.	⅛ Ducat	1673-98	*	40.00
61.	1/12 Ducat	ND. With blank Rev.		30.00

REBELLION OF THE MALCONTENTS, 1703-1707
Arms and date. Rev. Value in cartouche.

62.	5 Ducats	1704	1000.00

Arms. Rev. Madonna.

63.	1 Ducat	1704-07	*	150.00
64.	1 Ducat	1705. Square		400.00

JOSEPH I, 1705-1711

Ruler standing. Rev. Madonna.

65.	1 Ducat	1705-11	100.00

CHARLES VI, 1711-1740

Ruler standing. Rev. Madonna.

66.	1 Ducat	1712-40	*	125.00
67.	½ Ducat	1740		100.00
68.	¼ Ducat	1712-40		75.00

Bust. Rev. Madonna.

69.	1 Ducat	1736-40	125.00
70.	⅙ Ducat	1712-40	35.00
71.	⅛ Ducat	1739	35.00
72.	1/12 Ducat	1739	35.00

MARIA THERESA, 1740-1780

Ruler standing. Rev. Madonna.

73.	2 Ducats	1763-65	*	200.00
74.	1 Ducat	1741-65		125.00

Bust. Rev. Madonna.

75.	1 Ducat	1753-65	125.00

Old veiled bust. Rev. Madonna.

76.	1 Ducat	1765-80	125.00

JOSEPH II, 1765-1790
Ruler standing. Rev. Madonna.

77.	2 Ducats	1781-85	125.00
78.	1 Ducat	1781-85	100.00

LEOPOLD II, 1790-1792
Ruler standing. Rev. Madonna.

79.	1 Ducat	1790-92	100.00

JOSEPH II AND LEOPOLD II
Two busts. Rev. Inscription. On visit to the mines.

80.	1 Ducat	1764	300.00

FRANCIS II, 1792-1835
Ruler standing. Rev. Madonna.

81.	1 Ducat	1792-1835	75.00

FERDINAND I, 1835-1848
Ruler standing. Rev. Madonna.

82.	1 Ducat	1837-48. Latin legends	75.00
83.	1 Ducat	1848. Magyar legends	100.00

FRANCIS JOSEPH, 1848-1916
Ruler standing. Rev. Arms supported by angels.

84.	1 Ducat	1868-70. KB mm.	85.00
85.	1 Ducat	1868, 69. GYF mm.	65.00

Laureate head. Rev. Crowned arms.

86.	1 Ducat	1877-81	175.00

Laureate head. Rev. Arms and two values.

87.	8 Florins-20 Francs	1870-92. KB mm.	*	30.00
88.	8 Florins-20 Francs	1870, 71. GYF mm.		60.00
89.	4 Florins-10 Francs	1870-92. KB mm.	*	35.00
90.	4 Florins-10 Francs	1870. GYF mm.		75.00

Ruler standing. Rev. Arms.

91.	100 Korona	1907, 08		350.00
92.	20 Korona	1892-1916	*	27.50
93.	20 Korona	1914, 16. Slight change in arms		125.00
94.	10 Korona	1892-1915	*	25.00

Head. Rev. Coronation scene. On the 40th year of his reign.

95. 100 Korona 1907 .... 275.00

Crowned bust. Rev. Madonna and child. On the 1000th year of the Hungarian Kingdom.

96. 9 Ducats 1896 .... 1250.00

St. John. Rev. Lily. On the 1000th year of the Hungarian Kingdom.

97. 1 Goldgulden 1896 .... 275.00

CHARLES, 1916-1918
Head. Rev. Arms. Not placed in circulation.

98. 20 Korona 1918 .... **Rare**

REGENCY, 1919-1944

Arms. Rev. Value. Not placed in circulation.

99. 20 Pengo 1928, 29 ....*..... 2000.00
100. 10 Pengo 1928 .... 2000.00

B. People's Republic, 1945-

Bust of Liszt. Rev. Lyre.

101. 500 Florins 1961 .... 250.00
102. 100 Florins 1961 .... 75.00
103. 50 Florins 1961 .... 50.00

Bust of Bartok. Rev. Lyre.

104. 500 Florins 1961 .... 250.00
105. 100 Florins 1961 .... 75.00
106. 50 Florins 1961 .... 50.00

Bust of Nicholas Zrinyi. Rev. The defense of Szigetvar. On the 400th anniversary of the war against the Turks.

106a. 1000 Forint 1966 .... 350.00
106b. 500 Forint 1966 .... 150.00
106c. 100 Forint 1966 .... 50.00

Bust of Kodaly. Rev. Peacock. On the composer's 85th birthday.

106d. 1000 Forint 1967 .... 250.00
106e. 500 Forint 1967 .... 125.00

Bust of Dr. Ignaz Semmelweis. Rev. Arms. On the 150th anniversary of the birth of the obstetrician who conquered childbed fever.

106f. 1000 Forint 1968 .... 275.00
106g. 500 Forint 1968 .... 150.00
106h. 200 Forint 1968 .... 60.00
106i. 100 Forint 1968 .... 40.00
106j. 50 Forint 1968 .... 25.00

C. Cities of —

BATTHYANI

Princes —
CHARLES, 1764-1772

Bust. Rev. Arms.

107. 10 Ducats 1764 .... 1500.00
108. 5 Ducats 1764 .... 750.00
109. 1 Ducat 1764, 65 ....*...... 175.00

LOUIS, 1787-1806
Bust. Rev. Arms.

110.	10 Ducats 1788	1250.00
111.	5 Ducats 1789	500.00
112.	1 Ducat 1791	200.00

ESTERHAZY

Princes —

NICHOLAS, 1762-1790
Bust. Rev. Arms.

113.	1 Ducat 1770	300.00

KREMNITZ

St. George slaying dragon. Rev. Christ in boat. Struck during the period 1600-1800.

114.	10 Ducats ND	*	500.00
115.	6 Ducats ND		375.00
116.	5 Ducats ND		375.00
117.	3 Ducats ND		225.00
118.	2 Ducats ND		125.00
119.	1 Ducat ND		75.00

TRANSYLVANIA (SIEBENBURGEN)

Voivodes (Princes) of —

JOHN I ZAPOLYA, 1538-1540
Ruler standing. Rev. Madonna.

120.	1 Ducat 1540	125.00

St. Ladislas standing. Rev. Madonna.

121.	1 Ducat 1539, 40	125.00

Madonna. Rev. Arms.

122.	1 Ducat 1539	125.00

ISABELLA AND JOHN SIGISMUND, 1556-1559
Madonna. Rev. Arms.

123.	5 Ducats 1557	1500.00
124.	1 Ducat 1556-60	150.00
125.	½ Ducat 1558, 59	150.00
126.	¼ Ducat 1559	125.00

St. Ladislas. Rev. Arms.

127.	1 Ducat 1556	250.00

Arms. Rev. Legend.

128.	10 Ducats 1557	2000.00

129.	10 Ducats 1557. Square	2500.00
130.	5 Ducats 1557	1200.00

JOHN SIGISMUND, 1559-1571

Madonna. Rev. Arms.

131.	4 Ducats 1577. Thick flan.		1250.00
132.	2 Ducats 1562		400.00
133.	1 Ducat 1560-72	*	200.00

St. Ladislas standing. Rev. Arms.

134.	1 Ducat 1556-59	125.00

Arms and ISRV. Rev. Blank.

135.	10 Ducats 1562, 65	1500.00

STEPHAN BATHORI, 1571-1575
Madonna. Rev. St. Ladislas.

136.	1 Ducat 1572-79	150.00

CHRISTOPHER BATHORI, 1576-1581

Arms. Rev. Legend.

137.	10 Ducats 1577, 83	*	2000.00
138.	5 Ducats 1577, 83		1000.00
139.	4 Ducats 1577		800.00
140.	2 Ducats 1577		400.00
141.	1½ Ducats 1577		300.00

Madonna. Rev. Arms.

142.	1 Ducat 1579	200.00

Madonna. Rev. St. Ladislas.

143.	1 Ducat 1577-80	200.00

ELIZABETH BOCSKAI, 1577

Lion seated. Rev. Legend.

144.	10 Ducats 1577	*	2000.00
145.	5 Ducats 1577		1000.00
146.	3 Ducats 1577		600.00
147.	2 Ducats 1577		325.00

SIGISMUND BATHORI, 1581-1602
Bust. Rev. Eagle.

148.	10 Ducats 1598	2000.00
149.	9 Ducats 1598	2000.00

Bust. Rev. Arms supported by angels.

150.　10 Ducats 1590 ....· 2000.00

Madonna. Rev. St. Ladislas.

151.　5 Ducats 1590. Thick flan. 800.00
152.　1 Ducat 1581-97 ....* 150.00

St. Ladislas. Rev. Eagle.

153.　1 Ducat 1598 .... 150.00

Arms. Rev. Legend.

154.　10 Ducats 1583 ....· 1500.00

MOSES SZEKELY, 1602-1603

Two lions with sword. Rev. Legend.

155.　10 Ducats 1603 .... **Rare**

STEPHAN BOCSKAI, 1604-1606

Bust. Rev. Arm with sword.

156.　10 Ducats 1605 ....· 2000.00

Crossed swords. Rev. Double eagle. Struck by Rudolph II during siege of Hermannstadt.

157.　10 Ducats 1605 ....· 3500.00

Bust. Rev. Arms.

158.　10 Ducats 1606 .... 2000.00
159.　5 Ducats 1606 ....· 1000.00

Bust. Rev. Crossed swords.

160.　1 Ducat 1606 .,.............................. 275.00

Head with fur cap. Rev. Arms.

161.　2 Ducats 1606 .... 450.00
162.　1 Ducat 1606 ....* 250.00

Madonna. Rev. St. Ladislas.

163.　1 Ducat 1605, 06, 07, ND 175.00

Madonna. Rev. Arms.

164.　½ Ducat 1606 .... 125.00
165.　¼ Ducat 1606 .... 100.00

SIGISMUND RAKOCZI, 1607-1608

Bust. Rev. Legend.

166.　10 Ducats 1607 .... 2250.00

Bust. Rev. Eagle on castles.

167.　1 Ducat 1607, 08 .... 350.00

Madonna. Rev. Arms.

168.　¼ Ducat 1608 .... 100.00

GABRIEL BATHORI, 1608-1613
Bust. Rev. Three shields.

169.　10 Ducats 1609 .... 2000.00

Bust. Rev. Eagle.

170.　6 Ducats 1613. Thick flan. 1750.00
171.　1 Ducat 1611, 12, 13 ....* 200.00

Bust. Rev. Arms.

172.　2 Ducats 1610, 12 .... 400.00
173.　1 Ducat 1609-12, ND 200.00

Head with cap. Rev. Arms.

174.　1 Ducat 1613 .... 250.00

Bust. Rev. Crossed swords.

175.　1 Ducat 1613 .... 250.00

Madonna. Rev. St. Ladislas.

176.　1 Ducat 1609 .... 175.00

Three shields. Rev. Legend.

177.　10 Ducats 1611, 12, 13 .... 1500.00
178.　8 Ducats 1612 ....·1000.00

Madonna. Rev. Arms.

179.　½ Ducat 1612, 13 .... 90.00
180.　¼ Ducat 1610, 12, 13 .... 70.00

MICHAEL WEISS (1613)

Legend on each side.

181.　10 Ducats 1612 ....* 2500.00
182.　1 Ducat 1612, 13 .... 400.00

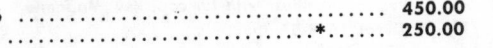

GABRIEL BETHLEN, 1613-1629
Bust with cap. Rev. Arms.

183.	2 Ducats 1613	400.00
184.	1 Ducat 1613-18	200.00

Bust with cap. Rev. Arm with sword.

185.	10 Ducats 1616	2500.00

Bust. Rev. Elaborate arms.

186.	1 Ducat 1618	225.00

Bust. Rev. Three shields.

187.	10 Ducats 1619	2500.00
188.	1 Ducat 1619	200.00

Bust. Rev. Arms.

189.	10 Ducats 1620, 21, 22, 28, ND	1500.00
190.	5 Ducats 1622	900.00
191.	3 Ducats 1627	600.00
192.	1 Ducat 1620, 22, ND ....*......	150.00

Bust. Rev. Madonna.

193.	1 Ducat 1620-27	150.00

Bust. Rev. Madonna in flames.

194.	2 Ducats 1628	500.00
195.	1 Ducat 1627, 28, 29	200.00

Madonna. Rev. Arms.

196.	1 Ducat 1627	175.00
197.	¼ Ducat 1619-27	60.00

CATHERINE BETHLEN, 1629-1630
Bust. Rev. Madonna.

198.	1 Ducat 1630	900.00

Bust. Rev. Arms.

199.	1 Ducat 1630	900.00

STEPHAN BETHLEN, 1630

Bust. Rev. Arms.

200.	1 Ducat 1630	900.00

GEORGE RAKOCZI I, 1630-1648

Bust. Rev. Legend.

201.	20 Ducats 1637, 39	Rare
202.	10 Ducats 1631, 36, 37, 39 ....*......	1750.00
203.	5 Ducats 1631, 36, 37, 39	900.00

Bust. Rev. Arms.

204.	10 Ducats 1645, 47	2000.00
205.	6 Ducats 1647	1250.00

Bust. Rev. Eagle and castles.

206.	2 Ducats 1632	600.00
207.	1 Ducat 1631-39	175.00

Bust with fur cap. Rev. Arms.

208.	10 Ducats 1646, 48	2000.00

Bust with fur cap. Rev. Eagle on castles.

209.	1 Ducat 1646	200.00

Bust with cap. Rev. Madonna.

210.	1 Ducat 1646, 48	150.00

Bust. Rev. Madonna.

211.	1 Ducat 1645, 48	150.00

Madonna. Rev. Arms.

212.	¼ Ducat 1642, 47	75.00

GEORGE RAKOCZI II, 1648-1660

Bust with fur cap. Rev. Arms.

213.	13 Ducats 1657. Square	Rare
214.	12 Ducats 1657. Square	Rare
215.	10 Ducats 1652, 57, 60. Square or hexagonal ..*......	3000.00
216.	10 Ducats 1648-60. Round	1500.00
217.	7 Ducats 1654	1500.00

Bust with fur cap. Rev. Madonna.

218.	1 Ducat 1648-57	150.00

Bust with fur cap. Rev. Eagle and castles.

219.	1 Ducat 1657	200.00
220.	1 Ducat 1657. Square	300.00

Madonna. Rev. Arms.

221.	¼ Ducat 1650, 53	75.00

ACHATIUS BARCSAI, 1658-1660

Bust. Rev. Arms.

222.	10 Ducats 1659, 60	2500.00
223.	10 Ducats 1659. Square or hexagonal	2000.00
224.	2 Ducats 1659	600.00
225.	1 Ducat 1659 ....*......	275.00

Arms. Rev. Legend.

226.	10 Ducats 1660	2500.00
227.	10 Ducats 1660. Square	2750.00
228.	9 Ducats 1660. Square	2500.00
229.	7 Ducats 1660. Square	2250.00
230.	5 Ducats 1660. Square	1750.00
231.	5 Ducats 1660	1700.00
232.	1 Ducat 1660	275.00

Arms on each side.

233.	10 Ducats 1660	2500.00

JOHN KEMENY, 1661-1662

Bust with fur cap. Rev. Arms.

234.	10 Ducats 1661 ....*......	3000.00
235.	5 Ducats 1661	1750.00
236.	3 Ducats 1661	1400.00
237.	2 Ducats 1661	1000.00
238.	2 Ducats 1661 Square	1200.00
239.	1 Ducat 1661	375.00

MICHAEL APAFI, 1661-1690

Bust with fur cap. Rev. Arms.
ROUND COINS

240.	100 Ducats 1677	Rare
241.	30 Ducats 1677, 83	Rare
242.	10 Ducats 1662-74	1750.00

243.	5 Ducats 1662-73	1100.00
244.	4 Ducats 1665	1000.00
245.	1 Ducat 1662, 82	350.00

SQUARE OR HEXAGONAL COINS

246.	10 Ducats 1662, 63, 75, 81 ....*......	2000.00
247.	6 Ducats 1668	1100.00
248.	4½ Ducats 1668	1100.00
249.	3 Ducats 1663	1000.00
250.	2 Ducats 1662, 68	600.00
251.	1 Ducat 1663, 68	300.00

Bust. Rev. Arms.
ROUND COINS

252.	10 Ducats 1672-89	1600.00
253.	5 Ducats 1677, 87	900.00
254.	4 Ducats 1677, 89	750.00
255.	1 Ducat 1673-90	200.00

SQUARE OR HEXAGONAL COINS

256.	25 Ducats 1687	Rare
257.	10 Ducats 1684, 89	2500.00
258.	6 Ducats 1686	1750.00
259.	5 Ducats 1689	1250.00
260.	4 Ducats 1678	900.00
261.	3 Ducats 1684	800.00
262.	2 Ducats 1689	600.00
263.	1 Ducat 1678-89	300.00

Bust in center within circle of ten other busts. Rev. Arms in center within circle of ten other arms.

264.	100 Ducats 1674, 75	Rare

EMERIC TOKELY, 1682-1690

Bust with fur cap. Rev. Arm with sword.

265.	10 Ducats 1683	2500.00
266.	8 Ducats 1683	1500.00
267.	4 Ducats 1683	900.00

Bust with fur cap. Rev. Arms.

268.	1 Ducat 1690	450.00

FRANCIS RAKOCZI II, 1704-1711

Arms. Rev. Palm tree.

269.	1 Ducat 1705	300.00

CHARLES VI, 1711-1740
Head. Rev. Arms.

270.	¼ Ducat ND	60.00

Arms. Rev. Globe.

271.	¼ Ducat ND	60.00

MARIA THERESA, 1740-1780
Arms. Rev. Value.

272.	¼ Ducat 1749	60.00
273.	⅛ Ducat 1778	60.00
274.	1/16 Ducat 1778	60.00

Bust. Rev. Arms.

275.	1 Ducat 1740-80	125.00

ICELAND

Head of Sigurdsson. Rev. Arms.

1. 500 Kronur 1961 .... 125.00

INDIA

A. British Sovereigns of —

WILLIAM IV, 1830-1837

Head. Rev. Lion and palm tree. Issued by the East India Company.

1. 2 Mohurs 1835 ....*...... 600.00
2. 1 Mohur 1835 .... 150.00

VICTORIA, 1837-1901

Head. Rev. Lion and palm tree. Issued by the East India Company.

3. 1 Mohur 1841 .... 200.00

Thin face with title of Queen. Rev. Value.

4. 1 Mohur 1862-70 ....*...... 125.00
5. 10 Rupees 1862-70 .... 75.00
6. 5 Rupees 1862-70 ....*...... 65.00

Plump face with title of Queen. Rev. Value.

7. 1 Mohur 1870 ....*...... 125.00
8. 10 Rupees 1870 .... 100.00
9. 5 Rupees 1870 .... 75.00

Thin face with title of Empress. Rev. Value.

10. 1 Mohur 1877-89 ....*...... 150.00
11. 5 Rupees 1879 .... 75.00

Plump face with title of Empress. Rev. Value.

12. 10 Rupees 1878, 79 .... 90.00
13. 5 Rupees 1879 .... 75.00

GEORGE V, 1910-1936

Head. Rev. Value.

14. 15 Rupees 1918 .... 125.00

Head. Rev. St. George. This is the same type as the English Pound but with the distinguishing Indian mint mark "I" on ground below horse.

15. 1 Pound 1918 .... 50.00

B. Private Tola Coinage of —

Gold coins issued by various Indian banking houses during the present generation. There are many varieties and the pieces may be round, square, diamond shaped, or scalloped. The Tola weighs a little more than 11.50 Grams and is thus similar to the Mohur. Tola coinage is undated.

16. 10 Tola piece 500.00
17. 5 Tola piece 350.00
18. 1 Tola piece 50.00
19. ½ Tola piece 40.00
20. ¼ Tola piece 35.00

C. Native States of —

AGRA

Indian legend on each side. Oblong shape.

21. 1 Mohur. About 1550-1600 .... 300.00

AJMIR AND DELHI

Goddess seated. Rev. Legend.

22. 1 Stater. About 1010-1160 .... 125.00

ARCOT

Persian legend on each side. Coinage of the East India Company in the name of Alamgir II of Hindustan. With dates from about 1172-1214 A.H. (1758-99).

23. 1 Mohur 65.00
24. ½ Mohur ....*...... 40.00
25. ¼ Mohur 25.00

ASSAM

Bengali legend on each side. Octagonal shaped coins struck during the period 1540-1820.

26. 1 Mohur ....*...... 100.00
27. ½ Mohur 65.00
28. ¼ Mohur 45.00
29. ⅛ Mohur 30.00
30. ¹⁄₁₆ Mohur 25.00
31. ¹⁄₃₂ Mohur 25.00

AWADH

Kings of —

GHAZI-UD-DIN-HAIDAR, 1819-1827

Persian legend. Rev. Two fish crowned, supported by tigers.

32. 1 Mohur 1234-1243 A.H. ....*...... 100.00
33. ¼ Mohur 1234-1243 A.H. 35.00

NAZIR-UD-DIN-HAIDAR, 1827-1837
Inscription. Rev. Arms.

34. 1 Mohur 1243-1253 A.H. 100.00

MOHAMMED ALI SHAH, 1837-1842

Persian legend. Rev. Two females standing and supporting crown.

35. 1 Mohur 1253-1258 A.H. 100.00

AMJAD ALI SHAH, 1842-1847

Persian legend. Rev. Umbrella over crown over fish.

36. 1 Mohur 1258-1262 A.H. 125.00
37. ½ Mohur 1258-1262 A.H. ....*...... 65.00

WAJID ALI SHAH, 1847-1856

Persian legend. Rev. Arms supported by mermaids holding clubs and banners.

38. 1 Mohur 1263-1272 A.H. ....*...... 125.00
39. ½ Mohur 1263-1272 A.H. ....*...... 65.00
40. ¼ Mohur 1263-1272 A.H. 50.00
41. ⅛ Mohur 1263-1272 A.H. 35.00

BAHAWALPUR

Bust of Rajah Sadik Mohammed V. Rev. Arms.

42. 1 Mohur 1343 A.H. (1925) 500.00

BAJRANGGARH

Indian legend on each side. Struck under Jai Singh.

43. 1 Mohur (1798-1818). Octagonal 250.00

BARODA

Bust of Gaikwar Sayaji Rao III (1875-1902). Rev. Legend. With dates from about 1940-1953 Samvat (1883-1896 A.D.).

44. 1 Mohur ....*...... 300.00
45. ⅓ Mohur 125.00
46. ⅛ Mohur ....*...... 85.00

BENARES

Persian legend on each side. Coinage of the East India Company in the name of Shah Alam II of Hindustan. With dates from about 1212-1235 A.H. (1797-1819).

47. 1 Mohur 100.00

BENGAL

Indian legend on each side. Royal coinage struck during the period 1302-1518.

48. 1 Mohur 75.00

Indian legend on each side. Coinage of the East India Company struck during the period 1750-1820.

49. 2 Mohurs 250.00
50. 1 Mohur 60.00
51. ¼ Mohur 40.00

BHARTPUR

Persian legend on each side. Rajah coinage struck during the period 1805-1823.

52. 1 Mohur 75.00

Crude head of Queen Victoria. Rev. Persian legend.

53. 1 Mohur ND. (About 1860) 175.00

BHOPAL

Persian legend on each side. Coinage of the Begums.

54. 1 Mohur (1840-1850) 85.00

BIKANIR

Bust of the Maharajah Sri Ganga Singhji. Rev. Value.

55. 1 Mohur 1994 Samvat (1937) ....*...... 225.00
56. ½ Mohur 1994 Samvat (1937) 150.00

BOMBAY

Arms of the English East India Company. Rev. "Bombay" and date.

57. 1 Mohur 1765 .... 600.00
58. ½ Mohur 1765 .... 300.00
59. ¼ Mohur 1765 .... 225.00

Persian legend on each side. Coinage of the East India Company in the name of Shah Alam of Hindustan.

60. 1 Mohur 1182 A.H. (1768) 85.00

Persian legend. Rev. English name, date and value.

61. 15 Rupees (1 Mohur) 1770 .... 750.00

BUNDI

Persian legend. Rev. Regnal year. Maharajah coinage struck during the period 1800-35.

62. 1 Mohur 85.00

CALCUTTA

Persian legend on each side with a large C on Rev. Coinage of the East India Company in the name of Shah Alam II of Hindustan.

63. 1 Mohur 1216 A.H. (1801) 150.00

CHEDI (WESTERN)

Goddess seated. Rev. Legend. Coinage of Governors struck during the period 1000-1100.

64. 1 Stater 100.00

CHOLAS

Ruler standing on each side. Crude tribal coinage struck during the period 1000-1300.

65. 1 Stater 125.00

COCHIN

Crude symbols on each side. Struck during the period 1740-80.

66. 1 Fanam 20.00

COROMANDEL COAST

Symbols on each side. Struck during the period 1700-1800.

67. 1 Fanam 20.00

CUTCH-BHUJ

MAHARAJAH PRAGMALJI II, 1860-1875

Persian legend with name of Queen Victoria, Christian date in Arabic numerals and value. Rev. Indian legend with Maharajah's name, Samvat date, and value.

68. 100 Kori 1866 ....*...... 200.00
69. 50 Kori 1873, 74 .... 150.00
70. 25 Kori 1862-70 .... 125.00

COOCH-BIHAR

Legend in square. Rev. Legend. Struck under Rajah Narendra Narayana, 1847-1863.

71. 1 Mohur 200.00

Arms supported by lion and elephant. Rev. Legend. Struck under Rajah Jitandra Narayana, 1912-1922.

72. 1 Mohur. Years 402, 404 (1912, 14) 375.00

DATIA

GOVIND SINGH, 1907-1948
Bust. Rev. Arms.

73. ½ Mohur ND 250.00

DELHI

Sultans of —

MOHAMMED I, 1193-1206
Indian legend within square on each side. With dates from about 589-602 A.H.

74. 1 Tanka. Large flan. Ghazni mint 300.00

Ruler on horse within circle. Rev. Legend.

75. 1 Tanka .... Unique

Crude figure of Lakshmi seated. Rev. Nagari legend.

76. ½ Tanka 125.00

SHAMS-UD-DIN ILTUTMISH, 1210-1235
Ruler on horse. Rev. Persian legend.

77. ½ Tanka ND .... Rare

ALA-UD-DIN MASUD, 1242-1246
Indian legend within square on each side. With dates from about 639-644 A.H.

78. 1 Mohur 300.00

NASIR-UD-DIN MAHMUD I, 1246-1266

Persian legend within circle on each side. With dates from about 644-664 A.H.

79. 1 Mohur 85.00

Indian legend within square on each side.

80. 1 Mohur 100.00

GHIYAS-UD-DIN BALBAN, 1266-1287

Persian legend within circle on each side. With dates from about 664-686 A.H.

81. 1 Mohur 75.00

KAIQUBAD, 1287-1290
Persian legend on each side.

82. 1 Mohur 100.00

JALAL-UD-DIN FIRUZ II, 1290-1296

Indian legend on each side. With dates from about 689-695 A.H.

83. 1 Mohur 75.00

ALA-UD-DIN MOHAMMED, 1296-1316
Persian legend on each side. With dates from about 695-715 A.H.

84. 1 Mohur. Round ....*...... 285.00
85. 1 Mohur. Square 125.00

SHIHAB-UD-DIN UMAR, 1316
Persian legend on each side.

86. 1 Mohur 715 A.H. 135.00

QUTB-UD-DIN MUBARAK, 1316-1320

Persian legend on each side. With dates from about 716-720 A.H.

87. 1 Mohur. Round 100.00
88. 1 Mohur. Square ....*...... 125.00
89. ⅓ Mohur. Square 65.00

NASIR-UD-DIN KHUSRU, 1320
Persian legend on each side.

90. 1 Mohur 720 A.H. 135.00

GHIYAS-UD-DIN TUGHLUK, 1320-1325
Persian legend on each side. With dates from about 720-725 A.H.

91. 1 Mohur 85.00

MOHAMMED III, 1325-1351

Arabic legend on each side. With dates from about 725-752 A.H.

92. 1½ Mohurs 150.00
93. 1　Mohur ....*...... 65.00
94. ½ Mohur ....*...... 40.00

FIRUZ III, 1351-1388

Persian legend on each side. With dates from about 752-790 A.H.

95. 1 Mohur 65.00

FATH KHAN, 1351-1388
(Son of Firuz III)
Persian legend on each side.

96. 1 Mohur 65.00

TUGHLUK II, 1388-1389
Persian legend on each side. With dates from about 790-791 A.H.

97. 1 Mohur 135.00

FIRUZ WITH ZAFAR, 1389
Persian legend on each side.

98. 1 Mohur 791 A.H. 125.00

ABU BAKR, 1389-1390
Persian legend on each side. With dates from about 791-793 A.H.

99. 1 Mohur 100.00

MOHAMMED IV, 1390-1393
Persian legend on each side. With dates from about 792-795 A.H.

100. 1 Mohur 85.00

MAHMUD II, 1393-1413
Persian legend on each side. With dates from about 795-815 A.H.

101. 1 Mohur 75.00

NUSRAT SHAH, 1395-1399
Persian legend on each side. With dates from about 779-802 A.H.

102. 1 Mohur 75.00

MUBARAK II, 1421-1434
Persian legend on each side. With dates from about 824-837 A.H.

103. 1 Mohur 75.00

MOHAMMED V, 1434-1445
Persian legend on each side. With dates from about 837-849 A.H.

104. 1 Mohur 75.00

SHER, 1538-1545
Persian legend on each side. With dates from about 945-952 A.H.

105. 1 Mohur 250.00

ISLAM, 1545-1552
Persian legend on each side. With dates from about 952-960 A.H.

106. 1 Mohur 250.00

MOHAMMED ADIL, 1552-1556

Persian legend on each side. With dates from about 960-964 A.H.

107. 1 Mohur 350.00

DIU

Portuguese Kings of —

JOHN V, 1706-1750

St. Thomas standing. Rev. Crowned arms. Crude style.

108. 5 Xerafins 1719 .... 275.00

JOSEPH I, 1750-1777

Crowned arms. Rev. Cross of St. Thomas. Crude style.

109.   10 Xerafins. Usually poorly dated 375.00

EAST INDIA COMPANY

(For other issues of the Company, see under British sovereigns of India. In addition, the Company struck native type coins at the mints of Arcot, Benares, Bengal, Bombay, Calcutta, Madras, Murshidabad and Surat, which see).

Arms supported by lions; English legend. Rev. Urdu legend.

110.   1 Mohur ND (1820) 75.00

Lion with crown on plain ground; English legend. Rev. Urdu legend.

111.   ½ Mohur ND (1820) 75.00
112.   ¼ Mohur ND (1820) ....*...... 50.00

Lion standing on shield; English legend. Rev. Urdu legend.

113.   ⅓ Mohur ND (1820) 75.00

GOA

A. Chiefs of —

Lion, sun and moon. Rev. Legend. Struck during the period 1185-1215.

114.   1 Pagoda ND 125.00

B. Portuguese Kings of —

MANUEL I, 1495-1521

MEA under crown. Rev. Globe.

115.   ½   Esphera   ND 325.00

JOHN III, 1521-1557

St. Thomas seated. Rev. Arms.

116.   1 Pardau San Tome ND 750.00

ALFONSO VI, 1656-1683

St. Thomas standing. Rev. Arms.

117.   1 Pardau San Tome ND 750.00

PETER, PRINCE REGENT, 1667-1683

St. Thomas standing. Rev. Arms.

118.   1 San Tome 1677, 80 .... 375.00

Arms. Rev. Cross of Jerusalem.

119.   1 Xerafin ND 75.00

JOHN V, 1706-1750
St. Thomas standing. Rev. Arms.

120.   1 San Tome 1719 .... 225.00

Arms. Rev. Cross of St. Thomas.

121.   12 Xerafins 1732 ....*...... 750.00
122.   10 Xerafins 1737 .... 750.00

Arms. Rev. Cross of Jerusalem.

123.   1 Xerafin 1715, 16, 18, 21 .... 150.00

JOSEPH I, 1750-1777

Arms. Rev. Cross of St. Thomas.

124.   12 Xerafins 1755-77 ....*...... 150.00
125.   8 Xerafins 1766, 71 .... 225.00
126.   4 Xerafins 1766, 68, 69, 77 .... 175.00
127.   2 Xerafins 1766, 68, 72, 74 .... 150.00

MARY I, 1777-1816

Arms. Rev. Cross of St. Thomas.

128.   12 Xerafins 1781-1806 .... 150.00
129.   8 Xerafins 1787, 95, 1805 .... 850.00
130.   4 Xerafins 1803-05 .... 850.00

JOHN, PRINCE REGENT, 1799-1816
Arms. Rev. Cross of St. Thomas.

131. 12 Xerafins 1808-15 .... 150.00

JOHN VI, 1816-1826
Arms. Rev. Cross of St. Thomas.

132. 12 Xerafins 1819, 25 .... 225.00

MARY II, 1834-1853

Arms. Rev. Cross of St. Thomas.

133. 12 Xerafins 1840, 41 .... 300.00

GUJARAT

*Persian legend on each side. Sultanate coinage struck during
the period 1410-1573.*

134. 1 Mohur ....*...... 125.00
135. ½ Mohur 100.00

GWALIOR

Turbaned bust of the Rajah Madho Rao III, 1886-1925. Rev. Arms.

136. ⅓ Mohur 1959 Samvat (1902) 225.00

HINDUSTAN

The coinage of the Mogul Emperors of Hindustan is the most extensive
and varied of Indian coinages. The largest gold coins of the entire
world were struck by these Emperors. The whereabouts of most of these
large coins is now unknown, but they are all reported as having been
seen in contemporary literature. The largest coin of all is the 200 Mohur
piece of Shah Jahan. The actual coin was last reported seen in India in
the early part of the 19th century, and a cast of the coin is now in the
British Museum (see the back page of the dust jacket).

The Mogul Emperors also issued the famous set of Zodiac Mohurs.
There are many variations of the Zodiac figures and the illustrations in
this book are of typical examples.

Mogul Emperors of —

HUMAYUN, 1530-1554

*Persian legend on each side. With dates from about 937-
960 A.H.*

137. ⅟₁₀ Mohur 40.00
138. ⅟₂₀ Mohur 30.00

AKBAR, 1556-1605
(Coinage with dates from about 963-1014 A.H.)

Persian legend on each side.

139.	100 Mohurs	Unknown
140.	50 Mohurs	Unknown
141.	20 Mohurs. Round	Unknown
142.	20 Mohurs. Square	Unknown
143.	5 Mohurs	3000.00
144.	2 Mohurs. Round	Unknown
145.	2 Mohurs. Square	Unknown
146.	1 Mohur. Round ....*......	85.00
147.	1 Mohur. Square ....*......	100.00
148.	1 Mohur. Oblong with scalloped corners ....*......	300.00
149.	½ Mohur. Lozenge shaped	225.00
150.	½ Mohur. Square	85.00
151.	¼ Mohur. Round	65.00
152.	¼ Mohur. Square	65.00
153.	⅟₁₀ Mohur	30.00
154.	⅟₂₀ Mohur	25.00

Persian legend within square on each side.

155. 1 Mohur 100.00

Persian legend within octagon on each side.

156. 1 Mohur 150.00

Hawk standing. Rev. Persian legend.

157. 1 Mohur 500.00

Duck standing. Rev. Persian legend.

158. 1 Mohur 500.00

*Male and female figures standing, the male holding bow and
arrows. Rev. Persian legend.*

159. ½ Mohur 475.00

JAHANGIR, 1605-1627
(Coinage with dates from about 1014-1037 A.H.)

Turbaned bust with or without fruit or goblet in front of face.
Rev. Lion to right or left under radiate sun.

160. 1 Mohur 500.00

King seated cross-legged. Rev. Persian legend.

161. ¼ Mohur 250.00

Small figure seated cross-legged. Rev. Lion under radiate sun.

162. 1 Mohur 850.00

Large figure seated cross-legged. Rev. Radiate sun in square
within panelled Persian legend.

163. 1 Mohur 850.00

Sign of the Zodiac as noted. Rev. Persian legend. The famous
Zodiac Mohurs.

164. 1 Mohur. Twins (Gemini) 700.00
165. 1 Mohur. Goat (Capricorn) 700.00
166. 1 Mohur. Scales (Libra) 700.00
167. 1 Mohur. Bull (Taurus) 700.00
168. 1 Mohur. Crab (Cancer) 800.00
169. 1 Mohur. Female (Virgo) 700.00
170. 1 Mohur. Ram (Aries) 800.00
171. 1 Mohur. Lion (Leo) 1000.00
172. 1 Mohur. Scorpion (Scorpio) 800.00
173. 1 Mohur. Archer (Sagittarius) 800.00
174. 1 Mohur. Water carrier (Aquarius) 1000.00
175. 1 Mohur. Fish (Pisces) 800.00

Persian legend on each side.

176. 5 Mohurs 2250.00
177. 1 Mohur. Round ....*...... 85.00
178. 1 Mohur. Square ....*...... 125.00

SHAH JAHAN, 1628-1658
(Coinage with dates from about 1037-1068 A.H.)
Persian legend on each side.

179. 1 Mohur. Round 85.00
180. 1 Mohur. Square 125.00
181. ½ Mohur 150.00

Persian legend within square on each side.

182. 200 Mohurs .... Unknown
183.   1 Mohur ....*...... 85.00

Persian legend within lozenge or diamond on each side.

184. 1 Mohur 85.00

Persian legend within circle on each side.

185. 1 Mohur 100.00

MURAD BAKHSH, 1658

Persian legend within square on each side.

186. 1 Mohur 1068 A.H. 175.00

AURANGZIB, 1659-1707
(Coinage with dates from about 1069-1118 A.H.)

Persian legend on each side.

187. 100 Mohurs .... Unknown
188.   1 Mohur 85.00
189.   ¼ Mohur ....*...... 40.00

Persian legend within square on each side.

190. 1 Mohur 100.00

AZAM SHAH, 1707
Persian legend on each side.

191. 1 Mohur 1118, 19 A.H. 175.00

KAM BAKHSH, 1708
Persian legend on each side.

192.　1 Mohur 1120 A.H. ....　225.00

SHAH ALAM BAHADUR I, 1707-1712

Persian legend on each side. With dates from about 1119-1124 A.H.

193.　1 Mohur. Usual size ....　85.00
194.　1 Mohur. Broad type ....*......　125.00

JAHANDAR, 1712
Persian legend on each side.

195.　1 Mohur 1124 A.H. ....　85.00

FARRUKH-SIYAR, 1713-1719

Persian legend on each side. With dates from about 1124-1131 A.H.

196.　1 Mohur ....　85.00
197.　¼ Mohur ....*......　30.00
198.　⅛ Mohur ....*......　25.00

RAFI-UD-DARJAT, 1719
Persian legend on each side.

199.　1 Mohur 1131 A.H. ....　300.00

SHAH JAHAN II, 1719
Persian legend on each side.

200.　1 Mohur 1131 A.H. ....　200.00

201.　The coin previously listed does not exist. ....　——

IBRAHIM, 1720
Persian legend on each side.

202.　1 Mohur 1132 A.H. ....　125.00

MOHAMMED SHAH, 1719-1748
Persian legend on each side. With dates from about 1131-1161 A.H.

203.　1 Mohur ....　85.00
204.　¼ Mohur ....　35.00
205.　1/64 Mohur ....　25.00

AHMED SHAH, 1748-1754
Persian legend on each side. With dates from about 1161-1167 A.H.

206.　1 Mohur ....　85.00
207.　1/64 Mohur. Rev. Blank ....　30.00

ALAMGIR II, 1754-1759
Persian legend on each side. With dates from about 1167-1173 A.H.

208.　1 Mohur ....　85.00
209.　¼ Mohur ....　50.00
210.　1/64 Mohur ....　20.00

Persian legend within square on each side.

211.　1 Mohur ....　100.00

SHAH JAHAN III, 1759-1760
Persian legend on each side.

212.　1 Mohur 1173, 74 A.H. ....　100.00

SHAH ALAM II, 1759-1806

Persian legend on each side. With dates from about 1173-1221 A.H.

213.　1 Mohur. Usual size ....*......　85.00
214.　1 Mohur. Broad type ....　200.00
215.　1/16 Mohur ....　40.00
216.　1/64 Mohur ....　25.00

Persian legend within circle on each side, the whole within a floral wreath formed by roses, thistles and shamrocks.

217.　1 Mohur ....　250.00

BIDAR BAKHT, PRETENDER, 1788
Persian legend on each side.

218.　1 Mohur 1202, 03 A.H. ....　135.00

HYDERABAD

Persian legend on each side. Coinage of the Nizams, struck during the period 1700-1902, and with dates from about 1114-1320 A.H.

219.　1 Mohur ....*......　90.00
220.　½ Mohur ....　75.00
221.　¼ Mohur ....　50.00
222.　⅛ Mohur ....　40.00
223.　1/16 Mohur ....　25.00

Persian type minaret or mosque. Rev. Legend. Struck under the Nizam Mir Mahbub, 1868-1911.

224.　1 Mohur 1321-29 A.H. (1903-11) ....*......　80.00
225.　½ Mohur 1321-29 A.H. (1903-11) ....　60.00
226.　¼ Mohur 1321-29 A.H. (1903-11) ....　45.00
227.　⅛ Mohur 1321-29 A.H. (1903-11) ....　35.00

Type similar to above but struck under the Nizam Mir Usman, 1911-1957.

228. 1 Mohur 1330-66 A.H. (1911-47) 100.00
229. ½ Mohur 1330-66 A.H. (1911-47) 70.00
230. ¼ Mohur 1330-66 A.H. (1911-47) 50.00
231. ⅛ Mohur 1330-66 A.H. (1911-47) 45.00

IKARI

Goddess seated. Rev. Legend. Coinage of Governors struck during the period 1500-1700.

232. 1 Pagoda ND 100.00

JAIPUR

Persian legend on each side. Maharajah coinage struck during the period 1800-1924.

233. 1 Mohur 75.00

JAISALMIR

Persian legend on each side. Rajah coinage struck during the period 1840-1870.

234. 1 Mohur 100.00

JAUNPUR

Persian legend on each side. Royal coinage struck during the period 1400-1500.

235. 1 Mohur 125.00

JEJAKABHUKTI (BUNDELKHAND)

Goddess seated. Rev. Legend. Coinage of Governors struck during the period 1055-1240.

236. 1 Stater 125.00

JIND

Indian legend on each side. Rajah coinage struck during the period 1840-1865.

237. 1 Mohur 100.00

JODHPUR

Persian legend. Rev. Arab legend. Rajah coinage struck during the period 1860-1912.

238. 1 Mohur 100.00

JUNAGARH

Urdu legend on each side. Struck under Nawab Bahadur Khan II.

239. 1 Kori 1309 A.H. (1891) ....*...... 225.00
240. ½ Kori 1309 A.H. (1891) 125.00

KALINGA

Recumbent bull. Rev. Date. Coinage of Governors struck during the period 1050-1150.

241. 1 Fanam 30.00

The Monkey god Hanuman. Rev. Blank.

242. 1 Fanam (1050-1150) 30.00

KALPI

Native legend on each side. Shah coinage struck during the period 1500-1600.

243. 1 Mohur. Square 150.00

KALYANI

Temple. Rev. Blank. Coinage of Governors struck during the period 1100-1200.

244. 1 Pagoda 85.00

The Monkey god Hanuman. Rev. Blank.

245. 1 Pagoda (1100-1200) 85.00

KANAUJ

King standing. Rev. Goddess. Royal coinage struck during the period 600-900.

246. 1 Stater 65.00

KASHMIR

King standing. Rev. Goddess seated. Royal coinage struck during the period 700-800.

247. 1 Stater 100.00

Indian legend on each side.

248. 1 Mohur (1450-1550) 75.00

KISHANGARH

Urdu legend on each side. Maharajah coinage struck during the period 1800-79.

249. 1 Mohur 100.00

KOTAH

Urdu legend on each side. Rajah coinage struck during
the period 1800-1900.

250. 1 Mohur	....	100.00
251. ½ Mohur	....	65.00

KULBARGA

Persian legend on each side. Bahmani coinage struck during
the period 1400-1500.

252. 1 Mohur	....	100.00

MADRAS

Urdu legend on each side. Coinage of the East India
Company struck during the period 1750-1820.

253. 1 Mohur	....	85.00
254. ½ Mohur	....	50.00
255. ⅓ Mohur	....	40.00

Vishnu seated. Rev. Star.

256. 1 Pagoda (1750)	....	65.00

Vishnu standing. Rev. Star.

257. 1 Pagoda (1750)	....	50.00

Vishnu standing. Rev. Grains.

258. 1 Pagoda (1750)	....	40.00

Three gods standing. Rev. Grains.

259. 1 Pagoda (1750)	....	50.00

Four-armed god. Rev. Grains.

260. 1 Pagoda (1750)	....	50.00

Siva and Parvati seated. Rev. Grains.

261. 1 Pagoda (1750)	....	50.00

Pagoda amid stars. Rev. Vishnu.

262. 2 Pagodas (1810)	....................................*......	125.00
263. 1 Pagoda (1810)	....................................*......	90.00
263a. ½ Pagoda (1811)	....	75.00

MAHAKOSALA

Rampant lion. Rev. Legend. Coinage of Governors struck
during the period 1140-1190.

264. 1 Stater	....	100.00

MALWA

Persian legend on each side. Royal coinage struck during the
period 1400-1600.

265. 1 Mohur. Round	....	150.00
266. 1 Mohur. Square	....................................*......	85.00
267. 1 Mohur. Octagonal	....	125.00

MANIPUR

Indian legend on each side. Rajah coinage struck during the
period 1760-1780.

268. 1 Mohur. Square	....	125.00
269. ½ Mohur. Square	....	85.00
270. ¼ Mohur. Square	....	65.00

MAHARASHTRA

Asoka Pillar. Rev. Lamp. On Inauguration of the State.

271. 1 Mudra 1960	....	750.00

MASULIPATAN

Three gods standing. Rev. Grains.

272. 1 Pagoda (1750)	....	25.00

MEWAR-UDAIPUR

State symbols on each side. Maharajah coinage struck during
the period 1825-1915.

273. 1 Mohur	....	100.00

Legend in two lines. Rev. Five characters in lobed circle.

274. 1 Mohur (1825-1915)	....	125.00

MOGUL EMPIRE

(See under Hindustan)

MURSHIDABAD

Urdu legend on each side, with oblique or straight milling
or with plain edge. Coinage of the East India Company
in the name of Shah Alam II of Hindustan. With dates
from about 1182-1204 A.H. (1768-1832).

₹75.	1 Mohur	..................................*......	100.00
₹76.	½ Mohur	....	50.00
₹77.	¼ Mohur	....	40.00
₹78.	⅛ Mohur	..................................*......	30.00
₹79.	1/16 Mohur	....	25.00

MYSORE

RAJAH RANADHIRA WODEYAR, 1638-1659
Vishnu seated. Rev. Legend.

280. 1 Fanam ND 20.00

SULTAN HAIDAR ALI, 1761-1782

Siva and Parvati seated. Rev. Initial on grains.

281. 1 Pagoda ND 50.00

Half-length figure of Vishnu. Rev. Initial on grains.

282. ½ Pagoda ND 75.00

SULTAN TIPOO, 1782-1799
(Coinage with dates from about 1197-1213 A.H.)
Persian legend on each side.

283.	1 Mohur	....	100.00
284.	½ Mohur	....	75.00
285.	1 Pagoda	....	40.00

Initial. Rev. Legend.

286.	1 Pagoda	..............................*......	50.00
287.	1 Fanam	....	25.00

RAJAH KRISHNA WODEYAR, 1799-1868
(Coinage with dates from about 1213-1285 A.H.)

Siva and Parvati seated. Rev. Legend.

288. 1 Pagoda ND 50.00

Persian legend on each side.

289.	1 Mohur	..............................*......	100.00
290.	½ Mohur	....	60.00
291.	1 Pagoda	..............................*......	60.00

NAWANAGAR

Bi-lingual legend on each side. Rajah coinage struck during the period 1300-1400.

292. ½ Mohur 50.00

Crude Persian legend on each side. Struck under Vibhaji II, 1852-1895.

293.	1 Kori	....	175.00
293a.	½ Kori	....	200.00

NEGAPATNAM

Crude four-armed god. Rev. Grains.

294. 1 Pagoda (1660-1780) 75.00

Vishnu standing. Rev. Grains.

295. 1 Pagoda (1660-1780) 50.00

Crude human figure. Rev. Legend and "OC" (East India Company).

296.	3 Fanams (1690-95)	....	100.00
297.	1 Fanam (1690-95)	....	50.00

ORISSA

Elephant. Rev. Scroll. Coinage of Governors struck during the period 1200-1400.

298. 1 Pagoda 125.00

Crude figure. Rev. Legend.

299.	1 Pagoda	....	65.00
300.	½ Pagoda	....	40.00

PATIALA

Native legend on each side. Rajah coinage struck during the period 1840-1900.

301. 1 Mohur 75.00

PONDICHERRY

(French Colony)
Crown and stars. Rev. Fleur-de-lis.

302. 1 Pagoda (1715-74) 150.00

Goddess. Rev. Symbol amid grains.

303. 1 Pagoda (1715-74) 50.00

Two goddesses. Rev. Symbol amid grains.

304. 1 Pagoda (1715-74) 50.00

Vishnu between two figures. Rev. Grains.

305. 1 Pagoda (1715-74) 50.00

PULICAT

(Dutch settlement on the Coromandel Coast)

Crude four-armed god. Rev. Legend.

306. 1 Pagoda (1646-1781) . . . . Unique

Crude symbol. Rev. Grains.

307. 1 Fanam (1646-1781) 50.00

PUNJAB

Persian legend on each side. Sikh coinage struck during the period 1750-1875.

308. 1 Mohur . . . .*. 100.00
309. 1 Rupee 1205 A.H. 15.00

RADHANPUR

Crude head of Queen Victoria. Rev. Urdu legend.

310. 1 Mohur (1860) 225.00

RAJKOT

Radiant sun. Rev. Arms and tridents.

311. 1 Mohur 1945 . . . . 600.00

SOUTH INDIA

 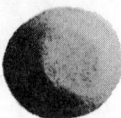

Lotus flower. Rev. Blank. Crude concave coins struck during the period 600-1000.

312. 1 Tanka 40.00

SURAT

Persian legend on each side. Coinage of the East India Company in the name of Shah Alam II of Hindustan. This issue was struck in 1825.

313. 1 Mohur . . . .*. 65.0
314. ½ Mohur 85.0
315. ¼ Mohur 40.0
316. ⅟₁₆ Mohur 30.0

Very small crowned head amid legend. Rev. Legend with date 1802 on small oval panel.

317. 1 Mohur 250.00
318. ¼ Mohur . . . .*. 150.00

TELLICHERRY

Native legend on each side.

319. 1 Pagoda (1806) 50.00

Native legend on each side with date on reverse.

320. ⅕ Rupee 1809 . . . . 100.00

TIPERAH

Native legend on each side. Rajah coinage struck during the period 1700-1800.

321. 1 Mohur 100.00

TONK

Persian legend on each side. Rajah coinage struck during the period 1834-1885.

322. 2 Mohurs . . . .*. 275.00
323. 1 Mohur 85.00

TRAVANCORE

Pellets and lines on each side.

324. 1 Fanam (1700-1880) 15.00

Pellets. Rev. Symbol.

325. 1 Fanam (1700-1880) 15.00

Crescent. Rev. Symbol.

326. 1 Fanam (1700-1880) 15.00

Symbol. Rev. Dots.

27. 1 Fanam (1700-1880) 15.00

Dagger. Rev. Heart.

28. 1 Fanam (1700-1880) 20.00

Bust of the Maharaja Sri Rama Varma, 1881-1924. Rev. Arms supported by elephants.

29. 1 Sovereign 1881 ....*...... 500.00
30. ½ Sovereign 1881 .... 675.00

Shell. Rev. Legend.

31. 2 Pagodas (1881-1924) 200.00
32. 1 Pagoda (1881-1924) ....*...... 125.00
33. ½ Pagoda (1881-1924) 85.00
34. ¼ Pagoda (1881-1924) 65.00

Shell. Rev. "R.V." and "1877" in wreath, "Travancore" above.

35. 2 Pagodas 1877 .... 300.00
36. 1 Pagoda 1877 .... 225.00

Native legend. Rev. Blank. Struck on smaller and thicker flans than preceding issues.

337. 2 Pagodas (1881-1924) ....*...... 150.00
338. 1 Pagoda (1881-1924) 100.00
339. ½ Pagoda (1881-1924) 65.00
340. ¼ Pagoda (1881-1924) 60.00

TUTICORIN

Crude symbols on each side.

341. 1 Fanam (1675-1760) 30.00

UJAIN

Native legend on each side. Rajah coinage struck during the period 1750-1800.

342. 1 Mohur 200.00

VENGI

Boar and umbrella. Rev. Blank. Coinage of Governors struck during the period 1000-1100.

343. 1 Pagoda 85.00

VIJAYANAGAR

God and Goddess seated. Rev. Legend. Royal coinage struck during the period 1400-1600.

344. 1 Pagoda ....*...... 50.00
345. ½ Pagoda 35.00

Deity seated. Rev. Legend.

346. 1 Pagoda 40.00

Eagle and elephants. Rev. Legend.

347. 1 Pagoda 85.00
348. ½ Pagoda ....*...... 65.00

Vishnu standing. Rev. Legend.

349. 1 Pagoda ....*...... 50.00
350. ½ Pagoda 30.00

IRELAND

English Kings of —

CHARLES I, 1626-1649

Weight 4 dwt. 7 gr. both sides. Inchiquin Money.

1. 1 Pistole ND .... Rare

ISRAEL

Israel was established as a republic in 1948. The 20 Pound piece is equivalent to the English Pound.

Small head of Herzl. Rev. Menorah

1. 20 Pounds 1960 .... 175.00

Small head of Weizmann. Rev. Menorah.

2. 100 Pounds 1962 .... 165.00
3. 50 Pounds 1962 ....*...... 85.00

Menorah. Rev. Cornucopia. On the National Bank Jubilee.

4. 50 Pounds 1964 .... 125.00

Emblem of the Israel Defense Forces. Rev. The Wailing Wall.
On Israel's victory in the six-day Middle East war.

5. 100 Pounds 1967 .... 275.00

Temple of Solomon. Rev. Panoramic view of Jerusalem. On
the 20th anniversary of independence.

6. 100 Pounds 1968 .... 225.00

Hebrew word "Shalom." Rev. Legend, helmet and sapling.
In memory of fallen comrades.

7. 100 Pounds 1969 .... 165.00

ITALY

Mints and mint marks or symbols for the Italian and Sardinian King-
doms during the period 1821-1878.
(Later coinage was struck only at the Rome Mint):—

R	mm for Rome
Eagles head	mm for Turin
Anchor	mm for Genoa
T and BN	mm for Turin
M and BN	mm for Milan

National Italian coinage from 1806 to 1927 was based first on th
French monetary system and later on the standard of the Latin Moneta
Union. The Italian gold Lira was subsequently re-valued and the fir
coins on the new standard were struck by the Vatican in 1929 and b
Italy in 1931.

The Italian series is second only to the German in its extent an
variety, since there was no truly national coinage until 1861. Prior
that time, Italy had a multitude of autonomous local coinages datin
back to about 600 A.D.

The Florentine Florin, the Genoese Genovino (and later Ducat) and th
Venetian Ducat (and later Zecchino) were the principal gold coins of th
late Middle Ages, 1200 and later. They were universally known an
respected .for the purity of their gold which was from about .990
1000 fine, and the size, weight and purity of these coins became th
prototypes for the principal part of later Continental coinage.

The enduring nature of the Ducat can be seen from the fact the
it was struck as an official government coin as recently as 1960. Th
country of issue was the Netherlands and it is interesting to note the
the specifications of the Ducat of 1960 were about the same as th
original Ducat which Venice introduced to the world about 1200.

A. Republic of —, 1797-1805

Head of Napoleon as founder and president. Rev. Value in
wreath or circle.

1. 1 Doppia 1803 (year 2) ....*......10,000.00
2. ½ Doppia 1803 (year 2) 8000.00

Head of Napoleon. Rev. Scales.

3. 20 Lire 1804 .... 5000.00

B. Kings of —, 1805-1814 and 1861-1945

NAPOLEON, 1805-1814

Head. Rev. Arms. Milan Mint with M mm.

4. 40 Lire 1807 .... 1250.00
5. 40 Lire 1808-14 ....*...... 150.00
6. 40 Lire 1808. Without M mm. 750.00
7. 20 Lire 1808-14 .... 80.00

(For French type coins struck at the Italian Mints, see
under France).

VICTOR EMANUEL II, 1861-1878

(For the earlier coins of this ruler, see under Sardinia and Emilia).

Head. Rev. Arms.

8.	100 Lire 1864. T mm.	2000.00
9.	100 Lire 1872, 78. R mm.	2500.00
10.	50 Lire 1864. T mm.	10,000.00
11.	20 Lire 1861-70. T mm.	35.00
12.	20 Lire 1870-78. R mm.	35.00
13.	20 Lire 1872-75. M mm. *	35.00
14.	10 Lire 1861. T mm.	2500.00
15.	10 Lire 1863-65. T mm. *	40.00
16.	5 Lire 1863, 65. T mm.	100.00

HUMBERT I, 1878-1900

Head. Rev. Arms.

17.	100 Lire 1880	6500.00
18.	100 Lire 1882, 83, 88, 91	1000.00
19.	50 Lire 1884, 88	800.00
20.	50 Lire 1891	4000.00
21.	20 Lire 1879-97 *	30.00

VICTOR EMANUEL III, 1900-1944

Head. Rev. Eagle. All coins of 1902, 1908, 1910 are rare.

22.	100 Lire 1903, 05	1400.00
23.	20 Lire 1902. With and without small anchor at bottom of Obv. indicating gold from Eritrea	2200.00
24.	20 Lire 1903, 05, 08, 10 *	150.00

Head. Rev. Allegorical scene. On the 50th year of the Kingdom.

25.	50 Lire 1911	200.00

Uniformed bust. Rev. Agricultural scene. The 1910, 1926, 1927 issues are rare.

26.	100 Lire 1910, 12, 26, 27	600.00
27.	50 Lire 1910, 12, 26, 27	150.00
28.	20 Lire 1910, 12, 26, 27 *	100.00
29.	10 Lire 1910, 12, 26, 27	500.00

Head. Rev. Fasces. On the first year of the Fascist march on Rome.

30.	100 Lire 1923	350.00
31.	20 Lire 1923 *	100.00

Small head. Rev. Naked male holding winged Victory. On the 25th year of reign and on the 10th year of entry into World War I.

32.	100 Lire 1925	700.00

Head. Rev. Italia on prow of ship.

33.	100 Lire 1931, 32, 33	175.00

Head. Rev. Figure holding Fasces.

34.	50 Lire 1931, 32, 33	125.00

Head right. Rev. Figure holding Fasces. After the conquest of Ethiopia, with the title of Emperor added to that of King.

35. 100 Lire 1936 ....*...... **1100.00**
36. 100 Lire 1937. Size reduced **2250.00**

Head left. Rev. Eagle over two medallions.

37. 50 Lire 1936 .... **750.00**

C. States and Cities of —

ACHAIA

Princes of —

ROBERT OF ANJOU, 1346-1364

Lily. Rev. St. John standing.

38. 1 Florin ND **1500.00**

AMADEUS VI OF SAVOY, 1367-1383
Helmeted arms. Rev. St. John.

39. 1 Florin ND **1500.00**

Arms. Rev. Cross.

40. 1 Scudo d'oro ND **4000.00**

LOUIS OF SAVOY, 1402-1418
Ruler on horse. Rev. Helmet.

41. 1 Florin ND **3000.00**

AMALFI

Rulers of —

PRINCE GUAIMARIO V AND MANSONE IV, 1042
Cufic legend on each side.

42. 1 Tari ND **400.00**

AUTONOMOUS, 1050-1100
Cufic legend on each side.

43. 1 Tari ND **150.00**

DUKE ROGER BORSA, 1085-1111
Cufic legend on each side.

44. 1 Tari ND **200.00**

GISULFO II, 1098
Head of St. Andrea. Rev. Cufic legend.

44a. 1 Tari ND **1900.00**

DUKE WILLIAM I, 1111-1127
W. Rev. Cross.

45. 1 Tari ND **200.00**

COUNT ROGER II, 1105-1154

R. Rev. Cross.

46. 1 Tari ND **200.00**

KING WILLIAM II, 1162-1189

W. Rev. Rex.

47. 1 Tari ND **300.00**

KING TANCRED, 1189-1194
ACD Monogram. Rev. Rex.

48. 1 Tari ND **300.00**

KING TANCRED AND WILLIAM, 1193
Rex and TCD Monogram. Rev. W.

49. 1 Tari ND **500.00**

KING HENRY VI, 1194-1197
Bust. Rev. Cross.

50. 1 Tari ND **600.00**

QUEEN CONSTANCE AND FREDERICK II, 1197-1198
Palm Tree. Rev. Cross.

51. 1 Tari ND **1500.00**

KING FREDERICK II, 1198-1250
FRE. Rev. Star.

52. 1 Tari ND **400.00**

F. Rev. Rex.

53. 1 Tari ND **500.00**

IMP. Rev. Cross Potent.

54. 1 Tari ND **600.00**

ANCONA

Anonymous Rulers of —

Knight standing. Rev. St. Quiriacus standing.

55. 2 Ducats ND (1500-1600) .... **Rare**
56. 1 Ducat ND (1500-1600) **2500.00**

(For additional coins of Ancona, see under Vatican-Ancona).

ANTIGNATE

Lords of —

JOHN BENTIVOGLIO II, 1494-1509
Bust with cap. Rev. Legend.

57. 4 Ducats 1494 .... **Rare**
58. ½ Ducat 1494 .... **2000.00**

Bust with cap. Rev. Arms.

59.   2 Ducats ND 1500.00
60.   1 Ducat ND ....* 2000.00

ARQUATA

Marcheses of —

JULIUS SPINOLA, 1681-1691
Bust. Rev. Arms.

61.   ½ Doppia 1681 .... 3000.00

GERARD SPINOLA, 1682-1694
Bust. Rev. Arms.

62.   1 Doppia 1682 .... 3000.00

ASTI

A. Kings of —

LOUIS XII OF FRANCE, 1498-1513
Crowned bust. Rev. Crowned arms.

63.   2 Ducats ND ....   Rare
64.   1 Ducat ND ....   Rare

Porcupine. Rev. Crowned arms.

65.   1 Ducat ND ....   Rare

B. Lords of —

CHARLES OF ORLEANS, 1407-1422 AND 1447-1465
Arms. Rev. Cross.

66.   1 Scudo d'oro ND 2000.00

LOUIS OF ORLEANS, 1465-1498
Ruler on horse. Rev. Arms.

67.   1 Ducat ND 1500.00

Arms. Rev. Cross.

68.   1 Scudo d'oro ND 3000.00

EMANUEL FILIBERT, 1542-1553
Arms. Rev. Cross.

69.   1 Scudo d'oro ND 1500.00

BARDI

Marcheses of —

FREDERICK LANDI, 1590-1627
Bust. Rev. St. Francis kneeling.

70.   5 Doppie 1622 .... 10,000.00

Bust. Rev. St. John standing.

71.   2 Doppie 1623 .... 6000.00

Bust. Rev. Double eagle in shield.

---

72.   2 Doppie ND ....* 5000.00
73.   1 Doppia ND ....* 4000.00

Bust. Rev. St. Theresa.

74.   1 Doppia ND .... Unknown

BARLETTA

Dukes of —

CHARLES I, 1266-1278

Bust. Rev. Arms.

75.   1 Real ND ....* 2500.00
76.   ½ Real ND ....   Rare

K. Rev. Arms.

77.   1 Tari ND 150.00

BELGIOJOSO

Princes of —

ANTHONY BARBIANO

Bust. Rev. Arms.

78.   1 Zecchino 1769 .... 1000.00

BELMONTE

Princes of —

ANTHONY PIGNATELLI

Bust. Rev. Arms.

79.   1 Zecchino 1733 .... 2500.00

BENEVELLO

Counts of —

JOHN ANTHONY FALLETTI, 1520-1544
Arms on cross. Rev. Eagle.

80.   1 Scudo d'oro ND 3000.00

BENEVENTUM

Dukes, and later, Princes of —

ANONYMOUS, 569-706
Bust. Rev. Cross.

81.	1 Solidus ND	250.00
82.	⅓ Solidus ND	150.00

ROMUALD II, 706-731

Bust. Rev. Cross.

83.	1 Solidus ND ....*......	300.00
84.	⅓ Solidus ND	150.00

AUDELAO, 731
Bust. Rev. Cross.

85.	1 Solidus ND	4000.00
86.	⅓ Solidus ND	2500.00

GREGORY, 732-739
Bust. Rev. Cross.

87.	1 Solidus ND	250.00
88.	⅓ Solidus ND	150.00

GODESCALCO, 739-742

Bust. Rev. Cross.

89.	1 Solidus ND ....*......	400.00
90.	⅓ Solidus ND	200.00

GISULF II, 742-751
Bust. Rev. Cross.

91.	1 Solidus ND	400.00
92.	⅓ Solidus ND	200.00

LUITPRAND AND SCAUNIPERGA, 751-755

Bust. Rev. Cross.

93.	1 Solidus ND ....*......	1500.00
94.	⅓ Solidus ND	650.00

LUITPRAND, 755-758
Bust. Rev. Cross.

95.	1 Solidus ND	350.00
96.	⅓ Solidus ND	200.00

Bust. Rev. Cross.

97.	1 Solidus ND ....*......	600.00
98.	⅓ Solidus ND	500.00

ARICHIS II, DUKE, 758-774
Bust. Rev. Cross.

99.	1 Solidus ND	350.00
100.	⅓ Solidus ND	150.00

ARICHIS II, PRINCE, 774-787

Bust. Rev. Cross.

101.	1 Solidus ND ....*......	200.00
102.	⅓ Solidus ND	80.00

GRIMOALD III, 788-806
Bust. Rev. Cross.

103.	1 Solidus ND. With monogram of Charlemagne	200.00
104.	1 Solidus ND. Without Monogram	160.00
105.	⅓ Solidus ND. With monogram of Charlemagne	100.00
106.	⅓ Solidus ND. Without monogram	80.00

SICO, 817-832
Bust. Rev. St. Michael.

107.	1 Solidus ND	250.00

Bust. Rev. Cross.

108.	⅓ Solidus ND	100.00

SICARDO, 832-839
Bust. Rev. Cross.

109.	1 Solidus ND	100.00
110.	⅓ Solidus ND	50.00

RADELCHIS, 839-851
Bust. Rev. Cross.

111.	1 Solidus ND	250.00

BERGAMO

CHARLEMAGNE, 773-800
Cross Potent. Rev. Cross and four globes.

112.	⅓ Solidus ND	3000.00

BOLOGNA

*(For additional coins struck at Bologna, see under Cispa-
dane Republic, Emilia and Vatican).*

A. Republic of —, 1376-1500

St. Peter standing. Rev. Lion.

113. 1 Bolognino d'oro ND 300.00

St. Peter seated. Rev. Lion.

114. 2 Bolognino d'oro ND 2000.00
115. 1 Bolognino d'oro ND 700.00

B. Governors of —

JOHN I BENTIVOGLIO, 1401-1402
St. Peter. Rev. Lion.

116. 1 Bolognino d'oro ND 500.00

PHILIP MARIA VISCONTI, 1438-1443
St. Peter. Rev. Lion.

117. 1 Florin ND .... Rare

JOHN II BENTIVOGLIO, 1463-1506
St. Peter. Rev. Lion.

118. 2 Bolognino d'oro ND 250.00
119. 1 Bolognino d'oro ND 500.00

CHARLES V OF SPAIN
Head. Rev. Pillars of Hercules.

120. 1 Imperial or 2½ Ducats 1530 .... Rare

BOZZOLO

Princes of —

JULIUS CAESAR GONZAGA, 1593-1609
Bust. Rev. Chameleon.

121. 5 Doppie (Gold Piastre) ND .... Rare
122. 1 Doppia ND 4000.00

Bust. Rev. Arms.

123. 1 Doppia ND 4000.00

Soldier. Rev. Arms.

124. 1 Ducat ND 2000.00

SCIPIO GONZAGA, 1609-1670
Arms. Rev. Crowned female.

125. 1 Doppia 1618 .... 3000.00

Bust. Rev. St. Peter kneeling before Christ.

126. 6 Doppie 1639 .... Rare
127. 4 Doppie 1639 .... Rare

Bust. Rev. Arms.

128. 5 Doppie ND .... Rare
129. 1 Doppia ND 2500.00

Bust. Rev. Two shields.

130. 1 Doppia ND 2500.00

Soldier. Rev. Tablet.

131. 1 Ducat ND 1200.00

Duke standing. Rev. Eagle.

132. 1 Ducat ND .... Rare

BRESCELLO

Lords of —

ALFONSO II D'ESTE, 1570-1595
Arms. Rev. Cross.

133. 1 Scudo d'oro ND 5000.00

BRINDISI

Kings of —

FREDERICK II, 1197-1250

Bust. Rev. Eagle.

134. 1 Augustalis ND 800.00
135. ½ Augustalis ND 750.00

Eagle in circle. Rev. Legend divided by cross.

136. 10 Tari ND 1000.00
137. 6 Tari ND ....* 600.00

CHARLES I OF ANJOU, 1266-1278
Bust. Rev. Arms.

138. 1 Real ND 2000.00

Ruler on horse. Rev. Cross.

139. 5 Tari ND 1500.00
140. 1 Tari ND 100.00

K. Rev. Cross.

141. Multiple Tari ND 200.00

142. The coin previously listed does not exist. .... —

Name. Rev. Cross.

143. Multiple Tari ND 250.00

CAGLIARI

Spanish Kings of —

CHARLES V
Arms. Rev. Cross.

144. 1 Scudo d'oro ND (1517-56) 1200.00

PHILIP V

Arms. Rev. Cross.

145. 1 Scudo d'oro 1701, 02, 03 .... 250.00

CHARLES III
Arms. Rev. Cross.

146. 1 Scudo d'oro 1710, 11, 12 .... 250.00

CAMERINO

Dukes of —

JOHN MARIA VARANO, 1511-1527

Bust. Rev. Arms.

147. 1 Ducat ND 2500.00

JULIA VARANO, 1527-1534
Head. Rev. Arms.

148. 1 Scudo d'oro ND 3000.00

Arms. Rev. Cross.

149. 1 Scudo d'oro ND 350.00

JULIA VARANO AND GUIDOBALD II DELLA ROVERE, 1534-1539

Arms. Rev. Cross.

150. 1 Scudo d'oro ND 350.00

CAMPI

Marcheses of —

CHARLES CENTURIONI, 1654-1663
Bust. Rev. Eagle.

151. 1 Doppia 1661 .... 3500.00

JOHN BAPTIST CENTURIONI, 1663-1715
Bust. Rev. Arms.

152. ½ Doppia 1668 .... 3000.00

Busts of John and his wife, Julia. Rev. Arms.

153. 1 Doppia 1668 .... 5000.00

CARMAGNOLA

Marcheses of —

LOUIS II DI SALUZZO, 1475-1504

Bust with cap. Rev. Arms.

154. 1 Doppia ND ....*...... 4000.00
155. 1 Ducat ND 3000.00

Bust with cap. Rev. Helmet.

156. 1 Ducat ND 3000.00

Busts of Louis and Margaret. Rev. Eagle.

157. 10 Scudi d'oro 1503 .... Rare

MICHAEL ANTHONY DI SALUZZO, 1504-1528

St. Constantine on horse. Rev. Cross.

158. 1 Scudo d'oro ND 850.00

St. Constantine. Rev. Helmet.

159. 1 Scudo d'oro ND 1500.00

Eagle. Rev. Cross.

160. 1 Scudo d'oro ND 1500.00

FRANCIS DI SALUZZO, 1529-1537
Arms. Rev. Cross.

161. 1 Scudo del sole ND 1500.00

GABRIEL DI SALUZZO, 1537-1548
Saint Constantine on horse. Rev. Helmeted shield.

162. 10 Scudi d'oro ND .... Rare

CASALE

Marcheses of —

WILLIAM I PALEOLOGO, 1464-1483
St. Theodore. Rev. Helmeted shield.

163. 1 Ducat ND 3000.00

WILLIAM II PALEOLOGO, 1494-1518
Bust with cap. Rev. Stag.

164. 4 Ducats ND .... Rare

Bust with cap. Rev. Arms.

165. 2 Ducats ND 8000.00

Bust. Rev. Plant.

166. 2 Ducats ND .... Rare

Arms. Rev. Cross.

167. 1 Scudo d'oro ND 5000.00

Double eagle. Rev. Cross.

168. 1 Scudo d'oro ND 600.00

BONIFACE II PALEOLOGO, 1518-1530
Bust with cap. Rev. Saint on horse.

169. 1 Ducat ND 5000.00

Double eagle. Rev. Cross.

170. 1 Scudo d'oro ND 800.00

JOHN GEORGE PALEOLOGO, 1530-1533
Double eagle. Rev. Cross.

171. 1 Scudo d'oro ND 3000.00

Arms. Rev. Cross.

172. 1 Scudo d'oro ND 3500.00

ANONYMOUS, 1500-1600
Double eagle. Rev. Cross.

173. 1 Scudo d'oro ND 2000.00

CHARLES V OF SPAIN, 1533-1536
Arms. Rev. Cross.

174. 1 Scudo d'oro ND 3500.00

FREDERICK II GONZAGA AND MARGARET PALEOLOGO, 1536-1540
Arms. Rev. Cross and initials.

175. 1 Scudo d'oro ND 5000.00

FRANCIS III GONZAGA AND MARGARET PALEOLOGO, 1540-1550

Arms. Rev. Cross and initials.

176. 1 Scudo d'oro ND 3000.00

WILLIAM GONZAGA AND MARGARET PALEOLOGO, 1550-1566

Arms. Rev. Cross and initials.

177. 1 Scudo d'oro 1563-67, ND 600.00

WILLIAM III GONZAGA, 1566-1587

Arms. Rev. Cross and initials.

178. 1 Scudo d'oro 1578, ND 250.00

Bust right or left. Rev. Arms.

179. 2 Doppie 1578-86, ND 1500.00
180. 1 Doppia 1578, ND ....*...... 2000.00

Bust. Rev. Cross.

181. 1 Scudo d'oro 1578-82 .... 2000.00

VINCENT I GONZAGA, 1587-1612

Bust. Rev. Arms.

182. 2 Doppie 1588-1601 .... 2500.00

Arms. Rev. Cross.

183. 1 Scudo d'oro ND 3000.00

Eagle. Rev. Ruler standing.

184. 1 Ducat ND 1500.00

FRANCIS IV GONZAGA, 1612-1613

Busts of Francis and Margaret. Rev. Flower.

185. 1 Doppia 1612 .... Rare

Cross. Rev. Arms on Mt. Olympus.

186. 1 Doppia 1612 .... 10,000.00

FERDINAND GONZAGA, 1613-1626

Bust. Rev. Arms.

187. 2 Doppie 1617, 21, ND 1500.00
188. 1 Doppia 1617, ND ....*...... 2000.00

Bust. Rev. Stag.

189. 5 Doppie ND .... Rare

VINCENT II GONZAGA, 1626-1627
Bust. Rev. Arms.

190. 2 Doppie 1627 .... 6000.00
191. 1 Doppia ND 6000.00

CHARLES I GONZAGA, 1627-1637
Bust. Rev. Arms.

192.	2 Doppie 1629, 31, 36	3000.00
193.	1 Doppia 1632	3000.00

CHARLES II GONZAGA, 1637-1655
Busts of Charles and Maria. Rev. Arms.

194.	2 Doppie ND	5000.00
195.	1 Doppia ND	5000.00

FERDINAND CHARLES GONZAGA, 1665-1708
Bust. Rev. Arms.

196.	2 Doppie	6000.00

CASTEL SEPRIO

DESIDERIUS, 757-773
Cross potent. Rev. Star.

197.	⅓ Solidus ND	2000.00

CHARLEMAGNE, 773-800
Cross potent. Rev. Cross and four globes.

198.	⅓ Solidus ND	2000.00

CASTIGLIONE DELLE STIVIERE

Princes of —

FRANCIS GONZAGA, 1593-1616
Bust. Rev. Arms.

199.	5 Doppie 1614	Rare
200.	½ Doppia ND	3000.00
201.	⅛ Doppia ND	800.00

FERDINAND GONZAGA, 1616-1678
Eagle. Rev. Soldier.

202.	1 Florin 1639	3000.00

St. Nazarius. Rev. Value.

203.	1 Florin ND	Rare

St. Ferdinandus. Rev. Value.

204.	1 Florin ND	Rare

Madonna. Rev. Value.

205.	1 Florin ND	Rare

Lion. Rev. Value.

206.	1 Florin ND	Rare

CASTIGLIONE DEI GATTI

Counts of —

HERCULES AND CORNELIUS PEPOLI, 1700

Tablet. Rev. Double eagle.

207.	1 Ducat ND	3000.00

ALEXANDER AND SICINIUS PEPOLI, 1703-1713
Tablet. Rev. Double eagle.

208.	1 Ducat ND	3000.00

CASTRO

Dukes of —

PETER LUIGI FARNESE, 1545-1547

Arms. Rev. Cross.

209.	1 Scudo d'oro ND	300.00

CHIVASSO

Marcheses of —

THEODORE I PALEOLOGO, 1307-1338
Lily. Rev. St. John.

210.	1 Florin ND	2000.00

CISPADANE REPUBLIC

Madonna. Rev. Trophies. Struck at Bologna.

211.	20 Lire or 1 Doppia 1797	Rare

CISTERNA

Princes of —

JAMES DAL POZZO, 1667-1677
Bust. Rev. Arms.

212.	10 Scudi d'oro 1677	Rare
213.	2 Doppie 1677	Rare

CORREGGIO

Princes of —

GILBERT, CAMILLO, AND FABRIZIO, 1569-1597
Eagle and arms. Rev. Madonna.

214.	1 Doppia ND	6000.00
215.	1 Scudo d'oro ND	4500.00

Eagle and arms. Rev. St. Quirinus.

216.	1 Scudo d'oro ND	700.00

Double eagle. Rev. St. Quirinus.

217.	1 Scudo d'oro ND	Rare

Arms. Rev. Young St. Quirinus in oval.

218.	1 Scudo d'oro ND	Rare

Soldier standing. Rev. Madonna.

219.	1 Ducat ND	Rare

Tablet. Rev. Madonna.

219a.	1 Ducat ND	Rare

CAMILLO AND FABRIZIO, 1580-1597
Arms. Rev. Bust of St. Quirinus.

220.   144 Soldi (Scudo d'oro) ND 3000.00

CAMILLO, 1597-1605

Ruler standing. Rev. Arms.

221.   1 Ducat 1599, ND 400.00

Ruler standing. Rev. Double eagle.

222.   1 Ducat ND 400.00

Ruler standing. Rev. Madonna.

223.   1 Ducat ND 350.00

SIRUS, 1605-1630
Soldier. Rev. Tablet.

224.   1 Ducat 1609 .... 400.00

CORTONA

LOMBARDIC PERIOD, 600-800
Cross. Rev. Legend.

225.   1/3 Solidus ND 1500.00

CREMONA

Lords of —

FRANCIS II SFORZA, 1521-1535
Saint standing. Rev. Serpent.

226.   1 Scudo d'oro ND .... Rare

CUNEO

SIEGE OF 1641
Arms. Rev. Column and flag.

227.   5 Doppie 1641 .... Rare
228.   1 Doppia 1641 .... Rare

DESANA

Counts of —

LOUIS TIZZONE II, 1510-1525
Bust. Rev. Arms.

229.   2 Ducats ND .... Rare

Arms. Rev. St. Peter seated.

230.   2 Scudi d'oro ND .... Rare
231.   1 Scudo d'oro ND 6000.00

Eagle. Rev. Cross.

232.   1 Scudo d'oro ND 6000.00

PETER BERARD, 1516-1529
Bust. Rev. Arms.

233.   1 Scudo d'oro ND .... Rare

Arms on cross. Rev. Cross.

234.   1 Scudo d'oro ND .... Rare

AUGUSTIN TIZZONE, 1559-1582
Bust. Rev. Arms.

235.   1 Doppia 1581 .... Rare

DELFINO TIZZONE, 1583-1598
Arms. Rev. St. Lawrence.

236.   1 Scudo d'oro ND 1200.00

ANTHONY MARIA TIZZONE, 1598-1641
Bust. Rev. Arms.

237.   2 Doppie ND 2500.00
238.   1 Doppia ND 2000.00
239.   1 Florin ND 1500.00

Bearded bust. Rev. Arms.

240.   2 Doppie ND .... Rare
241.   1 Doppia ND .... Rare

Head. Rev. Female at column.

242.   2 Doppie ND .... Rare

Head. Rev. St. Dorothea standing.

243.   1 Doppia ND 3000.00

Bust. Rev. Double eagle.

244.   1 Florin ND .... Rare

Bust. Rev. Arms

244a.   1 Florin ND 600.00

Arms. Rev. St. Peter.

245.   1 Florin ND .... Rare

Arms. Rev. Double eagle.

246.   1 Florin ND 1000.00
247.   1 Ducat ND 600.00

Arms. Rev. Cross.

248.   1 Scudo d'oro ND 600.00

Soldier standing. Rev. Tablet.

249.   1 Ducat 1603 .... 1000.00

Ruler standing. Rev. Tablet.

250.   1 Ducat ND 800.00

Arms. Rev. St. Catherine seated.

251.   1 Ducat ND 1000.00

Eagle. Rev. St. Lawrence.

252.   1 Ducat ND 1000.00

Double eagle. Rev. St. Louis standing.

253.   1 Ducat ND 1000.00

CHARLES JOSEPH FRANCIS TIZZONE, 1641-1676
Ruler standing. Rev. Tablet.

254.   1 Ducat ND 1000.00

Soldier standing. Rev. Tablet.

255.   1 Ducat ND 1000.00

EMILIA

VICTOR EMANUEL II, KING ELECT, 1859-1861

Head. Rev. Value in wreath. Bologna Mint with B mm.

256.	20 Lire 1860	6000.00
257.	10 Lire 1860 ....*......	750.00

FERRARA

Dukes of —

LIONEL D'ESTE, 1441-1450
Sail on mast. Rev. Christ.

258.   1 Ducat ND 5000.00

Pillow and helmet. Rev. Arms.

259.   ½ Ducat ND 5000.00

BORSO D'ESTE, 1450-1471
Christ. Rev. Arms.

260.   1 Ducat ND 5000.00

Bust. Rev. Christ.

261.   1 Ducat ND 10,000.00

HERCULES I D'ESTE, 1471-1475
Duke kneeling before saint. Rev. Christ.

262.   1 Doppia ND .... Rare

Head. Rev. Hercules and bull.

263.   1 Doppia ND 10,000.00

Head. Rev. Hercules and lion.

264.   1 Doppia ND .... Rare

Bust. Rev. Christ.

265.   1 Ducat ND 800.00

Duke standing. Rev. St. Maurelius seated.

266.   ½ Ducat ND 2000.00

Eagle. Rev. Animal.

267.   ½ Ducat ND 2000.00

ALFONSO I D'ESTE, 1505-1534

Plain or bearded bust. Rev. Christ and the Pharisee.

268.   2 Zecchini ND 10,000.00

Arms. Rev. Calvary cross.

269.   1 Scudo d'oro ND 200.00

HERCULES II D'ESTE, 1534-1559

Arms. Rev. Mary Magdalene at cross.

270.   1 Scudo d'oro 1534, ND 250.00

Bust. Rev. Hercules with lion skin.

271.   10 Scudi d'oro 1546 .... Rare

ALFONSO II D'ESTE, 1559-1597

Arms. Rev. Cross.

272.   1 Scudo d'oro 1576, ND 200.00

Duke standing. Rev. Arms.

273.   1 Ducat 1596, 97, ND 200.00

Bust. Rev. Eagle.

274.   ½ Ducat ND 2000.00

FLORENCE

A. Republic of —, 1189-1531

Lily. Rev. St. John.

275.	1 Florin ND (1252-1422) ....*......	120.00
276.	1 Florin ND. Broad type. (1422-1531)	200.00
277.	¼ Florin ND (1252-1422)	1000.00

Lily. Rev. St. John baptizing Christ.

278.	2 Florins ND (1504-31)	**Rare**

Arms. Rev. Cross. Struck during the Siege of Florence, 1530.

279.	1 Scudo d'oro ND	**Rare**

B. Tuscan Grand Dukes of —

ALEXANDER, 1531-1536

Arms. Rev. Cross.

280.	1 Scudo d'oro ND	200.00

COSIMO I, 1536-1574
Bust. Rev. Cross.

281.	1 Gold Piastre ND	**Rare**

Bust. Rev. St. John standing.

282.	1 Gold Piastre 1571, 72	**Rare**
283.	1 Ducat ND ....*......	**Rare**

Bust. Rev. St. John preaching to disciples.

284.	½ Gold Piastre 1571, 72	**Rare**

Arms. Rev. Cross.

285.	1 Gold Piastre ND	**Rare**
286.	1 Scudo d'oro ND ....*......	200.00
287.	½ Scudo d'oro ND	500.00

Bust of St. John. Rev. Arms.

288.	¼ Scudo d'oro ND	1000.00

FRANCIS I, 1574-1587
Bust. Rev. St. John standing.

289.	1 Gold Piastre (5 Doppia) 1574-84	**Rare**

Head. Rev. The Annunciation.

290.	1 Doppia 1580, 82 ....10,000.00

Arms. Rev. Cross.

291.	1 Scudo d'oro ND	500.00

FERDINAND I, 1587-1608
Bust. Rev. Bees in flight.

292.	14 Scudi d'oro 1587	**Rare**

Bust. Rev. The Annunciation.

293.	2 Doppie 1591	8000.00
294.	1 Doppia 1587-91	3000.00
295.	½ Doppia 1587, 93	2000.00

Bust. Rev. Cross of St. Stephan.

296.	½ Doppia 1587	4000.00

Bust. Rev. Cross.

297.	¼ Doppia ND ....*......	1500.00
298.	⅛ Doppia ND	1500.00

Bust. Rev. St. John baptizing Christ.

299.	1 Gold Piastre 1589, 92, 96	**Rare**

Lily. Rev. St. John standing.

300.	2 Ducats 1595	3000.00
301.	1 Ducat 1595, 96, 97, 1608 ....*......	300.00

Arms. Rev. Ornate cross.

302.	1 Doppia 1607	1200.00

Arms. Rev. Floriated cross.

303.	1 Scudo d'oro ND	250.00
304.	¼ Doppia ND	1000.00

Arms. Rev. Bust of St. John.

305.	⅛ Doppia ND	700.00

Arms. Rev. Cross of St. Stephan.

306.	⅛ Doppia ND	700.00

Arms. Rev. The Annunciation.

307.	1 Doppia 1588	2000.00

Arms. Rev. St. John seated.

308.	1 Florin 1588	2000.00

St. John standing. Rev. Cross of St. Stephan.

309.	1 Florin 1588	2000.00

COSIMO II, 1609-1621
Bust. Rev. St. John baptizing Christ.

310.	1 Gold Piastre 1610	Rare

Bust. Rev. Cross.

311.	¼ Doppia 1609	Rare

Arms. Rev. Cross.

312.	1 Doppia 1608, ND	400.00
313.	1 Scudo d'oro ND ....*......	1500.00

Lily. Rev. St. John standing.

314.	1 Florin 1608, 10, 11, 14	250.00

FERDINAND II, 1621-1670
Bust. Rev. St. John standing.

315.	1 Gold Piastre 1628	Rare

Arms. Rev. Cross.

316.	1 Doppia ND	300.00
317.	½ Doppia ND	700.00
318.	⅛ Doppia ND	800.00

Lily. Rev. St. John standing.

319.	1 Zecchino 1655, ND	400.00

Arms. Rev. Bust of St. John.

320.	¼ Doppia 1663, 68 ....*......	650.00
321.	⅛ Doppia ND	250.00

COSIMO III, 1670-1723

Arms. Rev. Cross.

322.	2 Doppie 1676	2000.00
323.	1 Doppia 1711, 16	1500.00
324.	½ Doppia ND ....*......	1000.00

Lily. Rev. St. John seated.

325.	1 Ruspone 1719	5000.00
326.	1 Florin 1712-23 ....*......	150.00

JOHN GASTON, 1723-1737

Lily. Rev. St. John seated.

327.	1 Ruspone 1724 ....*......	1500.00
328.	1 Zecchino 1723-36	100.00
329.	½ Zecchino 1726	1500.00

Lily. Rev. Bust of St. John.

330. ½ Zecchino 1726 .... 200.00

FRANCIS III, 1737-1765
Lily. Rev. St. John seated.

331. 1 Ruspone 1743-64 .... 450.00
332. 1 Zecchino 1737-43 .... 200.00

Head. Rev. Arms.

333. 1 Ducat 1738, 41 .... 3000.00

PETER LEOPOLD, 1765-1790

Lily. Rev. St. John seated.

334. 1 Ruspone 1765-90 .... 300.00
335. 1 Zecchino 1779-89 ....*...... 150.00

FERDINAND III, 1791-1801
Lily. Rev. St. John seated.

336. 1 Ruspone 1791-1801 .... 300.00
337. 1 Zecchino 1791- 97 .... 150.00

LOUIS I, 1801-1803
Lily. Rev. St. John seated.

338. 1 Ruspone 1801, 03 .... 450.00

CHARLES LOUIS AND MARIE LOUISE, 1803-1807

Lily. Rev. St. John seated.

339. 1 Ruspone 1803-07 .... 600.00

St. Zanobius kneeling before Christ. Rev. St. John standing.
Struck for the Levant.

340. 1 Zecchino ND 4000.00

FERDINAND III, 1814-1824
Lily. Rev. St. John seated.

341. 1 Ruspone 1815-23 .... 500.00
342. 1 Zecchino 1816, 21 .... 200.00

LEOPOLD II, 1824-1859

Lily. Rev. Arms.

343. 80 Florins or 200 Paoli 1827, 28 ..... 700.00

Lily. Rev. St. John seated.

344. 1 Ruspone 1824-36 .... 300.00
345. 1 Zecchino 1824-53 .... 200.00

(For the last coin of this type, see under Tuscany).

FORLI

Lords of —

HIERONYMUS RIARIO, 1480-1488
Double eagle. Rev. St. Mercurialus standing.

346. 1 Ducat 1480 .... Rare

FRINCO

Arms. Rev. Cross. Anonymous Princely coinage.

347. 1 Scudo d'oro ND (1581-1601) 5000.00

GAETA

Dukes of —

ALFONSO I, 1436-1458

Ruler on horse. Rev. Arms.

348. 1 Ducatone d'oro, ND (5.23 grams) ....*...... 2000.00
349. 1 Ducat ND 2000.00

GAZZOLDO

Counts of —

HANNIBAL DEGLI IPPOLITI, 1632-1666

Bust. Rev. St. Hippolitus.

350. 2 Doppie 1662 .... 6000.00

GENOA

A. Doges of —

The following coins are all of the same type and show a castle on the Obv. and a cross on the Rev. All are without dates.

ANONYMOUS DOGES, 1200-1350

351.	1 Genovino	......................*......	200.00
352.	1 Quartarola	....	150.00
353.	1 Soldo	......................*......	600.00

SIMON BOCCANEGRA, 1339-1344 AND 1356-1363

354.	1 Genovino	......................*......	250.00
355.	⅓ Genovino	....	250.00
356.	¼ Genovino	....	200.00

GABRIEL ADORNO, 1363-1370
357.	1 Genovino	....	300.00

DOMINIC DI CAMPOFREGOSO, 1370-1378
358.	1 Genovino	....	1200.00

ANTONIOTTO ADORNO, 1378
359.	1 Genovino	....	1500.00

NICHOLAS GUARCO, 1378-1383
360.	1 Genovino	....	400.00

LEONARD DI MONTALDO, 1383-1384
361.	1 Genovino	....	700.00

GEORGE ADORNO, 1413-1415
362.	1 Genovino	....	350.00

BARNABAS DI GOANO, 1415
363.	1 Genovino	....	900.00

THOMAS DI CAMPOFREGOSO, 1415-1421 (FIRST RULE)
364.	1 Ducat	....	250.00

PHILIP MARIA OF MILAN, 1421-1425
365.	1 Ducat	....	250.00

THOMAS DI CAMPOFREGOSO, 1436-1442 (SECOND RULE)
366.	1 Ducat. With "Dux XX."	....	1200.00
367.	1 Ducat. With "Dux XXI."	....	250.00

THE EIGHT CAPTAINS OF LIBERTY, 1442-1443
368.	1 Ducat	....	3000.00

RAFFAEL ADORNO, 1443-1447
369.	1 Ducat. With "Dux XXII."	....	600.00
370.	1 Ducat. With "Dux XXIII."	....	900.00
371.	½ Ducat	....	1600.00
372.	¼ Ducat	....	1800.00

JOHN CAMPOFREGOSO, 1447
373.	1 Ducat	....	1200.00
374.	½ Ducat	....	2000.00

LOUIS CAMPOFREGOSO, 1447-1450 AND 1461-1462
375.	1 Ducat. With "Dux XXV."	....	800.00
376.	1 Ducat. With "Dux XXVI."	....	Unknown

PETER CAMPOFREGOSO, 1450-1458
377.	1 Ducat	....	300.00

PROSPERO ADORNO, 1461
378.	1 Ducat	....	3200.00

PAUL CAMPOFREGOSO, 1463-1464
379.	1 Ducat	....	2800.00
380.	½ Ducat	....	3000.00

FRANCIS I OF MILAN, 1464-1466

381.	1 Ducat	......................*......	400.00
382.	½ Ducat	....	1200.00

GALEAZZO MARIA OF MILAN, 1466-1476
383.	1 Ducat	....	250.00
384.	½ Ducat	....	1000.00
385.	¼ Ducat	....	1500.00

PROSPERO ADORNO AND TWELVE CAPTAINS, 1478
386.	1 Ducat	....	4000.00

BAPTIST CAMPOFREGOSO, 1478-1483
387.	1 Ducat	....	300.00

PAUL CAMPOFREGOSO, 1483-1488
388.	1 Ducat. As Governor	....	3200.00
389.	1 Ducat. As Doge	....	700.00
390.	½ Ducat	....	3200.00

AUGUSTIN ADORNO, 1488-1489
391.	1 Ducat	....	2400.00

JOHN GALEAZZO OF MILAN, 1489-1494
392.	3 Ducats	....	8000.00
393.	2 Ducats	....	8000.00
394.	1 Ducat	....	500.00

LOUIS MARIA OF MILAN, 1494-1499
395.	1 Ducat	....	1200.00

ANTONIOTTO ADORNO, 1522-1527

396.	1 Ducat	....	500.00
397.	½ Ducat	....	800.00
398.	2 Scudi d'oro	....	3000.00
399.	1 Scudo d'oro	......................*......	250.00
400.	½ Scudo d'oro	....	800.00

B. French Kings of —
(Same type as above).

CHARLES VI, 1396-1409
401.	1 Genovino	....	1400.00
402.	⅓ Genovino	....	2000.00

CHARLES VII, 1458-1461
403.	1 Ducat	....	2200.00

LOUIS XII, 1499-1513
404.	1 Ducat	....	3200.00

Crowned arms of France with name of Genoa in title. Rev. Floriated cross.

405.	1 Ecu d'or ND	450.00

FRANCIS I, 1515-1528
Castle flanked by F and lis. Rev. Floriated cross.

406.	1 Ecu d'or ND	3200.00
407.	½ Ecu d'or ND	2500.00
408.	¼ Ecu d'or ND	Rare

Castle flanked by F and lis. Rev. Two F's and two lis in angles of floriated cross.

409.	1 Ecu d'or ND	3200.00
410.	The coin previously listed does not exist.	—

C. The Biennial Doges of —, 1521-1797

Castle. Rev. Cross.

411.	10	Scudi d'oro 1633	Rare
412.	1	Scudo d'oro 1541-55, ND	125.00
413.	½	Scudo d'oro 1541-55, ND	2000.00
414.	25	Doppie 1636	Rare
415.	12½	Doppie 1632, 34, 36, 37	12,000.00
416.	5	Doppie 1600-20	4000.00
417.	2½	Doppie 1596	Rare
418.	2	Doppie 1592-1638 *	1200.00
419.	1	Doppia 1557-1638	350.00
420.	½	Doppia 1557-1638	350.00
421.	¼	Doppia 1623-38	500.00
422.	⅛	Doppia 1623-38	400.00

Madonna. Rev. Cross.

423.	25	Doppie 1638-1714	Rare
424.	20	Doppie 1645	Rare
425.	12½	Doppie 1638-1711	12,000.00
426.	10	Doppie 1641-94	12,000.00
427.	5	Doppie 1640-97	4000.00
428.	4	Doppie 1720	3000.00
429.	2½	Doppie 1697	2000.00
430.	2	Doppie 1638-1722 *	2000.00
431.	1	Doppia 1640-1748	1000.00
432.	½	Doppia 1639-1749	450.00
433.	¼	Doppia 1641	450.00
434.	⅛	Doppia 1641	450.00

Doge kneeling before St. John. Rev. Christ.

435.	1 Zecchino ND	5000.00

Arms. Rev. St. George on horse.

436.	1 Zecchino 1718-23	2000.00
437.	½ Zecchino 1723	3000.00

Arms. Rev. St. John standing.

438.	1 Zecchino 1724-39 *	350.00
439.	½ Zecchino 1724-36	500.00

Arms supported by griffins. Rev. Madonna. The denominations do not appear on the first four pieces.

440.	100	Lire 1758-67	4000.00
441.	50	Lire 1758-67 *	3000.00
442.	25	Lire 1758-67	1500.00
443.	12½	Lire 1758-67	3000.00
444.	96	Lire 1792-97	500.00
445.	48	Lire 1792-97 *	400.00
446.	24	Lire 1792-95	850.00
447.	12	Lire 1793-95	1250.00

D. The Republic (Ligurian) of —

Liguria seated. Rev. Fasces.

448.	96	Lire 1798-1805 *	850.00
449.	48	Lire 1798, 1801, 04	1000.00
450.	24	Lire 1798	2800.00
451.	12	Lire 1798	2800.00

GORIZIA

Counts of —

HENRY II, 1304-1323
St. John. Rev. Lily.

452.	1 Florin ND	2000.00

ALBERT IV, 1338-1374
St. John. Rev. Lily.

453.	1 Florin ND	2000.00

HENRY III, 1338-1364
St. John. Rev. Lily.

454.	1 Florin ND	2000.00

MAINHARD, 1364-1385
St. John. Rev. Lily.

455.	1 Florin ND	2000.00

St. John. Rev. Arms.

456.	1 Florin ND	2000.00

GUASTALLA

Dukes of —

CAESAR I GONZAGA, 1557-1575
Arms. Rev. Cross.

457. 1 Scudo d'oro ND.................................. 1500.00

FERDINAND II GONZAGA, 1575-1630
Bust. Rev. The Annunciation.

458. 10 Doppie 1610 .... Rare

Ruler standing. Rev. Arms.

459. 1 Ducat ND 1500.00

Arms. Rev. Cross.

460. 1 Scudo d'oro ND 1500.00

GUBBIO

Lords of —

FRANCIS MARIA I DELLA ROVERE, 1508-1538
St. Ubaldus seated. Rev. Arms.

461. 1 Scudo d'oro ND 2000.00

FRANCIS MARIA II DELLA ROVERE, 1574-1634

Bust. Rev. Arms.

462. 1 Scudo d'oro ND 2000.00

IVREA

DESIDERIUS, 756-774
Monogram. Rev. St. Michael.

462a. ⅓ Solidus ND .... Rare

LEGHORN (LIVORNO)

Tuscan Grand Dukes of —

FERDINAND II, 1621-1670

Head. Rev. View of the Port of Leghorn.

463. 1 Ducat 1655, ND .... Rare

COSIMO III, 1670-1723

Ruler standing. Rev. Legend in tablet.

464. 1 Ducat 1674, 75, 76, 91 .... 700.00

Arms. Rev. Rose bush. These coins are also referred to as "Pezza d'oro della rosa".

465. The coin previously listed does not exist. .... ——
466. 1 Doppia or Rosina 1717, 18, 21 ....* 900.00
467. ½ Doppia or Rosina 1718, 20 .... 800.00

Bust. Rev. View of the Port of Leghorn.

468. 1 Ducat ND .... Rare

Ruler standing. Rev. Fame over globe.

469. 1 Ducat ND 3500.00

LOANO

Princes of —

JOHN ANDREW II, 1622-1640
Bust. Rev. Eagle.

470. 2 Doppie 1639 .... Rare
471. 1 Doppia 1639 .... 6000.00

Tablet Rev. Madonna.

472. 1 Ducat ND 3000.00

JOHN ANDREW III, 1654-1737
Bust. Rev. Arms and cross.

473. 1 Doppia 1665 .... Rare

LOMBARDY

Provisional Government of —

Italia standing. Rev. Value. Struck at Milan.

474. 40 Lire 1848 ....* 500.00
475. 20 Lire 1848 .... 400.00

LUCCA

A. Dukes of —

ANONYMOUS, 650-749
Monogram. Rev. Cross.

476. ⅓ Solidus ND 800.00

Star. Rev. Cross.

477. ⅓ Solidus ND 250.00

ASTOLF, 749-756
Rose. Rev. Cross.

478. ⅓ Solidus ND 600.00

Star. Rev. Cross.

479. ⅓ Solidus ND 2000.00

DESIDERIUS, 757-773
Star. Rev. Cross.

480. ⅓ Solidus ND 500.00

CHARLEMAGNE, 773-814
Bust. Rev. Star.

481. ⅓ Solidus ND 3000.00

Star. Rev. Cross.

482. ⅓ Solidus ND 500.00

FREDERICK II, 1190-1250

Bust of Christ facing or left. Rev. Monogram and name of Otto IV.

483. 1 Grosso d'oro ND 5000.00

ANONYMOUS, 1300-1350

Bust of Christ. Rev. St. Martin on horse.

484. 1 Florin ND 3000.00

B. Republic of —, 1369-1799

Bust of Christ. Rev. St. Peter.

485. 1 Florin ND (1387-1400) 5000.00

Bust of Christ. Rev. St. Martin on horse.

486. 1 Ducat ND (1400-1500) ....*...... 1000.00
487. 1 Zecchino 1572, ND 250.00

Arms. Rev. Bust of Christ.

488. 4 Scudi d'oro 1748 ....*..... 2000.00
489. 2 Scudi d'oro 1749, 50 .... 300.00
490. 1 Scudo d'oro 1552-1749, ND 200.00
491. ½ Scudo d'oro 1551, 52, ND 500.00

Head of Christ. Rev. Four letters crossed.

492. ½ Scudo d'oro ND 400.00

Arms. Rev. St. Paulinus seated.

493. 1 Doppia 1758 .... 2000.00

MACCAGNO

Counts of —

GIACOMO III MANDELLI, 1618-1645
Soldier. Rev. Arms.

494. 1 Ducat 1622, 23 .... 800.00

Saint with shield. Rev. Eagle.

495. 1 Ducat 1622 .... 800.00

Saint with shield. Rev. Orb.

496. 1 Ducat ND 800.00

St. Stephan kneeling. Rev. Arms.

497. 1 Ducat 1622 .... 800.00

Arms. Rev. Eagle.

498. 1 Ducat 1622, ND 800.00

Arms. Rev. Orb.

499. 1 Ducat 1622 .... 800.00

Ruler standing. Rev. Arms.

500. 1 Doppia ND 8000.00
501. 1 Ducat 1622, ND ....*...... 800.00

Ruler standing. Rev. Eagle.

502. 1 Ducat ND 800.00

Soldier. Rev. Tablet.

503. 1 Ducat 1623, ND 800.00

Madonna. Rev. Tablet.

504. 1 Ducat ND 800.00

Bust of Saint. Rev. Eagle.

505. 1 Ducat ND 800.00

Bust. Rev. Arms.

506. 1 Doppia 1625, ND 8000.00

Bust. Rev. Eagle.

507. 1 Ducat ND 800.00

Bust. Rev. Orb.

508. 1 Ducat ND 800.00

MANFREDONIA

MANFRED, 1258-1266

Eagle. Rev. Legend.

509. 10 Tari ND 1500.00
510. 8 Tari ND 1000.00
511. 6 Tari ND 600.00
512. 4 Tari ND ....* ... 300.00
513. 3 Tari ND 200.00

MANTUA

Marcheses, and later, Dukes of —

LOUIS II GONZAGA, 1445-1478

Bust. Rev. Sacred vessel.

514. 1 Ducat ND .... Rare

Ruler standing. Rev. St. George on horse.

515. 1 Ducat ND 2500.00

Sun. Rev. Sacred vessel.

516. ⅓ Ducat ND 1500.00

FREDERICK I GONZAGA, 1478-1484

Bust. Rev. Sacred vessel.

517. 1 Ducat ND .... Rare

FRANCIS II GONZAGA, 1484-1519

Bust. Rev. Arms.

518. 2 Ducats ND 6000.00

Bust. Rev. Crucible in flames.

519. 2 Ducats ND .... Rare
520. 1 Ducat ND ....* ... 2000.00

Bust with hat. Rev. Sacred vessel.

521. 1 Ducat ND 4500.00

Madonna. Rev. Altar.

522. ½ Ducat ND 3000.00

FREDERICK II GONZAGA, 1519-1540
Head. Rev. Ruler on horse.

523. 3 Ducats ND .... Rare
524. 2 Ducats ND 10,000.00

Head. Rev. St. Catherine.

525. 1 Ducat ND 3000.00

Head. Rev. Mt. Olympus.

526. 2 Ducats ND ....* ... 2500.00
527. 1 Ducat ND 4000.00

Arms. Rev. Christ and cross.

528. 1 Scudo d'oro ND 750.00

Madonna seated. Rev. Mt. Olympus.

529. ½ Ducat ND 3000.00

FRANCIS III GONZAGA, 1540-1550
Arms. Rev. Christ and cross.

530. 1 Scudo d'oro ND 1200.00

WILLIAM GONZAGA, 1550-1587
Arms. Rev. Christ and cross.

531. 1 Scudo d'oro 1555, ND 2000.00

Arms. Rev. Seated female.

532. 1 Scudo d'oro ND 900.00

Arms. Rev. Standing female.

533. 1 Ducat ND 4000.00

Arms. Rev. Cross and initials.

534. 1 Scudo d'oro ND 350.00

VINCENT I GONZAGA, 1587-1612

Bust. Rev. Arms.

535. 7 Doppie 1589 .... **Rare**
536. 4 Doppie 1590 .... 6000.00
537. 2 Doppie 1590, ND ....*...... 4000.00

Bust. Rev. Tree.

538. 2 Doppie 1590 .... **Rare**

Bust. Rev. St. George on horse.

539. 10 Doppie ND .... **Rare**

Bust. Rev. Arms on cross.

540. 2 Zecchini ND 6000.00

Ruler standing. Rev. Arms.

541. 1 Ducat 1595 .... 1000.00

Soldier standing. Rev. Arms.

542. 1 Ducat ND 300.00

Bust of Virgil. Rev. Half moon.

543. ⅛ Scudo d'oro ND 3500.00

Eagle. Rev. Compass and clock.

544. ¼ Ducat 1596 .... 500.00

Eagle. Rev. Crescent and legend.

545. ¼ Ducat 1596 .... 1500.00
546. ⅛ Ducat 1596 ....*... 800.00

FRANCIS IV GONZAGA, 1612
St. Andrew and St. Longinus. Rev. Arms.

547. 5 Doppie 1612 .... **Rare**

Bust. Rev. Arms.

548. 2 Doppie 1612 .... 10,000.00
549. 1 Doppia 1612 .... 10,000.00

FERDINAND GONZAGA, 1612-1626

Bust. Rev. Sun.

550. 12 Zecchini 1617 .... **Rare**
551. 6 Doppie 1613, 14, 15 .... 10,000.00
552. 4 Doppie ND ....*..... 7000.00

Bust. Rev. Two angels.

553. 2 Doppie 1613, 14, 15 ....*.... 2000.00
554. 1 Doppia 1614, 16 .... 3000.00

Bust. Rev. St. Andrew and St. Longinus.

555. 1 Doppia 1613 .... 4000.00

Bust. Rev. St. Longinus.

556. 1 Doppia 1616, ND 3500.00

Bust. Rev. Madonna.

557. 12 Doppie 1614 .... Rare
558. 6 Doppie 1614 .... 10,000.00

Bust right or left. Rev. Arms.

559. 6 Doppie 1616 .... 12,000.00
560. 2 Doppie 1621, ND ....*.... 1600.00
561. 1 Doppia 1617,.ND 3000.00
562. ½ Zecchino ND 2500.00

St. Andrew and St. Longinus. Rev. Arms.

563. 2 Doppie 1613 .... Rare

Arms on each side.

564. 6 Doppie 1620 .... Rare

Cardinal standing. Rev. Madonna.

565. 1 Scudo d'oro 1613, ND 4500.00

Madonna. Rev. Rose.

566. 1 Zecchino ND 1200.00

VINCENT II GONZAGA, 1626-1627

Bust. Rev. Arms.

567. 2 Doppie 1627 .... 4500.00

Legend. Rev. Ship.

568. 1 Scudo d'oro ND .... Rare

CHARLES I GONZAGA, 1627-1637

Bust. Rev. Sun in zodiac.

569. 8 Doppie 1628 .... 12,000.00
570. 6 Doppie 1628, 32 .... 12,000.00
571. 5 Doppie 1636 .... 12,000.00

Bust. Rev. Arms.

572.. 2 Doppie 1629, 31, 36 ....*.... 10,000.00
573. 1 Doppia ND 10,000.00

CHARLES II GONZAGA, 1637-1665

Busts of Charles and Maria. Rev. Madonna.

574. 12 Scudi d'oro ND .... Rare
575. 8 Doppie ND 12,000.00
576. 5 Doppie ND 10,000.00
577. 4 Doppie ND 10,000.00

Busts of Charles and Maria. Rev. Arms.

578. 2 Doppie ND 5000.00

Bust. Rev. Sun in shield.

579. 12 Scudi d'oro 1649 .... Rare
580. 10 Zecchini 1649 ....*...... Rare
581. 6 Doppie 1649 .... Rare

Bust. Rev. Arms.

582. 2 Doppie ND 7000.00
583. 1 Doppia ND .... Rare

FERDINAND CHARLES GONZAGA, 1665-1707

Busts of Ferdinand and Isabella Clara. Rev. Sun.

584.	12 Doppie 1666	Rare
585.	6 Doppie 1666	12,000.00
586.	5 Doppie 1666	10,000.00
587.	4 Doppie 1666	6000.00
588.	2 Doppie 1666 ....*.....	6000.00

Busts of Ferdinand and Isabella Clara. Rev. Madonna.

589.	6 Doppie 1666	12,000.00

Bust. Rev. Sun and rock.

590.	8 Doppie 1679	Rare

Bust. Rev. Arms.

591.	2 Doppie ND	Rare

MASSA DI LUNIGIANA

Dukes of —

ALBERIC CYBO MALUSPINA, 1559-1623

Bust. Rev. Arms.

592.	2 Doppie 1582, 88, 89, ND ....*......	2500.00
593.	1 Doppia 1588, ND	2000.00

Bust. Rev. Temple.

594.	2 Doppie 1588, ND	3000.00

Bust. Rev. Fire.

595.	1 Doppia ND	2000.00

Bust. Rev. Arms and eagle.

596.	2 Doppie 1593, 98, ND	3000.00
597.	1 Doppia 1593	2000.00

Arms. Rev. Eagle.

598.	1 Doppia ND	2000.00

Arms. Rev. Anvil.

599.	1 Scudo d'oro ND	2000.00

St. Peter. Rev. Arms.

600.	1 Scudo d'oro ND	2000.00

Arms. Rev. Cross.

601.	1 Scudo d'oro 1569, ND	2000.00

Arms. Rev. Pyramid.

602.	½ Scudo d'oro ND	2000.00

Arms. Rev. Rose Bush.

603.	½ Scudo d'oro ND	2000.00

CHARLES I CYBO MALUSPINA, 1623-1662
Bust. Rev. Arms.

604.	5 Doppie ND	6000.00

MASSA-LOMBARDY

Marcheses of —

FRANCIS D'ESTE, 1562-1578
Bust. Rev. Eagle.

605.	1 Scudo d'oro ND	6000.00

Eagle. Rev. Cross.

606.	1 Scudo d'oro ND	2500.00

MESSERANO

Princes of —

ANONYMOUS, 1492-1521
Madonna. Rev. St. Theomestus.

607.	1 Ducat ND	1000.00

Eagle. Rev. Cross.

608.	1 Scudo d'oro ND	3000.00

LOUIS II AND PETER LUCAS II, 1521-1528
Arms. Rev. Cross.

609.	1 Scudo d'oro ND	1600.00

LOUIS II, 1528-1532
Bust. Rev. Horse.

610.	1 Doppia ND	6000.00

Head. Rev. Arms.

611.	1 Ducat ND	4000.00

Head. Rev. St. Theonestus seated.

612.	1 Ducat ND	2500.00

Eagle. Rev. Cross.

613.	1 Scudo d'oro ND	800.00

PETER LUCAS II, 1528-1548
Eagle. Rev. Cross

614.	1 Scudo d'oro ND	1500.00

FILIBERT FERRERO, 1532-1559
Arms. Rev. Cross.

615.	1 Scudo d'oro ND	2000.00

BESSO FERRERO, 1559-1584
Bust. Rev. Arms.

616.	1 Doppia 1582	Rare

Arms. Rev. Cross.

617.	1 Scudo d'oro ND	1000.00

FRANCIS FILIBERT FERRERO, 1584-1629
Bust. Rev. Arms.

618.	1 Doppia 1594, ND	5000.00

Bust. Rev. The Annunciation.

619.	2 Doppie ND	Rare
620.	1 Doppia ND	Rare

Ruler standing. Rev. Arms on eagle.

621.	1 Ducat 1596, ND	1200.00

Ruler standing. Rev. Tablet.

622.	1 Ducat 1598	1200.00

PAUL BESSO FERRERO, 1629-1667
Bust. Rev. Arms.

623.	5 Doppie 1638	Rare
624.	1 Scudo d'oro 1640	2500.00

Soldier. Rev. Tablet.

625.	1 Ducat ND	1200.00

Tablet. Rev. Eagle.

626.	1 Ducat ND	1200.00

FRANCIS LOUIS FERRERO, 1667-1685
Bust. Rev. Arms.

627.	1 Doppia 1667	....	Rare

Bust. Rev. Four shields crossed.

628.	5 Doppie 1672	....	**Rare**

CHARLES BESSO FERRERO, 1685-1690
Bust. Rev. Arms.

629.	1 Doppia 1689	....	Rare

MESSINA

A. Norman Kings of —

ROGER II, 1102-1154
Cufic legend on each side.

630.	3 Tari ND	....	150.00
631.	2 Tari ND	....	60.00
632.	1 Tari ND	....	40.00

WILLIAM I, 1154-1166
Cufic legend on each side.

633.	2 Tari ND	....	70.00
634.	1 Tari ND	....	40.00

WILLIAM II, 1166-1189
Six globes. Rev. Cross.

635.	1 Tari ND	....	40.00

W. Rev. Star.

636.	1 Tari ND	....	40.00

Star. Rev. Cufic legend.

637.	3 Tari ND	...........................*......	100.00
638.	2 Tari ND	....	60,00
639.	½ Tari ND	....	40.00

TANCRED, 1190-1194
Globe. Rev. Cross.

640.	2 Tari ND	....	60.00
641.	1 Tari ND	....	40.00

B. German and Anjou Kings of —

HENRY VI OF HOHENSTAUFEN, 1194-1197
Bust. Rev. Cross and four globes.

642.	1 Tari ND	....	2000.00

E. Rev. Cross.

643.	1 Tari ND	....	100.00

HENRY VI AND FREDERICK II OF HOHENSTAUFEN, 1195
FE. Rev. Cross.

644.	3 Tari ND	....	150.00
645.	2 Tari ND	....	60.00
646.	1 Tari ND	....	90.00

Five globes. Rev. Cross.

647.	3 Tari ND	....	150.00

FREDERICK II OF HOHENSTAUFEN, 1198-1250
FRE. Rev. Cross.

648.	1 Tari ND	....	60.00

Cross on hill. Rev. Cross.

649.	1 Tari ND	....	100.00

Eagle. Rev. Cross.

650.	10 Tari ND	....	600.00
650a.	2 Tari ND	...........................*	100.00
651.	1 Tari ND	....	50.00

Five globes. Rev. Cross.

652.	1 Tari ND	....	50.00

CHARLES I OF ANJOU, 1266-1282
Bust. Rev. Arms.

653.	1 Real ND	....	4000.00

C. Spanish Kings of —

CONSTANCE AND PETER III OF ARAGON, 1282-1285

Arms. Rev. Eagle.

654.	1 Ducat or Oncia ND	....	1200.00

JAMES OF ARAGON, 1285-1296
Arms. Rev. Eagle.

655.	1 Ducat ND	....	Rare

FREDERICK III, 1296-1337
Arms. Rev. Eagle.

656.	1 Ducat ND	....	Rare

JOHN, 1458-1479
Ruler seated. Rev. Eagle.

657.	1 Real ND	....	650.00

FERDINAND II, 1479-1516
Bust. Rev. Eagle.

658.	2 Ducats ND	....	Rare

Ruler on throne. Rev. Eagle.

659.	1 Ducat ND	.......................*......	300.00
660.	½ Ducat ND	....	1200.00

CHARLES V, 1516-1556
Bust. Rev. Eagle.

661.	2 Ducats ND	....	Rare
662.	1 Ducat ND	....	Rare
663.	½ Ducat ND	....	Rare

Cross of St. Andrew. Rev. Shield.

664.	1 Scudo d'oro 1541-44	....	1000.00
665.	½ Scudo d'oro 1541-43	....	1000.00

Cross of St. Andrew. Rev. Eagle.

666. 1 Scudo d'oro 1544-54 ....*...... 1000.00
667. ½ Scudo d'oro 1544-51 .... 1000.00

PHILIP II, 1556-1598
Bust. Rev. Eagle.

668. 1 Scudo d'oro 1557 .... Rare

MILAN

A. Dukes of —

DESIDERIUS, 757-773
Cross. Rev. Star.

669. ⅓ Solidus ND 5000.00

CHARLEMAGNE, 774-814
Cross potent. Rev. Cross.

670. ⅓ Solidus ND 5000.00

Cross. Rev. Star.

671. ⅓ Solidus ND 5000.00

FIRST REPUBLIC, 1250-1310
Saints Protaxius and Gervasius standing. Rev. St. Ambrose standing.

672. 1 Florin ND 8000.00

Bust of St. Ambrose. Rev. M.

673. ½ Florin ND 350.00

LUCHINUS AND JOHN VISCONTI, 1339-1349
St. Ambrose seated. Rev. Dragon with shield.

674. 1 Florin ND 3500.00

GALEAZZO II AND BARNABAS VISCONTI, 1354-1378

Helmeted arms on each side.

675. 1 Florin ND 1000.00

GALEAZZO II VISCONTI, 1354-1378

Ruler on horse. Rev. Helmeted arms.

676. 1 Florin ND 500.00

BARNABAS VISCONTI, 1354-1385

Helmeted arms. Rev. Serpent and initials.

677. 1 Florin ND 1250.00

JOHN GALEAZZO VISCONTI, 1385-1402
Ruler on horse. Rev. Helmeted arms.

678. 1 Florin ND 800.00

Bust. Rev. Serpent.

679. 10 Florins ND .... Rare

JOHN MARIA VISCONTI, 1402-1412
Ruler on horse. Rev. Helmeted arms.

680. 1 Florin ND 3000.00

PHILIP MARIA VISCONTI, 1412-1447

Ruler on horse. Rev. Helmeted arms.

681. 1 Florin ND 250.00

SECOND REPUBLIC, 1447-1450
St. Ambrose standing. Rev. M.

682. 1 Florin ND 3200.00

FRANCIS I SFORZA, 1450-1466

Bust. Rev. Ruler on horse.

683. 1 Ducat ND 750.00

Ruler on horse. Rev. Helmeted arms.

684. 1 Ducat ND 4000.00

Ruler on horse. Rev. Serpent.

685. 1 Ducat ND 4000.00

GALEAZZO MARIA SFORZA, 1466-1476
Bust. Rev. Arms.

686. 10 Ducats ND .... Rare

Bust. Rev. Helmeted arms.

687. 2 Ducats ND 6000.00
688. 1 Ducat ND ....*...... 900.00

Bust. Rev. Lion.

689. 2 Ducats ND 5500.00

**BONA DI SAVOIA
AND JOHN GALEAZZO MARIA SFORZA, 1476-1481**
Bust on each side.

690. 2 Zecchini ND .... Rare

Bust. Rev. Lion.

691. 2 Zecchini ND 10,000.00

JOHN GALEAZZO MARIA SFORZA, 1481

Bust. Rev. Arms.

692. 10 Ducats ND .... Rare
693. 2 Ducats ND ....*...... 2500.00

JOHN GALEAZZO MARIA AND LOUIS MARIA SFORZA, 1481-1494
Bust on each side.

694. 10 Ducats ND .... Rare
695. 2 Ducats ND .... Rare

Bust of John. Rev. Arms.

696. 1 Ducat ND 6000.00

LOUIS MARIA SFORZA, 1494-1500

Bust. Rev. Ruler on horse.

697. 10 Ducats ND .... Rare
698. 2 Gold Testones ND ....*...... 3500.00

FRANCIS II SFORZA, 1522-1535
Bust. Rev. Bust of St. Ambrosius.

699. 10 Scudi d'oro ND .... Rare
700. 6 Scudi d'oro ND .... Rare

Ruler on horse. Rev. Arms.

701. 2 Scudi d'oro ND .... Rare

Arms. Rev. Cross.

702. 1 Scudo d'oro ND 1200.00

B. French Rulers of —

LOUIS XII, 1500-1513
Bust. Rev. Arms.

703. 10 Ducats ND .... Rare

Crowned bust. Rev. St. Ambrosius on horse.

704. 2 Ducats ND 10,000.00

St. Ambrosius seated. Rev. French coat-of-arms.

705. 2 Ducats ND 5000.00

FRANCIS I, 1515-1522
Armored bust. Rev. Crowned arms.

706. 2 Ducats ND .... Rare

*Crowned arms with small head of St. Ambrosius above. Rev.
Floriated cross.*

707. 1 Scudo d'oro ND 1200.00

C. Spanish Rulers of —

CHARLES V, 1534-1556
Bust. Rev. The Pillars of Hercules.

708. 2 Scudo d'oro ND 6000.00

PHILIP II, 1556-1598
Bust. Rev. Arms.

709. 3 Doppie 1555, 79, 82 ....10,000.00
710. 2 Doppie ND 5000.00
711. 1 Doppia ND 4000.00

Bust. Rev. St. Ambrosius on horse.

712. 2 Doppie 1562 .... 6000.00

Bust. Rev. Bust of St. Ambrosius.

713. 3 Doppie 1591 .... Rare

Bust. Rev. The Crucifixion.

714. 4 Doppie ND .... Rare

Radiate head right or left. Rev. Arms.

715. 2   Doppie 1562, 88, 95 .... 5000.00
716. 1   Doppia 1578-98, ND ....*..... 350.00
717. 1½ Scudi d'oro ND .... Rare
718. 1   Scudo d'oro ND 800.00

Arms. Rev. Cross.

719. 1 Scudo d'oro ND 1200.00

PHILIP III, 1598-1621

Bust. Rev. Arms.

720.	2 Doppie 1610, 17, ND	.....................*......	2500.00
721.	1 Doppia 1617, ND	....	2800.00

PHILIP IV, 1621-1665
Bust. Rev. City view.

722.	4½ Doppie 1630	....	Rare

Bust. Rev. Arms.

723.	20 Zecchini 1643	....	Rare
724.	2 Doppie 1630, ND	..................*......	800.00
725.	1 Doppia 1630, ND	....	2000.00

CHARLES II, 1665-1700

Busts of Charles and Maria Anna. Rev. Arms.

26.	2 Doppie 1666	....	Rare

Young bust. Rev. Arms.

27.	1 Doppia 1676	....	5000.00

Old bust. Rev. Arms.

28.	1 Doppia 1698	....	5000.00

D. Austrian Rulers of —

(For Austrian type coins struck at Milan with "M" mm, see under Austria. Italian type coins are listed here).

CHARLES VI, 1711-1740
Head. Rev. Arms.

29.	2 Scudi d'oro 1720, 24	....	4000.00

Head. Rev. Double eagle.

30.	1 Scudo d'oro 1723, 24	....	4000.00

Bust. Rev. Arms.

31.	12 Scudi d'oro ND	....	Rare

MARIA THERESA, 1740-1780
Bust. Rev. St. Ambrosius standing.

32.	1 Zecchino ND	....	Rare

Bust. Rev. Arms.

733.	2 Doppie 1778, 79	....	1400.00
734.	1 Doppia 1778, 79, 80	....	1000.00
735.	1 Zecchino 1778, 79, 80	...............*.....	500.00

JOSEPH II, 1780-1790

Bust. Rev. Legend. On his Inauguration.

736.	1 Doppia 1781	....	2000.00
737.	1 Zecchino 1781	........................*......	800.00

Bust. Rev. Arms.

738.	1 Doppia 1781-85	.......................*......	1000.00
739.	1 Zecchino 1781-88	....	500.00

FRANCIS II, 1792-1797

Bust. Rev. Legend. On his Inauguration.

740.	1 Doppia 1792	.........................*......	2000.00
741.	1 Zecchino 1792	....	800.00

MIRANDOLA

Dukes of —

JOHN FRANCIS PICO, 1499-1533
Book. Rev. The Resurrection.

742.	3 Zecchini ND	....	5000.00

Bust. Rev. The Resurrection.

743.	1 Doppia ND	....	2500.00

Plain bust right. Rev. St. Francis kneeling.

744.	1 Doppia ND	....	1250.00

Bust with hat to left. Rev. St. Francis kneeling.

745.	1 Doppia ND	....	2500.00

Bust with hat. Rev. Arms.

746. 1 Zecchino ND 2500.00

Head. Rev. Arms.

747. 1 Zecchino ND 2500.00

Head. Rev. Shield.

748. 1 Zecchino ND .... Rare

Head. Rev. Two Apostles standing.

749. 1 Zecchino ND 2500.00

Arms. Rev. Legend.

750. 1 Zecchino ND 500.00

GALEOTTO PICO II, 1533-1550
Arms. Rev. Cross.

751. 1 Scudo d'oro ND 1000.00

LOUIS PICO II, 1550-1568

Arms. Rev. Cross.

752. 1 Scudo d'oro ND ....*...... 275.00
753. ½ Scudo d'oro ND 800.00

GALEOTTO PICO III, 1568-1590
Arms. Rev. Cross.

754. 1 Scudo d'oro ND 1500.00

ALEXANDER PICO, 1602-1637
Bust. Rev. Arms.

755. 24 Scudi d'oro 1618 .... Rare

MODENA

Dukes of —

HERCULES I D'ESTE, 1471-1505
Head. Rev. St. Geminianus seated.

756. 1 Ducat ND 4000.00

Head with cap. Rev. St. Geminianus seated.

757. 1 Ducat ND 12,000.00

MAXIMILIAN I OF AUSTRIA, 1513-1514
Bust. Rev. St. Geminianus seated.

758. 1 Ducat ND 12,000.00

ALFONSO I D'ESTE, 1505-1534
Bust. Rev. St. Geminianus seated.

759. 1 Ducat ND 5000.00

Cross. Rev. St. Geminianus seated.

760. 1 Scudo d'oro ND 1500.00

HERCULES II D'ESTE, 1534-1559

Cross. Rev. St. Geminianus seated.

761. 1 Scudo d'oro ND 275.00

ALFONSO II D'ESTE, 1559-1597
Cross. Rev. St. Geminianus seated.

762. 1 Scudo d'oro ND 1000.00

CAESAR D'ESTE, 1598-1628

Ruler standing. Rev. Arms.

763. 1 Ducat 1598, 1600, ND ....*...... 200.00
764. ¼ Ducat ND .... Rare

Head. Rev. Patience standing.

765. 1 Doppia 1605, 09 .... 2000.00

Bust. Rev. Female standing.

766. 2 Doppie 1608 .... 4000.00

Bust. Rev. Soldier seated.

767. 4 Doppie 1612 .... 5000.00

Bust. Rev. Eagle.

768. 2 Doppie ND 1800.00

Arms. Rev. Cross.

769. 1 Scudo d'oro ND 1000.00

FRANCIS I D'ESTE, 1629-1658

Bust. Rev. Ship.

770. 24 Scudi d'oro 1631, ND .... Rare
771. 20 Scudi d'oro ND .... Rare
772. 16 Scudi d'oro 1631, ND .... Rare
773. 12 Scudi d'oro 1633, 46, ND .... Rare
774. 10 Scudi d'oro ND .... Rare
775. 8 Scudi d'oro 1631, 33, ND ....*...... 5000.00
776. 6 Scudi d'oro ND 3500.0

Bust. Rev. Madonna.

777.	8 Scudi d'oro 1631	....	**Rare**
778.	4 Scudi d'oro 1632, 34, ND	................*......	900.00
779.	2 Scudi d'oro 1631	....	1500.00

Bust. Rev. Arms.

780.	1 Doppia 1651	....	3000.00
781.	½ Doppia 1651	....	1000.00

Bust. Rev. Eagle.

782.	4 Scudi d'oro ND	....	3000.00
783.	2 Scudi d'oro ND	....	2000.00
784.	1 Scudo d'oro ND	....	800.00
785.	½ Scudo d'oro ND	....	600.00

Ruler standing. Rev. Tablet.

786.	1 Ducat 1649	....	1200.00

Ruler standing. Rev. Eagle.

787.	1 Doppia 1639	....	1500.00
788.	1 Ducat 1649	...................*......	1000.00

Ruler standing. Rev. Eagle with shield.

789.	1 Ducat 1649	....	1000.00

Legend. Rev. Eagle.

790.	5 Lire or ⅓ Scudo d'oro ND	....	250.00
791.	103 Soldi or ⅓ Scudo d'oro ND	............*......	150.00

ALFONSO IV D'ESTE, 1658-1662
Bust. Rev. Sword.

792.	12 Scudi d'oro 1659	....	Rare

Bust. Rev. Eagle.

793.	2 Doppie 1660	....	5000.00
794.	1 Doppia 1660, ND	....	3000.00

FRANCIS II D'ESTE, 1662-1694

Ruler standing. Rev. Eagle.

795.	1 Ducat ND	....	2000.00

MONTALCINO

SIENESE RULE, 1555-1559
Madonna. Rev. She-Wolf.

796.	4 Scudi d'oro 1556	....	6000.00

She-Wolf. Rev. Arms.

797.	1 Scudo d'oro 1556, 57, 58, 59	....	3000.00

S. Rev. Arms.

798.	½ Scudo d'oro ND	....	3500.00

MONTANARO

Abbots of —

BONIFACE FERRERO, 1529-1543
Arms. Rev. Cross.

799.	1 Scudo d'oro ND	....	3000.00

Eagle. Rev. Cross.

800.	1 Scudo d'oro ND	....	3000.00

SEBASTIAN FERRERO, 1546-1547
Bust. Rev. Arms.

801.	3 Scudi d'oro ND	....	Rare

Arms. Rev. Cross.

802.	1 Scudo d'oro ND	....	Rare

JOHN BAPTIST, 1581-1582
Soldier standing. Rev. Arms.

803.	2 Doppie ND	....	Rare
804.	1 Doppia ND	....	6000.00

Arms. Rev. Cross.

805.	1 Scudo d'oro ND	....	Rare

MUSSO

Marcheses of —

JOHN JAMES OF MEDICI, 1528-1530
Arms. Rev. Cross.

806.	1 Scudo d'oro ND	....	6000.00

Bust. Rev. Reclining figure.

807.	1 Zecchino ND	....	Rare

NAPLES

(KINGDOM OF THE TWO SICILIES; SEE ALSO SICILY)

A. Anjou Rulers of —

CHARLES I, 1266-1278

The Annunciation. Rev. Arms.

808. 1 Salut d'or ND ....*...... 300.00
809. ½ Salut d'or ND 3000.00

CHARLES II, 1285-1309
The Annunciation. Rev. Arms.

810. 1 Salut d'or ND 300.00

JOANNA I, 1343-1347
Ruler seated. Rev. Cross.

811. 1 Ducat ND 1200.00

St. John. Rev. Arms.

812. 1 Florin ND 450.00

JOANNA AND LOUIS, 1352-1362
St. John. Rev. Lily.

813. 1 Florin ND 600.00

LOUIS, 1382-1384
St. John. Rev. Arms.

814. 1 Florin ND 400.00

B. Aragon Rulers of —

ALFONSO I, 1442-1458

Ruler on horse. Rev. Arms.

815. 1 Ducatone ND (31 Millimetres) 700.00
816. 1 Ducat ND (27 Millimetres) ....*...... 450.00

FERDINAND I, 1458-1494
Crowned bust. Rev. Victory in chariot.

817. 5 Ducats ND .... Rare

Crowned bust. Rev. Arms.

818. 2 Ducats ND 10,000.00
819. 1 Ducat ND ....*...... 250.00

ALFONSO II, 1494-1495

Crowned bust. Rev. Arms.

820. 1 Ducat ND 500.00

FERDINAND II, 1495-1496

Crowned bust. Rev. Arms.

821. 1 Ducat ND 1250.00

FREDERICK III, 1496-1501

Crowned bust. Rev. Animal over shield.

822. 1 Ducat ND 1000.00

C. French Rulers of —

CHARLES VIII, 1495
Arms. Rev. Cross of Jerusalem.

823. 1 Scudo d'oro ND .... Rare

Arms between initials. Rev. Cross of Jerusalem in quadrilobe.

824. 2 Scudi d'oro ND .... Rare
825. 1 Scudo d'oro ND ....*...... Rare

LOUIS XII, 1501-1503

Crowned bust. Rev. Arms.

826. 1 Ducat ND 6000.00

D. Spanish Rulers of —

FERDINAND AND ISABELLA, 1504

Crowned busts facing each other. Rev. Arms.

827. 1 Zecchino ND 1250.00

FERDINAND THE CATHOLIC, 1504-1516

Crowned bust. Rev. Arms.

828.   1 Ducat ND 1000.00

CHARLES AND JOANNA, 1516-1519

Arms. Rev. Cross.

829.   1 Ducat ND 300.00

CHARLES V, 1519-1556

Bust. Rev. Peace standing.

830.   4 Scudi d'oro ND .... Rare
831.   2 Scudi d'oro ND ....*...... 750.00

Bust. Rev. Pallas seated.

832.   2 Scudi d'oro ND 2200.00

Crowned bust. Rev. Arms.

833.   1 Ducat ND 1800.00

Laureate head. Rev. Arms.

834.   1 Ducat ND 300.00

Arms. Rev. Cross.

835.   1 Scudo d'oro ND 125.00

PHILIP II, 1556-1598

Head. Rev. Arms.

836.   1 Scudo d'oro 1582, 97, ND 400.00

PHILIP III, 1598-1621

Radiate bust. Rev. Eagle.

837.   1 Scudo d'oro ND 10,000.00

Radiate bust. Rev. Arms.

838.   1 Scudo d'oro ND 3000.00

PHILIP IV, 1621-1665

Plain head right. Rev. Arms.

839.   2 Scudi d'oro 1626 .... Rare
840.   1 Scudo d'oro 1622-36 ....*...... 300.00

Armored bust left. Rev. Arms.

841.   1 Scudo d'oro 1642, 47 .... 1000.00

CHARLES II, 1667-1700

Bust. Rev. Arms.

842.   1 Ducat 1665 .... Rare

E. Bourbon Rulers of —

CHARLES, 1734-1759

Bust. Rev. Arms and value.

843.   6 Ducati 1749-55 ....*...... 200.00
844.   4 Ducati 1749-55 .... 200.00
845.   2 Ducati 1749-54 .... 200.00

FERDINAND IV (I), 1759-1825
(Ferdinand IV from 1759-1816 and Ferdinand I from 1817-1825).

Youthful bust. Rev. Arms.

846. 6 Ducati 1759-67 .... 120.00
847. 4 Ducati 1760-67 ....*...... 200.00
848. 2 Ducati 1762 .... 200.00

Older bust. Rev. Arms.

849. 6 Ducati 1768-81 ....*...... 120.00
850. 4 Ducati 1768-76 .... 200.00
851. 2 Ducati 1771 .... 200.00

Oldest bust. Rev. Arms.

852. 6 Ducati 1783, 84, 85 .... 700.00

Bust of Queen Maria Caroline. Rev. Two figures at altar.

853. 2 Ducati 1768 .... 700.00

Bust. Rev. Legend.

854. 2 Ducati 1772 .... 700.00

Crowned bust. Rev. Male standing at column.

855. 30 Ducati 1818 ....*...... 1200.00
856. 15 Ducati 1818 .... 800.00
857. 3 Ducati 1818 ....*...... 200.00

JOACHIM MURAT, 1808-1815
(Napoleonic Dynasty)

Head. Rev. Value.

858. 40 Franchi 1810 .... 12,000.00
859. 40 Lire 1813 .... 400.00
860. 20 Lire 1813 ....*...... 400.00
861. 20 Lire 1813. N mm 5000.00

FRANCIS I, 1825-1830

Head. Rev. Male standing at column.

862. 30 Ducati 1825, 26 .... 1500.00
863. 15 Ducati 1825 .... 10,000.00
864. 6 Ducati 1826 ....*..... 1500.00
865. 3 Ducati 1826 ....*..... 1200.00

FERDINAND II, 1830-1859

*Head with or without beard. Rev. Male standing at column
with or without wings.*

866. 30 Ducati 1831-56 ....*...... 1000.00
867. 15 Ducati 1831-56 ....*..... 1000.00
868. 6 Ducati 1831-56 ....*..... 400.00
869. 3 Ducati 1831-56 .... 300.00

NOVARA

Marcheses of —

PETER LUIGI FARNESE, 1538-1547

Arms. Rev. Cross.

870. 1 Scudo d'oro ND 5000.00

PADUA

FRANCIS I, 1355-1388
St. Prosdocimus. Rev. Arms.

871. 1 Ducat ND 5000.00

PALERMO

A. Fatimid Caliphs of —

AL QAYM, 934-945
Cufic legend on each side.

872. 1 Tari ND 65.00

EL HAKEM BIAMR ILAH, 996-1020

Cufic legend on each side.

873. 1 Tari ND 65.00

DHAER LEAZIZ DIN ILAH, 1020-1036
Cufic legend on each side.

874.   1 Tari ND 65.00

ANONYMOUS
ERTINA. Rev. Si Mirio.

875.   1 Tari ND (1020) 150.00

B. Kings of —

ROGER II, 1105-1154
Cufic legend on each side.

876.   2 Tari ND 100.00
877.   1 Tari ND 65.00

T. Rev. Cufic legend.

878.   1 Tari ND 65.00

WILLIAM II, 1166-1189
Cufic legend. Rev. Cross.

879.   1 Tari ND 65.00

FREDERICK II, 1198-1250
Eagle. Rev. Cross.

880.   2 Tari ND 100.00

CHARLES II, 1665-1700

Shield on breast of eagle. Rev. Small head in border under palms.

881.   1 Scudo Riccio 1697 ....   750.00

CHARLES III, 1720-1734
Head. Rev. View of Sicily.

882.   2 Ducati 1723 ....   Rare

Bust. Rev. Sceptre and sword above globe.

883.   4 Ducati 1727 ....   Rare
884.   2 Ducati 1727 ....   6000.00

Head. Rev. Phoenix.

885.   1 Oncia 1720-34 ....   120.00

CHARLES BOURBON, 1734-1759

Bust. Rev. Bourbon shield on eagle.

886.   2 Oncia 1734-54 ....   200.00

Bare head. Rev. Phoenix.

887.   1 Oncia 1734-59 ....   70.00

FERDINAND IV (III OF SICILY), 1759-1815

Radiate head. Rev. Triskelis.

888.   2 Oncia 1814 ....   2500.00

PARMA AND PIACENZA

(For the Papal coinage of Parma, see under Vatican-Parma).

A. Republic of —, 1448-1449

Christ and Madonna. Rev. St. John and St. Hillary standing.

889.   1 Ducat ND ....   Rare

B. Dukes of —

(Unless otherwise stated, all coins are for Parma. Those coins struck for Piacenza are so indicated at the end of the description).

OCTAVIUS FARNESE, 1547-1586

Arms. Rev. Security seated.

890.   1 Scudo d'oro 1552-57, ND ....* 600.00
891.   1 Scudo d'oro 1552. For Piacenza 1000.00

Pallas seated. Rev. Arms.

892.   ½ Scudo d'oro 1552, ND 1500.00

Head. Rev. She-wolf. For Piacenza.

893.   2 Doppie 1582, 86, 87, ND ....* 2500.00
894.   1 Doppia 1582, 85, 86, 89, ND 1200.00

ALEXANDER FARNESE, 1586-1591
Bust. Rev. The three Graces standing.

895.	7 Scudi d'oro 1588	**Rare**
896.	4 Doppie 1588	8000.00

Bust. Rev. Arms.

897.	2 Doppie ND	3000.00

Bust. Rev. Security standing.

898.	1 Doppia ND	3000.00

Bust. Rev. She-wolf. For Piacenza.

899.	2 Doppie 1590-99, ND	850.00

RANUCCIO FARNESE I, 1592-1622
Bust of Alexander Farnese. Rev. The three Graces standing.

900.	8 Scudi d'oro 1594	**Rare**

Ruler standing. Rev. Arms.

901.	1 Ducat 1602, 03	400.00

Ruler standing. Rev. Madonna.

902.	1 Ducat ND	1000.00

Bust. Rev. Ship. For Piacenza.

903.	2 Doppie 1592	2000.00

Bust. Rev. Wind blowing. For Piacenza.

904.	4 Doppie 1601	4000.00
905.	2 Doppie 1595, 1612, 13	2000.00
906.	1 Doppia 1595-1612 ....*.....	2000.00

Bust. Rev. She-wolf. For Piacenza.

907.	2 Doppie 1599-1622	850.00

Ruler standing. Rev. Tablet.

908.	1 Ducat 1601	**Rare**

ODOARDO FARNESE, 1622-1646

Bust. Rev. Madonna.

909.	8 Doppie 1639	**Rar**
910.	6 Doppie ND	**Rar**
911.	2 Doppie 1625, 39, ND ....*....	900.00
912.	1 Doppia ND	2200.00

Bust. Rev. Mars and Pallas standing.

913.	8 Doppie 1629	**Rar**

Bust. Rev. The three Graces standing.

914.	3 Doppie 1633	4000.00

Bust. Rev. Lily. For Piacenza.

915.	2 Doppie 1623, 24	**Ra**

Bust. Rev. St. Anthony on horse. For Piacenza.

916.	6 Doppie 1626, 29	**Rar**

Bust. Rev. She-wolf. For Piacenza.

917.	2 Doppie 1626, 31 ....*.....	800.0
918.	1 Doppia 1626	800.0

RANUCCIO FARNESE II, 1646-1694
Bust. Rev. Madonna.

919.	2 Doppie 1658, ND	2000.0

Bust. Rev. Saint standing.

920.	1 Doppia 1687	2000.0

Head. Rev. Windblowing.

921.	1 Doppia 1692	2000.0

Bust. Rev. Mars and Pallas standing.

922.	10 Doppie 1673	**Rare**
923.	8 Doppie 1660, 79	**Rare**

Bust. Rev. St. Anthony on horse. For Piacenza.

924.	10 Doppie 1676	**Rare**

FRANCIS FARNESE I, 1694-1727

Head. Rev. Arms.

925.   1 Doppia 1695 .... 3000.00

FERDINAND BOURBON, 1765-1802

Head. Rev. Arms.

926.   8 Doppie 1786-96 .... 1800.00
927.   6 Doppie 1786 .... 4000.00
928.   4 Doppie 1784-96 .... 1200.00
929.   3 Doppie 1786 .... 3500.00
930.   1 Doppia 1784-96 ....*..... 250.00
931.   ½ Doppia 1785 .... 150.00
932.   1 Zecchino 1784 .... 400.00

MARIE LOUISE, 1815-1847

Head. Rev. Arms.

933.   40 Lire 1815, 21 ....*...... 200.00
934.   20 Lire 1815, 32 .... 500.00

PASSERANO

ANONYMOUS, 1581-1598
Eagle. Rev. Cross.

935.   10 Scudi d'oro 1582 .... 12,000.00
Arms. Rev. Cross.

936.   2 Scudi d'oro 1597 .... Rare

PAVIA

Kings of —

ROTARI, 636-652
Bust. Rev. Victory standing.

937.   ⅓ Solidus ND 500.00

CUNIBERT, 686-700
Bust. Rev. St. Michael standing.

938.   ⅓ Solidus ND 500.00

Bust. Rev. Victory standing.

939.   ⅓ Solidus ND 500.00

LUITBERT, 700-701

Bust. Rev. St. Michael standing.

940.   ⅓ Solidus ND 500.00

ARIBERT, 701-712
Bust. Rev. St. Michael standing.

941.   ⅓ Solidus ND 500.00

LUITBRAND, 712-744
Bust. Rev. St. Michael standing.

942.   ⅓ Solidus ND 400.00

RACHIS, 744-749
Bust. Rev. St. Michael standing.

943.   ⅓ Solidus ND 3000.00

ASTOLF, 749-756
St. Michael standing. Rev. Christogram.

944.   ⅓ Solidus ND 2500.00

DESIDERIUS, 756-774
Cross. Rev. Star.

945.   ⅓ Solidus ND 2500.00

CHARLEMAGNE, 744-800
Cross. Rev. Star.

946.   ⅓ Solidus ND 3000.00

PHILIP MARIA, 1402-1412
Horseman. Rev. Arms.

947.   1 Florin ND 6000.00

FRANCIS I, 1447-1450
Ruler on horse. Rev. Crowned serpent.

948.   1 Ducat ND 6000.00

SIEGE OF PAVIA, 1524-1525
Legend. Rev. Legend incused. Square shape.

949.   1 Ducat 1524 .... 6000.00

PERUGIA

(Roman Republic, 1799).
Eagle facing, and below "Perugia." Rev. Value in wreath.

950.   1 Gold Scudo. Year VII (1799) .... Rare

(For additional coins of Perugia, see under Vatican).

PESARO

Dukes of —

JOHN SFORZA, 1489-1510
Bust. Rev. St. Paul standing.

951.   1 Zecchino ND 8000.00

CONSTANCE II SFORZA, 1510-1512
Arms. Rev. St. Paul standing.

952.   1 Scudo d'oro ND .... Rare

FRANCIS MARIA DELLA ROVERE, 1513-1538
Arms. Rev. St. Francis standing.

953.   1 Scudo d'oro ND 1800.00

Plan of fortress. Rev. St. Francis standing.

954.   1 Scudo d'oro ND 2000.00

GUIDOBALD II DELLA ROVERE, 1538-1574

Three pyramids. Rev. Legend.

955.	1 Ducat ND	....	1500.00
956.	½ Ducat ND	..............................*.....	1000.00

PIACENZA

DESIDERIUS, 756-774
Cross. Rev. Star.

956a. ⅓ Solidus ND .... Rare

PIOMBINO

Princes of —

NICHOLAS LUDOVISI, 1634-1665
Madonna. Rev. Arms.

957. 2 Doppie 1651 .... 5000.00
957a. 1 Doppia 1644 .... Rare

JOHN BAPTIST LUDOVISI, 1665-1699

Bust. Rev. Arms.

958. 1 Doppia 1695 .... Rare
959. 1 Zecchino 1695, 96 ....*..... 2500.00

PISA

A. Kings of —

ANONYMOUS, 650-749
Cross. Rev. Star.

960. ⅓ Solidus ND 2000.00

Star. Rev. Cross.

961. ⅓ Solidus ND 2500.00

ASTOLF, 749-756
Cross. Rev. Star.

962. ⅓ Solidus ND 2500.00

DESIDERIUS, 757-778
Cross. Rev. Star.

963. ⅓ Solidus ND 2500.00

CHARLEMAGNE, 774-800
Cross. Rev. Star.

964. ⅓ Solidus ND 1500.00

B. Republic of —

Madonna. Rev. Eagle.

965. 1 Zecchino ND (1313-1494) 1250.00

Madonna. Rev. Cross.

966. 1 Zecchino ND (1495-1509) 1250.00

C. French Rulers of —

CHARLES VIII, 1494-1495
Madonna and child. Rev. Crowned arms.

967. 1 Zecchino ND .... Rare

D. Tuscan Grand Dukes of —

FERDINAND I, 1587-1609
Madonna in clouds. Rev. Cross of Pisa.

968. 2 Doppie 1595 .... 1500.00
969. 1 Doppia 1595 .... 1000.00

FERDINAND II, 1621-1670

Madonna in clouds. Rev. Cross of Pisa.

970. 2 Doppie ND 2000.00
971. 1 Doppia 1641-55, ND ....*..... 500.00
972. ½ Doppia 1643, ND 200.00

COSIMO III, 1670-1723

Madonna in clouds. Rev. Cross of Pisa.

973. 1 Doppia ND 2000.00

PISTOIA

Rose. Rev. Cross.

974. ⅓ Solidus ND (700-800) 1500.00

POMBIA

DESIDERIUS, 756-774
Cross. Rev. Star.

974a. ⅓ Solidus ND 2500.00

POMPONESCO

Marcheses of —

JULIUS CAESAR GONZAGA, 1583-1593
Arms. Rev. Cross.

975. 1 Scudo d'oro ND .... Rare

PORCIA

Princes of —

HANNIBAL ALFONSO EMANUEL, 1704
Bust. Rev. Arms.

976. 1 Ducat 1704 .... Rare

RAVENNA

Kings of —

ASTOLF, 749-756
Bust. Rev. Cross.

977. 1 Solidus ND 3000.00
978. ⅓ Solidus ND 2000.00

REGGIO-EMILIA

Dukes of —

HERCULES I D'ESTE, 1471-1505
Hercules lifting Antaeus. Rev. St. Prospero standing.

979. 1 Ducat ND 3000.00

ALFONSO I D'ESTE, 1505-1534

Bust. Rev. St. Prospero seated.

980. 1 Ducat ND 6000.00

HERCULES II D'ESTE, 1534-1559

Arms. Rev. Christ with cross.

981. 1 Scudo d'oro 1550-58, ND 250.00

ALFONSO II D'ESTE, 1559-1597
Arms. Rev. Christ with cross.

982. 1 Scudo d'oro 1560-72 .... 250.00

Bust. Rev. Nude male with shield.

983. 2 Doppie 1567 .... Rare

Bust. Rev. Eagle.

984. 10 Scudi d'oro 1572 .... Rare

RETEGNO

Barons of —

ANTHONY THEODORE TRIVULZIO, 1676-1678
Ruler on horse. Rev. Bundle of corn ears.

985. 1 Zecchino 1676 .... 1200.00

Bust. Rev. Arms.

986. 10 Zecchini 1677 .... Rare

Soldier standing. Rev. Tablet.

987. 2 Ducats 1677 .... 2000.00
988. 1 Ducat 1677 .... 2200.00

ANTHONY CAIETAN TRIVULZIO, 1679-1705

Bust. Rev. Arms.

989. 10 Zecchini 1686 .... Rare

Soldier standing. Rev. Legend.

990. 2 Doppie ND .... Rare

Soldier standing. Rev. Tablet.

991. 2 Ducats 1686, ND ....*...... 1800.00
992. 1 Ducat 1686, ND 1200.00

ANTHONY PTOLEMY TRIVULZIO, 1708-1767

Bust. Rev. Arms.

993. 1 Ducat 1724, 26 .... 1250.00

RIFREDI

PISAN RULE, 1363
Madonna. Rev. Eagle.

994. 1 Zecchino ND 2500.00

ROME

(See Vatican).

RONCO

Marcheses of —

NAPOLEON SPINOLA, 1647-1672

Bust. Rev. Eagle.

995. 4 Ducats 1647 .... 5000.00
996. 1 Ducat 1668 ....*.... 3000.00

CHARLES SPINOLA
Bust. Rev. Eagle on arms.
997. 1 Doppia ND (1699) 4000.00

SABBIONETA

Dukes of —

VESPASIAN GONZAGA, 1562-1565
Arms. Rev. Cross.
998. 1 Scudo d'oro ND 2500.00

Head. Rev. Madonna.
999. ½ Scudo d'oro ND 2500.00

Three shields. Rev. Cross.
1000. 1 Scudo d'oro ND 3000.00

LUIGI CARAFA AND ISABELLA GONZAGA, 1591-1637
Madonna. Rev. Arms on eagle.
1001. 1 Ducat ND .,.................................... 3000.00

SALERNO

Princes of —

SICONOLFO, 839-849
Bust. Rev. Cross.
1002. 1 Solidus ND 400.00

GISULF I, 935-974

Cufic legend on each side.
1003. 1 Tari ND 150.00

GUAIMARIO IV, 999-1015
Cufic legend on each side.
1004. 1 Tari ND 150.00

ABU TAMIM MUSTANSIR, 1250

Cufic legend on each side.
1005. 1 Tari ND 250.00

GISULF II, 1052-1075
Latin and Cufic legends on each side.
1006. 1 Tari ND 200.00

ROBERT, 1059-1085

Cufic legend on each side.
1007. 1 Tari ND 250.00

ROGER II, 1127-1130
Cufic legend on each side.
1008. 1 Tari ND 150.00

WILLIAM II, 1166-1189

W. Rev. Star and Cufic legend.
1009. 1 Tari ND 200.00

TANCRED, 1189-1194
ACD REX. Rev. Cufic legend.
1010. 1 Tari ND 200.00

SAN GIORGIO

Marcheses of —

JOHN DOMINIC MILANO, 1732
Bust. Rev. Arms.
1011. 2 Zecchini 1732 .... Rare
1012. 1 Zecchino 1732 .... 2500.00

SAN JACOPO AL SERCHIO

FLORENTINE RULE, 1256
St. John standing, trefoil mm. Rev. Lily.
1013. 1 Florin ND 200.00

SARDINIA

(HOUSE OF SAVOY)

Counts, and later, Kings of —

AMADEUS VI, 1343-1383
Lily. Rev. St. John.
1014. 1 Florin ND 8000.00

AMADEUS VII, 1383-1391

Helmeted shield. Rev. St. John.
1015. 1 Florin ND 6000.00

Ruler on throne. Rev. Arms.
1016. 1 Florin ND 7500.00

Helmeted shield. Rev. Cross.
1017. 1 Scudo d'oro ND .... Rare

AMADEUS VIII (DUKE), 1391-1439

Ruler kneeling before St. Maurice. Rev. Helmeted shield.
1018. 1 Ducat ND 4000.00

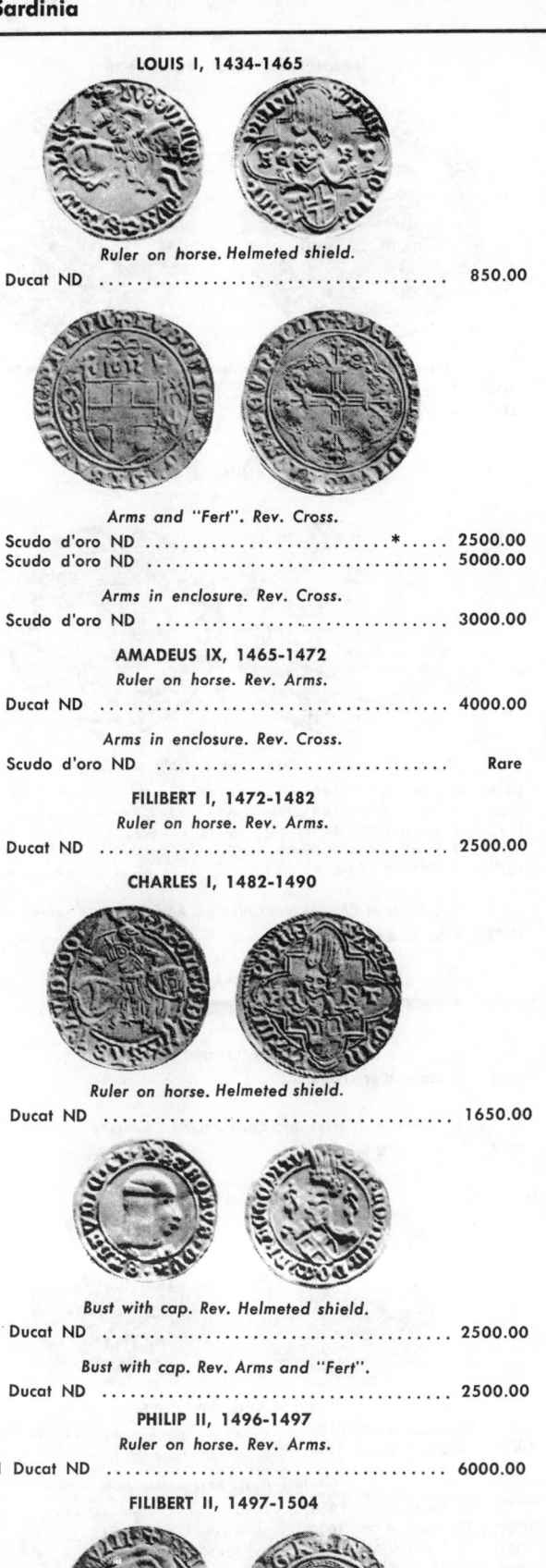

LOUIS I, 1434-1465

Ruler on horse. Helmeted shield.

1019. 1 Ducat ND 850.00

Arms and "Fert". Rev. Cross.

1020. 1 Scudo d'oro ND ....*..... 2500.00
1021. ½ Scudo d'oro ND 5000.00

Arms in enclosure. Rev. Cross.

1022. 1 Scudo d'oro ND 3000.00

AMADEUS IX, 1465-1472
Ruler on horse. Rev. Arms.

1023. 1 Ducat ND 4000.00

Arms in enclosure. Rev. Cross.

1024. 1 Scudo d'oro ND .... Rare

FILIBERT I, 1472-1482
Ruler on horse. Rev. Arms.

1025. 1 Ducat ND 2500.00

CHARLES I, 1482-1490

Ruler on horse. Helmeted shield.

1026. 1 Ducat ND 1650.00

Bust with cap. Rev. Helmeted shield.

1027. 1 Ducat ND 2500.00

Bust with cap. Rev. Arms and "Fert".

1028. 1 Ducat ND 2500.00

PHILIP II, 1496-1497
Ruler on horse. Rev. Arms.

1029. 1 Ducat ND 6000.00

FILIBERT II, 1497-1504

Bust with cap. Rev. Arms and "Fert".

1030.   The coin previously listed does not exist. .... ——
1031.   1 Ducat ND ....*.... 6000.00

CHARLES II, 1504-1553
Armored bust. Rev. Arms.

1032. 10 Ducats 1546 .... Rare

Crowned bust. Rev. Arms between two K's.

1033. 1 Ducat ND 6000.00

Bust with cap. Rev. Arms and "Fert".

1034. 1 Ducat ND .... Unknown

Ruler on horse. Rev. Arms.

1035. 1 Scudo d'oro ND 2500.00

Arms and "Fert". Rev. Cross.

1036. 1 Scudo d'oro ND 1800.00

Arms. Rev. Ornate cross.

1037. 1 Scudo d'oro ND 1800.00

Arms. Rev. St. Maurice on horse.

1038. 1 Scudo d'oro ND 2500.00

EMANUEL FILIBERT, 1553-1580
Arms. Rev. Cross.

1039. 1 Scudo d'oro ND. Broad type 1500.00

Arms and "Fert." Rev. Cross.

1039a. 1 Scudo d'oro ND. Broad type 1500.00

Oval shield. Rev. Cross.

1039b. 1 Scudo d'oro 1555-71 .... 350.00

Arms. Rev. Small cross on large cross.

1040. 1 Doppia 1576-80 .... 3000.00
1041. 1 Scudo d'oro 1570-80 ....*.... 600.00

Bust. Rev. Arms.

1042. 1 Doppia 1570-76 .... 2200.00

Armored bust. Rev. Elephant.

1043.	9 Lire ND	Rare

Busts of the Royal couple. Rev. Serpent.

1044.	3 Filibertos ND	Rare

CHARLES EMANUEL I, 1580-1630

Armored bust. Rev. Arms.

1045.	10 Ducats 1607-28	Rare
1046.	10 Scudi d'oro 1623	Rare
1047.	4 Scudi d'oro 1586, 87	8000.00
1048.	2 Doppie 1595, 98, 1601, ND	4000.00
1049.	1 Doppia 1580-1611, ND ....*....	1500.00

Bust. Rev. Cross.

1050.	1 Scudo d'oro 1627	Rare
1051.	½ Scudo d'oro 1627	Rare

Bust. Rev. Legend.

1052.	1 Scudo d'oro 1630	8000.00

Bust. Rev. Compass.

1053.	10 Scudi d'oro 1630	Rare

Arms. Rev. Cross.

1054.	1 Doppia 1581	3000.00
1055.	1 Scudo d'oro 1580-91	1500.00

Madonna. Rev. Arms.

1056.	1 Ducat 1601, 02	400.00

VICTOR AMADEUS I, 1630-1637
Bust. Rev. Three flags.

1057.	10 Scudi d'oro 1633	Rare
1058.	4 Scudi d'oro 1633, 34 ....10,000.00	
1059.	2 Doppie 1632	Rare

Bust. Rev. Arms.

1060.	30 Scudi d'oro 1635	Rare
1061.	20 Scudi d'oro 1635	Rare
1062.	10 Scudi d'oro 1633, 34, 35, 36 ....*....	Rare
1063.	4 Scudi d'oro 1634, ND	8000.00
1064.	1 Doppia ND	8000.00

Bust. Rev. Cross.

1065.	10 Scudi d'oro 1635	Rare

FRANCIS HYACINT, 1637-1638

Busts of Francis and his mother, Christina. Rev. Madonna.

1066.	8 Scudi d'oro ND	Rare
1067.	4 Scudi d'oro ND ....*....	8000.00

CHARLES EMANUEL II, 1638-1675

Busts of Charles and Christina to right or left. Rev. Arms.

1068.	20 Scudi d'oro 1641	Rare
1069.	10 Scudi d'oro 1641, 68	Rare
1070.	8 Scudi d'oro 1641, ND	Rare
1071.	4 Scudi d'oro 1639-48 ....*....	1000.00
1072.	1 Doppia 1640, 41	4000.00

Busts of Charles and Christina. Rev. Arms and value.

1073.	4 Scudi d'oro 1642	6000.00

Busts of Charles and Christina. Rev. Madonna.

1074.	8 Scudi d'oro ND	6000.00

Arms. Rev. Crossed initials.

1075.	1 Scudo d'oro ND	3000.00

Busts of Charles and Christina. Rev. Crossed initials.

1076.	½ Scudo d'oro ND	4000.00

Youthful bust. Rev. Arms.

1077.	10 Scudi d'oro 1639	Rare
1078.	4 Scudi d'oro 1639, 40 ....*....	8000.00

Mature bust. Rev. Arms.

1079.	40 Scudi d'oro 1656	Rare
1080.	30 Scudi d'oro 1656	Rare
1081.	20 Scudi d'oro 1649-71	Rare
1082.	10 Scudi d'oro 1649-71	Rare
1083.	4 Scudi d'oro 1649-54	8000.00
1084.	1 Doppia 1650-54	2000.00
1085.	½ Scudo d'oro 1649	Rare

Bust. Rev. Crossed initials.

1085a.	1 Doppia 1670	Rare
1086.	1 Scudo d'oro 1670	5000.00

Head. Rev. Arms.

1087. 1 Doppia 1675 .... 1500.00

Head. Rev. Cross.

1088. 1 Scudo d'oro ND .... Rare

VICTOR AMADEUS II, 1675-1730

Busts of Victor and Maria Joan. Rev. Arms.

1089. 5 Doppie 1675, 78 .... 8000.00
1090. 1 Doppia 1675-80 ....*..... 1000.00
1091. ½ Doppia 1675-79 .... 700.00

Busts of Victor and Maria Joan. Rev. Seated female and cherub.

1092. 2 Doppie 1675-77 .... 10,000.00

Youthful bust. Rev. Arms and lions.

1093. 20 Scudi d'oro 1684 .... Rare
1094. 10 Scudi d'oro 1680, 84 .... Rare

Ruler on horse. Rev. Justice standing.

1095. 5 Doppie 1694 .... Rare

Youthful bust. Rev. Arms.

1096. 2 Doppie 1680 .... Rare
1097. 1 Doppia 1680-82 .... 6000.00
1098. ½ Doppia 1680, 81 .... 5000.00

Older bust. Rev. Arms.

1099. 1 Doppia 1690-1706 .... Rare
1100. ½ Doppia 1692-1709 .... Rare

Older bust. Rev. Arms. With title of King of Sicily.

1100a. 1 Doppia 1714-18 .... 4500.00

CHARLES EMANUEL III, 1730-1773

Bust. Rev. Arms.

1101. 1 Doppia 1733-41 .... 6000.00
1102. ½ Doppia 1733-42 .... 4000.00

Head. Rev. Arms.

1103. 5 Doppie 1755-68 .... 5000.00
1104. 2½ Doppie 1755, 56, 57 .... 5000.00
1105. 1 Doppia 1755-69 .... 800.00
1106. ½ Doppia 1755-70 ....*..... 400.00
1107. ¼ Doppia 1755-58 .... 750.00

Bust. Rev. Oval shield of Sardinia.

1108. 5 Doppie 1768, 69 .... 6000.00
1109. 2½ Doppie 1768-71 ....*..... 2500.00
1110. 1 Doppia 1768-72 .... 450.00

Eagle. Rev. The Annunciation.

1111. 4 Zecchini 1745, 46 ....*..... 2600.00
1112. 1 Zecchino 1743-46 .... 400.00
1113. ½ Zecchino 1744-46 .... 300.00

Madonna. Rev. Angel.

1114. ⅛ Zecchino ND 3000.00
1114a. ⅛ Zecchino ND .... Rare

VICTOR AMADEUS III, 1773-1796

Head. Rev. Arms.

1115. 1 Doppia 1773-82 .... 2400.00
1116. ½ Doppia 1773-84 .... 1500.00
1117. ¼ Doppia 1773-85 .... 1000.00

Head. Rev. Eagle.

1118. 5 Doppie 1786 .... 4000.00
1119. 2½ Doppie 1786 .... 1500.00
1120. 1 Doppia 1786-96 .... 300.00
1121. ½ Doppia 1786-96 ....*..... 150.00
1122. ¼ Doppia 1786 ....*..... 300.00

Bust. Rev. Oval shield of Sardinia.

1123. 5 Doppie 1773-84 .... 5000.00
1124. 2½ Doppie 1773-84 .... 3000.00
1125. 1 Doppia 1773-86 ....*..... 1000.00

CHARLES EMANUEL IV, 1796-1802

Head. Rev. Eagle.

1126. 1 Doppia 1797-1800 ....*..... 900.00
1127. ½ Doppia 1797, 98 .... 650.00

VICTOR EMANUEL I, 1802-1821

Head. Rev. Eagle.

1128. 1 Doppia 1814, 15 .... 3500.00

Head. Rev. Square shield in circle.

1129. 20 Lire 1816-20 .... 175.00

Head. Rev. Oval shield within branches.

1130. 80 Lire 1821 ....*.... 5000.00
1131. 20 Lire 1821 .... 2000.00

CHARLES FELIX, 1821-1831

Head. Rev. Arms.

1132. 80 Lire 1823-31. Eagle's head mm. 250.00
1133. 80 Lire 1824-31. Anchor mm. ....*..... 250.00
1134. 40 Lire 1822-31. Eagle's head mm. 300.00
1135. 40 Lire 1825, 26. Anchor mm. 500.00
1136. 20 Lire 1821-31. Eagle's head mm. 80.00
1137. 20 Lire 1824-31. Anchor mm. 500.00

CHARLES ALBERT, 1831-1849

Head. Rev. Arms.

1138. 100 Lire 1832-44. Eagle's head mm. 250.00
1139. 100 Lire 1832-45. Anchor mm. ....*..... 250.00
1140. 50 Lire 1832-43. Eagle's head mm. 500.00
1141. 50 Lire 1833, 35, 41. Anchor mm. 700.00
1142. 20 Lire 1831-49. Eagle's head mm. 50.00
1143. 20 Lire 1831-49. Anchor mm. 50.00
1144. 10 Lire 1832-47. Eagle's head mm. 400.00
1145. 10 Lire 1833-47. Anchor mm. ....*..... 500.00

VICTOR EMANUEL II, 1849-1861

Head. Rev. Arms.

1146. 20 Lire 1850-61. Eagle's head mm. 45.00
1147. 20 Lire 1850-60. Anchor mm. ....*.... 45.00
1148. 20 Lire 1860. M mm. 120.00
1149. 10 Lire 1850-60. Eagle's head mm. 400.00
1150. 10 Lire 1850. Anchor mm. 800.00

(For the later coins of Victor Emanuel II, as King of all Italy, see under Italy, Kings of —).

SAVONA

St. John. Rev. Lily.

1151. 1 Florin ND (1350-96) 500.00

Madonna and child flanked by two lis. Rev. Eagle. Struck under Louis XII of France.

1152. 2 Ducats ND (1499-1510) .... Rare
1153. 1 Ducat ND (1499-1510) 6000.00

SAVOY, HOUSE OF

(See Sardinia).

SICILY

(See Messina and Palermo).

SIENA

A. Republic of —

S. Rev. Cross.

1154. 1 Florin ND (1340-1450) 1000.00
1155. 1 Sanese d'oro ND (1375-90) ....*..... 600.00
1156. 1 Ducat ND (1450-1550) 800.00
1157. ½ Ducat 1553-55, ND 1000.00
1158. ½ Scudo d'oro 1549-53 .... 1000.00

Madonna. Rev. Victory standing.

159. 2 Ducats ND .... **Rare**

She-wolf in shield. Rev. Cross.

160. 1 Scudo d'oro ND (1533-48) **800.00**

She-wolf. Rev. Cross.

161. 1 Scudo d'oro 1548-54, ND **1200.00**

Madonna. Rev. Cross.

162. 1 Scudo d'oro 1549 .... **1200.00**

Madonna. Rev. St. Victorius standing.

163. 3 Doppie 1550 .... **Rare**

B. Rulers of —

JOHN GALEAZZO, 1390-1404

S. Rev. Cross.

164. 1 Sanese d'oro ND **600.00**

COSIMO I, 1557-1574
Arms. Rev. Cross.

165. 1 Scudo d'oro ND **1200.00**

HENRY II OF FRANCE, 1547-1559
Madonna and child. Rev. She-wolf.

166. 4 Ecu d'or 1556 .... **Rare**

She-wolf. Rev. Band across oval shield.

167. 1 Ecu d'or 1557 .... **Rare**

S. Rev. Band across oval shield.

168. ½ Ecu d'or ND **3000.00**

SOLFERINO

Marcheses of —

CHARLES GONZAGA, 1643-1678
Bust. Rev. Arms.

169. 2 Florins ND **3000.00**

Ruler standing. Rev. Arms.

1170. 1 Ducat ND **2000.00**

SORAGNA

Princes of —

NICHOLAS MELI-LUPI, 1731-1741

Arms. Rev. Eagle.

1171. 1 Scudo d'oro 1731 .... **3500.00**

SUB-ALPINE REPUBLIC

Helmeted female head. Rev. Value and date. On the Victory of Marengo. Struck at Turin.

1172. 20 Francs. Years 9 and 10 (1800, 01) **425.00**

TASSAROLO

Counts of —

AUGUSTIN SPINOLA, 1604-1616
Bust. Rev. Arms.

1173. 5 Doppie 1604 .... **6000.00**
1174. 2 Doppie 1604 .... **3000.00**

Bust of Rudolph II. Rev. Eagle.

1175. 1 Ducat 1604 .... **3000.00**

Soldier standing. Rev. Tablet.

1176. 1 Ducat 1611, 12, ND **1600.00**

Soldier standing. Rev. Eagle.

1177. 1 Ducat ND **1000.00**

Soldier standing. Rev. Arms.

1178. 1 Ducat ND **1000.00**

Madonna. Rev. Arms.

1179. 1 Ducat 1614 .... **2500.00**

Eagle. Rev. St. Nicholas.

1180. 1 Doppia ND 3500.00

PHILIP SPINOLA, 1616-1688

Bust. Rev. Arms.

1181. 2 Doppie 1629 ....*..... 6000.00
1182. 1 Doppia 1630 .... 3000.00

Bust. Rev. St. Charles in fire.

1183. 2 Doppie 1640 .... 6000.00
1184. 1 Doppia 1640 .... 3000.00

Soldier standing. Rev. Eagle.

1185. 1 Ducat 1637 .... 1000.00

Soldier standing. Rev. Tablet.

1186. 1 Ducat ND 1000.00

Rose. Rev. Tablet.

1187. 1 Ducat ND 1200.00

Eagle Rev. Bishop.

1188. 2 Doppie ND 6000.00

TRENTO

Bishops of —

PETER VIGILIO, 1776-1796
Bust. Rev. Arms and eagle.

1189. 1 Ducat 1776 .... 1000.00

TRESANA

Marcheses of —

WILLIAM II, 1613-1651
St. Ladislas standing. Rev. Madonna.

1190. 1 Ducat 1620 .... 1000.00

St. Louis standing. Rev. Eagle.

1191. 1 Ducat ND 1000.00

Soldier standing. Rev. Tablet.

1192. 1 Ducat 1619 .... 1000.00

Arab legend on each side. Struck for use in the Levant.

1193. 1 Dinar ND 1000.0

TREVISO

DESIDERIUS, 757-773
Cross. Rev. Star.

1194. ⅓ Solidus ND 2500.0

TUSCANY

(For the coins of the Grand Dukes of Tuscany, see under Florence, Leghorn and Pisa).

Government of —

St. John seated. Rev. Lily. Struck at Florence.

1195. 1 Ruspone 1859 .... 1400.0

URBINO

Dukes of —

GUIDOBALD I, 1482-1508

Bust. Rev. Eagle and shield.

1196. 1 Ducat ND 4000.0

FRANCIS MARIA I, 1508-1538

Bust. Rev. Eagle and shield.

1197. 1 Ducat ND 1200.0

Helmeted bust. Rev. Eagle and shield.

1198. 1 Ducat ND 1500.0

LORENZO, 1516-1519
Bust. Rev. Arms.

1199. 1 Ducat ND .... 4000.

GUIDOBALD II, 1538-1574
Head. Rev. Arms.

1200. 4 Scudi d'oro ND .... 4000.

Bust. Rev. Legend.

1201. 1 Ducat ND 4000.00

Arms. Rev. The Annunciation.

1202. 1 Ducat ND 1500.00

St. Helen and cross. Rev. Arms.

1203. 1 Ducat ND 1250.00

Plant. Rev. Winged thunderbolt.

1204. ¼ Ducat ND 1000.00

FRANCIS MARIA II, 1574-1624

Bust. Rev. Arms.

1205. 20 Scudi d'oro 1604 .... Rare
1206. 10 Scudi d'oro 1603, 21 .... Rare
1207. 1 Scudo d'oro ND ....*..... 1500.00

Arms. Rev. Tree.

1208. 4 Scudi d'oro ND 3000.00
1209. 1 Scudo d'oro ND ....*..... 1800.00

St. Michael standing. Rev. Arms.

1210. 1 Scudo d'oro ND 600.00

St. Francis standing. Rev. Fortress.

1211. 1 Scudo d'oro ND 1200.00

VASTO

Marcheses of —

CAESAR D'AVALOS, 1704-1729

Bust. Rev. Arms.

1212. 20 Zecchini 1706 .... Rare
1213. 1 Zecchino 1706 .... 3500.00
1214. ½ Zecchino 1707 ....*..... 2500.00

VENICE

Doges of —

TYPE I

Doge kneeling before standing figure of St. Mark. Rev. Christ standing within stars. The following coins are undated.

JOHN DANDOLO, 1280-1289
1215. 1 Ducat 500.00

PETER GRADENIGO, 1289-1311
1216. 1 Ducat 100.00

MARINO ZORZI, 1311-1312
1217. 1 Ducat 900.00

JOHN SORANZO, 1312-1328
1218. 1 Ducat 100.00

FRANCIS DANDOLO, 1329-1339
1219. 1 Ducat 80.00

BARTHOLOMEW GRADENIGO, 1339-1342
1220. 1 Ducat 80.00

ANDREW DANDOLO, 1343-1354
1221. 1 Ducat 80.00

MARINO FALIER, 1354-1355
1222. 1 Ducat 2700.00

JOHN GRADENIGO, 1355-1356
1223. 1 Ducat 100.00

JOHN DELFINO, 1356-1361
1224. 1 Ducat 70.00

LORENZO CELSI, 1361-1365
1225. 1 Ducat 70.00

MARCO CORNER, 1365-1368
1226. 1 Ducat 80.00

ANDREW CONTARINI, 1368-1382
1227. 1 Ducat 70.00

MICHAEL MOROSINI, 1382
1228. 1 Ducat 600.00

ANTHONY VENIER, 1382-1400
1229. 1 Ducat 70.00

MICHAEL STENO, 1400-1413
1230. 1 Ducat 70.00

THOMAS MOCENIGO, 1414-1423
1231. 1 Ducat 80.00

FRANCIS FOSCARI, 1423-1457
1232. 1 Ducat 70.00

PASQUALE MALIPIERO, 1457-1462
1233. 1 Ducat 80.00

CHRISTOPHER MORO, 1462-1471
1234. 1 Ducat 100.00

NICHOLAS TRONO, 1471-1474
1235. 1 Ducat 1000.00

NICHOLAS MARCELLO, 1473-1474
1236. 1 Ducat ....* 2000.00

PETER MOCENIGO, 1474-1476
1237. 1 Ducat 2000.00

ANDREW VENDRAMIN, 1476-1478
1238. 1 Ducat 250.00

JOHN MOCENIGO, 1478-1485
1239. 1 Ducat 250.00

MARCO BARBARIGO, 1485-1486
1240. 1 Ducat 4000.00

AUGUSTIN BARBARIGO, 1486-1501
1241. 1 Ducat 100.00

LEONARDO LOREDANO, 1501-1521
1242. 1 Ducat 80.00
1243. ½ Ducat 600.00

ANTHONY GRIMANI, 1521-1523
1244. 1 Ducat 3500.00
1245. ½ Ducat 1500.00

ANDREW GRITTI, 1523-1539
1246. 1 Ducat 80.00
1247. ½ Ducat 850.00

PETER LANDO, 1539-1545
1248. 1 Ducat 90.00
1249. ½ Ducat 850.00

FRANCIS DONA, 1545-1553
1250. 1 Zecchino 80.00

MARC ANTHONY TREVISANI, 1553-1554
1251. 1 Zecchino 125.00
1252. ½ Zecchino 850.00

FRANCIS VENIER, 1554-1556
1253. 1 Zecchino 250.00
1254. ½ Zecchino 850.00

LORENZO PRIULI, 1556-1559
1255. 1 Zecchino 70.00
1256. ½ Zecchino 850.00

GIROLAMO PRIULI, 1559-1567
1257. 1 Zecchino 70.00
1258. ½ Zecchino 800.00

PETER LOREDANO, 1567-1570
1259. 1 Zecchino 70.00
1260. ½ Zecchino 800.00
1261. ¼ Zecchino 100.00

ALOIS MOCENIGO I, 1570-1577
1262. 2 Zecchini 2500.00
1263. 1 Zecchino 70.00

SEBASTIAN VENIER, 1577-1578
1264. 1 Zecchino 800.00
1265. ½ Zecchino 850.00
1266. ¼ Zecchino 500.00

NICHOLAS DAPONTE, 1578-1585
1267. 1 Zecchino 70.00
1268. ½ Zecchino 700.00
1269. ¼ Zecchino 600.00

PASQUALE CICOGNA, 1585-1595
1270. 1 Zecchino 70.00
1271. ½ Zecchino 850.00
1272. ¼ Zecchino 600.00

MARINO GRIMANI, 1595-1605
1273. 10 Zecchini 6500.00
1274. 1 Zecchino 70.00
1275. ½ Zecchino 150.00
1276. ¼ Zecchino 150.00

LEONARDO DONA, 1605-1612
1277. 15 Zecchini 6500.00
1278. 1 Zecchino 100.00
1279. ½ Zecchino 100.00
1280. ¼ Zecchino 100.00

MARC ANTHONY MEMMO, 1612-1615
1281. 1 Zecchino 300.00
1282. ½ Zecchino 300.00
1283. ¼ Zecchino 350.00

JOHN BEMBO, 1615-1618
1284. 1 Zecchino 500.00
1285. ½ Zecchino 1500.00
1286. ¼ Zecchino 1200.00

NICHOLAS DONA, 1618
1287. 1 Zecchino 1500.00
1288. ¼ Zecchino 1200.00

ANTHONY PRIULI, 1618-1623
1289. 5 Zecchini 5000.00
1290. 2 Zecchini 1200.00
1291. 1 Zecchino 70.00
1292. ½ Zecchino 100.00
1293. ¼ Zecchino 100.00

FRANCIS CONTARINI, 1623-1624
1294. 1 Zecchino 1300.00
1295. ½ Zecchino 1000.00
1296. ¼ Zecchino 600.00

JOHN CORNER I, 1625-1629
1297. 1 Zecchino 5000.00
1298. ½ Zecchino 1000.00
1299. ¼ Zecchino 1000.00

NICHOLAS CONTARINI, 1630-1631
1300. 25 Zecchini .... Ra
1301. 20 Zecchini 6500.00
1302. 15 Zecchini .... Ra
1303. 10 Zecchini 5000.00
1304. 5 Zecchini 5000.00
1305. 3 Zecchini 3000.00
1306. 2 Zecchini 4000.00
1307. 1 Zecchino 2000.00
1308. ½ Zecchino 1000.00
1309. ¼ Zecchino 800.00

FRANCIS ERIZZO, 1631-1646
1310. 1 Zecchino 70.00
1311. ½ Zecchino 200.00
1312. ¼ Zecchino 180.00

FRANCIS MOLIN, 1646-1655
1313. 20 Zecchini 6000.00
1314. 15 Zecchini 5000.00
1315. 12 Zecchini 4000.00
1316. 10 Zecchini 3500.00
1317. 7 Zecchini 3000.00
1318. 1 Zecchino 60.00
1319. ½ Zecchino 600.00
1320. ¼ Zecchino 400.00

CHARLES CONTARINI, 1655-1656
1321. 1 Zecchino 150.00
1322. ½ Zecchino 800.00
1323. ¼ Zecchino 700.00

FRANCIS CORNER, 1656

1324.	1 Zecchino	2000.00
1325.	½ Zecchino	1000.00

BERTUCCIO VALIER, 1656-1658

1326.	1 Zecchino	120.00
1327.	½ Zecchino	1000.00
1328.	¼ Zecchino	800.00

JOHN PESARO, 1658-1659

1329.	1 Zecchino	250.00
1330.	½ Zecchino	1000.00
1331.	¼ Zecchino	600.00

DOMINIC CONTARINI, 1659-1674

1332.	1 Zecchino	80.00
1333.	½ Zecchino	200.00
1334.	¼ Zecchino	150.00

NICHOLAS SAGREDO, 1675-1676

1335.	1 Zecchino	250.00
1336.	½ Zecchino	1000.00
1337.	¼ Zecchino	600.00

ALOIS CONTARINI, 1676-1684

1338.	1 Zecchino	70.00
1339.	½ Zecchino	1000.00
1340.	¼ Zecchino	250.00

MARC ANTHONY GIUSTIMANI, 1684-1688

1341.	1 Zecchino	80.00
1342.	½ Zecchino	400.00
1343.	¼ Zecchino	800.00

FRANCIS MOROSINI, 1688-1694

1344.	10 Zecchini	2500.00
1345.	8 Zecchini	3000.00
1346.	6 Zecchini	2500.00
1347.	1 Zecchino	80.00
1348.	½ Zecchino	500.00
1349.	¼ Zecchino	400.00

SILVESTER VALIER, 1694-1700

1350.	25 Zecchini	10,000.00
1351.	15 Zecchini	6000.00
1352.	12 Zecchini	6000.00
1353.	10 Zecchini	2500.00
1354.	1 Zecchino	80.00
1355.	½ Zecchino	500.00
1356.	¼ Zecchino	400.00

ALOIS MOCENIGO II, 1700-1709

1357.	10 Zecchini	2500.00
1358.	1 Zecchino	60.00
1359.	½ Zecchino	100.00
1360.	¼ Zecchino	80.00

JOHN CORNER II, 1709-1722

1361.	40 Zecchini	10,000.00
1362.	36 Zecchini	10,000.00
1363.	33 Zecchini	10,000.00
1364.	25 Zecchini	8000.00
1365.	20 Zecchini	6000.00
1366.	16 Zecchini	6000.00
1367.	15 Zecchini	5000.00
1368.	12 Zecchini	3000.00
1369.	10 Zecchini	2500.00
1370.	8 Zecchini	2500.00
1371.	2 Zecchini	1200.00
1372.	1 Zecchino	60.00
1373.	½ Zecchino	1000.00
1374.	¼ Zecchino	600.00

ALOIS MOCENIGO III, 1722-1732

1375.	60 Zecchini	10,000.00
1376.	50 Zecchini	10,000.00
1377.	10 Zecchini	2500.00
1378.	4 Zecchini	2500.00
1379.	1 Zecchino	60.00
1380.	½ Zecchino	100.00
1381.	¼ Zecchino	80.00

CHARLES RUZZINI, 1732-1735

1382.	10 Zecchini	3500.00
1383.	3 Zecchini	3000.00
1384.	1 Zecchino	80.00
1385.	½ Zecchino	100.00
1386.	¼ Zecchino	80.00

ALOIS PISANI, 1735-1741

1387.	40 Zecchini	10,000.00
1388.	30 Zecchini	8000.00
1389.	16 Zecchini	5000.00
1390.	10 Zecchini	3000.00
1391.	1 Zecchino	70.00
1392.	½ Zecchino	100.00
1393.	¼ Zecchino	80.00

PETER GRIMANI, 1741-1752

1394.	50 Zecchini	8000.00
1395.	28 Zecchini	6000.00
1396.	25 Zecchini	6000.00
1397.	22 Zecchini	5000.00
1398.	15 Zecchini	5000.00
1399.	10 Zecchini	4500.00
1400.	2 Zecchini	1500.00
1401.	1 Zecchino	70.00
1402.	½ Zecchino	100.00
1403.	¼ Zecchino	100.00

FRANCIS LOREDANO, 1752-1762

1404.	2 Zecchini	1500.00
1405.	1 Zecchino	70.00
1406.	½ Zecchino	100.00
1407.	¼ Zecchino	100.00

MARCO FOSCARINI, 1762-1763

1408.	1 Zecchino	100.00
1409.	½ Zecchino	150.00
1410.	¼ Zecchino	300.00

ALOIS MOCENIGO IV, 1763-1778

1411.	100 Zecchini	Rare
1412.	60 Zecchini	10,000.00
1413.	50 Zecchini	10,000.00
1414.	30 Zecchini	8000.00
1415.	25 Zecchini	6000.00
1416.	20 Zecchini	5000.00
1417.	18 Zecchini	4500.00
1418.	12 Zecchini	3500.00
1419.	10 Zecchini	3000.00
1420.	8 Zecchini	2500.00
1421.	1 Zecchino	50.00
1422.	½ Zecchino	80.00
1423.	¼ Zecchino	80.00

PAUL RAINIER, 1779-1789

1424.	55 Zecchini	6500.00
1425.	50 Zecchini	6500.00
1426.	40 Zecchini	6500.00
1427.	30 Zecchini	6000.00
1428.	24 Zecchini	6000.00
1429.	18 Zecchini	5000.00
1430.	12 Zecchini	2500.00
1431.	10 Zecchini	2000.00
1432.	8 Zecchini	2000.00
1433.	4 Zecchini	1500.00
1434.	1 Zecchino	90.00
1435.	½ Zecchino	80.00
1436.	¼ Zecchino	80.00

LOUIS MANIN, 1789-1797

1437.	105 Zecchini	12,000.00
1438.	50 Zecchini	8000.00
1439.	10 Zecchini	* 2500.00
1440.	9 Zecchini	2500.00
1441.	8 Zecchini	2000.00
1442.	6 Zecchini	2000.00
1443.	5 Zecchini	1800.00
1444.	2 Zecchini	800.00
1445.	1 Zecchino	60.00
1446.	½ Zecchino	80.00
1447.	¼ Zecchino	80.00

(For Austrian type coins struck at Venice and bearing the "V" mint mark, see under Austria.)

TYPE II

Cross. Rev. Lion in shield. The following coins are undated.

ANDREW GRITTI, 1523-1539

1448.	1 Scudo d'oro	100.00
1449.	½ Scudo d'oro	100.00

PETER LANDO, 1539-1545

1450.	1 Scudo d'oro	200.00
1451.	½ Scudo d'oro	1000.00

FRANCIS DONA, 1545-1553

1452.	1 Scudo d'oro	500.00
1453.	½ Scudo d'oro	1000.00

FRANCIS VENIER, 1554-1556

1454.	1 Scudo d'oro	600.00
1455.	½ Scudo d'oro	500.00

ANTHONY PRIULI, 1618-1623

1456.	2 Scudi d'oro	1400.00
1457.	1 Scudo d'oro	1600.00

FRANCIS CONTARINI, 1623-1624

1458.	2 Scudi d'oro *	500.00
1459.	1 Scudo d'oro	1000.00

JOHN CORNER I, 1625-1629

1460.	2 Scudi d'oro	750.00
1461.	1 Scudo d'oro	400.00

NICHOLAS CONTARINI, 1630-1631

1462.	2 Scudi d'oro	1000.00
1463.	1 Scudo d'oro	2000.00

FRANCIS ERIZZO, 1631-1646

1464.	2 Scudi d'oro	2000.00
1465.	1 Scudo d'oro	2500.00

FRANCIS CORNER, 1656

1466.	1 Scudo d'oro	3000.00

BERTUCCIO VALIER, 1656-1658

1467.	2 Scudi d'oro	3000.00

NICHOLAS SAGREDO, 1675-1676

1468.	2 Scudi d'oro	3000.00

SILVESTER VALIER, 1694-1700

1469.	2 Scudi d'oro	3000.00
1470.	1 Scudo d'oro	3000.00

JOHN CORNER II, 1709-1722

1471.	1 Scudo d'oro	3000.00

ALOIS MOCENIGO III, 1722-1732

1472.	½ Scudo d'oro	1500.00

CHARLES RUZZINI, 1732-1735

1473.	½ Scudo d'oro	1500.00

ALOIS PISANI, 1735-1741

1474.	2 Scudi d'oro	2500.00
1475.	½ Scudo d'oro	2000.00

PETER GRIMANI, 1741-1752

1476.	1 Scudo d'oro	2000.00

FRANCIS LOREDANO, 1752-1762

1477.	2 Scudi d'oro	2500.00
1478.	1 Scudo d'oro	2000.00
1479.	½ Scudo d'oro	1400.00

MARCO FOSCARINI, 1762-1763

1480.	2 Scudi d'oro	2500.00
1481.	1 Scudo d'oro	2000.00
1482.	½ Scudo d'oro	1400.00

ALOIS MOCENIGO IV, 1763-1778

1483.	2 Scudi d'oro	2000.00
1484.	1 Scudo d'oro	1500.00
1485.	½ Scudo d'oro	1000.00

PAUL RAINIER, 1779-1789

1486.	2 Scudi d'oro	2000.00
1487.	1 Scudo d'oro	1500.00
1488.	½ Scudo d'oro	1000.00

LOUIS MANIN, 1789-1797

1489.	2 Scudi d'oro	500.00
1490.	1 Scudo d'oro	300.00
1491.	½ Scudo d'oro	300.00

TYPE III

Doge kneeling before St. Mark seated. Rev. Lion. The following coins are undated.

LEONARDO DONA, 1605-1612

1492.	2 Ducats	3000.00
1493.	1 Ducat *	300.00
1494.	½ Ducat	250.00

NICHOLAS DONA, 1618

1495.	1 Ducat	3000.00

ANTHONY PRIULI, 1618-1623

1496.	1 Ducat	2000.00

JOHN CORNER I, 1625-1629

1497.	1 Ducat	3000.00

DOMINIC CONTARINI, 1659-1674

1498.	10 Ducats	3000.00

TYPE IV
Doge kneeling and lion. Rev. St. Justina standing.

LEONARDO DONA, 1605-1612

1499.	1 Ducat ND	2500.00

TYPE V
Doge kneeling before St. Mark. Rev. Christ on pedestal.

LEONARDO DONA, 1605-1612

1500.	1 Ducat ND	1000.00

TYPE VI

Lion on pedestal. Rev. Value. Struck under the Provisional Government of Venice.

1501.	20 Lire 1848	500.00

VENTIMIGLIA

Head of John VI. Rev. Arms.

1502.	2 Zecchini 1725	Rare

VERCELLI

DESIDERIUS, 757-773
Cross. Rev. Star.

1503. ⅓ Solidus ND .... Rare

Bust of Charles Emanuel of Sardinia. Rev. Legend. Siege Issue.

1503a. 4 Scudi d'oro 1617 .... Rare

Arms. Rev. Legend. Siege Issue.

1504. 1 Doppia 1638 .... 6000.00

VERONA

HENRY II, 1013-1024
Cross on each side.

1505. 1 Gold Denarius ND .... Rare

MAXIMILIAN I, 1509-1516

Bust. Rev. St. Zeno seated.

1506. 1 Ducat ND 12,000.00

VICENZA

DESIDERIUS, 756-774
Cross. Rev. Star.

1507. ⅓ Solidus ND .... Rare

JAMAICA

Gold coins of Spain or Spanish-American Mints counter-stamped GR (George III of England) in a circular depression.

1. 8 Escudos 1732-1820. .... 2000.00
2. 4 Escudos 1733-1820. .... 2000.00
3. 2 Escudos 1733-1820. ....*..... 1500.00
4. 1 Escudo 1733-1820. .... 1250.00
5. ½ Escudo 1744-1820. .... 1250.00

JAPAN

Emperors of —
A. Odd-Shaped Pieces of the Old Coinage

Oval shaped pieces averaging about 150 x 100 millimetres and characterized by seals punched into the metal and by legends applied with ink. The dates given are approximate.

OBANS OR 10 TAEL PIECES

1. Tensho Oban 1591. Diamond shaped seals .... Rare
2. Tensho Naga Oban 1591. Round seals .... Rare

3. Keicho Oban 1601 .... Rare
4. Genroku Oban 1695 .... Rare
5. Kyoho Oban 1725 .... 5000.00
6. Tempo Oban 1838 .... 7000.00
7. Manen Oban 1860 (Size 132 x 80) 3000.00

GORYOBAN OR 5 TAEL PIECES

Type similar to above but averaging about 90 x 50 millimetres and without the ink legends.

8. Tempo Goryoban 1837 .... 2000.00

KOBANS OR 1 TAEL PIECES

Type similar to above but averaging about 70 x 40 millimetres.

9. Keicho Koban 1601 .... 1750.00
10. Genroku Koban 1695 .... 2750.00
11. Hoei Koban 1710 .... 1750.00
12. Kyoho Koban 1716 ....*..... 1000.00
13. Genbun Koban 1736 .... 400.00
14. Bunsei Koban 1819 .... 400.00

15. Tempo Koban 1837 .... 300.00
16. Ansei Koban 1859 .... 1500.00
17. Manen Koban 1860 (Size 35 x 20) 200.00

NI-BU OR 2 BU PIECES

*Rectangular pieces averaging about 23 x 15 millimetres
and bearing legends and floral designs.*

18. Shinbun 2 Bu 1818 ....*...... 125.00
19. Sobun 2 Bu 1828 .... 100.00
20. Ansei 2 Bu 1856 .... 37.50
21. Manen 2 Bu 1860 ....*...... 50.00
22. Kaheishi 2 Bu 1868 .... 22.50

ICHI-BU OR 1 BU PIECES

Type similar to above but averaging about 18 x 10 millimetres.

23. Taiko 1 Bu 1591 ....*...... 1250.00
24. Keicho 1 Bu 1601 .... 150.00
25. Genroku 1 Bu 1695 .... 175.00
26. Hoei 1 Bu 1710 .... 150.00
27. Kyoho 1 Bu 1716 .... 75.00
28. Genbun 1 Bu 1736 .... 25.00
29. Bunsei 1 Bu 1819 .... 35.00
30. Tempo 1 Bu 1837 .... 35.00
31. Ansei 1 Bu 1859 .... 250.00
32. Manen 1 Bu 1860. (Size reduced) 175.00

NI-SHU OR 2 SHU PIECES

Type similar to above but averaging 13 x 8 millimetres.

33. Genroku 2 Shu 1695 .... 350.00
34. Tempo 2 Shu 1832 .... 10.00
35. Manen 2 Shu 1860 .... 12.50

IS-SHU OR 1 SHU PIECE

Type similar to above but averaging 10 millimetres square.

36. Bunsei 1 Shu 1824 .... 35.00

B. Round Pieces of the Old Coinage

Five characters around circle on each side. Size about 20 millimetres.

37. Taiko Gold coin 1591 .... 1250.00

Four characters around square central hole. Rev. Crest.

38. Eiraku Gold coin 1593 ....*...... 1250.00
39. Kanei Gold coin 1626 .... 600.00

*Legend and ornaments on each side. Issued by Koshu
Province about 1850.*

40. 1 Bu. Size 13 millimetres 150.00
41. 2 Shu. Size 11 millimetres 100.00
42. 1 Shu. Size 10 millimetres 100.00
43. ½ Shu. Size 8 millimetres 250.00
44. ½ Shu. Size 6 millimetres square 150.00

C. The Modern Coinage of Japan

The first modern gold coins of Japan were allied to the U. S. gold
standard but in 1897 the gold Yen was devalued by 50% and a new
coinage was issued to mark the change.

MUTSUHITO, 1867-1912
(The Meiji Era)

Dragon. Rev. Wreath over crossed banners.

45. 20 Yen. Years 3-13 (1870-80) 5000.00
46. 10 Yen. Years 4-13 (1871-80) 1000.00
47.   5 Yen. Years 3-30 (1870-97) ....*...... 450.00
48.   2 Yen. Years 3-13 (1870-80) 300.00

Japanese character. Rev. Wreath over crossed banners.

49. 1 Yen. Years 4-13 (1871-80) 150.00

*Radiant sun. Rev. Value in wreath. Reduced size coins struck
after revaluation of the gold yen in 1897.*

50. 20 Yen. Years 30-45 (1897-1912) 450.00
51. 10 Yen. Years 30-43 (1897-1910) ....*...... 250.00
52.   5 Yen. Years 30-45 (1897-1912) 250.00

YOSHIHITO, 1912-1926
(The Taisho Era)

Radiant sun. Rev. Value in wreath.

53. 20 Yen. Years 1-9 (1912-20) ....*...... 450.00
54.   5 Yen. Years 1, 2 (1912, 13) 300.00

HIROHITO, 1926-
(The Showa Era)
Radiant sun. Rev. Value in wreath.

55. 20 Yen. Years 5-7 (1930-32) 4000.00
56.   5 Yen. Year 5 (1930) 2500.00

JERUSALEM

(Including the Principality of Antioch and the Counties of Edessa and Tripoli).

Crusader Kings of —

BALDWIN I AND II, 1100-1131

Pseudo-Cufic legend on each side.

1.   1 Saracenic Bezant ND 200.00

BOHEMOND I AND II, 1098-1130

Pseudo-Cufic legend on each side, with the letter B on obverse and T on reverse. (Bohemond and Tancred)

2.   1 Saracenic Bezant ND 200.00

CONRAD AND CONRADIN, 1243-1268

Genuine Cufic legend on each side spelling out both the Christian date and phrases relating to Christianity.

3.   1 Bezant 1250-1259 .... 225.00

KATANGA

Bananas. Rev. Baluba cross.

1.   5 Francs 1961 .... 60.00

KOREA

Dragon. Rev. Value.

1. 20 Won 1906, 08, 09, 10 .... 4500.00
2. 10 Won 1906, 09 .... * 2000.00
3. 5 Won 1908, 09 .... 3000.00

KUWAIT

Value in Arabic in center circle. Rev. Dhow sailing left.

1.   5 Dinars 1961 .... 125.00

LATVIA (RIGA)

A. Archbishops of —

WILLIAM, 1554-1563
Bust. Rev. Arms.

1.   1 Ducat 1559 .... 2000.00

B. Polish Kings of —

STEPHAN BATHORI, 1576-1586

Bust. Rev. Riga City arms.

2. 10 Ducats 1586 .... * 7500.00
3. 5 Ducats 1586 .... 4000.00
4. 1 Ducat 1584, 85 .... 1750.00

SIGISMUND III, 1587-1632

Bust. Rev. Riga City arms.

5.   1 Ducat 1588, 94, 97, 99, 1619 .... 900.0

C. Swedish Kings of —

GUSTAVE ADOLPHE II, 1611-1632

Bust. Rev. Riga City arms.

6.	1 Ducat 1623	7500.00

CHRISTINA, 1632-1654
Facing bust. Rev. Riga City arms.

7.	6 Ducats 1644	3000.00
8.	5 Ducats 1644, 45	3000.00
9.	3 Ducats 1643	2500.00

Bust left. Rev. Riga City arms.

10.	1 Ducat 1644	1000.00

Bust right. Rev. Riga City arms.

11.	4 Ducats 1646	5000.00
12.	3 Ducats 1646	5000.00
13.	2 Ducats 1646 ....*......	2000.00
14.	1 Ducat 1646	1000.00

CHARLES X, 1654-1660

Bust. Rev. City view of Riga.

15.	6 Ducats 1654	4000.00
16.	5 Ducats 1654 ....*......	4000.00

CHARLES XI, 1660-1697

Bust. Rev. Riga City arms.

17.	2 Ducats 1667	1250.00
18.	1 Ducat 1664, 73 ....*......	800.00

CHARLES XII, 1697-1718

Bust. Rev. Riga City arms.

19.	1 Ducat 1701, 07	1000.00

LIECHTENSTEIN

The coinage from 1930 to 1952 was based on the Latin Monetary Union standard.

Princes of —

CHARLES, 1614-1627
Bust. Rev. Arms.

1.	10 Ducats 1616	4500.00
2.	6 Ducats 1617	2000.00
3.	5 Ducats 1615	2000.00
4.	4 Ducats 1618	1750.00
5.	3 Ducats 1614, 18	1250.00
6.	2 Ducats 1614, 16	850.00
7.	1 Ducat 1614, 17, 18	600.00

JOSEPH JOHN ADAM, 1721-1732
Bust. Rev. Arms.

8.	10 Ducats 1728	4000.00
9.	1 Ducat 1728, 29	600.00

JOSEPH WENZEL, 1748-1772

Armored bust. Rev. Arms.

10.	1 Ducat 1758	1500.00

FRANCIS JOSEPH I, 1772-1781

Bust. Rev. Arms.

11.	1 Ducat 1778	1200.00

JOHN II, 1858-1929

Head. Rev. Arms.

12.	20 Kronen 1898 ....*......	1000.00
13.	10 Kronen 1898 ....*......	1500.00
14.	10 Kronen 1900	750.00

LIECHTENSTEIN

FRANCIS I, 1929-1938

Head. Rev. Arms.

15.	20 Franken 1930	600.00
16.	10 Franken 1930	400.00

FRANCIS JOSEPH II, 1938-

Head. Rev. Arms.

17.	20 Franken 1946	125.00
18.	10 Franken 1946	100.00

Conjoined heads of the Prince and Princess. Rev. Arms.

19.	100 Franken 1952	1250.00
20.	50 Franken 1956 ....*.....	125.00
21.	25 Franken 1956	100.00

LITHUANIA

Polish Kings and Grand Dukes of —

SIGISMUND II, 1544-1572
Bust. Rev. Horseman.

1.	10 Ducats 1562	7500.00
2.	1 Ducat 1548-69	750.00

STEPHAN BATHORI, 1576-1586
Bust. Rev. Arms.

3.	1 Ducat 1586	2000.00

SIGISMUND III, 1587-1632

Bust. Rev. Arms.

4.	10 Ducats 1604-22	2000.00
5.	8 Ducats 1592	2000.00
6.	5 Ducats 1618-22 ....*.....	1250.00
7.	1 Ducat 1589, 90	1000.00

LADISLAS IV, 1632-1648
Bust. Rev. Arms.

8.	10 Ducats 1639	Rare

JOHN CASIMIR, 1648-1668

Bust. Rev. Horseman.

9.	1 Ducat 1666	1250.00
10.	½ Ducat 1664, 65	650.00

LIVONIA

A. Army Masters of —

WALTER, 1495-1535
Ruler standing. Rev. Madonna.

1.	10 Ducats 1525	3000.00

Ruler standing. Rev. Castle.

2.	2 Ducats 1528	1250.00

Madonna. Rev. Castle.

3.	1 Ducat 1528	700.00

Arms. Rev. Crossed keys.

4.	½ Ducat 1533	400.00

HERMAN, 1535-1549
Madonna. Rev. Arms.

5.	1 Florin 1535	900.00

WILLIAM, 1557-1559
Madonna. Rev. Arms.

6.	1⅓ Ducats 1558, 59	1250.00

GOTTHARD, 1559-1561

Armored bust. Rev. Christ over arms.

7.	2⅜ Ducats ND ....*.....	2000.00
8.	1⅜ Ducats ND	750.00

B. Swedish Rulers of —

CHRISTINA, 1632-1654

Facing bust. Rev. Arms.

9.	10 Ducats 1645	10,000.00
10.	2 Ducats 1646 ....*.....	1200.00
11.	1 Ducat 1645, 47, 48 ....*.....	500.00

Bust right. Rev. Arms.

12. 1 Ducat 1648 .... 1500.00

LUXEMBOURG

Grand Dukes of —

JOHN THE BLIND, 1310-1346
St. John. Rev. Lily.

1. 1 Florin ND 200.00

Ruler standing. Rev. Cross.

2. 1 Royal ND 1000.00

Ruler on throne. Rev. Cross.

3. 1 Ecu ND 750.00

CHARLES IV, 1346-1353
St. John. Rev. Lily.

4. 1 Florin ND 200.00

WENCESLAS I, 1353-1383

St. John. Rev. Lily.

5. 1 Florin ND 300.00

Ruler under dais. Rev. Arms.

6. 1 Florin ND .... Rare

WENCESLAS II, 1383-1419
St. John. Rev. Eagle.

7. 1 Florin ND 1200.00

JOHN OF BAVARIA AND ELIZABETH OF GOERLITZ, 1419-1425
St. Peter standing. Rev. Two shields.

8. 1 Florin ND 1500.00

PHILIP OF BURGUNDY, 1443-1467
St. Andrew with cross. Rev. Two shields.

9. 1 Florin ND 1000.00

PHILIP OF AUSTRIA, 1482-1506
St. Philip with shield. Rev. Cross.

10. 1 Florin 1502, ND 1500.00

PHILIP IV OF SPAIN, 1621-1665
Cross. Rev. Arms.

11. 1 Couronne d'or 1632 .... Rare

CHARLOTTE, 1919-1964

Conjoined heads of Prince Jean of Luxembourg and Princess Josephine Charlotte of Belgium. Rev. Arms; on their marriage. Although without a mark of value, this coin has the same specifications as the standard 20 Franc piece of the Latin Monetary Union.

12. (20 Francs) 1953 .... 60.00

MALAYA

Native legend on each side. Sultanate coinage struck during the period 1720-60.

1. 1 Mas ND. Octagonal 100.00

JOHORE

ABDUL JALIL, 1699-1719

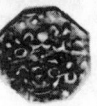

Inscription. Rev. Inscription.

2. 1 Kupang Mas. Round 100.00
3. 1 Kupang Mas. Octagonal 100.00

TRENGANU

ALFAHDIN SHAH (17th Century)

Inscription. Rev. Inscription.

4. 1 Mas ND (1600-1700) 100.00

MALTA

(The Knights of St. John of Jerusalem at Malta. For earlier coins of the Knights, see under Rhodes).

The coinage of both Malta and Rhodes was produced by the same order of Grand Masters; until 1530 at Rhodes and afterward at Malta.

Grand Masters of —

PHILIPPE VILLIERS, 1521-1534

Ruler kneeling before St. John. Rev. Christ standing.

1. 1 Zecchino ND 1000.00

Bust. Rev. Arms.

2.   1 Zecchino ND 3500.00

PETER DEL PONTE, 1534-1535
Ruler kneeling before St. John. Rev. Christ standing.

3.   1 Zecchino ND .... **Unique**

JOHN DE HOMEDES, 1536-1553
Ruler kneeling before St. John. Rev. Christ standing.

4.   1 Zecchino ND 900.00

JOHN DE LA VALLETTE, 1557-1568
Ruler kneeling before St. John. Rev. Christ standing.

5.   1 Zecchino ND 175.00

PETER DEL MONTE, 1568-1572

Ruler kneeling before St. John. Rev. Christ standing.

6.   1 Zecchino ND 175.00

JOHN DE LA CASSIERE, 1572-1581
Ruler kneeling before St. John. Rev. Christ standing.

7.   1 Zecchino ND 175.00

HUGH DE VERDALA, 1581-1595
Ruler kneeling before St. John. Rev. Christ standing.

8.   1 Zecchino ND 175.00

MARTIN GARZES, 1595-1601
Ruler kneeling before St. John. Rev. Christ standing.

9.   1 Zecchino ND 175.00

ALOFIUS DE WIGNACOURT, 1601-1622
Ruler kneeling before St. John. Rev. Christ standing.

10.   1 Zecchino ND 175.00

ANTHONY DE PAULE, 1623-1636
Ruler kneeling before St. John. Rev. Christ standing.

11.   1 Zecchino ND 675.00

JOHN PAUL LASCARIS, 1636-1657
Ruler kneeling before St. John. Rev. Christ standing.

12.   1 Zecchino ND 675.00

GREGORY CARAFFA, 1680-1690

Ruler kneeling before St. John. Rev. Arms.

13.   1 Zecchino ND 675.00

ADRIEN DE WIGNACOURT, 1690-1697

Ruler kneeling before St. John. Rev. Arms.

14.   4 Zecchini 1695 ....*...... 1500.00
15.   1 Zecchino 1691-96 .... 400.00

RAYMON PERELLOS, 1697-1720

Bust. Rev. Arms.

16.   4 Zecchini 1717, 18, 19 .... 1000.00

Ruler kneeling before St. John. Rev. Arms.

17.   10 Zecchini 1699 .... 6000.00
18.   4 Zecchini 1699, 1705 .... 1000.00
19.   1 Zecchino 1699, 1717, ND ....*...... 375.00

St. Michael. Rev. Arms.

20.   2 Zecchini ND 1000.00

MARCANTONIO ZONDADARI, 1720-1722
Bust. Rev. Legend.

21.   4 Zecchini 1721 .... 1800.00

Bust. Rev. Arms.

22.   4 Zecchini 1722 .... 1800.00

Ruler kneeling before St. John. Rev. Arms.

23.   1 Zecchino 1722 .... 425.00

ANTHONY DE VILHENA, 1722-1736

Bust. Rev. Arms.

24.	12 Zecchini 1725	....	4500.00
25.	10 Zecchini 1722	....	3000.00
26.	4 Zecchini 1722-28	....	1000.00
27.	2 Zecchini 1723-28	.........................*......	700.00

Ruler kneeling before St. John. Rev. Arms.

28.	1 Zecchino 1723, 24, 25, 28	....	300.00

EMANUEL PINTO, 1741-1773

Bust. Rev. Arms.

29.	10 Zecchini 1742, ND	....	1750.00
30.	5 Zecchini 1742, ND	....	900.00
31.	4 Zecchini 1742, ND	......................*......	750.00
32.	2 Zecchini 1742, ND	......................*......	325.00
33.	1 Zecchino 1742, ND	....	150.00

Bust to right or left. Rev. Arms on cross.

34.	20 Scudi 1764, 65, 70, 72	....	400.00

St. John standing. Rev. Two shields.

35.	20 Scudi 1764	....	450.00

St. John standing. Rev. Arms.

36.	10 Scudi 1756, 61, 62, 63	....	175.00
37.	5 Scudi 1756	.............................*......	150.00

FRANCIS XIMINES, 1773-1775

Bust in circle. Rev. Two shields.

38.	20 Scudi 1773	....	500.00
39.	10 Scudi 1773	.............................*......	400.00

Bust not in circle. Rev. Two shields.

40.	10 Scudi 1774	....	250.00

Bust not in circle. Rev. Arms on cross.

41.	20 Scudi 1774	....	425.00
42.	10 Scudi 1774	.............................*......	225.00

EMANUEL DE ROHAN, 1775-1797

Bust. Rev. Two shields.

43.	20 Scudi 1778, 81, 82	....	325.00
44.	10 Scudi 1778, 82	.......................*......	175.00
45.	5 Scudi 1779	............................*......	150.00

FERDINAND DE HOMPESCH, 1797-1799

St. John standing. Rev. Arms on double eagle. Although dated 1778, this coin is attributed to Hompesch.

46.	20 Scudi 1778	....	3000.00

THE SIEGE OF MALTA, 1798-1800

Oblong gold Ingot struck by General Vaubois, French defender of the island, during the blockade by the British. Rampant lion. Rev. Value. Size 25 x 20 Millimetres.

47.	17 Scudi, 3 Tari, 5 Grani ND	....	Unique

MARTINIQUE

Gold coins of Brazil or Portugal counterstamped with "22" or "20" (for karats) and a small eagle.

1.	6400 Reis 1727-1804.	..........................*......	350.00
2.	3200 Reis 1727-1786.	....	500.00
3.	4000 Reis 1707-1817.	....	250.00
4.	1000 Reis 1752-1787.	....	300.00
5.	400 Reis 1725-1796.	....	350.00
6.	½ Escudo 1752-1796.	....	350.00

MEXICO

Mints and mint marks:—

Mo	mm for Mexico City
A or As	mm for Alamos
C or Cn	mm for Culican
Ca or Ch	mm for Chihuahua
Do	mm for Durango
Eo Mo	mm for Tlalpan
Ga	mm for Guadalajara
GC	mm for Guadelupe y Calvo
Go	mm for Guanajuato
Ho	mm for Hermosillo
O or Oa	mm for Oaxaca
Pi	mm for San Luis Potosi
Zs	mm for Zacatecas

The early gold coins of Mexico are known as "cobs", because of their irregular shape, and pieces with a decipherable date are worth twice as much or more than specimens without dates. Full round coins of Philip V, before 1732, are worth three to four times more than the cob specimens. There are five known reverses for the coins of Philip V.

The Escudo system, inherited from the Spanish Kings, was continued under the Republic as late as the 1870's. The Peso, from 1870 to 1905, varied little from that of U.S. gold coinage, the Peso almost being equal to the Dollar. In 1905, the Gold Peso was devalued about one half and the first coins on the new standard appeared in 1905.

The 50 Peso piece or Centennario was struck as a regular circulating medium until 1931. This and other Mexican gold coins minted in the 1940's and later were struck mainly to satisfy the world wide demand for gold coins.

A. Spanish Kings of —

(All coins are from the Mexico City Mint, unless otherwise noted)

CHARLES II, 1665-1700
Arms. Rev. Cross. Cob type.

1.	8 Escudos 1691-1700. Full round type	....	Rare
2.	8 Escudos 1679-1701	....	2500.00
3.	4 Escudos 1695, 1701	....	1500.00
4.	2 Escudos 1701	....	750.00
5.	1 Escudo 1695, 97, 98, 1701	....	800.00

PHILIP V, 1700-1746

Arms. Rev. Cross.

6.	8 Escudos 1702-32. Cob type	....	2000.00
7.	8 Escudos 1702-32. Full round type	....	Rare
7a.	4 Escudos 1713-15. Cob type	....	1500.00
7b.	2 Escudos 1700-15. Cob type	....	350.00
7c.	1 Escudo 1711-15. Cob type	....	200.00

Bust. Rev. Arms.

8.	8 Escudos 1732-47	....	700.00
9.	4 Escudos 1732-46	....	600.00
10.	2 Escudos 1732-46	....	300.00
11.	1 Escudo 1732-46	...................*......	225.00

LOUIS I, 1724
Arms. Rev. Cross.

12.	8 Escudos 1725. Cob type	....	Rare
12a.	8 Escudos 1725. Full round type	....	Rare

FERDINAND VI, 1746-1760

Large bust. Rev. Arms.

13.	8 Escudos 1747	..............................*......	1000.00
14.	4 Escudos 1747	....	1500.00
15.	2 Escudos 1747	....	600.00
16.	1 Escudo 1747	....	500.00

Small bust in high relief. Rev. Arms. The value does not appear on the coins dated from 1752-56.

17.	8 Escudos 1748-56	....	650.00
18.	4 Escudos 1748-56	........................*......	850.00
19.	2 Escudos 1748-56	....	350.00
20.	1 Escudo 1748-56	....	200.00

Re-designed bust in lower relief. Rev. Arms.

21.	8 Escudos 1757-59	....	600.00
22.	4 Escudos 1757-59	........................*......	800.00
23.	2 Escudos 1757-59	....	300.00
24.	1 Escudo 1756-59	....	200.00

CHARLES III, 1759-1788

Small bust. Rev. Arms.

25.	8 Escudos 1760, 61	........................*......	700.00
26.	4 Escudos 1760, 61	....	1000.00
27.	2 Escudos 1760, 61	....	500.00
28.	1 Escudo 1760, 61	....	300.00

Large bust. Rev. Arms.

29.	8 Escudos 1762-71	....	650.00
30.	4 Escudos 1764-71	....	1250.00
31.	2 Escudos 1763-71	.........................*	400.00
32.	1 Escudo 1762-71	....	300.00

Older bust of different style. Rev. Arms.

33.	8 Escudos 1772-88	....	275.00
34.	4 Escudos 1772-88	.........................*	425.00
35.	2 Escudos 1772-88	....	200.00
36.	1 Escudo 1772-88	....	150.00

CHARLES IV, 1788-1808

Bust of the previous king, Charles III, with name as "Carol IV." Rev. Arms.

37.	8 Escudos 1789, 90	.........................*	325.00
38.	4 Escudos 1789, 90	....	600.00
39.	2 Escudos 1789, 90	....	300.00
40.	1 Escudo 1789, 90	....	200.00

Similar to above type but with name as " Carol IIII."

41.	8 Escudos 1790	....	400.00
42.	4 Escudos 1790	....	500.00

Bust. Rev. Arms.

43.	8 Escudos 1791-1808	....	225.00
44.	4 Escudos 1792-1808	....	350.00
45.	2 Escudos 1791-1808	.........................*	150.00
46.	1 Escudo 1792-1808	....	100.00

FERDINAND VII, 1808-1822

Large armored bust. Rev. Arms.

47.	8 Escudos 1808-12	.........................*	225.00
48.	4 Escudos 1808-12	....	400.00
49.	1 Escudo 1809-12	....	125.00

Large uniformed bust. Rev. Arms.

50.	8 Escudos 1813. Ga mm.	.................*	3000.00
51.	4 Escudos 1812. Ga mm.	....	Rare

Laureate head. Rev. Arms.

52.	8 Escudos 1814-21. Mo mm.	....	225.00
53.	8 Escudos 1821. Ga mm.	.................*	750.00
54.	4 Escudos 1814-20	....	500.00
55.	2 Escudos 1814-20	....	175.00
56.	1 Escudo 1814-20	....	125.00
57.	½ Escudo 1814-20	....	100.00

Draped bust. Rev. Arms.

58.	8 Escudos 1821. Ga mm.	....	750.00

B. Emperors of —

AUGUSTIN ITURBIDE I, 1822-1823

Head. Rev. Eagle on cactus.

59. 8 Escudos 1822 .... 500.00

Head. Rev. Arms.

60. 8 Escudos 1823 .... 500.00
61. 4 Escudos 1823 ....*..... 500.00

MAXIMILIAN I, 1864-1867

Head. Rev. Arms.

62. 20 Pesos 1866 .... 500.00

C. Republic of —

Hand with Liberty Cap over book. Rev. Eagle facing left.
The so-called "Hooked neck" or profile eagle.

63. 8 Escudos 1823 .... 1500.00

Hand with Liberty Cap over book. Rev. Eagle facing right.

8 ESCUDOS

64.	Mo	mm. 1824-70	175.00
65.	A	mm. 1864-72	1000.00
66.	C	mm. 1846-70 ....*....	175.00
67.	Ca	mm. 1841-71	250.00
68.	Do	mm. 1832-70	250.00
69.	Eo Mo	mm. 1828-30	2750.00

70.	Ga	mm. 1825-63	750.00
71.	GC	mm. 1844-53	500.00
72.	Go	mm. 1828-70	150.00
73.	Ho	mm. 1863-73	475.00
74.	O	mm. 1859-69	500.00
75.	Zs	mm. 1858-71	300.00
76.	Cn	mm. 1860	350.00

(Note: Pi mm., San Luis Potosi, none struck)

4 ESCUDOS

77.	Mo	mm. 1825-70	300.00
78.	C	mm. 1846-70	800.00
79.	Do	mm. 1832-70	600.00
80.	Eo Mo	mm. 1827-30	Unknown
81.	Ga	mm. 1823-70	1000.00
82.	GC	mm. 1843-52	1000.00
83.	Go	mm. 1828-70	350.00
84.	Ho	mm. 1861-73	850.00
85.	O	mm. 1861	Rare
86.	Zs	mm. 1824-70	750.00

2 ESCUDOS

87.	Mo	mm. 1825-70	100.00
88.	C	mm. 1846-70	250.00
89.	Do	mm. 1824-70	500.00
90.	Eo Mo	mm. 1828-30	1500.00
91.	Ga	mm. 1825-70	225.00
92.	GC	mm. 1843-52	500.00
93.	Go	mm. 1828-70	150.00
94.	Ho	mm. 1861-73	500.00
95.	O	mm. 1858-70	Unknown
96.	Zs	mm. 1824-70	300.00

1 ESCUDO

97.	Mo	mm. 1825-70	60.00
98.	C	mm. 1846-70	75.00
99.	Do	mm. 1832-70	95.00
100.	Eo Mo	mm. 1828-30	Unknown
101.	Ga	mm. 1833-70	75.00
102.	GC	mm. 1843-52	175.00
103.	Go	mm. 1825-70	100.00
104.	Ho	mm. 1861-73	Unknown
105.	O	mm. 1858-70	Unknown
106.	Zs	mm. 1824-70	125.00

½ ESCUDO

107.	Mo	mm. 1825-70	35.00
108.	A	mm. 1862-72	225.00
109.	C	mm. 1846-70	50.00
110.	Ca	mm. 1831-70	75.00
111.	Do	mm. 1824-70	50.00
112.	Eo Mo	mm. 1828-30	1000.00
113.	Ga	mm. 1825-70	50.00
114.	GC	mm. 1843-52	100.00
115.	Go	mm. 1825-70	35.00
116.	Ho	mm. 1861-73	225.00
117.	O	mm. 1858-70	125.00
118.	Zs	mm. 1824-70	75.00

Scales and Liberty Cap. Rev. Eagle.

20 PESOS

119.	Mo	mm. 1870-1905 ....*......	275.00
120.	As	mm. 1876-78, 88	900.00
121.	Ch	mm. 1872-95	500.00
122.	Cn	mm. 1870-1905	300.00
123.	Do	mm. 1870-80	400.00
124.	Go	mm. 1870-1900	250.00
125.	Ho	mm. 1875, 88	900.00
126.	Oa	mm. 1870-72, 88	500.00
127.	Zs	mm. 1871-89	450.00

10 PESOS

128.	Mo mm. 1870-1905	200.00
129.	As mm. 1873-95	350.00
130.	Ch mm. 1884, 88	600.00
131.	Cn mm. 1877-1903	250.00
132.	Do mm. 1872-83	200.00
133.	Ga mm. 1870-81, 91	350.00
134.	Go mm. 1872, 87, 88	225.00
135.	Ho mm. 1876, 78, 80, 81	300.00
136.	Oa mm. 1870-86	225.00
137.	Pi mm. 1888	Rare
138.	Zs mm. 1871-95	200.00

5 PESOS

139.	Mo mm. 1870-1905	150.00
140.	As mm. 1873-78	350.00
141.	Ch mm. 1888	500.00
142.	Cn mm. 1873-1903	150.00
143.	Do mm. 1877-79	150.00
144.	Go mm. 1871, 87, 88, 93	125.00
145.	Ho mm. 1874, 77, 88	225.00
146.	Oa mm. 1870-93 ....Unknown
147.	Zs mm. 1874-92	150.00

Eagle. Rev. Value.

2½ PESOS

148.	Mo mm. 1870-92	150.00
149.	As mm. 1888	750.00
150.	Ch mm. 1870-95 ....Unknown
151.	Cn mm. 1893	175.00
152.	Do mm. 1870-95 ....Unknown
153.	Go mm. 1871, 88	175.00
154.	Ho mm. 1874, 88	500.00
155.	Oa mm. 1870-93 ....Unknown
156.	Zs mm. 1872, 73, 75, 88-90	150.00

1 PESO

157.	Mo mm. 1870-1905 ....*......	75.00
158.	As mm. 1888	250.00
159.	Ch mm. 1888	500.00
160.	Cn mm. 1873-1905	75.00
161.	Go mm. 1871, 80, 88, 90, 92, 94-1900	75.00
162.	Ho mm. 1875	200.00
163.	Oa mm. 1870-93 ....Unknown
164.	Zs mm. 1872, 88-90	75.00

D. Estados Unidos Mexicanos

Head of Hidalgo to left. Rev. Eagle.

165.	10 Pesos 1905	200.00
166.	10 Pesos 1906-08, 10, 16, 17, 19, 20, 59	25.00
167.	5 Pesos 1905	200.00
168.	5 Pesos 1906, 07, 10, 18-20, 55 ....*......	12.50
169.	2½ Pesos 1918-20, 44-48 ....*......	15.00

Eagle. Rev. Value in wreath.

170.	2 Pesos 1919, 20, 44-48	10.00

Aztec Calendar stone. Rev. Eagle.

171.	20 Pesos 1917-21, 59	50.00

Winged Victory. Rev. Eagle. The so-called Centenario. The denomination does not appear on the coins dated 1943.

172.	50 Pesos 1921-31, 44-47	95.00
173.	50 Pesos 1943	110.00

E. Revolutionary Period, 1913-1916

OAXACA STATE

Head of Juarez. Rev. Liberty Cap over scales.

174.	60 Pesos 1916	3500.00

Head of Juarez. Rev. Value in wreath. Struck in low grade gold.

175.	20 Pesos 1915 ....*......	250.00
176.	10 Pesos 1915	150.00
177.	5 Pesos 1915	150.00

MOLDAVIA

Princes of —

JOHN HERACLIDES
Crowned head. Rev. Arms.

1.	1 Ducat 1563	2250.00

MONACO

The coinage from 1838 to 1904 was based on the French monetary system and the Latin Monetary Union standard.

Princes of —

LUCIANO, 1505-1523
Crowned arms. Rev. Cross.

1. 1 Scudo d'oro ND 6000.00

HONORE II, 1604-1662

Bust. Rev. Cross of initials.

2. 2 Doppia 1649, 50 .... 3000.00
3. 1 Doppia 1648-60 ....*..... 2000.00
4. ½ Doppia 1650 .... 1750.00

Bust. Rev. Crowned initial.

5. 2 Doppia 1656 .... 4000.00
6. 1 Doppia 1656, 61 .... 2250.00

Bust. Rev. Arms.

7. 5 Doppia 1649 .... 7500.00

LOUIS I, 1662-1701
Bust. Rev. Two L's.

8. 4 Ducats 1663, 64 .... 4000.00

HONORE V, 1819-1841

Head. Rev. Arms with supporters. These coins were not placed in circulation.

9. 40 Francs 1838 .... 1250.00
10. 20 Francs 1838 ....*...... 1000.00

CHARLES III, 1856-1889

Head. Rev. Arms.

11. 100 Francs 1882, 84, 86 .... 225.00
12. 20 Francs 1878, 79 ....*...... 85.00

ALBERT, 1889-1922

Head. Rev. Arms. The 20 Franc piece was not placed in circulation.

13. 100 Francs 1891-1904 ....*..... 175.00
14. 20 Francs 1892 .... 500.00

LOUIS II, 1922-1949
(Souvenir gold coins struck from dies also used for minor coins).
Large bust. Rev. Arms.

15. 20 Francs 1947. Normal thickness 275.00
16. 20 Francs 1947. Double thickness 275.00
17. 10 Francs 1946. Normal thickness 175.00
18. 10 Francs 1946. Double thickness 225.00

Head. Rev. Arms.

19. 5 Francs 1945. Normal thickness 225.00
20. 5 Francs 1945. Double thickness 275.00
21. 2 Francs ND (1943) 150.00
22. 1 Franc ND (1943) 150.00

RAINIER III, 1949-
(Souvenir gold coins struck from dies also used for minor coins).

Head. Rev. Horseman.

23. 100 Francs 1950. Normal thickness ....*..... 200.00
24. 100 Francs 1950. Double thickness 225.00
25. 50 Francs 1950. Normal thickness 175.00
26. 50 Francs 1950. Double thickness 200.00

Head. Rev. Arms.

27. 20 Francs 1950. Normal thickness ....*..... 150.00
28. 20 Francs 1950. Double thickness 175.00
29. 10 Francs 1950. Normal thickness ....*..... 125.00
30. 10 Francs 1950. Double thickness 150.00

New type head. Rev. Arms. Of smaller size than previous issues of this value.

31. 100 Francs 1956 .... 125.00

MONTENEGRO

This country issued gold coins in one year only, 1910, and these pieces conformed to the standards of the Latin Monetary Union.

Kings of —

NICHOLAS I, 1860-1918

Plain head to right. Rev. Arms.

1. 100 Perpera 1910 .... 1250.00
2. 20 Perpera 1910 ....*...... 200.00
3. 10 Perpera 1910 ....*...... 175.00

Laureate head to left. Rev. Arms. On the 50th year of both his reign and marriage.

4. 100 Perpera 1910 .... 1250.00
5. 20 Perpera 1910 ....*...... 200.00
6. 10 Perpera 1910 ....*...... 150.00

MOROCCO

Arab legend on each side. Sultanate coinage struck during the period 1600-1750. With dates from about 1009-1164 A.H.

1. 1 Dinar 60.00
2. ½ Dinar 40.00

Arab legend within star on each side. Struck during the period 1750-1860. With dates from about 1164-1277 A.H.

3. 1 Dinar 80.00

Arab legend. Rev. "1201". Struck at Madrid.

4. 10 Mizquals 1201 A.H. (1786 A.D.) 600.00

Six-pointed star. Rev. Value and date. Struck under French influence and the equivalent of the 20 Franc piece. This coin was not placed in circulation.

5. 4 Ryals 1297 A.H. (1879 A.D.) 1500.00

MOZAMBIQUE

Portuguese Kings of —

JOSEPH I, 1750-1777

Arms. Rev. Cross in quadrilobe.

1. 4000 Reis 1755 ....*...... 700.00
2. 2000 Reis 1755 .... 550.00
3. 1000 Reis 1755 .... 550.00

MARY II, 1834-1853

"M" in enclosure with various punches and stamps. Rev. Value.

4. 2½ Maticaes ND. Rectangular bar 250.00
5. 1¼ Maticaes ND. Rectangular bar 175.00

MUSCAT AND OMAN

SAID BIN TAIMUR
Crossed daggers. Rev. Value.

1. 15 Rials 1381 A.H. (1962) 150.00

NEPAL

Kings of —

(The Nepalese Mohar is equal to about ½ of the Indian Mohur. Generally, the 2 and 1 mohar pieces are of the same size and can be distinguished by different thickness and weight. The Rupee is equal to about 2 mohars.)

Square and legend. Rev. Circle and legend. Issued from about 1750-1880 and with Saka dates from about 1670-1802.

1. 4 Mohars 300.00
2. 2 Mohars ....*...... 150.00
3. 1 Mohar 100.00

Inscription in star. Rev. Inscription.

4. ½ Mohar 1731 (1809 A.D.) 100.00

Inscription around triangle. Rev. Inscription around trident.

5. 1 Mohar ND (1809) 250.00

Legend and symbols on each side.

6. ½ Mohar ....*...... 60.00
7. ¼ Mohar ....*...... 40.00
8. ⅛ Mohar 25.00
9. 1/16 Mohar 25.00
10. 1/32 Mohar 25.00
11. 1/64 Mohar 25.00

PRITHVI, 1881-1911

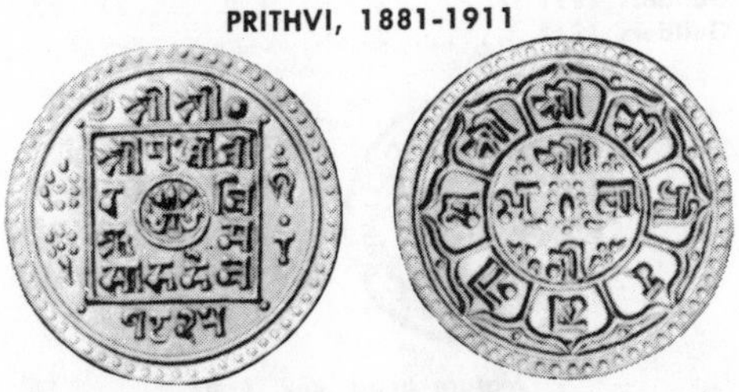

Square between small and large circle. Rev. Circle within panelled legend. With Saka dates from 1803-1833 (1881-1911 A.D.). Up to Saka 1823 (1901 A.D.) the coinage is with plain edge. After Saka 1824 the coinage is with reeded edge and is of much finer workmanship.

12. 4 Mohars ....*...... 250.00
13. 2 Mohars 150.00
14. 1 Mohar 80.00

Legend and symbols on each side.

15. ½ Mohar 60.00
16. ¼ Mohar 45.00
17. ⅛ Mohar 30.00
18. 1/16 Mohar 25.00
19. 1/32 Mohar 25.00
20. 1/64 Mohar 25.00
21. 1/128 Mohar 20.00

TRIBHUBANA, 1911-1954

Type similar to above. With Samvat dates from 1969-1995 (1912-1938 A.D.).

22. 2 Mohars ....*...... 175.00
23. 1 Mohar 90.00
24. ½ Mohar 50.00

Type similar to above.

25. 2 Rupees 2005 (1948 A.D.) 200.00
26. 1 Rupee 1995-2005 (1938-1948 A.D.) 100.00
27. ½ Rupee 1995-2005 (1938-1948 A.D.) 50.00
28. ¼ Rupee 1995 (1938 A.D.) 25.00

Head of Tribhubana. Rev. Mountain and rising sun in wreath.

29. 1 Rupee 2010 (1953 A.D.) 125.00
30. ½ Rupee 2010 1953 A.D.) 65.00
31. ¼ Rupee 2010 (1953 A.D.) 30.00
32. ⅛ Rupee 2010 (1953 A.D.) 20.00

MAHENDRA, 1955-

Square between small and large circle. Rev. Circle within panelled legend.

33. 2 Rupees 2012 (1955 A.D.) 85.00
34. 1 Rupee 2012, 19 (1955, 62 A.D.) 40.00
35. ½ Rupee 2012, 19 (1955, 62 A.D.) 22.50
36. ¼ Rupee 2012 (1955 A.D.) 17.50
37. ⅛ Rupee 2012 (1955 A.D.) 15.00

Plumed crown. Rev. Legend with sword and wreath. On Mahendra's coronation.

38. 1 Rupee 2013 (1956 A.D.) 125.00
39. ½ Rupee 2013 (1956 A.D.) 65.00
40. ⅛ Rupee 2013 (1956 A.D.) 27.50

NETHERLANDS

Mint and mint marks:—Torch or lis for Utrecht; B for Brussels.

Early Dutch coins were adaptations of types existing in Spain, England, France and the Holy Roman Empire.

The Guilder as a true Dutch denomination was first introduced about 1680 in Zeeland. The Guilder is sometimes also called a Florin.

A. Kings of —

LOUIS NAPOLEON, 1806-1810

Head. Rev. Arms.

1. 20 Guilders 1808, 10 .... 2000.00
2. 10 Guilders 1808, 10 ....*... 1500.00
3. 1 Ducat 1809, 10 ....*... 125.00

Head. Rev. Knight standing.

4. 1 Ducat 1808, 09 .... 225.00

Knight standing. Rev. Square tablet.

5. 2 Ducats 1806, 07, 08 ....*... 250.00
6. 1 Ducat 1806, 07, 08 .... 75.00

NAPOLEON, 1810-1814
(For French type coins struck in the Netherlands, see under France).

WILLIAM I, 1813-1840

Head. Rev. Arms.

7. 10 Guilders 1818-40, Torch or lis mm. ....*...... 150.00
8. 10 Guilders 1824-29. B mm. 125.00
9. 5 Guilders 1827. Torch mm. 125.00
10. 5 Guilders 1826, 27. B mm. 100.00

WILLIAM II, 1840-1849

Head. Rev. Arms flanked by value.

11. 10 Guilders 1842 .... 1000.00
12. 5 Guilders 1843 .... 400.00

Head. Rev. Arms in wreath. Trade coins called "Negotie-penning". The denomination is expressed by the weight of the coin in grams and may be found on the Rev.

13. 20 Guilders or 13.458 Grams 1848 .... 1400.00
14. 10 Guilders or 6.729 Grams 1848 ....*...... 1000.00
15. 5 Guilders or 3.3645 Grams 1848 .... 850.00

WILLIAM III, 1849-1890

Head. Rev. Arms in wreath. Trade coins or "Negotiepenning".

16. 20 Guilders or 13.458 Grams 1850, 51, 53 ....*...... 1200.00
17. 10 Guilders or 6.729 Grams 1850, 51 .... 500.00
18. 5 Guilders or 3.3645 Grams 1850, 51 .... 450.00

Head. Rev. Arms flanked by value.

19. 10 Guilders 1875-89 .... 30.00

WILHELMINA, 1890-1948

Girl head with long flowing hair. Rev. Arms. The first two dates are rare.

20. 10 Guilders 1892 .... 1500.00
21. 10 Guilders 1895 ....*...... 1000.00
22. 10 Guilders 1897 .... 65.00

Large youthful head with coronet. Rev. Arms.

23. 10 Guilders 1898 .... 100.00

Small older head with coronet. Rev. Arms.

24. 10 Guilders 1911-17 .... 30.00
25. 5 Guilders 1912 .... 60.00

Mature head. Rev. Arms.

26. 10 Guilders 1925-33 .... 25.00

B. United Provinces of —, 1576-1795

(The Issues of the United Provinces were succeeded by those of the Batavian Republic, which see).

Heads of Ferdinand and Isabella of Spain. Rev. Arms on eagle. The coins were struck about 1590 and are undated.

No.	Province	Denomination		Price
27.	CAMPEN.	2 Ducats		275.00
28.		1 Ducat		100.00
29.	GELDERLAND.	2 Ducats		500.00
30.	OVERYSSEL.	2 Ducats		275.00
31.		1 Ducat		125.00
32.	WESTFRISIA.	2 Ducats		300.00
33.	ZEELAND.	2 Ducats	*	300.00
34.		1 Ducat		125.00
35.	ZWOLLE.	2 Ducats		275.00
36.		1 Ducat		100.00

Bust of Philip II of Spain. Rev. Arms. The coins were struck about 1590 and are undated.

37.	GELDERLAND.	1 Real d'Or ....*......	275.00
38.		1 Real d'Or. "England" in title	350.00
39.		½ Real d'Or	125.00
40.		½ Real d'Or. "England" in title	350.00
41.	HOLLAND.	1 Real d'Or	300.00
42.		½ Real d'Or. Bust left	150.00
43.		½ Real d'Or. Bust right	500.00
44.	OVERYSSEL.	½ Real d'Or	200.00

Royal figure in ship. Rev. Rose or sun in center of crowns.

45.	CAMPEN.	1 Noble ND (1600)	275.00
46.		½ Noble ND (1600)	175.00
47.		¼ Noble ND (1600)	650.00
48.	FRISIA.	1 Noble ND (1600)	900.00
49.		½ Noble ND (1600)	750.00
50.	GELDERLAND.	2 Nobles ND	1500.00
51.		1 Noble 1579, ND	500.00
52.		½ Noble 1579, ND	300.00
53.	'S-HEERENBERG.	1 Noble ND	Rare
54.	OMMELANDEN.	1 Noble 1579, ND	Rare
55.	OVERYSSEL.	1 Noble 1583, ND ....*......	250.00
56.		¼ Noble 1583, 85, ND	400.00
57.	UTRECHT.	1 Noble 1579	750.00
58.		1 Noble ND (1600)	250.00
59.		½ Noble 1579	575.00
60.		½ Noble ND (1600)	150.00
61.		¼ Noble 1579	400.00
62.	ZEELAND.	1 Noble 1583, 84, 85, ND	250.00
63.		½ Noble 1583, 85, ND	200.00

Knight in ship holding seven shields. Rev. Rose and bundle of arrows.

64.	ZEELAND.	1 Noble 1586	1250.00
65.		½ Noble 1587, 93, 94, 95	400.00

Royal figure seated. Rev. Arms within rose.

66.	CAMPEN.	8 Nobles or 4 Souverain d'or ND (1600)	Rare
67.		2 Nobles or 1 Souverain d'or ND (1600)	2000.00

Arms. Rev. Cross.

68.	BATENBURG.	1 Cruzado ND	400.00
69.	GELDERLAND.	2 Florins 1577, 78	400.00
70.	HOLLAND.	1 Couronne d'Or 1576, 80, ND	250.00
71.	UTRECHT.	1 Couronne d'Or 1573-80, ND	275.00
72.		2 Florins 1577	600.00

Double eagle. Rev. Five shields.

73.	FRISIA.	1 Florin 1617, 18, 19	100.00

Double eagle. Rev. Arms.

74.	FRISIA.	1 Florin 1618, 19	400.00

Orb. Rev. Three shields.

75.	CAMPEN.	1 Florin ND (1612-19)	150.00

Royal figure standing. Rev. Legend (plain or in tablet).

76.	CAMPEN.	2 Ducats 1650-58 ....*......	250.00
77.		1 Ducat 1596-1676	100.00
78.	DEVENTER.	2 Ducats 1662, 66	575.00
79.		1 Ducat 1603-66	150.00
80.	ZWOLLE.	2 Ducats 1655, 56, 62	250.00
81.		1 Ducat 1630-76, ND .....*......	100.00

Royal figure standing. Rev. Three shields.

82.	CAMPEN.	1 Florin 1597	150.00

Royal figure standing. Rev. Arms.

83.	WESTFRISIA.	1 Ducat 1587-1605	100.00

Royal figure standing. Rev. Madonna.

84.	GELDERLAND.	1 Ducat ND (1591)	150.00
85.	OVERYSSEL.	1 Ducat ND (1579)	100.00
86.	UTRECHT.	1 Ducat 1591. Figure between V-D ..	500.00
87.	ZWOLLE.	1 Ducat ND (1600)	100.00

William the Silent standing. Rev. Legend.

88.	HOLLAND.	1 Ducat 1583	1000.00

Knight standing with shield. Rev. Tablet.

89.	FRISIA.	1 Ducat 1604, 05	250.00

Knight standing. Rev. Tablet.

90.	FRISIA.	2 Ducats 1612, 61	....	400.00
91.		1 Ducat 1586-1693	....	100.00
92.	GELDERLAND.	2 Ducats 1656-1761	....	250.00
93.		1 Ducat 1586-1792	....	90.00
94.	HOLLAND.	2 Ducats 1645-1793	....	200.00
95.		1 Ducat 1586-1791	......*.....	60.00
96.	OVERYSSEL.	1 Ducat 1593-1773	....	80.00
97.	UTRECHT.	2 Ducats 1652-1794	......*.....	200.00
98.		1 Ducat 1587-1794	....	50.00
99.	WESTFRISIA.	2 Ducats 1660-1780	....	225.00
100.		1 Ducat 1607-1780	....	75.00
101.	ZEELAND.	2 Ducats 1646-84	....	250.00
102.		1 Ducat 1586-1763	....	80.00

Knight standing. Rev. Circle of shields.

103.	ZEELAND.	30 Guilders 1683, 84, 86, 87	......	1000.00

Knight standing. Rev. Arms.

104.	ZEELAND.	10 Ducats 1682-87	....	1500.00

Knight standing between F-D. Rev. Shield.

105.	FRISIA.	1 Ducat ND (1600)	....	550.00

Horseman. Rev. Arms. Early style.

106.	FRISIA.	2 Cavaliers 1583. Small type	......	600.00
107.		1 Cavalier 1582-99. Small type	....	200.00
108.		1 Cavalier 1607-28. Large type	....	500.00
109.		½ Cavalier 1585. Small type	....	250.00
110.		½ Cavalier 1620-44. Large type	....	350.00
111.	GELDERLAND.	1 Cavalier 1582, ND. Small type	..	450.00
112.		1 Cavalier 1606-28. Large type	....	500.00
113.		½ Cavalier 1607-44	....	250.00
114.	HOLLAND.	1 Cavalier 1606-32	......*.....	500.00
115.		½ Cavalier 1606-45	....	225.00
116.	OVERYSSEL.	1 Cavalier 1582	....	900.00

117.		1 Cavalier 1607-20. Large type	....	600.00
118.		½ Cavalier 1606-16	....	250.00
119.	UTRECHT.	1 Cavalier 1606-25	....	500.00
120.		½ Cavalier 1607-44	......*.....	225.00
121.	WESTFRISIA.	1 Cavalier 1621-27	....	425.00
122.		½ Cavalier 1621-44	....	250.00
123.	ZEELAND.	1 Cavalier 1606-44	....	400.00
124.		½ Cavalier 1610-48	....	250.00
125.	ZWOLLE.	½ Cavalier 1644	....	350.00

Horseman. Rev. Arms. Modern style.

126.	GELDERLAND.	14 Guilders 1750-62	....	200.00
127.		7 Guilders 1750-62	......*.....	125.00
128.	GRONINGEN.	14 Guilders 1761	....	200.00
129.		7 Guilders 1761	....	125.00
130.	HOLLAND.	14 Guilders 1749-63	....	200.00
131.		7 Guilders 1749-63	....	125.00
132.	OVERYSSEL.	14 Guilders 1760-63	....	225.00
133.		7 Guilders 1760-63	....	140.00
134.	UTRECHT.	14 Guilders 1749-63	......*.....	200.00
135.		7 Guilders 1749-63	....	125.00
136.	WESTFRISIA.	14 Guilders 1749-63	....	200.00
137.		7 Guilders 1749-63	....	125.00
138.	ZEELAND.	14 Guilders 1760-64	....	200.00
139.		7 Guilders 1760-64	....	125.00

C. Cities and States of —

AMSTERDAM

Knight standing. Rev. Tablet and city shield.

140.	5 Ducats 1673	....	450.00
141.	4 Ducats 1673	....	400.00
142.	3 Ducats 1673	....	400.00
143.	1 Ducat 1673	....	150.00

BAAR

Three shields. Rev. Arms on cross.

144.	1 Florin 1445	....	500.00

BATAVIAN REPUBLIC

Knight standing. Rev. Tablet. This type was continued under the Kings of the Netherlands.

145.	2 Ducats 1795-1805	............*......	275.00
146.	1 Ducat 1795-1805	....	75.00

BATENBURG

Barons of —

ANONYMOUS, 1516-1525
St. John. Rev. Orb.

147.	1 Florin ND	550.00

THIERRY II, 1432-1456
St. Peter. Rev. Floriated cross.

148.	1 Peter d'or ND	2000.00

WILLIAM, 1556-1573
St. Stephen. Rev. Eagle shield.

149.	2 Ducats ND	425.00
150.	1 Florin ND	175.00

Christ and Pharisee. Rev. Arms.

151.	2 Ducats ND	900.00

St. Victor standing. Rev. Madonna.

152.	1 Ducat ND	150.00

Bust of Ferdinand. Rev. Madonna.

153.	1 Ducat ND	150.00

St. Michael. Rev. Ship.

154.	1 Angel 1561, 62, ND	300.00
155.	½ Angel 1562	700.00

Serpent on cross. Rev. Floriated cross.

156.	1 Couronne d'or ND	400.00

Arms. Rev. Cross. Portuguese style.

157.	1 Cruzado ND	425.00

HERMAN THIERRY, 1573-1612

Ruler standing. Rev. Arms.

158.	1 Ducat 1577, 78, 79	200.00

Arms. Rev. Cross.

159.	1 Couronne d'or ND	500.00

Knight standing. Rev. Madonna.

160.	1 Ducat 1579, ND	200.00

Knight. Rev. Lion.

161.	1 Ducat ND	300.00

St. Victor standing. Rev. Arms.

162.	1 Ducat ND	350.00

St. John. Rev. Arms.

163.	1 Florin ND	350.00

CAMPEN

St. John. Rev. Orb.

164.	1 Florin ND (1525)	250.00

Emperor Maximilian seated. Rev. Arms.

165.	1 Real ND	2500.00

St. Nicolas. Rev. Orb.

166.	1 Florin ND	700.00

DEVENTER

St. Lebuin. Rev. Orb.

167.	1 Florin 1488	250.00
168.	1 Florin ND	200.00

Eagle. Rev. Orb.

169.	1 Florin 1523	125.00

Double eagle. Rev. Arms.

170.	1 Florin 1600	275.00
171.	1 Florin ND (1612-37)	100.00

DEVENTER - CAMPEN - ZWOLLE

Orb. Rev. Three or four shields.

172.	1 Florin 1546, ND	200.00

Double eagle. Rev. Three helmeted shields.

173.	1 Florin 1568-79	275.00

Royal figure standing. Rev. Three shields and orb.

174.	1 Florin 1557	300.00

DUURSTEDE

Head of Madelinus. Rev. Cross.

175.	1 Triens ND (650-750 A.D.)	200.00

FRANEKER

St. John. Rev. Orb.

176.	1 Florin 1491, 92, ND	300.00

FRIESLAND

Counts of —

GEORGE AND HENRY, 1500-1504
St. John. Rev. Orb.

177. 1 Florin ND 575.00

GEORGE, 1504-1515
St. John. Rev. Orb.

178. 1 Florin ND 575.00

St. Bonifacius. Rev. Arms.

179. 1 Florin ND 425.00

GELDERLAND

Dukes of —

EDWARD, 1361-1371
Lamb. Rev. Cross.

180. 2 Mouton d'ors ND 2250.00
181. 1 Mouton d'or ND 1750.00

Lion. Rev. Cross.

182. 1 Lion d'or ND 2500.00

MECHTELD, 1371-1379
Bust under dais. Rev. Two shields.

183. 1 Florin ND 1250.00

MARIE, 1361-1399
Bust under dais. Rev. Arms.

184. 1 Florin ND 250.00

Arms. Rev. Cross.

185. 1 Couronne d'or ND 400.00

WILLIAM I, 1377-1402
Bust under dais. Rev. Arms.

186. 1 Florin ND 125.00

St. John. Rev. Arms.

187. 1 Florin ND 450.00

Figure in ship. Rev. Cross.

188. 1 Noble ND 1600.00
189. ½ Noble ND 1400.00

Ruler on throne. Rev. Cross.

190. 1 Chaise d'or ND 1700.00

REINALD IV, 1394-1402
St. John. Rev. Five shields.

191. 1 Florin ND. Struck in Venray 700.00
192. 1 Florin ND 125.00

St. John. Rev. Two shields.

193. 1 Florin ND. Struck in Nymegen 575.00

Angel. Rev. Madonna.

194. 1 Florin ND 500.00

Arms. Rev. Horseman.

195. 1 Florin ND 700.00

Bust under dais. Rev. Two shields.

196. 1 Florin ND 750.00

St. Peter. Rev. Five shields.

197. 1 Florin ND 800.0

ARNOLD, 1423-1473
Ruler standing. Rev. Four shields.

198. 1 Florin ND 225.0

St. John. Rev. Five shields.

199. 1 Florin ND 600.00

St. John. Rev. Arms.

200. 1 Florin ND 70.00

St. John. Rev. Five shields.

201. 1 Florin ND 250.0

Horseman. Rev. Arms.

202. 2 Florins (Cavalier d'or) ND .... Rare
203. 1 Florin ND 125.00
204. ½ Florin ND 900.00

Arms on cross. Rev. Three shields.

205. 1 Florin ND 700.00

CHARLES I, 1473-1477
St. Andrew. Rev. Arms.

206. 1 Florin ND 225.00

CHARLES II (MINORITY), 1477-1479
St. John. Rev. Four shields.

207. 1 Florin ND. Struck in Roermond 450.00

PHILIP THE FAIR (MINORITY), 1482-1494
St. Andrew. Rev. Arms on cross.

208. 1 Florin ND 900.00

Ruler on throne. Rev. Crowned Arms.

209. 1 Real 1487 .... 4500.00

Ruler in ship. Rev. Cross.

210. ½ Noble 1488 .... 1500.00

CHARLES II, 1492-1538
St. John. Rev. Arms.

211. 1 Florin ND 75.00

Horseman. Rev. Arms.

212. 1 Florin ND 85.00

Christ. Rev. Three shields.

213. 1 Florin ND 550.00

Christ. Rev. Four shields.

214. 1 Florin ND 700.00

CHARLES V OF SPAIN, 1543-1555
Bust with sword and sceptre. Rev. Arms on eagle.

215. 1 Real d'or ND 350.00
216. 1 Florin ND 300.00

Arms. Rev. Cross.

217. 1 Couronne 1544, 45, 55 .... 150.00

PHILIP II OF SPAIN, 1555-1579
St. Andrew. Rev. Arms.

218. 1 Florin 1568 .... 450.00

Arms between P-P. Rev. Cross.

219. 1 Couronne 1571, 72, 73, 75 .... 375.00

GRONINGEN

St. John. Rev. Orb.

220. 1 Florin 1488, ND 450.00

St. John. Rev. Double eagle.

221. 1 Florin 1591 .... 350.00

St. Martin. Rev. Orb.

222. 1 Florin ND 125.00

Double eagle. Rev. Orb.

223. ½ Florin 1492 .... 700.00

'S-HEERENBERG

Counts of —

OSWALD, 1511-1546

St. John. Rev. Four shields.

224. 1 Florin ND 500.00

WILLIAM IV, 1546-1586

St. Michael. Rev. Ship.

225. 1 Angel ND 275.00

Bust of St. Oswald. Rev. Madonna.

226. 1 Ducat ND 275.00

St. Oswald standing. Rev. Arms.

227. 1 Ducat ND 400.00
228. 1 Ducat 1577 .... 500.00

St. Oswald standing. Rev. Madonna.

229. 1 Ducat ND 400.00

FREDERICK, 1577-1580
Horse carriage. Rev. Cross.

230. 1 Pistolet 1578, 79, ND 300.00

St. Pancras standing. Rev. Madonna.

231. 1 Florin 1578, 79 .... 500.00

St. Pancras standing. Rev.. Lion.

232. 1 Ducat ND 400.00

St. Pancras standing. Rev. Arms.

233. 1 Ducat 1578 .... 500.00

St. Martin. Rev. Arms.

234. 1 Florin 1577 .... 600.00

HERMAN FREDERICK, 1627-1631
Bust. Rev. Four shields.

235. 1 Florin ND 600.00

Eagle. Rev. Arms.

236. 1 Florin ND 600.00

St. Stephen. Rev. Arms.

237. 1 Florin ND 115.00

HOLLAND

Counts of —

WILLIAM V, 1350-1389
Lamb. Rev. Cross.

238. 2 Mouton d'ors ND 1000.00
239. 1 Mouton d'or ND 700.00

Ruler on throne. Rev. Cross.

240. 1 Chaise d'or ND 300.00

Ruler standing. Rev. Arms.

241. 1 Florin ND 100.00

Horseman. Rev. Cross.

242. 1 Rider ND 700.00

ALBERT, 1389-1404
Ruler on throne. Rev. Cross.

243. 1 Chaise d'or ND 250.00

Two lions with shield. Rev. Cross.

244. 1 Chaise d'or ND 1500.00

Ruler standing. Rev. Arms.

245. 1 Florin ND 200.00

Arms. Rev. Cross.

246. 1 Couronne d'or ND 800.00

WILLIAM VI, 1404-1417
Ruler on throne. Rev. Cross.

247. 2 Chaise d'ors ND .... Rare
248. 1 Chaise d'or ND 175.00
249. ½ Chaise d'or ND 175.00
250. ⅓ Chaise d'or ND 200.00

JOHN, 1421-1425
Ruler on throne. Rev. Cross.

251. 1 Chaise d'or ND 225.00
252. ½ Chaise d'or ND 250.00

St. John. Rev. Five shields.

253. 1 Florin ND 110.00

PHILIP THE GOOD, 1425-1428 (AS HEIR)
Ruler on throne. Rev. Cross.

254. 1 Chaise d'or ND 150.00
255. ½ Chaise d'or ND 125.00

PHILIP THE GOOD AND JACQUELINE, 1428-1433
Ruler on throne. Rev. Cross.

256. 1 Chaise d'or ND 200.00
257. ½ Chaise d'or ND 175.00

PHILIP THE GOOD, 1433-1467 (AS COUNT)

Lion. Rev. Arms.

258. 1 Lion d'or ND 250.00
259. ⅔ Lion d'or ND ....*...... 500.00

St. Andrew. Rev. Arms.

260. 1 Florin ND 500.00

Knight on horse. Rev. Arms on cross.

261. 1 Rider ND ....*...... 250.00
262. ½ Rider ND 400.00

MARY, 1477-1482
St. Andrew. Rev. Arms.

263. 1 Florin ND 500.00

MAXIMILIAN AND PHILIP, 1482-1494
Ruler on throne. Rev. Crowned arms.

264. 1 Real d'or 1487 .... 2750.00

Ruler on ship. Rev. Arms on cross.

265. 1 Noble ND ....*...... 1700.00
266. ½ Noble 1488 .... 500.00

St. Andrew. Rev. Arms.

267. 1 Ducat 1487, 89 .... 1000.00

PHILIP THE FAIR, 1496-1506
St. Philip. Rev. Cross.

268. 1 Florin ND 100.00
269. ½ Florin ND 225.00

Full length figure. Rev. Arms on cross.

270. 1 Florin ND 225.00

CHARLES V OF SPAIN, 1515-1555
St. Philip. Rev. Cross.

271. 1 Florin ND 100.00
272. ½ Florin ND 450.00

Bust with sword and orb. Rev. Arms on eagle.

273. 1 Real d'or ND ....*...... 275.00
274. 1 Florin ND 100.00

Arms. Rev. Eagle in shield.

275. ½ Real d'or ND 125.00

Cross. Rev. Arms.

276. 1 Couronne d'or 1543-46, ND 125.00

PHILIP II OF SPAIN, 1555-1581
St. Andrew standing. Rev. Arms.

277. 1 Florin 1567, 68, 69 .... 275.00

Cross. Rev. Arms.

278. 1 Couronne d'or 1576, 80, ND 350.00

MIDDELBURG

Legend in circle. Rev. Blank. Square siege coins.

279. 4 Ducats 1573 .... 700.00
280. 2 Ducats 1573 .... 350.00
281. 1 Ducat 1573, 74 ....*...... 200.00

NYMEGEN

St. Stephen standing. Rev. Arms.

282. 2 Ducats ND (1500-56) ....*...... 275.00
283. 1 Florin ND (1499-1525) 150.00

Bust of Charles V of Spain. Rev. St. Stephen.

284. 1 Ducat ND 600.00

Bust of Emperor Ferdinand. Rev. St. Stephen.

285. 1 Ducat 1558 .... 600.00

St. Stephen seated. Rev. Three shields and orb.

286. 1 Florin 1557 .... 600.00

Arms. Rev. Double eagle.

287. 1 Florin 1569, 1602, 20 .... 700.00

OVERYSSEL

CHARLES V OF SPAIN, 1515-1555
Arms on cross. Rev. Arms.

288. ½ Real ND. Mintmark C on cross 700.00

Bust. Rev. Arms on double eagle.

289. 1 Florin ND. Mintmark C on cross 550.00

ROERMOND

St. John. Rev. Lily.

290. 1 Florin ND (1343-61) 500.00

UTRECHT

Bishops of —

ARNOLD, 1371-1378
St. Martin in dais. Rev. Arms.

291. 1 Florin ND 1000.00

FLORIS, 1379-1393

Bust in dais. Rev. Two shields.

292. 1 Florin ND 350.00

Bust in dais. Rev. Eagle on shield.

293. 1 Florin ND 350.00

Ruler seated. Rev. Cross.

294. 1 Chaise d'or ND 625.00

FREDERICK, 1394-1423
St. Peter. Rev. Four shields.

295. 1 Florin ND 500.00

St. Peter. Rev. Five shields.

296. 1 Florin ND 500.00

St. John. Rev. Arms.

297. 1 Florin ND 75.00

St. John. Rev. Three shields.

298. 1 Florin ND 500.00

St. John. Rev. Four shields.

299. 1 Florin ND 400.00

ZWEDER, 1425-1426
St. John. Rev. Five shields.

300. 1 Florin ND 750.00

RUDOLPH (BISHOP-ELECT), 1426-1433
St. Martin. Rev. Arms.

301. 1 Florin ND 200.00

St. John. Rev. Arms.

302. 1 Florin ND 400.00

St. John. Rev. Four shields.

303. 1 Florin ND .... Rare

Two shields. Rev. Eagle.

304. 1 Florin ND 450.00

RUDOLPH, 1433-1455
St. Martin. Rev. Arms.

305. 1 Florin ND 75.00

WALRAVEN, 1433-1450
St. Martin. Rev. Arms.

306. 1 Florin ND 850.00

DAVID, 1455-1496
St. Martin. Rev. Arms.

307. 1 Florin ND 75.00

King David behind shield. Rev. Ornate floriated cross.

308. 1 Harpe d'or ND 300.00

Half length bust with harp. Rev. Arms.

309. ½ Florin 1492 .... 425.00

King David seated. Rev. Arms.

310. 1 Florin 1492 .... 300.00

Christ seated. Rev. Four shields.

311. 1 Florin ND 250.00

ENGELBERT, 1481-1483
St. Martin. Rev. Arms.

312. 1 Florin ND 700.00

FREDERICK, 1496-1516
St. John. Rev. Five shields.

313. 1 Florin ND 125.00

Christ seated. Rev. Four shields.

314. 1 Florin ND 700.00

Bishop seated. Rev. Arms on cross.

315. 1 Florin ND 700.00

PHILIP, 1517-1524
Seated figure. Rev. Arms.

316. 1 Florin ND 425.00

PHILIP II OF SPAIN, 1555-1579
St. Andrew. Rev. Arms.

317. 1 Florin 1568 .... 600.00

VIANEN

Barons of —

HENRY, 1556-1568
St. Michael. Rev. Arms on ship.

318. 1 Angel ND 275.00

Arms. Rev. Cross.

319. 1 Couronne d'or ND 1100.00

Bust of St. Henry. Rev. Madonna.

320. 1 Ducat ND 200.00

St. John. Rev. Four shields.

321. 1 Florin ND 500.00

ZWOLLE

St. Michael. Rev. Orb.

322. 1 Florin ND (1488-1519) 150.00

Double eagle. Rev. Helmeted arms.

323. 1 Florin ND (1590-1612) 125.00

NETHERLANDS EAST INDIES

A. Java Coinage

Symbol. Rev. Incuse square. Struck during the Hindu period, 896-1158. The largest piece weighs about 10 grams.

1. 96 Krisnalas ND	....	500.00
2. 24 Krisnalas ND	..........................*......	85.00
3. 12 Krisnalas ND	....	85.00
4. 6 Krisnalas ND	....	70.00

"B" (Batavia) counterstamped on Dutch ducats during the period 1686-1700.

5. 1 Ducat. Dates before 1700 .... 600.00

Dutch lion in square counterstamped on Japanese gold Kobans of the Keicho era, 1596-1614.

6. 1 Koban ND 2000.00

"Java" (in Arabic) counterstamped on the obverse of Dutch ducats during the period 1753-1761.

7. 1 Ducat. Dates before 1761 .... 200.00

Native legend with Christian date. Rev. Native legend. The "Rupee" (also known as mohur) coinage was struck from dies that were also used for silver coins. The issues from 1808-1816 were struck under foreign occupation; under the French from 1808-1811, and under the British from 1811-1816.

8. 2 Java Ducats 1746, 47, 48	....		700.00
9. 1 Java Ducat 1744, 45, 46	...............*		500.00
10. 2 Gold Rupees 1783	....		800.00
11. 1 Gold Rupee 1766-97	................*		600.00
12. ½ Gold Rupee 1766-1807	.............*		300.00
13. ¼ Gold Rupee 1766	....		500.00
14. 1 Gold Rupee 1808-16	....		400.00
15. ½ Gold Rupee 1813-16	....		400.00

B. Sumatra Coinage

Native legend on each side. Struck under the Sultans of Atjeh during the period 1297-1760.

16. 1 Mas ND 50.00

C. Coinage under the Kingdom of the Netherlands

Knight standing. Rev. Legend in square tablet. This type was struck exclusively for use in the East Indies beginning in 1814. They were also used as trade coins among the Dutch banks. The type does not change from ruler to ruler.

17. 1 Ducat 1814-40. (William I). Utrecht Mint. Torch mm. ..		40.00
18. 1 Ducat 1824-30. Brussels Mint. Palm branch mm.	......	100.00
19. 1 Ducat 1841. (William II)	....	55.00
20. 2 Ducats 1854, 67. (William III)	....	750.00
21. 1 Ducat 1849-85. (William III)	....	55.00
22. 1 Ducat 1894-1937. (Wilhelmina)	....	25.00
23. 1 Ducat 1960. (Juliana)	....	50.00

NEWFOUNDLAND

Head of Queen Victoria of Great Britain. Rev. Value and date.

1. 2 Dollars 1865-88 (1880 Rare) 95.00

NORWAY

A. Danish Kings of —

FREDERICK III, 1648-1670

Crowned bust facing. Rev. Lion.

1. 1 Ducat 1660 .... 1250.00

Laureate bust. Rev. Lion.

2. 1 Portugaloser 1665, 68, 69 .... 5500.00
3. 2 Ducats 1665 ....*...... 1500.00
4. 1 Ducat 1665, 68, 69 .... 750.00
5. ½ Ducat 1666, ND 500.00

CHRISTIAN V, 1670-1699

Laureate bust. Rev. Lion.

6. 4 Ducats 1671 .... 3000.00
7. 3 Ducats 1671, 73, 77 .... 1500.00
8. 2 Ducats 1673, ND ....*...... 1200.00
9. 1 Ducat 1673, ND 575.00
10. ½ Ducat ND 450.00

Laureate head. Rev. Lion. Thick flan.

11. 2 Ducats ND 700.00

Ruler on horse. Rev. Lion.

12. 3 Ducats 1673 .... 1250.00

Crowned C5 and lion. Rev. Long cross.

13. 1 Louis d'or 1673, 84, 85 ....*...... 1200.00
14. ½ Louis d'or 1684, 85 .... 800.00

B. Swedish Kings of —

OSCAR II, 1872-1905

Head. Rev. Lion shield and two values.

15. 5 Species-20 Kroner 1874, 75 .... 100.00
16. 2½ Species-10 Kroner 1874 .... 125.00

Head. Rev. Lion shield.

17. 20 Kroner 1876-1902 .... 75.00
18. 10 Kroner 1877, 1902 .... 95.00

C. Independent Kings of —

HAAKON VII, 1905-1957

Crowned head. Rev. St. Olaf standing.

19. 20 Kroner 1910 .... 125.00
20. 10 Kroner 1910 .... 150.00

PARAGUAY

Lion seated before pole bearing the Liberty Cap. Rev. Justice seated. This coin was not placed in circulation.

1. 4 Pesos 1867 .... 6000.00

Lion standing before pole bearing the Liberty Cap. Rev. Value in wreath, star above.

2. 5 Pesos 1873 .... 7500.00

Bust of Stroessner. Rev. Lion seated before pole bearing the Liberty Cap. Only 50 pieces were struck for presentation purposes.

3. 10,000 Guaranies 1968 .... Rare

PERSIA (IRAN)

Shahs of —

It will be noted that the Shahs did not picture themselves on their coinage until recent times, the first portrait piece appearing in 1854.

ISMAIL I, 1502-1524

Arab legend on each side. With dates from about 907-930 A.H.

1. 1 Ashrafi ....*...... 85.00
2. ¼ Ashrafi 60.00

TAHMASP I, 1524-1576
Arab legend on each side. With dates from about 930-984 A.H.

3. 1 Ashrafi 125.00
4. ⅔ Ashrafi 100.00

MOHAMMED KHUDABANDA, 1578-1587
Arab legend on each side. With dates from about 985-996 A.H.

5. 1½ Ashrafi 150.00
6. 1 Ashrafi 85.00

ABBAS I, 1587-1629
Arab legend on each side. With dates from about 996-1038 A.H.

7. 2 Ashrafis 150.00
8. 1 Ashrafi 125.00
9. ½ Ashrafi 50.00

HUSSEIN, 1694-1722
Arab legend on each side. With dates from about 1105-1135 A.H.

10. 1 Ashrafi 60.00

TAHMASP II, 1722-1731

Arab legend on each side. With dates from about 1135-1144 A.H.

11. 1 Ashrafi 60.00

ASHRAF, 1725-1729
Arab legend on each side. With dates from about 1137-1142 A.H.

12. 1 Ashrafi 75.00

ABBAS III, 1731-1736
Arab legend on each side. With dates from about 1144-1148 A.H.

13. 1 Ashrafi 50.00

NADIR, 1736-1747

Arab legend on each side. With dates from about 1148-1158 A.H.

14. 1 Ashrafi ....*...... 50.00
15. 2 Mohurs 150.00
16. 1 Mohur ....*...... 60.00

RUKH, 1748-1750
Arab legend on each side. With dates from about 1161-1163 A.H.

17. 1 Mohur 90.00

KERIM KHAN, 1750-1779

Arab legend on each side. With dates from about 1163-1193 A.H.

18. 1 Mohur ....*...... 50.00
19. ½ Mohur 40.00
20. ¼ Mohur 30.00

Arab legend. Rev. Legend in star shaped pattern.

21. 1 Mohur 125.00

MOHAMMED HASAN KHAN, 1750-1759

Arab legend on each side. With dates from about 1163-1172 A.H.

22.   1 Mohur 60.00
23.   ¼ Mohur 45.00

ABUL FATH KHAN, 1779

Arab legend on each side.

24.   ¼ Mohur 1193 A.H. 150.00

SADIK KHAN, 1779-1782

Arab legend on each side. With dates from about 1193-1196 A.H.

25.   1 Mohur 60.00
26.   ¼ Mohur 40.00

ALI MURAD KHAN, 1779-1785

Arab legend on each side. With dates from about 1193-1199 A.H.

27.   1 Mohur 60.00
28.   ¼ Mohur 40.00

JAAFAR KHAN, 1785-1789

Arab legend on each side. With dates from about 1199-1203 A.H.

29.   1 Mohur 60.00

LUTFALI KHAN, 1789-1794

Arab legend on each side. With dates from about 1203-1209 A.H.

30.   ¼ Mohur 50.00

AKA MOHAMMED KHAN, 1794-1797

Arab legend. Rev. Embellished legend with date in panel.

31.   1 Toman 1209 A.H. (1794 A.D.) 175.00

FATH ALI, 1797-1834

Arab legend on each side. With dates from about 1212-1250 A.H.

32.   5 Tomans 225.00
33.   2 Tomans 100.00
34.   1 Toman ....*...... 50.00
35.   ½ Toman 40.00
36.   ⅔ Toman 40.00
37.   ⅓ Toman 25.00

Ruler on horse. Rev. Legend.

38.   2 Tomans 1239 A.H. (1823 A.D.) 400.00
39.   ⅔ Toman 1236 A.H. (1820 A.D.) 200.00

Ruler seated on throne. Rev. Legend in panel or star as indicated.

40.   ½ Toman 1249 A.H. (1833 A.D.). Panel 100.00
41.   ½ Toman 1249 A.H. (1833 A.D.). Star 125.00

MOHAMMED, 1834-1848

Lion. Rev. Legend in square.

42.   ½ Toman 1262 A.H. (1846 A.D.) 60.00

Arab legend on each side.

43.   ½ Toman 1250-1264 A.H. (1834-48 A.D.) 40.00

HASAN SALAR, REBEL, 1848-1850

Arab legend on each side.

44.   ½ Toman 1265 A.H. (1848 A.D.) 100.00

NASREDIN, 1848-1896

(The coinage of this ruler is dated from 1265-1314 A.H.).

Arab legend on each side in either a circle, square or octogram.

45.   1 Toman ....*...... 40.00
46.   ½ Toman 30.00
47.   ¼ Toman 20.00

Toughra in wreath. Rev. Legend in wreath.

48.   2 Tomans 1281 A.H. (1864 A.D.) 275.00

Half-length uniformed bust facing. Rev. Legend.

49.   2 Tomans 1271 A.H. (1854 A.D.) ....*...... 125.00
50.   1 Toman 1273-91 A.H. (1856-74 A.D.) ....*...... 60.00
51.   ⅕ Toman 1274 A.H. (1857 A.D.) 20.00

Lion. Rev. Legend in wreath or circle.

52.	10 Tomans	....	450.00
53.	5 Tomans	.............................*......	350.00
54.	2 Tomans	....	110.00
55.	1 Toman	....	55.00
56.	½ Toman	....	35.00
57.	⅕ Toman	....	20.00

Bust. Rev. Legend in wreath or circle.

58.	25 Tomans	....	1500.00
59.	20 Tomans	....	700.00
60.	10 Tomans	.............................*......	525.00
61.	5 Tomans	....	250.00
62.	2 Tomans	.............................*......	100.00
63.	1 Toman	....	70.00
64.	½ Toman	....	40.00
65.	⅕ Toman	....	20.00

MUZAFFAREDIN, 1896-1907

(The coinage of this ruler is dated from 1314-1325 A.H.).

Uniformed bust with plumed hat. Rev. Legend in wreath.

66.	10 Tomans	....	700.00
67.	5 Tomans	....	400.00
68.	2 Tomans	.............................*......	85.00
69.	1 Toman	.............................*......	50.00
70.	½ Toman	....	35.00
71.	⅕ Toman	....	25.00

Same type as above but with Persian characters at each side of bust on Obv. On his birthday.

72.	2 Tomans 1322 A.H. (1904 A.D.)	..............*......	125.00
73.	1 Toman 1322 A.H. (1904 A.D.)	....	200.00

Lion. Rev. Legend in wreath.

74.	10 Tomans	....	700.00
75.	5 Tomans	....	350.00
76.	1 Toman	.............................*......	40.00
77.	½ Toman	....	30.00
78.	⅕ Toman	....	20.00

MOHAMMED ALI, 1907-1909

Uniformed bust with plumed hat. Rev. Lion.

79.	5 Tomans 1324, 26 A.H. (1907, 09 A.D.)	....	750.00

Uniformed bust with plumed hat. Rev. Legend in wreath.

80.	2 Tomans 1326, 27 A.H. (1908, 09 A.D.)	....	300.00
81.	1 Toman 1326, 27 A.H. (1908, 09 A.D.)	.......*......	125.00
82.	½ Toman 1326 A.H. (1908 A.D.)	.............*......	80.00
83.	⅕ Toman 1326 A.H. (1908 A.D.)	....	60.00

Lion. Rev. Legend in wreath.

84.	1 Toman 1324 A.H. (1907 A.D.)	....	50.00
85.	½ Toman 1324 A.H. (1907 A.D.)	....	35.00

AHMED, 1909-1925

(The coinage of this ruler is dated from 1327-1344 A.H.).

Lion. Rev. Legend.

86.	10 Tomans	....	600.00
87.	5 Tomans	....	200.00
88.	1 Toman	....	35.00
89.	½ Toman	....	25.00
90.	⅕ Toman	....	20.00

Bust with plumed hat. Rev. Legend.

91.	10 Tomans	....	500.00
92.	2 Tomans	....	75.00
93.	1 Toman	.............................*......	40.00
94.	½ Toman	....	30.00
95.	⅕ Toman	....	25.00

Bust with plumed hat. Rev. Lion. On the 10th year of reign.

96.	10 Tomans 1337 A.H. (1919 A.D.)	....	500.00
97.	5 Tomans 1337 A.H. (1919 A.D.)	.............*......	300.00
98.	2 Tomans 1337 A.H. (1919 A.D.)	....	75.00
99.	1 Toman 1337 A.H. (1919 A.D.)	....	45.00

RIZA KHAN PAHLEVI, 1925-1941

(The Persian calendar was changed during this reign, causing 1304 A.H. to fall in 1926 A.D.)

Lion. Rev. Legend.

100.	5 Pahlevi 1305 A.H. (1927 A.D.)	75.00
101.	2 Pahlevi 1305 A.H. (1927 A.D.)	40.00
102.	1 Pahlevi 1305 A.H. (1927 A.D.)	30.00
103.	1 Toman 1305 A.H. (1927 A.D.) ....*......	50.00

Bust with plumed hat. Rev. Legend.

104.	5 Pahlevi 1306-08 A.H. (1928-30 A.D.) ....*......	80.00
105.	2 Pahlevi 1306, 08 A.H. (1928, 30 A.D.) ......*......	45.00
106.	1 Pahlevi 1306, 08 A.H. (1928, 30 A.D.)	35.00

Head left with military cap. Rev. Lion.

107.	1 Pahlevi 1310 A.H. (1932 A.D.)	200.00
108.	½ Pahlevi 1310-15 A.H. (1932-36 A.D.)	100.00

MOHAMMED RIZA PAHLEVI, 1942-

Lion. Rev. Legend.

109.	1 Pahlevi 1320-27 A.H. (1942-49 A.D.)	25.00
110.	½ Pahlevi 1322-27 A.H. (1944-49 A.D.)	20.00

Head. Rev. Lion. These coins appear in red gold.

111.	5 Pahlevi 1340 A.H. (1962 A.D.)	200.00
112.	2½ Pahlevi 1340 A.H. (1962 A.D.)	125.00
113.	1 Pahlevi 1328-40 A.H. (1950-62 A.D.) ......*......	25.00
114.	½ Pahlevi 1328-40 A.H. (1950-62 A.D.) ......*......	20.00
115.	¼ Pahlevi 1328-40 A.H. (1950-62 A.D.)	15.00
116.	¼ Pahlevi 1338-40 A.H. (1960-62 A.D.) large flan.	20.00

Bust. Rev. Inscription. Commemorative.

117.	2½ Pahlevi 1338 A.H. (1960 A.D.)	150.00

Bust of Shah and Farah Diba. Rev. Inscription. On marriage.

118.	5 Pahlevi 1339 A.H. (1961 A.D.)	250.00

PERU

Mints and mint marks:—L, LM, ME or monogram for Lima; C or CO for Cuzco. Like the Mexican Centennario, the gold coinage of 1950-1964 was struck to satisfy the demand for gold coins. Since 1862 Peru has used four standards in the minting of its gold coins. These standards are: the French monetary system for Soles of 1863, the English Pound for the Libra denominations 1898-1964, the U.S. gold Dollar for the 50 Soles (equivalent to 20 Dollars) 1930-1931, and the current price of gold at $35.00 per ounce for Soles minted since 1950.

A. Spanish Kings of —

CHARLES II, 1665-1700

Pillars and date. Rev. Cross. Cob type.

1.	8 Escudos 1696-1701 ....*......	1500.00
2.	4 Escudos 1696-1701	2000.00
3.	2 Escudos 1696-1701. L mm	500.00
4.	2 Escudos 1698. C mm	750.00
5.	1 Escudo 1696-1701. L mm	500.00
6.	1 Escudo 1698. C mm	600.00

PHILIP V, 1700-1746

Pillars and date. Rev. Cross. Cob type.

7.	8 Escudos 1702-46	600.00
8.	4 Escudos 1702-46	800.00
9.	2 Escudos 1702-46 ....*......	500.00

Crude castle. Rev. Cross.

10.	1 Escudo 1702-46	500.00

LOUIS I, 1724
Pillars and date. Rev. Cross. Cob type.

11.	8 Escudos 1724, 25	3000.00

FERDINAND VI, 1746-1760

Pillars and date. Rev. Cross. Cob type.

12.	8 Escudos 1747-50 ....*......	700.00
13.	4 Escudos 1747-50	1250.00
14.	2 Escudos 1747-50	450.00
15.	1 Escudo 1747-50	350.00

Large bust with flowing wig. Rev. Arms with value.

16. 8 Escudos 1751, 52, 53 .... 375.00
17. 4 Escudos 1751, 52 .... 900.00
18. 2 Escudos 1751, 52, 53 ....*..... 400.00
19. 1 Escudo 1751, 52 .... 225.00

Smaller bust. Rev. Arms without value.

20. 8 Escudos 1754-60 ....*..... 450.00
21. 4 Escudos 1757, 58 .... 900.00
22. 2 Escudos 1758, 59 .... 400.00
23. 1 Escudo 1754, 57, 59 .... 300.00

CHARLES III, 1759-1788

Small armored bust. Rev. Arms.

24. 8 Escudos 1761, 62 .... 500.00
25. 4 Escudos 1761, 62 .... 1000.00
26. 2 Escudos 1761, 62 ....*..... 450.00
27. 1 Escudo 1761, 62 .... 250.00

Large bust. Rev. Arms without value.

28. 8 Escudos 1763-72 .... 450.00
29. 4 Escudos 1769, 70 .... 1500.00
30. 2 Escudos 1765-72 .... 275.00
31. 1 Escudo 1766-72 ....*..... 200.00

Bust. Rev. Arms with value.

32. 8 Escudos 1771-89 ....*..... 250.00
33. 4 Escudos 1777-88 .... 450.00
34. 2 Escudos 1772-89 .... 200.00
35. 1 Escudo 1772-89 .... 125.00

CHARLES IV, 1788-1808

Bust of the previous King, Charles III. Rev. Arms.

36. 8 Escudos 1789, 90, 91 .... 250.00
37. 4 Escudos 1789, 91 ....*..... 575.00
38. 2 Escudos 1790, 91 .... 250.00
39. 1 Escudo 1789, 90, 91 .... 150.00

Bust. Rev. Arms.

40. 8 Escudos 1792-1807 .... 200.00
41. 4 Escudos 1792-1807 .... 450.00
42. 2 Escudos 1792-1808 ....*..... 175.00
43. 1 Escudo 1792-1808 .... 125.00

FERDINAND VII, 1808-1824

Bust in uniform. Rev. Arms.

44. 8 Escudos 1808-12 ....*..... 500.00
45. 4 Escudos 1810, 11 .... 1200.00
46. 2 Escudos 1810, 11 .... 400.00
47. 1 Escudo 1810, 12 .... 250.00

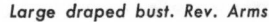

Large draped bust. Rev. Arms.

48. 8 Escudos 1812 .... 500.00
49. 4 Escudos 1812 .... 750.00

Small draped bust. Rev. Arms.

50. 8 Escudos 1812, 13, 14 ....*..... 300.00
51. 4 Escudos 1812, 13 .... 600.00
52. 2 Escudos 1812, 13 .... 300.00
53. 1 Escudo 1812, 13 .... 200.00

Laureate head. Rev. Arms.

54.	8 Escudos 1814-21. ME mm. ....*.....	225.00
55.	8 Escudos 1824. CO mm.	750.00
56.	4 Escudos 1814-21	400.00
57.	2 Escudos 1814-21	225.00
58.	1 Escudo 1814-21	125.00
59.	½ Escudo 1815-21	150.00

B. Republic of —

Llama, tree and cornucopia. Rev. Wreath and place of minting.

60.	½ Escudo 1826. Cuzco	100.00
61.	½ Escudo 1827-56. Lima ....*......	75.00

Liberty standing holding shield and pole; the place of minting in the legend. Rev. Arms.

62.	8 Escudos 1826-55. Lima	300.00
63.	8 Escudos 1826-55. Cuzco	350.00
64.	4 Escudos 1828-55. Lima ....*.....	175.00
65.	2 Escudos 1828-55. Lima	125.00
66.	1 Escudo 1826-55. Lima	50.00
67.	1 Escudo 1830-46. Cuzco	75.00

Liberty seated facing left. Rev. Arms.

68.	8 Escudos 1862, 63	250.00
69.	4 Escudos 1863	1000.00
70.	20 Soles 1863 ....*......	200.00
71.	10 Soles 1863	125.00
72.	5 Soles 1863	100.00

Indian head. Rev. Arms.

73.	1 Libra 1898-1964 ....*.....	35.00
74.	½ Libra 1902-64	25.00
75.	⅕ Libra 1906-64	20.00

Arms. Rev. Motto.

76.	5 Soles 1910	20.00

Head of the Inca Indian Chief, Manco Capoc. Rev. Inca emblems.

77.	50 Soles 1930-31 (rare), 67, 68	150.00

Liberty seated facing right. Rev. Arms.

78.	100 Soles 1950-64 (1952, 58 rare)	100.00
79.	50 Soles 1950-64 (1952, 58 rare)	75.00
80.	20 Soles 1950-64 (1952, 58 rare) ....*......	25.00
81.	10 Soles 1956-64 ....*......	15.00
82.	5 Soles 1956-64	10.00

Replica of the first Peruvian coin, an 8 Reales. Rev. Arms. On the 400th anniversary of the Lima Mint.

83.	100 Soles 1965 ....*......	125.00
84.	50 Soles 1965	75.00

Arms. Rev. Winged Victory. On the centennial of the defeat of the Spanish fleet in the naval battle of 1866.

85.	100 Soles 1966	....	125.00
86.	50 Soles 1966	....	75.00

C. Republican States of —

NORTH PERU

Liberty standing holding shield and pole. Rev. Arms and "Estado Nor Peruano".

87.	8 Escudos 1838	...............................*......	2500.00
88.	4 Escudos 1838	....	4000.00
89.	2 Escudos 1838	....	1500.00
90.	1 Escudo 1838	....	750.00

SOUTH PERU

Sun over flags and "Estado Sud Peruano". Rev. Volcano and castle and below "Federacion".

91.	8 Escudos 1837	....	450.00

Obv. similar to above but with legend "Repub. Sud Peruano". Rev. similar to above but with Confederacion".

92.	8 Escudos 1837, 38, 39	....	500.00

Radiant sun. Rev. Value in wreath.

93.	1 Escudo 1838	....	125.00
94.	½ Escudo 1838	....	75.00

PHILIPPINE ISLANDS

Spanish Rulers of —

ISABELLA II, 1833-1868

Head. Rev. Arms.

1.	4 Pesos 1861-68	.............................*......	200.00
2.	2 Pesos 1861-68	.............................*......	100.00
3.	1 Peso 1861-68	....	60.00

ALFONSO XII, 1875-1886

Head. Rev. Arms.

4.	4 Pesos 1882, 85	....	350.00

POLAND

Other coins of the Kings of Poland will be found under Danzig, Latvia, Lithuania and Germany-Elbing.

A. Kings of —

LADISLAS LOKIETEK, 1306-1333
King on throne. Rev. St. Stanislas.

1.	1 Ducat ND	....	Rare

SIGISMUND I, 1506-1548
Bust. Rev. Arms.

2.	1 Ducat 1528-48	....	500.00

STEPHAN BATHORI, 1576-1586
Bust. Rev. Arms.

3.	1 Ducat 1586	....	1750.00

SIGISMUND III, 1587-1632

Bust. Rev. Arms.

4.	100 Ducats 1621	....	Rare
5.	90 Ducats 1621	....	Rare
6.	60 Ducats 1621	....	7500.00

7. 20 Ducats 1614, 17 .... 2500.00
8. 10 Ducats 1588-1628, ND 1250.00
9. 5 Ducats 1596-1623 ....*...... 850.00
10. 4 Ducats 1611, 12 .... 850.00
11. 3 Ducats 1612 .... 500.00
12. 2 Ducats 1610 .... 400.00
13. 1 Ducat 1588-1630, ND ....*...... 150.00

LADISLAS IV, 1632-1648

Bust. Rev. Arms.

14. 10 Ducats 1635, 36 .... 1750.00
15. 5 Ducats 1642, 45, 47 .... 1000.00
16. 1 Ducat 1639-44 ....*...... 175.00

JOHN CASIMIR, 1648-1668

Bust. Rev. Arms.

17. 10 Ducats 1661 .... 2000.00
18. 5 Ducats 1649-52, ND 900.00
19. 2 Ducats 1650-67 ....*...... 450.00
20. 1 Ducat 1649-62 ....*...... 225.00
21. ½ Ducat 1653-62, ND 125.00

Bust. Rev. Eagle.

22. 2 Ducats 1650 .... 500.00

Ruler standing. Rev. Arms.

23. 1 Ducat 1649 .... 425.00

MICHAEL KORYBUT, 1669-1673

Bust. Rev. Arms.

24. 2 Ducats 1671 .... 1000.00

JOHN III SOBIESKI, 1674-1696

Bust. Rev. Arms.

25. 2 Ducats ND 650.00
26. 1 Ducat 1682, 83 ....*...... 450.00

AUGUST II AND AUGUST III, 1697-1763
(See under Germany-Saxony).

STANISLAS AUGUST, 1764-1795

Head. Rev. Arms.

27. 3   Ducats 1794 ....*...... 700.00
28. 1½ Ducats 1794 .... 450.00
29. 1   Ducat 1765. Armored bust 600.00

Initials on star. Rev. Arms.

30. 1 Ducat 1766 .... 600.00

Head. Rev. Value in square.

31. 1 Ducat 1766-79 .... 200.00

Ruler standing. Rev. Value in square.

32. 1 Ducat 1766, 67, 70, 71, 72 .... 250.00

Head. Rev. Legend.

33. 1 Ducat 1780-95 .... 175.00

B. Russian Czars of —

ALEXANDER I, 1815-1825

Plain head. Rev. Eagle.

34. 50 Zloty 1817-19. Oblique milling ....*...... 300.00
35. 25 Zloty 1817-19. Oblique milling 200.00
36. 50 Zloty 1819-23. Straight milling 300.00
37. 25 Zloty 1820-25. Straight milling ....*...... 200.00

Laureate head. Rev. Value and date in wreath.

38. 50 Zloty 1827-29 .... 375.00
39. 25 Zloty 1828-33 .... 225.00

NICHOLAS I, 1825-1855

Eagle. Rev. Two values as indicated.

40. 20 Zloty-3 Roubles 1834-40. St. Petersburg mm * 125.00
41. 20 Zloty-3 Roubles 1841. St. Petersburg mm .... Rare
42. 20 Zloty-3 Roubles 1834-40. Warsaw Mint 750.00

C. Revolution 1830-1831

Knight standing. Rev. Tablet. Dutch type coin bearing the mint mark of a small eagle.

43. 1 Ducat 1831 .... 125.00

D. Republic of —

Crowned head of Boleslaus. Rev. Eagle. On the 900th Anniversary of Poland.

44. 20 Zloty 1925 .... 85.00
45. 10 Zloty 1925 .... 65.00

E. Cities of —

GNESEN

Bishops of —

STANISLAUS SZEMBEK, 1706-1721

Bust. Rev. Arms.

46. 1 Ducat 1721 .... 750.00

KRAKAU

Bishops of —

CAJETAN SOLTYK, 1759-1782

Bust. Rev. Legend.

47. 1 Ducat 1762 .... 500.00

THORN

Polish Kings of —

SIGISMUND III, 1587-1632

Bust. Rev. Arms.

48. 1 Ducat 1630 .... 225.00

City view. Rev. Legend.

49. 5 Ducats 1629 .... 1000.00

LADISLAS IV, 1632-1648

Bust. Rev. Arms.

50. 1 Ducat 1633-48 .... 225.00

JOHN CASIMIR, 1648-1668

Bust. Rev. Arms.

51. 2 Ducats 1660-68 ....* 375.00
52. 1 Ducat 1649-67 .... 225.00

Bust. Rev. City view.

53. 5 Ducats 1655, 59 ....* 1000.00
54. 4 Ducats 1655 .... 1000.00
55. 3 Ducats 1655 .... 750.00

MICHAEL KORYBUT, 1669-1673

Bust. Rev. Arms.

56. 2 Ducats 1671 .... 1000.00

332

Bust. Rev. City view.

57. 2 Ducats 1670, ND 500.00

AUGUST II OF SAXONY, 1697-1733

Bust. Rev. Arms.

58. 1 Ducat 1702 .... 375.00

WARSAW

Saxon Grand Dukes of —

FREDERICK AUGUST

Head. Rev. Arms.

59. 1 Ducat 1812, 13 .... 225.00

PORTUGAL

Other coins of the Portuguese Kings will be found under Brazil, India-Diu, India-Goa and Mozambique. The only appearance of mint marks on Portuguese coins took place in the period 1712-1722 at which time L was used for Lisbon and P for Porto.

Kings of —

SANCHO I, 1185-1211

Ruler on horse. Rev. Cross of five shields with a star in each angle.

1. 1 Morabitino ND 750.00

ALFONSO II, 1211-1223

Ruler on horse. Rev. Cross of five shields with three stars and a cross in angles.

2. 1 Morabitino ND 9000.00

SANCHO II, 1223-1248

Ruler on horse. Rev. Cross of five shields.

3. 1 Morabitino ND 5000.00

ALFONSO III, 1248-1279

Ruler on horse. Rev. Cross of five shields.

4. 1 Morabitino ND 2500.00

PEDRO I, 1357-1367

(Dobras and Half Dobras are mentioned in contemporary documents as existing, but no specimen of either coin has yet been discovered.)

FERDINAND, 1367-1383

Ruler standing. Rev. Ornate floriated cross in quadrilobe.

5. 1 Dobra ND 2250.00

Ruler standing. Rev. Cross of five shields in circle.

6. 1 Dobra ND .... *...... 1250.00
7. ½ Dobra ND 9000.00

DUARTE, 1433-1438

Crowned E in octolobe. Rev. Crowned shield.

8. 1 Escudo ND .... Unique

ALFONSO V, 1438-1481

Arms. Rev. Cross in ornamental frame.

9. 1 Cruzado ND 300.00

Crown over ALFQ. Rev. Shield.

10. 1 Escudo ND 3500.00

Crowned shield. Rev. Castle. Struck for Ceuta.

11. ½ Escudo ND .... Unique

Crowned shield. Rev. Quartered arms. Struck for Toro.

12. 1 Escudo ND .... Unique

JOHN II, 1481-1495

Ruler on throne. Rev. Shield.

13. 1 Justo ND 2000.00

Ruler standing. Rev. Shield.

14. 1 Justo ND 4000.00

Hand holding sword. Rev. Arms.

15. ½ Justo ND 500.00

Arms. Rev. Cross in ornamental frame.

16. 1 Cruzado ND 200.00

MANUEL, I, 1495-1521

Arms. Rev. Cross.

17. 1 Portuguez (10 Ducats) ND 2000.00
18. 1 Cruzado ND ....*...... 200.00
19. ¼ Cruzado ND 4500.00

JOHN III, 1521-1557
Arms. Rev. Cross.

20. 1 Portuguez ND 3000.00
21. 1 Cruzado ND 225.00

Arms. Rev. Cross of Calvary.

22. 1 Calvario ND 175.00

St. Vincent standing. Rev. Arms.

23. 1 San Vincente ND ....*...... 350.00
24. ½ San Vincente ND 300.00

SEBASTIAN, 1557-1578

St. Vincent standing. Rev. Arms.

25. 1 San Vincente ND 350.00
26. ½ San Vincente ND ....*...... 400.00

Arms. Rev. Cross of Jerusalem.

27. 1 Engenhoso 1562, 63, 65, ND. (Long cross) ..*...... 400.00
28. ½ Engenhoso ND. (Long cross) 3000.00
29. 500 Reis (1 Cruzado) ND. (Short cross) ....*...... 125.00

HENRY I, 1578-1580

Arms. Rev. Cross of Jerusalem.

30. 500 Reis ND. (1 Cruzado) 1500.00

THE GOVERNORS, 1580

Arms. Rev. Cross of Jerusalem.

31. 1 Cruzado ND 2250.00

ANTONIO I, 1580-1583
Arms. Rev. Cross of Jerusalem.

32. 500 Reis ND. (1 Cruzado) 6000.00

Arms. Rev. Floriated cross. Struck for the Azores.

33. 2000 Reis ND 4000.00
34. 1000 Reis ND 2000.00

Arms. Rev. Cross of St. George. Struck for the Azores.

35. 1000 Reis ND 6000.00

PHILIP I OF SPAIN, 1580-1598
Arms. Rev. Cross of St. George.

36. 4 Cruzados ND 3000.00
37. 2 Cruzados ND 1500.00
38. 1 Cruzado ND 1500.00

Arms. Rev. Cross of Jerusalem.

39. 500 Reis ND 4000.00

PHILIP II OF SPAIN, 1598-1621

Arms. Rev. Cross of St. George.

40. 4 Cruzados ND 900.00
41. 2 Cruzados ND 1250.00
42. 1 Cruzado ND ....*...... 1250.00

PHILIP III OF SPAIN, 1621-1640

Arms. Rev. Cross of St. George.

43.	4 Cruzados ND	...............................*	700.00
44.	2 Cruzados ND	....	1250.00
45.	1 Cruzado ND	....	1250.00

JOHN IV, 1640-1656

Arms. Rev. Cross of St. George.

46.	4 Cruzados 1642-52	.........................*	850.00
47.	2 Cruzados 1642, 46, 47	....	700.00
48.	1 Cruzado 1642, 47	....	900.00

Laureate bust. Rev. Arms on cross. This coin was not placed in circulation.

| 49. | 4 Cruzados 1650 | ....Unknown |

ALFONSO VI, 1656-1683

(4 and 2 Cruzado pieces were struck, but all known specimens are counterstamped. They are listed under Brazil).

Arms. Rev. Cross of Jerusalem. 1000 Reis pieces were also struck, but all known pieces are counterstamped. They are listed under Brazil.

| 50. | 4000 Reis 1663 | .... | 1750.00 |
| 51. | 2000 Reis 1663 | .... | 1500.00 |

PETER, PRINCE REGENT, 1667-1683

Arms. Rev. Cross in quadrilobe.

52.	4400 Reis 1668-74	.............................*	800.00
53.	2200 Reis 1668, 69, 74	....	900.00
54.	1100 Reis 1668, 71	....	1100.00

Arms. Rev. Cross.

55.	4000 Reis 1677-82	....	300.00
56.	2000 Reis 1677-81	....	225.00
57.	1000 Reis 1677-81	.........................*	300.00

PETER II, 1683-1706
Arms. Rev. Cross.

58.	4000 Reis 1688-1706	....	200.00
59.	2000 Reis 1683-1704	....	175.00
60.	1000 Reis 1683-1706	....	100.00

JOHN V, 1706-1750

Bust. Rev. Arms. The 24 and 16 Escudo pieces were not placed in circulation.

61.	24 Escudos 1731	....	Rare
62.	16 Escudos 1731	....	Rare
63.	8 Escudos 1717-32	....	550.00
64.	4 Escudos 1722. L mm.	....	550.00
65.	4 Escudos 1723-50. No mm.	....................*	225.00
66.	2 Escudos 1722. L mm.	....	525.00
67.	2 Escudos 1723-50. No mm.	....	150.00
68.	1 Escudo 1722. L mm.	....	250.00
69.	1 Escudo 1723-49. No mm.	....	75.00
70.	½ Escudo 1722. L mm.	....	65.00
71.	½ Escudo 1723-50. No mm.	....	50.00

Arms. Rev. Cross. The 8000 Reis piece was not placed in circulation.

72.	8000 Reis 1711	....	Rare
73.	4000 Reis 1707-22. No mm.	....	175.00
74.	4000 Reis 1712, 13, 14. P mm.	....	325.00
75.	2000 Reis 1707-25. No mm.	....	100.00
76.	2000 Reis 1713, 14. P mm.	.....................*	325.00
77.	1000 Reis 1707-47. No mm.	....	75.00
78.	1000 Reis 1713. P mm.	....	450.00

Cross. Rev. crown over name.

| 79. | 400 Reis 1717-48 | .... | 30.00 |

JOSEPH I, 1750-1777

Bust. Rev. Arms.

80.	4 Escudos 1750-76	....	175.00
81.	2 Escudos 1751-76	.........................*	225.00
82.	1 Escudo 1751-76	....	100.00
83.	½ Escudo 1751-76	....	40.00

Arms. Rev. Cross.

84. 1000 Reis 1749-69 .... 40.00

Cross. Rev. Crown over name.

85. 400 Reis 1752-76 .... 25.00

MARY I AND PETER III, 1777-1786

Conjoined Busts. Rev. Arms.

86. 4 Escudos 1778-85 ....* 200.00
87. 2 Escudos 1778, 84 .... 175.00
88. 1 Escudo 1777-85 .... 100.00
89. ½ Escudo 1777-84 .... 50.00

Arms. Rev. Cross.

90. 1000 Reis 1777-84 .... 40.00

Cross. Rev. Crown over name.

91. 400 Reis 1777-85 .... 50.00

MARY I, 1786-1816

Bust with widow's veil. Rev. Arms.

92. 4 Escudos 1786, 87 .... 175.00
93. 1 Escudo 1787 .... 225.00
94. ½ Escudo 1787, 88 ....* 225.00

Bust with ornamental headdress. Rev. Arms.

95. 4 Escudos 1789-99 ....* 175.00
96. 2 Escudos 1789 .... 250.00
97. 1 Escudo 1789-96 .... 100.00
98. ½ Escudo 1789-96 .... 50.00

Arms. Rev. Cross.

99. 1000 Reis 1787, 89, 92 .... 40.00

Cross. Rev. Crown over name.

100. 400 Reis 1787-96 .... 35.00

JOHN, PRINCE REGENT, 1799-1816

Bust. Rev. Plain arms.

101. 4 Escudos 1802 .... 450.00

Bust. Rev. Ornamental arms.

102. 4 Escudos 1804-17 .... 200.00
103. 2 Escudos 1805, 07 .... 250.00
104. 1 Escudo 1807 ....* 200.00
105. ½ Escudo 1805, 06, 07 .... 75.00

Cross. Rev. Crown over name.

106. 400 Reis 1807 .... 100.00

JOHN VI, 1816-1826

Bust. Rev. Arms.

107. 4 Escudos 1819-24 .... 200.00
108. 2 Escudos 1818-22 ....* 165.00
109. 1 Escudo 1818, 19, 21 .... 175.00
110. ½ Escudo 1818-21 .... 85.00

Arms. Rev. Cross.

111. 1000 Reis 1818, 19, 21 .... 150.00

Cross. Rev. Crown over name.

112. 400 Reis 1818-21 .... 75.00

PETER IV, 1826-1828

Laureate head. Rev. Arms.

113. 4 Escudos 1826-28 .... 250.00
114. 2 Escudos 1827 ....* 275.00

MICHAEL I, 1828-1834

Small laureate bust. Rev. Arms in clinging palms.

115.	4 Escudos 1828 ....*	450.00
116.	2 Escudos 1828	275.00

Large laureate bust with collar. Rev. Arms in spreading palms.

117.	4 Escudos 1830, 31, 32 ....*	400.00
118.	2 Escudos 1830, 31	300.00

MARY II, 1834-1853

Head with upswept hair. Rev. Arms.

119.	4 Escudos 1833	500.00

Draped bust with diadem. Rev. Arms.

120.	4 Escudos 1833, 34, 35	325.00

Head. Rev. Arms.

121.	5000 Reis 1836-51 ....*	150.00
122.	2500 Reis 1836-53	100.00
123.	1000 Reis 1851	65.00

During this reign, the Brazilian 20,000 Reis pieces of the Minas Mint, 1724-27, were counterstamped with the arms of Portugal, giving these coins a decreed legal value of 30,000 Reis.

124.	20,000 Reis 1724-27. Counterstamped	900.00

PETER V, 1853-1861

Head. Rev. Arms. The 10,000 Reis piece was not placed in circulation.

125.	10000 Reis 1861	**Rare**
126.	5000 Reis 1860, 61 ....*	125.00
127.	2000 Reis 1856-60	75.00
128.	1000 Reis 1855	60.00

LOUIS I, 1861-1889

Young head. Rev. Small arms in palms.

129.	5000 Reis 1862, 63 ....*	85.00
130.	2000 Reis 1864, 65, 66	50.00

Older head. Rev. Large draped arms.

131.	10000 Reis 1878-89 ....*	175.00
132.	5000 Reis 1867-89	85.00
133.	2000 Reis 1868-88	65.00

Head. Rev. Value.

134.	1000 Reis 1879	**Rare**

CHARLES I, 1889-1908
Head. Rev. Arms. This coin was not placed in circulation.

135.	5000 Reis 1895	**Rare**

Republic, 1910-1926

Seated female. Rev. Arms. This coin was not placed in circulation.

136.	5 Escudos 1920	**Rare**

RHODES

(The Knights of St. John of Jerusalem at Rhodes)

Most of the coinage is of Venetian style and type.

Grand Masters of —

DIEUDONNE DE GOZON, 1346-1353

Ruler kneeling before St. John. Rev. Angel seated on Sepulcher of Christ.

1.	1 Zecchino ND	1500.00

PIERRE DE CORNILLAN, 1354-1355

Ruler kneeling before St. John. Rev. Angel seated on Sepulcher of Christ.

2. 1 Zecchino ND 2250.00

ANTOINE FLUVIAN, 1421-1437

Ruler kneeling before St. John. Rev. Christ standing.

3. 1 Zecchino ND 1500.00

JACQUES DE MILLY, 1454-1461

Ruler kneeling before St. John. Rev. Christ standing.

4. 1 Zecchino ND 1500.00

JEAN BAPTIST ORSINI, 1467-1476

Ruler kneeling before St. John. Rev. Christ standing.

5. 1 Zecchino ND 500.00

PIERRE D'AUBUSSON, 1476-1503

Ruler kneeling before St. John. Rev. Christ standing.

6. 1 Zecchino ND 300.00

EMERIC D'AMBOISE, 1503-1512

Arms. Rev. Lamb

7. 2 Ducats ND 2250.00
8. 1 Ducat ND ....*...... 2250.00

Ruler kneeling before St. John. Rev. Christ standing.

9. 1 Zecchino ND 275.00

FABRIZIO DEL CARRETTO, 1513-1521

Bust with cap. Rev. Arms. (This may be a medal).

10. 10 Zecchini ND .... **Rare**

Ruler kneeling before St. John. Rev. Christ standing.

11. 1 Zecchino ND 275.00

PHILIPPE VILLIERS

At Rhodes 1521-1522 and at Malta 1530-1534.

(For the coinage of this Grand Master and of his successors see under Malta).

ROUMANIA

The entire gold coinage of Roumania is based on the Latin Monetary Union standard. The 12½ Lei piece of 1906 is the only example of this denomination in the Union's coinage. The 50, 25 and 12½ Lei pieces struck in 1906, and the 50 and 25 Leis of 1922 are broad and thin and are struck in imitation of Ducat coinage to represent the equivalent of 4, 2 and 1 Ducat pieces. The commemorative coins of 1939 and 1940 (numbers 13-20) are rare and seldom appear.

Kings of —

CAROL I, 1866-1914

Young head with side whiskers. Rev. Value.

1. 20 Lei 1867, 68 .... 600.00

Older head with whiskers. Rev. Value.

2. 20 Lei 1870 .... 90.00

Head. Rev. Arms.

3. 20 Lei 1883-90 .... 45.00

Old head of 1906. Rev. Young head of 1867. On the 40th year of reign.

4. 100 Lei 1906 ....*...... 400.00
5. 20 Lei 1906 .... 75.00

Uniformed bust. Rev. Ruler on horse. On the 40th year of reign.

6. 50 Lei 1906 .... 200.00

Uniformed bust. Rev. Eagle. On the 40th year of reign.

7.   25   Lei 1906 .... 125.00
8.   12½ Lei 1906 ....*...... 65.00

FERDINAND I, 1914-1927

Head. Rev. Arms. On his Coronation.

9. 100 Lei 1922 ....*...... 475.00
10. 20 Lei 1922 .... 100.00

Crowned bust. Rev. Crowned bust of Marie. On his Coronation.

11. 50 Lei 1922 .... 300.00
12. 25 Lei 1922 ....*...... 175.00

CAROL II, 1930-1940
Commemorative Coins on the Centennial of Birth of Carol I.

Head. Rev. Large arms.

13. 100 Lei 1939 .... 450.00
14. 20 Lei 1939 ....*...... 125.00

Head. Rev. Angel over shield.

15. 100 Lei 1939 .... 500.00

Head. Rev. Eagle over shield.

16. 20 Lei 1939 .... 125.00

Commemorative Coins on the 10th year of his Reign.

Head and legend within ornamental circle. Rev. Small
crown over large monogram.

17. 100 Lei 1940 .... 550.00
18. 20 Lei 1940 ....*...... 125.00

Head and legend only. Rev. Large crown over small monogram.

19. 100 Lei 1940 .... 450.00
20. 20 Lei 1940 .... 125.00

MICHAEL I, 1940-1947

Conjoined heads of three Roumanian Kings, with dates
1601, 1918, 1944. Rev. Eagle within circle of shields.
Although without the mark of value, this coin has the
same specifications as the standard 20 Lei coin.

21. (20 Lei) 1944 .... 35.00

RUSSIA

Most of the early gold coins (numbers 1-61) exist as later re-strikes.
Russia affords us the only example of platinum coins actually being
struck for circulation, and the 12, 6 and 3 Rouble coins of this metal
are highly prized.

At the time platinum was discovered in the Ural Mountains it was worth
so much less than gold that a 3 Rouble platinum coin weighing 10.3600
grams was the equal of a 3 Rouble gold coin weighing only 3.4900
grams. As a matter of fact, gold coins began to be counterfeited in
platinum or struck in platinum at government mints (unofficially) from
original dies. The platinum coins were then gold plated, and since
platinum is slightlly denser than gold and passes the same chemical
tests as gold does, the gilded coins became indistinguishable from all-
gold coins. These platinum coins are also highly prized.

The 3 Rouble gold piece struck from 1869 to 1885 is the Russian
equivalent of the 1 Ducat. The 10 and 5 Rouble pieces struck from
1886 to 1894 and then re-valued in 1897 to 15 and 7½ Roubles, were
struck according to the Latin Monetary Union standard and are equal
to 40 and 20 Franc pieces.

Czars of —

VLADIMIR, 978-1015
Bust. Rev. Bust of Christ.

1.   1 Solidus ND 5000.00

IVAN III, 1462-1505
Hungarian state emblem. Rev. St. Vladislav.

1a. 1 Ducat 1484. Hermitage Museum .... Unique

IVAN IV, THE TERRIBLE, 1533-1584
Eagle on each side.

1b.	5 Ducats ND	Rare

Eagle. Rev. Legend.

2.	4 Gold Kopecks ND	3000.00
3.	2 Gold Kopecks ND	2250.00
4.	1 Gold Kopeck ND	1500.00
5.	½ Gold Kopeck ND	1000.00

THEODORE, 1584-1598
Eagle. Rev. Legend.

6.	1 Ducat ND	1500.00

Ruler on horse. Rev. Legend.

7.	1 Ducat ND	1500.00
8.	⅔ Ducat ND	1000.00

BORIS GODUNOV, 1598-1605
Bust with sceptre. Rev. Eagle.

9.	1 Ducat ND	4500.00

DEMETRIUS (PRETENDER), 1604-1606
Bust with sceptre. Rev. Eagle.

10.	12 Ducats ND	Rare

Eagle on each side.

11.	10 Ducats ND	Rare
12.	1½ Ducats ND	1500.00

Ruler on horse. Rev. Legend.

13.	1 Gold Kopeck ND	1000.00
14.	½ Gold Kopeck ND	900.00

BASIL SHUISKY, 1606-1610
St. George. Rev. Eagle.

15.	5 Ducats ND	Rare
16.	1 Ducat ND	2250.00

Eagle. Rev. Legend.

17.	1 Gold Kopeck ND	900.00

Ruler on horse. Rev. Legend.

18.	1 Gold Kopeck ND ....*......	900.00
19.	½ Gold Kopeck ND	750.00

LADISLAS, 1610-1612

Ruler on horse. Rev. Legend.

20.	1 Gold Kopeck ND	750.00

MICHAEL, 1613-1645

Eagle on each side.

21.	3 Ducats ND ....*.....	1500.00
22.	2 Ducats ND	1000.00
23.	1 Ducat ND	600.00
24.	⅔ Ducat ND	600.00

Eagle. Rev. Legend.

25.	1½ Gold Kopecks ND	750.00

Ruler on horse. Rev. Legend.

26.	1 Gold Kopeck ND ....*......	750.00
27.	½ Gold Kopeck ND	600.00

ALEXIUS, 1645-1676
Eagle on each side.

28.	10 Ducats ND	Rare
29.	3 Ducats ND	3000.00
30.	2 Ducats ND	3000.00
31.	1 Ducat ND	2250.00

Bust with sceptre. Rev. Bust of Christ.

32.	4 Ducats ND	Rare
33.	2 Ducats ND	Rare

Eagle. Rev. Legend.

34.	⅔ Ducat ND	900.00
35.	½ Ducat ND	900.00
36.	⅓ Ducat ND	600.00
37.	1 Gold Kopeck 1654, ND ....*......	750.00
38.	½ Gold Kopeck ND	450.00

THEODORE ALEXEIVITCH, 1676-1682

Eagle on each side.

39.	1 Ducat ND	1000.00

SOPHIA, REGENT FOR PETER I, 1682-1689

Bust of Sophia. Rev. Busts of Peter I and Ivan V.

40.	5 Ducats ND ....*......	7500.00
41.	3 Ducats ND	3000.00
42.	2 Ducats ND	1500.00
43.	1 Ducat ND ....*.....	1000.00
44.	⅔ Ducat ND	900.00
45.	½ Ducat ND	600.00
46.	1 Gold Kopeck ND ....*......	600.00

Eagle. Rev. Legend.

47.	4 Ducats ND	1000.00

Eagle on each side.

48.	2 Ducats ND	1000.00
49.	1½ Ducats ND	750.00
50.	1 Ducat ND	600.00

IVAN V, REGENT FOR PETER I, 1682-1689
Eagle on each side.

51.	9 Ducats ND	Rare
52.	6 Ducats ND	Rare

Ruler on horse. Rev. Legend.

53.	½ Gold Kopeck ND	450.00

PETER I, THE GREAT, 1682-1725

Bust. Rev. Eagle.

54.	12 Ducats 1702. Dated March 1	6000.00
55.	10 Ducats 1702. Dated March 1	4000.00
56.	8 Ducats 1702. Dated February 1	3000.00
57.	8 Ducats 1702. Dated March 1	3500.00
58.	6 Ducats 1702. Dated February 1	2700.00
59.	5 Ducats 1702. Dated February 1	2500.00
60.	4 Ducats 1714 ....*......	2250.00
61.	3 Ducats 1702. Dated February 1	1750.00
62.	2 Ducats 1701, 14	1500.00
63.	1 Ducat 1701-07. Date in Slavic numerals	700.00
64.	1 Ducat 1710-16. Date in Cardinal numerals ..*......	550.00

Bust. Rev. St. Andrew.

65.	2 Roubles 1718-25	300.00

Bust. Rev. Ruler on horse.

66.	1 Ducat 1708	750.00

Crown on cushion. Rev. Crown and legend. On the Coronation of Catherine I.

67.	1 Ducat 1724	400.00

CATHERINE I, 1725-1727

Bust. Rev. St. Andrew.

68.	2 Roubles 1726, 27	800.00

PETER II, 1727-1730

Bust. Rev. Eagle.

69.	1 Ducat 1729	750.00

Crown on pedestal. Rev. Crown over legend. On his Coronation.

70.	1 Ducat 1728	450.00

Bust. Rev. St. Andrew.

71.	2 Roubles 1727, 28	400.00

ANNE, 1730-1740

Bust. Rev. Eagle.

72.	1 Ducat 1730, 38, 39	750.00

Crown. Rev. Legend. On her Coronation.

73.	1 Ducat 1730	350.00

Knight standing. Rev. Tablet. Dutch type.

73a.	1 Ducat 1735-1849	100.00

Crowned bust. Rev. Eagle and trophies. On the Peace with Turkey.

74.	1 Ducat 1739	450.00

Crowned bust. Rev. Legend. On her death.

75.	1 Ducat 1740	450.00

ELIZABETH, 1741-1762

Bust. Rev. St. Andrew.

76.	2 Ducats 1749, 51 ....*......	900.00
77.	1 Ducat 1749-53	300.00

Bust. Rev. Eagle.

78.	2 Ducats 1747-51	500.00
79.	1 Ducat 1742-57 ....*......	350.00
80.	5 Roubles 1755	800.00
81.	2 Roubles 1756-58	175.00
82.	1 Rouble 1756-58	125.00

Bust. Rev. Crowned initials.

83.	½ Rouble or Poltina 1755, 56	100.00

Bust. Rev. Eagle to left on clouds. This issue was not placed in circulation.

84.	2 Roubles 1756	600.00
85.	1 Rouble 1756	400.00

Bust. Rev. Cross of four shields.

86.   20 Roubles 1755 ....*..... 6000.00
87.   10 Roubles 1755-59 ....*   900.00
88.   10 Roubles 1757. Larger bust 1000.00
89.   5 Roubles 1755-59 .... 600.00

Tomb. Rev. Crown over legend. On her death.

90.   1 Ducat 1761 .... 375.00

PETER III, 1762

Bust. Rev. Cross of four shields.

91.   10 Roubles 1762   .... 1200.00
92.   5 Roubles 1762   ....*   650.00

Bust. Rev. Eagle.

93.   1 Ducat 1762 .... 750.00

CATHERINE II, THE GREAT, 1762-1796

Bust. Rev. Cross of four shields.

94.   10 Roubles 1762-96 ....*...... 375.00
95.   5 Roubles 1762-96 .... 225.00

Bust. Rev. Eagle.

96.   10 Ducats 1762 .... 4000.00
97.   2 Ducats 1796 .... 750.00
98.   1 Ducat 1762-96 .... 250.00
99.   2 Roubles 1766-86 ....*..... 200.00
100.   1 Rouble 1779 .... 150.00

Bust. Rev. Crowned initials.

101.   ½ Rouble or Poltina 1777, 78 .... 75.00

Crown. Rev. Legend. On her Coronation.

102.   1 Ducat 1762 .... 225.00

Bust. Rev. Flying eagle.

103.   1 Ducat 1766 .... 225.00

Ceres seated. Rev. Caduceus. On the Peace with Turkey.

104.   1 Ducat 1774 .... 225.00

Olive Branch. Rev. Legend. On the Peace with Sweden.

105.   1 Ducat 1790 .... 225.00

PAUL I, 1796-1801

Cross of four crowned initials. Rev. Tablet.

106.   5 Roubles 1798-1801 ....*...... 400.00
107.   1 Ducat 1797 .... 450.00

Eagle. Rev. Tablet.

108.   1 Ducat 1796 .... 500.00

ALEXANDER I, 1801-1825

Cross of four shields. Rev. Legend.

109.   10 Roubles 1802-05, 09 ....*...... 700.00
110.   10 Roubles 1806 .... 1250.00
111.   5 Roubles 1802-05 .... 450.00
112.   5 Roubles 1806 .... Rare

Eagle. Rev. Legend in wreath.

113.   5 Roubles 1817-25 .... 150.00

Knight standing. Rev. Tablet. Dutch type.

114.   1 Ducat 1807-25 .... 100.00

NICHOLAS I, 1825-1855

Conjoined busts of the Czar and Czarina. Rev. As indicated. These coins were not placed in circulation.

115.   10 Roubles 1836. Rev. Initials 1250.00
116.   10 Roubles 1836. Rev. Value and date ....*...... 1750.00

Eagle. Rev. Legend in four lines.

117. 5 Roubles 1826-31 .... 125.00

Eagle. Rev. Value and date.

118. 5 Roubles 1832-55 ....*...... 85.00
119. 5 Roubles 1842-49. Warsaw mint 500.00

Eagle. Rev. Value and date. With additional legend indicating gold from the Kolywan Mines.

120. 5 Roubles 1832 ....:..... 500.00

Eagle. Rev. Value and date.

121. Platinum 12 Roubles 1830-45 .... 2500.00
122. Platinum 6 Roubles 1829-45 .... 1250.00
123. Platinum 3 Roubles 1828-45 ....*...... 300.00

124. (The coin previously listed here is now No. 73a.) .... —

ALEXANDER II, 1855-1881

Eagle. Rev. Value. The 25 Rouble piece was not placed in circulation.

125. 25 Roubles 1876 .... 2500.00
126. 5 Roubles 1855-81 ....*...... 60.00
127. 3 Roubles 1869-80 .... 100.00
128. 3 Roubles 1881 .... Rare

ALEXANDER III, 1881-1894

Eagle. Rev. Value.

129. 5 Roubles 1881-85 ....*...... 60.00
130. 3 Roubles 1881-85 .... 60.00

Head. Rev. Eagle.

131. 10 Roubles 1886-94 ....*..... 225.00
132. 5 Roubles 1886-94 ....*...... 40.00

NICHOLAS II, 1894-1917

Head. Rev. Eagle in circle, legend around. These coins were not placed in circulation.

133. 37½ Roubles or 100 Francs 1902 ....*..... 3000.00
134. 25   Roubles or 2½ Imperials 1896, 1908 .... 2500.00
135. 10   Roubles or 1 Imperial 1895-97 .... 1000.00
136. 5   Roubles or ½ Imperial 1895-96 ....*...... 750.00

Head. Rev. Eagle.

137. 15   Roubles 1897 .... 75.00
138. 7½   Roubles 1897 .... 60.00
139. 10   Roubles 1898-1911 .... 35.00
140. 5   Roubles 1897-1911 ....*...... 17.50

SOVIET UNION

Sower scattering seed. Rev. Hammer and Sickle.

141. 10 Roubles or 1 Chervonetz 1923 .... 350.00

SAINT MARTIN

Gold coins of Brazil counterstamped on Obv. with "22" or "20" (for karats), a small H and a small negro head.

1. 6400 Reis 1727-1804 .... 1000.00

SAINT VINCENT

Gold coins of Brazil counterstamped three times along the outer edge of the Obv. with an S and usually with a plugged hole in the center.

1. 6400 Reis 1787-1804 .... 1000.00

SALVADOR

Liberty head. Rev. Arms.

1.	20	Pesos 1892	1000.00
2.	10	Pesos 1892	750.00
3.	5	Pesos 1892 ....*....	500.00
4.	2½	Pesos 1892	300.00

Conjoined heads of Alvarada (1525) and Quinonez (1925). Rev. Arms. On the 400th year of Salvador.

5. 20 Colones 1925 .... 900.00

SAN MARINO

St. Marinus standing. Rev. Three towers.

1. 20 Lire 1925 .... 400.00
2. 10 Lire 1925 .... 350.00

SAUDI ARABIA

Arab legend in circle on each side.

1. 1 Saudi Pound 1370 A.H. (1951) 25.00

Palm tree over crossed swords. Rev. Value and date.

2. 1 Saudi Pound 1377 A.H. (1957-58) 25.00

(Note: For the gold coins struck at the Philadelphia Mint, see under United States of America, following the 50 Dollar gold pieces).

SCOTLAND

Kings of —

DAVID II, 1329-1371
Ruler in ship. Rev. Ornate cross.

1. 1 Noble ND .... Rare

ROBERT III, 1390-1406

Crowned shield. Rev. St. Andrew with long cross.

2. 1 Lion ND ....*...... 200.00
3. ½ Lion or Demy ND 150.00

Crowned shield. Rev. St. Andrew with short cross.

4. 1 Lion ND 200.00

Crowned shield within border. Rev. St. Andrew with long cross.

5. ½ Lion or Demy ND 350.00

Crowned shield. Rev. St. Andrew without cross.

6. 1 Lion ND 200.00

Shield. Rev. Cross of St. Andrew.

7. ½ Lion or Demy ND 150.00

JAMES I, 1406-1437

Lion in square. Rev. Cross of St. Andrew in border.

8. 1 Demy ND 100.00
9. ½ Demy ND ....*...... 200.00

JAMES II, 1437-1460

Lion in square. Rev. Cross of St. Andrew in border.

10. 1 Demy ND 125.00

Crowned shield. Rev. St. Andrew with cross.

11. 1 Lion ND ....*...... 200.00
12. ½ Lion ND 300.00

Shield and value. Rev. Cross with thistles in angles.

24. 20 Shillings or 1 Crown. ND 150.00

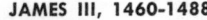

JAMES III, 1460-1488

Ruler on horse. Rev. Shield on long cross.

13. 1 Rider ND ....*...... 300.00
14. ½ Rider ND ....*...... 400.00
15. ¼ Rider ND 750.00

Bust with hat. Rev. Arms.

25. 1 Bonnet Piece ND ....*...... 850.00
26. ⅔ Bonnet Piece ND 1000.00
27. ⅓ Bonnet Piece ND 1250.00

MARY, 1542-1567

Unicorn. Rev. Star with wavy rays.

16. 1 Unicorn ND ....*...... 200.00
17. ½ Unicorn ND 200.00

Crowned shield. Rev. Floriated cross.

28. 1 Abbey Crown or 20 Shillings ND 350.00

JAMES IV, 1488-1513

Unicorn. Rev. Star with wavy rays.

18. 1 Unicorn ND 200.00
19. ½ Unicorn ND ....*...... 250.00

Crowned shield. Rev. Crown over MR or Maria monogram.

29. 20 Shillings 1543 ....*...... 500.00
30. 1 Lion or 44 Shillings 1553 .... 450.00
31. ½ Lion or 22 Shillings 1553 ....*...... 450.00

Crowned shield between M and R. Rev. Crown over Maria monogram.

32. 1 Lion 1557 .... 650.00

Crowned shield. Rev. St. Andrew with cross.

20. 1 Lion ND ....*...... 400.00
21. ½ Lion ND 600.00

JAMES V, 1514-1542

Bust. Rev. Crowned shield.

33. 3   Pounds or 1 Ryal 1555-58 ....*...... 1500.00
34. 1½ Pounds or ½ Ryal 1555-58 .... 1500.00

Unicorn. Rev. Star.

22. 1 Unicorn ND ....*...... 250.00
23. ½ Unicorn ND 400.00

Busts of Mary and Francis of France facing each other.
Rev. Floriated cross.

35. 1 Ducat or 60 Shillings 1558 .... **Rare**

Shield. Rev. Cross of four crowned M's.

36. 1 Crown 1561-65 .... **Rare**

JAMES VI, 1567-1625

Half length figure. Rev. Shield.

37. 20 Pounds 1575, 76 .... **4500.00**

Youthful bust. Rev. Shield between divided date.

38. 1 Ducat (4 Pounds or Noble) 1580 .... **1500.00**

Lion holding sword and sceptre. Rev. Cross of four IR's.

39. 1 Lion Noble 1582-89 .... **1500.00**
40. ⅔ Lion Noble 1582-89 ....*...... **2000.00**
41. ⅓ Lion Noble 1582-89 .... **Rare**

Shield on ship. Rev. Cross in embellished border.

42. 1 Thistle Noble 1588, 89 .... **400.00**

Bust with high hat. Rev. Seated lion.

43. 1 Hat Piece 1591-94 .... **1500.00**

Ruler on horse. Rev. Crowned shield.

44. 1 Rider 1593-1601 ....*...... **250.00**
45. ½ Rider 1593-1601 .... **500.00**

Sword and sceptre. Rev. Crowned shield.

46. 1 Sword and Sceptre Piece 1601-04 ....*...... **125.00**
47. ½ Sword and Sceptre Piece 1601-04 .... **125.00**

Crowned bust with orb and sceptre. Rev. Arms.

48. 1 Unite (20 Shillings or 1 Sceptre) ND **175.00**

Crowned bust. Rev. Arms.

49. 2 Crowns or ½ Unite ND **400.00**
50. 1 Britain Crown ND ....*...... **200.00**
51. ½ Crown ND ....*...... **150.00**

Crowned thistle. Rev. Crowned rose.

52. 1 Thistle Crown ND **150.00**

CHARLES I, 1625-1649

Bust of James with orb and sceptre but with name and initials of Charles. Rev. Arms.

53. 1 Unite ND 200.00

Crowned bust of James. Rev. Arms. With name and initials of Charles.

54. 2 Crowns or ½ Unite ND ....*...... 750.00
55. 1 Britain Crown ND 200.00

Bust of Charles with orb and sceptre. Rev. Arms. Briot's coinage.

56. 1 Unite ND 250.00

Bust of Charles. Rev. Arms. Briot's coinage.

57. 2 Crowns or ½ Unite ND ....*...... 250.00
58. 1 Britain Crown ND 400.00
59. ½ Crown ND 175.00

WILLIAM II (III OF ENGLAND), 1694-1702

Bust with small rising sun below. Rev. Arms.

60. 1 Pistole 1701 ....*...... 500.00
61. ½ Pistole 1701 .... 500.00

SERBIA

19th century Serbian coinage is based on the Latin Monetary Union standard.

Kings of —

STEPHAN DUSHAN, 1331-1355
Standing royal couple. Rev. Christ seated.

1. 3 Ducats ND 5000.00

STEPHAN UROSH, 1346-1370
Ruler on horse. Rev. Helmet and insignia.

2. 1 Solidus or Ducat ND 2250.00

MILAN OBRENOVICH IV, 1868-1889

Head by Tasset with full title in legend. Rev. Value.

3. 20 Dinars 1879 .... 75.00

New head by Scharff with short title. Rev. Value.

4. 20 Dinars 1882 .... 70.00
5. 10 Dinars 1882 .... 60.00

SIAM

Kings of —

A. Gold Bullet Money of the Bangkok Dynasty

A roughly round shaped piece of gold, a portion of which dimples back on itself. The clear portion of the "Bullet" bears a mark which has been counterstamped on it and identifies it. The various marks used by the respective Kings are described below. These issues are without dates.

PRA NANG KLAO, 1824-1851
Palace mark (A crude gateway).

1. 1 Tical 450.00
2. ⅛ Tical 225.00
3. 1/16 Tical 175.00

Crude flower mark.

4. ⅛ Tical 175.00

Three leaves of the bale-fruit tree.

5. ⅛ Tical 175.00

MONGKUT, 1851-1868
Marks of the Chakra and the Siamese Crown.

6. 4 Ticals 550.00
7. 2 Ticals 400.00
8. 1 Tical 350.00
9. ½ Tical 175.00
10. ¼ Tical 115.00
11. 1½ Ticals. Elliptical shape 850.00

SIAM (continued)

Waterpot mark.

12.	¼ Tical	....	115.00
13.	⅛ Tical	....	90.00
14.	¹⁄₁₆ Tical	....	85.00

B. Conventional or Standard Gold Coins

The conventional or standard gold coins are of far greater scarcity than the earlier bullet money.

FIRST ISSUE OF MONGKUT (1863)

Crown between umbrellas with a few leaf scrolls in the field. Rev. Elephant in beaded circle within a chakra with narrow spokes.

15.	8 Ticals ND	........................*	350.00
16.	4 Ticals ND	........................*	250.00
17.	2 Ticals ND	....	150.00

SECOND ISSUE OF MONGKUT (1864)

Crown between umbrellas with flamboyant leaves in the field. Rev. Elephant in ornamental circle within a chakra with wide spokes. The coins of this issue are the same size as the corresponding silver coins of these values.

18.	2 Ticals ND	........................*	5000.00
19.	1 Tical ND	....	1650.00
20.	½ Tical ND	....	1100.00
21.	¼ Tical ND	....	500.00
22.	⅛ Tical ND	....	350.00
23.	¹⁄₁₆ Tical ND	....	150.00

MISCELLANEOUS ISSUES OF MONGKUT
Large crown between flower sprays. Rev. Legend.

24.	2 Ticals ND	....	400.00

Chakra over crown flanked by waterpots. Rev. Blank.

25.	2 Ticals ND	....	400.00

CHULALONGKORN, 1868-1910

Bust. Rev. Crown and umbrellas.

26.	2 Ticals ND	....	150.00

SIERRA LEONE

Lion's head. Rev. Map and value. On the 5th anniversary of independence.

1.	1 Golde 1966	....	250.00
2.	½ Golde 1966	....	125.00
3.	¼ Golde 1966	....	75.00
4.	Palladium 1 Golde 1966	....	500.00
5.	Palladium ½ Golde 1966	....	250.00
6.	Palladium ¼ Golde 1966	....	125.00

SINGAPORE

Crest of the Republic. Rev. Raffles lighthouse.

1.	150 Dollars 1969	....	100.00

SOUTH AFRICA

Only 837 specimens were struck of the Burgers Pound of 1874. The ½ Pound of 1893 is very rare, as are also the English type Pounds and ½ Pounds of 1923 and 1924. South Africa became a republic in 1961 and adopted the decimal system for its coinage. The 2 Rand denomination is equivalent to the Pound.

A. Presidents of —

Head of Thomas Francois Burgers. Rev. Arms.

1.	1 Pound 1874	....	1500.00

Head of Krueger. Rev. Arms.

2.	1 Pound 1892-1900	........................*	80.00
3.	½ Pound 1892-97	....	60.00

ZAR in script letters. Rev. EEN POND. The so-called Veld Pound struck at Pilgrims Rest.

4. 1 Pound 1902 .... 800.00

B. British Sovereigns of —

GEORGE V, 1910-1936

Head. Rev. St. George. This is the same type as the English Pound but with the distinguishing South African mint mark SA on ground below horse.

5. 1 Pound 1923-32 .... 25.00
6. ½ Pound 1923-26 .... 25.00

GEORGE VI, 1937-1952

Head. Rev. Springbok.

7. 1 Pound 1952. Proof 85.00
8. ½ Pound 1952. Proof 50.00

ELIZABETH II, 1952-1960

Head. Rev. Springbok.

9. 1 Pound 1953-60. Proof 75.00
10. ½ Pound 1953-60. Proof 50.00

C. Republic of, 1960 —

Bust of Riebeck. Rev. Springbok.

11. 2 Rand 1961- ....*...... 45.00
12. 1 Rand 1961- 35.00

Bearded bust of President Paul Kruger (1883-1902). Rev. Springbok. Without the mark of value. Intended as a trade coin for distribution through banks outside South Africa.

13. 1 Krugerrand 1967- 65.00

SPAIN

Mints and mint marks:—

S	mm for Seville
M or MD	mm for Madrid
B or BA	mm for Burgos or Barcelona
C Crowned	mm for Cadiz
C Plain	mm for Catalonia
G	mm for Granada
T	mm for Toledo
V	mm for Valencia
Aqueduct	mm for Segovia

Geographically, Spanish coinage is the most universal in the annals of world numismatics. At one time or another, Spain had control over much of the world and her coinage followed the course of empire.

The Spanish series is, therefore, the most far flung of all national coinages, extending beyond the borders of Continental Spain into the following areas:

Europe: Portugal; Belgium (see Brabant and Flanders); France (see Besancon, Dole, Navarre, Provence and Rousillon); Italy (see Cagliari, Messina, Milan and Naples); Netherlands (see Gelderland, Holland, and United Provinces).

America: Bolivia, Chile, Colombia, Guatemala, Mexico and Peru.

Orient: Philippine Islands.

The Spanish and Spanish-American gold Doubloon was the most popular coin of its day. Most of the coinage was struck from gold mined in the American colonies.

After the Escudo-Real standard was abandoned about 1850, Spain adopted the Latin Monetary Union standard and the first coin on the new standard was struck in 1870.

(The Houses of Castile and Leon)
A. Kings of —

ALFONSO VIII, 1158-1214

Arab legend on each side with the addition of "ALF" on Obv. Struck in the style of the Arab Dinars of the period.

1. 1 Maravedi ND 300.00

ALFONSO X, 1252-1284

Castle. Rev. Lion.

2. 1 Dobla ND 375.00

ALFONSO XI, 1312-1350
Castle. Rev. Lion.

3. 1 Dobla ND 900.00

PETER I, 1350-1369

Crowned bust. Rev. Arms.

4.	12 Doblas ND	4500.00
5.	10 Doblas ND	3500.00
6.	1 Dobla ND ....*..	450.00
7.	20 Maravedis ND	375.00

Castle. Rev. Lion.

8.	1 Dobla ND	300.00
9.	20 Maravedis ND	225.00

HENRY II, 1368-1379

Ruler on horse. Rev. Arms.

10.	1 Dobla ND	600.00

HENRY III, 1390-1406
Castle. Rev. Lion.

11.	1 Dobla ND	600.00

JOHN II, 1406-1454

Shield. Rev. Arms.

12.	1 Dobla de la Banda ND	200.00

HENRY IV, 1454-1474
Castle. Rev. Lion.

13.	1 Dobla ND	150.00
14.	½ Dobla ND	550.00

Ruler on throne. Rev. Arms.

15.	5 Enriques or 5 Doblas ND	Rare
16.	1 Enrique or Dobla ND ....*....	350.00
17.	½ Enrique or ½ Dobla ND	300.00

Shield. Rev. Arms.

18.	1 Dobla de la Banda ND	375.00

ALFONSO DE AVILA, 1465-1468
Ruler on horse. Rev. Arms.

19	1 Dobla ND	550.00
20	½ Dobla ND	375.00

FERDINAND V AND ISABELLA I, 1476-1516

Crowned busts facing each other. Rev. Arms on eagle.

21.	50 Excelentes ND. S mm.	Rare
22.	20 Excelentes ND. S mm.	Rare
23.	10 Excelentes ND. S or G mm.	Rare
24.	4 Excelentes ND. B mm. ....*.....	750.00
25.	4 Excelentes ND. Aqueduct mm.	850.00
26.	2 Excelentes ND. B mm.	325.00
27.	2 Excelentes ND. G mm.	250.00
28.	2 Excelentes ND. S mm.	250.00
29.	2 Excelentes ND. T mm. ....*.....	250.00
30.	2 Excelentes ND. Aqueduct mm.	325.00
31.	2 Excelentes ND. C mm.	250.00
32.	2 Ducats ND. S mm.	250.00

Crowned busts facing each other. Rev. Arms without eagle.

33.	1 Excelente ND. C mm. (Cuenca)	350.00
34.	1 Excelente ND. G mm.	225.00
35.	1 Excelente ND. S mm. ....*....	200.00
36.	1 Excelente ND. T mm.	225.00
37.	1 Castellano ND. S mm.	225.00
38.	1 Castellano ND. T mm.	225.00
39.	½ Castellano ND. S mm.	200.00
40.	½ Castellano ND. T mm.	200.00
41.	1 Ducat ND. S mm.	225.00

Crowned figures seated on thrones. Rev. Two shields on eagle.

42.	4 Ducats ND. S mm.	3000.00

Crowned F. Rev. Crowned Y.

43.	½ Excelente ND. B mm.	400.00
44.	½ Excelente ND. S mm.	175.00

CHARLES I AND JOHANNA, 1516-1556

Crowned arms. Rev. Cross.

45.	1 Escudo ND. S mm. ....*......	125.00
46.	1 Escudo ND. Aqueduct mm.	150.00

PHILIP II, 1556-1598

Crowned arms. Rev. Cross. With or without poorly showing dates.

47.	4 Escudos ND. S mm. ....*	375.00
48.	4 Escudos 1591. M mm.	600.00
49.	4 Escudos 1597. BA mm.	600.00
50.	2 Escudos ND. B mm.	350.00
51.	2 Escudos ND. M mm.	350.00
52.	2 Escudos ND. G mm.	175.00
53.	2 Escudos ND. S mm.	125.00
54.	2 Escudos ND. T mm.	175.00
55.	1 Escudo ND. T, G mm.	175.00
56.	1 Escudo ND. S mm.	100.00

PHILIP III, 1598-1621

Arms. Rev. Cross. The cobs with or without poorly showing dates.

57.	100 Escudos 1618	Rare
58.	8 Escudos ND. MD mm. Cob type	500.00
59.	8 Escudos 1614. Aqueduct mm. Modern style	1500.00
60.	8 Escudos ND. T mm. Cob type	900.00
61.	4 Escudos ND. Cob type	450.00
62.	4 Escudos 1607, 11. Aqueduct mm. Modern style	900.00
63.	2 Escudos 1611. S mm. Cob type	200.00
64.	2 Escudos 1610. Aqueduct mm. Modern style	600.00
65.	2 Escudos 1616. MD mm.	350.00
66.	1 Escudo 1607, 08. Aqueduct mm. Modern style *	225.00
67.	1 Escudo 1611. Cob type	125.00

Crowned arms. Rev. Cross with castles and lions in the angles. Struck from dies used for the silver 50 Real coin.

68.	Gold 50 Reales 1620	Rare

PHILIP IV, 1621-1665

Arms. Rev. Cross. The cobs with or without poorly showing dates.

69.	100 Escudos 1633	Rare
70.	8 Escudos 1630-61. M or MD mm. Cob type	1000.00
71.	8 Escudos 1627-65 S mm. Cob type	800.00
72.	8 Escudos 1627-55. Aqueduct mm. Modern style *	2500.00
73.	4 Escudos 1638-44. MD mm. Cob type	400.00
74.	4 Escudos 1631-59. S mm. Cob type	300.00
75.	4 Escudos 1655. Aqueduct mm. Modern style	850.00
76.	2 Escudos 1640-61. S mm. Cob type	225.00
77.	2 Escudos ND, 1625. B mm. Cob type	325.00
78.	2 Escudos 1652. Aqueduct mm. Modern style	700.00
79.	1 Escudo 1646. MD mm. Cob type	125.00
80.	1 Escudo 1639. Aqueduct mm. Cob type	125.00

Crowned arms. Rev. Cross with castles and lions in the angles. Struck from dies used for the silver 50 Real coin.

81.	Gold 50 Reales 1626	Rare

CHARLES II, 1665-1700

Arms. Rev. Cross. The cobs with or without poorly showing dates.

82.	8 Escudos 1697. B mm. Cob type	700.00
83.	8 Escudos Poorly dated. MD mm. Cob type	1500.00
84.	8 Escudos 1668-99. S mm. Cob type	900.00
85.	8 Escudos 1699, 1700. S mm. Modern style	950.00
86.	8 Escudos 1682-87. Aqueduct mm. Modern style ..*	750.00
87.	4 Escudos. Poorly dated. MD mm. Cob type	250.00
88.	4 Escudos 1699, 1700. S mm. Modern style	450.00
89.	4 Escudos 1687. Aqueduct mm. Modern style	700.00
90.	2 Escudos 1699. S mm.	350.00
91.	2 Escudos 1683. Aqueduct mm. Modern style	600.00
92.	1 Escudo 1689. MD mm. Cob type	225.00
93.	1 Escudo 1672-1700. S mm. Cob type	100.00
94.	1 Escudo 1683. Aqueduct mm. Modern style	200.00

PHILIP V, 1700-1746

Bust with long hair. Rev. Arms.

95.	8 Escudos 1728-30. M mm.	800.00
96.	8 Escudos 1729-38. S mm. ....*	450.00
97.	4 Escudos 1732-34. M mm.	375.00
98.	4 Escudos 1729, 30, 33. S mm.	325.00
99.	2 Escudos 1729-34. M mm.	125.00
100.	2 Escudos 1730-42. S mm. ....*	175.00
101.	1 Escudo 1729-42. M mm.	75.00
102.	1 Escudo 1729, 31, 33. S mm.	100.00
103.	½ Escudo 1738-46. M mm.	50.00
104.	½ Escudo 1738-45. S mm.	50.00

Arms. Rev. Cross. The cobs with or without poorly showing dates.

105.	8 Escudos 1719-27. M mm.	1250.00
106.	8 Escudos. Poorly dated. M or MD mm. Cob type.	**Rare**
107.	8 Escudos 1708-23. Aqueduct mm	750.00
108.	8 Escudos 1701-29 S mm	500.00
109.	4 Escudos 1710, 19. M mm.	400.00
110.	4 Escudos 1701-29. S mm.	300.00
111.	4 Escudos 1740. S mm. Cob type	450.00
112.	4 Escudos 1707. V mm.	750.00
113.	2 Escudos 1707. V mm.	650.00
114.	2 Escudos 1721. M mm.	300.00
115.	2 Escudos 1701-26. S mm.	200.00
116.	2 Escudos 1719. S mm. Cob type	150.00
117.	1 Escudo 1723. M mm.	150.00
118.	1 Escudo 1701-21. S mm.	125.00
119.	1 Escudo 1736. S mm. Cob type	100.00

LOUIS I, 1724

Arms. Rev. Cross.

120.	8 Escudos 1724. Aqueduct mm.	3500.00
121.	4 Escudos 1724. Aqueduct mm. ....*..	2000.00
122.	2 Escudos 1724. S mm. Cob type	450.00
123.	2 Escudos 1724. S mm. Modern style	1250.00

FERDINAND VI, 1746-1759

Bust. Rev. Arms.

124.	8 Escudos 1747, 48. S mm.	1250.00
125.	8 Escudos 1747, 49, 50. M mm.	1000.00
126.	4 Escudos 1748. M mm. ....*..	1250.00
127.	2 Escudos 1749. M mm.	500.00

Plain head. Rev. Arms.

128.	2 Escudos 1749. S mm.	250.00
129.	½ Escudo 1746-59. M mm.	45.00
130.	½ Escudo 1746-58. S mm. ....*..	45.00

Arms. Rev. Cross. Cob type.

131.	8 Escudos 1752, 55. S mm.	500.00
132.	2 Escudos 1751, 54. S mm.	150.00

CHARLES III, 1759-1788

Bust or plain head. Rev. Arms.

133.	½ Escudo 1759-71. M mm. ....*..	50.00
134.	½ Escudo 1759-71. S mm.	50.00

Young bust. Rev. Arms.

135.	8 Escudos 1760. M mm.	1000.00
136.	4 Escudos 1761. M mm.	750.00

Older bust. Rev. Arms.

137.	8 Escudos 1772-88. M mm.	300.00
138.	8 Escudos 1762-88. S mm. ....*..	300.00
139.	4 Escudos 1773-88. M mm.	200.00
140.	4 Escudos 1772-87. S mm.	225.00
141.	2 Escudos 1773-88. M mm.	75.00
142.	2 Escudos 1776, 79, 87, 88. S mm.	125.00
143.	1 Escudo 1772-88. M mm.	40.00
144.	1 Escudo 1773-87. S mm.	55.00
145.	½ Escudo 1772-88. M mm.	25.00
146.	½ Escudo 1773-88. S mm.	25.00

CHARLES IV, 1788-1808

Bust. Rev. Arms.

147.	8 Escudos 1788-1806. M mm	275.00
147a.	8 Escudos 1790, 91. S mm	1750.00
148.	4 Escudos 1788-1803. M mm	175.00
148a.	4 Escudos 1801, 08. S mm	1500.00
149.	2 Escudos 1789-1808. M mm.	75.00
150.	2 Escudos 1790-1808. S mm.	80.00
151.	1 Escudo 1789-1801. M mm.	35.00
152.	½ Escudo 1788-96. M mm.	30.00

JOSEPH NAPOLEON BONAPARTE, 1808-1814

Head. Rev. Arms. All with M mm.

153.	320 Reales 1810, 12. Laureate head ....*..	900.00
154.	80 Reales 1809, 10. Plain head	200.00
155.	80 Reales 1811, 12, 13. Laureate head	175.00

FERDINAND VII, 1808-1833

Broad draped bust. Rev. Arms.

156.   2 Escudos 1808, 09. S mm. 125.00

Draped laureate bust. Rev. Arms.

157.   8 Escudos 1811. C mm. 800.00
158.   2 Escudos 1811. C mm. ....*...... 200.00
159.   2 Escudos 1813. M mm. 200.00
160.   2 Escudos 1809. S mm. 225.00

Laureate bust with high collar. Rev. Arms.

161.   2 Escudos 1812-14. M mm. 250.00

Plain or laureate head. Rev. Arms. The large plain C mm.
is for Catalonia. The small crowned C mm. is for Cadiz.

162.   8 Escudos 1813, 14. Large C mm. 1400.00
163.   8 Escudos 1814-20. M mm. 300.00
164.   4 Escudos 1814-24. M mm. ....*...... 150.00
165.   2 Escudos 1811-14. Crowned C mm. 150.00
166.   2 Escudos 1811, 12, 13, 14. Large C mm. 325.00
167.   2 Escudos 1813-33. M mm. 75.00
168.   2 Escudos 1815-33. S mm. 75.00
169.   1 Escudo 1817. M mm. 65.00
170.   ½ Escudo 1817. M mm. 50.00

Plain older head. Rev. Arms.

171.   320 Reals 1822, 23. M mm 600.00
172.   160 Reals 1822. M mm. ....*..... 300.00
173.   80 Reals 1822, 23. M mm. 125.00
174.   80 Reals 1823. B mm. 125.00
175.   80 Reals 1823. S mm. 300.00

ISABELLA II, 1833-1868

Head right with hair combed up. Rev. Arms.

176.   80 Reals 1836-48. B mm. ....*...... 85.00
177.   80 Reals 1834-48. M mm. 85.00
178.   80 Reals 1836-48. S mm. 95.00

Head left with hair combed down. Rev. Arms.

179.   1 Doblon or 100 Reals 1850, 51. M mm. ......*...... 150.00
180.   1 Doblon or 100 Reals 1850. B mm. 200.00

Head left with hair combed down. Rev. Arms in palms.

181.   100 Reals 1854, 55 .... 125.00

Draped laureate bust. Rev. Arms in palms.

182.   100 Reals 1856-62 ....*...... 75.00
183.   40 Reals 1861, 62, 63 .... 60.00
184.   20 Reals 1861, 62, 63 .... 50.00

Draped laureate bust. Rev. Draped arms. The 10 Escudos
value is equal in size and weight to the 100 Reals value.

185.   100 Reals 1863, 64 .... 90.00
186.   40 Reals 1864 .... 75.00
187.   10 Escudos 1865-68 ....*...... 60.00
188.   4 Escudos 1865-68 .... 50.00
189.   2 Escudos 1865 .... 40.00

PROVISIONAL GOVERNMENT, 1870

Hispania standing. Rev. Arms.

190.   100 Pesetas 1870 .... Rare

AMADEO I, 1871-1873

Head. Rev. Arms.

191.	100 Pesetas 1871	......................................*......	4000.00
192.	25 Pesetas 1871	....	2250.00

ALFONSO XII, 1874-1885

Young head. Rev. Arms.

193.	25 Pesetas 1876-80	....	50.00
194.	10 Pesetas 1878	....	40.00

Older bearded head. Rev. Arms.

195.	25 Pesetas 1881-85	....	50.00

ALFONSO XIII, 1886-1931

Large baby head. Rev. Arms.

196.	20 Pesetas 1889, 90	....	85.00

Child head with curly hair. Rev. Arms.

197.	20 Pesetas 1892	....	200.00

Juvenile head. Rev. Arms.

198.	100 Pesetas 1897	....	400.00
199.	20 Pesetas 1899	...........................*......	75.00

Uniformed bust. Rev. Arms.

200.	20 Pesetas 1904	....	200.00

B. Cities and Kingdoms of —

ARAGON

Kings of —

PETER IV, 1336-1387

St. John standing. Rev. Lily.

201.	1 Florin ND	...............................*......	175.00
202.	½ Florin ND	....	300.00
203.	¼ Florin ND	....	300.00

JOHN I, 1387-1396

St. John standing. Rev. Lily.

204.	1 Florin ND	....	125.00
205.	½ Florin ND	....	275.00

MARTIN, 1396-1410

St. John standing. Rev. Lily.

206.	1 Florin ND	....	125.00
207.	½ Florin ND	....	200.00

FERDINAND I, 1412-1416

St. John standing. Rev. Lily.

208.	1 Florin ND	....	350.00
209.	½ Florin ND	....	300.00

ALFONSO V, 1416-1458

St. John standing. Rev. Lily.

210.	1 Florin ND	....	200.00
211.	½ Florin ND	....	175.00

JOHN II, 1458-1479

Crowned bust. Rev. Shield and dragon.

212.	1 Timbre ND	....	1750.00

Crowned bust. Rev. Crowned arms.

213.	1 Florin ND	....	275.00
214.	¼ Florin ND	....	375.00

FERDINAND II, 1479-1516

Crowned bust. Rev. Crowned arms.

215.	4 Ducats ND. Bust left	....	1500.00
216.	2 Ducats ND. Bust left	....	1200.00
217.	1 Ducat ND. Bust right	...........................*......	450.00

CHARLES AND JOHANNA, 1516-1555

Crowned busts facing each other. Rev. Arms.

218.	50 Ducats 1520	Rare
219.	20 Ducats 1520, ND	Rare
220.	2 Ducats ND ....*......	600.00

BARCELONA

Arms. Rev. Value. Siege coin of the Napoleonic Wars.

221.	20 Pesetas 1812, 13, 14	200.00

CATALONIA

Barcelona Mint

Princes of —

BERENGUER RAMON I, 1018-1035
Arab legend in circle within Latin legend. Rev. Arab legend.

222.	1 Mancuso ND	1000.00

PEDRO OF PORTUGAL, 1464-1466
Crowned bust facing. Rev. Arms.

223.	1 Pacifico or Ducat ND	1000.00
224.	½ Pacifico or ½ Ducat ND	1000.00

RENE OF ANJOU, 1466-1472

Crowned bust facing. Rev. Arms.

225.	1 Pacifico or Ducat ND ....*......	450.00
226.	½ Pacifico or ½ Ducat ND	600.00
227.	¼ Pacifico or ¼ Ducat ND	175.00

FERDINAND II, 1479-1516

Crowned bust. Rev. Arms.

228.	4 Principats or 4 Ducats ND	1500.00
229.	2 Principats or 2 Ducats ND	1200.00
230.	1 Principat or Ducat ND ....*......	450.00
231.	½ Principat or ½ Ducat ND	300.00

CHARLES AND JOHANNA, 1516-1558

Crowned busts facing each other. Rev. Arms.

232.	2 Principats 1542, ND	900.00

Initials I and C in circle. Rev. Arms.

233.	½ Principat ND	150.00

PHILIP III, 1598-1621

Bust. Rev. Arms.

234.	⅓ Trentin 1618	375.00

PHILIP IV, 1621-1665
Bust. Rev. Arms.

235.	⅓ Trentin 1625	500.00

Busts of Ferdinand and Isabella facing each other. Rev. Arms.

236.	1 Trentin 1622-32, ND	450.00
237.	½ Trentin 1626, 30, ND ....*......	375.00

PRIVATE ISSUE, 1900
Empty throne. Rev. St. George slaying dragon. Private contribution coins without denomination but corresponding to the contemporary Spanish gold coins.

238.	(100 Pesetas) 1900	225.00
239.	(20 Pesetas) 1900	60.00

LEON

Kings of —

FERDINAND II, 1157-1188
Crowned bust. Rev. Lion and globe.

240.	1 Maravedi ND	1200.00

ALFONSO IX, 1188-1230

Crowned bust. Rev. Lion walking.

241.	1 Maravedi Alfonsi ND	500.00

MAJORCA

Kings of —

PETER IV, 1343-1387

Ruler on throne. Rev. Cross potent.

242.	1 Gold Real ND	........................* 400.00
243.	½ Gold Real ND	.... 300.00
244.	¼ Gold Real ND	.... 200.00
245.	⅛ Gold Real ND	.... 150.00

FERDINAND II, 1479-1516

Bust. Rev. Arms.

246.	1 Ducat ND	.... 400.00

CHARLES I, 1516-1556

Bust. Rev. Arms.

247.	1 Ducat ND	.... 400.00

PHILIP III, 1598-1621

Arms. Rev. Square shield.

248.	4 Escudos ND	.... 400.00
249.	2 Escudos ND	.....................* 250.00
250.	1 Escudo ND	.... 400.00

PHILIP IV, 1621-1665
Arms. Rev. Square shield.

251.	4 Escudos 1648, ND	.... 500.00

Crowned bust. Rev. Arms.

252.	2 Ducats ND	.... 1000.00

CHARLES II, 1665-1700

Arms. Rev. Square shield.

253.	4 Escudos 1698	.....................* 400.00
254.	2 Escudos ND, 1689	.... 250.00
255.	1 Escudo 1689, 98	.... 300.00
256.	½ Escudo 1695	.... 250.00

PHILIP V, 1700-1746

Bust. Rev. Arms.

257.	2 Escudos 1723, 26	.... 250.00

Bust. Rev. Arms and tree.

258.	2 Escudos ND	.... 250.00
259.	1 Escudo ND	.... 250.00

Arms. Rev. Square shield.

260.	4 Escudos 1704	.... 600.00
261.	2 Escudos 1704	.... 400.00

CHARLES III, 1700-1724
Arms. Rev. Shield.

262.	1 Escudo ND	.... 300.00

VALENCIA

Kings of —

ALFONSO V OF ARAGON, 1416-1458

Dragon over shield. Rev. Square shield.

263.	1 Timbre or ⅔ Ducat ND	...............* 200.00
264.	½ Timbre ND	.... 200.00

JOHN II, 1458-1479

Bust facing. Rev. Arms.

265.	1 Ducat ND	.... 300.00

FERDINAND AND ISABELLA, 1479-1504

Crowned heads facing each other. Rev. Arms.

266.	4 Ducats ND	.... 1250.00
267.	2 Ducats ND	.... 750.00
268.	1 Ducat ND	....................* 300.00

Initials F and I crowned. Rev. Arms.

269.	½ Ducat ND	.... 125.00

FERDINAND II, 1504-1516

Bust right or left. Rev. Square shield.

270.	4 Ducats ND	....	500.00
271.	2 Ducats ND	....*	300.00
272.	1 Ducat ND	....	200.00
273.	½ Ducat ND	....	150.00

Initial F. Rev. Arms.

274.	½ Ducat ND	....	100.00

CHARLES I, 1517-1556

Bust. Rev. Square shield.

275.	4 Ducats ND	....	1200.00
276.	2 Ducats ND	.............................*	300.00
277.	1 Ducat ND	....	500.00

Cross of Jerusalem. Rev. Square shield.

278.	4 Corona or 4 Ducats ND	....	400.00
279.	2 Corona or 2 Ducats ND	....	500.00
280.	1 Corona or Ducat ND	...................*	200.00

PHILIP II, 1556-1598

Cross of Jerusalem. Rev. Square shield.

281.	4 Escudos ND	....	800.00

PHILIP IV, 1621-1665

Cross of Jerusalem. Rev. Square shield.

282.	1 Escudo ND or poorly dated	....	400.00

CHARLES II, 1665-1700

Cross of Jerusalem. Rev. Square shield.

283.	1 Escudo 1695	....	200.00

Dragon over shield. Rev. Square shield.

284.	1 Escudo ND	....	100.00

SWEDEN

This section in the catalogue is devoted to the coinage struck in Sweden proper. Additional coins of the Swedish Kings will be found under Esthonia, Latvia, Livonia and in Germany under Augsburg, Bremen and Verden, Elbing, Erfurt, Furth, Hesse-Cassel, Mayence, Nuremberg, Osnabruck, Pomerania, Stettin and Wurzburg.

Sweden was on the Ducat standard as late as 1868. After that, a brief coinage was made on the Latin Monetary Union and a Carolin or 10 Franc piece was struck from 1868 to 1872. The modern coinage of Sweden is based on the standards of the Scandinavian Monetary Union, to which Denmark and Norway also subscribed.

Kings of —

ERIC XIV, 1560-1568

Head. Rev. Jehova in Hebrew characters over Sceptre.

1.	1 Goldgulden 1568	....	3500.00

JOHN III, 1568-1592

Bust in circle. Rev. Heart shaped shield within inscribed circle.

2.	20 Ducats or 2 Portugalosers ND	....	Unique
3.	10 Ducats or 1 Portugaloser ND	....	8000.00
4.	5 Ducats or ½ Portugaloser or 2 Rosenobles ND *......		5000.00

Bust in circle. Rev. Christ over shield.

5.	5 Ducats or ½ Portugaloser or 2 Rosenobles 1576	......	7500.00

Crowned sheaf with value and date. Rev. Arms in circle.

6.	48 Marks 1590	....	Rare
7.	24 Marks 1590	....	Rare
8.	12 Marks 1590	....	Rare

Crowned sheaf and value. Rev. Three crowns and date.

9.	6 Marks 1590, 91	....	2500.00

Rampant lion in circle. Rev. Three crowns and value.

10.	3 Marks 1590	....	1250.00

Crowned bust. Rev. Quartered arms.

11.	1 Hungarian Gulden 1569, 73	....	2500.00

Crowned bust. Rev. Shield with three crowns.

12.   1 Crown Gulden 1569, 70 .... 2000.00

CHARLES IX, 1560-1611
Bust. Rev. Value.

13.   8 Marks 1587, 89, 99, 1603. Square 2250.00

Laureate or crowned bust. Rev. Arms.

14. 16 Marks 1606-11 .... 2500.00

Bust. Rev. Crown over three shields.

15.   6 Marks 1609 .... 750.00

Sheaf. Rev. Hebrew "Jehova."

16. 10 Marks 1610. Square 3000.00
17.   5 Marks 1610, 11. Square 1750.00

GUSTAVE II ADOLPHE, 1611-1632
Bust. Rev. Arms.

18. 16 Marks 1615, 24 .... 3750.00

Sheaf Rev. Hebrew "Jehova."

19. 10 Marks 1616, 26. Square ....*...... 2500.00
20.   5 Marks 1612. Square 2000.00

Bust. Rev. Arms supported by lions.

21.   5 Ducats 1620 .... 5000.00

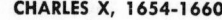

Bust. Rev. Arms.

22. 10 Ducats 1654 .... Rare
23.   1 Ducat 1654-60, ND ....*...... 3000.00

CHARLES XI, 1660-1697

Bust right. Rev. Arms.

24.   1 Ducat 1662-65 .... 1100.00

Bust or head left. Rev. Cross of arms.

25.   1 Ducat 1666-69 .... 900.00

Laureate bust left. Rev. Crown over linked C's.

26.   1 Ducat 1670-76, ND 900.00

Plain bust left. Rev. Crown over linked C's.

27.   1 Ducat 1677 .... 900.00

Plain bust right. Rev. Crown over linked C's.

28.   1 Ducat 1677-95 ....*...... 700.00
29. ¼ Ducat 1692 .... 200.00

Head right. Rev. Legend. From gold of the Dalarna Mines.

30.   1 Ducat 1695 .... 1750.00

CHARLES XII, 1697-1718

Bust with long hair. Rev. Crown over linked C's.

31. 2 Ducats 1702, 04 ....*...... 2000.00
32. 1 Ducat 1697-1707 .... 700.00
32a. 1 Ducat 1708-16 (Short hair) 750.00
33. ½ Ducat 1701 .... 350.00
34. ¼ Ducat 1700 .... 275.00

Bust with short hair. Rev. Crown over linked C's.

35. 1 Ducat 1718 .... 750.00

ULRICA ELEONORA, 1719-1720

Bust. Rev. Arms.

36. 2 Ducats 1719 .... 550.00

Bust. Rev. Crown over linked UE.

37. 1 Ducat 1719, 20 .... 475.00

FREDERICK I, 1720-1751

Bust. Rev. Crown over linked FR or FF.

38. 1 Ducat 1720-28 .... 450.00

Bust. Rev. Cross of four F's.

39. 1 Ducat 1728, 29, 32 .... 450.00
40. ¼ Ducat 1730, 33, 40 .... 150.00

Bust. Rev. Crowned shield.

41. 1 Ducat 1734-50 .... 450.00
42. ½ Ducat 1735, 38 .... 300.00

Bust. Rev. Crowned shield with sun rising from bottom left. From gold mined in China.

43. 1 Ducat 1738-50 .... 500.00

Bust. Rev. Crowned shield, and below, the small arms of Smaland, indicating gold from the Adelfors Mines.

44. 1 Ducat 1741-50 .... 750.00
45. ½ Ducat 1741, 46, 47 .... 400.00

ADOLPHE FREDERICK, 1751-1771

Head. Rev. Crowned shield.

46. 1 Ducat 1751-71 ....*...... 700.00
47. ½ Ducat 1754, 55 .... 325.00
48. ¼ Ducat 1754, 55 .... 175.00

Head. Rev. Crowned shield and legend indicating gold from the Dalarna Mines.

49. 1 Ducat 1751, 54 .... 1000.00

Head. Rev. Crowned shield, and below, the small arms of Smaland, indicating gold from the Adelfors Mines.

50. 1 Ducat 1752-70 .... 950.00

GUSTAVE III, 1771-1792

Head. Rev. Crowned shield.

51. 1 Ducat 1771-92 .... 600.00

Head. Rev. Crowned shield, and below, the small arms
of Smaland, indicating gold from the Adelfors Mines.

52. 1 Ducat 1771-86 .... 950.00

GUSTAVE IV ADOLPHE, 1792-1809

Head. Rev. Crowned shield.

53. 1 Ducat 1793-98 .... 400.00

Armored bust. Rev. Crowned shield.

54. 1 Ducat 1799-1809 .... 275.00

Head. Rev. Crowned shield, and below, the small arms
of Smaland, indicating gold from the Adelfors Mines.

55. 1 Ducat 1796 .... 1100.00

Armored bust. Rev. Similar to above.

56. 1 Ducat 1801 .... 775.00

Armored bust. Rev. Crowned shield, and below, the small
arms of Dalarna, indicating gold from the Dalarna Mines.

57. 1 Ducat 1804 .... 850.00

CHARLES XIII, 1809-1818

Head with title as King of Sweden. Rev. Crowned shield.

58. 1 Ducat 1810-14 .... 300.00

Head with title as King of Sweden and Norway. Rev.
Crowned shield.

59. 1 Ducat 1815, 16, 17 .... 225.00

Head. Rev. Crowned shield, and below, the small arms
of Dalarna, indicating gold from the Dalarna Mines.

60. 1 Ducat 1810 .... 700.00

CHARLES XIV, 1818-1844

Head. Rev. Crowned shield.

61. 1 Ducat 1818-29 .... 225.00

Head. Rev. Arms.

62. 4 Ducats 1837-43 ....*...... 650.00
63. 2 Ducats 1830-43 .... 600.00
64. 1 Ducat 1830-43 .... 200.00

OSCAR I, 1844-1859

Head. Rev. Arms.

65. 4 Ducats 1846, 50 ....*...... 1500.00
66. 2 Ducats 1850, 52, 57 ....*...... 600.00
67. 1 Ducat 1844-59 .... 175.00

CHARLES XV, 1859-1872

Head. Rev. Arms.

68. 1 Ducat 1860-68 .... 150.00

Head. Rev. Crowned shield. With two values as indicated.

69. 1 Carolin-10 Francs 1868-72 .... 100.00

OSCAR II, 1872-1907

Head. Rev. Arms.

70. 20 Kronor 1873-1902 ....*...... 125.00
71. 10 Kronor 1873-1901 .... 80.00

Head. Rev. Value.

72. 5 Kronor 1881-1901 .... 75.00

GUSTAVE V, 1907-1950

Head. Rev. Arms.

73. 20 Kronor 1925 .... 375.00

Head. Rev. Value.

74. 5 Kronor 1920 .... 75.00

SWITZERLAND

Switzerland, though small in area, has produced a body of coinage that for historical interest, variety of type and numismatic value, rivals that of any major power of the world, past or present.

A. Confederation of —

Cross on shield. Rev. Value. Not placed in circulation.

1. 20 Francs 1871 .... 2000.00

Girl head. Rev. Cross on shield. Not placed in circulation.

2. 20 Francs 1871 .... 3500.00

Helvetia seated. Rev. Value and date. Not placed in circulation.

3. 20 Francs 1873. Two dots and mintmark ...*......... 1000.00
4. 20 Francs 1873. Two dots, no mintmark 1500.00

Girl head. Rev. Cross on shield.

5. 20 Francs 1883, 86, 89-96 ....*...... 50.00
6. 20 Francs 1888 .... 1800.00

Girl head against Alps background. Rev. Cross on shield.

7. 20 Francs 1897-1949 ....*...... 17.50

Girl head against Alps background. Rev. Value and date.

8.	100 Francs 1925	....	1800.00
9.	10 Francs 1911	....	100.00
10.	10 Francs 1912-22	....	35.00

Rifleman standing. Rev. Oval shield. On the Fribourg Shooting Festival.

11.	100 Francs 1934	....	800.00

Rifleman kneeling. Rev. Legend over shield. On the Lucerne Shooting Festival.

12.	100 Francs 1939	....	250.00

B. Cantons, Ecclesiastical Princes and Cities of —

APPENZELL (INNER-RHODEN)

St. Mauritius standing. Rev. Legend in cartouche.

13.	1 Ducat 1737	...........................*......	3000.00
14.	1 Ducat 1739	....	Rare

BASEL

Coinage as a mint of the Holy Roman Empire.

Madonna standing. Rev. Orb. With the name of Sigismund.

15.	1 Goldgulden ND. (1419-33). As King	....	200.00
16.	1 Goldgulden ND. (1433-37). As Emperor	....	200.00
17.	1 Goldgulden ND. Without his name	..........*......	500.00

Madonna standing. Rev. Orb. With the name of Albert II.

18.	1 Goldgulden ND. (1437-39)	....	600.00

Madonna standing. Rev. Orb. With the name of Frederick III.

19.	1 Goldgulden ND. (1440-51). As King	....	250.00
20.	1 Goldgulden ND. (1451-93). As Emperor	....	200.00
21.	1 Goldgulden ND. With Weinsberg shield	....	300.00
22.	1 Goldgulden 1491, 92, 93	....	1000.00

Madonna standing. Rev. Orb. With the name of Maximilian I.

23.	1 Goldgulden 1502, 03. With Weinsberg shield	....	1200.00
24.	1 Goldgulden 1505-09. With Konigstein-Munzenberg shield	...................................*......	800.00

City Coinage

Madonna standing, Basel arms at feet. Rev. Orb. With the name of Pope Julius II.

25.	1 Goldgulden 1512. Museum of Basel	....	Unique

Madonna standing. Rev. Arms on cross. With the name of Pope Julius II.

26.	1 Goldgulden 1513	....	1000.00

Madonna standing. Rev. Arms on cross. With the name of Maximilian I.

27.	1 Goldgulden 1516	....	900.00

Madonna standing. Rev. Arms on cross. With the name of the City of Basel.

28.	1 Goldgulden 1520, 21	....................*......	900.00
29.	1 Goldgulden 1524, 25, 28, 33, 38, 39	....	1500.00

Arms. Rev. Double eagle.

30.	4 Ducats ND (about 1570)	....	Rare

Arms on cartouche. Rev. Orb.

31.	2 Goldgulden ND. (17th Century)	....	1200.00
32.	1 Goldgulden ND. (17th Century)	....	350.00

Basilisk with arms. Rev. Orb.

33.	2 Goldgulden ND. (17th Century)	....	1400.00

Basilisk with arms. Rev. Double eagle.

34.	2 Goldgulden ND. (17th Century)	....	1600.00

Arms on cartouche. Rev. Liberty cap on pole.
35. 2 Goldgulden ND. (18th Century) 1200.00
36. 1 Goldgulden ND. (18th Century) 350.00

Northern view of the city. Rev. Basilisk and arms within eight shields.
37. 25 Ducats ND. (1700-10) .... Rare
38. 20 Ducats ND. (1700-10) .... Rare
39. 15 Ducats ND. (1700-10) ....*...... Rare

Northeastern view of the city. Rev. Basilisk holding shield with eight small arms.
40. 12 Ducats ND. (1700-30) 4500.00
41. 10 Ducats ND. (1700-30) 3500.00

Northwestern view of the city. Rev. Two basilisks holding arms.
42. 8 Ducats ND. (about 1700) 3500.00

Northeastern view of the city. Rev. Arms within eight shields.
43. 6 Ducats ND. (17th Century) 3000.00

Northwestern view of the city. Rev. Arms within eight shields.
44. 4 Ducats ND. (17th Century) ....*...... 2500.00
45. 3 Ducats ND. (17th Century) 2200.00
46. 2 Ducats ND. (17th Century) 1500.00

Legend on cartouche. Rev. Basilisk with arms.
47. 2 Ducats ND. (18th Century) 1500.00
48. 1 Ducat ND. (18th Century) ....*...... 800.00
49. ½ Ducat ND. (18th Century) 1000.00

Arms in cartouche. Rev. Double eagle.
50. 1 Ducat ND. (1620-50) 700.00

Legend in square cartouche. Rev. Arms in oval cartouche.
51. 1 Ducat ND. (17th Century) 750.00

Basilisk and oval shield. Rev. Value and name.
52. ½ Ducat ND. (1750-80) 400.00
53. ¼ Ducat ND. (1750-80) 300.00

Arms on cross. Rev. Double eagle.
54. 1 Goldgulden 1621, 22 ....*...... 1000.00
55. 1 Goldgulden 1623 .... Rare

Arms on cartouche. Rev. Double eagle.
56. 1 Ducat 1640 .... 900.00

Legend on cartouche. Rev. Basilisk with arms.
57. 1 Ducat 1653 .... 1000.00

Legend on cartouche. Rev. Arms. Angel's head above.
58. 10 Ducats 1676 .... Rare

Eastern view of the city. Rev. Basilisk with arms.

59.	20 Ducats 1741	6000.00
60.	12 Ducats 1741	5000.00
61.	10 Ducats 1741	4000.00
62.	8 Ducats 1741	3300.00
63.	6 Ducats 1741	2800.00
64.	5 Ducats 1740	*......2000.00
65.	4 Ducats 1740	1800.00
66.	3 Ducats 1740	1600.00

Northwestern view of the city. Rev. Basilisk with arms, shields below.

67.	2 Ducats 1743	1400.00
68.	1 Ducat 1743	*......1300.00
69.	⅔ Ducat 1743	1000.00

Value on drapery, liberty cap above. Rev. Basilisk with arms.

70.	2 Ducats ND. (1750-1800)	1000.00

Denomination in wreath. Rev. Arms, liberty cap above.

71.	2 Ducats 1795	**Rare**

Arms, liberty cap above. Rev. Tripod.

72.	1 Duplone 1795	900.00

Arms, liberty cap above. Legend in wreath.

73.	1 Duplone 1795, 96	650.00

"Show Pieces" of Basel

Basilisk with arms and eight shields. Rev. Plancus standing.

74.	12 Ducats ND. (17th Century)	3000.00
75.	8 Ducats ND. (17th Century)	*......2800.00
76.	6 Ducats ND. (17th Century)	2400.00

Northern view of the city. Rev. Plancus standing.

77.	3 Ducats ND. (17th Century)	**Rare**

Double eagle. Rev. Plancus standing.

78.	1 Ducat ND. (1620-50)	750.00

Northwestern view of the city. Rev. Hen.

79.	3 Ducats ND. (17th Century)	550.00

Western view of the city behind arms held by griffins. Rev. Hen.

80.	10 Ducats ND. (17th Century)	3000.00
81.	6 Ducats ND. (17th Century)	*......2500.00
82.	5 Ducats ND. (17th Century)	2000.00

Northern view of the city. Rev. The Adoration by the shepherds.

83.	3 Ducats ND. (1680-1700)	500.00
84.	2 Ducats ND. (1680-1700)	400.00

Northern view of the city. Rev. The Adoration by the three Magi.

85.	3 Ducats ND. (1680-1700)	500.00
86.	2 Ducats ND. (1680-1700)	*......400.00

The Adoration by the shepherds. Rev. The Adoration by the three Magi.

87.	3 Ducats ND. (1680-1700)	500.00
88.	2 Ducats ND. (1680-1700)	400.00

BERNE

One-headed eagle over arms. Rev. St. Vincent standing.
89. 4 Goldgulden 1492 ....*...... 6000.00
90. 3 Goldgulden 1492 .... 5000.00
91. 2 Goldgulden 1492 .... 4500.00

Two-headed eagle over arms. Rev. St. Vincent standing.
92. 2 Ducats 1600 ....*...... 1750.00
93. 1 Ducat 1600 ....*...... 1200.00
94. ½ Ducat 1601 .... 1300.00

Bear and two-headed eagle below seven shields, within circle of 20 shields. Rev. St. Vincent standing.
95. 10 Ducats 1501 .... 7000.00
96. 9 Ducats 1501 .... 6500.00
97. 8 Ducats 1501 .... **Rare**
98. 6 Ducats 1501 ....*..... 5500.00
99. 5 Ducats 1501 .... 5000.00

Arms. Rev. St. Peter standing.
100. 1 Goldgulden ND. (1479-1500) 3000.00

Arms. Rev. Bust of St. Vincent.
101. 1 Goldgulden ND. (1500-30) .... **Rare**

Two-headed eagle over arms. Rev. Orb with name of Frederick II.
102. 1 Goldgulden ND. (16th Century) 2500.00
103. 1 Goldgulden 1590, 94 .... **Rare**

Eagle over arms. Rev. Cross.
104. 2 Goldgulden ND. (1490-1550) .... **Rare**
105. 1 Goldgulden ND. (1490-1550) .... **Rare**
106. ½ Goldgulden ND. (1490-1550) .... **Rare**
107. ½ Goldgulden 1554, 56, 62, 90 .... **Rare**

Arms. Rev. Eagle with name of Frederick II.
108. 1 Goldgulden 1530. Swiss National Museum. .... **Unique**
109. 1 Goldgulden 1537, 39. Single head eagle ....*...... 3000.00
110. 1 Goldgulden 1566. Double eagle .... **Rare**

Arms. Rev. Cross.
111. 4 Ducats ND. (16th Century) .... **Rare**

Arms. Rev. Legends as illustrated.
112. 3 Ducats ND. (16th Century). Legend in seven lines *... 5000.00
113. 3 Ducats ND. (16th Century). Circular legend ......*... **Rare**
114. 2 Ducats ND. (16th Century). Legend in seven lines 3500.00

Arms. Rev. Double eagle.
115. 3 Ducats 1659 .... 3000.00
116. 2 Ducats 1658 .... 2500.00
117. 2 Ducats ND. (1645-1665) 2800.00
118. 1 Ducat 1658 ....*...... 1400.00

Arms supported by bear and lion. Rev. Crowned cartouche supported by bears.
119. 4 Ducats ND. (about 1700) 3000.00

Arms. Rev. Value and date between branches.
120. 2 Ducats 1679 .... 1500.00
121. 1 Ducat 1679 .... 1200.00
122. 1 Ducat 1679. (Rev. Cartouche) 1300.00

Bear and lion holding arms. Rev. Legend and value in cartouche with floral wreath.

123. 12 Ducats 1681 .... 7000.00
124. 10 Ducats 1681 .... 6500.00
125. 4 Ducats 1680, 84. Without floral wreath on Rev. *...... 3000.00

Crown over two shields and value. Rev. Male and female holding drapery.

126. 3 Ducats 1680, 84, 97, 1707 ....*...... 1800.00
127. 3 Ducats 1699 (one shield on Obv.) 2000.00
128. 3 Ducats 1734 (cartouche on Rev.) 2000.00

Crowned arms on branches. Rev. Legend in cartouche.

129. 3 Ducats 1734 .... 2200.00

Arms. Rev. Male and female holding drapery.

130. 2 Ducats 1698 .... 1500.00
131. 1 Ducat 1697, 1718 .... 800.00

Crowned arms supported by bear and lion. Rev. View of the city, with small arms above.

132. 10 Ducats ND. (1680-1720) 7000.00

Crowned arms on branches. Rev. Legend in cartouche.

133. 10 Ducats ND. (18th Century) 6000.00
134. 8 Ducats ND. (18th Century) 5000.00
135. 6 Ducats ND. (18th Century) ....*..... 3800.00
136. 4 Ducats ND. (18th Century) 2800.00
137. 4 Ducats ND. (18th Century). Value on Rev. 2800.00

Arms supported by bear and lion. Rev. Male and female at altar.

138. 10 Ducats ND. (1700-1710) 6000.00
139. 8 Ducats ND. (1700-1710) .... Rare
140. 7 Ducats ND. (1700-1710) .... Rare
141. 6 Ducats ND. (1700-1710) 3800.00
142. 5 Ducats ND. (1700-1710) 3000.00
143. 4 Ducats ND. (1700-1710) ....*...... 2200.00

Crowned arms. Rev. Male and female at altar.

144. 5 Ducats ND. (18th Century) 3000.00
145. 4 Ducats ND. (18th Century) 2200.00

Bear holding arms in circle of shields. Rev. Male and female at altar.

146. 8 Ducats ND. (1700-1710). She-bear nursing .... Rare
147. 5 Ducats 1700, ND. (1700-1710) 3000.00
148. 4 Ducats ND. (1700-1710) 2300.00

Bear in cartouche. Rev. Angel with shield.

149. 1 Ducat 1696 .... 1200.00

Arms supported by bear and lion. Rev. Bear holding shield.

150. 6 Ducats 1701 .... 3500.00
151. 5 Ducats 1701 .... 3000.00
152. 4 Ducats 1701 ....*...... 2500.00

Two lions holding arms and cap. Rev. Legend and value on shield.

153.   2 Ducats 1703, 19, 27, 71 .... 1200.00

Arms. Rev. Cross.

154.   ½ Ducat 1718 ....   500.00
155.   ½ Ducat 1781 ....   **Rare**
156.   ¼ Ducat 1707, 31, 66, 77, 78, 81, ND. (1800) ..*......   450.00

Crowned arms. Rev. Legend and value in cartouche.

157.   3 Ducats 1772 .... 1800.00
158.   2 Ducats 1789 ....*..... 1200.00
159.   1 Ducat 1725, 41, 88, 89, ND. (1772) ....*.....   550.00
160.   ½ Ducat 1714, 17, 19 ....   300.00

Crowned arms. Rev. Value and date in wreath, legend around.

161.   8 Ducats 1796 .... 4500.00
162.   8 Ducats 1798 ....   **Rare**
163.   6 Ducats 1796 .... 4200.00
164.   4 Ducats 1796, 98 .... 2800.00
165.   4 Ducats 1825 .... 3400.00
166.   2 Ducats 1796 ....*..... 1000.00
167.   1 Ducat 1793 (Oval shield) Rare; 94 ....*......   600.00

Crowned arms. Rev. Legend in wreath.

168.   2 Duplones 1793-96 ....   800.00
169.   1 Duplone 1793-96 ....*......   500.00

Crowned arms. Rev. Warrior standing.

170.   6 Duplones or 12 Ducats 1795. (Struck from thaler
      dies). ....   **Rare**
171.   4 Duplones or 8 Ducats 1797 .... 4000.00
172.   2 Duplones 1794, 96, 97, 98 ....*..... 1500.00
173.   1 Duplone 1793, 97, 1819, 29 .... 1000.00
174.   ½ Duplone 1797 ....   500.00

*Arms. Rev. Crowned monogram. Without the mark of value
and not placed in circulation.*

175.   (10 Francs) ND. (About 1810) 3000.00

CHUR

A. Bishops of —

PETER II, 1581-1601

Bust of St. Luke. Rev. Double eagle.

176.   7 Ducats ND 4000.00

JOHN V, 1601-1627

Bust of St. Luke. Rev. Double eagle.

177.   7 Ducats 1613 .... 3000.00
178.   7 Ducats 1615 .... 3500.00
179.   7 Ducats ND ....*..... 2200.00
180.   1 Goldgulden ND. (Name of Matthias) 400.00
181.   1 Goldgulden ND. (Name of Ferdinand II) 700.00

Arms. Rev. Double eagle.

182.   2 Ducats ND ....   **Rare**

JOSEPH, 1627-1635
Arms. Rev. Double eagle.

182a.   1 Ducat ND ....   **Rare**

JOHN VI, 1636-1661
Arms. Rev. Double eagle.

183.   1 Ducat 1636, 49, 52 ....   **Rare**

ULRIC VI, 1661-1692
Arms. Rev. Double eagle.

184.	6 Ducats 1664	Rare
185.	1 Ducat 1664	Rare

ULRIC VII, 1692-1728
Arms. Rev. Double eagle.

186.	10 Ducats 1720	Rare

Arms. Rev. Bust of St. Luke.

187.	1 Ducat 1693	Rare
188.	1 Ducat 1697. (broad flan)	Rare
189.	1 Ducat 1713	2400.00

JOSEPH BENEDICT, 1728-1754

Bust. Rev. Arms.

190.	10 Ducats 1736, 37	Rare
191.	8 Ducats 1747	3800.00
192.	7 Ducats 1749 . . . .*.	3500.00
193.	6 Ducats 1749	Rare
194.	5 Ducats 1749	3000.00
195.	1 Ducat 1749	1200.00

JOHN ANTHONY, 1755-1777

Arms. Rev. Madonna.

196.	1 Ducat 1767 . . . . 1500.00

B. City of —

Bust of St. Luke. Rev. Double eagle.

197.	1 Goldgulden ND (Name of Ferdinand II)	1000.00

St. Luke standing. Rev. Double eagle.

198.	1 Goldgulden 1618 (Name of Matthias)	1500.00

Arms. Rev. Double eagle.

199.	2 Ducats 1633. (Name of Ferdinand II)	3200.00
200.	1 Ducat 1634, 36, 37 (Name of Ferdinand II)	1600.00
201.	1 Ducat 1638, 39, 41, 42, 44 (Name of Ferdinand III)	1500.00

EINSIEDELN

Abbots of—

BEATUS, 1780-1808
Arms. Rev. Madonna of Einsiedeln.

202.	1 Ducat 1783	900.00

FISCHINGEN

Abbots of—

FRANCIS, 1688-1728

Arms. Rev. St. Ida with stag.

203.	2 Ducats 1726. Thick flan . . . .*.	1800.00
204.	1 Ducat 1726	1300.00

FRIBOURG

Eagle over fortress. Rev. Floriated cross.

205.	2 Florins 1597. Swiss National Museum	Unique
206.	1 Florin 1594, 97 . . . .*.	2400.00
207.	1 Florin 1599	1700.00
208.	1 Florin 1619, 20	Rare
209.	½ Florin ND. (About 1510)	1400.00
210.	½ Ecu d'or 1610. 2.18 g. Berne Museum	Unique

Eagle over fortress. Rev. Bust of St. Nicholas.

211.	1 Florin 1587 . . . .*.	2000.00
212.	1 Florin 1594	Rare

Eagle over fortress. Rev. St. Nicholas standing.

213.	1 Ducat ND. (About 1550)	2300.00

Eagle over fortress. Rev. Cross in quadrilobe.

214.	1 Quadruple or 2 Duplones 1622	Rare
215.	1 Duplone or 1 Pistole 1622	Rare
216.	1 Duplone or 1 Pistole 1635 ....*......	1700.00

Arms. Rev. Sun.

228.	1 Ecu d'or au Soleil ND. (1540-50)	4000.00
229.	3 Pistoles 1771 ....*......	1000.00
230.	1 Small Pistole of 35 Florins	
	1752-55, 57, 58, 62, 70 ....*......	400.00

GENEVA

Arms. Rev. Value.

231.	20 Francs 1848	550.00
232.	10 Francs 1848	650.00

Double eagle and arms. Rev. Sun.

217.	1 Quadruple 1635, 37, 38, 40-42, 44-46 ......*......	2000.00
218.	1 Ecu-Pistolet 1562-68, 74-76, 80-83, 85, 86, 1634	500.00
219.	1 Ecu-Pistolet 1569, 78, 79	Rare
220.	1 Pistole 1634, 36, 38-42	1500.00

Double eagle over arms. Rev. Quadrilobe.

221.	1 Pistole 1594. (Struck from 3 Sols dies)	Unique

GRISONS

Canton of —

Three shields. Rev. Value.

233.	16 Francs 1813	3500.00

Double eagle. Rev. Legend in tablet.

222.	2 Ducats 1654, 58-60, 62, 63, 66	1800.00
223.	2 Ducats 1656, 57, 64, 90 ....*......	1300.00
224.	1 Ducat 1644, 46, 48-51, 54	650.00
225.	1 Ducat 1647, 52, 67	Rare

HALDENSTEIN

Barons of —

THOMAS I, 1609-1628
Bust. Rev. Double eagle.

234.	7 Ducats 1617	5000.00
235.	4 Ducats 1617	4500.00
236.	2 Ducats 1617	Rare

Arms. Rev. Double eagle.

226.	1 Large Pistole of 40 Florins 1722, 24	650.00
227.	1 Small Pistole of 35 Florins 1772	650.00

Double eagle. Rev. Ruler kneeling before seated Christ.

237.	1 Goldgulden ND	700.00

Double eagle. Rev. Ruler kneeling before standing Christ.

238.	1 Goldgulden 1618	....	**Rare**
239.	1 Goldgulden ND	....	1400.00

JULIUS OTTO I, 1628-1666
Ruler standing. Rev. Double eagle.

240.	1 Ducat 1638, 42, 49	....	1800.00

THOMAS II, 1667
Bust facing. Rev. Double eagle.

241.	1 Ducat 1667	....	**Rare**

GUBERT, 1733
Bust. Rev. Arms.

242.	6 Ducats 1733	....	**Rare**
243.	5 Ducats 1733	....	**Rare**
244.	1 Ducat 1733	....	**Rare**

THOMAS III, 1747-70
Bust. Rev. Arms.

245.	1 Ducat 1767	....	**Rare**

HELVETIAN REPUBLIC

Warrior standing. Rev. Value.

246.	32 Francs 1800	...........................*......	3000.00
247.	16 Francs 1800	....	1200.00

LAUSANNE

Bishops of —

BENOIT, 1476-1491
Bust. Rev. Arms.

248.	1 Ducat ND. Lausanne Museum	....	**Unique**

AYMON, 1491-1517
Bust. Rev. Arms.

249.	1 Ducat ND	....	2000.00

LUCERNE

Eagle over arms. Rev. Bust of St. Leodegar.

250.	4 Ducats ND. (16th Century)	...................*......	5000.00
251.	3 Ducats ND. (16th Century)	....	**Rare**

Eagle over arms. Rev. Bust of St. Leodegar facing.

252.	4 Ducats ND	....	**Rare**
253.	2 Ducats 1603	....	**Rare**

Arms. Rev. St. Leodegar standing.

254.	6 Ducats 1698	....	3500.00
255.	5 Ducats 1698	....	3000.00
256.	4 Ducats 1698	....	2000.00

Value in cartouche. Rev. St. Leodegar and St. Maurice standing.

257.	1 Ducat ND. (1695-1700)	....	1200.00

Double eagle over arms. Rev. Bust of St. Leodegar facing.

258.	1 Ducat 1639	....	1000.00

Crowned arms. Rev. St. Leodegar and Church.

259.	2 Ducats 1675. (Broad flan)	....	2000.00

Warrior with shield seated. Rev. St. Leodegar seated.

260.	5 Ducats 1695	....	**Rare**
260a.	4 Ducats 1695 (Berne Museum)	....	**Unique**
261.	2 Ducats 1695	....	3000.00

St. Leodegar seated. Rev. Legend in cartouche.

262.	10 Ducats 1714	....	**Rare**
263.	5 Ducats 1714	....	3500.00

Arms. Rev. Legend in cartouche.

264.	5 Ducats 1714	....	3200.00

St. Leodegar standing. Rev. Value in cartouche.

265.	3 Ducats 1714	....	2000.00
266.	2 Ducats 1714	...............................*....	1250.00
267.	1 Ducat 1715	....	1000.00
268.	1 Ducat 1725	....	1250.00

Arms supported by wild men. Rev. Value.

269.	5 Ducats 1741	....	3800.00
270.	4 Ducats 1741	....	3200.00
271.	3 Ducats 1741	....	2750.00
272.	2 Ducats 1741	...............................*....	1200.00
273.	1 Ducat 1741	................................*....	800.00

Crowned arms. Rev. Value in wreath.

274.	24 Munzgulden 1794, 96	..................*......	1500.00
275.	12 Munzgulden 1794, 96	....	700.00

Crowned arms. Rev. Warrior seated.

276.	20 Francs 1807	....	1200.00
277.	10 Francs 1804	...............*......	450.00

MESOCCO

Marcheses of —

GIAN GIACOMO, 1487-1518
Arms: Three crosses. Rev. Cross.

278.	1 Scudo d'oro del sole ND	....	1750.00

Arms: Lily of France. Rev. Cross.

279.	1 Scudo d'oro del sole ND	....	Rare

Arms: Three scallops. Rev. Cross.

280.	1 Scudo d'oro del sole ND	....	Rare

Orb. Rev. Madonna.

281.	1 Zecchino ND. City Museum, Brescia, Italy	......	Unique

MURI

Abbots of —

PLACIDUS, 1684-1723
Bust. Rev. View of the Abbey.

282.	5 Ducats 1720	....	2500.00

Bust. Rev. Arms of the Zurlauben family.

283.	1 Ducat 1720	....	800.00

NEUCHATEL

Counts of —

HENRY I, 1575-1595
Bust. Rev. Arms.

284.	1 Ecu Pistolet	....	Unique

HENRY II, 1595-1663
Bust. Rev. Arms.

285.	2 Pistoles 1603	....	Rare
286.	2 Pistoles 1618	....	Rare

Bust right. Rev. Arms.

287.	2 Pistoles 1631. Berne Museum	....	Unique

MARIE, 1694-1707

Bust. Rev. Arms.

288.	4 Pistoles 1694. Neuchatel Museum	....	Unique
289.	2 Pistoles 1694	...............*......	4500.00

Cross of four M's, "16" (Kreuzer) in center. Rev. Arms.

290.	1 Pistole (2 Ducats) 1694. Neuchatel Museum	....	Unique
291.	½ Pistole (1 Ducat) 1694	....	Rare

(For the gold coins struck by the kings of Prussia for Neuchatel, see under Germany-Prussia.)

OBWALDEN (UNTERWALDEN)

Arms. Rev. St. Nicholas von der Flue standing.

292.	8 Ducats 1728	....	Rare

Double eagle with arms of Obwalden. Rev. Legend in rectangular cartouche.

293.	1 Ducat 1726	....	1500.00

Legend in rectangular cartouche. Rev. St. Nicholas von der Flue standing.

294.	1 Ducat 1726	....	750.00

Legend in cartouche. Rev. St. Nicholas von der Flue kneeling to right.

295.	5 Ducats 1732	Rare
296.	1 Ducat 1725	Rare
297.	1 Ducat 1730	900.00
298.	1 Ducat 1743 ....*	500.00
299.	1 Ducat 1787 (St. Nicholas to left and facing)	600.00
300.	1 Ducat 1787. "Niederberger"—restrike by Durussel	275.00

Arms. Rev. St. Nicholas kneeling slightly to left.

301.	1 Ducat 1774	1500.00

RHEINAU

Abbots of —

GEROLD II, 1697-1735

Arms. Rev. View of the Abbey.

302.	1 Ducat 1710	1200.00

Bust. Rev. Arms.

303.	2 Ducats 1723	1500.00

Arms. Rev. St. Fintan standing.

304.	2 Ducats 1723 ....*	1400.00
305.	1 Ducat 1723	1000.00

ST. GALLEN

A. City of —

Bear. Rev. Double eagle.

306.	4 Ducats 1620. Square. Museum of St. Gallen	Unique
307.	3 Ducats 1618, 19. Museum of St. Gallen	Unique
308.	2 Ducats 1621 ....*	1700.00

B. Abbots of —

BEDA, 1767-1796

Arms. Rev. St. Gallus on throne.

309.	1 Ducat 1773 ....*	1400.00
310.	1 Ducat 1774. (Date on Obv.)	1200.00

Arms. Rev. Bear with stick of firewood.

311.	1 Ducat 1781	1000.00

SCHAFFHAUSEN

Ram jumping out from city gate. Rev. Double eagle.

312.	20 Ducats 1656	Rare
313.	1 Goldgulden 1622	Rare

Arms. Rev. Double eagle.

314.	1 Ducat 1633 ....*	850.00
315.	1 Ducat 1657 (overstruck on 1633 Ducat), ND (1658) ..	1000.00

SCHWYZ

Crowned double eagle over arms. Rev. Floriated cross. Struck at Bellinzona, 1510-20.

316. 1 Scudo d'oro ND .... **Rare**

St. Martin on horseback, and beggar. Rev. Madonna.

317. 1 Ducat ND (1621), 1653 ....*...... 1500.00
318. 1 Ducat 1674 .... **Rare**

Lion holding shield. Rev. Legend.

319. 1 Ducat ND (1779), 1781, 88, 90 .... 1200.00

Lion holding shield. Rev. Legend.

320. 1 Ducat 1844 .... 1300.00

SION (WALLIS)

Bishops of —

HILDEBRAND, 1565-1604

Floriated cross. Rev. St. Theodul over arms.

321. 1 Ducat ND 2500.00

ADRIEN III, 1640-1646

Mitre and crosier over arms of Riedmatten. Rev. Eagle over arms of Wallis. Struck from Kreuzer dies.

322. 1 Ducat ND 2500.00

SOLOTHURN

Eagle over arms. Rev. Bust of St. Ursus. Struck from Dicken dies.

323. 3 Ducats ND. (16th Century) .... **Rare**

Arms. Rev. St. Ursus standing in oval trilobe.

324. 1 Ducat 1630. Museum of Berne .... **Unique**
325. ½ Ducat 1630 ....*...... **Rare**

Double eagle and arms. Rev. St. Ursus standing in oval trilobe.

326. 1 Ducat ND (about 1630) .... **Unique**

Crowned arms. Rev. St. Ursus standing.

327. 1 Ducat 1768 .... 2000.00
328. 2 Duplones 1787, 96 .... 1400.00
329. 2 Duplones 1797, 98 .... 1300.00
330. 1 Duplone 1787, 96, 97 ....*...... 800.00
331. 1 Duplone 1798 .... 900.00
332. ½ Duplone 1787, 96 ....*...... 500.00
333. ¼ Duplone 1789, 96 .... 225.00

Crowned oval shield. Rev. St. Ursus standing.

333a. 32 Franken 1813 .... **Rare**
334. 16 Franken 1813 .... 2500.00
335. 8 Franken 1813 .... 2500.00

URI

Floriated cross over arms. Rev. St. Martin on horseback and beggar.

336. 1 Pistole ND. Small size. (17th Century) ....*...... 1200.00
337. 1 Pistole 1613. Large size .... **Rare**

Legend and value. Rev. St. Martin standing and beggar.

338. 1 Ducat 1701 .... **Rare**
339. 1 Ducat 1704 (overstruck on 1701 Ducat) 1800.00

Arms. Rev. St. Martin on horseback and beggar.

340. 1 Ducat 1720 .... 900.00
341. 1 Ducat 1736 (overstruck on 1720 Ducat) ......*...... 700.00

URI, SCHWYZ AND UNTERWALDEN

Three shields, double eagle and crossed keys. Rev. Floriated cross. Presumably struck at Bellinzona before 1520. Only a rubbing of this piece is known.

342. 1 Scudo d'oro ND .... —

Same Obv. as above. Rev. St. Martin on horseback and beggar. Struck at Bellinzona.

343. 1 Ducat ND (about 1520) .... **Rare**

Double eagle over three arms. Rev. Floriated cross. Naples type, struck at Altdorf.

344. 1 Gold Krone ND (about 1561) ....*...... 5500.00
345. 1 Gold Krone 1556 .... **Unique**

Three arms in triangular composition. Rev. Floriated cross. Struck from Broad-Batzen dies.

346. 1 Pistole 1569. Museum of Berne .... **Unique**

URI AND UNTERWALDEN

Crowned double eagle over two arms. Rev. Floriated cross. North Italian type, struck at Bellinzona after 1508.

347. 1 Scudo d'oro ND 5500.00

ZUG

Arms. Rev. Crowned double eagle. Struck from ⅛ Assis dies.

348. ⅛ Ducat ND. (17th Century) .... **Rare**

Bust of St. Oswald. Rev. Double eagle and arms.

349. 1 Ducat 1691. Museum of Winterthur .... **Unique**
350. 1 Goldgulden 1615 .... **Unique**

Arms. Rev. Legend.

351. 1½ Ducats 1692 .... **Rare**

Arms. Rev. Value.

352. ½ Ducat 1692 .... 800.00

ZURICH

Eagle and large arms. Rev. Charlemagne on throne.

353. 1 Goldgulden ND (about 1510) 1800.00

Arms in trilobe. Rev. Double eagle in shield. Gothic script.

354. 1 Goldgulden 1526 .... 3000.00
355. 1 Goldgulden 1527 ....*...... 2500.00

Two lions with three shields and crown. Rev. Circle of nine shields around arms of Zurich. "Schnabeltaler" dies.

356. 10 Ducats 1559 ....*...... 6000.00
357. 9 Ducats 1559 .... 5000.00
358. 8 Ducats 1559 .... 4500.00

Arms on double eagle. Rev. Floriated cross.

359. 1 Gold Krone ND (about 1560) ....*...... 1800.00
360. 1 Gold Krone 1631 .... 2200.00
361. ½ Gold Krone ND (about 1560) ....*...... 600.00

Eagle and small Zurich shield. Rev. Charlemagne on throne.

362. 1 Goldgulden ND (about 1600) ....*...... 2000.00
363. 1 Goldgulden ND (about 1600). Charlemagne
 on double trilobe .... **Rare**
364. ½ Goldgulden ND (about 1600) .... **Unique**

Small Zurich shield in quadrilobe. Rev. Crowned double eagle.

365. 1 Goldgulden 1622 .... 1500.00

Eagle and shield. Rev. Charlemagne with orb standing right.

366. 1 Ducat ND (about 1600) 1250.00

Double-headed eagle and shield. Rev. Charlemagne standing with sword, facing.

367. ½ Ducat ND. (End of 16th Century). Broad flan 1500.00

Charlemagne on throne. Rev. Saints Regula and Felix standing and carrying their heads.

368. 1 Ducat ND (about 1607) 1500.00

Legend in wreath. Rev. Charlemagne on throne.

369. 2 Ducats ND (about 1620) 2000.00
370. 1 Ducat ND (about 1620) ....*...... 1200.00

Lion with shield. Rev. Double eagle.

371. 4 Ducats 1624 ....*...... 3000.00
372. 4 Ducats 1622. (From ½ Taler dies) .... Rare
373. 4 Ducats 1629 .... Rare
374. 2 Ducats 1624 .... 2000.00
375. 2 Ducats 1629. (Date in exergue on Rev.) 2000.00

Warrior standing. Rev. Legend in wreath.

376. ½ Ducat 1639 ....*...... 600.00
377. ¼ Ducat 1639 .... 700.00

Large arms between branches. Rev. Legend. Struck from 20 Schilling dies.

378. 2 Ducats ND. (17th Century) .... Rare

Two lions holding arms and wreath. Rev. Crowned double eagle.

379. 4 Ducats 1640, 41 .... 3000.00
380. 2 Ducats 1641 ....*...... 1500.00

Legend in wreath. Rev. Two lions and one shield.

381. 1 Ducat 1641, 43 .... 1000.00

Legend in wreath. Rev. Two lions and two shields.

382. 1 Ducat 1646, 48 (Rare), 49, 50 .... 1000.00

Legend in wreath. Rev. Lion and arms.

383. 4 Ducats 1666 .... Rare
384. 2 Ducats 1673. (IUSTICIA ET CONCORDIA) 1500.00
385. 1 Ducat ND, 1645, 61, 62, 73 (Rare), 80, 84, 97 *...... 1000.00
386. ½ Ducat 1641, 45, 49, 51, 66, 70 .... 175.00
387. ¼ Ducat 1645, 49 .... 100.00

Date in wreath. Rev. Lion and arms.

388. ½ Ducat 1671, 77, 92, 1702 ....*.... 225.00
389. ¼ Ducat 1671, 77, 92, 1702 .... 100.00

 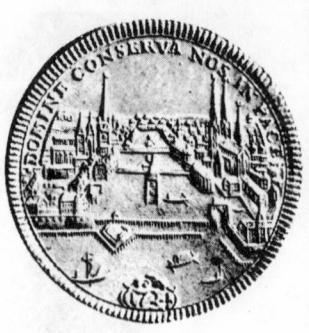

Two lions and arms. Rev. Western view of the city.

400. 10 Ducats 1724, 25 ....*...... 6000.00
401. 8 Ducats 1723 .... Rare

Two lions holding two shields and wreath. Rev. Legend in cartouche.

390. 15 Ducats 1649 .... 6000.00
391. 8 Ducats 1646 .... 4500.00
392. 6 Ducats 1647 ....*...... 3500.00

Two lions and arms. Rev. Legend in cartouche.

402. 2 Ducats 1707-76. 1707 is Rare 800.00

Legend in wreath. Rev. Arms in cartouche.

393. 1 Ducat 1651 .... 1000.00

Arms. Rev. Date in wreath.

394. ½ Ducat 1654, 62 .... 200.00
395. ¼ Ducat 1654, 66 .... 100.00

Lion and arms. Rev. Legend in wreath or cartouche.

403. 1 Ducat 1705-1810 ....*...... 350.00
404. ½ Ducat 1707-76. 1723 is Rare ....*...... 125.00
405. ¼ Ducat 1707-67 .... 75.00

Lion and shield. Rev. Western view of the city.

396. 10 Ducats ND. (17th Century). Northern view
        of the city within bulwarks 6000.00
396a. 8 Ducats 1739 .... Rare
397. 6 Ducats 1739 .... Rare
398. 5 Ducats 1720, 24, 30 (rare), 33, 40, 53 .... 4000.00
399. 4 Ducats 1720, 28 .... Rare

Bust of Zwingli to left. Rev. Legend. On the Reformation.

406. 1 Ducat 1719 .... 225.00

Bust of Zwingli to right. Rev. Legend. On the Reformation.

407. 1 Ducat 1819 .... 200.00

SYRIA

Eagle. Rev. Legend in rectangular panel.

1.	1 Pound 1950	60.00
2.	½ Pound 1950	30.00

TANGIER

Hercules standing. Rev. Legend, weight and fineness. A private bank issue of Tangier.

1.	1 Hercules ND (1954)	100.00

TIBET

Tibetan style lion. Rev. stylized design in circle.

1.	20 Srangs 1917-20	375.00

TIERRA DEL FUEGO

Julius Popper, who struck these coins, was a South American adventurer. This coinage may be considered as a territorial issue of Argentina.

The name Popper centered over crossed hammers and pick axe. Rev. Value in circle.

1.	5 Gramos 1889	1000.00
2.	1 Gramo 1889	300.00

TRANQUEBAR

Danish Kings of —

CHRISTIAN VII, 1766-1808

Monogram. Rev. The God Swami.

1.	1 Pagoda ND	250.00

TUNIS

A. Beys of —

MOHAMMED, 1854-1858 AND SADIK, 1859-1882

Three line Arab legend in open wreath. Rev. Arab date and value.

1.	100 Piastres 1272-85 A.H. (1855-68) ....*		200.00
2.	80 Piastres 1272 A.H. (1855)		175.00
3.	50 Piastres 1272-89 A.H. (1855-72)		150.00
4.	40 Piastres 1272 A.H. (1855)		150.00
5.	25 Piastres 1270-98 A.H. (1853-81)		75.00
6.	20 Piastres 1272 A.H. (1855)		75.00
7.	10 Piastres 1272-88 A.H. (1855-71)		50.00
8.	5 Piastres 1281-89 A.H. (1864-72)		30.00

B. French Protectorate of —

The only 10 Franc piece that it is normally possible to obtain is dated 1891. All other dates are very rare.

New type legend in closed wreath. Rev. Arab date and value.

9.	25 Piastres 1300 A.H. (1882)	125.00

French value. Rev. Arab value and date. Two denominations appear on this coin, the old Tunisian value of 25 Piastres and the new French equivalent of 15 Francs.

10.	15 Francs-25 Piastres 1300-07 A.H. (1882-89). No mm. ...	125.00
11.	15 Francs-25 Piastres 1308, 09 A.H. (1890, 91). A mm. *..	150.00

Arab legend in wreath. Rev. French name, value and date.
Very small amounts were coined of the 20 Franc pieces of 1894-96, 1902, 05-28 and of the 10 Franc pieces from 1892-1928.

12.	20 Francs 1891-1928 ....*		25.00
13.	10 Francs 1891-1928		30.00

Arab legend in vertical panel. Rev. Value and date in circle.

14. 100 Francs 1930-37 .... 60.00

Arab legend in vertical panel. Rev. Large date. Without the mark of value, although the coins have the same specifications as the preceeding issues. Only about 30 pieces were struck in each year.

15. (100 Francs) 1938-55 .... 250.00

TURKESTAN, CHINESE

Native legend on each side. Struck during the period 1865-1877 by the rebel, Yakub Beg. With dates from about 1283-1294 A.H.

1. 1 Tilla 150.00

Four Chinese characters in circle. Rev. Dragon, and in English, "Sungarei . . . 2 Mace".

2. 2 Mace (1906) .... Rare

Dragon. Rev. Four Chinese characters in circle.

3. 2 Mace (1907) ....*...... 400.00
4. 1 Mace (1907) 300.00

TURKEY

As is typical of the Arab-Asian Empires (which see) the coinage of the Ottoman Sultans was of the same general type over a period of about 400 years. It was, therefore, not felt necessary to describe the coinage of each Sultan, since such a catalogue would be more a chronological list of names than of coin types.

A. Ottoman Sultans of —

MOHAMMED II, 1451, TO MUSTAFA IV, 1808

Arab legend on each side. This general type was used by the Sultans from 1451 to 1808; with dates from about 943-1223 A.H.

1. 1 Sequin ....*...... 30.00
2. ½ Sequin 20.00
3. ¼ Sequin 15.00

AHMED III, 1703, TO MAHMUD II, 1839

Toughra as main motif. Rev. Arab legend. This general type was used by the Sultans from 1703 to 1839; with dates from about 1116-1254 A.H.

4.   6   Sequins 350.00
5.   5   Sequins 150.00
6.   4   Sequins 300.00
7.   3   Sequins 85.00
8.   2   Sequins 65.00
9.   1½ Sequins 65.00
10. 1   Sequin ....*...... 25.00
11. ½   Sequin 20.00
12. ¼   Sequin 15.00

ABDUL MEJID, 1839-1861
Toughra and value in plain field. Rev. Legend and date.

13. 1 Sequin 1255-59 A.H. (1839-43) 35.00
14. ½ Sequin 1255-59 A.H. (1839-43) 25.00
15. ¼ Sequin 1255-59 A.H. (1839-43) 20.00

Toughra and regnal date. Rev. Legend and accession date. All coins bear the accession date 1255 in Arabic numerals, in addition to other numerals for the regnal year, which indicate the precise date of coinage.

16. 500 Piastres 300.00
17. 250 Piastres ....*...... 150.00
18. 100 Piastres 40.00
19.   50 Piastres 30.00
20.   25 Piastres 25.00
21.   10 Piastres 20.00
22.   5 Piastres 15.00

Type as above but with the name of the city of Adrianople added to the legend on coins with regnal date 8, thus commemorating the Sultan's visit to that city.

22a. 100 Piastres 85.00
22b.   50 Piastres 65.00

ABDUL AZIZ, 1861-1876

Same type as above but with the accession date 1277.

23.	500 Piastres	150.00
24.	250 Piastres	125.00
25.	100 Piastres ....*	30.00
26.	50 Piastres	25.00
27.	25 Piastres	20.00
28.	10 Piastres	15.00

Type as above but with the name of the city of Brousse added to the legend on coins with regnal dates 1 or 2, thus commemorating the Sultan's visit to that city.

28a.	100 Piastres	75.00
28b.	50 Piastres	50.00
28c.	25 Piastres	35.00

MURAD V, 1876

Toughra and regnal year 1. Rev. Legend and accession date 1293.

29.	100 Piastres	175.00
30.	50 Piastres	100.00
31.	25 Piastres	65.00

ABDUL HAMID II, 1876-1909
Standard Gold Coins

Same type as above and with the accession date, 1293. The coins occur in two varieties: (1) Regnal years 1-6 have a flower to the right of the toughra; (2) regnal years 7-34 have the inscription "al-Ghazi" (i.e., fighter of infidels) in place of the flower.

32.	500 Piastres	150.00
33.	250 Piastres	125.00
34.	100 Piastres	25.00
35.	50 Piastres	25.00
36.	25 Piastres	20.00

De Luxe Gold Coins

Toughra. Rev. Legend. Ornamental wreath on each side. With accession date 1293. Although very large and quite thin, these coins are of standard weight.

37.	500 Piastres	250.00
38.	250 Piastres ....*	200.00
39.	100 Piastres	100.00
40.	50 Piastres	75.00
41.	25 Piastres	50.00

MOHAMMED V, 1909-1918
Standard Gold Coins

Same type as previous issues but with the accession date 1327. The coins occur in two varieties: (1) Regnal years 1-6 have the inscription "Rashad" (the Sultan's name) to the right of the toughra; (2) regnal years 7-10 have "al-Ghazi" instead of "Rashad."

42.	500	Piastres ....*	150.00
43.	250	Piastres	75.00
44.	100	Piastres	22.50
45.	50	Piastres	17.50
46.	25	Piastres	15.00
47.	12½	Piastres	10.00

Type as above but with the name of a city added to the legend on coins with regnal dates 1, 2 or 3. The following cities may be read in Arabic on the coins, which thus commemorate the Sultan's visit to that city:—Adrianople, Brousse, Kossova, Monastir, Salonica.

48.	500	Piastres	250.00
49.	250	Piastres	150.00
50.	100	Piastres	75.00
51.	50	Piastres	50.00
52.	25	Piastres	35.00
53.	12½	Piastres	25.00

De Luxe Gold Coins

Group of military weapons. Rev. Legend. With accession date 1327.

54.	500	Piastres ....*	350.00
55.	250	Piastres	125.00
56.	100	Piastres	100.00
57.	50	Piastres	50.00
58.	25	Piastres	30.00

MOHAMMED VI, 1918-1921
Standard Gold Coins

Same type as previous issues but with the accession date 1336.

59.	500 Piastres	225.00
60.	250 Piastres	125.00
61.	100 Piastres	50.00
62.	50 Piastres	40.00
63.	25 Piastres	25.00

De Luxe Gold Coins

Same general type as the previous issue of De Luxe Gold Coins but with the accession date 1336.

64.	500 Piastres	375.00
65.	250 Piastres	150.00
66.	100 Piastres	100.00

67. 50 Piastres 50.00
68. 25 Piastres 30.00

B. Republic of —

I. REGULAR ISSUES
Standard Gold Coins

Star, legend and Mohammedan year within crescent. Rev. Legend and corresponding Christian year (in Arabic numerals).

69. 500 Piastres 1926-29 ....*...... 250.00
70. 250 Piastres 1926-28 .... 150.00
71. 100 Piastres 1926-28 .:............................. 75.00
72. 50 Piastres 1926-28 ..:............................ 60.00
73. 25 Piastres 1926-29 .... 40.00

De Luxe Gold Coins

Sunburst and crescent. Rev. Date and wreath. As the de luxe coins of the Sultans, these pieces are highly decorative. They are very large and thin but of standard weight.

74. 500 Piastres 1927, 28 .... 325.00
75. 250 Piastres 1927, 28 .... 150.00
76. 100 Piastres 1927, 28 ....*...... 100.00
77. 50 Piastres 1927, 28 .... 60.00
78. 25 Piastres 1927, 28 .... 40.00

II. SPECIAL COMMEMORATIVE ISSUES
The following coins do not bear the marks of value but are of the same sizes and weights as the previous issues.

PRESIDENT KEMAL ATATURK
Standard Gold Coins

Head and below "Ankara". Rev. Legend and date 1923, with two additional numerals below, which must be added to 1923 to determine the exact year of issue.

79. 500 Piastres 1943- 100.00
80. 250 Piastres 1943- 65.00
81. 100 Piastres 1943- ....*...... 27.50
82. 50 Piastres 1943- 15.00
83. 25 Piastres 1943- 10.00

De Luxe Gold Coins

Head in circle of stars. Rev. Legend in circle of stars, date below.

84. 500 Piastres 1942-51, 60 ....*...... 100.00
85. 250 Piastres 1942-51, 60 .... 65.00
86. 100 Piastres 1942-51, 57, 59 .... 27.50
87. 50 Piastres 1942-51, 61 .... 15.00
88. 25 Piastres 1942-51, 61 .... 10.00

PRESIDENT ISMET INONU
Standard Gold Coins

Head and below "Ankara". Rev. Legend and date 1923, with two additional numerals below, which must be added to 1923 to determine the exact year of issue.

89. 500 Piastres 1943-49 ....*...... 125.00
90. 250 Piastres 1943-49 .... 65.00
91. 100 Piastres 1943-49 .... 30.00
92. 50 Piastres 1943-49 .... 20.00
93. 25 Piastres 1943-49 .... 15.00

De Luxe Gold Coins

Head in wreath. Rev. Legend and date.

94. 500 Piastres 1943-47 .... 150.00
95. 250 Piastres 1944-47 .... 75.00
96. 100 Piastres 1944-47 ....*...... 45.00
97. 50 Piastres 1944-47 .... 25.00
98. 25 Piastres 1944-47 .... 20.00

UNITED STATES OF AMERICA

Mints and mint marks:—

Without mint mark for Philadelphia (Pennsylvania)
C   mm for Charlotte (North Carolina)
CC   mm for Carson City (Nevada)
D   mm for Dahlonega (Georgia, 19th century)
D   mm for Denver (Colorado, 20th century)
O   mm for New Orleans (Louisiana)
S   mm for San Francisco (California)

The initial gold coinage, 1795-1834, was of sterling purity, .916 ⅔ Fine. In 1834, the fineness was reduced to .899¼ and at the same time, the weight of the coins themselves was also reduced, the 5 Dollar piece, for example, going from 135 to 129 grains, and the 2½ Dollar piece in proportion. In 1837, the fineness was increased to .900, at which point it remained until the end of gold coinage in 1933. United States gold coins dated before 1808 do not show the mark of value. The Philadelphia Mint coined 20 Dollar gold pieces dated 1933, but this date is not listed in the catalogue since the coins were not released officially and possession of this one date is illegal.

There is also in existence, a large amount of so-called coins of ¼, ½ and 1 Dollar denominations. Most of these coins are octagonal and they are sometimes called California gold coins or charms. They were privately struck in California or other western areas until the early years of this century. They are not included in this book since they do not form a part of regular U. S. coinage. On the other hand, the coinage of Territorial and Pioneer Gold, privately minted, has been included because these pieces are collected for their historic interest.

A. Coinage of the Official U. S. Government Mints

(The valuations are for the commonest date of the respective mint.)

1 DOLLAR

Liberty Head. Rev. Value. Small size.

1.	No mm. 1849-54	70.00
2.	C mm. 1849-53	150.00
3.	D mm. 1849-54 ....*......	200.00
4.	O mm. 1849-53	70.00
5.	S mm. 1854	135.00

Small Liberty Head with feather head-dress. Rev. Value. Large size.

6.	No mm. 1854, 55	175.00
7.	C mm. 1855	250.00
8.	D mm. 1855 ....*......	1400.00
9.	O mm. 1855	175.00
10.	S mm. 1856	185.00

Large Liberty Head with feather head-dress. Rev. Value. Large size.

11.	No mm. 1856-89	80.00
12.	C mm. 1857, 59	185.00
13.	D mm. 1856-61	300.00
14.	S mm. 1857-60, 1870 ....*......	110.00

For the Louisiana Purchase Exposition.

15.	1903. Head of Jefferson	100.00
16.	1903. Head of McKinley	100.00

For the Lewis & Clark Exposition.

17.	1904, 05. Head on each side	350.00

For the Panama-Pacific Exposition.

18.	1915. Panama Canal Laborer	85.00

For the McKinley Memorial.

19.	1916, 17. Head of McKinley	90.00

For the Grant Memorial.

20.	1922. Head of Grant	325.00
21.	1922. Same but with star on Obv.	300.00

2½ DOLLARS (QUARTER EAGLES)

(The reverses bear various types of eagles.)

Liberty Head without stars.

22.	No mm. 1796	5500.00

Liberty Head with stars.

23.	No mm. 1796-98, 1802, 04-07	1000.00

Draped bust of Liberty with round cap.

24.	No mm. 1808	4500.00

Liberty Head with round cap.

25. No mm. 1821, 1824-27 ....*...... 1000.00
26. No mm. 1829-34. Size reduced 600.00

Liberty Head with ribbon and without motto on Rev.

27. No mm. 1834-39 ....*...... 80.00
28. C mm. 1838, 39 .... 200.00
29. D mm. 1839 .... 210.00
30. O mm. 1839 .... 135.00

Liberty Head with Coronet.

31. No mm. 1840-1907 ....*...... 70.00
32. No mm. 1848-"Cal" over eagle 3000.00
33. C mm. 1840-44, 46-52, 54-56, 58, 60 .... 125.00
34. D mm. 1840-57, 59 .... 125.00
35. O mm. 1840, 42, 43, 45-47, 50-52, 54, 56, 57 .... 75.00
36. S mm. 1854, 56-63, 65-73, 75-79 .... 70.00

Indian Head with designs and legends incused.

37. No mm. 1908-15, 26-29 .... 50.00
38. D mm. 1911, 14, 25 ....*...... 52.50

For the Panama-Pacific Exposition.

39. 1915. Columbia on mythical sea horse 350.00

For the Philadelphia Sesquicentennial.

40. 1926. Liberty standing. Rev. Independence Hall 75.00

3 DOLLARS

Liberty Head with feather head-dress. Rev. Value and date.

41. No mm. 1854-89 ....*...... 300.00
42. D mm. 1854 .... 1750.00
43. O mm. 1854 .... 300.00
44. S mm. 1855-57, 60, 70 .... 300.00

4 DOLLARS (STELLA)

Liberty Head with flowing hair. Rev. Star.

45. No mm. 1879, 80 .... Rare

Liberty Head with coiled hair. Rev. Star.

46. No mm. 1879, 80 .... Rare

5 DOLLARS (HALF EAGLES)
(The reverses bear various types of eagles.)

Liberty Head with small eagle.

47. No mm. 1795-98 .... 1500.00

Liberty Head with large, heraldic eagle.

48. No mm. 1795, 1797-1807 .... 500.00

Draped bust of Liberty with round cap.

49. No mm. 1807-12 .... 425.00

Liberty Head with round cap.

50. No mm. 1813-29 .... 500.00
51. No mm. 1829-34. Size reduced 900.00

Liberty Head with ribbon and without motto on Rev.

52. No mm. 1834-38 ....*...... 100.00
53. C mm. 1838 .... 375.00
54. D mm. 1838 .... 325.00

Liberty Head with coronet and without motto on Rev.

55. No mm. 1838-65 ....*...... 75.00
56. C mm. 1839-44, 46-61 .... 200.00
57. D mm. 1839-61 .... 225.00
58. O mm. 1840-47, 51, 54-57 .... 135.00
59. S mm. 1854-66 .... 100.00

Liberty Head with coronet and with motto on Rev.

60. No mm. 1866-1908 ....*...... 57.50
61. O mm. 1892-94 .... 100.00
62. S mm. 1866-88, 92-1906 .... 57.50
63. CC mm. 1870-84, 90-93 .... 85.00
64. D mm. 1906, 07 .... 57.50

Indian Head with designs and legends incused.

65. No mm. 1908-15, 1929 ....*...... 65.00
66. O mm. 1909 .... 400.00
67. S mm. 1908-16 .... 65.00
68. D mm. 1908-11, 1914 .... 65.00

10 DOLLARS (EAGLES)
(The reverses bear various types of eagles.)

Liberty Head with small eagle.

69. No mm. 1795-97 .... 1250.00

Liberty Head with large heraldic eagle.

70. No mm. 1797-1801, 03, 04 .... 700.00

Small Liberty Head without motto on Rev.

71. No mm. 1838, 39 .... 400.00

Large Liberty Head without motto on Rev.

72. No mm. 1840-65 ....*...... 60.00
73. O mm. 1841-60 .... 65.00
74. S mm. 1854-66 .... 65.00

Liberty Head with motto on Rev.

75. No mm. 1866-1907 ....*...... 60.00
76. O mm. 1879-83, 88, 92-95, 97, 99, 1901, 03, 04, 06 .... 65.00
77. S mm. 1866-74, 76-89, 92-1903, 05-07 .... 60.00
78. CC mm. 1870-84, 90-93 .... 90.00
79. D mm. 1906, 07 .... 60.00

Indian Head without motto on Rev.

80. No mm. 1907. With period before and after the Rev.
    legend **2000.00**
81. No mm. 1907, 08. Without periods ....* **90.00**
82. D mm. 1908 .... **100.00**

Liberty Head with motto on Rev., and "Twenty Dollars."

94. No mm. 1877-1907 ....* **95.00**
95. S mm. 1877-85, 1887-1907 .... **95.00**
96. CC mm. 1877-79, 82-85, 89-93 .... **175.00**
97. D mm. 1906, 07 .... **100.00**

Indian Head with motto on Rev.

83. No mm. 1908-15, 26, 32, 33 ....* **90.00**
84. S mm. 1908-16, 20, 30 .... **90.00**
85. D mm. 1908-11, 14 .... **90.00**

Liberty standing (St. Gaudens type) with date in Roman Numerals.

98. No mm. 1907. Very high relief (concave) and very
    wide edge .... **Rare**
99. No mm 1907. Normal high relief with wire or
    flat edge ....* **1000.00**

20 DOLLARS (DOUBLE EAGLES)
(The reverses bear various types of eagles.)

Liberty Head without motto on Rev.

86. No mm. 1850-65 ....* **100.00**
87. No mm. 1861. Rev. by Paquet .... **Rare**
88. O mm. 1850-61 .... **150.00**
89. S mm. 1854-66 .... **100.00**
90. S mm. 1861. Rev. by Paquet .... **Rare**

Liberty standing with date in usual numerals and without motto on Rev.

100. No mm. 1907, 08 ....* **95.00**
101. D mm. 1908 .... **95.00**

Liberty Head with motto on Rev., and "Twenty D.".

91. No mm. 1866-76 ....* **95.00**
92. S mm. 1866-76 .... **95.00**
93. CC mm. 1870-76 .... **110.00**

Liberty standing with motto on Rev.

102. No mm. 1908-15, 20-29, 31, 32 .... **95.00**
103. S mm. 1908-11, 13-16, 20, 22, 24-27, 30 ......* **95.00**
104. D mm. 1908-11, 13, 14, 23-27, 31 .... **95.00**

50 DOLLARS

For the Panama-Pacific Exposition.
Head of Minerva. Rev. Owl.

105.	1915. Round coin	5500.00
106.	1915. Octagonal coin ....*......	4500.00

GOLD COINAGE FOR FOREIGN COUNTRIES
(Gold coins struck at the Philadelphia Mint in 1945 and 1946 for use in Saudi Arabia.)

Weight and fineness in three line rectangular tablet. Rev. Eagle and "U.S. Mint, Philadelphia, U.S.A."

107.	4 Saudi Pounds ND ....*......	175.00
108.	1 Saudi Pound ND	40.00

B. Coinage of the Territorial and Private Mints

(Pioneer Gold)

BALDWIN & CO.

San Francisco, California

Horseman with lariat. Rev. Eagle.

109.	10 Dollars 1850	7500.00

"Baldwin & Co" on head band of liberty. Rev. Eagle.

110.	5 Dollars 1850	900.00
111.	10 Dollars 1851	3000.00
112.	20 Dollars 1851	6000.00

AUGUST BECHTLER

Rutherford, North Carolina

Value and legend. Rev. Weight and legend. The coins are undated but were struck from 1831 to 1842.

113.	1 Dollar ND. One variety ....*......	150.00
114.	5 Dollars ND. Three varieties	400.00

CHRISTOPHER BECHTLER

Rutherford, North Carolina

Value and legend. Rev. Weight and legend. The coins are undated but were struck from 1831 to 1842.

115.	1	Dollar ND. Four varieties	150.00
116.	2½	Dollars ND. Seven varieties ....*......	450.00
117.	5	Dollars ND. Six varieties	400.00
118.	5	Dollars August 1, 1834. Two varieties ......*......	400.00

BLAKE & CO.

Sacramento, California
Stamping machine. Rev. Value and legend.

119.	20 Dollars 1855	Rare

BLAKE & AGNELL

Sacramento, California
Square shaped ingot with name, weight, fineness and value stamped on both sides.

120.	$23.30 1855	Rare

EPHRAIM BRASHER

New York

Radiant sun over mountains. Rev. Eagle with "EB" punched on either the wing or breast. The famous Brasher Doubloon.

121.	Doubloon 1787 ....*..... Very Rare
122.	½ Doubloon 1787 .... Unique

Cross of Jerusalem and "EB" punch mark. Rev. Pillars with "Brasher" below. An imitation of a Lima Mint 8 Escudos dated 1742.

123.	8 Escudos or Doubloon (1787)	Rare

CALIFORNIA & SIERRA CO.

California

Rectangular ingot with various punch marks and lettered edges.

124. $36.57 1860 .... Rare

CINCINNATI MINING & TRADING CO.

San Francisco, California

Indian Head. Rev. Eagle.

125. 5 Dollars 1849 .... Rare
126. 10 Dollars 1849 .... Rare

CLARK, GRUBER & CO.

Denver, Colorado

View of Pikes Peak. Rev. Eagle.

127. 10 Dollars 1860 ....*...... 1500.00
128. 20 Dollars 1860 .... 4500.00

"Clark & Co." on head band of Liberty. Rev. Eagle.

129. 2½ Dollars 1860 .... 400.00
130. 5 Dollars 1860 .... 500.00

"Pikes Peak" on head band of Liberty. Rev. Eagle.

131. 2½ Dollars 1861 .... 375.00
132. 5 Dollars 1861 ....*...... 450.00
133. 10 Dollars 1861 .... 450.00
134. 20 Dollars 1861 .... 1500.00

J. J. CONWAY & CO.

Georgia Gulch, Colorado

*Name of company. Rev. Value and "Pikes Peak". Undated
but struck in 1861.*

135. 2½ Dollars ND .... Rare
136. 5 Dollars ND .... Rare
137. 10 Dollars ND .... Rare

DUBOSQ & CO.

San Francisco, California

"Dubosq & Co." on head band of Liberty. Rev. Eagle.

138. 5 Dollars 1850 .... Rare
139. 10 Dollars 1850 .... Rare

DUNBAR & CO.

San Francisco, California

"Dunbar & Co." on head band of Liberty. Rev. Eagle.

140. 5 Dollars 1851 .... Rare

AUGUSTUS HUMBERT

U.S. Assayer of gold, San Francisco, California.

Eagle. Rev. Four line legend in tablet.

141. 10 Dollars 1852 ....*...... 500.00
142. 20 Dollars 1852 .... 1250.00

 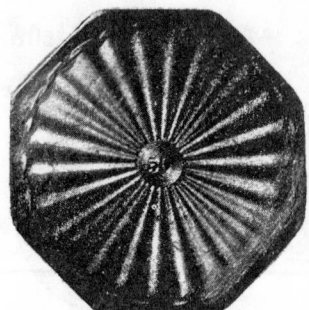

*Eagle. Rev. Small 50, star or circle in center of reverse.
Octagonal shaped with lettered edge.*

143. 50 Dollars 1851. Five varieties 2250.00

 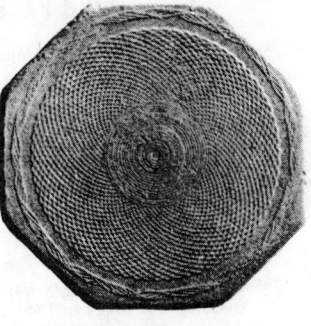

Eagle. Rev. Machine made criss-cross of circular lines. Octagonal shaped with reeded edge.

144. 50 Dollars 1851, 52. Three varieties 1750.00

KELLOGG & CO.

San Francisco, California

"Kellogg & Co." on head band of Liberty. Rev. Standard Eagle.

145. 20 Dollars 1854, 55 .... 450.00

Obv. Similar to above. Rev. Eagle holding shield.

146. 50 Dollars 1855 .... Rare

KELLOGG & HEWSTON

San Francisco, California

Rectangular ingot with various punch marks and name along edge.

147. $49.50 ND. (1860) .... Rare

F. D. KOHLER

State Assayer, San Francisco and Sacramento, California
Rectangular gold ingots bearing name, weight, fineness and value.

148. $36.55 1850 .... Rare
149. $37.31 1850 .... Rare
150. $40.07 1850 .... Rare
151. $41.68 1850 .... Rare
152. $45.34 1850 .... Rare
153. $50.00 1850 .... Rare
154. $54.09 1850 .... Rare

MASSACHUSETTS & CALIFORNIA CO.

San Francisco, California

Arms supported by bear and stag. Rev. Value in wreath.

155. 5 Dollars 1849. Four varieties .... Rare

MINERS BANK

San Francisco, California

Name and value. Rev. Eagle.

156. 10 Dollars 1849 .... 2250.00

MOFFAT & CO.

San Francisco, California

"Moffat & Co." on head band of Liberty. Rev. Eagle.

157. 5 Dollars 1849, 50 .... 300.00
158. 10 Dollars 1849, 52 .... 500.00
159. 20 Dollars 1853 ....*...... 600.00

Rectangular ingots bearing legends, values and weights.

160. $ 9.43 ND (1849-1853) .... Unique
161. $14.25 ND (1849-1853) .... Unique
162. $16.00 ND (1849-1853) .... Rare

THE MORMONS

Salt Lake City, Utah

Eye and Bishop's Mitre. Rev. Clasped hands.

163. 2½ Dollars 1849 .... 700.00
164. 5 Dollars 1849, 50 ....*...... 500.00
165. 10 Dollars 1849 ....*...... Rare
166. 20 Dollars 1849 ....*...... 6500.00

Lion. Rev. Beehive on breast of eagle.

167.   5 Dollars 1860 .... 1100.00

NORRIS, GRIEG & NORRIS

San Francisco, California

Eagle. Rev. Legend.

168.   5 Dollars 1849. Plain or reeded edge 750.00

OREGON EXCHANGE CO.

Oregon City, Oregon

Beaver and initials. Rev. Legend.

169.   5 Dollars 1849 .... 2000.00
170. 10 Dollars 1849 .... Rare

J. S. ORMSBY

San Francisco, California

"J.S.O." Rev. Value. Undated but struck in 1849.

171.   5 Dollars ND .... Rare
172. 10 Dollars ND ....*...... Rare

PACIFIC CO.

San Francisco, California

Liberty Cap. Rev. Eagle.

173.   5 Dollars 1849 ....*...... Rare
174. 10 Dollars 1849 .... Rare

JOHN PARSONS & CO.

Tarryall Mines, Colorado

Stamping machine. Rev. Eagle and "Pikes Peak Gold." Undated but struck in 1861.

175.   2½ Dollars ND .... Rare
176.   5   Dollars ND .... Rare

Rectangular ingot bearing name and various legends.

177. 20 Dollars 1860 .... Unique

SHULTS & CO.

San Francisco, California

"Shults & Co." on head band of Liberty. Rev. Eagle.

178.   5 Dollars 1851 .... Rare

TEMPLETON REID

Lumpkin County, Georgia

Legend on each side.

179.   2½ Dollars 1830 .... Rare
180.   5   Dollars 1830 .... Rare
181. 10   Dollars 1830 .... Rare
182. 10   Dollars ND .... Rare

TEMPLETON REID

San Francisco, California
Legend on each side.

183. 10 Dollars 1849 .... Rare
184. 25 Dollars 1849 ....Unknown

UNITED STATES ASSAY OFFICE OF GOLD

San Francisco, California

Eagle. Rev. Legend in tablet.

185. 10 Dollars 1852, 53. Two varieties ....*...... 500.00
186. 20 Dollars 1853. Two varieties 500.00

 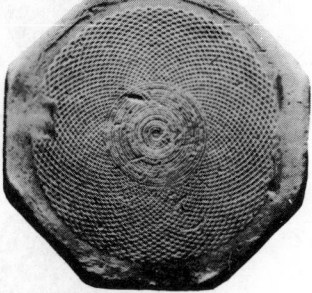

Eagle. Rev. Machine made criss-cross of circular lines. Octagonal shaped.

187. 50 Dollars 1852. Two varieties 1750.00

WASS, MOLITOR & CO.

San Francisco, California

"W.M. & Co." on head band of Liberty. Rev. Eagle.

188. 5 Dollars 1852 .... 600.00
189. 10 Dollars 1852, 55. Two varieties ....*...... 700.00
190. 20 Dollars 1855. Two varieties 1200.00

Liberty head. Rev. Name and value.

191. 50 Dollars 1855 .... 4000.00

URUGUAY

Arms. Rev. Value in wreath. These coins were not placed in circulation.

1. 40 Reales 1854 .... Rare
2. 1 Doblon 1870 ....*...... Rare
3. 5 Pesos 1870 .... Rare
4. 2 Pesos 1870 .... Rare
5. 1 Peso 1870 .... Rare

Head of Artigas. Rev. Value and dates 1830 and 1930. On the Centennial of the Republic. 100,000 were reported struck, but only 14,415 were issued.

6. 5 Pesos 1930 .... 150.00

VATICAN CITY (ROME)

Papal coinage closely follows Italian issues insofar as coinage standards are concerned.

Popes of —

A. Coinage struck at Rome

POPULAR GOVERNMENT, 1305
Arms. Rev. St. John.

1. 1 Florin ND .... Rare

JOHN XXII, 1316-1334
INNOCENT VI, 1352-1362
URBAN V, 1362-1370
CLEMENT VII, 1378-1394
(See under France-Avignon).

THE ROMAN SENATE, 1350-1439

Senator kneeling before St. Peter. Rev. Christ.

2. 1 Ducat ND 120.00

ALEXANDER V, 1409-1410
JOHN XXIII, 1410-1415
MARTIN V, 1421-1428
(See under Vatican-Bologna).

EUGENE IV, 1431-1447

Arms. Rev. St. Peter.

3. 1 Ducat ND 800.00

NICHOLAS V, 1447-1455
Crossed Keys. Rev. St. Peter and St. Paul.

4. 3 Ducats ND .... Rare

Keys. Rev. Pope seated.

5. 1 Ducat ND .... Rare

Arms. Rev. St. Peter.

6. 1 Ducat ND 200.00

CALIXTUS III, 1455-1458

Arms. Rev. St. Peter in ship.

7. 1 Ducat ND 500.00

Arms. Rev. St. Peter standing.

8. 1 Ducat ND 400.00

Arms. Rev. St. Peter and St. Paul.

9. 1 Ducat ND 400.00

PIUS II, 1458-1464
St. Peter and St. Paul. Rev. Ship at Sea.

10. 2 Ducats ND .... Rare

Arms. Rev. Ship at sea.

11. 1 Ducat ND .... Rare

Arms. Rev. St. Peter.

12. 1 Ducat ND 300.00

PAUL II, 1464-1471
Christ and St. Peter. Rev. Eight apostles.

13. 4 Ducats 1464, 65 .... Rare

Arms. Rev. Christ and St. Peter.

14. 1 Ducat 1464 .... 2000.00

Arms. Rev. Pope kneeling before St. Peter.

15.   2 Ducats ND ....*...... Rare
15a. 1 Ducat 1464, ND 2000.00

Arms. Rev. Pope kneeling before Christ.

16. 1 Ducat ND 700.00

Arms. Rev. St. Peter.

17. 2 Ducats ND .... Rare
18. 1 Ducat ND 300.00

Arms. Rev. Two apostles.

19. 1 Ducat ND 300.00

Arms. Rev. St. Veronica.

20. 1 Ducat ND 600.00

SIXTUS IV, 1471-1484
Christ and St. Peter in landscape. Rev. Apostles in ship.

21. 10 Ducats 1475 .... Rare

Arms. Rev. Christ and St. Peter.

22. 2 Ducats ND .... Rare

Arms. Rev. St. Peter in ship.

23. 1 Ducat 1475, ND 250.00

Arms. Rev. Pope kneeling before Christ.

24. 1 Ducat ND 3000.00

Arms. Rev. Two apostles.

25. 1 Ducat ND 400.00

INNOCENT VIII, 1484-1492

Arms. Rev. St. Peter in ship.

26. 1 Ducat ND 250.00

Arms. Rev. Two apostles.

27. 1 Ducat ND 400.00

ALEXANDER VI BORGIA, 1492-1503
Bust. Rev. Arms.

28. 3 Ducats 1495, 1500 .... Rare

Arms. Rev. St. Peter in ship.

29. 5 Ducats ND .... Rare
30. 2 Ducats ND ....*...... 750.00
31. 1 Ducat ND 250.00

Two apostles. Rev. Legend.

32. 1 Ducat ND 3000.00

PIUS III, 1503
Arms. Rev. St. Peter in ship.

33. 1 Ducat ND .... Rare

JULIUS II, 1503-1513
Bust. Rev. Pastoral scene.

34. 4 Ducats ND .... Rare

Bust. Rev. St. Peter seated.

35. 3 Ducats ND .... Rare

Bust. Rev. Two apostles in ship.

36. 2 Ducats ND 4000.00

Bust. Rev. Two apostles kissing.

37. 2 Ducats ND 8000.00

Bust. Rev. St. Peter in ship.

38. 2 Ducats ND 6000.00

Arms. Rev. Two apostles in ship.

39. 2 Ducats ND 2000.00
40. 1 Ducat ND ....*...... 250.00

Arms. Rev. St. Peter in ship.

41. 2 Ducats ND 1500.00
42. 1 Ducat ND 250.00

LEO X, 1513-1521

Bust. Rev. The three Magi.

43. 2½ Ducats ND ....*...... 6000.00
44. 2   Ducats ND 8000.00

Arms. Rev. Two apostles in ship.

45. 2 Ducats ND 1500.00
46. 1 Ducat ND ....*...... 700.00

Arms. Rev. Two apostles standing.

47. 1 Ducat ND 400.00

Arms. Rev. St. Peter in ship.

48. 1 Ducat ND 400.00

SEDE VACANTE, 1521

Arms. Rev. St. Peter in ship.

49. 1 Ducat ND 2500.00

ADRIAN VI, 1522-1523

Arms. Rev. St. Peter in ship.

| 50. | 2 Ducats ND | ....*...... | 4000.00 |
| 51. | 1 Ducat ND | .... | 1200.00 |

CLEMENT VII, 1523-1534

Birth of Christ. Rev. Pope opening the Holy Door.

| 52. | 5 Zecchini 1525 | .... | Rare |

Bust. Rev. Angel and St. Peter.

| 53. | 2 Ducats ND | .... | Rare |

Bust. Rev. Christ standing.

| 54. | 2 Ducats ND | .... | Rare |

Pope and Emperor Charles V standing. Rev. Two apostles.

| 55. | 2 Ducats ND | .... | Rare |

Arms. Rev. Two apostles.

| 56. | 3 Ducats ND | .... | Rare |

Arms. Rev. Two apostles in ship.

| 57. | 2 Ducats ND | .... | 3000.00 |

Arms. Rev. St. Peter.

| 58. | 2 Ducats ND | .... | 3000.00 |

Arms. Rev. St. Peter in ship.

| 59. | 2 Ducats ND | ....*...... | 1000.00 |
| 60. | 1 Ducat ND | .... | 300.00 |

Arms. Rev. St. Peter seated.

| 61. | 2 Ducats ND | .... | 6000.00 |

PAUL III, 1534-1549

Bust. Rev. St. Peter in ship.

| 62. | 2 Ducats ND | .... | 4000.00 |

Arms. Rev. St. Paul in ship.

| 63. | 1 Ducat ND | .... | 2000.00 |

Arms. Rev. St. Peter in ship.

| 64. | 1 Ducat ND | .... | 500.00 |

Arms. Rev. St. Paul standing. There are several varieties of the standing figure.

| 65. | 1 Scudo d'oro ND | .... | 150.00 |

JULIUS III, 1550-1555

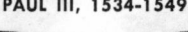

Bust. Rev. St. Peter in ship.

| 66. | 1 Ducat 1551 | .... | 5000.00 |

Arms. Rev. St. Peter.

| 67. | 1 Scudo d'oro ND | .... | 3000.00 |

Arms. Rev. The Holy Door.

| 68. | 1 Scudo d'oro 1550 | .... | 3500.00 |

Arms. Rev. Bust of Christ.

| 69. | 1 Scudo d'oro 1551, 52, ND | .... | 800.00 |

SEDE VACANTE, 1555

Arms. Rev. St. Peter.

| 70. | 1 Scudo d'oro 1555 | .... | 4000.00 |

PAUL IV, 1555-1559

Arms. Rev. St. Paul.

| 71. | 1 Scudo d'oro ND | .... | 5000.00 |

Arms. Rev. St. Peter.

| 72. | 1 Scudo d'oro ND | .... | 5000.00 |

SEDE VACANTE, 1559

Arms. Rev. St. Peter.

| 73. | 1 Scudo d'oro 1559 | .... | 3000.00 |

PIUS IV, 1559-1565
(See under Vatican-Bologna).

PIUS V, 1566-1572
Bust. Rev. St. Peter in ship.

| 74. | 2 Ducats 1566 | .... | Rare |
| 75. | 1 Ducat ND | .... | 6000.00 |

Arms. Rev. St. Peter kneeling before Christ.

| 76. | 4 Scudi d'oro ND | .... | Rare |

GREGORY XIII, 1572-1585
Bust. Rev. The Holy Door.

| 77. | 1 Scudo d'oro 1575 | .... | Rare |

Bust. Rev. Charity standing.

78. 1 Scudo d'oro 1576 ....   **Rare**

Bust. Rev. Christ and two apostles in ship.

79. 1 Doppia 1578 ....   **Rare**

Arms. Rev. St. Peter.

80. 1 Scudo d'oro 1581, ND 4000.00

Bust. Rev. Madonna seated.

81. 1 Scudo d'oro ND 3000.00

Bust. Rev. St. Paul.

82. 1 Scudo d'oro ND 3000.00

Arms. Rev. The Holy Door.

83. 1 Scudo d'oro 1575 .... 3000.00

Arms. Rev. St. Peter in ship.

84. 1 Scudo d'oro 1575, 76 .... 3000.00

Arms. Rev. Bust of Christ.

85. 1 Scudo d'oro 1577-82, ND 800.00

SIXTUS V, 1585-1590

Arms. Rev. Bust of Christ.

86. 1 Scudo d'oro 1585, 87, 88 .... 2000.00

Arms. Rev. St. Peter.

87. 1 Scudo d'oro 1585 .... 2000.00

SEDE VACANTE, 1590
Arms. Rev. St. Peter and angel.

88. 4 Scudi d'oro 1590 ....   **Rare**

Arms. Rev. Roma seated.

89. 1 Scudo d'oro 1590 ....   **Rare**

Arms. Rev. Bust of Christ.

90. 1 Scudo d'oro 1590 ....   **Rare**

URBAN VII, 1590
GREGORY XIV, 1590-1591
(See under Vatican-Bologna).

SEDE VACANTE, 1591

Arms. Rev. David with harp.

91. 4 Scudi d'oro 1591 ....   **Rare**

INNOCENT IX, 1591-1592
(See under Vatican-Bologna).

CLEMENT VIII, 1592-1605
Bust. Rev. Justice standing.

92. 4 Scudi d'oro 1598 ....   **Rare**

Bust. Rev. The Church seated.

93. 4 Scudi d'oro ND ....   **Rare**

Bust. Rev. The Lateran Church.

94. 1 Scudo d'oro ND ....   **Rare**

Arms. Rev. The Church seated.

95. 1 Scudo d'oro ND 4000.00

Arms. Rev. Pope kneeling.

96. 1 Scudo d'oro ND 4000.00

Arms. Rev. Dove.

97. 1 Scudo d'oro ND 4000.00

SEDE VACANTE, 1605
Arms. Rev. The Church seated.

98. 4 Scudi d'oro 1605 ....   **Rare**
99. 1 Scudo d'oro 1605 ....   **Rare**

PAUL V, 1605-1621

Bust. Rev. St. Paul seated.

100. 4 Scudi d'oro 1606, 07 .... 2800.00

Bust. Rev. St. Paul standing.

101. 4 Scudi d'oro 1609 .... 2800.00
102. 1 Scudo d'oro 1617 ....*...... 650.00

Arms. Rev. Bust of St. Paul.

103. 4 Scudi d'oro 1608, 09 .... 2500.00
104. 1 Scudo d'oro 1607, 15 ....*...... 750.00

Arms. Rev. Busts of St. Peter and St. Paul.

105. 1 Scudo d'oro 1609 .... 800.00

Arms. Rev. St. Paul standing.

106. 2 Scudi d'oro ND 2000.00

Arms. Rev. St. Paul seated.

107. 4 Scudi d'oro 1617 .... 2500.00
108. 1 Scudo d'oro 1606, 11 ....*..... 600.00

GREGORY XV, 1621-1623

Bust. Rev. Madonna standing.

109. 1 Scudo d'oro 1622 .... 2500.00

Bust. Rev. Church of St. Mary the Major.

110. 1 Scudo d'oro 1622 .... 3000.00

Arms. Rev. Madonna standing.

111. 4 Scudi d'oro ND ....*..... 5500.00
112. 2 Scudi d'oro ND 4500.00

Arms. Rev. St. Paul standing.

113. 2 Scudi d'oro ND 4500.00

SEDE VACANTE, 1623
Arms. Rev. Christ standing.

114. 4 Scudi d'oro 1623 .... 6500.00
114a. 2 Scudi d'oro 1623 .... 6000.00

URBAN VIII, 1623-1644

Bust. Rev. The Holy Door.

115. 1 Scudo d'oro 1625 .... 1200.00

Bust. Rev. Madonna standing.

116. 4 Scudi d'oro 1634 .... 5000.00
117. 1 Scudo d'oro 1627-36, ND ....*..... 1200.00

Bust. Rev. St. Michael standing.

118. 4 Scudi d'oro 1634 .... 5500.00
119. 1 Scudo d'oro 1629, 36 .... 1200.00

Bust. Rev. Bust of Christ.

120. 1 Scudo d'oro 1630 .... 1200.00

Arms. Rev. Madonna standing.

121. 2 Scudi d'oro 1624 .... 4000.00
122. 1 Scudo d'oro 1642, 43, ND 1200.00

Arms. Rev. Busts of St. Peter and St. Paul.

123. 2 Scudi d'oro 1624 .... 4500.00

Arms. Rev. The Holy Door.

124. 1 Scudo d'oro 1625 .... 1000.00

Arms. Rev. Bust of St. Paul.

125. 1 Scudo d'oro 1627 .... 1000.00

Arms Rev. St. Michael standing.

126. 1 Scudo d'oro 1642, 43, ND 1000.00

INNOCENT X, 1644-1655
Bust. Rev. Arms.

127. 4 Scudi d'oro 1647 .... 10,000.00

Bust. Rev. The Holy Door.

128. 4 Scudi d'oro 1650 .... 8000.00

Arms. Rev. Bust of St. Peter.

129. 2 Scudi d'oro 1652 .... 6000.00
130. 1 Scudo d'oro 1644, 52 ....*..... 2500.00

Arms. Rev. Madonna standing.

131. 1 Scudo d'oro 1645, 52 .... 2500.00

Arms. Rev. The Holy Door.

132. 2 Scudi d'oro 1651 .... 6000.00

SEDE VACANTE, 1655

Arms. Rev. Dove.

133. 4 Scudi d'oro 1655 .... 6000.00
134. 2 Scudi d'oro 1655 ....*..... 4500.00

ALEXANDER VII, 1655-1667

Arms. Rev. Money chest.

135. 4 Scudi d'oro ND 10,000.00

Arms. Rev. Legend.

136.	2 Scudi d'oro ND ....*......	8000.00
137.	1 Scudo d'oro ND	2500.00

SEDE VACANTE, 1667
Arms. Rev. Dove.

138.	1 Scudo d'oro 1667	3500.00

CLEMENT IX, 1667-1669

Arms. Rev. Madonna.

139.	4 Scudi d'oro ND ....*......	8000.00
140.	2 Scudi d'oro ND	3000.00
141.	1 Scudo d'oro ND	1800.00

SEDE VACANTE, 1669
Arms. Rev. Dove.

142.	4 Scudi d'oro 1669	6000.00
143.	2 Scudi d'oro 1669	4000.00
144.	1 Scudo d'oro 1669	2500.00

CLEMENT X, 1669-1676

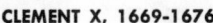

Bust. Rev. St. Peter.

145.	2 Scudi d'oro 1670	3500.00

Arms. Rev. St. Venantius.

146.	2 Scudi d'oro ND	3500.00

Bust. Rev. King David.

147.	4 Scudi d'oro 1673	6000.00

Arms. Rev. The Holy Door.

148.	1 Scudo d'oro 1675	1600.00

Arms. Rev. King David.

149.	4 Scudi d'oro ND	5500.00

Arms. Rev. St. Peter and St. Paul.

150.	2 Scudi d'oro ND	3500.00

Arms. Rev. St. Peter.

151.	1 Scudo d'oro ND	1600.00

Arms. Rev. Madonna.

152.	1 Scudo d'oro ND	1600.00

INNOCENT XI, 1676-1689

Bust. Rev. Madonna and four saints.

153.	4 Scudi d'oro 1676, 77	6500.00

Bust. Rev. Holy figure among clouds.

154.	4 Scudi d'oro 1678	6500.00

Bust. Rev. Legend.

155.	4 Scudi d'oro 1681, 82, 85	6500.00

Arms. Rev. Religion seated.

156.	2 Scudi d'oro 1678	3500.00

Arms. Rev. Legend.

157.	4 Scudi d'oro 1687	5000.00
158.	2 Scudi d'oro 1677-87	3500.00
159.	1 Scudo d'oro 1684, ND ....*......	1000.00

Arms. Rev. Madonna.

160.	1 Scudo d'oro ND	1000.00

Arms. Rev. Bust of Madonna.

161.	1 Scudo d'oro ND	1000.00

Arms. Rev. Bust of St. Peter.

162.	1 Scudo d'oro ND	1000.00

SEDE VACANTE, 1689
Arms. Rev. Dove.

163.	4 Scudi d'oro 1689	6500.00

ALEXANDER VIII, 1689-1691

Bust. Rev. St. Peter and St. Paul.

164. 4 Scudi d'oro 1689 .... 5500.00

Bust. Rev. The Church standing.

165. 16 Scudi d'oro 1690 .... **Rare**

Bust. Rev. Two oxen.

166. 4 Scudi d'oro 1690 .... 4500.00

Bust. Rev. St. Bruno.

167. 4 Scudi d'oro 1690 .... 5500.00

Bust. Rev. St. Magnus and St. Bruno.

168. 4 Scudi d'oro 1690 .... 5500.00

Arms. Rev. St. Bruno.

169. 2 Scudi d'oro 1689 .... 3500.00

Arms. Rev. St. Peter.

170. 1 Scudo d'oro 1689 .... 1250.00

Arms. Rev. Busts of St. Peter and St. Paul.

171. 1 Scudo d'oro 1690 .... 750.00

Arms. Rev. Altar.

172. 2 Scudi d'oro 1690 .... 4000.00

SEDE VACANTE, 1691

Arms. Rev. Dove.

173. 2 Scudi d'oro 1691 .... 6000.00

INNOCENT XII, 1691-1700

Bust. Rev. Fountain.

174. 4 Scudi d'oro 1694 .... 4500.00

Bust. Rev. Noah's Ark.

175. 2 Scudi d'oro 1697 .... 3500.00

Bust of St. Peter. Rev. Arms.

176. 1 Scudo d'oro 1691, 92 .... 1500.00
177. ½ Scudo d'oro 1694 .... 700.00

Arms. Rev. St. Paul.

178. 2 Scudi d'oro 1692 .... 3500.00

Arms. Rev. Plant.

179. 1 Scudo d'oro 1694 .... 3000.00

Arms. Rev. The Holy Door.

180. 2 Scudi d'oro 1699 .... 3500.00
181. 1 Scudo d'oro 1700 .... 1500.00
182. ½ Scudo d'oro 1694 .... 1200.00

Arms. Rev. Corn ears in vessel.

183. 1 Scudo d'oro 1697 .... 800.00

SEDE VACANTE, 1700
Arms. Rev. Dove.

184. 1 Scudo d'oro 1700 .... 2500.00

CLEMENT XI, 1700-1721

Bust. Rev. The Holy Door.

185.   2 Scudi d'oro 1700 .... 2000.00

Bust. Rev. Piety and Discord.

186.   4 Scudi d'oro 1706 ....10,000.00

Bust. Rev. Arms.

187.   1 Scudo d'oro 1710 .... 1500.00

Bust. Rev. Star over sea.

188.   ½ Scudo d'oro 1716 .... 2000.00

Bust. Rev. Bust of St. Peter.

189.   ½ Scudo d'oro 1717 .... 300.00

Bust. Rev. Legend.

190.   2 Scudi d'oro 1710, 14 .... 3500.00

Bust of St. Paul. Rev. Arms.

191.   2 Scudi d'oro 1702, 05 .... 3500.00
192.   1 Scudo d'oro 1702-09 ....*...... 600.00

Arms. Rev. Madonna.

193.   4 Scudi d'oro 1706 .... 6000.00

Arms and globe. Rev. Legend.

194.   2 Scudi d'oro 1706 .... 3500.00

Arms. Rev. Anchor.

195.   1 Scudo d'oro 1706 .... 1300.00

Arms. Rev. Charity standing.

196.   4 Scudi d'oro 1707 .... 6000.00

Arms. Rev. Three females.

197.   4 Scudi d'oro 1707 .... 6500.00

Arms. Rev. St. Francis kneeling.

198.   2 Scudi d'oro 1707 .... 4000.00

Arms. Rev. St. Francisca.

199.   2 Scudi d'oro 1709 .... 4000.00

Arms. Rev. Bust of St. Peter.

200.   ½ Scudo d'oro 1709, 16, 17 .... 300.00

Arms. Rev. Various legends.

201.   2 Scudi d'oro 1712 .... 3500.00
202.   1 Scudo d'oro 1711-18 ....*...... 800.00
203.   ½ Scudo d'oro ND 300.00

Arms. Rev. Bow and arrow.

204.   1 Scudo d'oro 1716 .... 1200.00

Arms. Rev. Religion seated.

205.   1 Scudo d'oro 1718 .... 800.00

Arms. Rev. Faith standing.

206.   1 Scudo d'oro 1718 .... 800.00

Arms. Rev. Olive tree.

207.   1 Scudo d'oro 1720 .... 1200.00

Three mountains. Rev. Star over sea.

208.   ½ Scudo d'oro 1706 .... 800.00

SEDE VACANTE, 1721
Arms. Rev. Dove.

209.   2 Scudi d'oro 1721 .... 4000.00
210.   1 Scudo d'oro 1721 .... 1800.00

INNOCENT XIII, 1721-1724

Bust. Rev. Eagle.

211. 1 Scudo d'oro 1724 .... 1500.00

Arms. Rev. Legend.

212. 1 Scudo d'oro 1722 .... 1250.00

Arms. Rev. Eagle.

213. ½ Scudo d'oro 1724 .... 1000.00

SEDE VACANTE, 1724
Arms. Rev. Dove.

214. 1 Scudo d'oro 1724 .... 3000.00

BENEDICT XIII, 1724-1730

Arms. Rev. The Holy Door.

215. 2 Scudi d'oro 1725 .... 4000.00
216. 1 Scudo d'oro 1725 ....*...... 1500.00

The Church seated. Rev. Rose and value.

217. 1 Zecchino 1729 .... 800.00

SEDE VACANTE, 1730
Arms. Rev. Dove.

218. 2 Scudi d'oro 1730 .... 4000.00

Arms on cross and value. Rev. The Church seated.

219. 1 Zecchino 1730 .... 1500.00

CLEMENT XII, 1730-1740

Bust. Rev. Various legends.

220. 1 Scudo d'oro 1735, 38, 39 .... 350.00

Arms. Rev. The Church seated.

221. 2 Zecchini 1731, 39 ....*...... 2500.00
222. 1 Zecchino 1738, 39, ND 200.00
223. ½ Zecchino 1739 .... 125.00

Arms. Rev. Legend.

224. 1 Scudo d'oro 1734, 35 .... 350.00

Legend. Rev. Bust of St. Peter.

225. ¼ Zecchino ND 400.00

SEDE VACANTE, 1740
Arms. Rev. The Church seated.

226. 2 Zecchini 1740 .... 2000.00
227. 1 Zecchino 1740 .... 500.00
228. ½ Zecchino 1740 .... 500.00

Legend. Rev. Bust of St. Peter.

229. ¼ Zecchino 1740 .... 200.00

BENEDICT XIV, 1740-1758

Arms. Rev. The Church seated.

230. 2 Zecchini 1748 ....*...... 1200.00
231. 1 Zecchino 1740-56, ND 100.00
232. ½ Zecchino 1740-55 .... 80.00

Legend. Rev. Bust of St. Peter.

233. ¼ Zecchino 1741, ND 50.00

Arms. Rev. Bust of St. Peter.

234. ¼ Zecchino 1751 .... 50.00

SEDE VACANTE, 1758
Arms. Rev. The Church seated.

235. 1 Zecchino 1758 .... 650.00

CLEMENT XIII, 1758-1769

Arms. Rev. The Church seated.

236. 2 Zecchini 1759, 66 ....*...... 600.00
237. 1 Zecchino 1758-69 .... 100.00
238. ½ Zecchino 1758, 67 .... 100.00

SEDE VACANTE, 1769
Arms. Rev. The Church seated.

239. 1 Zecchino 1769 .... 600.00

CLEMENT XIV, 1769-1774

Arms. Rev. The Church seated.

240. 1 Zecchino 1769-73 ....*...... 120.00
241. ½ Zecchino 1769 .... 100.00

SEDE VACANTE, 1774
Arms. Rev. The Church seated.

242. 1 Zecchino 1774 .... 300.00

PIUS VI, 1774-1799
Arms. Rev. The Church seated.

243. 1 Zecchino 1775-84 .... 120.00
244. ½ Zecchino 1796 .... 250.00

Lily. Rev. St. Peter seated.

245. 2 Doppia or 60 Paoli 1776, 77 ....*...... 1250.00
246. 1 Doppia or 30 Paoli 1776-91 .... 200.00
247. ½ Doppia or 15 Paoli 1776-87 .... 150.00

PIUS VII, 1799-1823

Arms. Rev. St. Peter seated.

248. 1 Doppia 1800-23. R mm. ....*...... 125.00
249. 1 Doppia 1815-21. B mm. 250.00

SEDE VACANTE, 1823

Arms. Rev. St. Peter seated.

250. 1 Doppia 1823. R mm. 1250.00
251. 1 Doppia 1823. B mm. ....*...... 1200.00

LEO XII, 1823-1829

Bust. Rev. Faith standing.

252. 2 Zecchini 1828. R mm. 1500.00

Arms. Rev. Faith seated.

253. 2 Zecchini 1824, 25. R mm. 1200.00

Arms. Rev. St. Peter seated.

254. 1 Doppia 1823, 29. R mm. ....*...... 600.00
255. 1 Doppia 1824. B mm. 650.00

SEDE VACANTE, 1829

Arms. Rev. St. Peter seated.

256. 1 Doppia 1829. R mm. ....*...... 1250.00
257. 1 Doppia 1829. B mm. 650.00

PIUS VIII, 1829-1830
Bust. Rev. St. Peter and St. Paul standing. Without the mark of value.

258. 20 Scudi 1830. B mm. .... Rare

SEDE VACANTE, 1830

Arms. Rev. Dove.

259. 1 Doppia 1830. R mm. 1500.00

GREGORY XVI, 1831-1846

Bust. Rev. St. Peter and value.

260. 1 Doppia 1833, 34. R mm. ....*...... 800.00
261. 1 Doppia 1834. B mm. 500.00

Bust. Rev. St. Peter and St. Paul.

262. 5 Scudi 1834. R mm. 6000.00

Bust. Rev. Value.

263.	10	Scudi 1835-45 R mm.	700.00
264.	10	Scudi 1835-45. B mm.	800.00
265.	5	Scudi 1835-46. R mm.	600.00
266.	5	Scudi 1835-43. B mm.	650.00
267.	2½	Scudi 1835-45. R mm.	300.00
268.	2½	Scudi 1835-46. B mm. ....*......	400.00

SEDE VACANTE, 1846

Arms. Rev. Dove.

269. 5 Scudi 1846. R mm. 2000.00

PIUS IX, 1846-1878

Bust. Rev. Value.

270.	10	Scudi 1850, 56. R mm.	2200.00
271.	5	Scudi 1846-54. R mm.	900.00
272.	5	Scudi 1846. B mm.	1000.00
273.	2½	Scudi 1848-63. R mm. ....*......	125.00
274.	2½	Scudi 1854-59. B mm.	150.00
275.	1	Scudo 1853-57. R mm. Small size	120.00
276.	1	Scudo 1853, 54. B mm. Small size ......*......	150.00
277.	1	Scudo 1858-65. R mm. Large size	120.00
278.	100	Lire 1866, 68, 69	2000.00
279.	50	Lire 1868, 70	2000.00
280.	20	Lire 1866-70 ....*......	100.00
281.	10	Lire 1866, 67, 69	350.00
282.	5	Lire 1866, 67 ....*......	900.00

PIUS XI, 1922-1937

Bust. Rev. Christ standing.

283.	100 Lire 1929-35 ....*......	225.00
284.	100 Lire 1933 (1934). On the Holy Year and showing both dates	125.00
285.	100 Lire 1936, 37. Size reduced. 1937 rare date	175.00

PIUS XII, 1939-1958

Bust. Rev. Christ standing.

286. 100 Lire 1939, 40, 41 .... 250.00

Bust. Rev. Charity seated with children.

287.	100 Lire 1942-47 ....*......	400.00
288.	100 Lire 1948-49	175.00

Crowned bust. Rev. Opening of the Holy Door. On the Holy Year of 1950.

289. 100 Lire 1950 .... 225.00

Bust. Rev. Charity standing.

290. 100 Lire 1951-56 .... 300.00

Bust. Rev. Arms.

291. 100 Lire 1957-58 .... 175.00

JOHN XXIII, 1958-1963

Bust. Rev. Arms.

292. 100 Lire 1959 .... 500.00

B. Papal Coinage struck outside of Rome

These issues are distinguishable from those of the Rome Mint by differences of type, legend or arms.

Arms. Rev. St. Peter and St. Paul.

302. 1 Ducat ND 2000.00

ANCONA

SIXTUS IV, 1471-1484
Arms. Rev. St. Peter and St. Paul.

293. 1 Ducat ND 1500.00

INNOCENT VIII, 1484-1492
Arms. Rev. St. Peter in ship.

294. 1 Ducat ND 1500.00

Arms. Rev. Two saints.

295. 1 Ducat ND 1500.00

ALEXANDER VI BORGIA, 1492-1503
Arms. Rev. St. Peter.

296. 1 Ducat ND 1500.00

ADRIAN VI, 1522-1523
Knight on horse. Rev. St. Quiriacus.

303. 1 Ducat ND 5000.00

Arms. Rev. Two saints.

304. 1 Ducat ND 5000.00

CLEMENT VII, 1523-1534
Knight on horse. Rev. St. Quiriacus.

305. 1 Ducat ND 3000.00

Arms. Rev. Two saints.

306. 1 Ducat ND 2500.00

Arms. Rev. Cross.

307. 1 Scudo d'oro ND 2000.00

ANONYMOUS COINAGE, 1500-1600
Knight on horse. Rev. St. Quiriacus.

308. 2 Ducats ND 2000.00
309. 1 Ducat ND 1200.00

GREGORY XIII, 1572-1585
Bust. Rev. The Holy Door.

310. 1 Scudo d'oro 1575 .... 3500.00

Arms. Rev. St. Peter in ship.

297. 1 Ducat ND 700.00

Knight on horse. Rev. St. Quiriacus.

298. 1 Ducat ND 2500.00

JULIUS II, 1503-1513

Bust. Rev. Charity standing.

311. 1 Scudo d'oro ND 3500.00

Arms. Rev. St. Peter in ship.

299. 1 Ducat ND 1800.00

LEO X, 1513-1521

Knight on horse. Rev. St. Quiriacus.

300. 2 Ducats ND ....*...... 5000.00
301. 1 Ducat ND 1500.00

Arms. Rev. Charity standing.

312. 1 Scudo d'oro ND 2000.00

SIXTUS V, 1585-1590
Arms. Rev. Legend.

313. 2 Scudi d'oro 1585 .... 3500.00

Arms. Rev. Madonna.

314. 4 Scudi d'oro 1586 ....   Rare

Arms. Rev. Cross.

315. 2 Scudi d'oro 1586 .... 3500.00
316. 1 Scudo d'oro 1586 ....*...... 2500.00

AVIGNON

(See under France-Cities).

BOLOGNA

ALEXANDER V, 1409-1410
Sun and shield. Rev. Uncertain.

317.	2 Zecchini ND	....	**Rare**

St. Peter. Rev. Arms.

318.	1 Bolognino d'oro ND	....	4500.00

JOHN XXIII, 1410-1415

Arms. Rev. St. Peter.

319.	1 Bolognino d'oro ND	....	2500.00

MARTIN V, 1421-1428
Lion. Rev. St. Peter.

320.	1 Bolognino d'oro ND	....	1000.00

Arms. Rev. St. Peter.

321.	1 Bolognino d'oro ND	....	2000.00

ANONYMOUS COINAGE, 1350-1450

Lion. Rev. St. Peter.

322.	1 Bolognino d'oro ND	....	500.00

EUGENE IV, 1431-1447

Arms. Rev. St. Peter.

323.	1 Ducat ND	....	2000.00

PIUS II, 1458-1464
Lion. Rev. St. Peter.

324.	1 Ducat ND	....	3000.00

PAUL II, 1464-1471
Arms. Rev. St. Peter.

325.	1 Ducat ND	....	3000.00

Lion. Rev. St. Peter.

326.	1 Ducat ND	....	2000.00

SIXTUS IV, 1471-1484
Arms. Rev. St. Peter.

327.	1 Ducat ND	....	3000.00

INNOCENT VIII, 1484-1492
Arms. Rev. St. Peter.

328.	1 Ducat ND	....	3000.00

Lion. Rev. St. Peter.

329.	1 Ducat ND	....	2000.00

ALEXANDER VI BORGIA, 1492-1503

Arms. Rev. St. Peter.

330.	1 Ducat ND	....	300.00

PIUS III, 1503
Arms. Rev. St. Peter.

331.	1 Ducat ND	....	**Rare**

JULIUS II, 1503-1513
Arms. Rev. St. Peter.

332.	1 Ducat ND	....	250.00

Bust. Rev. St. Petronius seated.

333.	2 Scudi d'oro ND	..................*	**Rare**
334.	1 Scudo d'oro ND	....	5000.00

LEO X, 1513-1521
Bust. Rev. St. Petronius seated.

335.	2 Ducats ND	....	**Rare**

Bust. Rev. St. Peter.

336.	1 Ducat ND	....	**Rare**

Arms. Rev. St. Peter.

337.	1 Ducat ND	....	250.00

Lion. Rev. St. Peter.

338.	1 Ducat ND	....	500.00

CLEMENT VII, 1523-1534
Bust of St. Petronius. Rev. Legend.

339.	10 Ducats 1529	....	**Rare**
340.	3 Ducats 1529	....	**Rare**

Lion. Rev. St. Peter.

341. 1 Ducat ND 600.00

Arms. Rev. Cross.

342. 1 Scudo d'oro ND ....*...... 250.00
343. ½ Scudo d'oro ND 700.00

PAUL III, 1534-1549

Arms. Rev. Cross.

344. 1 Scudo d'oro ND 250.00

JULIUS III, 1550-1555
Arms. Rev. Cross.

345. 1 Scudo d'oro ND 500.00
346. ½ Scudo d'oro ND 1000.00

PAUL IV, 1555-1559

Arms. Rev. Cross.

347. 1 Scudo d'oro ND 500.00

PIUS IV, 1559-1565
Arms. Rev. Cross.

348. 1 Scudo d'oro ND 600.00

PIUS V, 1565-1572

Arms. Rev. Cross.

349. 1 Scudo d'oro ND ....*...... 600.00
350. ½ Scudo d'oro ND 1000.00

GREGORY XIII, 1572-1585
Arms. Rev. Cross.

351. 1 Scudo d'oro ND 600.00

SIXTUS V, 1585-1590

Arms. Rev. Cross.

352. 2 Scudi d'oro ND ....*...... 2000.00
353. 1 Scudo d'oro ND 600.00

URBAN VII, 1590 (13 DAYS)

Arms. Rev. Cross.

354. 2 Scudi d'oro ND 8000.00

GREGORY XIV, 1590-1591

Arms. Rev. Cross.

355. 2 Scudi d'oro ND 4000.00

INNOCENT IX, 1591-1592
Arms. Rev. Cross.

356. 2 Scudi d'oro ND 10,000.00

CLEMENT VIII, 1592-1605
Arms. Rev. Cross.

357. 2 Scudi d'oro 1559, ND 5000.00

ANONYMOUS COINAGE, 1500-1600
St. Peter. Rev. Lion.

358. 1 Bolognino d'oro ND 500.00

INNOCENT X, 1644-1655
Arms. Rev. Cross.

359. 4 Scudi d'oro 1651, 54 .... 4000.00
360. 2 Scudi d'oro 1654 .... 2500.00
361. 1 Scudo d'oro 1654 .... 1000.00

ALEXANDER VII, 1655-1667

Arms. Rev. Cross.

362. 4 Scudi d'oro 1655-66 ....*...... 1800.00
363. 2 Scudi d'oro 1655-66 .... 1200.00
364. 1 Scudo d'oro 1655-66 .... 700.00

CLEMENT IX, 1667-1669
Arms. Rev. Cross.

365.	4 Scudi d'oro 1667	6000.00
366.	2 Scudi d'oro 1667	4500.00
367.	1 Scudo d'oro 1667	4000.00

CLEMENT X, 1669-1676
Arms. Rev. Cross.

368.	8 Scudi d'oro 1671	Rare
369.	4 Scudi d'oro 1673	Rare
370.	2 Scudi d'oro 1673	Rare
371.	1 Scudo d'oro 1671	Rare

CLEMENT XI, 1700-1721
Arms. Rev. Cross.

372.	2 Scudi d'oro 1713, 14, ND	Rare
373.	1 Scudo d'oro 1713	Rare

CLEMENT XII, 1730-1740
Arms. Rev. Cross.

374.	1 Scudo d'oro 1732, 36	3000.00

Lion. Rev. Two shields.

375.	1 Zecchino 1737, 38	2000.00

SEDE VACANTE, 1740
Lion. Rev. Two shields.

376.	1 Zecchino 1740	1500.00

BENEDICT XIV, 1740-1758

Bust. Rev. Felsina standing.

377.	2 Zecchini 1741, 42	3000.00
378.	1 Zecchino 1741, 42 ....*......	1500.00

Bust. Rev. Legend.

379.	10 Scudi d'oro 1756, 57	Rare

Lion. Rev. Two shields.

380.	1 Zecchino 1746	1200.00

Arms. Rev. Cross.

381.	1 Zecchino 1751	2000.00

382.	The coin previously listed does not exist.	—

CLEMENT XIV, 1769-1774

Lion. Rev. Two shields.

383.	1 Zecchino 1771	1200.00

PIUS VI, 1774-1799

Lily. Rev. Two shields.

384.	4 Doppia 1786, 87	700.00
385.	2 Doppia 1778-96. (60 Paoli)	450.00
386.	1 Doppia 1778-92. (30 Paoli) ....*	150.00
387.	½ Doppia 1778-91. (15 Paoli)	150.00

Lily. Rev. Arms.

388.	½ Doppia 1778	300.00

Bust. Rev. Temple.

389.	1 Zecchino 1782	1200.00

Arms. Rev. St. Petronius over two shields.

390.	10 Zecchini 1786, 87	1600.00
391.	5 Zecchini 1787	1500.00
392.	2 Zecchini 1786, 87	1000.00
393.	1 Zecchino 1778-87, ND ....*......	500.00
394.	½ Zecchino 1786	800.00
395.	100 Bolognini (Scudo d'oro) ND	Rare

(Later coinage of the Bologna Mint is of the same type as that of the Rome Mint and will be found under Vatican-Rome described with "B mm").

CAMERINO

PAUL III, 1534-1549

Arms. Rev. St. Paul.

396.	1 Scudo d'oro ND	2000.00

FERRARA

PAUL V, 1605-1621

Bust. Rev. St. George and St. Maurelius.

397. 4 Scudi d'oro 1620 .... Rare

FOLIGNO

PAUL II, 1464-1471

Arms. Rev. St. Peter kneeling before Christ.

398. 1 Zecchino ND .... Unknown

LEO X, 1513-1521
Lion. Rev. St. Peter and St. Paul.

399. 2 Scudi d'oro ND 6000.00

Arms. Rev. St. Felician.

400. 1 Ducat ND .... Rare

MACERATA

SIXTUS IV, 1471-1484
Arms. Rev. St. Peter.

401. 1 Ducat ND 2000.00

INNOCENT VIII, 1484-1492

Arms. Rev. St. Peter in ship.

402. 1 Ducat ND 1500.00

ADRIAN VI, 1522-1523
Arms. Rev. St. Peter in ship.

403. 1 Ducat ND 3000.00

MODENA

LEO X, 1513-1521

Bust. Rev. St. Geminianus seated.

404. 1 Ducat ND 8500.00

ADRIAN VI, 1522-1523
Bust. Rev. St. Geminianus seated.

405. 1 Ducat ND .... Rare

CLEMENT VII, 1523-1534

Bust. St. Geminianus seated.

406. 1 Ducat ND 2500.00

Arms. Rev. St. Geminianus seated.

407. 1 Ducat ND 1200.00

PARMA

JULIUS II, 1503-1513
St. John and St. Hillary. Rev. Christ and Madonna.

408. 1 Ducat ND .... Rare

ADRIAN VI, 1522-1523
St. John and St. Hillary. Rev. Christ and Madonna.

409. 1 Zecchino ND .... Rare

CLEMENT VII, 1523-1534
Arms. Rev. Christ and Madonna.

410. 2 Ducats 1526 .... Rare

Arms. Rev. Madonna.

411. 1 Ducat ND .... Rare

PAUL III, 1534-1549

Arms. Rev. Pallas seated.

412. 1 Scudo d'oro ND 400.00

Arms. Rev. Cross.

413. ½ Scudo d'oro ND 2000.00

PERUGIA

LEO X, 1513-1521
Arms. Rev. Griffin.

414. 1 Zecchino ND 4000.00

St. Herculanus. Rev. Griffin.

415. 1 Zecchino ND 4000.00

PAUL III, 1534-1549

Arms. Rev. Griffin and shield.

416. 1 Scudo d'oro ND 2500.00

Arms. Rev. Griffin in square.

417. 1 Scudo d'oro ND 2500.00

JULIUS III, 1550-1555
Arms. Rev. Cross.

418. 1 Scudo d'oro ND .... Rare

PIACENZA

ADRIAN VI, 1522-1523
Bust. Rev. Legend.

419. 1 Doppia ND .... Rare

Bust. Rev. Keys.

420. 1 Zecchino ND .... Rare

CLEMENT VII, 1523-1534

Bust. Rev. St. Anthony on horse.

421. 1 Zecchino ND 10,000.00

PAUL III, 1534-1549

Arms. Rev. Cross.

422. 1 Scudo d'oro ND ....*...... 200.00
423. ½ Scudo d'oro ND .... Rare

RAVENNA

LEO X, 1513-1521

Arms. Rev. St. Appolinaris.

424. 1 Zecchino ND 5000.00

SPOLETO

PAUL II, 1464-1471

Arms. Rev. St. Peter.

425. 1 Ducat ND 5000.00

VENEZUELA

Venezuelan coinage is based on the Latin Monetary Union standard. The 100, 50 and 5 Bolivar pieces of 1875 are of exceptional rarity and are specimen proofs marked "ESSAI."

Head of Bolivar. Rev. Arms. The values are expressed on the Rev. by the weight of the coins in grams.

1. 100 Bolivares 1875 (32.2580 Grams) .... Rare
2. 100 Bolivares 1886-89 (32.2580 Grams) ....*...... 325.00
3. 50 Bolivares 1875, 88 (16.1290 Grams) .... Rare
4. 25 Bolivares 1875 (8.0645 Grams) 175.00
5. 20 Bolivares 1879-1912 (6.4516 Grams) 55.00
6. 10 Bolivares 1930 (3.2258 Grams) ....*..... 50.00
7.   5 Bolivares 1875 (1.6129 Grams) .... Rare

WALLACHIA

Voivods of —

MICHAEL THE BRAVE, 1600-1601

Bust with furred hat. Rev. Legend.

. 10 Ducats 1600 ....* 5000.00
. 5 Ducats 1600 ....* 3000.00

CONSTANTINE BRENCOVAN, 1688-1714

Bust with furred hat. Rev. Arms. On the 25th year of reign.

. 5 Ducats 1713 .... 3000.00

YEMEN

AHMED HAMID AL-DIN, 1948-1963

Inscription on crescent. Rev. Inscription.

. 1 Imadi 1377 A.H. (1958) ....* 500.00
. ½ Imadi 1370 A.H. (1951) 250.00
. ¼ Imadi 1370-77 A.H. (1951-58) 150.00

YUGOSLAVIA

A. Kings of —

ALEXANDER I, 1921-1934

Head. Rev. Value and date.

1. 20 Dinars 1925 .... 85.00

Conjoined heads of the King and Queen. Rev. Eagle.

2. 4 Ducats 1931, 32, 33 .... 225.00

Head. Rev. Eagle.

3. 1 Ducat 1931, 32, 33 .... 50.00

B. Cities of —

RAGUSA (DUBROVNIK)

St. Blasius standing. Rev. Christ amid stars.

4. 1 Gold Perper or 2 Doppia 1618, 83 .... 2500.00

LAIBACH (LJUBLIANA)

Bishops of —

THOMAS GRONN, 1599-1630
Two shields. Rev. Legend.

5. 3 Ducats 1599 .... 1250.00

ZANZIBAR

The two gold coins are of extraordinary rarity. The author knows of only four specimens of the 5 Rial piece and only one of the 2½ Rial piece which was last noted in 1938. The coins were struck at the Brussels Mint.

SULTAN SA'ID, 1870-1888

Arab legend. Rev. Arab legend and date, with value in Christian numerals.

1. 5 Rials 1299 A.H. (1881) 1500.00
2. 2½ Rials 1299 A.H. (1881) 2000.00

RECENT ISSUES OF
GOLD COINS
of the WORLD
STARTING WITH 1960

Supplement

RECENT ISSUES OF GOLD COINS OF THE WORLD
STARTING WITH 1960

Since 1960 many nations have manufactured gold coins exclusively for collectors and not for circulation. The question of whether or not to include these coins in the book has posed a problem since there is no unanimity of opinion among numismatists regarding their status as coins. The publisher has decided to include all of the recent issues of non-circulating legal tender coins in the book. Depending on what series was involved, they have sometimes been included in the main body of the book, and at other times, in this section.

Among the factors which were taken into consideration in determining whether to place a coin in the main body of the book or in this section, were the following: the previous coinage history of the country; whether or not it had previously issued gold coins; whether or not it was also manufacturing minor coins exclusively for collectors rather than as coin of the realm; whether or not the legends and designs on the gold coins were in keeping with the traditional coinage designs of the country; and whether or not the coins were being distributed by the government, by a bank or by a private sales agency.

Publication of the issues contained in this section does not constitute a recommendation, but rather a desire on the part of the publisher to make this book as complete as possible.

ALBANIA

(For previous issues, see pages 26, 27.)

Different obverses as indicated. Rev. Arms.

18.	500 Leks 1968. Bust of Skanderbeg	275.00
19.	200 Leks 1968. Woman's head	140.00
20.	100 Leks 1968. Girl picking fruit	70.00
21.	50 Leks 1968. Fortress and viaduct	35.00
22.	20 Leks 1968. Sword and helmet in wreath	20.00

ANGUILLA

Different obverses as indicated. Rev. Arms.

1.	100 Dollars 1967. People in circle	200.00
2.	20 Dollars 1967. Two mermaids	40.00
3.	10 Dollars 1967. Underwater scene	20.00
4.	5 Dollars 1967. Church	15.00

BAHAMAS

1967. See page 50.

BAHRAIN

1968. See page 50.

BERMUDA

1970. See page 59.

BHUTAN

Bust of Maharaja Jigme Wangchuk. Rev. Sacred thunderbolt on Buddhist wheel of life.

1.	5 Sertums 1966	300.00
2.	2 Sertums 1966	100.00
3.	1 Sertum 1966	50.00
4.	Platinum 5 Sertums 1966	Rare
5.	Platinum 1 Sertum 1966	Rare

BIAFRA

Arms. Rev. Eagle in wreath. On the 2nd anniversary of independence.

1.	25 Pounds 1969	225.00
2.	10 Pounds 1969	100.00
3.	5 Pounds 1969	65.00
4.	2 Pounds 1969	35.00
5.	1 Pound 1969	20.00

BOTSWANA

Portrait of President Seretse Khama. Rev. Arms.

1.	10 Thebes 1966	40.00

BULGARIA

1963, 64. See page 70.

BURUNDI

Uniformed bust of King Mwambutsa IV. Rev. Arms. Independence commemorative.

1. 100 Francs 1962 .... 150.00
2. 50 Francs 1962 .... 75.00
3. 25 Francs 1962 .... 35.00
4. 10 Francs 1962 .... 20.00

(Description not available.)

5. 100 Francs 1965 .... 100.00
6. 50 Francs 1965 .... 60.00
7. 25 Francs 1965 .... 30.00
8. 10 Francs 1965 .... 15.00

CAMEROUN

Bust of President El Hadj Ahmadou Ahidjo. Different reverses as indicated. On the 10th anniversary of independence.

1. 20,000 Francs 1970. Coat of arms 225.00
2. 10,000 Francs 1970. Two elk 115.00
3. 5000 Francs 1970. Official seal of Cameroun 60.00
4. 3000 Francs 1970. Horns of elk 35.00
5. 1000 Francs 1970. Geometric design 15.00

CANADA

1967. See page 70.

CENTRAL AFRICAN REPUBLIC

Bust of President Jean Bedel Bokassa. Different reverses as indicated.

1. 20,000 Francs 1970. Native food products. 225.00
2. 10,000 Francs 1970. UN symbol and 3 co-joined female heads 115.00
3. 5000 Francs 1970. Olympic wrestlers 60.00
4. 3000 Francs 1970. Martin Luther King 35.00
5. 1000 Francs 1970. Coat of arms 15.00

CHAD

The following issues were all released in 1970.

Head of President Tombalbaye. Rev. Arms. On the 10th anniversary of independence.

1. 20,000 Francs 1970 .... 225.00

Uniformed bust of General De Gaulle. Rev. Arms above Cross of Lorraine.

2. 10,000 Francs 1960 .... 115.00

Head of General Leclerc. Rev. Palm trees, buildings and arms.

3. 5000 Francs 1941 .... 60.00

Head of Governor Eboue. Rev. Map and arms.

4. 3000 Francs 1940 .... 35.00

Head of Commandant Lamy. Rev. Nude girl and arms.

5. 1000 Francs 1900 .... 15.00

CHILE

(For previous issues, see pages 71-73.)

Different obverses as indicated. Rev. Arms.

57. 500 Pesos 1967. Liberty head and flag 300.00
58. 200 Pesos 1967. O'Higgins and San Martin on horseback.. 150.00
59. 100 Pesos 1967. Liberty head and coining machine 80.00
60. 50 Pesos 1967. Bust of O'Higgins 40.00

CHINA

1965, 66. See pages 73 and 74.

COLOMBIA

(For previous issues, see pages 74-76)

Head of Pope Paul VI. Rev. Arms and value. On the 39th International Eucharistic Congress of Bogota.

112. 1500 Pesos 1968 .... 225.00
113. 500 Pesos 1968 .... 100.00
114. 300 Pesos 1968 .... 75.00
115. 200 Pesos 1968 .... 40.00
116. 100 Pesos 1968 .... 20.00

Uniformed bust of Bolivar. Different reverses as indicated.

117. 1500 Pesos 1969. Bust of Santander 200.00
118. 500 Pesos 1969. Bust of Rondon 75.00
119. 300 Pesos 1969. Bust of Anzoategui 50.00
120. 200 Pesos 1969. Bust of Soublette 30.00
121. 100 Pesos 1969. Bust of Paris 20.00

CONGO

Military bust of President Joseph Kasavubu. Rev. Elephant. On the 5th anniversary of independence.

1. 100 Francs 1965 .... 100.00
2. 50 Francs 1965 .... 50.00
3. 25 Francs 1965 .... 30.00

Military bust of Kasavubu. Rev. Palm trees.

4. 20 Francs 1965 .... 20.00
5. 10 Francs 1965 .... 15.00

COSTA RICA

(For previous issues, see pages 76 and 77.)

Different obverses as indicated. Rev. Arms.

23. 1000 Colones 1970. Map, waves, sun and mountains ...... Rare
24. 500 Colones 1970. Bust of Jesus Jimenez 225.00
25. 200 Colones 1970. Juan Santamaria and cannon 100.00
26. 100 Colones 1970. Native art 50.00
27. 50 Colones 1970. Figure on globe 25.00

EGYPT

1960, 64, 68, 70. See pages 91 and 92.

EQUATORIAL GUINEA

"Jules Rimet" soccer cup and scenic views of various countries. Rev. Arms above crossed tusks.

1. 1000 Pesetas 1970 .... ——

Different obverses as indicated. Rev. Arms above crossed tusks. On the centennial of Rome as a capital city.

2. 750 Pesetas 1970. Roma standing .... ——
3. 750 Pesetas 1970. Forum and Coliseum .... ——
4. 750 Pesetas 1970. Roma seated .... ——
5. 750 Pesetas 1970. Winged head of Roma .... ——

ETHIOPIA

(For previous issues, see pages 92 and 93.)

Bust of Haile Selassie. Rev. Arms. On his 75th birthday.

30. 200 Dollars 1966 .... 225.00
31. 100 Dollars 1966 .... 115.00
32. 50 Dollars 1966 .... 60.00
33. 20 Dollars 1966 .... 25.00
34. 10 Dollars 1966 .... 15.00

FUJAIRAH

Different obverses as indicated. Rev. Arms.

1.	200 Riyals 1968. Bust of Alsharqi	150.00
2.	100 Riyals 1968. Heads of Apollo 11 astronauts	65.00
3.	100 Riyals 1968. Heads of Apollo 12 astronauts	65.00
4.	50 Riyals 1968. Olympic rings, torch and legend	35.00
5.	25 Riyals 1968. Bust of President Nixon	20.00

(Description not available.)

6.	100 Riyals 1970	——
7.	100 Riyals 1970	——
8.	100 Riyals 1970	——

GABON

Head of President Leon Mba. Rev. Arms. Dated 1960 but struck and released in 1965 to commemorate independence.

1.	100 Francs 1960	125.00
2.	50 Francs 1960	60.00
3.	25 Francs 1960	25.00
4.	10 Francs 1960	15.00

Bust of President Bongo. Different reverses as indicated.

5.	20,000 Francs 1969. Apollo 11 on launching pad	225.00
6.	10,000 Francs 1969. Apollo 11 landing on moon	115.00
7.	5000 Francs 1969. Tribal masks	60.00
8.	3000 Francs 1969. Arms	35.00
9.	1000 Francs 1969. Woodcutter	15.00

GREAT BRITAIN

1962—. See page 226.

GREECE

1967. See page 227.

GUINEA

Different obverses as indicated. Rev. Arms.

1.	10,000 Francs 1969. Bust of Ahmed Sekou Toure	165.00
2.	5000 Francs 1969. Views of Munich and other Olympic sites	80.00
3.	2000 Francs 1969. Apollo 11 landing on moon	40.00
4.	1000 Francs 1969. Conjoined heads of John Kennedy and Robert Kennedy	20.00

Different obverses as indicated. Rev. Arms.

5.	2000 Francs ND (1970). Apollo 12 in flight	——
6.	2000 Francs ND (1970). Apollo 13 insignia	——

HAITI

Series A. (.900 fine gold).

Different obverses as indicated. Rev. Arms.

1.	1000 Gourdes 1968. Bust of Duvalier	600.00
2.	200 Gourdes 1968. Native running with machete	200.00
3.	100 Gourdes 1968. Girl holding machete	100.00
4.	50 Gourdes 1968. Voodoo dancer	50.00
5.	20 Gourdes 1968. Native holding machete	20.00

Series B. (.585 fine gold).

Different obverses as indicated. Rev. Arms.

6.	500 Gourdes 1968. Three artists	325.00
7.	250 Gourdes 1968. Bust of Christophe	150.00
8.	60 Gourdes 1968. Bust of Petion	40.00
9.	40 Gourdes 1968. Bust of Dessalines	25.00
10.	30 Gourdes 1968. The Citadelle	20.00

HUNGARY

1961, 66-68. See page 233.

ICELAND

1961. See page 238

INDONESIA

Different obverses as indicated. Rev. Bird flanked by BI monogram (Bank of Indonesia).

1.	25,000 Rupiah 1970. Bust of Suharto	——
2.	20,000 Rupiah 1970. Deity	——
3.	10,000 Rupiah 1970. Balinese dancer	——
4.	5000 Rupiah 1970. Idol	——
5.	2000 Rupiah 1970. Plumed bird	——

ISLE OF MAN

Head of Queen Elizabeth II. Rev. Arms in shield. On the 200th anniversary of England's purchase of the Isle of Man.

1.	5 Pounds 1965	250.00
2.	1 Pound 1965	60.00
3.	½ Pound 1965	30.00

ISRAEL

1960-69. See pages 251 and 252.

IVORY COAST

Bust of President Felix Houphouet Boigny. Rev. Arms.

1.	100 Francs 1966	——
2.	50 Francs 1966	——
3.	25 Francs 1966	——
4.	10 Francs 1966	——

JORDAN

Bust of King Hussein, Different reverses as indicated.

1.	25 Dinars 1969. Dome of the Rock	225.00
2.	10 Dinars 1969. Bust of Pope Paul VI	100.00
3.	5 Dinars 1969. Treasury Building	60.00
4.	2 Dinars 1969. Forum of Jepagh	25.00

KATANGA

1961. See page 301.

KENYA

Bust of President Jomo Kenyatta. Different reverses as indicated.

1.	500 Shillings 1966. Mt. Kenya	200.00
2.	250 Shillings 1966. Cockerel	100.00
3.	100 Shillings 1966. Kenyatta's fly whisk	40.00

KUWAIT

1961. See page 301.

LAOS

Bust of King Sri Savang Vatthana. Rev. Three-headed elephant. On the king's coronation.

1.	80,000 Kip 1971	250.00
2.	40,000 Kip 1971	125.00
3.	20,000 Kip 1971	75.00
4.	8,000 Kip 1971	35.00
5.	4,000 Kip 1971	20.00

LESOTHO

Bust of King Moshoeshoe in tribal regalia. Rev. Arms.

1.	4 Maloti 1966	175.00
2.	2 Maloti 1966	100.00
3.	1 Maloti 1966	50.00

Head of undraped King Moshoeshoe. Rev. Arms. Patterns. Only seven pattern sets were prepared.

4.	20 Maloti 1966	Rare
5.	10 Maloti 1966	Rare
6.	4 Maloti 1966	Rare
7.	2 Maloti 1966	Rare

Bust of King Moshoeshoe in tribal regalia. Different reverses as indicated. To commemorate the work of the F.A.O. (Food and Agriculture Organization) of the United Nations.

8.	20 Maloti 1969. Sheep	225.00
9.	10 Maloti 1969. Water buffalo	125.00
10.	4 Maloti 1969. Ram	75.00
11.	2 Maloti 1969	40.00
12.	1 Maloti 1969	25.00

LIBERIA

Head of President Tubman. Rev. Arms and value.

1.	20 Dollars 1964. Red gold	50.00
2.	20 Dollars 1964. Yellow gold	250.00

Head of President Tubman. Rev. Providence Island.

3.	25 Dollars 1965	60.00

(Description not available.)

4.	30 Dollars 1965	75.00
5.	12 Dollars 1965	30.00

LIECHTENSTEIN

(For previous issues, see pages 302 and 303.)

Head to right. Rev. Arms. On 100th anniversary of Landesbank. Not released for circulation.

22.	50 Franken 1961	60.00
23.	25 Franken 1961	35.00

MALI

Head of President Modibo Keita. Rev. (Description not available).

1.	100 Francs 1967	100.00
2.	50 Francs 1967	60.00
3.	25 Francs 1967	30.00
4.	10 Francs 1967	15.00

MALTA

(For previous issues, see pages 304-306.)

Sovereign Military Order of Malta.

(Description not available.)

48.	10 Scudi 1961-63	——
49.	5 Scudi 1961-63	——

Uniformed facing bust of Grand Master De Mojana. Rev. Crowned quartered arms of the Order.

50.	10 Scudi 1964-66	——

Uniformed facing bust of Grand Master De Mojana. Rev. St. John the Baptist handing pennon of the Order to kneeling Grand Master.

51.	5 Scudi 1964-66	——

Uniformed profile bust of Grand Master De Mojana. Rev. Crowned quartered arms of the Order.

52.	10 Scudi 1967, 68	——

Uniformed profile bust of Grand Master De Mojana. Rev. St. John the Baptist handing pennon of the Order to kneeling Grand Master.

53.	5 Scudi 1967, 68	——

Uniformed bust of Grand Master. Rev. St. John the Baptist handing pennon of the Order to kneeling Grand Master.

54.	10 Scudi 1969	——

Uniformed bust of Grand Master. Rev. Crowned Maltese cross.

55.	5 Scudi 1969, 70	——

Uniformed bust of Grand Master. Rev. St. John the Baptist holding pennon of the Order.

56.	10 Scudi 1970	——

MONACO

(For previous issues, see page 311.)

Conjoined heads of Prince Rainier and Princess Grace. Rev. Crowned arms. On their 10th wedding anniversary.

32.	200 Francs 1966	150.00

MUSCAT AND OMAN

1962. See page 312.

NETHERLANDS EAST INDIES

1960. See page 322.

NICARAGUA

Bust of poet Ruben Dario. Rev. Arms within triangle. On the the centenary of the poet.

1.	50 Cordobas 1967	125.00

NIGER

Bust of President Hamani. Rev. Arms flanked by flags. Issued in 1965 on the 5th anniversary of independence.

1.	100 Francs 1960	90.00
2.	50 Francs 1960	50.00
3.	25 Francs 1960	25.00
4.	10 Francs 1960	15.00

(Description not available.)

5.	100 Francs 1968	90.00
6.	50 Francs 1968	50.00
7.	25 Francs 1968	25.00
8.	10 Francs 1968	15.00

PARAGUAY

1968. See page 324.

PERSIA

1960-62. See page 327.

PERU

1960-68. See pages 229 and 330.

PHILIPPINES

(For previous issues, see page 330.)

Head of Pope Paul VI. Rev. Head of President Ferdinand E.
Marcos. On the Pope's visit to the Philippines.

5.	1 Piso 1970	——

RAS AL KHAIMA

Different obverses as indicated. Rev. Legend and value. On
the centenary of Rome as a capital city.

1.	200 Riyals 1970. Romulus, Remus and wolf	——
2.	150 Riyals 1970. Liberty standing; a building; Romulus, Remus and wolf	——
3.	100 Riyals 1970. World War I victory	——
4.	75 Riyals 1970. The city of Rome	——
5.	50 Riyals 1970. The kingdom of Italy	——

RHODESIA

Head of Queen Elizabeth II. Different reverses as indicated.
On the first anniversary of independence.

1.	5 Pounds 1966. Arms	250.00
2.	1 Pound 1966. Lion with elephant tusk in forepaw	60.00
3.	10 Shillings 1966. Sable antelope	40.00

RWANDA

Bust of President Gregoire Kayibanda. Rev. Arms. Independence commemorative.

1.	100 Francs 1961	75.00
2.	50 Francs 1961	40.00
3.	25 Francs 1961	25.00
4.	10 Francs 1961	15.00

SENEGAL

(Description not available.)

1.	100 Francs 1968	100.00
2.	50 Francs 1968	60.00
3.	25 Francs 1968	35.00
4.	10 Francs 1968	20.00

SHARJAH

Different obverses as indicated. Rev. Palm tree above crossed
flags.

1.	200 Riyals 1970. Head of Khalid bin Mohamed Al-Qasimi	——
2.	100 Riyals 1970. Bust of Napoleon	——
3.	100 Riyals 1970. Bust of Bolivar	——
4.	50 Riyals 1970. "Jules Rimet" soccer cup and globe	——
5.	25 Riyals 1970. Mona Lisa	——

SIERRA LEONE

1966. See page 348.

SINGAPORE

1969. See page 348.

SOMALIA

Bust of President Osman. Rev. Arms. On the 5th anniversary
of independence.

1.	500 Shillings 1965	225.00

2.	200 Shillings 1965	100.00
3.	100 Shillings 1965	50.00
4.	50 Shillings 1965	25.00
5.	20 Shillings 1965	15.00

Arms. Different reverses as indicated. On the 10th anniversary of independence.

6.	500 Shillings 1970. Building	225.00
7.	200 Shillings 1970. Camel	100.00
8.	100 Shillings 1970. Girl carrying fruit	50.00
9.	50 Shillings 1970. Man holding vase	25.00
10.	20 Shillings 1970. Stylized atomic symbol	15.00

SOUTH AFRICA

1960—. See page 349.

SOUTH KOREA

Different obverses as indicated. Rev. Arms.

1.	25,000 Won 1970. King Sejong the Great	Rare
2.	20,000 Won 1970. Crown of Silla Dynasty	235.00
3.	10,000 Won 1970. President Chung Hee Park	125.00
4.	5000 Won 1970. Turtle ship	65.00
5.	2500 Won 1970. Queen Sunduk	35.00
6.	1000 Won 1970. Great South Gate	15.00

SWAZILAND

Head of King Sobhuza II. Rev. Arms. Independence commemorative.

1.	1 Lilangeni 1968	200.00

THAILAND

Head of Queen Sirikit. Rev. Queen's initials and floral
wreath. On her 36th birthday.

1.	600 Baht 1968	70.00
2.	300 Baht 1968	35.00
3.	150 Baht 1968	20.00

TONGA

Standing figure of Queen Salote Tupou III. Rev. Arms.

1.	1 Koula 1962	125.00
2.	½ Koula 1962	65.00
3.	Platinum 1 Koula 1962	Rare
4.	Platinum ½ Koula 1962	Rare

Bust of Queen Salote Tupou III. Rev. Arms.

5.	¼ Koula 1962	40.00
6.	Platinum ¼ Koula 1962	Rare

Bust of King Taufa'ahau Tupou IV. Rev. Arms. On the king's
coronation.

7.	Palladium 1 Hau 1967	200.00
8.	Palladium ½ Hau 1967	100.00
9.	Palladium ¼ Hau 1967	60.00

Bust of Tupou IV. Rev. Arms. On the king's 50th birthday.

10.	Palladium 1 Hau 1968	200.00
11.	Palladium ½ Hau 1968	100.00
12.	Palladium ¼ Hau 1968	60.00

TUNISIA

Head of President Habib Bourguiba. Rev. Minaret of Grand
Mosque at Kairouan. On the 10th anniversary of the
Republic.

1.	40 Dinars 1967	225.00
2.	20 Dinars 1967	125.00
3.	10 Dinars 1967	65.00
4.	5 Dinars 1967	35.00
5.	2 Dinars 1967	15.00

TURKEY

960, 61. See page 380.

UGANDA

Different obverses as indicated. Rev. Arms.

1.	1000 Shillings 1969. Bust of Pope Paul VI	500.00
2.	500 Shillings 1969. Pope Paul VI on globe	225.00
3.	100 Shillings 1969. Pope Paul VI on map of Africa	50.00
4.	50 Shillings 1969. Martyrs' shrine	25.00

YEMEN ARAB REPUBLIC

(For previous issues, see page 407.)

Arms. Different reverses as indicated.

4.	50 Ryals 1969. Lion	—
5.	30 Ryals 1969. Head of Azzubairi	—
6.	20 Ryals 1969. Apollo 11 moon landing	—
7.	20 Ryals 1969. Camel	—
8.	10 Ryals 1969. Gazelles	—
9.	5 Ryals 1969. Falcon head	—

YUGOSLAVIA

(For previous issues, see page 407.)

Bust of President Tito. Rev. Arms. On the 25th anniversary of the Council of National Liberation.

6.	1000 Dinars 1968	275.00
7.	200 Dinars 1968	60.00

People holding flags; above, a panoramic view of the town of Jajce. Rev. Arms.

8.	500 Dinars 1968	130.00
9.	100 Dinars 1968	30.00

Appendix

THE PRINCIPAL GOLD COINS OF THE WORLD
Their weight, fineness, and original exchange value.

The tables below will show the relationship to each other in terms of U. S. gold dollars of the principal gold coins of the world.

The period of time used in arriving at the original exchange value is the so-called "Golden Age" of gold coinage—most of the 19th century and until the outbreak of World War I in 1914. It was during this period that a true international gold standard was in existence.

This standard came to an unofficial end in 1914 and to an official end in 1933, when following an outbreak of universal monetary failures, the world price of gold was raised to $35.00 per ounce.

During this stable period of about 100 years, the face value of U.S. gold coins was based on the legal value of $20.67183 per ounce of pure or fine gold. The original exchange values listed below are in terms of U.S. gold dollars based on U.S. gold coins struck during the period of 1837-1933.

For those gold coins of the world struck before 1837 or after 1933, the values have been determined by judging the weight and fineness of the coins as though they had been struck during the period 1837-1933. To find the present gold value multiply the fine gold weight in grams by $1.125.

In consulting these tables it should be borne in mind that the fractions or multiples of a given gold coin are always in exact proportion as regards weight and value.

The original exchange values are approximate to the nearest cent—a fraction of ½ Cent or more has been carried to the next cent, and a lesser fraction to the preceding cent.

Some coinages that were struck over a century or more inevitably tend to show variations in weight, fineness or both and the figures given below for such coinages are for typical or average specimens of the coins in question.

Table I is confined to those coins of the same denomination and value but of different national origin which circulated in many countries over a long period of time, enjoying international acceptance.

Table II shows the principal gold coins of specific countries.

TABLE I

In this table especially (because the coinages extended over hundreds of years), the figures in the Gram and fineness columns are approximate and are for average, familiar specimens.

Name of Coin	Where Circulated and Ultimate Dates of Coinage	Weight of Coin in Grams	Purity or Fineness	Original Value in U.S. Gold Dollars
THE DINAR	**Africa and Asia, 660-1902**			
3 Dinars		12.6000	.975	$ 7.80
2 Dinars		8.4000	.975	5.20
1 Dinar		4.2000	.975	2.60
½ Dinar		2.1000	.975	1.30
¼ Dinar		1.0500	.975	.65
THE DUCAT	**All Europe, 1280-1960**			
100 Ducats		350.0000	.986	229.00
50 Ducats		175.0000	.986	114.50
20 Ducats		70.0000	.986	45.80
10 Ducats		35.0000	.986	22.90
5 Ducats		17.5000	.986	11.45
4 Ducats		14.0000	.986	9.16
3 Ducats		10.5000	.986	6.87
2 Ducats		7.0000	.986	4.58
1 Ducat		3.5000	.986	2.29
½ Ducat		1.7500	.986	1.15
¼ Ducat		.8750	.986	.58
⅛ Ducat		.4375	.986	.29
1/16 Ducat		.2188	.986	.15
1/32 Ducat		.1094	.986	.08

Name of Coin	Where Circulated and Ultimate Dates of Coinage	Weight of Coin in Grams	Purity or Fineness	Original Value in U.S. Gold Dollars
THE ESCUDO	**Spain and Spanish-America, 1598-1873**			
8 Escudos		27.0000	.875	$16.00
4 Escudos		13.5000	.875	8.00
2 Escudos		6.7500	.875	4.00
1 Escudo		3.3750	.875	2.00
½ Escudo		1.6875	.875	1.00
THE FLORIN	**All Europe, 1200-1896** Similar to the Ducat.			
THE GOLDGULDEN	Same as the Florin			
THE MOHUR	**Asia, 1200-1947**			
	See Table II, under India			
THE POUND	**British Empire, 1817-1964**			
	See Table II, under Great Britain			
THE SEQUIN	**Ottoman Empire, 1451-1839**			
	See Table II, under Turkey			

TABLE II

Country and Denomination	Period of Coinage	Weight of Coin in Grams	Purity or Fineness	Original Value in U.S. Gold Dollars
AFGHANISTAN				
5 Amani	1921	22.7500	.900	$13.50
2 Amani	1921-1924	9.1000	.900	5.40
1 Amani	1919-1932	4.5500	.900	2.70
½ Amani	1921-1928	2.2750	.900	1.35
ALBANIA				
100 Francs	1926-1938	32.2580	.900	19.29
50 Francs	1938	16.1290	.900	9.65
20 Francs	1926-1938	6.4516	.900	3.86
10 Francs	1927	3.2258	.900	1.93
ARGENTINA				
5 Pesos	1881-1896	8.0645	.900	4.82
2½ Pesos	1881-1884	4.0322	.900	2.41
AUSTRIA				
1 Souverain d'or or Sovrano	1781-1800	11.0600	.919	6.86
½ Souverain d'or or Sovrano	1781-1800	5.5300	.919	3.43
1 Sovrano	1820-1856	11.3320	.900	6.86
½ Sovrano	1820-1856	5.6660	.900	3.43
1 Krone	1858-1866	11.1110	.900	6.66
½ Krone	1858-1866	5.5550	.900	3.33
8 Florins-20 Francs	1870-1892	6.4516	.900	3.86
4 Florins-10 Francs	1870-1892	3.2258	.900	1.93
100 Corona	1908-1915	33.8753	.900	20.26
20 Corona	1892-1916	6.7750	.900	4.05
10 Corona	1892-1912	3.3375	.900	2.03
100 Schillings	1926-1938	23.5240	.900	14.12
25 Schillings	1926-1938	5.8810	.900	3.53
BELGIUM				
100 Francs	1853-1912	32.2580	.900	19.29
40 Francs	1834-1841	12.9032	.900	7.72
25 Francs	1847-1850	8.0645	.900	4.82
20 Francs	1835-1914	6.4516	.900	3.86
10 Francs	1849-1912	3.2258	.900	1.93
BOLIVIA				
35 Grams Pure Gold	1952	38.9000	.900	23.30
14 Grams Pure Gold	1952	15.5600	.900	9.31
7 Grams Pure Gold	1952	7.7800	.900	4.65
3½ Grams Pure Gold	1952	3.8900	.900	2.33
BRAZIL				
20,000 Reis	1724-1727	53.6000	.916⅔	32.77
10,000 Reis	1724-1727	26.8000	.916⅔	16.38
4,000 Reis	1703-1727	10.7200	.916⅔	6.54
2,000 Reis	1703-1727	5.3600	.916⅔	3.27
1,000 Reis	1708-1727	2.6800	.916⅔	1.64
400 Reis	1725-1730	1.0720	.916⅔	.65

(The above six coins were struck under the national system and bear the cross of Jerusalem. The first three coins below were struck under the colonial system and bear a plain cross, except for the dates from 1823 to 1833 of the 4,000 Reis piece, which show the Brazilian emperor.)

Country and Denomination	Period of Coinage	Weight of Coin in Grams	Purity or Fineness	Original Value in U.S. Gold Dollars
4,000 Reis	1695-1833	8.2000	.916⅔	4.93
2,000 Reis	1695-1793	4.1000	.916⅔	2.47
1,000 Reis	1696-1787	2.0500	.916⅔	1.24
12,800 Reis	1727-1733	28.6000	.916⅔	17.47
6,400 Reis	1727-1833	14.3000	.916⅔	8.74
3,200 Reis	1727-1786	7.1500	.916⅔	4.37
1,600 Reis	1727-1784	3.5750	.916⅔	2.19
800 Reis	1727-1786	1.7875	.916⅔	1.10
400 Reis	1730-1734	0.8938	.916⅔	.55
20,000 Reis	1849-1922	17.9296	.916⅔	10.93
10,000 Reis	1849-1922	8.9648	.916⅔	5.46
5,000 Reis	1854-1859	4.4824	.916⅔	2.73
BULGARIA				
100 Leva	1894-1912	32.2580	.900	19.29
20 Leva	1894-1912	6.4516	.900	3.86
10 Leva	1894	3.2258	.900	1.93

Country and Denomination	Period of Coinage	Weight of Coin in Grams	Purity or Fineness	Original Value in U.S. Gold Dollars
BURMA				
4 Rupees	1852-1878	2.8000	.900	1.70
2 Rupees	1852-1878	1.4000	.900	.85
1 Rupee	1852-1878	.7000	.900	.43
CANADA				
10 Dollars	1912-1914	16.7185	.900	10.00
5 Dollars	1912-1914	8.3592	.900	5.00
CHILE				
10 Pesos	1853-1890	15.2000	.900	9.15
5 Pesos	1858-1873	7.6000	.900	4.58
2 Pesos	1857-1875	3.0400	.900	1.84
1 Peso	1860-1873	1.5200	.900	.92
20 Pesos	1896-1917	11.9500	.916⅔	7.30
10 Pesos	1895-1901	5.9900	.916⅔	3.65
5 Pesos	1895-1900	2.9900	.916⅔	1.83
100 Pesos	1926-1955	20.3397	.900	12.20
50 Pesos	1926	10.1698	.900	6.10
20 Pesos	1926	4.0680	.900	2.44
CHINA				
20 Dollars-Republic	1919	14.8000	.900	9.00
10 Dollars-Republic	1916-1919	7.4000	.900	4.50
10 Dollars-Yunnan	1919	9.0000	.900	5.40
5 Dollars-Yunnan	1919	4.5000	.900	2.70
COLOMBIA				
20 Pesos	1859-1877	32.2580	.900	19.29
10 Pesos	1856-1877	16.1290	.900	9.65
5 Pesos	1856-1885	8.0645	.900	4.82
2 Pesos	1856-1876	3.2258	.900	1.93
1 Peso	1856-1878	1.6129	.900	.96
10 Pesos	1919-1924	15.9761	.916⅔	9.73
5 Pesos	1913-1930	7.9881	.916⅔	4.87
2½ Pesos	1913-1928	3.9940	.916⅔	2.43
COSTA RICA				
10 Pesos	1870-1876	14.3000	.875	8.60
5 Pesos	1867-1875	7.1500	.875	4.30
2 Pesos	1866-1876	2.8600	.875	1.72
1 Peso	1864-1872	1.4300	.875	.86
20 Colones	1897-1900	15.5600	.900	9.31
10 Colones	1897-1900	7.7800	.900	4.65
5 Colones	1899-1900	3.8900	.900	2.33
2 Colones	1897-1928	1.5560	.900	.93
CUBA				
20 Pesos	1915-1916	33.4370	.900	20.00
10 Pesos	1915-1916	16.7185	.900	10.00
5 Pesos	1915-1916	8.3592	.900	5.00
4 Pesos	1915-1916	6.6872	.900	4.00
2 Pesos	1915-1916	3.3436	.900	2.00
1 Peso	1915-1916	1.6718	.900	1.00
DANISH WEST INDIES				
10 Daler-50 Francs	1904	16.1290	.900	9.65
4 Daler-20 Francs	1904-1905	6.4516	.900	3.86
DANZIG				
25 Gulden	1923-1930	7.9881	.916⅔	4.87
DENMARK				
2 Christian d'or	1826-1870	13.3000	.903	8.00
1 Christian d'or	1775-1869	6.6500	.903	4.00
20 Kroner	1873-1931	8.9606	.900	5.36
10 Kroner	1873-1917	4.4803	.900	2.68
DOMINICAN REPUBLIC				
30 Pesos	1955	29.6220	.900	17.85
ECUADOR				
10 Sucres	1899-1900	8.1360	.900	4.87
1 Condor	1928	8.3592	.900	5.00
EGYPT				
500 Piastres	1861-1960	42.5000	.875	24.70
100 Piastres	1839-1960	8.5000	.875	4.94
50 Piastres	1839-1958	4.2500	.875	2.47
20 Piastres	1923-1938	1.7000	.875	.99
10 Piastres	1839-1909	.8500	.875	.49
5 Piastres	1839-1909	.4250	.875	.25
10 Pounds	1964	52.0000	.875	30.26
5 Pounds	1964	26.0000	.875	15.13

Country and Denomination	Period of Coinage	Weight of Coin in Grams	Purity or Fineness	Original Value in U.S. Gold Dollars
ETHIOPIA				
1 Wark	1931	About 7.0000	.900	4.10
½ Wark	1931	About 3.5000	.900	2.05
FINLAND				
20 Markkaa	1878-1913	6.4516	.900	3.86
10 Markkaa	1878-1913	3.2258	.900	1.93
200 Markkaa	1926	8.4210	.900	5.10
100 Markkaa	1926	4.2105	.900	2.55
FRANCE (Until 1803, the figures are an average of familiar pieces)				
1 Ecu d'or	1266-1641	3.4000	.963	2.25
1 Chaise d'or	1285-1422	4.7000	1.000	3.15
1 Royal d'or	1285-1461	4.2000	1.000	2.81
1 Lion d'or	1328-1350	4.9000	1.000	3.28
1 Pavillion d'or	1328-1350	5.1000	1.000	3.42
1 Ange d'or	1328-1350	7.2500	1.000	4.86
1 Franc a Cheval	1350-1461	3.8900	1.000	2.61
1 Mouton d'or	1350-1422	4.7000	1.000	3.15
1 Franc a Pied	1350-1380	3.8200	1.000	2.56
1 Salut d'or	1380-1461	3.8900	1.000	2.61
1 Heaume d'or	1380-1422	5.1000	.916⅔	3.12
1 Henry d'or	1550-1559	3.6000	.958	2.28
2 Louis d'or	1640-1792	13.40-17.20	.916⅔	8.10-10.40
1 Louis d'or	1640-1793	6.70- 8.60	.916⅔	4.05- 5.20
½ Louis d'or	1640-1784	3.35- 4.30	.916⅔	2.03- 2.65
100 Francs	1855-1913	32.2580	.900	19.29
50 Francs	1855-1904	16.1290	.900	9.65
40 Francs	1803-1839	12.9039	.900	7.72
20 Francs	1803-1914	6.4516	.900	3.86
10 Francs	1854-1914	3.2258	.900	1.93
5 Francs	1854-1889	1.6129	.900	.96
100 Francs	1929-1936	6.5500	.900	3.94
GERMAN EAST AFRICA				
15 Rupees	1916	7.5000	.900	4.48
GERMAN NEW GUINEA				
20 Marks	1895	7.9650	.900	4.76
10 Marks	1895	3.9825	.900	2.38
GERMANY				
20 Marks	1871-1915	7.9650	.900	4.76
10 Marks	1872-1914	3.9825	.900	2.38
5 Marks	1877-1878	1.9913	.900	1.19
10 Taler	1742-1857	13.3000	.900	7.96
5 Taler	1699-1856	6.6500	.900	3.98
2½ Taler	1699-1855	3.3200	.900	1.99
1 Carolin	1726-1782	9.7000	.770	4.90
½ Carolin	1726-1737	4.8500	.770	2.45
¼ Carolin	1726-1736	2.4250	.770	1.23
10 Gulden	1819-1842	6.8500	.904	4.16
5 Gulden	1819-1835	3.4250	.904	2.08
1 Krone	1857-1870	11.1110	.900	6.66
½ Krone	1857-1869	5.5550	.900	3.33
1 Pistole	Same as the 5 Taler piece above			
1 Frederick d'or (or other name)	Same as the 5 Taler piece above			
GHANA				
5 Pounds	1960	15.976	.916⅔	9.75
GREAT BRITAIN (Until 1663, the figures are an average of familiar pieces)				
1 Noble	1327-1483	8.0000	.975	5.30
1 Angel	1422-1625	5.0000	.958	3.20
1 Ryal	1485-1625	13.0000	.958	8.25
1 Sovereign	1485-1625	12.0000	.958	7.65
1 George Noble	1509-1547	4.5000	.916⅔	2.75
3 Pounds (Triple Unite)	1642-1644	27.0000	.916⅔	16.50
20 Shillings (1 Unite or Laurel)	1603-1663	9.0000	.916⅔	5.50
2 Crowns or 10 Shillings	1603-1663	4.5000	.916⅔	2.75
1 Crown or 5 Shillings	1509-1663	2.2500	.916⅔	1.38
½ Crown or 2½ Shillings	1509-1625	1.1250	.916⅔	.69
5 Guineas	1668-1777	41.7500	.916⅔	25.50
2 Guineas	1664-1777	16.7000	.916⅔	10.20
1 Guinea	1663-1813	8.3500	.916⅔	5.10
½ Guinea	1669-1813	4.1750	.916⅔	2.55
⅓ Guinea	1797-1813	2.7834	.916⅔	1.70
¼ Guinea	1718-1762	2.0875	.916⅔	1.28
5 Pounds	1820-1953	39.9403	.916⅔	24.33
2 Pounds	1820-1953	15.9761	.916⅔	9.73
1 Pound	1817-1964	7.9881	.916⅔	4.87
½ Pound	1817-1953	3.9940	.916⅔	2.43
GREECE				
100 Drachmae	1876	32.2580	.900	19.29
50 Drachmae	1876	16.1290	.900	9.65
40 Drachmae	1852	12.9039	.900	7.72
20 Drachmae	1833-1884	6.4516	.900	3.86
10 Drachmae	1876	3.2258	.900	1.93
5 Drachmae	1876	1.6129	.900	.96
GUATEMALA				
20 Pesos	1869-1878	32.2580	.900	19.29
16 Pesos	1863-1869	25.8078	.900	15.44
10 Pesos	1869	16.1290	.900	9.65
8 Pesos	1864	12.9039	.900	7.72
5 Pesos	1869-1878	8.0645	.900	4.82
4 Pesos	1861-1869	6.4516	.900	3.86
2 Pesos	1859	3.2258	.900	1.93
1 Peso	1859-1860	1.6129	.900	.96
4 Reales (½ Peso)	1859-1864	.8065	.900	.48
20 Quetzals	1926	33.4370	.900	20.00
10 Quetzals	1926	16.7185	.900	10.00
5 Quetzals	1926	8.3592	.900	5.00
HEJAZ				
1 Dinar	1923	7.2166	.916⅔	4.39
HUNGARY				
8 Florins-20 Francs	1870-1892	6.4516	.900	3.86
4 Florins-10 Francs	1870-1892	3.2258	.900	1.93
100 Korona	1907-1908	33.8753	.900	20.26
20 Korona	1892-1916	6.7750	.900	4.05
10 Korona	1892-1915	3.3375	.900	2.03
ICELAND				
500 Kronur	1961	8.9604	.900	5.36
INDIA				
200 Mohurs	1628-1658	2332.0000	.916⅔+	1,416.00
100 Mohurs	1556-1707	1166.0000	.916⅔+	708.00
5 Mohurs	1556-1627	58.3000	.916⅔+	35.40
2 Mohurs	1556-1835	23.3200	.916⅔	14.16
1 Mohur	1200-1947	11.6600	.916⅔	7.08
½ Mohur	1200-1947	5.8300	.916⅔	3.54
¼ Mohur	1200-1947	2.9150	.916⅔	1.77
⅛ Mohur	1200-1947	1.4575	.916⅔	.89
1/16 Mohur	1500-1820	.7288	.916⅔	.45
1/32 Mohur	1500-1820	.3644	.916⅔	.23
10 Rupees (⅔ Mohur)	1862-1879	7.7740	.916⅔	4.72
5 Rupees (⅓ Mohur)	1820-1879	3.8870	.916⅔	2.36
15 Rupees	1918	7.9881	.916⅔	4.87
1 Pagoda (crude style)	1200-1868	3.0000	.800	1.60
(The following for Cutch-Bhuj)				
100 Kori	1866	18.7000	.916⅔	11.35
50 Kori	1873-1874	9.3500	.916⅔	5.68
25 Kori	1862-1870	4.6750	.916⅔	2.84
(The following for Madras; modern style coinage)				
2 Pagodas	(1810)	5.8500	.916⅔	3.56
1 Pagoda	(1810)	2.9250	.916⅔	1.78
(The following for Travancore)				
2 Pagodas	1877-1924	5.1000	.916⅔	3.12
1 Pagoda	1877-1924	2.5500	.916⅔	1.56
½ Pagoda	1881-1924	1.2750	.916⅔	.78
¼ Pagoda	1881-1924	.6375	.916⅔	.39
ISRAEL				
100 Pounds	1962	26.6800	.916⅔	16.25
50 Pounds	1962-1964	13.3400	.916⅔	8.13
20 Pounds	1960	7.9880	.916⅔	4.87

Country and Denomination	Period of Coinage	Weight of Coin in Grams	Purity or Fineness	Original Value in U.S. Gold Dollars
ITALY				
100 Lire	1832-1927	32.2580	.900	19.29
80 Lire	1821-1831	25.8078	.900	15.44
50 Lire	1832-1927	16.1290	.900	9.65
40 Lire	1806-1848	12.9039	.900	7.72
20 Lire	1800-1927	6.4516	.900	3.86
10 Lire	1832-1927	3.2258	.900	1.93
5 Lire	1863-1865	1.6129	.900	.96
100 Lire	1931-1936	8.7990	.900	5.25
50 Lire	1931-1936	4.3995	.900	2.63

(The following for Florence:

80 Florins = 10 Zecchini = 200 Paoli = 133⅓ Lire)

80 Florins	1827-1828	32.6180	1.000	21.66
1 Ruspone (3 Zecchini)	1719-1859	10.4610	1.000	6.93
1 Zecchino	1712-1853	3.4870	1.000	2.31

(The following for Naples: 30 Ducati = 10 Ducats = 10 Oncie)

6 Ducati	1749-1785	8.8200	.875	5.12
4 Ducati	1749-1782	5.8800	.875	3.42
2 Ducati	1749-1772	2.9400	.875	1.71
30 Ducati	1818-1856	37.8670	.996	25.00
15 Ducati	1818-1856	18.9330	.996	12.50
6 Ducati	1826-1856	7.5730	.996	5.00
3 Ducati	1818-1856	3.7860	.996	2.50

(For the following, please see Table I)

1 Doppia	1280-1815	Equal to 2 Ducats	
1 Florin	1250-1500	Equal to 1 Ducat	
1 Scudo d'oro	1300-1750	Equal to 1 Ducat	
1 Zecchino	1500-1800	Equal to 1 Ducat	
1 Genovino	1200-1415	Equal to 1 Ducat	

Country and Denomination	Period of Coinage	Weight of Coin in Grams	Purity or Fineness	Original Value in U.S. Gold Dollars
JAPAN				
20 Yen	1870-1880	33.3332	.900	19.94
10 Yen	1871-1880	16.6666	.900	9.97
5 Yen	1870-1897	8.3333	.900	4.98
2 Yen	1870-1880	3.3333	.900	1.96
1 Yen	1871-1880	1.6666	.900	.98
20 Yen	1897-1932	16.6666	.900	9.97
10 Yen	1897-1910	8.3333	.900	4.98
5 Yen	1897-1930	4.1666	.900	2.49
KOREA				
20 Won	1906-1910	16.6666	.900	9.97
10 Won	1906-1909	8.3333	.900	4.98
5 Won	1908-1909	4.1666	.900	2.49
KUWAIT				
5 Dinars	1961	13.5715	.916⅔	8.27
LIBERIA				
20 Dollars	1964	18.6500	.900	11.16
LIECHTENSTEIN				
20 Kronen	1898-1900	6.7750	.900	4.05
10 Kronen	1898-1900	3.3375	.900	2.03
100 Franken	1952	32.2580	.900	19.29
20 Franken	1930-1946	6.4516	.900	3.86
10 Franken	1930-1946	3.2258	.900	1.93
50 Franken	1956-1961	11.2900	.900	6.84
25 Franken	1956-1961	5.6450	.900	3.42
LUXEMBOURG				
20 Francs	1953	6.4516	.900	3.86
MALTA				
20 Scudi	1764-1778	16.0000	.840	9.00
10 Scudi	1756-1782	8.0000	.840	4.50
5 Scudi	1756-1779	4.0000	.840	2.25
MEXICO				
20 Pesos	1870-1905	33.8400	.875	19.72
10 Pesos	1870-1905	16.9200	.875	9.86
5 Pesos	1870-1905	8.4600	.875	4.93
2½ Pesos	1870-1893	4.2300	.875	2.47
1 Peso	1870-1905	1.6900	.875	.99
50 Pesos	1921-1947	41.6666	.900	24.90

Country and Denomination	Period of Coinage	Weight of Coin in Grams	Purity or Fineness	Original Value in U.S. Gold Dollars
20 Pesos	1917-1959	16.6666	.900	9.97
10 Pesos	1905-1959	8.3333	.900	4.98
5 Pesos	1905-1955	4.1666	.900	2.49
2½ Pesos	1918-1948	2.0833	.900	1.25
2 Pesos	1919-1948	1.6666	.900	1.00
MONACO				
100 Francs	1882-1904	32.2580	.900	19.29
40 Francs	1838	12.9039	.900	7.72
20 Francs	1838-1892	6.4516	.900	3.86
MONTENEGRO				
100 Perpera	1910	32.2580	.900	19.29
20 Perpera	1910	6.4516	.900	3.86
10 Perpera	1910	3.2258	.900	1.93
MOROCCO				
4 Ryals	1879	6.4516	.900	3.86
MUSCAT				
15 Rials	1962	7.9878	.916⅔	4.87
NEPAL				
4 Mohars	1750-1938	23.0500	.916⅔	14.00
2 Mohars	1750-1938	11.5250	.916⅔	7.00
1 Mohar	1750-1938	5.7625	.916⅔	3.50
½ Mohar	1750-1938	2.8813	.916⅔	1.75
¼ Mohar	1750-1911	1.4406	.916⅔	.88
⅛ Mohar	1750-1911	.7203	.916⅔	.44
1/16 Mohar	1750-1911	.3602	.916⅔	.22
1/32 Mohar	1750-1911	.1801	.916⅔	.11
1/64 Mohar	1750-1911	.0901	.916⅔	.06
NETHERLANDS				
20 Guilders	1808-1810	13.6500	.916⅔	8.34
10 Guilders	1808-1810	6.8250	.916⅔	4.17
20 Guilders	1848-1853	13.4580	.900	8.04
10 Guilders	1818-1933	6.7290	.900	4.02
5 Guilders	1826-1912	3.3645	.900	2.01
14 Guilders	1749-1764	9.9300	.916⅔	6.10
7 Guilders	1749-1764	4.9650	.916⅔	3.05
NEWFOUNDLAND				
2 Dollars	1865-1888	3.2828	.916⅔	2.00
NORWAY				
20 Kronor	1874-1910	8.9606	.900	5.36
10 Kronor	1874-1910	4.4803	.900	2.68
PERSIA				
1 Ashrafi	1500-1750	3.5000	.975	2.25
25 Tomans	1848-1896	71.9252	.900	43.00
20 Tomans	1848-1896	57.4880	.900	34.40
10 Tomans	1848-1925	28.7440	.900	17.20
5 Tomans	1848-1925	14.4372	.900	8.60
2 Tomans	1848-1925	5.7489	.900	3.44
1 Toman	1848-1927	2.8744	.900	1.72
½ Toman	1848-1925	1.4372	.900	.86
⅕ Toman	1848-1925	.5749	.900	.34
5 Pahlevi	1927-1930	9.5000	.900	5.66
2 Pahlevi	1927-1930	3.8000	.900	2.26
1 Pahlevi	1927-1930	1.9000	.900	1.13
5 Pahlevi	1961-1962	40.6799	.900	24.35
2½ Pahlevi	1961-1962	20.3399	.900	12.17
1 Pahlevi	1932-1962	8.1000	.900	4.80
½ Pahlevi	1932-1962	4.0500	.900	2.40
¼ Pahlevi	1950-1962	2.0250	.900	1.20
PERU				
20 Soles	1863	32.2580	.900	19.29
10 Soles	1863	16.1290	.900	9.65
5 Soles	1863	8.0645	.900	4.82
1 Libra	1898-1964	7.9881	.916⅔	4.87
½ Libra	1902-1964	3.9940	.916⅔	2.43
⅕ Libra	1906-1964	1.5976	.916⅔	.97
50 Soles	1930-1931	33.4370	.900	20.00
100 Soles	1950-1964	46.8071	.900	28.00
50 Soles	1950-1964	23.4035	.900	14.00
20 Soles	1950-1964	9.3614	.900	5.60
10 Soles	1956-1964	4.6807	.900	2.80
5 Soles	1956-1964	2.3404	.900	1.40

Country and Denomination	Period of Coinage	Weight of Coin in Grams	Purity or Fineness	Original Value in U.S. Gold Dollars
PHILIPPINE ISLANDS				
4 Pesos	1861-1882	6.7600	.875	3.86
2 Pesos	1861-1868	3.3800	.875	1.93
1 Peso	1861-1868	1.6900	.875	.96
POLAND				
50 Zloty	1817-1829	9.8000	.916⅔	6.04
25 Zloty	1817-1833	4.9000	.916⅔	3.02
20 Zloty-3 Roubles	1834-1840	3.4500	.980	2.26
20 Zloty	1925	6.4516	.900	3.86
10 Zloty	1925	3.2258	.900	1.93
PORTUGAL				
4 Cruzados	1580-1652	14.0000	.986	9.15
2 Cruzados	1580-1647	7.0000	.986	4.58
1 Cruzado	1438-1647	3.5000	.986	2.29
4,000 Reis	1663-1722	10.7200	.916⅔	6.54
2,000 Reis	1663-1725	5.3600	.916⅔	3.27
1,000 Reis	1663-1821	2.6800	.916⅔	1.64
400 Reis	1717-1821	1.0720	.916⅔	.65
8 Escudos	1717-1732	28.6000	.916⅔	17.47
4 Escudos	1722-1835	14.3000	.916⅔	8.74
2 Escudos	1722-1831	7.1500	.916⅔	4.37
1 Escudo	1722-1821	3.5750	.916⅔	2.19
½ Escudo	1722-1821	1.7875	.916⅔	1.10
5,000 Reis	1836-1851	9.5600	.916⅔	5.92
2,500 Reis	1838-1853	4.7800	.916⅔	2.96
1,000 Reis	1851	2.3900	.916⅔	1.48
10,000 Reis	1878-1889	17.7300	.916⅔	10.81
5,000 Reis	1860-1889	8.8600	.916⅔	5.40
2,000 Reis	1856-1888	3.5400	.916⅔	2.16
1,000 Reis	1855-1879	1.7700	.916⅔	1.08
ROUMANIA				
100 Lei	1906-1940	32.2580	.900	19.29
50 Lei	1906-1922	16.1290	.900	9.65
25 Lei	1906-1922	8.0645	.900	4.82
20 Lei	1867-1944	6.4516	.900	3.86
12½ Lei	1906	4.0323	.900	2.41
RUSSIA (From 1718 to 1825, Rouble gold coinage was of variable weight or fineness)				
25 Roubles	1876	32.7000	.916⅔	19.90
10 Roubles	1836	13.0800	.916⅔	7.96
5 Roubles	1826-1885	6.5400	.916⅔	3.98
3 Roubles	1869-1885	3.9000	.916⅔	2.38
12 Roubles-Platinum	1830-1845	41.5000	1.000	9.52
6 Roubles-Platinum	1829-1845	20.7500	1.000	4.76
3 Roubles-Platinum	1828-1845	10.3750	1.000	2.38
10 Roubles	1886-1894	12.9039	.900	7.72
5 Roubles	1886-1894	6.4516	.900	3.86
15 Roubles	1897	12.9039	.900	7.72
7½ Roubles	1897	6.4516	.900	3.86
37½ Roubles	1902	32.2580	.900	19.29
25 Roubles	1896-1908	32.2580	.900	19.29
10 Roubles	1898-1923	8.6026	.900	5.15
5 Roubles	1897-1910	4.3013	.900	2.57
SALVADOR				
20 Pesos	1892	32.2580	.900	19.29
10 Pesos	1892	16.1290	.900	9.65
5 Pesos	1892	8.0645	.900	4.82
2½ Pesos	1892	4.0323	.900	2.41
20 Colones	1925	15.5600	.900	9.31
SAN MARINO				
20 Lire	1925	6.4516	.900	3.86
10 Lire	1925	3.2258	.900	1.93
SAUDI ARABIA				
1 Saudi Pound	1951-1957	7.9881	.916⅔	4.87
SERBIA				
20 Dinars	1879-1882	6.4516	.900	3.86
10 Dinars	1882	3.2258	.900	1.93
SIAM				
8 Ticals	1851-1868	7.8400	.900	4.50
4 Ticals	1851-1868	3.9200	.900	2.25
2 Ticals	1851-1907	1.9600	.900	1.13
SOUTH AFRICA, REPUBLIC				
2 Rand	1961-1964	7.9881	.916⅔	4.87
1 Rand	1961-1964	3.9940	.916⅔	2.43
SPAIN				
10 Doblas	1350-1369	34.9000	.986	22.84
5 Doblas	1454-1474	22.5000	.986	14.70
1 Dobla	1252-1474	4.5000	.986	2.94
½ Dobla	1454-1474	2.2500	.986	1.47
1 Excelente	1476-1516	Equal to 1 Ducat		
Escudo Coinage	1516-1833	See Table I with following exceptions regarding fineness.		
Escudo Coinage	1516-1772	—	.916⅔	—
Escudo Coinage	1773-1785	—	.900	—
Escudo Coinage	1786-1833	—	.875	—
320 Reales	1810-1823	27.0000	.875	15.54
160 Reales	1822	13.5000	.875	7.72
80 Reales	1809-1848	6.7500	.875	3.86
100 Reales or 10 Escudos	1850-1868	8.3500	.900	4.97
40 Reales or 4 Escudos	1861-1868	3.3400	.900	1.98
20 Reales or 2 Escudos	1861-1865	1.6700	.900	.99
100 Pesetas	1870-1897	32.2580	.900	19.29
25 Pesetas	1871-1885	8.0645	.900	4.82
20 Pesetas	1889-1904	6.4516	.900	3.86
10 Pesetas	1878	3.2258	.900	1.93
SWEDEN				
1 Carolin or 10 Francs	1868-1872	3.2258	.900	1.93
20 Kronor	1873-1925	8.9606	.900	5.36
10 Kronor	1873-1901	4.4803	.900	2.68
5 Kronor	1881-1920	2.2401	.900	1.34
SWITZERLAND				
20 Francs	1871-1947	6.4516	.900	3.86
10 Francs	1911-1922	3.2258	.900	1.93
100 Francs	1925	32.2580	.900	19.29
100 Francs	1934	25.9000	.900	15.50
100 Francs	1939	17.5000	.900	10.50
50 Francs	1955	11.2900	.900	6.84
25 Francs	1955	5.6450	.900	3.42
6 Duplones	1794	45.8400	.900	27.60
4 Duplones	1797-1798	30.5600	.900	18.40
2 Duplones	1793-1798	15.2800	.900	9.20
1 Duplone	1787-1829	7.6400	.900	4.60
½ Duplone	1787-1796	3.8200	.900	2.30
¼ Duplone	1789-1796	1.9100	.900	1.15
32 Franken	1800	15.2800	.900	9.20
16 Franken	1800-1813	7.6400	.900	4.60
8 Franken	1813	3.8200	.900	2.30
24 Munzgulden	1794-1796	15.2800	.900	9.20
12 Munzgulden	1794-1796	7.6400	.900	4.60
20 Francs (Geneva)	1848	7.6000	.750	3.86
10 Francs (Geneva)	1848	3.8000	.750	1.93

(Other denominations are similar to those of France, Germany or Italy)

Country and Denomination	Period of Coinage	Weight of Coin in Grams	Purity or Fineness	Original Value in U.S. Gold Dollars
SYRIA				
1 Pound	1950	6.7500	.900	4.06
½ Pound	1950	3.3750	.900	2.03
TUNIS				
100 Piastres	1855-1864	19.4920	.900	11.90
80 Piastres	1855	15.5936	.900	9.52
50 Piastres	1855-1867	9.7460	.900	5.95
40 Piastres	1855	7.7968	.900	4.76
25 Piastres	1857-1882	4.8730	.900	2.98
20 Piastres	1855	3.8984	.900	2.38
10 Piastres	1855-1871	1.9492	.900	1.19
5 Piastres	1864-1872	.9746	.900	.60
20 Francs	1891-1928	6.4516	.900	3.86
15 Francs	1886-1891	4.8387	.900	2.90
10 Francs	1891-1928	3.2258	.900	1.93
100 Francs	1930-1955	6.5500	.900	3.94
TURKEY				
5 Sequins	1703-1839	15.0000	.800	8.00
4 Sequins	1703-1839	12.0000	.800	6.40
3 Sequins	1703-1839	9.0000	.800	4.80
2 Sequins	1703-1839	6.0000	.800	3.20

Country and Denomination	Period of Coinage	Weight of Coin in Grams	Purity or Fineness	Original Value in U.S. Gold Dollars
1 Sequin	1451-1839	3.0000	.800	1.60
½ Sequin	1451-1839	1.5000	.800	.80
¼ Sequin	1451-1839	.7500	.800	.40
500 Piastres	1839-1960	36.0829	.916⅔	21.98
250 Piastres	1839-1960	18.0414	.916⅔	10.99
100 Piastres	1839-1959	7.2166	.916⅔	4.40
50 Piastres	1839-1961	3.6083	.916⅔	2.20
25 Piastres	1839-1961	1.8041	.916⅔	1.10
12½ Piastres	1909-1918	.9021	.916⅔	.55
10 Piastres	1839-1876	.7216	.916⅔	.44
5 Piastres	1839-1861	.3608	.916⅔	.22

UNITED STATES

Country and Denomination	Period of Coinage	Weight of Coin in Grams	Purity or Fineness	Original Value in U.S. Gold Dollars
50 Dollars	1915	83.5920	.900	50.00
20 Dollars	1850-1933	33.4370	.900	20.00
10 Dollars	1795-1804	17.4957	.916⅔	10.68
10 Dollars	1838-1933	16.7185	.900	10.00
5 Dollars	1795-1833	8.7479	.916⅔	5.34
5 Dollars	1837-1929	8.3592	.900	5.00
4 Dollars	1879-1880	6.6872	.900	4.00
3 Dollars	1854-1889	5.0154	.900	3.00
2½ Dollars	1796-1833	4.3740	.916⅔	2.67
2½ Dollars	1837-1929	4.1796	.900	2.50
1 Dollar	1849-1889	1.6718	.900	1.00
4 Saudi Pounds	1945-1946	31.9522	.916⅔	19.48
1 Saudi Pound	1945-1946	7.9881	.916⅔	4.87

URUGUAY

Country and Denomination	Period of Coinage	Weight of Coin in Grams	Purity or Fineness	Original Value in U.S. Gold Dollars
5 Pesos	1930	8.4800	.916⅔	5.20

VATICAN

Country and Denomination	Period of Coinage	Weight of Coin in Grams	Purity or Fineness	Original Value in U.S. Gold Dollars
4 Doppia	1786-1787	21.8000	.900	13.04
2 Doppia	1776-1777	10.9000	.900	6.52
1 Doppia	1776-1834	5.4500	.900	3.26
½ Doppia	1776-1787	2.7250	.900	1.63
10 Scudi	1835-1856	17.3000	.900	10.36
5 Scudi	1835-1854	8.6500	.900	5.18
2½ Scudi	1835-1863	4.3250	.900	2.59
1 Scudo	1853-1865	1.7300	.900	1.04
100 Lire	1866-1870	32.2580	.900	19.29
50 Lire	1868-1870	16.1290	.900	9.65
20 Lire	1866-1870	6.4516	.900	3.86
10 Lire	1866-1869	3.2258	.900	1.93
5 Lire	1866-1867	1.6129	.900	.96
100 Lire	1929-1935	8.7990	.900	5.25
100 Lire	1936-1959	5.2000	.900	3.18

(Other denominations are the same as those of Italy)

VENEZUELA

Country and Denomination	Period of Coinage	Weight of Coin in Grams	Purity or Fineness	Original Value in U.S. Gold Dollars
100 Bolivares	1875-1889	32.2580	.900	19.29
50 Bolivares	1875-1888	16.1290	.900	9.65
25 Bolivares	1875	8.0645	.900	4.82
20 Bolivares	1879-1912	6.4516	.900	3.86
10 Bolivares	1930	3.2258	.900	1.93
5 Bolivares	1875	1.6129	.900	.96

YUGOSLAVIA

Country and Denomination	Period of Coinage	Weight of Coin in Grams	Purity or Fineness	Original Value in U.S. Gold Dollars
20 Dinars	1925	6.4516	.900	3.86

ZANZIBAR

Country and Denomination	Period of Coinage	Weight of Coin in Grams	Purity or Fineness	Original Value in U.S. Gold Dollars
5 Rials	1881	8.3592	.900	5.00
2½ Rials	1881	4.1796	.900	2.50

WEIGHTS AND MEASURES

A. The purity or fineness of gold coins

The fineness of gold coins ranges from about .750 fine to 1000 fine or pure gold.

Chemically pure, unalloyed gold is considered to be 1000 fine or 24 karats. The term "Fine gold" as used in banking and government circles refers to gold of 1000 fineness.

24 Karats	=	1000	Fine
23 Karats	=	.958⅓	Fine
22 Karats	=	.916⅔	Fine
21 Karats	=	.875	Fine
20 Karats	=	.833⅓	Fine
18 Karats	=	.750	Fine
14 Karats	=	.583⅓	Fine

It will be noted that .900 fine gold (the standard of U.S. gold coins and of most other countries) would be about 21.6 Karats.

B. The weight of gold coins

The troy and metric systems are used in weighing gold coins or precious metals in general. The weight of gold coins is usually expressed in grams.

1	Troy Ounce	=	31.103½ Grams
1	Troy Ounce	=	480 Grains
1	Troy Ounce	=	20 Pennyweight
12	Troy Ounces	=	1 Troy Pound
32.15	Troy Ounces	=	1 Kilogram
1	Gram	=	15.432 Grains
1	Gram	=	0.643 Pennyweight
1,000	Grams	=	1 Kilogram
24	Grains	=	1 Pennyweight
5,760	Grains	=	1 Troy Pound
15,432	Grains	=	1 Kilogram
240	Pennyweight	=	1 Troy Pound
643.01	Pennyweight	=	1 Kilogram
1	Kilogram	=	2.68 Troy Pounds

Comparisons of Grains and Grams

Grains		Grams
1	=	.0648
10	=	.648
15.432	=	1
20	=	1.30
25	=	1.62
35	=	2.27
50	=	3.24
75	=	4.86
100	=	6.48
125	=	8.10
150	=	9.72
175	=	11.34
200	=	12.96
250	=	16.20
300	=	19.44
350	=	22.68
400	=	25.92
450	=	29.16
500	=	32.40
1000	=	64.80

Equivalents of the Troy and Avoirdupois systems

(The Troy Pound consists of 12 Ounces; the Avoirdupois Pound of 16 Ounces.)

Avoirdupois		Troy or Metric	
1	Ounce	=	437.50 Grains
1	Ounce	=	18.2291 Pennyweight
1	Ounce	=	28.3495 Grams
1	Ounce	=	0.9114 Ounce
1	Ounce	=	0.0625 Pound
1	Pound	=	7,000 Grains
1	Pound	=	291.666 Pennyweight
1	Pound	=	14.5833 Ounces
1	Pound	=	453.5926 Grams
35.2740	Ounces	=	1 Kilogram
2.2046	Pounds	=	1 Kilogram

C. Inches and Millimeters

The diameter or size of coins is usually expressed in millimeters. The table below shows the relationship between the millimeter scale and the more familiar inch scale.

Inches	Millimeters
¼	6.35
½	12.70
¾	19.05
1	25.40
1¼	31.75
1½	38.10
1¾	44.45
2	50.80

THE MOHAMMEDAN CALENDAR

This table shows the Christian or A.D. years of corresponding Mohammedan or A. H. years, and will enable one to ascertain at a glance the correct Christian year of those Afro-Asian coins which are dated according to the Mohammedan Calendar.

Year 1 A.H. of this Calendar began on July 16, 622 A.D. (A.H. is Anno Hegira, meaning in the year of Mohammed's flight from Mecca to Medina.)

A. H.	A. D.		A. H.	A. D.		A. H.	A. D.		A. H.	A. D.
1	622		1000	1591		1200	1785		1300	1882
10	631		1010	1601		1210	1795		1305	1887
20	640		1020	1611		1215	1800		1310	1892
30	650		1030	1620		1220	1805		1315	1897
40	660		1040	1630		1225	1810		1320	1902
50	670		1050	1640		1230	1814		1325	1907
60	679		1060	1650		1235	1819		1330	1911
70	689		1070	1659		1240	1824		1335	1916
80	699		1080	1669		1245	1829		1340	1921
90	708		1090	1679		1250	1834		1345	1926
100	718		1100	1688		1255	1839		1350	1931
200	815		1110	1698		1260	1844		1355	1936
300	912		1120	1708		1265	1848		1360	1941
400	1009		1130	1717		1270	1853		1365	1946
500	1106		1140	1727		1275	1858		1370	1950
600	1203		1150	1737		1280	1863		1375	1956
700	1300		1160	1747		1285	1868		1380	1961
800	1397		1170	1756		1290	1873		1385	1965
900	1494		1180	1766		1295	1878		1390	1970
			1190	1776						

FOREIGN LANGUAGE NUMERALS

	1	2	3	4	5	6	7	8	9	0	10	100
CHRISTIAN	1	2	3	4	5	6	7	8	9	0	10	100
ARABIC - TURKISH	١	٢	٣	٤	٥	٦	٧	٨	٩	٠	١٠	١٠٠
ARABIC - PERSIAN			٣	۴	۵							
SIAMESE	๑	๒	๓	๔	๕	๖	๗	๘	๙	๐	๑๐	๑๐๐
INDIAN	९	२	३	४	५	६	७	८	९	०	१०	
CHINESE, JAPANESE, KOREAN, ANNAMESE (NEW)	一	二	三	四	五	六	七	八	九	〇	十	百
CHINESE, JAPANESE, KOREAN, ANNAMESE (OLD)	壹	貳	叁	肆	伍	陸	柒	捌	玖	〇	拾	
AMHARIC	፩	፪	፫	፬	፭	፮	፯	፰	፱	·	፲	፻
ADDITIONAL NEW CHINESE	½ 半	1,000 千	10,000 万									G.C.H.

Chart courtesy of Gilbert C. Heyde, F.R.N.S

423

GENERAL REFERENCES

From the hundreds of books and catalogues consulted in the preparation of this work, the following are suggested as general sources of reference.

AFGHANISTAN. Wilson, London, 1841.

AMERICAS, THE. References are for all countries in The Americas. Raymond, "The Gold Coins of North and South America", New York, 1937; Raymond, "Standard Catalogue of United States Coins", New York, 1954; Yeoman, "A Guide Book of United States Coins", Racine, 1964; Santos Leitao, "Brazil Coinage", Rio de Janeiro, 1960; Vidal Quadras, "Collection of Spanish Gold Coins", Barcelona, 1892; Tolra, "Collection of Spanish Gold Coins", Barcelona, 1936; Christensen, "The Ubilla-Echevez Collection", Hoboken, 1964.

ANNAM. Schroeder, Berlin Museum, 1898.

ARAB-ASIAN EMPIRES. Berlin Museum, 1898 and British Museum, 1941, 1956 for Arab-Byzantine and Arab-Sassanian issues.

AUSTRALIA. Deacon, Melbourne, 1952.

AUSTRIA. Miller-Aichholz, Vienna, 1948; Cejnek, Vienna, 1935; Horsky Collection, Frankfurt, 1910; Jaeckel, Basel, 1956; Bernhart and Roll (For Salzburg), Munich, 1930.

BELGIUM. Dupriez, Brussels, 1949; Gaillard, Ghent, 1854; Nussbaum; Delmonte, Amsterdam, 1964.

BULGARIA. Ljubica, Zagreb, 1875.

CEYLON. Codrington, Colombo, 1924.

CHINA. Kann, Hong Kong, 1954.

CYPRUS. Schlumberger, Paris, 1877.

DANZIG. Hutten-Czapski, St. Petersburg, 1871.

DENMARK. Schou, Copenhagen, 1926.

ETHIOPIA. Anzani, Rome, 1926.

FRANCE. Ciani, Paris, 1926; F. Poey d'Avant, Paris, 1838; La-Faurie, Paris, 1951, 1956; Monsieur V. Guilloteau, Paris, 1943.

GERMANY. General reference works consulted:—Jaeger, Basel, 1956; Kohler, Hannover, 1759; Soothe, Hamburg, 1784; Reimmann, Frankfurt, 1892; Rudolph, Dresden, 1911.

Specialized reference works consulted:

City	Author	Place and Date
Aachen	Menadier	Berlin 1913
Anhalt	Mann	Hannover 1907
Augsburg	Forster	Leipzig 1910, 1914
Baden	Wielandt	Karlsruhe 1955
Bamberg	Heller	Bamberg 1839
Bavaria	Beierlein	Munich 1894, 1900, 03, 06
Bentheim	Kennepohl	Frankfurt 1927
Brandenburg-Franconia	Schroetter	Halle 1927, 29
Bremen	Jungk	Bremen 1875
Brunswick	Fiala	Prague 1910
Cologne	Noss	Cologne 1926
Dortmund	Meyer	Vienna 1883
Eichstadt	Gebhardt	Halle 1924
Einbeck	Buck	Leipzig 1939
Emden	Knyphausen	Hannover 1872
Erfurt	Leitzman	Weissensee 1864
Frankfurt	Joseph and Fellner	Frankfurt, 1896, 1903
Fulda	Schneider	Fulda 1826
Hamburg	Gaedechens	Hamburg 1850
Hanau	Suchler	Hanau 1897
Hesse	Hoffmeister	Hannover 1880 and Prince Alexander, Darmstadt, 1877-85
Hildesheim	Buck	Leipzig 1937
Julich Cleve Berg	Noss	Munich 1929
Lauenburg	Schmidt	Ratzeburg 1884 and Dorfmann, Ratzeburg, 1940
Lippe	Grote	1867
Lubeck	Behrens	Berlin 1905
Magdeburg	Schroetter	Magdeburg 1909
Mansfeld	Tornau	Prague 1937
Mayence	Prince Alexander	Darmstadt 1882
Mecklenburg	Evers	Schwerim 1799
Minden	Stange	Munster 1913
Moers	Noss	Munich 1927
Munster	Niessert	Coesfeld 1839, 1841
Nassau	Isenbeck	Wiesbaden 1890
Nordhausen	Lejeune	Dresden 1910
Nuremberg	Kellner	Grunwald 1957
Oettingen	Loeffelholz	Oettingana 1883
Osnabruck	Kennepohl	Munich 1938
Paderborn	Weingartner	Munster 1882
Palatinate	Noss	Munich 1938 and Exter, Zweibrucken, 1759, 1775
Prussia	Schroetter	Berlin 1902-25 and Bahrfeldt, Halle, 1913
Quedlinburg	Duning	Quedlinburg 1886
Rantzau	Meyer	Vienna 1882
Ratzeburg	Bahrfeldt	Schwerin 1913
Regensburg	Plato	Regensburg 1779
Reuss	Schmidt and Knab	Dresden 1907
Rosenberg	Friedensburg and Seger	Breslau 1901
Rostock	Grimm	Berlin 1905
Salm	Joseph	Frankfurt 1914
Saxony	Tentzel	Dresden 1705, 1714 and Baumgarten, Dresden 1812
Schauenburg	Weinmeister	Berlin
Schleswig-Holstein	Lange	Berlin 1908, 1912
Schwarzburg	Fischer	Heidelberg 1904
Silesia	Friedensburg and Seger	Breslau 1901
Solms	Joseph	Frankfurt 1912
Speyer	Harster	Speyer 1882
Stolberg	Frederick	Dresden 1911
Stralsund	Bratring	Berlin 1907
Teutonic Order	Waschinski	Gottingen 1952
Treves	Noss	Bonn 1916
Ulm	Binder	Stuttgart 1846
Wallenstein	Meyer	Vienna 1886
Wismar	Grimm	Berlin 1897
Worms	Joseph	Darmstadt 1906
Wurttemberg	Ebner	Stuttgart 1910-1915

GREAT BRITAIN. Brooke, London, 1932; Seaby, London, 1965; Spink, London, 1950.

HOLY ROMAN EMPIRE. Same as Austria.

HUNGARY. Same as Austria and Rethy, Budapest, 1899. For Transylvania: Resch, Hermannstadt, 1901.

INDIA. Calcutta Museum, 1906; Delhi Museum, 1936; British Museum, 1892; Marsden, London, 1823; Meili Collection of Schulman, Amsterdam, 1910.

ISRAEL. Kadman, Tel-Aviv, 1963.

ITALY. "Corpus Nummorum Italicorum" by King Victor Emanuele III, Rome, 1910-1943.

JAPAN. Jacobs and Vermuele, New York, 1953.

JERUSALEM. Schlumberger, Paris, 1877.

MALTA. Schembri, London, 1910.

NETHERLANDS. Stephanik, Amsterdam, 1904; Schulman, Amsterdam, 1946.

NETHERLANDS EAST INDIES. Netcher, Batavia, 1863; Bucknill, London, 1931; Scholten-Schulman, Amsterdam, 1953.

POLAND. Hutten-Czapski, St. Petersburg, 1871.

PORTUGAL. Vaz, Lisbon, 1948; Batalha-Reis, Lisbon, 1956.

RHODES. Schlumberger, Paris, 1877.

RUSSIA. Schubert, St. Petersburg, 1855; Severin, New York, 1958; Spassky, Amsterdam, 1967.

SCOTLAND. Stewart, London, 1955.

SERBIA. Ljubica, Zagreb, 1875.

SIAM. Le May, Bangkok, 1932.

SOUTH AFRICA. Kaplan, Germiston, 1950.

SPAIN. Vidal Quadras, Barcelona, 1892; Tolra, Barcelona, 1936; Lopez-Chaves and Yriarte, Madrid, 1968.

SWEDEN. Levin, Stockholm, 1887; Brunn Collection, Frankfurt, 1914; Gluck-Hesselblad, Stockholm, 1953 .

TUNIS. Monsieur V. Guilloteau, Paris, 1943.

TURKEY. British Museum, 1883.

VATICAN. "Corpus Nummorum Italicorum" by King Victor Emanuele III, Rome, 1910-1943.